ISLAMIC ALGORITHMS

Also Available from Bloomsbury:

Muslims Making British Media, Carl Morris

Cyber Muslims, Edited by Robert Rozehnal

The Bloomsbury Handbook of Muslims and Popular Culture, Edited by Hussein Rashid and Kristian Petersen

ISLAMIC ALGORITHMS

Online Influence in the Muslim Metaverse

Gary R. Bunt

BLOOMSBURY ACADEMIC
LONDON • NEW YORK • OXFORD • NEW DELHI • SYDNEY

BLOOMSBURY ACADEMIC
Bloomsbury Publishing Plc, 50 Bedford Square, London, WC1B 3DP, UK
Bloomsbury Publishing Inc, 1359 Broadway, New York, NY 10018, USA
Bloomsbury Publishing Ireland, 29 Earlsfort Terrace, Dublin 2, D02 AY28, Ireland

BLOOMSBURY, BLOOMSBURY ACADEMIC and the Diana logo are trademarks of Bloomsbury Publishing Plc

First published in Great Britain 2024
Paperback edition published 2026

A catalogue record for this book is available from the British Library.

Names: Bunt, Gary R., author.
Title: Islamic algorithms: online influence in the Muslim metaverse / Gary R. Bunt.
Description: 1st. | New York: Bloomsbury Academic, 2024. | Includes bibliographical references and index.
Identifiers: LCCN 2023041052 (print) | LCCN 2023041053 (ebook) | ISBN 9781350418264 (hardback) | ISBN 9781350418301 (paperback) | ISBN 9781350418288 (ebook) | ISBN 9781350418271 (pdf)
Subjects: LCSH: Islam–Computer network resources. | Social media–Religious aspects–Islam. | Mass media–Religious aspects–Islam. | Islam–21st century. | Islam in mass media.
Classification: LCC BP185.7 .B863 2024 (print) | LCC BP185.7 (ebook) | DDC 297.2/7–dc23/eng/20230921
LC record available at https://lccn.loc.gov/2023041052
LC ebook record available at https://lccn.loc.gov/2023041053

ISBN: HB: 978-1-3504-1826-4
PB: 978-1-3504-1830-1
ePDF: 978-1-3504-1827-1
eBook: 978-13504-1828-8

Typeset by Deanta Global Publishing Services, Chennai, India

For product safety related questions contact productsafety@bloomsbury.com.

To find out more about our authors and books visit www.bloomsbury.com and sign up for our newsletters

For my inspirational family

CONTENTS

Acknowledgements viii
Note on the transliteration ix

INTRODUCTION: INTO MUSLIM METAVERSES 1

Chapter 1
ISLAMIC ALGORITHMS: TRANSMISSION, INFLUENCE, DESIGN 9

Chapter 2
BEFORE MUḤAMMAD 35

Chapter 3
MUḤAMMAD AND DIGITAL INFLUENCE 47

Chapter 4
CYBER REPRESENTATION: THE PROPHET'S FAMILY, PROXIMITY AND SUCCESSION 57

Chapter 5
CIE LEGAL: DIGITAL SUNNI INFLUENCES, LAW AND AUTHORITY 75

Chapter 6
AHL AL-BAYT, SHĪʿĪSM AND IMAMATES IN CYBERSPACE 105

Chapter 7
SHĪʿĪSM – AYATOLLAHS IN DIGITAL ZONES 129

Chapter 8
SUFI PATHWAYS IN MUSLIM METAVERSES 143

Chapter 9
MEDIA OFFENSIVE: DOOMSCROLLERS, DIGITAL CONTENT, INFLUENCERS AND E-JIHĀD 173

Chapter 10
PROCESSING ISLAM: CONTEMPORARY INFLUENCES AND INFLUENCERS IN EVOLVING MUSLIM METAVERSES 193

Chapter 11
ISLAMIC ALGORITHMS AND META MUSLIM FUTURES 223

Notes 231
Index 307

ACKNOWLEDGEMENTS

This book would not have been written without the help of many people and avatars in digital spaces, metaverses and closer to home.

I appreciated the insights of students, postgraduates and staff at the University of Wales Trinity Saint David, especially Ibrahim Abusharif, Fleur Allen, Maggie Webster and others who have discussed their research in related areas. I particularly enjoyed exploring the ups and downs of studying cyber-Islam with colleagues from the ESRC *Digital British Islam* project: Muhammed Alamgir Ahmed, Sariya Contractor-Cheruvallil, Khadijah Elshayyal, Sadek Hamid, Laura Jones and Frédéric Volpi have offered new perspectives into our developing field. The same is true for my many colleagues in the CHANSE *Digital Islam Across Europe* project, especially Anna Grasso.

I am indebted to the organisers of and participants in numerous UK and international workshops and conferences I participated in, online and in-person, providing safe spaces to test-drive theories and ideas. The readers of this book's drafts gave thoughtful and detailed advice that contributed to this final version. Particular thanks are due for the support of Lalle Pursglove, Emily Wootton and the Bloomsbury team. I have worked with many other editors, academics and readers on my research over the years, all of whom have contributed to my approach to this present book.

This book came together during the Covid-19 crisis. My wife, Yvonne, provided insights and a sense of perspective during this unusual time. My son Kane maintained a virtuoso long-distance music soundtrack alongside informed political analysis and detailed technological knowledge. My mother, Elizabeth, continues her enthusiastic support of my work while remarkably producing her own book during this period. Other family members, along with friends, maintained encouragement and interest.

Despite the input of all the above, this book's contents and shortcomings remain my responsibility.

Gary R. Bunt
Lampeter

NOTE ON THE TRANSLITERATION

A transliteration system is used in this book, as numerous Islamic terms and proper names are in the text. These terms and names with diacritics may help readers seek further information and definitions in specialist sources. At the same time, hopefully, they will not impede non-specialist readers outside of the multiple fields associated with the study of Islam. The system was adapted using general principles from the *Encyclopaedia of Islam: New Edition* (Leiden: E.J. Brill, 1960), along with Ian Richard Netton's model within *A Popular Dictionary of Islam* (London: Curzon Press, 1991), both of which I have applied in previous books. Quotations from the internet and textual sources retain original transliterations; proper names maintain locally applied spellings and transliterations; common anglicized spellings of Islamic terms are applied where relevant (e.g. 'mosque' for *masjid/mas*dj*id*). Islamic English is a complex area open to discussion regarding boundaries and spellings, but less common terms have general definitions in parentheses in this book. *VirtuallyIslamic.com* contains a lexicon of terminology from the book.

INTRODUCTION

INTO MUSLIM METAVERSES

When visiting Jakarta's Istiqlal Mosque in 2019, I was struck by how digital interfaces were being used to access Islamic content. Individuals in the main multi-level prayer area offered *duʿāʾ* (prayer) using their smartphones to guide them through recitation. In contrast, others in a study group of elders worked on their iPads in the mosque, consulting religious texts and playing recitations. It was an oasis of calm compared with the multi-lane traffic chaos and noise outside. Inside the vast hall, amidst prayers (and extensive building work, including installation of high-tech multimedia systems), people sat in meditative silence scrolling through their phones – although it was not possible to determine from a distance whether the content was 'religious' in orientation. Watched over by a digital clock indicating prayer times and a computer-linked *minbar* (raised lectern for delivery of sermons) this integration or blended approach towards technology and Islam suggests a sophisticated consumption pattern reflective of other internet use areas. It made me consider how, in the future, internet usage and Islam will shift and merge in line with technological developments. If there is further integration and seamless online and offline religious activity, is there scope for Islam within iterations of virtual reality and prospective metaverses?

Muslim metaverses in which digital nomads traverse interactive and immersive zones of religious knowledge, information and authority and 'sit' at the feet of scholars in virtual mosques could become the latest form of Cyber Islamic Environments. These online worlds could have information marketplaces and back alleys built on the foundations of today's digital constructs, networks and identities. There is a paramount need for communities and observers to understand existing online activities, as part of strategies to build and respond to the shifting parameters of Muslim digital worlds, in which algorithms and undercurrents of influence draw audiences into the proximity of diverse understandings of Islam.

To explore these questions, *Islamic Algorithms* explores the intersection between the internet and religious understanding represented by diverse Islamic influences over space and time, which could form a central zone with Muslim metaverses. This includes key formative and influential figures (and their representatives) whose presence online maintains their legacy in digital formats, as well as those contemporaneous individuals ('influencers') who have developed extensive digital audiences for their interpretive approaches towards Islam and Muslim lifestyles through online activities. Whether contemporary or historical, these figures comprise the different forms of influence discussed in this book. They are not equally weighted in terms of status in Islamic contexts. Readers may have their own list of Islamic influences – given that a complete list across cultures, contexts and history would require multiple encyclopaedic volumes.

In *Islamic Algorithms*, the continually evolving umbrella term 'Cyber Islamic Environments' (henceforth, CIEs) is applied. First introduced in 2000, it reflects on the diversity between and within different zones in various iterations of cyberspace over time. Multiple formats and religious zones are featured in my initial definition.[1] This term evolved in line with technological shifts and their applications in diverse Muslim contexts but has not yet become redundant given inherent flexibility in encompassing complex digital media forms from multiple content providers who define themselves as 'Muslims'. There may be scope for updated terminology, but CIEs provide continuity with past iterations and versions of online concepts associated with online Islam dating back to (at least) the 1990s. It reflects multifaceted and varied Muslim world views, presenting reference points of identity within conceptualizations of Islam. In *iMuslims*, I suggested that 'The source encoding of such environments follows specific protocols of identity with particular Islamic reference points, including essential beliefs shared by the majority of Muslims. The encoding is refined and in some cases hacked to engineer manifestations of Muslim understandings that adapt to networks, contexts, histories, and contemporary issues.'[2]

While technology has shifted, the essential aspects of this definition remain. The term has been used across my work to explore different impacts and influences across Islamic knowledge economies, especially the ways in which conventional models of understanding have had to adapt to more open-source models of interpretation and knowledge development. While not assuming the impact is universal, the internet has in some contexts had a transformational effect on how Muslims practice and mediate Islam, how Islam is represented to wider audiences and how Muslim societies represent themselves.

The 'iMuslims' term has been applied across diverse internet media for religious understandings, identity affiliations and network connexions. This reflected exponential growth in internet technologies (including mobile phone technologies) and gradual increases in digital access in synchronization with rapid growth in online Islamic discourse. iMuslims acted synonymously for 'cyber-Muslims' but referred to a broader sense of information technology, searchability and interactivity, where multiple programs linked together (in products such as iPhones) applying the 'mercurial i' as a prefix. The continuity of shifting technology and increasingly creative online use means this is a continually shifting field of study, with real-world impact.

Increasingly, where there is access to technology and the requisite digital skills, online content is integrated into everyday religious activities. There is continuity between pre-digital practices and understandings and their online manifestations. This has been significant for dispersed communities and individuals connecting with their peers across diverse locations. This does not suggest that the essence of

Islam has changed, but the ways it is articulated and practised may be calibrated in line with digital content and integrated into many aspects of religious activities. Technology is blended into lifestyles in increasingly seamless ways, from the *Fajr* prayers of dawn through to the final fixed *ʿIshāʾ* prayer.

Islamic Algorithms raise issues of how (or whether) digital content is embedded in contemporary understandings of Islam and its dissemination – where online content can impact analogue Islamic contexts. In part, this can be through algorithms, positioned here as a metaphor for subsets of influences and in their computer language context. Islamic algorithms drive and dictate interpretations and discussions across different digital contexts – from the simplest cell phone to high-end computers, drawn upon by users whose world views are increasingly shaped by digital interfaces, including the search for religious knowledge. Algorithms underpin search hierarchies and the most basic applications. They represent the encoding of core online content (in the context of this book), the architecture of CIEs and inform future online iterations of Islam on the internet – including 'Muslim metaverses'. By discussing and seeking to understand these building blocks and influences, the book will demonstrate the essential role of CIEs in impacting contemporary understandings of religion, politics, ethics, ritual and practice. This is integral to developing holistic knowledge about modern Muslim discourse, across digital worlds and interfaces, where Islamic algorithms impact influence and understanding for a variety of users.

Islamic Algorithms is underpinned by long-standing research interest in Islam, Muslims and the internet. It emerged from the fields of religious studies and the study of Islam, so comes with a particular interest in how religious identities, rituals, authority and practice are impacted by online developments. This research has involved many hours of online observation and archiving/capturing of CIEs in diverse formats, from reading multiple Q&A websites to 'doom scrolling' e-jihād activities. A key element was exploring how the interpretation of Islam represented itself online and how the dynamics of digital discourse started to impact the interpretation of Islam itself. Exploring CIEs helps us to understand the diverse strands of identities, influences and affiliations represented in Islam in general and in digital contexts.

My current technology used for research across multiple devices and clouds is a space-age leap from the first basic computers I used in the late 1970s (not for research), a world of floppy disks, green command lines, monochrome screens, daisy-wheel printers and clunky beige computers. This technology is now showcased in the Science Museum. The emergence of email via ARPANET and Graphical User Interfaces (GUIs) in the 1980s were big leaps in terms of computer use. Into the mainstream came early personal computers such as the Apple Macintosh and various DOS Windows operating systems: the ability to click on icons using a mouse and use multiple windows and folders on a screen may seem basic today, but it was a game changer for computer users, and the focal point of technological battles as Apple and Microsoft slugged it out for dominance in computer consumer markets. In terms of electronic communication using these and other computers prior to the internet, from the late 1970s Bulletin

Board Systems (BBS) using dial-up modems were being used within thousands of electronic communities focused on specific issues – including religion and politics.[3]

The growth in computer availability and internet access stimulated the development of early websites and discussion groups in the mid-1990s on the 'new' browsers such as Netscape and Mosaic. Pages and websites devoted to Islam emerged online as early portals to religious knowledge and opinion. The technology used by Muslims in cyberspace changed over time, from the early online communities in chat rooms and mailing lists (often in English) facilitated by Muslim students studying and working primarily in technologically connected Western contexts. These were text-only and frequently dense discussions, projecting the complexities of Muslim world views and political opinions without filters and – at times – regard for copyright (cut-and-pasted from other sources). In the early period access often required the use of a computer lab, with personal connected computers being more the domain of hobbyists until technology became more accessible and user-friendly.

There was the early excitement of encountering the Qurʾān online in a digital format, with recitation sound files, scanned images and text-dense files of translated chapters and verses. It took time to load in my rural Wales location but heralded a transformative phase in Muslim online developments. Searchable, easy-to-download and circulate content on Islam represented 'cutting edge' activities going beyond text-only materials, demonstrating the abilities of information technology literate students and professionals involved in content creation and delivery. Nascent online communities engendered new identities and networks in response to communication opportunities stimulated by increased access to (and improved navigation of) the internet.

The range of content in this early phase included some Qurʾān and ḥādīth databases alongside early portals, innovative in providing a gateway for Muslims who were early technology adopters.[4] FTP (File Transfer Protocol) access restricted materials to image-heavy content before the emergence of browsers such as Mosaic, Netscape and Internet Explorer. In the pre-Google era, search engines such as W3Catalog, Lycos, WebCrawler, MetaCrawler and Dogpile became tools of choice when surfing the internet. Search was predicated on early algorithmic equations, which shifted and evolved over time. Permutations of Internet Relay Chat, message boards, email lists and forums had been active in Islamic-related fields since the 1980s, focused on a technologically literate audience with access to the internet. The relationships and dynamics between authorities and their audiences shifted in line with technological and media transformations, a theme which was picked up by academics across disciplinary perspectives (discussed further in Chapter 1).[5]

In the Islamic Studies' lecture rooms in the 1990s, digital sources started being cited in (still handwritten) student essays, with in-class conversations inspired by online content – often to the detriment of readings of print media. When I started researching issues associated with Islam and the internet in the 1990s, it was possible to collect and publish principal links and websites relating to Islam onto a few pages of hypertext markup language (HTML), aggregated on the *Islamic Pathways* website.[6] This helped students navigate this new territory and even included a technical explanation of *how* they should access the internet.

In earliest academic presentations of online Islamic content in the 1990s, it was necessary to explain to audiences exactly what the internet *was* and how a browser functioned. Conference rooms lacked computers and online connectivity. In a pre-PowerPoint era, overhead projectors and transparencies facilitated the sessions![7] Working out how to study this new phenomenon also presented specific challenges, especially from a religious studies and methodological perspective. These included explaining it to non-digitally literate colleagues who expected more traditional scholarly routes of investigation in my field. Before broadband, downloading content took an age on basic modems and phone lines. CIEs were functional and available, but a world away from current iterations in terms of technology and interfaces.

Nowadays, contemporary CIEs transcend technology, from basic interfaces to interactive devices, all informed by algorithms and influences. *Islamic Algorithms* will demonstrate the multiple ways Islam can be mediated online and chart the way forward as CIEs edge into metaverse territories.

Into the metaverse

Discussion and hype concerning the introduction of a 'Metaverse' will introduce further terminological and methodological challenges to research in this area, in zones where wearable devices and digitally constructed 'realities' are taken to further levels; 'meta' in relation to religion may have a more significant association with the metaphysical realms discussed later in this book. A Muslim Metaverse (or multiple metaverses) linking these elements together may be an aspiration for some developers. The notion of an immersive and interoperable form of CIEs will be built in part on the foundations of digital content discussed in this book. This infrastructure of materials is open to upgrading into integrated online realities, 'lived' by connected individuals, whose Islamic lifestyles may be predicated by digital influences and influencers within the complex and 'messy' milieu of CIEs.

Metaverses form part of future online contexts, within understandings of immersive 'Web3' contexts. Beyond the hype, parallels are drawn between the internet and the metaverse, which can be synonymous:

> To help you get a sense of how vague and complex a term 'the metaverse' can be, here's an exercise: Mentally replace the phrase 'the metaverse' in a sentence with 'cyberspace.' Ninety per cent of the time, the meaning won't substantially change. That's because the term doesn't really refer to any one specific type of technology, but rather a broad (and often speculative) shift in how we interact with technology. And it's entirely possible that the term itself will eventually become just as antiquated, even as the specific technology it once described becomes commonplace.[8]

The term metaverse is consequently difficult to define. It means different things to different technology developers and theorists. Rather than a singularity, a complex multiplicity of possibilities, encompassing highly immersive virtual reality gaming environments and parallel virtual worlds generating their own economies and societal perspectives. Technology platforms are making substantial investments in their versions of metaverses, including the development of complex and diffuse virtual reality spaces, along with the hardware and financial systems to make metaverses function.[9] However, at the time of writing, the full technological potential of immersive metaverses remains on the drawing board. Virtual reality headsets which would be used to interact with forms of metaverse content are a niche product. If metaverse concepts become mainstream, then specific strategies will have to be adopted to accommodate developing (virtual) realities. This includes approaches by Islamic platforms and influencers seeking to develop or maintain their presence online.

In anticipation of projected potential, the word 'Meta' was appropriated and utilized by Facebook as part of a rebranding exercise in 2021, to encompass a variety of current projects, alongside its aspiration for a presence in the metaverse.[10] Herman Narula notes that analyses of potential metaverses are problematic, given that the term is difficult to define: 'Outdated or superficial visions of virtual worlds and the metaverse tend to focus on the what, but not the why; the thing, but not its purpose; the opportunities that will be made available to us in embodied digital spaces, but not the reasons why we would want to pursue them in the first place.'[11]

Back in 2000, I discussed early iterations of CIEs and Islamic 'virtual worlds' in *Virtually Islamic*, when online interfaces were clunky and interactions extremely slow. There was limited multimedia, search was restricted and a high proportion of the content was text and photos. By contrast, in terms of Islam, our discussion of Muslim metaverse(s) might represent the latest iteration of CIEs. Their rationale would have continuity with previous 'versions' of the internet, in that they are a means to search for God, understand Islam and link up with like-minded Muslim individuals and networks – albeit in a more 'immersive' fashion.

This echoes questions as to whether it is possible for an individual to have a 'religious experience' in a metaverse? Would the metaverse engender greater proximity to the divine? This might underpin the rationale for wanting to develop Muslim metaverses in the first place. At present, we can look at the potential content and dominant influences that would conceivably form part of any Muslim metaverse. The envisaged Islamic metaverse futures may resemble science fiction at present, but its primary content basis, knowledge and influences are already in place, which can be embedded into the next generation of CIEs – whatever shapes and structures the technologies emerge into.

The interfaces to search for Islam may change, but a proportion of the essential source code is in the system, grounded in the algorithms that pervade and impact upon CIEs. It is these issues which will be explored in the book, alongside a survey of influences and influencers which would underpin projected metaverses. This is approached through a series of thematic snapshots of key influences, figures, issues and themes impacting the development of Muslim societies past and present

– captured and discussed as indicators of the state and structures of CIEs, while recognizing that content and technology are fluid – with potential to reconfigure, realign, disappear and be repacked across formats, contexts and languages. In part, zeitgeist and continued daily monitoring and content capture across multiple channels informs the content of this book, while recognizing that this process is not automated or team-driven – rather the activity of a single researcher wresting with other demands of academia. Many themes discussed in the book have the potential for further in-depth analysis and discussion, and it is hoped that readers will be encouraged to engage in their own explorations of CIE strands. The book was written in part during the Covid-19 pandemic, which itself became a particular driver for Muslim online activities seeking to respond to the crises and its impact on ritual, practice and societies. This extraordinary episode caused many organizations to reappraise their approaches towards online activities, while influencers and others sought to fill the information vacuum at a time when many people were spending much more time online during various lockdowns. With further potential shifts in internet usage and applications in line with expanding use of artificial intelligence and the projected developments (or hype) surrounding metaverses, this book provides an opportunity to reappraise the influences and content bound to inform the algorithms underpinning our digital worlds.

Book outline

Each chapter can be read separately and out of sequence. This is particularly relevant when reading a searchable e-Book edition. A linear reading seems anachronistic when discussing digital content, but readers can also use the index to explore specific themes and content.

For traditional readers, the following sequence applies:

Chapter 1 unpacks ideas about religious influences and influencers, including the roles of algorithms as sources of connectivity and controversy; it explores existing sources relating to the study of Islam, Muslims and cyberspace. Chapter 2 looks at influences before the emergence of Prophet Muḥammad, including the roles of other prophets in articulating Islamic value systems. Chapter 3 focuses on Muḥammad's representation in cyberspace. Chapter 4 discusses the digital manifestations of the Prophet's family members and descendants and the influential authority figures who followed Muḥammad. Chapter 5 unpacks ideas of religious influence in Sunni contexts over space, time and within CIEs. Chapter 6 discusses how the Shīʿa Ahl al-Bayt and the Imamates resonate in cyberspace through to the present day. Chapter 7 explicitly focuses on Ayatollahs and their online presence. Chapter 8 delves into 'Sufi' esoteric dimensions of digital Islam, where the metaverse(s) interlock with the metaphysical. The micro-area of jihād, which has a specific resonance in CIEs, is unpacked in Chapter 9. The book then looks in Chapter 10 at different forms of contemporary influencers online, selecting examples and case studies from diverse themes and contexts. Chapter 11 draws together some conclusions about influence and influencers in CIEs, projected

Muslim metaverses and their implications and provides suggestions for future exploration in the field.

Readers may wish to consult *virtuallyislamic.com* for book-related links and further content, including its blog, a full bibliography, lexicon and URL listing. Feedback is also welcome via the website.

Conclusion

Islamic Algorithms explores the role of influence in Islamic historical and contemporary settings by reviewing the state of play of significant figures over space and time and how their voices resonate digitally across the internet. It also explores different forms of contemporary influence and influencers, across social media and digital platforms, in ways which relate directly to impacting individuals and societies regarding their practice and understanding of Islam. It looks at the influences that might act as undercurrents to underpin different concepts and frameworks associated with ideas of Muslim metaverses while recognizing that they are ambiguous and open to multiple definitions. This discussion contains 'snapshots' of key drivers and activities, which seek to open the academic area further to consideration of Islamic influence, algorithms and Muslim metaverses.

Chapter 1

ISLAMIC ALGORITHMS

TRANSMISSION, INFLUENCE, DESIGN

In this chapter, ideas surrounding algorithms are introduced in the context of cyber-Islamic environments. The intention is to show how understanding of digital Islam can be shaped by artificial intelligence and how this forms part of a wider picture of knowledge acquisition and influence in digital Muslim contexts. The chapter looks at how notions of influence and influencers are defined. It also introduces significant theoretical approaches and influences shaping this book's background.

Calibrating Islamic Algorithms

The human element is significant within the context of this book, where algorithms are impacted by the influences over space and time which have contributed to knowledge and conversations about Islam and Muslims. This factor is inherent within Islamic algorithms where searchability, influence, interfaces, location, key concepts and words come together to form strings of results for iMuslims seeking knowledge about Islam. In earlier books, I referred to the famous saying of the Prophet (*ḥādīth*), often translated as 'Seek knowledge even if you have to go as far as China' – which itself has been subject to some conjecture as to its veracity and authenticity, in part because of its weak *isnād*.[1] There is no doubt that whatever the authenticity of his *ḥādīth*, the notion of seeking knowledge is incumbent on all Muslims. Now the seeking takes place online, going 'further' than China (although often using Chinese-built technology), into the digital depths of information oceans. Algorithms may, in part, guide these seekers of knowledge now and in future metaverses.

Algorithms are a significant pivot across CIES. The term 'algorithm' may be applied in this book as a metaphor for subsets of influences (and influencers) that impact Islamic understandings, as well as in its mathematical frameworks. It seems appropriate in the context of this volume that the term 'algorithm' derived from the Persian mathematician and theorist Muḥammad ibn Mūsā al-Khwarizmi (*c.*780–850 CE), who drew on mathematical antecedents from Babylonia, India and Persia while working in Baghdad during the time of the Abbasid Caliphate.[2] In this book, on a technical level the term 'algorithm' can represent a procedure applied for the location of data, drawing on different mathematical processes to retrieve data from hierarchical structures, dependent on the input of the searcher, the input of the specific data creator and the functions of digital interfaces. Algorithms are parts of everyday life, such as machine-learning algorithms that do not depend on human programmers and classic algorithms that require a programmer's input and (hopefully) logic to produce results.

Algorithms result from human input and calculation over time, including potential errors and bias as part of the inherent data sets. The 'deep learning' parameters of extensive multimedia data sets can build on specific assumptions as part of its source code. Uncritical use of systems can be predicated on casual and distorted inputting and categorizing of data by humans whose inherent biases may impact results.[3]

Artificial intelligence and CIEs

Artificial Intelligence (AI) raises concerns when exploring the veracity of information in general, and in the context of this book, on Islam and Muslims in particular. A key question is how (or whether) AI shapes perspectives and approaches towards Islam and Muslims, from those within diverse Muslim communities and contexts, as well as those looking in from outside. Generic questions about AI's influence across societal and cultural contexts can be introduced as a focal point for understanding the ways in which CIEs operate and evolve. Non-human autonomous systems are impacting across societies, working and learning through algorithmic programming which is predicated on datasets and information inputted by humans. High-level AI includes the ways in which search engines operate, drawing on diverse sources and analytical approaches to provide answers to queries and aid in decision-making. AI evolves in multiple forms to perform different tasks and objectives dependent on the 'training' they might receive.[4]

It has been suggested that the term 'artificial intelligence' is inherently problematic and mythologized, particularly around science-fiction depictions, and that the misunderstanding of the term(inology) can lead to its mismanagement. Jaron Lanier indicates that AI programs such as ChatGPT are 'an innovative form of social collaboration . . . Seeing AI as a way of working together, rather than a technology for creating independent, intelligent beings, may make it less mysterious – less like HAL 9000 or Commander Data. But that's good, because mystery only makes mismanagement more likely'.[5] Lanier suggests that we should adopt a more human-centric approach towards AI, beyond sensationalistic headlines, and this is worthy of consideration within approaches towards CIEs and Muslim metaverses.

Keeping these caveats in mind, AI can incorporate and perpetuate inherent biases (from all perspectives). It does not indicate the provenance or veracity of information provided. There were no footnotes or endnotes in the AI language bot

ChatGPT at the time of writing. While this situation might change as AI develops, this is problematic if the readers suspend or do not have critical perspectives and take AI content at face value. 'Information' generated about Islam scraped by AI from disparate sources and taken at face value potentially adds to the 'fake news' and distortions. AI impacts on how Islam is mediated through CIEs, in part via the algorithms impacting on search and knowledge acquisition. Awareness of this is relevant when exploring Islam and Muslims in cyberspace.

Unmediated views can be generated and disseminated rapidly in multiple versions via ChatBots, building on patterns of digital propagation that can spread rapidly without editorial control or management. While this might have some positive aspects within Islamic contexts, this might also include anti-Muslim prejudice, or content intended to generate intra-Muslim conflict. It could also promote a specific world view with an effect amplified (in search parameters) through its repeated presence across multiple online channels, which can impact on algorithmic function when page hierarchies influence search results. Search can also be influenced by AIs measuring what the individual has inputted into search engines before: 'An entirely predictably life isn't worth living. But algorithmic induction can lead to a kind of information determinism, in which our past clickstreams entirely decide our future. If we don't erase our Web histories, in other words, we may be doomed to repeat them.'[6]

The idea that computers in general and, in particular, AI may be infallible does not necessarily reflect the reality: 'Claims about "superhuman" accuracy and insight, paired with the inability to fully explain how these results are produced, form a discourse about AI that we call enchanted determinism.'[7] The 'magic' surrounding perceptions of AI and potential metaverses removes the human element and adds to an over-hyping of the potential of information technology. There are specific issues of accuracy in AI in general: science-fiction writer Ted Chiang suggested that OpenAI's ChatGPT's content was analogous to a lossless compressed image, in which small elements of the image were subtlety degraded:

> Think of ChatGPT as a blurry jpeg of all the text on the Web. It retains much of the information on the Web, in the same way that a jpeg retains much of the information of a higher-resolution image, but, if you're looking for an exact sequence of bits, you won't find it; all you will ever get is an approximation. But, because the approximation is presented in the form of grammatical text, which ChatGPT excels at creating, it's usually acceptable.[8]

This is significant, if one is 100 per cent reliant on AI answers, that there can be this margin of error. In conjunction with this, there are concerns of AI tools being subject to 'hallucinations' or fabricated responses to questions, requiring the development of different training models and strategies to pre-empt these difficulties.[9] There are particular implications for any person reliant on AI for religious advice, where there is potential for hallucination-influenced error. Alongside disinformation and determining the veracity in general of online content, this aspect of AI becomes an important further issue for consideration.

Taking some steps back from the 'hype' surrounding AI can be relevant, especially when considering CIEs and the roles of iMuslims, which include the individuals responsible for inputting information about Islam into websites, apps and other interfaces. This notion of human fallibility has some resonance in Islamic contexts in terms of source veracity issues associated with *ḥādīth*. The importance of strong *isnād* or chain of transmission is fundamental to their reliability as sources, linked to the reputations of the promulgator of a saying or action of the Prophet Muḥammad.

The notion of Islamic algorithms refers here to how individuals might 'locate' an aspect of Islam through a digital interface and how this is influenced by the creation of specific data structures and relationships. It does not suggest that Allāh might have any direct input into the searching processes, although individuals with more fatalistic approaches to divine interactions and predestination may seek to differ. This could open a discussion that has existed since the emergence of Islam and has been a cause of splits in interpretation and approaches over history (beyond the scope of this book).

As a side note, inevitably there have been discussions as to whether AI is 'permissible' within Islamic contexts, which might be a moot point, given the ubiquity of AI and algorithms within CIE contexts. As with other areas of interpretation, there will be nuance in understandings, given that aspects of AI can have benefit to humanity and positively impact on public welfare and interests (*al-maslaha* in a religious legalistic context) – but that those aspects which lead to 'un-Islamic' prohibited activities would be forbidden.[10] Junaid Qadir and Amana Raquib researched into the Islamic ethical principles associated with AI and expressed concerns about (a lack of) Muslim representation in the design and implementation of different AI forms.[11] The impact of AI in Muslim contexts has been the subject of philosophical speculation, focused on the diverse approaches towards machine learning, and AI's implications in terms of creation, the soul and AI's impact on humanity.[12]

Influences, influencers and interfaces

Individual 'influences' from contemporary or historical contexts represent 'intermediaries' to aspects of religious knowledge, including spiritual and religious figures and thinkers, legal interpreters, political voices and – in online contexts – iMuslims across generations whose actions in CIEs impact on Islamic activities and performance. Influencers can also impact this equation. 'Influence' itself is difficult to quantify and may be subtle or overt, based on long-standing interactions or something that has immediate effect (or points in between).

An 'influencer' is an individual with the potential capacity to use online channels to cause others to 'buy into' a product or message. The term has become synonymous with social media. Analysis of different hierarchies and forms of influencers suggests an evolving term, associated with marketing and delivery of messages by individuals, organizations and institutions. 'Macro influencers' often have millions of followers and celebrity status. Cornwell and Katz suggest: 'there are micro influencers, more often regular people who have gained a following through their expertise or passion on a topic. Finally, we have nano influencers, with much smaller followings but often a niche interest that makes them extremely persuasive to those who follow them.'[13]

While this approach was developed around commercial marketing, it is still relevant to deconstruct and consider the nuanced approaches to the 'influencer' term. The micro and nano categories are most relevant when looking at 'Islamic influencers', especially the sense of persuasion and projection of expertise that accompanies these online voices. The term 'Islamic influencer' is applied here in contemporary contexts to represent a (Muslim) individual or organization whose application of social media presents, propagates and markets religiously oriented content across diverse platforms and interests, whether subtle or overt, at times with a commercial edge to output. There are shades of influence here to incorporate multifaceted elements such as religious interpretation, propagation, authority, political understandings and cultural outlooks. It is recognized that the hierarchy and definition of Islamic influencers could be further broken down and categorized (beyond this book's remit).

As with other zones of CIEs over the years, the individual influencer may project a specific Islamic identity, ethos and expertise in their own terms through language, imagery and links to other content and may or may not be connected directly to a specific religious organization or interpretative framework in an 'official' capacity. There are issues of connectivity within local, regional and global contexts – where the impact of the local 'analogue' interfaces may also be significant adjuncts to notions of online identity – but may also be entirely separate, distinct and counter to local narratives and expectations of religious identity and knowledge. Influences (if not 'influencers') also include those figures from religious, historical and cultural pasts who have impacted Islamic understandings – and whose thoughts now resonate in cyberspace.

The choices of figures and networks discussed in this book represent a cross-section of influences and content available, with the recognition that there are many other critical figures across diverse cultural and religious contexts that could be discussed. The intention here is to demonstrate the different ways that online Islamic influences occur across multiple sectors. The figures selected are a sample snapshot of the multiple nodes of interpretation, authority, influence and religious knowledge available across CIEs. There is scope for deeper research on online influence in its multiple forms by teams of specialists, an activity currently under-represented in academic discourse. Capturing and analysing this contributes to the understanding of contemporary Islamic movements and influences, as well as the pulses of knowledge impacting individuals and communities.

Across the divides: Accessing CIEs

There are substantial differences in terms of internet access between and within Muslim population zones. While the focus of this work is *not* on the Middle

East and North Africa (MENA), forms of access can vary substantially between different nations: for example, according to a McKinsey survey, the United Arab Emirates had 204 mobile subscriptions per 100 people in 2022, compared with Egypt's sixty-nine mobile subscriptions; mobile subscriptions in UAE were three times that of Egypt. Their survey of Saudi Arabia, Egypt and UAE indicated that online consumption was predominantly mobile apps.[14] Growth in bandwidth use in 2021 increased in the Arab States compared with the Asia Pacific region.[15] However, there are disparities in access between zones with substantial Muslim populations: the MENA region had 46 per cent mobile internet connectivity in 2021; Sub-Saharan Africa had 22 per cent; South Asia had 41 per cent. This can be compared with North America (83 per cent) and Europe and Central Asia (78 per cent).[16]

Outside of the MENA region, other Muslim-majority zones have varying levels of internet access and usage: Indonesia, for example, had 204 million people (out of a 270 million population) classified as online in 2021. Mobile usage was a key factor, with an average in 2019 of eight and a half hours of daily internet use across the population; neighbouring Malaysia had an average of nine hours and ten minutes. UAE, Saudi Arabia, Egypt and Turkey also featured in the 'Top 20' of mobile usage.[17] There may also be disparities between Muslims in 'minority' contexts and wider populations, where factors such as access, digital literacy, poverty and socio-economic exclusion impact on forms of online access. However, factors such as age can also impact the disparity of access: for example, an analysis of Muslims in England and Wales based on the 2011 Census saw only 33 per cent of Muslims over sixty-five years of age used the internet, in comparison with 60 per cent of people aged over sixty-five who did not identify as Muslim.[18]

The continued digital divide is a crucial reference point within any discussions on CIEs, and while access levels and connectivity trends suggest global increases and improvements, these are not universal. Digital influence is in line with connectivity and of course, it should not be assumed that online users are focused on religious content. The complexity of content associated with religion is a small, significant component of much broader digital media consumption patterns in Muslim population zones.

CIE source code

Islamic Algorithms develops theoretical approaches presented in my other books, with some adaptations and updates below, but readers may also wish to consult these earlier volumes. This section provides an overview of significant works proven relevant to approaches towards studying the internet in general, religion and the internet, and Islam and the internet. These formative discussions and key works influenced my interdisciplinary and multidisciplinary approaches towards understanding and interpreting diverse forms of online Islam:

A critical starting point was Marshall McLuhan's (1911–80) analysis, which famously focused on 'the medium being the message'. His prescient discussions, especially in the pre-internet 1960s, determined how different media forms were impacting societies within the notion of a 'global village', while exploring audience responses and levels of participation across media forms from print to television.[19] McLuhan's approaches continue to resonate, stimulating the media studies field, while also being the subject of critiques recognizing his key works as inevitably dated products of the 1960s, with some methodological deficiencies.[20]

Diverse digital media have shaped the formulation of influences in CIEs across various formats and increasingly integrated to overarching media strategies. Approaches to this present book were impacted by Jean Baudrillard's (1927–2007) exploration of how 'hyperreality' and its impacts on postmodern perceptions of the world have implications in how we understand ideas about cyberspace, while Michel Foucault's (1926–84) work on knowledge construction is also pertinent in terms of its role in societal control. Roland Barthes' (1915–80) approach to the analysis of symbols is relevant within religious contexts, even though it predates digital contexts.[21]

In any discussion of media's impact on public opinion, Jürgen Habermas (1929–) is a reference point in exploring the public sphere, the information flow and media's shaping of public opinion. Habermas' studies focused on the seventeenth- and eighteenth-century European salon cultures and have been open to critiques associated with a perceived passive reception of media content. They remain a relevant touchstone in some cyber-Islamic contexts, especially when considering how information flows and how media institutions influence issues of opinion and control. Technology can have an impact when applied towards objectives, including developing understandings and perspectives within audiences. Habermas originally wrote in a pre-digital context, so subsequent dynamic changes in information access and availability challenge his notion of the public sphere. Concepts regarding passive consumption have adjusted with the interactivity of web media. These notions are relevant in the context of CIEs, where online content seeks to impact opinion and control but also opens the public sphere to new influences outside traditional interpretative frameworks.[22]

Howard Rheingold's (1947–) discussions on virtual communities and internet connectivity on the prototype Whole Earth 'Lectronic Link community of 1980s San Francisco also stimulated my early research on Islam and the internet. Viewed through the prism of our current digital connectivity, ideas contained within this period can seem somewhat idealistic and even quaint. Rheingold percipiently predicted potential harmful elements associated with computer-mediated communication. The internet's rapid shifts into a commercial entity had resonance within CIEs. Anyone who lived through the transition from the emergence of personal computers and the 28k dial-up modem to broadband, FTP to browser and deskbound to mobile computing will reflect on how rapid the shift felt. The culture accompanying it witnessed similar transitions in audience expectations and technological interfaces.

Challenges of an increasingly networked world were analysed by Manuel Castells (1942–) especially the influence of political and commercial interests on network infrastructures and the exclusion of individuals from communication opportunities. Such control can be at a state level, through censorship and filtering.

Still, it can equally result from cultural restrictions on internet usage, even in an age of increased digital literacy and networking access. Internet access restrictions continue for individuals and communities within and between CIEs.[23]

There is relevance in focusing on specific studies associated with media, religion and the internet. These chart significant developments over time, so that older volumes can – in some cases – effectively become historical snapshots capturing activities and perspectives from formative periods. Approaching this field has required the development of specific methodological approaches, which continue to evolve in line with research forms and technological shifts. Examples include works by Stewart M. Hoover and Lynn Schofield Clark (together and separately), which engaged in significant methodological concerns associated with studies of religions and media. This includes analysis of the impact of radio and television broadcasts in disseminating religious content and how messages shifted in line with media requirements (the media shaping the message).[24]

Studying religions on the internet

In the late 1990s, towards the mid-2000s, an increasing number of academic works emerged relating specifically to religion and the internet, intersecting with my own research. The academic field opened up with these contributions and conversations: Jeffrey K. Hadden and Douglas E. Cowan's edited publication in 2000 brought together approaches to the subject area, including cutting-edge theoretical material and contributions from early theorists in this developing field. Significant edited collections of associated studies further refined methods and approaches.[25] Greater granulation of content appeared within the variety of studies that contribute to understanding religion and the internet, including guides to online resources associated with religions and cyberspace.[26]

There have been multiple shifts in methodological approaches towards multidisciplinary studies of digital religions, which draw on diverse methods in order to map the fields and provide analytical platforms, utilizing different technological approaches.[27] The University of Heidelberg introduced the *Journal of Religions on the Internet* in 2005, featuring significant works by scholars on different religious perspectives which contributed to methodological approaches. Detailed studies of specific religions and the diversity of sacred (and other) online phenomena included Heidi Campbell's study of Christian communities online, Christopher Helland's studies of Buddhism and Douglas Cowan's analysis of cyber-paganism. Campbell continued extensive work in the field with a blend of online and print publications, including work focused on responses to Covid-19. The *Journal of Religion, Media and Digital* published widely on religions and their digital manifestations.[28] The utilization of multiple platforms for presenting religious content has been explored through theories of 'hypermediation' of religion, emphasizing the speed of religious processes and practices.[29]

Ruth Tsuria and Heidi Campbell's 2022 edited volume on digital religion unpacked digital religion in terms of significant themes of religion, ritual, identity, community, authority and embodiment – all of which being relevant to this present book. The extending sophistication and granularity of studies associated with digital religion in general mark a shift away from earlier 'pioneer' efforts at seeking to respond to the dramatic new electronic frontiers presented by the internet from the mid-1990s onwards. The studies of digital religion have evolved and shifted, partially in line with technological changes, but also in relation to different disciplinary and interdisciplinary approaches and focal points. Campbell notes that 'Although the subject of digital religion can and should be studied through different disciplinary lenses, it also requires a "space" of its own.'[30] This is a significant point in relation to digital religion in general, but – of course – it can also be further compartmentalized into the studies on digital Islam, in which this book seeks to make a contribution.

Interpreting digital Islam and Muslims

This section looks at the specific disciplinary and methodological variations concerning the study of digital Islam and Muslims, which have had an impact on my own work. I have been fortunate to meet and collaborate with several of the following people at conferences or through publication projects who have been involved during this formative period of the study of digital Islam. They provide evidence of diverse methodological approaches, often with an emphasis on recording and analysing online activities, and exploring the impact of the internet across Muslim contexts:

Key to this development was the work of Jon Anderson, who presented formative perspectives in the construction of paradigms associated with diverse aspects of Muslim activities, specifically in the Middle East. This included approaches towards the significant early developments on the Internet of Muslim actors and an analysis of the diffuse associated communication patterns of access, interpretation and curation of online content. Anderson explored how pioneering developments in public spheres implemented ideas of religious authority, circumnavigating some of them (at the time) more mainstream voices and institutions.[31]

Specialists in the study of Islam have contributed to the field, reflecting diverse disciplinary perspectives and interests, and cross-fertilizing the field of digital Islam with extensive disciplinary experience across Islamic studies. Bruce B. Lawrence's reflections on the significance of his own identity in its impact on his research echo my own. As an academic who is not Muslim but has studied Islam for over thirty-five years, from a 'white British' middle-class background working in the relatively privileged context of a university in west Wales, clearly, these factors inform my approaches to the subject area.[32] Lawrence's approaches towards Islamic civilizations (as cultures over space and time) and cosmopolitanism are particularly relevant to exploring Islam and cyberspace. There is an emphasis on the relevance of studying interconnectivity at both global and local levels (and points in between), where identities and concerns are 'messy' rather than clear-cut binaries; simple dichotomies of 'traditional' and 'modern' do not apply.

The need for empathetic imagination and critical scrutiny is appropriate when unpacking CIEs, which are open to analysis by 'insiders' and 'outsiders' (perhaps simplistic descriptors for more complex identities).[33] The de-centring of studying Islam and Muslims away from focusing on the MENA region, which has been a feature of some of Lawrence's own output, is also relevant to my approach.[34] Lawrence's reflections on the impact of the internet on diverse aspects of Islamic understanding include discussion on aspects of Sufi understanding and reflections on Allāh through ninety-nine names and the pronoun *hu* or *huwa*.[35] The work of Lawrence and cooke (together and separately) demonstrates a conscious academic approach towards the internet's impact on forms of Muslim discourse, recognizing its continuity with pre-existing histories and networks, which may be mirrored in cyberspace while new forms of identities and authority emerge within digital construct.[36] In an Afterword echoing the themes of cooke and Lawrence's 2005 *Muslim Networks* edited volume, Taieb Belghazi noted that: 'Muslim identities are not fixed along clearly demarcated lines that disallow negotiations, ambivalence, hybridity and vernacular cosmopolitanisms. Muslims try to reinvent and reinterpret their traditions and their communities through the adoption of network technologies, even when the modernity that promotes these technologies is made the object of attack.'[37]

Notions of cosmopolitanism are associated with the fluid and messy notions of identities across religions, cultures, knowledge and languages. Lawrence has theorized on and reframed ideas of the term 'Islamicate Cosmopolitan', reflecting on Marshall Hodgson's formative work. Lawrence has explored this in wider discussions about 'Islamicate' and 'Persianate' elements, and the construction of multiple historical global networks which transcend binary and essentialized understandings of Islamic beliefs and perspectives while incorporating 'hybrid traces' of Islam and synergy with 'non-Muslim' factors. In a discussion on religious labels and their utility (or a need for re-evaluation) Lawrence draws on the following definition of 'Islamicate' (influenced by Hodgson): 'it draws on Muslim/Islamic antecedents but out of an expansive reservoir of human experience and expression that exceeds religion. It is not secular but centripetal, always attracting a mixture of elements that are both religious and cultural'.[38] This factor can be seen in aspects of cyber-Islamic discourse and has a bearing on future constructs of Muslim metaverses. Digital Islam constructs challenge uniform perceptions of Islam and Muslims by reflecting (for those who wish to explore them) the complex and myriad networks and ideas of Islam and Muslims. This is particularly important when looking at ideas of 'influence' and 'influencers', in terms of their articulation of knowledge, authority and (in some cases) power. Traditional labels such as 'Islamic' and 'Muslim' are utilized in this book for reasons of clarity, with an awareness that they can be open to scrutiny and have associated complexities.

This sense of continuity between and within identities and networks is significant when considering contemporary understandings of Islam, Muslims and the internet. They are tacked in various ways in multiple other works, which should also be acknowledged in their valuable approaches towards different aspects of CIEs, showing complex, refined and imaginative methods of capturing and interpreting digital Islam. Many critical studies emerged on the interactions between the media, Muslims and society, which identified the internet as a significant channel for diverse forms of Muslim communication, integrated into other forms of dialogue and interaction.[39] Studies on the media, including the internet, explore their impact on the Middle East.[40] Some scholars applied fieldwork to interpret notions of political liberalization in Arabic-speaking contexts and their relationship with online content.[41] This has included the use of social media by diverse religious authority figures competing with each other across political, ideological and religious divides – while it also became a significant channel for accessing worldviews for observers, researchers and commentators.[42]

Work on religion and spirituality in networking includes analysing how anonymity has been applied for Islamic purposes.[43] There has been a detailed analysis of the formation of fatwas and counselling advice on the (then) prominent Islamic website Islam Online during the 2000s, which also provides an invaluable snapshot of its activities and approaches during this significant period of digital developments.[44] The journal *CyberOrient* is a consistent channel for papers discussing aspects of digital activities associated with Islamic contexts.[45] These works are important in representing the multidisciplinary and interdisciplinary nature of work associated with digital Islam, which of necessity employ diverse skills and methodological approaches in gathering and interpreting a range of content. While operating in the intersection between the study of religion and the study of Islam (themselves complex and multidisciplinary), this book seeks to draw in other relevant disciplinary approaches in formulating an understanding of CIEs.

The range of research on Islam and the internet encompasses surprisingly diverse subject areas: a study of Islamic emoticons goes beyond traditional scholarship of Islam, in showing how the digital Muslim symbols impact on computer-mediated human interaction.[46] The celebration of the Prophet Muḥammad's *mawlid* (birthday) is not a universally accepted practice but is one where online activities provide one marker towards participation in (or opposition to) associated ritual practices.[47] The role of mystical expression (under the 'Sufi' banner) and its articulation online has also formed part of research projects.[48] These are important outlets for personal and collective religious expression, which have a basis in historical, cultural and religious influences. Many are represented online, particularly relevant for dispersed communities or those operating in contexts where these practices are discouraged or forbidden. This adds impact to some of the influences and influencers discussed in this book who reach out to those whose mediation of their religious identities may be proscribed.

There have been several studies on internet impact embedded into wider studies on practice and ritual. Studies of specific applications offer a granulation and focal point for developing knowledge of CIEs, especially in ritual moments in the sacred Islamic calendar.[49] This includes publications by Sophia Rose Arjuna on the computer-mediated Ḥajj and the marketing approaches towards forms of spirituality (which can spill over into online contexts). The emergence of entrepreneurial CIE elements shows the development of apps facilitating prayer,

Islamic finance and marriage.[50] Robert Rozehnal focused on a specific sector of digital activities associated with mystical Sufi practices in a granulated study which could act as a template for similar studies on specific strands of religious understanding.[51] Wendy Bellar studied the ways in which ritual practices had the potential to be impacted by app use, given the increasing prevalence of such content on mobile devices.[52]

Research has also developed focused on specific personalities online: Nabil Echchaibi explored media forms impacted on focal points of religious authority, shifting from analogue to digital, with an attendant emphasis on new 'celebrity' religious figures.[53] Sana Patel surveyed significant ideas associated with the mediation of religious authority and focused on authenticity issues for audiences. In fieldwork in Canada, she noted that CIE users are nuanced and discerning in their consumption of Islamic online media. 'Celebrity imams' (effectively 'influencers') can have a role in validating authenticity – but may be challenged by audiences in terms of the legitimacy of their message. Patel explores how the dynamics towards religious authority have changed in line with online influencers, whose impact is directly linked to social media activity, in turn generating substantial audiences for their 'in-person' activities.[54] The influence of structures built up around religious personalities go beyond the studios and desktops of their organizations and teams, impacting grassroots activities and understandings of Islam, with asynchronous impact as well as simultaneous synchronous resonance. Yvonne Howard-Bunt interprets this as a 'pendulum' between on- and offline, real and digital impact.[55]

Granulated studies on aspects of digital religious practices and their impact are produced in international contexts. For example, Indonesian academia took this up as a significant driver and challenge, with numerous papers on aspects of online Islam produced, reflecting Indonesian state interest and high levels of digital interconnectivity in urban contexts.[56] A 2019 conference brought many Indonesian scholars together to discuss the impact of digital technologies on religion and society, endorsed by the presence of the Minister of Religious Affairs.[57] The detailed attention being paid to online Islamic activities in the most populous Muslim-dominated nation is extremely relevant, not only for informing and influencing national discourses about religious issues but as a way of soft-power regional projection into regional and global contexts. The focus on micro-issues in Indonesian CIEs by academics is being utilized to develop comprehensive and regulated state-informed approaches towards religious practice and identities, countering perspectives which emerge outside of the specific structures of Muslim understandings in Indonesia. The complexity of this discourse is approached within this book.

Studies have focused on specific regions in terms of approaches to CIEs: journalist Hussein Kesvani delved into the British Muslim experience, utilizing online activity as a measure of exploring identities across diverse contexts.[58] Sadek Hamid surveyed aspects of the internet's impact on religious-political movements in the UK.[59] Ibrahim Abusharif examined religious authority through the matrix of Salafi-Sufi contestation, particularly in the UK, drawing on digital media utilization for analytical discussion, especially relating to differences in ideals of religious practice.[60] A study by Shaheen Whyte looked at religious authority in the context of Muslims in Australia, determining how key figures utilize digital platforms to project religious knowledge and influence, drawing on fieldwork and a survey to establish findings.[61] Muslims in the minority context of Korea were analysed by Farrah Sheikh, with a focus on converts and their applications of the internet and social media as a means of developing identities, networks and conversations in the face of anti-Muslim prejudice and misunderstandings.[62] It is important to acknowledge these and other works which offer specific focal points on aspects of CIEs while recognizing that it is also relevant to 'connect the dots' between and within broader Islamic frameworks. The relationships micro-contexts have with the digital influences discussed in this book can demonstrate their relevance and impact, which through CIEs offers potential wider audiences for traditional and other Islamic understandings packages in websites, apps, social media and iterations of understandings informed by algorithms – such as AI and metaverse constructs.

Significant research projects associated with Islam and the internet contributed to the discourse on key issues. The *Canadian Muslims Online* project drew on scholars from across Canada to explore Muslim identities in digital frameworks, discussing religious authority and inter-religious/intrafaith issues.[63] In Western Europe, the *Mediating Islam in the Digital Age* multi-institutional project focused on developing research in studying Islam and Muslims on the internet through a substantial training programme.[64] In 2022, as principal investigator on the *Digital British Islam* project, I commenced collaboration with academic partners to develop an understanding of the complexities of Muslim online use in the UK, including archiving, interviews, a survey and interactions with Muslim communities and individuals – in an initiative to develop a fuller understanding of the complexities of CIEs in UK contexts.[65] I also contributed as co-investigator for the *Digital Islam Across Europe* project, working with international partners on digital issues specific to different European Muslim communities.[66]

Some religious institutions started developing their responses to Islam and cyberspace, notably the Iranian Office of Islamic Studies in Cyberspace, founded in 2018 in Qom.[67] This is significant in providing a dedicated 'insider' perspective from the governmental position in the Islamic Republic of Iran. Their activities include seminars, publications, analysis and social media in Farsi, Arabic and English. The Shīʿa context became an area of specific academic exploration, including how technologies influenced religious leadership.[68] Some of that discourse is represented in this book, which seeks to counter 'Sunni-dominant' themes that predominate many conversations about contemporary Islam, which have a bearing on the framing of Islam and Muslims across digital constructs.

Gender issues demonstrate multiple themes, including how gender-specific approaches impact on interpretation issues and *ijtihād* within online discussions.[69] While I have investigated aspects of gender and Islam, I am convinced that this was a subject best left to female researchers (Muslim and others) who have created extensive and essential work in this still under-represented field. Anna Piela's comprehensive study of women and the internet explored methodological considerations and specific issues as they manifested themselves online, while her later work on the 'digital niqabosphere' explored how niqab-wearing women used different online platforms to explore identities and lifestyles and exchange their experiences with others – including of 'conversion' to Islam.[70] Through social media, Muslim women develop relationships very different to the analogue world.[71] Eva Nisa unpacked this in an online discussion of the roles of Indonesian female scholars and religious authority during the Covid-19 pandemic.[72] Nisa also looked at the relationship between online activism and gender issues across diverse religious perspectives, suggesting the continuity of a 'gendered' internet.[73]

The Muzmatch app and its impacts on religious identity were addressed by Farah Hasan, drawing on ethnographic research.[74] Ruqaiyyah Pramiyanti and Alila Kauser's research separately explored hijab representation on Instagram.[75] Gender underpins so much of online discourse, especially in themes associated with influence and influencers in CIEs, which is especially important in countering prevalent stereotypes and assumptions about Muslim women (generated inside and outside of Islamic frameworks), where the complex affiliations, identities and religious understandings are articulated in positive narratives for multiple audiences. This book explores these themes to a degree in sections on particular influences, alongside contemporary influential conversations on gender issues in CIEs.

Rozehnal's edited book *Cyber Muslims* investigated diverse academic approaches to Islam, Muslims and the internet. This includes interdisciplinary work on religious authority, identities, rituals and authenticity in cyber-Islamic contexts, focusing on gender concerns.[76] Specific consideration was given to the diversity of identities and approaches towards cyber-Islamic environments, from young Muslims and Sufi shaykhs to Latinx Muslims – demonstrating new frontiers and potential areas for research. There was also an assessment of specific media forms, including religious apps and platforms such as Instagram.[77] Rozehnal makes important points about the different ways in which academic approaches shift across diverse disciplinary perspectives when looking at online Islamic activities, emphasizing an increasing granularity which has resonance with Tsuria and Campbell's discussion about developments in wider fields of the study of digital religion.[78] Diversity of identities is particularly important to recognize, rather than uniformity across time, location and history: CIEs reflect this messy complexity, and through my discussion of the diversity of influences informing online expression (and algorithms) it is intended that this book provides further emphasis on the granularity of Islam and Muslims, countering reductive stereotyping.

Despite these many studies and publications, readers must avoid assumptions that the internet is impactful in every context and take care with implied efficacy and impact.[79] Political-religious elements relating to online activities hold significance in complex shifting contemporary Muslim contexts. Numerous studies seek to increase understanding of the real-world impact of online activities, reflecting ongoing and intensive fieldwork, together with regional specialisms.[80] In zones with high-tech connectivity levels, the dynamics impacting change in the Arabic world are substantial.[81] Internet change agents influenced Muslim political contexts and social movements such as the so-called 'Arab Spring', which became a focus of analysis on relationships between social media technologies and revolutionary movements.[82] Specific regional studies emerged which contributed to the understanding of different aspects of cyberactivism in the winter after the 'Arab Spring', such as the protests in Bahrain analysed by Nada Alwadi and Sahar Khamis.[83] This interest has intensified, where political discussions appear online in real time, and protests (which may have a religious element) are live-streamed. Islam is not just an Arab issue, so research in this field must represent the international diversity of religious expression and understanding.[84] This book acknowledges the significance of digital developments in the MENA regions, recognizes the ambiguity of the term 'Middle East' and seeks to ensure that populations and developments outside of MENA are fully represented. In particular, the voices and developments associated with Muslims in minority contexts are important to these influence equations, in the ways they reach out to broader Muslim networks and influences, while also generating their own impact through online discourse that might increase their representation and impact across diverse global contexts.

The fields of study associated with the study of CIEs continue to shift, with increases in granulated studies from across different disciplinary areas contributing to our understanding of networks, discourse, authority and the real-world impact of digital Islamic expression. As technologies continue to develop and shift (through every update of your mobile device!), this represents a challenge to our understanding that this book seeks to address. Methodologies also shift to respond to these changes, especially in capturing the discourse and the everyday information flows that inform discussions – but may seem ephemeral to their creators. There's no permanent record of the internet in its entirety, although the Internet Archive and some national archives have attempted to capture online discourse. Any 'relics' may be lost on servers for future generations, fragmented, erased or difficult to access. The sheet quantity of the information flow also makes recording and analysing a challenge, particularly when it is being put down in printed form. In order to keep up with developments in CIEs, methodological innovation must combine with technological investment and academic training to ensure that the complexities of CIEs are captured for analysis, from metadata to the metaverse, and that the tools exist for comprehensive interpretation from diverse perspectives in the fields. The continued work of scholars discussed in this section offers a way forward to the development of sustainable and granulated approaches towards the study of CIEs.

E-jihād zones and CIEs

The focus of Islam and the internet is often disproportionately placed on aspects of militaristic jihād, ignoring key drivers of religious practice, identity and authority – including the roles of influencers in CIEs. Militaristic jihād-oriented online discourse (electronic jihād or e-jihād, in its multifarious forms) proportionally distorted the CIE field for some observers, a small component in a much more substantial and varied set of online networks, affiliations and voices associated with articulating Muslim identities and knowledge. Clearly it is necessary to acknowledge its online impact, without distorting the influence or conflating it necessarily with other zones of Islamic digital activities. My tendency has been to compartmentalize militaristic jihād in my writing, as a small component in a much larger picture. There is substantial specialism on jihād in general, which increasingly incorporates the online components of its impact.

In observing and monitoring constant shifts in CIEs, often about specific concerns and issues which emerged since the late 1990s, awareness developed of the increasingly innovative and digitally literate applications being utilized by digital natives. It was embedded in content from platforms and organizations – alongside individuals and groups who established their own novel outlets online. The separation between online and offline became increasingly anachronistic, with mobile devices coupled with enhanced digital literacy and access making the internet a natural zone for elements of Muslims' lives. This was particularly obvious when looking at e-jihād and its presentation by diverse advocates, radicalizing influences and supporters. This ranges from individuals using their smartphones 'in the field' to those armchair e-jihād advocates generating supportive memes and online content thousands of miles from the front lines, whose motivations could be complex and diverse.

Investigations on jihād-oriented online activities have tracked numerous movements and platforms.[85] Valuable materials focused on specific contexts and regions, with a subtext of how the internet informed and stimulated e-jihād developments. This includes analysis specific to conflicts within specific regions.[86] This work is discussed in the relevant chapter below.

Configuring personal approaches to CIEs

Given thirty years of observing different iterations of online Islamic content, inevitably methods and tactics towards materials have shifted over time, from casual early interest through to more precise and focused readings. My approach has been grounded in chronicling and mapping key online developments in cyber-Islamic environments, including discussion on UK Muslim activities online before the 2000 publication of *Virtually Islamic*.[87] I'd been looking at materials from Bulletin Board Systems and Chat Rooms from the early 1990s, following channels which articulated diverse interpretations of Islam (usually in English) for group members. I was working on my PhD about (pre-digital) Islamic religious authority at the time, so became naturally interested in the developing voices emerging on the internet. These were augmenting and/or challenging existing authority media structures associated with print media, audio (especially radio and cassette content) and analogue and satellite television programmes. It was a natural transition to start a more systemized approach towards information capture as I recognized its increasing significance, especially when students started citing materials derived from internet sources.[88]

I archived content on floppy disks and (in less environmentally conscious days) by printing it out and filling numerous filing boxes with online materials. At the same time, I had been coding and developing websites since the mid-1990s, building partly on computer experience from a pre-academic media career. One driver was the ambition to capture and analyse the phenomena associated with cyber-Islamic activities, which were constantly shifting, mutating and disappearing. *Virtually Islamic* surveyed significant online activities in what now looks more like a history of Muslim cyberspace during that period. It provided an opportunity to frame this material, primarily through a study of religions approach (reflecting my academic background) and focusing on the phenomena associated with CIEs. There was a sharp personal learning curve in terms of developing systems for categorization and preservation of data, especially when materials would appear and disappear with regularity online.

Time has moved on in terms of exponential technological developments, matched by a content delivery curve in which competing voices took advantage of the new technologies to mark their presence on the internet. With this, my methodological approaches have (hopefully) evolved through personal activities and the practices of others in related fields. This approach includes different ways of chronicling, capturing and analysing data, which I continue to learn about and develop, especially in content analysis and data visualization (part of future projects). I seek to describe CIEs through specific examples across diversity of expression, focused in part on key influential figures and factors through overviews and case studies. A particular interest is the nature of online religious authorities and their impact across the complexities of online environments which have adapted and mutated over time in line with technological developments.

This research included snapshots of specific periods and phases, from the emergence of Islam on the internet onward. The formative phase was covered by *Virtually Islamic*, post-9/11 contexts explored in *Islam in the Digital Age*, the emergence of forms of social media ('Web 2.0') and their implications features in *iMuslims* and increased Islamic digital activities across multiple platforms featured in *Hashtag Islam*. I focused on specific themes in individual chapters in edited books, such as explorations of the digital Qurʾān, online sacred space and cyber religious authority. Approaches to methodological concerns have developed, including recording and observing online materials. One consistent element has been grounding the work in the intersected zone(s) of religious and Islamic studies. These works reflect changes in technology and interface dynamics, which have shifted substantially from the early days of discussing CIEs.[89]

The approach includes daily monitoring of online developments impacting Muslim contexts, focusing on significant digital channels across social media and the web. When a specific story or theme 'breaks', a detailed capture of content is undertaken, with pages archived and stored for further use. My blogs and social media often make a basic record of these developments, and at times these can develop into specific subsets of pages and links online, in line with awareness that content frequently disappears or updates.[90] It is not possible to capture everything (!) given that this is an individual effort (part of a working day), but it is possible to generate a sense of developments and trends which can be further built upon in later research (with the benefit of hindsight).

The influences selected for *Islamic Algorithms* represent key figures that have made an impact in Muslim histories, cultures, societies and religious developments – while recognizing that these are a snapshot of much broader and more complex networks and influences. The issue of representing these influences was deemed significant, as they inform much of contemporary Muslim discourse, and consequently their digital representation impacts on how Islam and Muslim societies are represented online – especially when content is being scraped and repurposed by AI programs and apps such as ChatGPT. The shape of future iMuslim discourse can be impacted by internet searches through such apps answering questions about multiple aspects of Islam, even though the veracity of this information may be filtered and subject to other influences, such as malign online content and disinformation. External perceptions and readings of Islam are also subject to these influences, which will inform the algorithms underpinning the internet, including projected metaverse constructs.

Approaching religious authorities

The projection of Islamic authority requires time and resources, particularly if an individual or group seeks to develop interactive and responsive digital spaces where affiliations and memberships can be engineered and maintained. Many CIEs fell by the wayside over the years, with their megabytes of opinions, knowledge and information deleted or fragmented. The online marketplace for ideas stretches into micro-areas and back channels of discourse and interpretation. As with other sectors of the internet, the 'long tail' of micro-demand enables the location of highly specialized perspectives and 'products'; this includes networks of individuals sharing a specific set of interpretative values which they may not be able to express in their local, analogue context.[91] At the most basic level, this can include allegiance to a prohibited political-religious perspective or online observance of religious practices and rituals that are not permitted or encouraged in local mosques.

Digital material seeks to attract attention immediately before an individual swipe through to other content. Attention spans in digital spaces waver, especially with contesting distractions available for consumers when messaging alerts and pop-ups interfere with content consumption (including during the research for this book!). Marketing is key. Affiliation and continuity with pre-digital Muslim networks and interests can be a significant drawing factor, albeit in a reframing of knowledge and identity in a digital context. There is a maintenance of themes too. Advocates of diverse religious perspectives have recognized these factors. The spectrum of authority, from *jihād*-oriented content to Sufi ritual performance, relies on non-static, dynamic content conscious of the different online consumption patterns, interfaces and influences in the contested marketplace. 'Influencers' have roles to play, attracting and maintaining loyal audiences and followers across platforms through regularly updated content.

These updates can be in multiple forms and have continuity with pre-digital contexts. Definitions and approaches towards religious authority can vary, with differing hierarchical and linear models seeking to encompass diversities of approaches (which are explored later in this book). Within a Sunni 'orthodox' context, the notion of religious authority values being transmitted from generation to generation through chains of scholarship has been an important one. This relates to the preservation of knowledge and concepts associated with *ijtihād*, which represents 'exerting oneself to the utmost degree to understand *sharīʿa* through disciplined judgement', *sharīʿa* being seen as divine law as articulated in the Qurʾān and interpreted by human beings to contribute to Islamic law or jurisprudence (*fiqh*).[92] The term *ijtihād* has been defined and applied in many ways, with complex differences in definition, which frequently emerge on the internet. This includes the production of *fatāwā* or legal opinions based on religious grounds under the authority of religious scholars who may be representing specific organizations, governments or platforms.[93]

This continuity of transmitted knowledge and opinions acquired substantial impetus when information could be shared not just through face-to-face communication but also, first, through emergence of printing and then the development of other forms of media. The arrival of the internet impacted the levels of networking and dissemination of religious influences within a contested Islamic knowledge marketplace, especially in terms of immediacy and sharing. The multiple distribution patterns of *fatāwā* were discussed in different contexts and timeframes by Muhammad Khalid Masud, Brinkley Messick and David Powers in *Islamic Legal Interpretation*, demonstrating the diverse approaches to the phenomena and their articulation across media – although its publication in the mid-1990s predated the mass impact of the internet as a dissemination tool.[94]

Diverse factors have impacted the distribution system of influence, *fatāwā* and religious authority, including historical patterns of political-religious leadership and guidance. Several factors contributed to the development of specific movements and notions of 'reform' in this context, whose story now incorporates digital interfaces. While it is impossible to generalize, some factors suggest a commonality. These can include responses towards the imposition of 'alien' ways of life, in which religious answers are sought to societal changes – related to shifting political-religious systems, population shifts, economics, identity crises, or the 'shock of the new'. Max Weber (1864–1920) saw a relationship between religion and economic activity, especially in a world becoming more secularized.[95] Over time, the wealth of some sectors has driven and accelerated digital developments, especially in perceptions of global religious authority emanating from nations such as Iran and Saudi Arabia.

When societies respond to specific pressures (at local, regional and global levels), these may necessitate the development of new affiliations, forms of social support and responses drawing on religious rhetoric. These elements occur in a digital context. In Islam, political-religious influence is associated (by commentators and participants) with factors such as nationalism, religious symbols, religious activities, modern values and secularism. These can feed into notions of authority and identity, with contemporary digital frameworks referencing historical patterns and influences. Movements provide comprehensive alternative structures, utilizing religious language and political ideology, which can also play out online. Influence and leadership, in the context of Islam, have often been charismatic, male and authoritarian. These factors can also play out in CIEs, where there is scope for more female voices, including scholars, authorities and other forms of religious influence.

The rhetoric draws upon religious language, ideals and an interpretation of belief systems (idealized, suiting an objective). Movements link to regional concerns, nationalism, or universally identified with 'religion' (or an interpretation of religion). The language evokes God and Prophet(s) within a supportive framework. Intermediaries are required to approach all powerful deities, which Ernest Gellner (1925–95) described as 'a hierarchical, specialised class of religious personnel'.[96] These religious personnel now have an online representation, with gatekeepers, site developers and content creators interlocked with the output of influences (past and present) and in some cases 'influencers' in a projection of iMuslims in CIEs.

Muḥammad and CIEs

Notions of influence and authority in Islam – digital or analogue – lead back to a single source: the Prophet Muḥammad. The paradigm includes the idealized qualities of Muḥammad as a pragmatic leader, especially his decision-making based on contextual Divine Revelation (Qurʾān) and the example of sayings and actions. This formative period in Islam's development presents a model in which all facets of life are to be encompassed by Islamic practices and principles (ultimately), especially those established within Medinan society after the Hijrah. The Hijrah ('migration') marks Muḥammad's journey to Yathrib in 622 CE and the establishment of a proto-Muslim community in the city – subsequently renamed Medina. This community was small and (according to tradition) open to Muḥammad's introduction of practices to loyal followers despite warfare and external resistance. Critical to this transition was the notion of Arab identity, language and culture, focusing on an extraordinary individual.

Following Muḥammad's death in 632 CE, Muslim societies inevitably divided, especially as Islam expanded into different environments where expectations and cultural practices differed. The shift away from the desert-urban society of the Arabian Peninsula towards Syria and Egypt, for example, encompasses the integration of other cultures, languages and traditions drawn into an 'Islamic' or 'Muslim' identity (however tokenistic or practical for individuals and communities). Practices established in Medina, often based on pre-existing principles, could not necessarily easily be exported successfully to Syria, Egypt or other locations further afield. What is suggested is the pragmatic aspect of Islam and the adaptability of religious-political systems (while following the 'roots' of religion), resulting in variations in interpretation, legal differences and diversity of practice.

Critics suggest the past can be (re-)interpreted, and the 'mythologisation' of history can be difficult to reconcile with the present realities. They indicate that

– while the Qur'ān remains unchanged in substance and content – fabrication and manipulation of interpretation, and scholarship associated with the strategic adjustment of the discourse (whether deliberate or not), make an impact.[97] Rather than a singularity, there are multiple interpretative approaches towards the Qur'ān, reflecting complex and diverse religious, historical, linguistic, cultural, intellectual and/or philosophical approaches and influences, which play out online.[98] The Qur'ān has become a digital phenomenon in which silicon sūras (*suwar*) and *āya* apps flow between and within CIEs. Ideals of social unity can be reconciled to 'utopian' ideologies and the need to distinguish between romantic political arguments and specific programmes of action.[99] This recalibration is part of cyber-Islamic discourse, as will be seen across diverse sectors of Muslim understandings online. It forms part of a discussion on how religious authority has projected itself online while referencing traditional practices and notions of the sacred. New forms of a 'public sphere' relating to Islam have evolved.[100] Within contemporary contexts, this has facilitated increased levels of 'shopping around' for religious opinions in some contexts, where digital platforms and accessibility can be facilitated, often mediated by algorithms and other forms of online influence.[101]

Religious influence online

Influence is built and developed across and within categories of interpretation, context, origins and historical patterns – from the emergence of the Qur'ān through to Islamic expansion in space and time. The power dynamics of CIEs incorporate specific influences and ideas explored in this book. Religious authority and influence take diverse forms. Some underlying archetypal patterns can relate to context and combinations of other factors and influences – traditional, historical, cultural, genealogical, linguistic, interpretative and, in contemporary contexts, technological.

Digitalization has influenced the spread of religious knowledge and information, especially through enhanced text searchability. Algorithms have always maintained an influence. Key terms could be located through different search forms, extending from general search engines such as Google to text-specific and e-book searches. Searchability enables the isolation of particular terms and concepts and their rapid identification. The price of those using digital sources in a rapid fashion may be that they do not acquire the more profound knowledge of their complexity and depth that might be acquired through the use of 'analogue' texts. Through algorithms underpinning search engines, the ability to seek a religious opinion, scrape specific data and then copy and paste it has seen some 'opinions' promulgated out of context and rapidly distributed through social media. Different search engines extend the options and searchable opportunities through multiple interfaces and different search parameters, including 'deep search' and archive search options. The search for content has gone beyond Google: ByteDance's TikTok search algorithm became dominant within 'Generation Z' markets, stressing its immediacy and precision in directing users to specific content.[102] However, Google maintains overall influence across search globally (beyond the TikTok app) through its range of products and services.[103]

The enablement of armchair scholars is not a new phenomenon. It has mutated into keyboard scholars and digital authorities with varying levels (and in some cases degrees) of knowledge and experience. The diversity of religious opinions is not necessarily a negative one. Still, it does challenge and, in some way, supersede some of the long-standing traditions associated with knowledge acquisition and religious authority. Algorithms can be unreliable. When watching Egyptian devotional music from al-Azhar, and being enraptured by its spirituality, my numinous moment was lost by the sudden intervention of a right-wing politician advertising financial products. The transcendent moment shattered, leading me to reflect instead on the vagaries of algorithms.[104]

If an individual is not required to complete a specific degree, study for an *ijaza* (proof of learning with a specific scholar) or undertake training before they can go online to present their religious ideas, that can be an attractive proposition for some. This can be coupled with incorporating high levels of web literacy and the knowledge to design pages, site architecture and social media sites to aid navigation and attract traffic and clickthrough. Their embedding of content into systems can impact deep learning about Islam, with the potential for human error (as with all input). The human programming methodology may require uncritical cut-and-paste from other sites and forums with inherent issues of disinformation, bias and lack of objectivity.

The absence of critical response or reasoning into the equations and their application in algorithms might directly impact and create bias in the system, which no amount of processing power can challenge once embedded into and transmitted across deep learning systems. They become part of search parameters and results. Integrating new notions of religious understanding and knowledge approaches into systems opens opportunities for creativity and societal development, especially when responding to unprecedented situations or issues. This response is on YouTube and other channels such as Snapchat and TikTok. This is a means to open approaches away from the status quo and the perceived moribund nature of religious authorities. It is a way of subverting tradition and presenting ideas unfiltered by barriers associated with the layers of generational transmission, which have not necessarily reflected on contemporary issues or dealt with specific issues of modernity.

There are discussions exploring the pros and cons of machine learning and AI as part of Islamic decision-making contexts, with advocates reflecting dystopian and utopian perspectives (and points in between).[105] Over the years, many of these issues have ended up being discussed online, where digital native utopians have been challenged by the establishment with less technically inclined dystopian visions. The period surrounding the emergence of widespread internet usage saw a particular focus on this. At the same time, the perceived intrusion of digital devices into everyday religious life has suggested a challenge to 'traditional' Islamic values. The embedding of the articulation of these values within digital devices has countered some of these arguments.

The most challenging questions of the age can require some form of religious response. This phenomenon predates the internet. Print newspaper columns, for example, answered readers' religious questions in many Muslim contexts. Many of these columns ultimately made it online. In the 1990s, I noted that scholars generally were increasingly utilizing fax machines and tentative online fora to disseminate and discuss religious opinions and ideas. The internet (capitalized at the time as an entity) amplified the process, in a rise of religious authority content transcending different internet media. Over time, adopting the latest forms of worldwide web-based technologies in line with technological advancement has seen authorities and individuals presenting their religious opinions in multimedia formats, shaping the reduced digital divide with increased technology access.

When exploring notions of Islamic influences in digital contexts, one must also reflect on the diverse networks associated with Shīʿīsm, where authority frameworks can differ substantially between them within different contexts. They do share specific significant figures emerging out of the Prophet's family, many of which have a particular representation. The line of imams represents idealized religious authority. Many of these figures and their families are represented online, with content focusing on their various pilgrimage sites and shrines. These form independent but influential sets of hubs from which religious authority can emanate and whose supporters often (in contemporary contexts) promote through the application of digital spaces. Some Shīʿa networks are proactive, especially those international in scope where specific hubs have their nodes in different locations. Still, they can share a relevant virtual space if they face persecution within contexts that are not always amenable to or sympathetic towards forms of Shīʿīsm. Digital media are applied to share representations of specific ritualistic events, such as the passion plays associated with various martyrs, the rituals related to pilgrimage, and sites linked to the imams, notably in Karbala and Iran, but also many other locations. Shīʿa Muslims can face extensive persecution in some zones, where they are deemed 'outside of Islam' because of their strong focus on 'alternative' forms of religious practice and the veneration of specific religious figures. This perspective has led to condemnation and, in some cases, the suggestion that they are *kuffār* – rejecters of Islam.

Within Shīʿa Islam, the generation of religious authority has different dimensions, including how *fatāwā* works. They are the subject of traditional Islamic education in seminary and university contexts. In many cases, *fatāwā* are granulated, specific to circumstances and can be binding on individuals in areas of personal law and practice. Still, the availability of the principal source materials in digital form is also having an impact, with algorithmic searchability and a reduced digital divide being key drivers opening the sources to other forms of readership previously restricted because of limitations of access, expense and barriers to knowledge. Access to the content is impacted by censorship, blocked services, password requirements and other impediments.

Persecution of Shīʿa Muslims in Iraq and Syria by the so-called 'Islamic State' – especially in the 2010s – saw executions and the destruction of Shīʿa religious sites. In the same period, there were bombings of the Shīʿa Muslim mosques and other sites in Pakistan. This antipathy and aggression also play out online, fuelled by rhetoric in chat rooms and on social media, and backed up in some cases by 'justification' from religious scholars making pronouncements on the internet and through other channels (discussed in Chapter 9). Combined with political and cultural factors, this is a heady and dangerous equation for those groups that do not fall within the accepted parameters of belief, including those with esoteric tendencies that suggest through their practices, they can acquire greater proximity to the Divine and other 'conventional' Muslims.

There is a tendency towards a reductive simplification between and within 'Sunni' and 'Shīʿa' Islam, facilitated by advocates of division, academics and other commentators. This phenomenon belies the complexities of identities, knowledge and approaches towards religion over time – often seen in online contexts. Assertion of dominance goes both ways, and Shīʿīsm is reflected within its majority contexts as presenting similar justifications in some cases as to the efficacy and authority of its messages. Online channels reinforce these tropes, using the imagery of specific influences such as ʿAlī, Ḥasan and Ḥusayn and the Prophet's family to generate enthusiasm and affinity through specific symbolism (discussed in detail in Chapter 6).[106] The language draws on sources specific to Shīʿīsm and the legal and religious messages from authorities, such as scholars and Ayatollahs (discussed in Chapter 7). Adherence generates substantial online content that presents the authorities as definitive voices to create affinity and authority online through social media and other channels.

It is not intended here to essentialize terms such as 'Sunni', 'Shīʿa' or 'Sufi', and it is acknowledged that there is an interplay between and within these categories. Relationships at times play out online, including key influential figures who appear across different categories. While acknowledging this complexity, it is helpful to delineate between these zones in terms of organizing a book of this nature, especially in helping readers who are less familiar with the nuanced understandings within the Islam matrix.

There is a long line of Islamic influences, with a continuity going back to the Prophet. In a way, the role of area specialists working on digital content is to provide that extra level of granularity and knowledge so that these figures can be unpacked and analysed in the necessary detail. There is potential to determine how they impact real-world knowledge and development in what has been described as a 'digital-analogue pendulum' of communication.[107] Each analogue community (and microcosm within it) will have different digital influences. In contrast, in national and global contexts, evolving networks of influences have emerged in response to the increasingly granulated demands for (Islamic) goods and services.

The reduced digital divide, cheaper devices and increased digital literacy across Muslim zones have heightened demands for influencer content, whether pure text or sophisticated AI, conditioned partly on location and affiliation within the competitive marketplace. Attention spans have diminished in these zones, where mundane content competes with the spiritual, and religion is one node in complex digital worlds. This authority also extends to deceased scholars whose adherents project them 'from the grave' so that their message can still be heard, including film clips where available and photographs, audio recordings, statements and textual sources. I was struck by the strength of this rhetoric when playing audio clips of significant but now deceased Egyptian preachers to students. These mosque recordings are sourced from the same cassette tapes that generations of Egyptian taxi drivers and shop owners have played in decades gone by.[108]

It may not always be safe in some contexts to listen to such content. People may have different devices for specific purposes, with choices and attitudes cloaked by Virtual Private Networks (VPNs), especially in locations where internet monitoring, filtering and control intensifies. This is particularly pertinent where users hide their online religious choices when they go against the norms of their local societies. The utilization of these sources facilitates the exploration of other cultural and religious attitudes and boundaries. Developing the appropriate skills for these activities can incorporate visits to the dark web through the Tor browser and other tools.[109] The dark web is associated with criminality. It is also a 'safe space' and a facilitation tool to avoid censorship by anonymizing IP addresses. This zone includes sectors of Islamic cyber expression, including those evading political-religious control; this sector incorporates 'jihād' oriented activities as much as more pacific forms of Muslim political-religious expression.

The presence of key figures and influences can form a significant entry point into these networks of religious authority, especially when they are designed along the lines of usability and effective design for mobile devices, rather than simply being a data dump of a scanned book. These factors of design and interpretation can be enhanced for the user when accompanied by commentaries from scholars and authorities explaining the critical issues in a dynamic and lively way, using language which is understandable and accessible. It is one thing for these materials to be online. Still, it is another for them to be read or consumed (depending on format) in a competitive information marketplace, not just for Islamic content but for other forms of digital materials as well.

Alternative approaches towards information consumption are found in CIEs. The rendering of episodes in Islamic history through computer-generated modelling, such as significant battles, along with the presentation of ritualistic performance content online, can be evocative for users and offer an entry point into more profound and granulated forms of religious expression. In their own rights, they can also attract attention and, in some cases, bring in financial and religious influence. Their online presence offers a helpful entry point, especially for those persecuted or unable to approach conventional religious channels. They also provide a way through which others can learn of specific religious city values. Sharing of this content by detractors and opponents can harm content providers. Censorship can impinge on the distributed messages, especially when they might have some form or political-religious subtext.

Content providers bring their understandings, theories, perspectives and biases. Some textual sources, such as e-books and documents, are reproduced in a digital format. Others further represent sources through multimedia interfaces in a way that takes advantage of the medium, offering compelling communication experiences that match those of content providers in other online zones. Remember that the contestation is not just the religious materials, given the numerous distractions that exist online in different zones. Materials include the production of apps for specific Islamic purposes, such as reading the Qur'ān, determining prayer direction and generating reminders of prayer times. This raises important questions of how (or whether) the apps inform religious practices and whether there is an integration of apps and associated devices specifically into ritual.[110]

Conclusion

Religion forms a microelement of much broader content consumption patterns and distractions online, which purveyors of cyber-Islamic content must compete with at various levels so that their message reaches its intended audiences. AI algorithms impact on these processes, as the latest in a long line of influences on discourse, knowledge consumption and understanding. The notion of influence in *Islamic Algorithms* crosses historical, religious and cultural divides as pulses of knowledge, whose impact is subtle rather than overt – and is not always recognized contemporaneously (or positively) by an influence's peers. An influence may be subject to forms of revisionism and idealization over time, interpreted by societies to drive specific cultural, political and religious agendas. It is not the purpose here to measure the status of specific influences or make value judgements as to impact, and those influences presented are examples that may only affect specific sectors of Muslim understandings over time.

These influences form part of the digital information *souq* or marketplace of ideas and knowledge. The next chapters show that key influences and ideas about Islam form part of the knowledge marketplace which will impact on future Muslim metaverses.

Chapter 2

BEFORE MUḤAMMAD

This chapter introduces significant Islamic influences that emerged before the time of Prophet Muḥammad, including the roles of other prophets in articulating Islamic value systems. These figures form part of knowledge frameworks and interpretative approaches, with a renewed presence across digital constructs.

Search engines and algorithms can turn up some interesting results. Perhaps surprising to some online users, part of the framework for searches about Islam is the presence of figures that predate Muḥammad from a pre-Islamic Online Milieu. Some of these are part of the lines of Judeo-Christian prophets who form part of Islam's heritage and who feature significantly in the Qur'ān. Others are more ethereal entities. Online, they are debated and discussed with profiles, sermons and apps pointing back in time to figures whose actions and practices have a direct and profound influence on contemporary Islam. Algorithms will point online users to different interpretations of many of these, demonstrating the complexities of sources and ideas and the different approaches to ideas about Islam that these can raise. How users mediate these complex ideas is significant, especially when gatekeepers point towards alternative understandings.

The sample of critical figures and entities discussed here will engender a sense of how they impact contemporary formulations of Islamic understanding, especially in digital contexts. They are integral to interpretations of Islam in terms of approaches to religious discourse, ritual and practice – and form part of the structure of the Qur'ān. This includes the jinn and angels of various descriptions whose histories are seen as part of the cosmology of Islam but predate the emergence of Muḥammad. Some figures go beyond neat categorization: the shayṭān – possibly the most negative potential 'influencer' according to Islamic sources – is in various forms and guises. It is intriguing to see that these esoteric entities have a presence online, although there are different emphases on their representation and within the discussion.

Jinn

Ethereal and derived from fire, the jinn have an important role within Islam – and can also be found in cyberspace. They have a 'voice' in the Qur'ān and listen to its recitation; in Islamic traditions, encounters between Muḥammad and jinn form part of the narrative surrounding the Prophet's life. They also helped prophets and historical figures, according to the Qur'ān, including Sulaymān's building of the Jerusalem Temple. The jinn feature in the Qur'ān (in which they have a *sūrah* or chapter named after them) which discusses their creation and how they have different tribes, practices and conduct. In the biographical sources of Muḥammad's life, he is said to have been observed by the jinn on his travels who heard his recitation.[1]

Jinn are the subject of legends which go beyond the contexts of Islam, into pre-Islamic folklore and superstition. The resonance of this can be found in the amulets and talismans found in contemporary societies and sold online today – along with the prayers and recitations which either encourage protective jinn or expel those who are more worrisome. The jinn are represented online through diverse channels. Mystical understandings of Islam under the banner of Sufism have a role – in the discussion on the feeding of anger that jinn undertake.[2]

Going beyond the encounters within the Qur'ān, articulated in the eponymous Sūra and other sections, this takes readers towards explorations of 'the supernatural'. The Islamic world is full of jinn, some better behaved than others. They are the subjects of religious opinions and fatwas, offering advice and protective prayers.[3] The presence of mischievous entities has led to an entire online and commercial sector seeking to 'exorcise' their presence. Algorithms on jinn will take online surfers beyond the Disneyfication of 'genies', supernatural Marvel cinematic renderings or the *Arabian Nights'* styled depictions, into areas that are equally disturbing and controversial in scope.

Shayṭān

The *shayṭān* are everywhere, including on the internet. Some interpreters might think the internet embodies the influence of the shayṭān and that algorithms direct people into their negative digital clutches. Be that as it may, the shayṭān's presence forms part of online discourse, as a warning to humanity, but the term's meaning can be ambiguous. The term '*shayṭān*' can refer to specific jinn, while 'satans' (*shāyiṭin*) can also inspire artists as 'familiar spirits'. Although its origins link to Hebrew terminology, the term has several meanings.[4] They negatively impact people, bringing disease and misfortune – although not all are 'evil'. In some traditions, specific amulets can ward off these influences, and tradition suggests they are powerless during Ramadan (at least for those who do not break the fast).

The 'chief *shayṭān*' is Iblīs, whose refusal to bow to 'Ādam resulted in his casting out of heaven.[5] The importance of Iblīs within the narrative is also stressed online, given his sense of superiority over other creatures and the constant whispering temptations he puts in their path.[6] In popular tradition, Iblīs instils a propensity towards sinful behaviour into humans at birth. Iblīs' role as a negative influence is paramount when he whispers into human ears. The presence of an angel and a shayṭān accompanying every human adds to the negative impact. Their religious practices can help prevent temptation, with the disobedient Iblīs seen as the epitome of evil, being against Allāh and humanity. A reminder of this occurs in hajj when the ritual of stoning pillars at Minā traditionally represents Ibrāhīm's stoning of Shayṭān.

The presence of Iblīs and the *shāyiṭin* in CIEs appears in numerous contexts, where countering their negative influence forms a subtext in advice delivered to Muslims online, for example, in online Q&A websites, sermons and other indicators of good practice. The stoning at Minā appears in hajj apps and advice online. Some authorities have seen the internet itself as having inherently 'satanic' aspects to it. The levels to which this opinion is endorsed (or not) are significant. It depends on the specific platforms' world view and content providers. The calibration of esoteric dimensions can vary substantially. YouTube has specific prayers utilized to counter the negative aspects of jinn and *shāyiṭin* (acknowledging that not all elements are necessarily harmful). This approach goes beyond simply listening to recitations and into zones of online learning.[7]

A taxonomy of jinn is discussed online, often as a 'warning' or admonition for individuals, with appropriately disturbing imagery better placed in a Hollywood film.[8] Warnings take a sensational and disturbing turn with a discussion by Ustadh Tim Humble on 'A Jinn Rapes Her Every Night!' This explains how to counter such attacks (on males and females) by using oils, removing things that attract *shāyiṭin* (such as TVs and music) and performing specific supplications.[9] Other videos seek to counter ideas associated with exorcism and the 'industry' that surrounds these rituals and processes, which some see as outside of the pale of Islamic convention and practice.[10] There is a commercial edge to the promotion and sale of talismans which seek to prevent the impact of jinn, with items preventing the 'evil eye' available on eBay, Amazon and other channels.[11] Online zones offer various talismans, amulets and other devices to purchase online.[12] Attributing specific behaviours to jinn can mask significant mental health issues, especially when 'treatments' take the form of exorcisms or other non-clinical practices, which in some cases have resulted in poor outcomes for their subjects.[13]

Efforts to keep such influences away from humanity form part of online discourse, from the constant reflection in prayer and good practice to cultural-religious interpretations of popular religious beliefs. Online exorcisms, the purchase of amulets and specific talisman practices form a subtext to cyber-Islamic environments – especially in efforts to remove the presence of jinn and shayṭān from people's lives. Over time this has included videos which appeared to show 'exorcisms' and 'possessions' of individuals by jinn. 'Therapies' have been offered online to present jinn, offering insights into the mediation between these beliefs and online activities, including using the Qur'ān to combat these influences. Skype videos demonstrated these procedures. Related services were online.[14]

Angels

Type 'Islam angels' into a search engine, click on images and a host of historical and contemporary renderings are generated, from stylized AI artworks to Persian manuscript illustrations. These are all attempts to render the spiritual entities described in complex detail across Islamic sources. Angels (*malā'ikah*) permeate the Qur'ān, from the first Revelation received from Allāh via the Angel Jibrīl (Gabriel) to the numerous encounters Muḥammad and other prophets have over time. They also feature in other sources, especially narratives associated with the Prophet receiving Revelation and episodes within his life – emerging in *aḥādīth* and biographical sources. Again, different typologies are associated with angels, with significant angels named. The hierarchy shows angels with different qualities and personalities, from Isrāfīl, the angel associated with death, whose trumpet blowing occurs on the Day of Judgement (Qiyāmah), to Mīkhā'īl, deemed a friend to humanity. Nakīr and Munkar seek answers from the soul regarding behaviour, while al-Katibun and al-Kiram record individual deeds. Angels feature specifically in the Night Journey (discussed below) and accounts of the projected Day of Judgement.

Cyberspace also features angels as part of the Islamic algorithms. Suppose an algorithm is an instruction that solves a problem. In that case, angels' contextual emergence at times of crisis to articulate the response to a problem (an answer that has come from Allāh) forms a crucial component of any equation. Muḥammad's encounters with Jibrīl are not the only ones he has with angels, given that there is a hierarchy in Islamic interpretations of angels with different roles and responsibilities. Jibrīl also encounters other religious figures, such as John the Baptist's father Zachariah and mother Elizabeth, to whom Jibrīl announced the birth of their son, as well as foretelling the birth of Jesus to Mary.

Angels have a specific role for every individual, observing good and bad deeds. Angels also figure in Qur'ānic accounts with other prophets, for example, Ibrāhīm. Angels appear in battles, assisting Muḥammad and his forces. Angels also intercede in so-called mystical experiences, bringing individuals closer to Muḥammad or Allāh, thus promoting their religious and spiritual credibility. In biographies of 'saints', angels may appear. They feature in Islam-influenced art. Various angels demonstrate other forms of intellect and aspects of Allāh's attributes.

Representing beings made of light who are unseen may present some logistical difficulties, but this does not impact unduly on their representation online, which can draw specifically on traditional artistic renderings of angels – such as those in Persian miniature art. They can also feature in memes reflecting angels' traditional roles or focus on a specific angel in the hierarchy.[15] Video effects can augment a traditional sermon on angels, such as a discussion on 'The Birth & Death Of Angel Jibreel', which discusses the size of angels and Jibrīl's appearance (with 600 wings) drawing on ḥādīth sources, as well as exploring the interactions between angels and other prophets.[16] The miraculous interventions of angels and their roles are explored through discussion on ḥādīth sources by Omar Suleiman, especially when they disguise themselves in human forms.[17]

Angels have a specific role within Sufism in poetry, ritual practice, art and religious expression. This function links to specific religious thinkers over time who may have had interactions themselves. Jalāl al-Dīn Muḥammad Rūmī's poetry and associated quotations on angels form a part of popular culture that goes beyond

Islamic frameworks. This phenomenon is especially prevalent on Instagram and Pinterest, where concise quotes and associated images are appropriate for Rumi's work on angels and multiple other themes. These may draw on various artistic influences well beyond traditional Islamic frameworks.[18]

Algorithms take those searching for angels across the complexities of interpretations and esoteric understanding associated with Islam, in the language of Revelation and poetry. These descriptions informed artistic depictions of angels, which are not universally endorsed across the Islamic spectrum, due to aniconism presenting limitations of artistically rendering physical and ethereal forms. This has not inhibited their depiction on AI artistic platforms, as well as their symbolic representation in digital art patterns. As intermediaries between humanity and the divine, angels play an influential role in approaches towards Islam, especially in its esoteric dimensions as articulated in cyberspace.

ʾĀdam and Hawwāʾ

Humanity's origin story forms part of the algorithmic search matrix: in Islam, ʾĀdam represents the first human being, similar to Judeo-Christian accounts encapsulated in Genesis. The Qurʾān reflects aspects of the creation story, although Eve (Hawwāʾ) is unnamed. Eve was created from a rib. In the Qurʾān, Iblīs is seen as tempting ʾĀdam and Eve with the forbidden fruit, causing their recognition of nakedness and expulsion from the Garden of Eden.[19]

This theme is represented in online discussions about Hawwāʾ and feeds into the explorations of gender issues and questions about the status of women that can be found across online fora. Discussion about ʾĀdam offers insight into other dimensions of faith associated with Islam. While ʾĀdam is the primordial (hu) man and the first Prophet on earth, there is a *ḥādīth* which states that Muḥammad pre-existed ʾĀdam and Creation. Muḥammad has a status as *al-Insān al-Kāmil*, the perfect human being, a concept explored in the work of Ibn ʿArabī and significant within Sufi understandings of Islam. In Shīʿīsm, the concept also extends to the imamate, discussed later in this book.

The notion of sin (and whether it is 'original') appears in online discussions and clearly can be a contentious term.[20] ʾĀdam and Eve are presented as absent of sin in some sources despite their fall. Online in exegetical discussions, this references the fall as being a 'slip' and a 'disappointment'.[21] Traditional accounts have different intended audiences, from child-level upwards, including cartoon representations of ʾĀdam. Iblīs is represented as the black 'satan' or shayṭān, with angels as white characters.[22] Many dimensions of the accounts associated with ʾĀdam are online. The story featured in online lectures, such as that of Abu Bakr Zoud, who notes that ʾĀdam is the only Prophet whose sin is discussed in the Qurʾān.[23] Lectures explore the specific features of accounts, such as Sheikh Shady Alsuleiman, considering the great ages people reached (according to tradition) during the time of ʾĀdam.[24]

In Shīʿīsm, Sayed Ammar Nakshawani discusses the complexity of the accounts surrounding ʾĀdam and issues surrounding some of the most ambiguous matters.

He argues that there were thousands of '’Ādams' over time and that there were lifeforms before humanity (including jinn).[25] The significance of the creation story links to the other entities referred to in the creation story, including the jinn and angels – created simultaneously alongside humanity.

Nūḥ (Noah)

Complex traditions and content relating to Nūḥ can be found online. Nūḥ features throughout the Qur'ān, with a specific sūra named after him. The message of Nūḥ has a resonance with Noah in the Old Testament, with its emphasis on him telling the people about Allāh and seeking to steer them away from idolatry. The narrations on Nūḥ incorporate references to the Qur'ān and other sources, reflecting traditional print sources. Commonalities exist between Sunni and Shī'a accounts.[26] Shī'a sources also incorporate accounts specifically from traditions associated with the imams; Imam Ja'far al-Ṣādiq (*c.*702–65) stated that the Ark circled the Ka'bah several times and performed the trotting ritual; the Ark was also said to contain the body of 'Ādam. Some of these traditions are absent from Sunni frameworks, which present their perspectives on the events surrounding Nūḥ.[27]

Interpretation of Nūḥ also leads to online discussions on whether the biblically described Flood matches that within Islamic sources and also that Qur'ān exegesis can fit contemporary scientific evidence on the Flood with specific aspects of Qur'ān-ic understanding (in contradiction to biblical accounts).[28] Online speculation surrounds the Ark's location(s), with expositions on Mount Judi (Ararat) in Turkey.[29] Nūḥ's final resting place is a matter of consideration. Searches come up with several results on this subject, with 'Alī's mosque in Najaf, Iraq, being one contender, in line with Shī'a thought that 'Ādam and Nūḥ are buried next to 'Alī. Other possible locations are in Lebanon, Turkey and a zone contested by Azerbaijan and Armenia. All areas have websites presenting their case, including travel agents offering visits and official sources amplifying their 'authentic' positions.[30]

Ibrāhīm

It is interesting to see the significance Ibrāhīm (Abraham) has as an influence in cyberspace, reflecting that he is a crucial prophetic reference point in Islam, especially through his association with the building of the Ka'bah and the associated accounts. *Al-Baqarah*, the Qur'ān's second sūra, refers to the 'religion of Abraham'. Practices Allāh had commanded were to be instituted in the Ka'bah (Allāh's sacred house) in Mecca. Later scholars trace the origins back to the beginning of Creation. According to popular Muslim tradition, 'Ādam built the Ka'bah as a copy of the heavenly house of Allāh. Its destruction during Nūḥ's

Flood left only the foundation. The Qur'ān says that Ibrāhīm and his son Ismā'īl built the shrine.

Key events surrounding Ibrāhīm and his family are reflected annually in the hajj and the minor pilgrimage, the *'umrah*. Consequently, explanations of the events are prevalent on accounts explicitly associated with the hajj, including those incorporated in pilgrimage apps. These offer step-by-step searchable guidance on every stage of the hajj, linked to GPS, enabling specific instructions related to the location of the individual pilgrim. In the past, mobile phone technology use was discouraged in the precincts of the Ka'bah. Now the use has religious and logistical implications and relevance for authorities.[31] Ibrāhīm's ritual practices, including a sacrifice, are also represented in charitable zones of Islamic cyberspace, where his story encourages donations for Qurbani to Islamic charities.[32] The integration of technology into key religious practices, specifically associated with Ibrāhīm, can also be seen at the organizational stage – where artificial intelligence is applied to organize and manage key aspects of pilgrimage, in particular crowd management.[33]

In the precincts of the Ka'bah, Ibrāhīm is represented through a station or *maqām*, said to contain his footprint. It represents a point where he prayed or where he stood when constructing the Ka'bah walls. This area symbolizes a significant ritual point in the hajj, represented online in photographs taken by pilgrims and others. Pinterest, for example, contains numerous images of the *maqām*. Some have a commercial edge (hyper-) linked to travel companies offering pilgrimage packages.[34]

'Abrahamic' practices link Judaism, Christianity and Islam. As with other prophets, there can be a contestation of 'ownership' and interpretation between supporters of specific world views, along with dialogue opportunities. This can include discussions comparing the perceptions of Ibrāhīm in biblical and Islamic sources.[35] As part of a series on pre-Islamic prophets, American imam Shabir Ally noted the ritual importance of Ibrāhīm in prayer while also exploring questions as to whether Ibrāhīm existed. He used Torah and New Testament sources to do this, alongside Qur'ān materials.[36] A commentary on Ibrāhīm by Nouman Ali Khan reflects on Ibrāhīm in the context of interfaith issues, including his destruction of idols.[37]

Shī'a perspectives on Ismā'īl, Isḥāq and Ibrāhīm are unpacked in commentaries on the Qur'ān and long lectures (taken from broadcasts). The Ahl ul-Bayt (and the line of 'Alī) indicate that the Qur'ān refers directly to Ismā'īl. Sayed Ammar Nakshawani uses colloquial English in his discussion, discussing generational differences towards Islam and reflecting on how participation in hajj is imperative and for the 'correct' reasons (not just for the hajji title).[38]

Mūsā (Moses)

Mūsā ibn 'Imrān's position as a pivotal figure in CIEs reflects the parallels commentators draw between the accounts of his life and that of Muḥammad. Online discussions reflect on Mūsā's reception of Revelation and responses to pressures on his community. The biblical Exodus becomes analogous to the *hijrah* in the Qur'ān. Mūsā and Muḥammad also meet during the miraculous journey

(Isrā᾽) between Mecca and Jerusalem made by Muḥammad and the subsequent ascension (Miʿrāj) through the seven heavens. Muḥammad negotiates the number of prayers through discussion with Mūsā, who shows him the seven heavens and hell during this Night Journey. Consequently, with over 120 references to Mūsā in the Qur᾽ān, there are numerous digital angles on his role and symbolism.[39]

There is an impact on religious practice, too, such as the ʿĀshūrā᾽ fasting day on the tenth Muḥarram to mark Mūsā leading the Israelites from the Pharaoh. According to some interpretations, the stand that Mūsā takes became a model for Muḥammad's actions against his opponents. At the same time, it also influences later interpretations of militaristic jihād. These themes play out online, including very detailed online narratives focused on Mūsā in diverse formats from various ideological positions. This dynamic includes different forms of 'Salafi' websites which can inform political-religious interpretations based on notions of 'renewal' and 'reform' of Islam.[40] Mūsā's story lends itself to animation, sermons and feature-length expositions. Some have higher production values, such as the animated Arabic and English 'Chronicles of Musa' series.[41] In Sufism, key figures such as Rūmī and Ibn ʿArabī refer to Mūsā in their reflections on the spiritual journey.

In Shīʿa thought, the relationship that Mūsā has with his brother Hārūn (Aaron) is analogous to that of Muḥammad's relationship with his son-in-law ʿAlī ibn Abī Ṭālib. This theme emerges from a specific ḥādīth in which Muḥammad designated ʿAlī as his successor and responded to ʿAlī 's assertion that he was being 'left behind' with women and children during a military option. There are various versions of this ḥādīth, 'Will you not be pleased that you will be to me like Aaron to Moses?'[42] This saying reminds people of the relationship between Mūsā and Hārūn, who would deputize for his brother in his absence. In Shīʿa sources, where emphasis on the selection of ʿAlī as the designated success is integral to beliefs, there is attention to the references to Mūsā and Hārūn in the Qur᾽ān. This focus represents a source of contention between Sunni and Shīʿa interpretations of sources over time, amplified in cyberspace. [43]

The themes also form a foundation of Shīʿa-Sunni contestations in other zones of cyberspace – where the tone can become more vitriolic. These include long tracts where different sides in cyberspace engage in 'scholarly' disputation on each other's posts. For example, Answering-Ansar Unveiled explores the ḥādīth associated with Hārūn and its Shīʿa interpretation, negating the assertions of specific parallels made on the site Answering-Ansar: 'Answering-Ansar has nothing to refute it. Trying to refute it, it further increases the problems for itself.'[44] The mission of Answering-Ansar Unveiled is to counter the statements of the Answering-Ansar website, which later became ShiaPen.[45]

There are gentler assertions on the ḥādīth and its veracity, which can draw on other internet sources to back up their points of view.[46] Others note perceived 'parallels' such as Mūsā having descendants who became religious authorities: 'The progeny of Moses produced Imams/Prophets/Leaders to guide mankind. Similarly, the progeny of Muḥammad bore 12 Imams, whose duty is the same.'[47] Coincidentally the observance of ʿĀshūrā᾽ as a commemoration for Mūsā's victory over Pharaoh has a further layer of significance for Shīʿa Muslims, as it is marked as the day Ḥusayn was killed at the Battle of Karbala.

Al-Khiḍr

The esoteric dimensions of Islam form an important subtext to Islamic cyberspace, particularly in the case of al-Khiḍr: The Qurʾān describes Mūsā's encounter with a 'Servant of Allāh', which leads to a series of esoteric episodes where the Servant takes actions Musa cannot understand (despite his questions). There is a greater divine purpose, explained by the Servant later on. The Servant is not given a name in the Sūra, *al-Kahf*. However, in later interpretations, he is described as al-Khiḍr ('the green one'), a provider of esoteric wisdom – a focal point for later mystically oriented understanding of Islam articulated by various Sufi orders. Al-Khiḍr features in ḥādīth narratives, one linking him with annually meeting Ilyās (Elijah) in Jerusalem for the month of Ramadan, in which encounters al-Khiḍr's presence leads to the greening of barren land. Sufi sources reference Al-Khiḍr, indicating he is part of various Sufi *tariqah* as well as aiding those on the mystical pathways.[48]

Al-Khiḍr is part of the explanations for the qualities of specific days provided online, attributed to Ibn ʿArabī, which guides in interpreting esoteric attributes, planetary alignments, mystical letters and divine attributes: Thursday aligns with Mūsā and Al-Khiḍr.[49] The subject of Al-Khiḍr and his relationship with Mūsā is unpacked through online sermons and analyses, often in conjunction with discussions about Musa's role in other religious frameworks (and to position it within Islam). Naqshbandi Shaykh Abdulkerim el Kibrisi breaks down the events as represented in sources about Al-Khiḍr, with an interpretation of the esoteric dimensions and clarifying differentials between prophethood and hidden knowledge.[50] Muḥammadan Way Sufi Center has several presentations on Al-Khiḍr, with versions for children as well as expositions from scholars.[51] Al-Khiḍr is explained through various Sufi commentaries over time. Representations of Al-Khiḍr from Persian and other miniatures are online.

Al-Khiḍr also has a role to play in Shīʿism; he has encounters with ʿAlī to instruct him about extra prayers, which would help in attacking the Antichrist due to appear on the Day of Judgement. Al-Khiḍr also meets with ʿAlī, Ḥasan and Ḥusayn to confirm Muḥammad's prophethood.

ʿĪsā (Jesus)

The prominent presence of ʿĪsā (Jesus) in CIEs may surprise some unfamiliar with Islam, but it reflects several references specifically to him in the Qurʾān, as well as the presence of Christianity during the time of Muḥammad. Biographical sources describe how Muḥammad encountered Christian monks in his youth while trading across the Arabian Peninsula towards Syria. In the emergence of Islam, Christians in Ethiopia offered refuge to members of the nascent Muslim community. The

Islamic nature of ʿĪsā is distinct from its representation in Christian sources, as ʿĪsā is a human being born of Maryam (consequently, he is also known as ʿĪsā Ibn Maryam), albeit one who could present miraculous interventions.

Maryam is significant as a figure of discussion in Islamic contexts; the Qurʾān mentions her birth while the Annunciation story features in a portion of the Qurʾān (Sūra Maryam, 19). ʿĪsā's birth and the events surrounding it, including the miraculous provision of sustenance, are described in the Qurʾān, emphasizing differentials between the Islamic and Gospel versions of the stories. There is no mention of a father. As al-Masīḥ, 'the Messiah', Jesus has a special status as a Nabī (Prophet) and Rasūl (Messenger), which he pronounced from his cradle.[52] ʿĪsā is not subject to crucifixion within Islamic interpretations; another person died who was 'made' to resemble ʿĪsā. According to tradition, he will kill al-Dajjāl or the 'Antichrist' on the Day of Judgement, setting in motion further processes leading to a single religion (Islam). ʿĪsā was another figure that Muḥammad encountered directly on the Night Journey and Ascension from Mecca to al-Quds (Jerusalem) and then to the seven heavens – where he met all the prophets.

Along with other traditional readings and references in other sources, ninety-three verses in the Qurʾān refer directly to ʿĪsā. Elements in the Qurʾān relating to ʿĪsā suggests, in part, a correlation with Christian Gospels. ʿĪsā is said to predict the coming of Muḥammad.[53] In commentaries (including those featured online), Christianity has a role on the developmental path towards its perfection in the form of 'Islam', which irons out inconsistencies of perceived logic and outlook in various interpretations of Christian faiths.[54] Several religious opinions pay attention to the qualities of Jesus, before and after his death.[55]

The developed empathy towards ʿĪsā reflected online offers a significant route for enhancing Christian-Muslim relations, presenting clarification of positions and suggested commonalities. ʿĪsā is naturally a focal point for Christian-Muslim discussions, but these can go into polemical areas. Algorithms generated by deep searches take surfers to detailed Qurʾānic discussions of ʿĪsā's qualities. Symbolic elements have online representation: here you can find the Umayyad Mosque in Damascus' minaret, the point where ʿĪsā will return on the Day of Judgement to hunt down al-Dajjāl or the Antichrist. Online sources stress ʿĪsā's qualities which are visible on this Day.[56] These complexities feature in a children's story, explaining how Maryam could conceive without being touched by a man.[57] Full-length feature films and animations provide Islamic perspectives on ʿĪsā. The 2007 Iranian film 'The Messiah' was available for streaming on unofficial outlets.[58] A wealth of traditions from Shīʿa sources stress ʿĪsā's relationship to the imamate.[59] The significance of iconography in Shīʿism features digital representations of ʿĪsā, including with Shīʿa imams.[60]

Sufi cyberspace (discussed further in Chapter 8) explains how the miracles associated with ʿĪsā have a particular resonance in esoterically oriented areas of Islamic thought and beliefs, in line with Muḥammad's attributed miracles stressed in some biographical sources. There is also the ascetic dimension of aspects of mystical practices, aligned with aspects of ʿĪsā's life, where episodes in his life link to specific stations in Sufism, marking the spiritual journey(s) towards ultimate knowledge and annihilation in Allāh.

One Naqshbandi Sufi interpretation explores the Gospels, highlighting specific verses and linking them to the states on the pathway to 'truth'.[61] There are also discussions on the permissibility (or not) within Sufi interpretations to observe the birthday of ʿĪsā (and other prophets); marking the birth of ʿĪsā is different from the Christian festivities of Christmas, and the specific date is not known.[62] Naqshbandi online sources stress the qualities and attributes of ʿĪsā, especially their articulation online. Sufilive showed Naqshbandi leader Mawlana Shaykh Nazim Adil Sultanul Awliya emphasizing ʿĪsā's words, as articulated in the Qurʾān.[63] Sermons discuss specific miraculous stories associated with ʿĪsā.[64]

As a significant figure in Islam and a precursor to Muḥammad, ʿĪsā has a considerable role in cyber-Islamic contexts. Quotations from the Qurʾān associated with ʿĪsā form a central part of galleries on Pinterest, along with more apologetic quotes, especially in terms of proving one specific world view as superior over another concerning ʿĪsā. These channels are informed by mission and propagation subtexts. These quotations can form part of the process of encouraging individuals to convert or revert from Christianity to Islam by emphasizing ʿĪsā's qualities. Online posters stress that an individual's love for ʿĪsā is enhanced through following Islam. ʿĪsā represents a significant influence in Christian and Muslim online space, with considerable intersection between these interests.

Conclusion

These primary figures are integral to the perception of Islam and the influences impacting Muslims in digital contexts. They form part of dimensions of religious expression and understanding encompassing experiential and ritualistic digital elements. Any knowledge of Islam must reference these key entities and figures to form a holistic understanding of the dynamics of digital Muslim life. Early prophets, angels, jinn and even a shayṭān (in various forms) can inhabit cyberspace (and potential metaverses). They form part of Islamic algorithm equations, impacting how searches reveal information about Islam and inform perceptions of Islam. Networks of ethereal entities – the jinn in the machine – may seem particularly appropriate in hyper-reality contexts and meta-constructs, especially given the amorphous nature of potential metaverses.

The cosmology of Islam is complex, and many other entities, figures and individuals exert influence in cyberspace. The chronology of Islam did not start with Muḥammad; rather, it extends back to creation, where all the significant prophets and figures from Judeo-Christian sources were seen as part of Islam's linear development as a religion. Muḥammad's encounters in biographical and traditional sources reflect these influences and interactions, searchable across space and time and regarded with reverence and respect by Muslims. CIEs extend this narrative, relevant in linking concepts and entities together while also presenting them to audiences via multimedia interfaces.

Chapter 3

MUḤAMMAD AND DIGITAL INFLUENCE

If one were to develop a list of key Islamic influences, then Muḥammad ibn ʿAbd Allāh's (570–632 CE) legacy as manifested online would place him at the top. This chapter focuses specifically on how Muḥammad is represented in digital constructs, which retain his status and legacy and negotiate sensitivity in handling the complexities of representation and understanding.

Searching for the Prophet

Muḥammad's responses to major episodes in his prophetic career are significant and influential, impacted directly in some cases by Revelation. There is a continuity of preservation and propagation, from the formative phase of Islam's development to contemporary times, within various media. The presence of Muḥammad in any envisioned Muslim metaverse will be built in part on the current complexity of influences, algorithms and content in CIEs. Given that the pictorial depiction of Muḥammad (and other figures) is discouraged in many Islamic traditions, this 'representation' will have to draw on textual and other sources which possess their own digital influence in CIEs.

Muḥammad's legacy presents an implicit influence and presence in any Muslim metaverse. As an exemplary model of interpretive practice and the individual chosen by God to be a Prophet, Muḥammad's sayings and actions were recorded by generations of followers as a guide to understanding aspects of Revelation that were not explicit or clear. The science associated with these interpretations, based on reasoning and gathering of compendia of small details related to his life, forms part of the scholarship model associated with the ḥādīth and Sunnah (sayings and actions), referred to when doubts have emerged over understanding and practice.

Various degrees of authenticity are associated with these sources, recorded in extensive collections, which can present diverse outlooks and approaches towards Islam. These sources were memorized by scholars over the centuries, forming part of other interpretive works, including commentaries on the Qur'ān, legalistic sources, histories and biographies. The knowledge contained within these sources was taught at seminaries positioned in many Muslim contexts and passed down through generations of scholars. This development informed broader audiences through their presence in sermons, legal decisions and Islamic education for the masses. The printing press's introduction led to the sources' compilation, editing and distribution, with extracts appearing in guidance texts and forming part of the mass media distribution.

The internet was an effective outlet for making sources cost-effectively available to wider audiences; a key factor was searchability concerning keywords which meant that readers could seek out prophetic sayings and responses to specific issues electronically. In a way, digital media was a natural place for such activity, with the production of CD-ROMs containing various collections as well as online databases. This development was significant in the 1990s when translated versions of sources appeared on Islamic websites, such as English language Muslim student associations' sites in the United States. These took advantage of searchability even in a pre-browser context, enhanced with internet browsers' emergence in the mid-1990s, making sources more accessible to people lacking access to the multivolume sets, who lacked the time, energy or money to explore extensive printed copies. This technological access opened the biographical sources to new audiences, although there may have been issues with the veracity of materials, depending on how they were inputted and referenced; they lend themselves to academic environments that themselves were geared around the emphatic need for accurate references so that the chains of transmission incorporated within the ḥādīth could be meticulously reproduced.[1]

One result of this was that individuals who had not formally trained in interpretive sciences applied search tools to traverse the sources, especially when looking for responses to issues linked to the practice of the Prophet, without the necessity of interacting with a scholar formally trained in the field. These short-circuited traditional roots of religious authority also meant that sensitive questions that people could not ask about Muḥammad locally could be addressed online. Over time this phenomenon expanded with the introduction of question-and-answer websites and resources, enabling interaction with scholars and trained individuals (in most cases) online. This development did not negate traditional routes of approaching the resources but, in some ways, may have even opened them up to wider audiences, especially in minority contexts among emerging computer-literate generations, for whom it was increasingly natural to go online to locate answers to critical questions.

The presence of prophetic announcements plays out in contemporary religious discourse and is effective across diverse formats beyond web browsers to incorporate apps, social media and other 'always on' technology. The quest for immediacy in terms of responses is shifting the religious discourse and interaction dynamic. At the same time, traditional ideas of petitioning the scholar remain, with face-to-face interaction (on or offline); there is an increasing digital subtext to ideas about religious authority. This underlying theme emphatically became the case when exploring the presence of Muḥammad online, especially as his sayings and actions inform so much of Islamic discourse. He is a continual figure of reference as the medium of the Divine Revelation received from God by the angel Jibrīl, rather than the origin of the Revelation. His specific qualities and exemplary status, emphasized in different degrees depending on the interpretive framework, find a place on the internet.

YouTube discussions and online groups centred around Muḥammad emphasize this status as much as reproduced texts and sources; specific materials designed for online consumption form part of this equation, relevant as content providers operate in a competitive marketplace, where they are buying influence and impact of their pronouncements. Simply reproducing text from the print source may be insufficient; online sources explicitly designed for digital consumption across platforms hold more attraction for users, where reading patterns and attention spans may differ. Materials may also take on a multimedia edge through animation, graphical interfaces, interactive experiences and video. Consumption reflects content users' world views, but equally, it can expose the consumer to new influences and ideas, with the concept of 'shopping around' for a religious opinion or interpretation being a practical option. This opinion perusal includes how the prophetic sources are mediated and interpreted, influenced by the religious, linguistic and cultural values associated with specific interpretations, which can also hold connotations shaped for political agendas.

Applying a search engine to seek basic knowledge associated with the Prophet can alert the reader to a multitude or a cacophony of different voices and opinions. This information overload, on the one hand, exposes the reader to a range of options, but these might be challenging and confusing, necessitating detailed research rather than providing an instant answer. Content providers presenting themselves as the 'go-to' source for information or a mediation point may offer their adherents a shortcut that already relates to the current world view. It may also subtly reshape it. Occasionally, this reshaping may go against the traditional values of a community network. This has been responsible for the political-religious framing of opinions which have led to so-called radicalization, in some cases associated with platforms associated with al-Qaeda and the 'Islamic State'. They form part of the marketplace of ideas and available information open to all web users, primarily focused on Muhammad.

Muḥammad is a constant factor within this framework of shopping around for opinions. Online content brings diverse understandings. Some textual sources are simply reproduced in a digital format, such as e-books and documents. Others further represent these sources through multimedia interfaces in a way that takes advantage of the medium and offers a practical communication experience for content use. Remember that the contestation is not just the religious materials, given the numerous distractions that exist online in different science. Religion forms part of a much broader content consumption pattern.

Aḥādīth databases

Consider the sayings and actions of Muḥammad: a simple online search for '*hadith*' (without transliteration marks) will be subject to variables based on location, browser, search engine, interface, time, metadata and search history. The contestation for authority means that the design of sites focuses on ensuring content reaches as substantial audiences as possible through the implementation of metadata which informs the search engine, along with the linkages between them with insights that can boost their rankings.

One 2020-page search included listings of significant sources, some available commercially, along with links to various databases. The same pages led to online videos where aspects of these sources were explained in videos by prominent influential 'authorities', including Nouman Ali, Shabir Ally and Omar Suleiman; a video explaining how to use a ḥādīth app also emerged.[2] There were links to generic definitions from Wikipedia and Encyclopaedia Britannica at the top level.[3] The videos can incorporate a question-and-answer discussion, in which a presenter talks to a scholar rather than simply listening to a lecture. This format lends itself to television-style interaction. Searching the videos also opens discussions, especially when contesting perspectives make comments that dispute the findings within the video. This dynamic includes the rejection of ḥādīth outright by some who suggest that the Qur'ān alone is sufficient and that ḥādīth sources include elements of conjecture and fragmentation.

The searchability facilitated by the digitization of ḥādīth sources offers a different dimension to approaching these sources. Multivolume printed versions can be accessed through thematic indexes, may be organized on a subject-by-subject basis, with similar ḥādīth (with minor differences in their content or *isnad* authority transmission chains) highlighted for scholarly interpretation. Learning these sources (by rote) and discussing them in scholarly disputation and analysis can form part of a 'traditional' Islamic education, mediated by a scholar whose credentials are often linked to an Islamic institution, with in-depth knowledge of each ḥādīth's veracity, its *isnad* and its relative strength or weakness.[4] This is a well-established pattern, which has in part been subverted by easier non-specialist access to ḥādīth content through electronic interfaces. There are mixed views as to this 'opening up' of ḥādīth sources.

The online collections have their foundations in the 1990s compilation of ḥādīth sources by the University of Southern California-Muslim Students Association (USC-MSA), part of a compendium which also included translations of the Qur'ān.[5] This site was a ground-breaking initiative in bringing ḥādīth sources to broader English-speaking international audiences with a user-friendly interface. In a way this provided the 'source code' underpinning other aspects of CIEs. While the original site is now unavailable directly, it was mirrored across the internet and adjusted over time in terms of correcting typographical errors and textual omissions. This development meant that websites applied it as part of their online databases to present the significant collections of ḥādīth in digital form; in some ways, these reflect their print origins as they are copies of printed texts. All are searchable, meaning readers can quickly locate keywords and authoritatively reference related sayings.[6] This site was a scholarly and technical approach to sources. Efforts to make it more interactive and accessible during the same source material were made, including the development of ḥādīth apps discussed later in this book.[7] It was ground-breaking in its approach, offering a template for future ḥādīth databases, while also representing a learning curve in terms of developmental issues and source continuity.

Observers have suggested, however, that no single comprehensive and reliable ḥādīth database has been developed to date, although 'authenticity' and 'veracity' are in the eyes of the beholder (or authority concerned), and there are technical restrictions associated with digitization, verification and responses to the integration of ḥādīth into artificial intelligence contexts.[8] Despite these limitations, it can be seen across diverse Islamic frameworks that ḥādīth sources underpin discussions across historical and contemporary contexts and are referred to within multiple CIE locations. Audiences include consumers and users of the multiple apps of Islamic sources who may refer to digital devices in the quest to answer religious questions or verification of action. Determining popularity can be problematic, but one indicator may be via metrics on app stores, where some ḥādīth apps have acquired over half a million downloads.[9] This may be a small number relative to the global Muslim population. 'Authenticity' is a key issue: a Shīʿa ḥādīth database app, containing traditions associated with the Shīʿa imams (discussed later in this book), received anti-Shīʿa negative feedback for containing 'fabricated' content.[10] These contested ideas about 'authenticity' are considered in later chapters.

Biography

Muḥammad's web presence extends to biographical sources (*Sīra*), offering a narrative combining ḥādīth and Sunnah sources with a 'historical' timeline, providing a traditional linear approach to the Prophet's life. There is a crowded marketplace of content, so accessing these materials can be linked to the underlying algorithms and metadata of specific sites and products. Some combine a variety of materials and approaches. As well as reproducing media from other sources, such as textual sources, cinematic biographies and audio accounts. Muḥammad's life features in specific online tools. AlphaApps' *The Seerah of Prophet Muḥammad* had its content approved by Awqaf Abu Dhabi and National Media Council UAE, providing a religiously sanctioned approach to its app's multimedia narrative. Commissioned music and graphics gave the material a unique interface for a young audience.[11]

Numerous audio-only interpretations emerged from various perspectives (not complementary to each other) across multiple platforms: Taimiyyah Zubair, the daughter of Islamic scholar Farhat Hashmi, produced her audio Seerah app in 2019.[12] Zimbabwean scholar and self-styled 'motivational speaker' Ismail bin Musa Menk's interpretation of the biography of Muḥammad could be sourced on Spotify. Menk has been accused by critics of being a 'Salafi', which he disputes, although he trained as a Deobandi.[13] Controversially, on Google Play, an audio life of the Prophet featured Anwar al-Awlaki's narrative; he was the influential American-born al-Qaeda advocate 'martyred' by a drone in 2011.[14]

The Prophet's representation shows diverse interpretation aspects across the Islamic spectrum. Complex frameworks of understanding from historical and cultural models have a digital edge. This representation can include ideas related to the mystical approaches and dimensions, often articulated within the esoteric Sufi framework(s). These can also integrate philosophical systems and understandings and unique articulations of meaning.

The cyber Mi'raj

The representation of specific episodes in Muḥammad's life marked out in the biographical sources are significant in their own right. One episode is representative in that it encompasses many facets of Islam, Muslims and Muḥammad: the Mi'raj (Night Journey). Muḥammad is said to have journeyed on the mystical animal Burāq (accompanied by Jibrīl) from the precincts of Mecca to Jerusalem in a single night – a journey deemed impossible given it took many days by camel. He then ascends to the heavens (Isrā'), where he encounters previous prophets and angels and negotiates the number of prayers with Mūsā. This sequence of events features in the Qur'ān, in Sūra Isrā', and in biographical sources as episodes which confirm Muḥammad's position as the last (and most significant) Prophet in a line going back through Judeo-Christian tradition to 'Ādam.

In popular culture, the Night Journey is represented in many ways, not least when Burāq images are found on trucks and buses as a symbol for safe travel. This phenomenon is on several picture boards, such as Pinterest, which demonstrate the historical and cultural representations of the Burāq – from Persian miniatures to contemporary art.[15] Elsewhere scientific justification for the Night Journey is presented online, linking to understandings of black holes and relevant verses from the Qur'ān, suggesting Muḥammad went into a black hole to make the journey in a single night.[16]

The integration of traditional sources, including Muḥammad's biographical *Sīra*, alongside ḥādīth sources, provides an online diagrammatic synthesis – and an opportunity to pay for the illumination of the Dome of the Rock (worth 1,000 prayers) – through a charitable donation to the Muslim Hands website. This site maps the different journey points based on ḥādīth narratives indicating the stops Burāq made on the journey. Muḥammad was encouraged to pray in Medina, at Mount Sinai (where he speaks to Mūsā), Bethlehem, Mūsā's grave and finally at the point of ascension in al-Aqṣā (Jerusalem).[17] This fusion of prophetic narrative and charity online is not unique to this website.

There are several animated versions of the narrative aimed at younger audiences. A contribution from Iqra Cartoons includes a Burāq depiction more in line with the style of 'My Little Pony' than its mythical depiction in Islamic sources, where a child narrates the story to an audience while also referencing a *tafsīr* (Qur'ānic commentary) by Ibn Kathīr (1300–73), a prominent scholar of Islamic sources famous for his work on the Qur'ān.[18] By contrast, a sermon by Yusuf al-Qadhi received over a million views as a soundtrack for a combination of captioned and illustrated content, reflecting the themes of the Night Journey. This familiar format is on other online platforms, where sermons form the basis of illustrated films, avoiding facial features or depictions of the Prophet. In some of these lectures, there is only one image.[19] Recorded *khuṭbah* can also discuss Mi'raj online, such as that of British scholar Abdal

Hakim Murad, illustrating episodes of the Night Journey. The Cambridge Central Mosque media team filmed Murad's sermon in its environmentally friendly mosque (and promoted it through social media channels following the speech).[20]

Search algorithms will lead surfers to different readings of the Miʿraj. For example, a videoed sermon by the Shīʿa preacher Syed Ammar Nakshawani discussed the scholars who believe there were different journeys and also reflected on the Shīʿa sources which explain the fundamental role of the Miʿraj in Muslim beliefs.[21] Other Shīʿa sermons unpack alternative perspectives.[22] Shīʿism's diversity features within understandings of Muḥammad's role as part of the wider prophetic family or Ahl al-Bayt.[23] While these can draw from sources and interpretations associated with Sunni traditions, they also spawned other materials which emphasize specific Shīʿa values and world views.

The Night Journey is a focal point in esoteric dimensions of Islam, which include interpretations under the 'Sufi' banner (which, as Chapter 8 will show, is complex and diverse). This zone contains an imaginative and attention-grabbing sermon entitled 'Intergalactic Gateway to Heaven via Jacob's Ladder' by Shaykh Mirahmadi on the Muḥammadan Way website, which emphasizes how meditation allows an individual to move outside of their body in an analogous way to Muḥammad's journey.[24] SufiLive, a channel with a sustained online presence across diverse media, goes inside a mosque to capture Shaykh Hisham Kabbani and his audience members in a discussion on the mystical dimensions of the Night Journey. Video proximity to Kabbani and others is a feature, especially where recitation from the Qurʾān forms part of the sequence. Talking directly to the camera, Kabbani creates an intimate perspective.[25]

Perennial Wisdom presents a different approach from its t-shirt-wearing Indonesian presenter Angga Arifka. With a more informal approach and using quotes from the Qurʾān along with images of the Sufi poet Rūmī (discussed in Chapter 8) to discuss Miʿraj, Arifka unpacks diverse interpretations and philosophical systems. This is from a series of lectures on Sufi-associated themes, with notes from academic works by Western and other scholars.[26]

When building a picture of Muḥammad's life through online sources, numerous other events could be investigated in-depth as they inform CIEs in terms of content, purpose and the broader expression of Islam. It is relevant to examine other aspects of Muḥammad's prophetic experience, particularly his presence in battles. This feature is synonymous with articulating the (lesser) jihād, representing the militaristic striving in the name of God; the episodes associated with Muḥammad and military activity appear in voluminous detail.[27] One significant military encounter is discussed below, relevant in its influence on understanding jihād and the ways in which its presentation can inform readers and seekers of religious knowledge in this complex zone:

Badr online

The Battle of Badr (624 CE) shows Muḥammad and his small band of followers facing significant and unexpected military Meccan non-Muslim forces in the second year following the establishment of the nascent Muslim city-state of Medina. Despite the fear within Muḥammad's forces – and the assertion of certain followers that they were only bound to protect Muḥammad in the confines of the city – according to tradition, his leadership inspired the forces to beat a Meccan army. Within the biographical sources and the Qur'ān, accounts of Badr suggest that Muḥammad saw Jibrīl and that angels on horseback assisted the Medinan forces. A miraculous sword features in battle. The concept of martyrdom is stressed, given the significant number of casualties. Within the body of *rajaz* poetry based on an account of warfare, there are stories of one-to-one combat and reports of family clashes between Muslims and their non-Muslim relations. In the aftermath, there is clarification (through Revelation) about spoils and captives. The theme from Badr is that Allāh assists Muslims, even when faced with overwhelming odds, and the victory was confirmation of Muḥammad's prophecy and his belief in a single God. This victory also demonstrates a level of prestige.

Badr is a significant reference point in the development of Islam. Defeat in this battle would negatively impact Islam's expansion and progress. Consequently, it is represented extensively online, not just in the various textual accounts and references available in Islamic sources. Inevitably it has become a reference point in e-jihad-oriented contexts too. A more traditional approach is contained in a video from OnePath Network, which explored lessons derived from the event and its aftermath.[28] A sermon by Sheikh Shady Alsuleiman, an Australian imam, has been used as the basis of a video containing a range of images and clips 'depicting' the events of Badr.[29] References to Badr come from incongruous sources, including a gaming company, which provided a detailed video account of the battle from a military perspective (while promoting their game 'Conqueror's Blade'). This game seemed to rely on several Muslim traditional accounts.[30]

Moustapha Akkad's 1976 feature film 'The Message' depicts Badr in epic detail with a basis in Islamic sources. An extract in a YouTube clip had over four million views (2022). Filmed in separate Arabic and English versions simultaneously, some saw 'The Message' as a vital propagation source, despite the Hollywood roots of its stars.[31] In contrast, a children's account of Badr produced by Iqra also uses traditional sources and represents key figures (blurred out for etiquette regarding the representation of the human form). The miraculous intervention of Muḥammad and one thousand angels is emphasized, and there is some (cartoon) blood, especially when Muḥammad's enemies are vanquished.[32] The Badr site features a page on Islamic Landmarks, showing significant battle locations. It features as a destination on TripAdvisor, highlighting the Masjid Badar (Mosque of Badr).[33] Videos from the Badr site are presented online by visitors on road trips, tourist sites and video blogs: Shaykh Amer Jamil from Scotland provides a brief on-site narrative of Badr's significance; A3's travelogue takes viewers on a tour of the Badr Mosque and its surrounding area.[34] A multitude of digital resources show Badr's implications as a transitional point in Islam's development, emphasizing the complexities of different interpretations and approaches to episodes in Muḥammad's life.

Conclusion

When looking at influences, the incorporation of other historical figures associated with Muḥammad is crucial. Members of the Prophet's family, his companions and the subsequent caliphate assumed the mantle of authority after the death of Muḥammad. The legitimacy of succession became a contentious subject area, which features within online dimensions and sources. Their legitimacy and roles reflect a much more comprehensive and long-standing historical conversation which has taken place regarding the development of Islam and the notions associated with different forms of religious authority and legitimacy. These have become incredibly influential in how the Qur'ān was collected, edited and disseminated. It had an impact relating to legitimacy concepts within a legalistic framework. A collection of the sayings and actions of the Prophet led in part to the development of various legal 'schools', which became the foundations of Islamic jurisprudence represented within the Sunni orthodox framework. These elements underpin the algorithms and coding which guide iMuslims towards specific Islamic sources and interpretations This authority and influence are the subjects of the following chapters.

Chapter 4

CYBER REPRESENTATION

THE PROPHET'S FAMILY, PROXIMITY AND SUCCESSION

This chapter explores the roles of different members of Muḥammad's family, especially how they are influential within CIEs. The chapter also looks at those who succeeded Muḥammad as leaders within the new Muslim community (not necessarily unconnected to his family). Each figure could be unpacked in further detail as the subject of individual studies to determine the complexities of online representation and authority within various Islamic constructs. In line with the previous chapter, some of them have roles in articulating traditional readings of the life of Muḥammad and in the attendant sources associated with this.

The Prophet's family

Representation and historical readings of the Prophet's family have become not only an issue but also a focal point for conflict. These underlying conflicts can impact perceptions when discussing the role of influences over history. They also play out online, suggesting a continuity of themes, prejudices and attitudes between different zones on the Islamic spectrum. Specific protocols and sensitivities surround the depiction of the family, especially in online contexts, including issues of boundaries surrounding their physical representation and depiction. The role of social media and online media also means that minority positions and less mainstream perspectives have a voice. Determining how this contributes to the cacophony of opinions is a complex process. It is relevant to consider how these opinions and their rapid circulation online can inflame prejudices and ideas about other interpretations and lead to real-world conflicts. This factor is particularly pertinent when considering the role of the Prophet's family and descendants.

The following section looks at some of the key figures that influenced the development of Islam from various perspectives. These zones are particularly complex as their biographies can vary depending on the writer. Divisions between and within Shīʿīsm and Sunni Islam, for example, represent these key figures differently. Online this means that their roles as influences are contested, with competition for ownership of actions, events and individuals. One must question the relationship between the historical and virtual figures. The idealized attributes in many traditional sources play out online differently, amplified through social media applications. This is not to say that traditional educational methods are still not applied but locating these views in the mainstream can be problematic. The scholars of religion may be in one silo, but mainstream society may not have that depth of knowledge about key individuals, so they may go online to seek out information if it is not readily available in their location.

Khadīja

According to tradition, Muḥammad's first wife Khadīja bint Khuwaylid (555–619) played a significant role in the initial development of Islam, recognizing his initial Revelation on Mount Hirā᾿ as a prophetic sign and supporting him during difficult times when he started to preach the message he received, initially to a largely hostile audience in Mecca. Khadīja represents an assertive businesswoman with her networks of trade and influence prior to her initial meeting with Muḥammad – who became her employee before marrying his older boss.

Unsurprisingly a range of digital religious perspectives and interests present interpretations of her life, drawing on traditional sources and readings while integrating exemplary practices attributed to her. Khadīja is often seen as the first person to accept Islam as a religion (after Muḥammad). Her life story appears in sermons and lectures: Yaqeen Institute presents her story in a discussion by Sh. Omar Suleiman, sees her life as a series of 'firsts' concerning her history, 'Muḥammad's first love', and a reflection of a 'perfect' practitioner of faith. Her shared ancestry with Muḥammad is stressed in the lecture's extended history of antecedents.[1] Suleiman also provides another lecture on Khadīja, in a shorter format, recorded outdoors: the language is more conversational and colloquial, full of anecdotes based on traditional sources.[2] An approach suitable for younger audiences is presented in an animated format, although it includes details of Khadīja's first two marriages (which both ended in the death of her husbands); it draws on traditional sources but (leaving the merits of the story aside) its presentation probably would not compete with more dynamic animation.[3]

The dry lecture format can be compared with the Shīʿa Ahlulbayt documentary, which utilizes graphics, various 'talking head' scholars, drawings, music and depictions of seventh-century Arabia. One speaker, Sheikh Ali Kourani, stresses that she is not only 'mother of all believers' but 'grandmother of all the Imams' – that being the line of religious authority in which Shīʿism places a specific emphasis. The documentary explores her role as a businesswoman, demonstrating links with other locations in the Arabian Peninsula and also that she put all her resources into supporting Muḥammad and Islam. However, the video lacks female voices as commentators (only in a dramatized voiceover of Khadīja discussing marriage to relatives and her daughter Fāṭimah talking to Muḥammad). These sections (drawn from other sources) also include graphics showing Khadīja, although – in line with interpretations of physical depictions – in this case, her face is not 'revealed' (other Shīʿa sources do present idealized portraits of key figures).[4]

Biographies come in many forms, including from Shīʿa sources, with different emphases regarding influences and authorities. The focal point may be the *ḥādīth* (or variants thereof), which refers to the relevance of ʿAlī ibn Abī Ṭālib – seen as an especially pivotal figure in Shīʿīsm (being 'the party of ʿAlī'). Khadīja has her biography interpreted in diverse ways synthesizing various sources, for example, in an accessible version for non-specialists by Yasin T. Al-Jibouri, which features on the Ahlul Bayt Digital Islamic Library Project's Al-Islam pages as an e-book.[5] A less conventional approach to Khadīja can be found on Pinterest, for example, on a board which draws together various quotations and sayings attributed to her.[6] She represents a role model for contemporary society, with one pin stating: 'In a world full of Kardasians, Aspire to be like a Khadija.'[7] Hadith of the day focuses on Khadīja. Textually based, focusing on detailed sources, this is more of a traditional essay on Khadīja and her attributes, based on prophetic biographical sources. These pages emphasize Khadīja's role as a receptive audience of the first Revelation and a protector of Muḥammad. [8]

How is Khadīja represented in cyberspace, and what does digital media bring to her biography? When represented on Pinterest, there is more of a multimedia emphasis. The cinematic depictions offer a depth and a dimension that goes beyond reading a text, allowing for an imaginative interplay between traditional sources and cinematic imagery. Audiences for this material vary, focusing on providing introductory information, sources and context. The presentation in a basic cartoon format provides one such entry point.

Given that the emphasis within much online media is around Muhammed, figures associated with him from his life story can be marginalized or have the role of bit players, even within cyberspace. There is scope for expanding the dynamic nature of this type of content to provide higher levels of interactivity and potential audience interest in figures, especially females, who can have a role in terms of being receptors for propagation information and focal points for powerful narratives. This factor can apply to others within the Prophet's household, many of whom have traditions and biographies attributed to them in different forms.

The Muzlimah marriage app is one channel through which it presents biographical information about Khadīja. This intersection between a contemporary online approach to marriage with a commercial edge and an accessible biography that is informed and critical (but not overly referenced!) is significant. Khadīja was, after all, a businesswoman who might appreciate the utilization of her life story for the 'halal' purpose of encouraging marriage. The article sits in a blog on various issues and adjacent to links for the Muzlimah app, combining marketing with propagating an interpretation of Islam.[9] There is a business model for creating, distributing, marketing and selling Islamic apps.

This intersection between technology and traditional values is fascinating on many levels, especially utilizing biographical sources to promote specific aspects of Islam through online interfaces. There may be a relationship between the exemplary models presented by key figures and their use as attributes to attract individuals towards religious beliefs, practices and values. The extent to which an online interface can do this is impossible to quantify, especially in a competitive marketplace for ideas, products and attention spans. This approach is also relevant when looking at other key figures associated with Muḥammad, especially those within his close circle.

ʿĀʾishah

Every wife of Muḥammad who followed Khadīja has specific attributes and merits associated with biographical sources and traditions. It is interesting to consider one in particular within an online context because she has been a focal point for anti-Muslim prejudice through readings and perhaps misreading of her life story: ʿĀʾishah bint Abī Bakr (613/4–678) is a significant figure within Muslim traditional frameworks, in fact, she is seen as a critical source of the sayings of Muḥammad, as well as being an observer of many of the important events within his life, specifically in the latter phases. Therein lies the controversy because she was, according to tradition, betrothed to Muḥammad at a very young age. For detractors (including online) this is seen as a factor that links to child marriage and child abuse.

Controversy surrounded ʿĀʾishah due to unfounded allegations of a relationship linked to a scandal known as the 'Necklace', which led to Revelation demanding witnesses for alleged adultery and castigation for those who promoted rumours and slander without substantiation. This latter element is perhaps very relevant within a social media context, given the prevalence of fake news and negativity online. As the daughter of the first caliph ʾAbū Bakr (573–634), who was one of Muḥammad's closest allies, her posthumous status is impacted by later perspectives on the caliphate and her roles and political-religious associations after Muḥammad's death. The life of ʿĀʾishah has been used by those seeking to present negative images of Islam. It is helpful to examine the presentation of her life and how these allegations feature within cyber-Islamic contexts.

The question of her marriage is one that particularly exercises online commentators. Egypt's Dar ul-Ifta alludes to the issue, focusing on Muḥammad's moral qualities and the contractual qualities of the marriage (in the tribal Quraysh context of the seventh century), noting the variations in age from different sources.[10] About Islam focuses on the relationship as an example of romantic love.[11] The article does not refer to the more negative aspects that can be associated with ʿĀʾishah.

One apologetic video from Muslim Central suggests that the child marriage practice was being viewed through 'post-modern' lenses, suggesting it was the values of the age that permitted the marriage at the age of nine (confirming it with specific *ḥādīth* sources). 'Orientalistic' perspectives were said to be behind the negative presentation of the marriage. It also drew on comparisons with historical marriage practices from other cultures and traditions, reinforcing its perspective through the use of animated graphics. The video received substantial positive feedback for its 'clarity' on YouTube.[12]

Islamic Awareness is critical of other Muslim perspectives and apologetics when pushing back the age of ʿĀʾishah:

> This evidence having been established, there doesn't seem much room for debate about ʿĀʾishah's age amongst believing Muslims. Until someone proves that in the Arabic language '*nine years old*' means something other than '*nine years old*', then we should all be firm in our belief that she was '*nine years old*' (as if there's a reason or need to believe otherwise!?!). In spite of these facts, there are still some Muslim authors that have somehow (?) managed to push ʿĀʾishah's age out to as far as '*fourteen or fifteen years old*' at the time of her marriage to the Prophet[(P)]. It should come as no surprise, however, that none of them ever offer any proof, evidence or references for their opinions.[13]

Opinions on this issue go way beyond cyberspace, with a comparative apologetic approach drawing on historical examples of marriage from Christian and Jewish traditions and contemporary examples from the United States.[14] One commentator notes: 'It's also worth noting that while the Prophet's marriage comes under scrutiny by Western critics, he could legally have married Lady ʿĀʾishah – having the full support of her family – right here in America (recall that in many states there is no age limit for marriage; only parental and/or judicial support is needed).'[15]

The status of ʿĀʾishah is significant within Islam not just because of her marriage and the controversies surrounding it but in other areas of her life where she was the subject of accusations and conjecture. Numerous biographical sources reflect these factors in different ways, which can help explain to readers specific portions from the Qurʾān, which often refer to the episode of 'the necklace', which presented multiple issues relevant for later interpretations.[16] According to tradition, ʿĀʾishah was part of a caravan, which she departed to locate a lost necklace; she met with a man from outside her group or family circle who helped her get back to her travelling party. This episode led to rumour and conjecture in Mecca because of alleged adultery or inappropriate contact. It was of great concern to Muḥammad, who initially expected a Revelation response in order that he could deal with the situation. Initially, this did not appear, 'evidence' that Revelation did not appear 'on demand', with sources suggesting that it was a month before there was a declaration of innocence. This pause emphasizes the Prophet's humanity, according to some sources.[17]

Ultimately Revelation was received relating to slander and, separately, the criteria for establishing adultery necessitating the presence of four witnesses. Specific issues also emerged regarding Muḥammad's doubts associated with ʿĀʾishah in the light of these accusations. These principles are important ones within ideas of contemporary Islamic interpretation as they have become part of legalistic frameworks, applied in contexts where rumour and conjecture can damage an individual's reputation. Revelation restored ʿĀʾishah's reputation. Muḥammad confronted the issue of how to deal with those individuals who had circulated the slanderous accusations. It was to form a precedent for others in the future regarding their behaviour in similar circumstances. Inevitably, online, this is another area of dispute which can also be a means of attacking Islam in general and the Prophet in particular.

In some religious and cultural contexts, infidelity is a capital crime, so establishing the grounds for cases requires precision. However, such punishments can be seen as controversial and inhumane in a contemporary context and would not be universally applied. As a basis for legal interpretation and approaches towards divorce, however, the principles can be seen as applicable, especially concerning the necessity of acquiring witnesses for the substantiation of an allegation of adultery. Sources also derived a positive spin on the outcome: 'The incident became the cause of some very important additions to the social law and injunctions of Islam. Through these the Muslims received such Commandments from Allah by which the Muslim society can be kept clean and protected against the creation and propagation of moral evils, and if at all they arise, they can be corrected promptly.'[18]

The potential influence of online content concerning ʿĀʾishah and the episode surrounding her is interesting to consider. Those seeking quick and easy answers to complex questions often go online to get information and responses that can act as an appropriate precedent for action and behaviour. The influence of figures such as ʿĀʾishah can have a bearing on contemporary societies in this regard where she is held as a role model and key source for information about the early period of Islam.

A variety of sources present ʿĀʾishah in a positive light, drawing on traditional interpretations to approach these important questions. ʿĀʾishah's role as a conduit for traditional practising behaviour also means that she has a dominant voice in Islamic discourse. This factor is also linked to her reputation as a daughter of ʾAbū Bakr, reinforcing her position. There are other dimensions to the understanding of ʿĀʾishah, reflected in CIEs: ʿĀʾishah is revered as a scholar of traditions associated with the Prophet, especially by legally included institutions such as Egypt's Dar ul-Ifta, which highlights her use of independent reasoning (*ijtihād*), high levels of knowledge on Islamic matters and interpretation issues and her intellect exercised in the fifty years following Muḥammad's death.[19]

Within Shīʿa contexts, attacks on ʿĀʾishah are part of the intra-Muslim conflict, where the detractors of Shīʿīsm suggest that the negative perceptions are based on slanderous, '*kuffār*' (non-believer') positions which hide the identities of those who made the slanderous comments. It is interesting that these concepts now form part of Sunni-Shīʿa conflicts in some contexts, linking them back to the clash between the first Umayyad Caliph Muʿāwiya Abī Sufyān (d.680) and ʿAlī ibn Abī Ṭālib – Muʿāwiya interpreted as the advocate of ideologies which attacked the Ahl al-Bayt (interpreted as the descendants of the Prophet). This element reflects, in particular, the attitudes of certain 'Salafi' and Deobandi Muslims who went against other Sunni attitudes seen as more accommodating towards Shīʿīsm.[20] However, there have also been accusations that Shīʿa Muslims have been opposed to ʿĀʾishah due to her position as the daughter of the first caliph and that she denied ʿAlī ibn Abī Ṭālib's caliphate. There are also suggestions that she fabricated *aḥādīth*. Accusations are made based on Shīʿa *aḥādīth* that she (alongside another wife, Ḥafṣah) sought to poison Muḥammad.[21] Such intra-Muslim dialogues focused on the Prophet's wives belie broader issues represented online in chatrooms and discussion groups, where animosity is featured towards and between diverse strands of Islamic interpretation. Other channels seek to refute such accusations, using Islamic sources and seeking evidence-based responses.[22]

ʿĀʾishah was opposed to the caliph ʿUthmān, although she disapproved of his murder. A subsequent power struggle saw her fight (and lose) against ʿAlī in the battle of the Camel (656), with prominent followers on either side killed, in a dispute that has been read in diverse ways by Sunni and Shīʿa sources. This episode caused conflict between Muḥammad's surviving family (including his wives) as part of a power struggle over the succession. In Shīʿīsm, there is a tension between ʿĀʾishah's role with Muḥammad, and the later conflict with ʿAlī, meaning that her status is not as exalted as it is in Shīʿīsm (in general). However, ʿAlī reconciled with ʿĀʾishah after the battle, as she was secluded from further political activity (and was prevented from remarriage due to her status). These factions and fractures play out online.

ʿĀʾishah's position in Islam – and especially in her representation in CIEs – makes her a critical reference point when searching for information about different aspects of Islam. Search query algorithms on complex and multiple themes will point towards her, particularly in controversial matters, where she may be used by detractors of Islam in terms of her early age marriage. ʿĀʾishah's political activities are a further focal point, retrospectively as a key player in the conflicts surrounding community leadership(s) after Muḥammad's death. As a source of knowledge for some interpreters, the traditions associated with her are embedded in multiple *aḥādīth* databases, forming an essential part of search results for those seeking specific information and advice.

The Prophet's other wives

Alongside Khadīja and ʿĀʾishah, it is relevant to consider the roles of Muḥammad's other wives within the discussion of influential figures. The marriages also raise polygamy issues and its legitimacy (or not) in Islam and whether Muḥammad had a special status regarding marriages. While considerable attention focuses on Khadīja and ʿĀʾishah, there is also an opportunity to explore the digital presence of Muḥammad's eleven other wives. These were marriages for multiple reasons. They could be strategic in that they brought alliances with significant families. They could be compensatory in that they were marriages of the wives of those who had fallen husbands who had died in battles. The political alliances could stretch across borders and religions. Marriages could also be based on desire. Some of Muḥammad's other wives are discussed below, in terms of their digital impact:

Algorithms and deep searching on Muḥammad's other wives will demonstrate a spectrum of qualities and issues relevant to understanding different aspects of Islam, which can form exemplary models and constructs for audiences: for example, Sawda bint Zamʿa (570/80–674?), an early convert to Islam, is significant because she was concerned about being divorced from Muḥammad due to her age, and it was said that he desired this, leading to Revelation emerging to support *her* position.[23] Sawda relinquished her time and sexual relations with the Prophet, establishing a precedent that provided practices for subsequent generations in matters of marriage and relationships, with a positive spin in some interpretations countering patriarchal assumptions regarding sexuality and age.[24] Online, these details permeate lectures and sermons, often as part of a series on the Prophet's wives, frequently narrated by males.[25] The principles associated with Sawda's physical separation from Muḥammad are relevant for questions of divorce, which feature extensively in online Q&A sites, in which surfers send in their questions to authorities for consideration and a religious opinion. Some of the responses focus on the emulation of Sawda's 'ideal' domestic nature.[26]

Other wives have specific roles in Islam's formative development: Ḥafṣah bint ʿUmar (*c*.605–65) is emphasized in online sources as a literate person who memorized the Qurʾān. According to tradition, it was Ḥafṣah's collection of various folios and manuscripts (brought together by Zayd bin Thābit) that led to the first physical recension of the Qurʾān. Some point to Ḥafṣah exploring interpretations of the Qurʾānic Revelations as they emerged.[27] Ḥafṣah is a protector of the Qurʾān from external parties who sought to acquire it for nefarious purposes. Wives can also be cast in a more negative light. Some aspects of Shīʿīsm represent Ḥafṣah in a more negative light; an anti-Shīʿa site (with the misleading title TwelverShia .net) suggests that Shīʿa Muslims condemn Ḥafṣah for (allegedly) conspiring against Muḥammad's daughter Fāṭimah with regards to an inheritance and intra-wife jealously leading to accusations of Ḥafṣah seeking to poison Muḥammad (alongside ʿĀʾishah).[28] This application of Ḥafṣah as a means of condemning Shīʿīsm is an unusual one.

As a model for behaviour, Ḥafṣah's role presents qualities of trustworthiness, studious ability, resilience and devotion in various hagiographic sources.[29] These may draw on traditional works for their readings of Ḥafṣah and her status alongside other wives, including her (possible) role as a compiler of the Qurʾān, reinforcing women's role in early Islam.[30] Some place a greater emphasis on her role than others.[31]

Other wives also play roles in delivering and protecting Islamic sources: Hind bint ʾAbī ʾUmayyah (d.680), known by the *kunya* ʾUmm Salama, is a significant source of *aḥādīth*, and has importance in Shīʿīsm due to her role in raising Muḥammad's daughter, Fāṭimah. ʾUmm Salama is a widely cited source of nearly four hundred *aḥādīth*, collected in the *ʾUmm Salama Musnad*; Shīʿa sources emphasize her proximity to Muḥammad's family and descendants at critical episodes in their lives (and deaths).[32] Online, her quotations and prayers are widely available from Sunni and Shīʿa platforms.[33] ʾUmm Salama was the last of Muḥammad's wives to die, living until the age of eighty-four (according to some sources), some fifty-two years after marrying Muḥammad. Online, the Sufi Chishti Order connects ʾUmm Salama (and other prominent Muslim females) to its line.[34] Muslims for Progressive Values cite the case of ʾUmm Salama as having a *mukhanath* or 'effeminate' friend who was 'accepted' by Muḥammad, significant in explorations of gender, Islam and sexuality. She features extensively on Islam Q&A sites as a frequently referenced source in response to specific questions seeking fatwas.[35]

Muḥammad's wives can also impact other areas of Islam, such as inter-religious relations: Rayhāna bint Zayd (d.631) was a freed Jewish enslaved person who eventually converted to Islam and married Muḥammad. The actual marriage is seen as contentious, as is the issue of whether she remained an enslaved person. Rayhāna was a member of the Banu Qurayza tribe, which allegedly broke a covenant with the Medina Muslim community, which led to the slaughter of several hundred prisoners. Traditions suggest that despite this, Rayhāna provided Muḥammad with insights into Judaism (at a time when he sought to encourage Jewish tribes to convert to Islam). Inevitably Rayhāna is a focal point for some online Jewish voices and their historical readings of Islam. There is minimal discussion on Rayhāna online. She is a discussion point for issues associated with slavery and Jewish-Muslim relations. Apologetic sites contest anti-Muslim opinions in the difficult reconciliation of seventh-century Arabian values with those of the contemporary world.[36] While Rayhāna does not have a specific influence on these events, she is a specific reference point and presence stimulating online dialogues and conversations.

Those seeking links between Judaism and Islam may come across Ṣafiyya bint Ḥuyayy (*c.*610/14–664/72), a further wife of Muḥammad to emerge from a Jewish background. She was a member of the Banū Naḍīr Jewish tribe whose father was executed at the Battle of the Trench, while her first husband died after a significant defeat of Jewish tribes at the Battle of Kaybar in 629. A dream that suggested a forthcoming marriage of Ṣafiyya to Muḥammad has specific mystical implications for those within the more esoteric zones of Islamic interpretation, in which dream interpretation has importance.[37] Sources suggest that – as a captive – Ṣafiyya did not have the option of consent in the marriage arrangements and that her dowry was simply her freedom.[38] Other sites may apply this to promote Muḥammad's role as an equitable individual who cared for his wives.[39] Ṣafiyya's case is used to cast negative aspersions on Islam and Muslims while also being a focal point for anti-Semitism. Other sources suggest that it reinforces Judaism's status in Islam. In Morocco, Sufis regard Ṣafiyya as a *murshida* ('guide') and Torah teacher, whose status is exemplified in digital contexts.[40]

The role of wives from diverse religious backgrounds offers an interesting dynamic to ideas about interfaith issues. A further example is Mariyāh al-Qibtiyya (d.627), an enslaved Christian Egyptian who converted to Islam (alongside her sister), having been 'gifted' to Muḥammad by the Archbishop of Alexandria. She married Muḥammad and gave birth to a son, Ibrāhīm, who died in infancy (as had Qāsim and ʿAbd Allāh, his sons with Khadīja). Mariyāh's significance in terms of online perceptions is associated with this tragedy and her perceived piety – especially concerning her Christian background.[41] Mariyāh also countered jealousy from other wives, especially ʿĀʾishah; some suggest that ʿĀʾishah was responsible for rumours that Mariyāh was not married to Muḥammad – but was a concubine, albeit with high status.[42] Some sites assert this position in discussions on Christian-Muslim relations (given the permissibility of Muslim men having Christian wives).[43] Other sites suggest that her status was 'upgraded' from concubine to wife when she gave birth to Ibrāhīm.[44] This issue has also become a focal point for those seeking to critique Islam and disparage Muḥammad, often using the content of various Islam websites to construct their arguments, resulting in online counterarguments.[45]

Those searching for the spiritual qualities of Muḥammad's wives may be directed to Zaynab bint Jaḥsh (*c*.590–640), whose online links focus on her perceived emphasis on piety and poverty. A first cousin of Muḥammad, she lost previous husbands in battles prior to marrying Muḥammad's adopted son Zayd ibn Ḥāritha (also known as Zayd ibn Muḥammad). Adopted sons in traditional pre-Islamic Arabic contexts were regarded in the same ways as biological sons. Zaynab also raises issues regarding divorce, as she sought divorce from Zayd, raising complex issues associated with the permissibility of divorce. The emergence of Revelation in the Qur'ān answered key questions on these issues associated with divorces relating to the wives of adopted sons and changed the status of foster sons.[46] It is unusual because it is a piece of Revelation that mentions one of Muḥammad's companions (Zayd) by name. The sequence of events led to criticism from some sectors critical of Muḥammad and Islam at the time.[47] The nature of adoption changed in Islam during this sequence of events.[48] These elements are significant reference points for those seeking answers on critical aspects of Islamic personal law.

Zaynab becomes a reference point concerning divorce practices, as her divorce was 'heavenly decreed', something she reminded the other wives of Muḥammad.[49] The nature of the divorce becomes a contentious subject on Q&A sites, especially given the different interpretations and emphases on various sources, including the need to justify approaches to Muḥammad that did not apply to others due to his special prophetic status.[50] Complex issues associated with Zaynab feature on video sermons too, including those collected from diverse sources (repeating some content); one YouTube video on Zaynab includes bizarre musical organ accompaniment.[51] These concerns cross over into Shīʿīsm and are applied to condemn some of the sources associated with depictions of Muḥammad in Sunni Islam – such as traditions indicating 'human' desires in the case of Zaynab. Sayed Hossein Al Qazwini's YouTube video stresses the veracity of Shīʿa opinions and sources over Sunni traditions in this matter.[52] This is significant for those comparing intra-Islamic positions on personal law issues which can have real-life implications when interpreted analogously.

Ramla bint Abī Sufyān (*kunya*: ʾUmm Ḥabība) came from a complex background, as her father was Muḥammad's principal adversary in the Quraysh tribe, ʾAbū Sufyān. After her husband Ubayd-Allah died in Abyssinia in 627, Muḥammad proposed marriage to ʾUmm Ḥabība. The marriage ceremony took place from a distance, as Muḥammad was in Mecca, and ʾUmm Ḥabība in Abyssinia, with the Abyssinian ruler paying her dowry. In contemporary contexts, this is an interesting precedent, as it suggests, especially in the online context, that ʾUmm

Ḥabība's 'distance marriage' could be a precedent for online 'distance marriages' when parties to the marriage are in different places. ʾUmm Ḥabība is seen online as standing up to challenges from her tribe the Quraysh (including her father).[53] The political implications of her marriage clearly impact Islam's development.

Muḥammad's wives are significant figures to consider as they provide some exemplary models utilized in sermons and lectures as behaviour patterns. Within the biography of the Prophet, they also add to the richness of detail relating to his life and times, which can stress human qualities and how – according to tradition – he negotiated complex relationships. These are all themes which can play out in cyberspace: the names are familiar to people from their inclusion in narratives and histories. They are essential concerning gender roles, especially as they can present the impression of strong women with negotiating powers which influence the behaviour of Muḥammad and within traditions are seen as providing him with high levels of support and comfort at critical times.

Bilāl

It is possible to discuss hundreds of other figures outside of the immediate family concerning the early development of Islam. It is not possible to represent them all here, but there is one figure that is important to explore in this section concerning its impact in online discourse: Bilāl ibn Rabāḥ (580–640) has a prominent and complex role in the development of Islam; a freed enslaved person of black African heritage, he achieved prominence as the first muezzin, calling to prayer the early Muslim community. He succeeded on the battlefield, notably in revenge against his former torturers and tormentors who had demanded his departure from Islam by placing stones on his chest in the burning sun. These deprivations and Bilāl's later success make him a significant figure for those facing adversity for their beliefs, mainly the enslaved, and becoming a symbol for those of shared heritage over distance and time who were to become Muslim. His story is shared across children's videos, academic analysis and opinion pieces as a profound symbol against injustice and inequality.[54] During the 2020 #BlackLivesMatter campaigns, Bilāl's symbolism took on extra resonance in the United States, especially as a symbol against racism (as reflected in Muḥammad's defence of Bilāl and advocation of equality as represented in his Final Sermon).[55]

The significance of his role as a muezzin makes Bilāl a focal point of religious practice and an essential zone of online activities; in Sunni practice, the methodology for the call to prayer (*adhān*) came from a figure dressed in green through a dream by Muḥammad's follower ʿAbd Allāh bin Zaid. He was told to pass it on to Bilāl, the possessor of the loudest voice.[56] Shīʿa sources believe that the call to prayer was received directly by Muḥammad. *Adhān* app developers use Bilāl's name in apps that calculate prayer times and directions.[57] App stores provide many variants of prayer apps and associated content. Bilāl's name is on many apps, religiously oriented and otherwise, including a biography.[58] An intriguing Bilāl Ethiopian app provides Amharic *nashīd* renditions (devotional songs) and Qurʾān recordings.[59]

'Bilāl' is represented on video extracts from Moustapha Akkad's 1976 film 'The Message', with millions of YouTube views. One channel had numerous positive references to #BlackLivesMatters in its comments.[60] Bilāl was also the subject of a 1973 film *Hazreti Bilāl-i Habesi*, now widely available online, having achieved millions of hits.[61] An animated film *Mu'āwiya: A New Breed of Hero*, developed in Dubai by Barajoun Entertainment, generated substantial attention online with its trailers (and subsequent availability through streaming channels): 'Inspired by true events, this is a story of a real hero who earned his remembrance in time and history.' It received mixed feedback online too from Muslim audiences for its representation of early Meccan society and the levels of violence depicted in the film.[62] The movie also spawned an app and game.[63] Bilāl represents a significant figure of influence across diverse cyber-Islamic contexts, relevant to multiple audiences and influential in campaigns as a symbol against deprivations and adversity.

Succeeding Muḥammad

I have taught early Islam courses from the start of my academic career. It has been interesting to see how digital content integrated traditional sources into narratives about Muḥammad and those who followed him. These have often featured in student essays and dissertations, which have broadened the scope of materials relevant for discussions about this phase in Islam's history, especially when giving access to complex and detailed sources. This development has impacted student perceptions of Islam, especially when they have looked at the concept of the caliphate:

The individuals who followed Muhammad as leaders of the new Muslim community have a significant role in CIEs, exemplars of behaviour and advocates for Islam. It is essential to consider the roles of the first caliphs who naturally get the highest level of attention within a Sunni cyber context. This factor is associated with notions of religious authority and lines of influence emanating from the Prophet – but based around the designated successors, and military and community leaders within contesting zones of leadership. There were differing interpretations of who should lead the community at the time. These opinions feature in traditional and historical interpretations over time (linked to political, linguistic and cultural factors). Echoes of the disputations and conflicts play out in cyberspace, the latest iteration of bodies of works discussing religious and historical readings of events. Representations of individuals are also crucial in providing exemplars of patterns of behaviour and paradigms of practice to follow. The qualities projected on these individuals through their digital portrayal act as reminders for each of *'al-'Ashara al-Mubashshara'* – ten companions of Muḥammad said to be destined for paradise, according to a ḥādīth which named them. The ten includes subsequent three caliphs ('Umar, 'Uthmān and 'Ali) alongside other companions (Ṭalḥa ibn 'Ubayd Allāh, Zubayr ibn al-'Awwām, 'Abd al-Raḥmān ibn 'Awf, Sa'd ibn Abī Waqqās, Sa'īd ibn Zayd, 'Abū 'Ubayda,

ʿĀmir ibn ʿAbd Allah ibn al-Jarrāḥ) who were close to Muḥammad and were specifically mentioned in the ḥādīth. The succession is a contentious area within Islam, with various parties vying for control. ʾAbū Bakr's status as a successor is exemplified in Sunni sources but disputed in Shīʿa interpretations. He acquired his position (in Sunni perspective) after discussion and consensus within the Medina community after Muḥammad's death. This status is in line with his representation in sources as one of '*al-ʿAshara al-Mubashshara*'.

Within Sunni traditional contexts, the first three *al-Khulafāʾ al-Rāshidūn* or 'rightly guided caliphs' are considered to be ʾAbū Bakr (d. 634), ʿUmar (d. 644) ʿUthmān (d. 656) and ʿAlī (d.661). A committee selected these Companions of the Prophet from Muḥammad's Meccan kinfolk and – according to tradition – were judged eligible according to criteria based on acceptance of the Qurʾān and the Sunnah and membership of Muḥammad's Quraysh tribe. The first caliphs began to have practices and precedents attributed to them. While the process of Islam's expansion continued certain flaws, administrative problems and defeats led to suggestions that the caliphs' status was unfounded.

The ultimate sovereign in Islam is God: Muḥammad was Allāh's 'vice-regent' on earth (*caliph* – successor and deputy). After Muḥammad died in 632, there was the question of who would lead the Muslim community. Muḥammad was the Final Prophet – therefore, no more prophets would come to lead the community. There was a need for leadership to preserve Revelation and enable Islam to develop and spread further (keeping the momentum established by Muḥammad). There was also the need for an arbiter of disputes and the maker of community decisions.

The contestation of dynastic leadership led to a series of civil wars, as different parties asserted themselves and sought control of the Muslim community. Leadership was contested, with sources indicating factionalization and conflict. Sources present versions of events associated with the succession. On Muḥammad's death, there was a fear that the tribal alliances he had engendered would dissolve – and that the unity of the Muslim community would fracture (further). Assertions from supporters of Muḥammad's follower ʾAbū Bakr and Muḥammad's son-in-law ʿAlī separately suggested that both were advanced for the position by Muḥammad. ʾAbū Bakr and ʿUmar were associated with Muḥammad through marriage and clan ties. This contestation is a significant feature of online content associated with both parties and their successors.

ʾAbū Bakr was active as caliph between 632 and 634 and affirmed this authority with military campaigns, projecting Islam into (and beyond) the frontier regions of empires. Consolidation processes known as *ridda* wars maintained the expansive momentum of the Muslim community and Islam, which was drawn northwards to richer Syria and Iraq, conquering Arabia and entering Palestine. As an early convert to Islam, ʾAbū Bakr held authority in Mecca that influenced others towards affiliation with the 'new' religion. His proximity to Muḥammad during significant events highlights his role, such as when he helped Muḥammad escape persecution on route to establishing the first Muslim state in Yathrib (later known as *Madīnat al-Nabī* or the 'Prophet's city', shortened to Madīna or Medina). The marriage of ʾAbū Bakr's daughter ʿĀʾishah to Muḥammad strengthened his position, alongside his prowess in significant battles – leading to him presiding over the first Islamic pilgrimage (Ḥajj) in Muḥammad's absence. ʾAbū Bakr's significant role included instigating the collection of the Qurʾān towards the development of a definitive collected edition (*muṣḥaf*) completed after his death.

ʿUmar ibn al-Khaṭṭāb (r. 634–44) led the expansive Muslim state in its conquest of Damascus in 636. A ten-year period of expansion embraced the Arabian Peninsula, parts of the former Sasanian Empire and Byzantine Syrian and Egyptian provinces. The focal shift towards the Mediterranean world took advantage of vacuums of power and control caused by agricultural system problems, economic challenges, epidemics and protracted conflicts. Shared religious values between Christian and Jewish populations and Arab Muslims aided transitions in some contexts, motivated by precedent and the status of these *Ahl al-Kitāb* ('People of the Book') in Muslim societies; changes in rulers might not impact the grassroots level. Arab Muslim forces took advantage of these opportunities, utilizing military skills and experience of fighting in other zones, with logistics centred around effective long-distance campaigning using camels. Over time, conquests and capitulations led to the expansion of Arabic language usage for everyday and religious purposes. Religion played a part in motivations for some fighters, while it became a convenient banner for acquiring spoils and status for others.

One would expect this expansive phase in Islamic history to project well on ʿUmar in his online representation, especially in Sunni contexts. Shīʿa commentators are less favourable, suggesting conspiracies against ʿAlī ibn Abī Ṭālib led by ʿUmar. They would be less than enthusiastic about the 30-part TV series about ʿUmar promoted online (and archived). Originally produced by Saudi channel MBC (with headquarters in Dubai) and Qatar Television, the series was available via the long-standing portal IslamiCity and through other unofficial channels such as Vimeo, where enthusiasts had uploaded it. Less anticipated, perhaps, was the reaction of Sunni Islamic authorities to the original TV series, condemned in a *fatwā* or religious opinion as 'sinful' by al-Azhar for its representation of historical figures and receiving similar negative feedback from Saudi religious authorities.[64] Pirated copies were on eBay. Its extensive biographical approach, big budget and level of historical detail mark this period drama out, alongside high production values and echoes of 'Game of Thrones' in its battle depictions.[65]

The programme also received negative feedback from some because it depicted other Islamic figures, including ʿAlī. However, it was dubbed, translated into several languages and broadcast internationally. Through the fusion of broadcast media and the internet, a figure such as ʿUmar acquires a substantial new profile and status. Other interpretations might cast a more negative light on the person who planned (before becoming Muslim) to assassinate Muḥammad and also attacked family members for reading the Qurʾān before hearing its recitation and converting. He is a redemptive figure. One online chaplaincy saw him as a figure who could influence prisoners to change their ways and become Muslim.[66] The death of ʿUmar at the hands of a knife assassin marks him as a martyr (to some), with a series of traditions drawn from his sayings just after the attack, including advice relating to funerary arrangements and bequests (that informed later practices).[67]

The third caliph, ʿUthmān ibn ʿAffān ibn Abī al-ʾĀs (644–56), was an early convert to Islam from a prosperous family that had supported Muḥammad. Like ʿAli, he was a son-in-law of Muḥammad, having first married Ruqayyah bint Muḥammad (who died during the period of the Battle of Badr) and then ʾUmm Kulthūm bint Muḥammad (who died prior to her father, in 630). ʿUthmān kept a relatively low profile during the Prophet's lifetime, only gaining political ascendancy after Muḥammad's death. The bubbling tensions and conflicts of earlier caliphates re-emerged after ʿUmar's assassination. ʿUthmān's conciliatory position, according to some sources, sought to bring together contesting factions in an environment where tensions heightened during the further expansion of the Muslim state.

ʿUthmān's control saw expansion into zones including Egypt and North Africa and consolidation over recently conquered Persia territories. The conquests eastwards in Herat and Balkh in modern-day Afghanistan in 651 created a route for ultimate further expansion in the Indian subcontinent. ʿUthmān sanctioned an epic victory against Byzantine forces under Gregory the Patrician in 651. Muslim-controlled naval forces opened the Mediterranean to ʿUthmān's forces, utilizing a new Muslim capital in Damascus. Incursions into al-Andalus established a foothold that ultimately led to the conquest of the Iberian Peninsula.

Criticism of ʿUthmān's administrative qualities is countered by those who see an astute financial manager who encouraged the development of coins inscribed in Arabic. His religious initiative to develop the recension of the Qurʾān (which bears his name) means that his reputation continues to resonate over time, at least among Sunnis. They recognize this action (Shīʿa Muslims do not acknowledge ʿUthmān's role).

ʿUthmān's selection of members of his own Umayyad clan as provincial governors created resentment and opposition in Medina from the sons of companions and ʿĀʾishah – and in Kufa and Fustat. The resentment of Meccan domination of Medina in tribal affairs, and the atmosphere of nepotism went against principles articulated in the Qurʾān. ʿUthmān's murder in 656 is associated with administrative issues in Egypt and a complex set of rivalries, which resulted in a coup in Egypt that ʿUthmān could not suppress. Rebellious contingents from Basra, Kufa and Egypt sought to overthrow and kill ʿUthmān, ultimately resulting in a siege in Medina (ʿAli's sons Ḥasan and Ḥusayn guarded ʿUthmān). Despite this, the rebels breached the house's security and killed ʿUthmān (although his family defended him). He was buried as a 'martyr'.

ʿUthmān death split the Muslim community, essentially creating fractures that led to the development of Shīʿa factions under ʿAli and his family line and the separate caliphate under Muʿāwiya ibn Abī Sufyān. The claimant to the title of the caliph was (ʿUthmān's brother-in-law) ʿAli, the Quraysh early convert to Islam and a cousin of Muḥammad who had married Muḥammad's daughter Fāṭimah bint Muḥammad. ʿUthmān's clan and others disputing the election's validity opposed ʿAli.

Given these complex circumstances, naturally, there are different emphases on ʿUthmān online. Islamic Guidance presents Mufti Menk's sermon with a hagiographic account of his life, illustrated by orientalist paintings, over the narration drawn from a sermon.[68] Another YouTube film shows Menk behind the lectern.[69] Sermons on ʿUthmān have made it into audiobook format.[70] Children's stories reflect traditional sources about ʿUthmān, including an animated story which focused on his modesty, piety and early life as a trader (with a blurred image representing ʿUthmān). The cartoon characters appear as 'white European', unrepresentative of ethnic groups in the Arabic peninsular. The gory details of ʿUthmān's death were (understandably) avoided.[71] Online, there remains substantial discussion on ʿUthmān's death and the reasons for the conflicts between companions and other parties, impacting contemporary perceptions of Islam.[72] A vital element of these discussions is the role of ʿAli (explored in Chapter 6).

The lives of all these and other *al-ʿAshara al-Mubashshara* figures play out as influential figures within cyberspace, with lectures and videos devoted to their activities and actions as the lives of Muḥammad's companions (*Ṣaḥābah*).[73] Long discourses on each are online, going into exhaustive detail on these and other figures.[74] The ten's military and political influence is exemplified in descriptions based on *aḥādīth* and other sources, including biographical materials associated with Muḥammad. Infographics link the ten together too. The tombs of some of these figures became shrines (with 'Islamic State' targeting some of them). Their influence extends beyond the Arabian Peninsula (Waqqās has a shrine in China). The roles of these and other companions would fill multiple volumes, given their influence and impact on later developments of Islam, especially in terms of the aḥādīth and principles associated with their interpretation and practice. The ten's presence online allows for deeper exploration and distribution of information relating to their roles and status, specifically in association with Muḥammad during his lifetime and in the phases after his death.

Conclusion

Many of the figures surrounding Muḥammad have significant roles as exemplary figures, which plays out online in terms of their depiction and implicit influence on Muslim societies. Their representation has a central role in CIEs and could become a focal point of any metaverse construct. This is significant among those zones that observe the caliphate's principles, relevant as role models and preservers of the nascent religion and its expansion into broader contexts. Contrasting perspectives and degrees of influence across contexts can make generalization problematic. This early generation of influences provides further stability and understanding of Islam, especially for those seeking contextual meanings and 'historical' readings alongside traditional understandings. Sources claim to provide a chronology and authentic meaning to these figures online, reflecting traditional and other materials. This is relevant for those wanting to return to the 'original interpretations' and understandings of Islam from the time of the Prophet and the immediate companions, meaning that these figures impact legalistic and traditional readings of Islamic sources and practices. There is an interplay here between these figures and those associated with the Prophet's family, including the Ahl al-Bayt. Combined with diverse historical readings, these complex connections and networks play out in cyberspace.

The figures surrounding Muḥammad are by no means peripheral to the development of Islam and have a role to play within the digital hierarchies of CIEs, where they play roles as purveyors of tradition and examples of behaviour. As such, they form a major part of the subtexts of interpretation and understanding, especially when looking at the complexities of interpretation issues and their approaches within digital constructs. These figures are influences and link directly to powerful narratives of behaviour and practice, a relevant point for the following chapter. It is interesting to consider the myriad complex roles of the wives within discussions about contemporary Islam, as many of the episodes associated with them can be analogous to modern concerns and agendas. The differing perspectives can also be seen in important figures often linked to the political and religious contexts in which they operated and subsequently influenced over generations. Perceptions are based on traditional sources which may have been embellished or edited over time but form part of a hypertext reality that informs contemporaneous discussion and debate.

Chapter 5

CIE LEGAL

DIGITAL SUNNI INFLUENCES, LAW AND AUTHORITY

The chapter explores how figures with influence in pre-digital frameworks maintain a reference point and have a presence within online contexts. They form part of ongoing discussions about the essence of Islam and have a pervading digital impact which has been reinforced through online media development – which not only maintains a legacy but creates new audiences for their opinions and religious perspectives. These influences will impact future Muslim metaverse contexts and CIEs, with audiences in some cases far greater in terms of numbers than previous generations, especially in terms of the translation and repurposing of their work across multimedia. The metaverse marketplace of ideas and influence is based on the foundations of many of the individuals discussed below, alongside their 'schools' and supporters. The impact of figures discussed below is also linked to their position in Sunni legalistic contexts, which are significant in many Muslim societies as reference points for decision-making and interpretation, especially based on precedent and analogy. Concepts associated with the pragmatic interpretation of Islam in the light of contemporary circumstances (*ijtihād*) are particularly relevant in CIEs. Other frameworks feature elsewhere in this book.

The Sunni online equation

Discourse on 'Islamic law' has underpinned much of cyber-Islamic activities across formats and networks. While it is not assumed here that all Muslims observe a specific, codified approach towards 'Islamic law', approaches towards it may inform development and activities within any projected Muslim metaverse, in terms of appropriate behaviour and development of permissible content. The digitization of this system on one level facilitates comprehensive access to knowledge and opinion, but it can also generate confusion. The configuration of search parameters and algorithms impact specifically on these zones of religious authority online.

Defining 'Sunni' frameworks

The chapter's focus on Sunni contexts looks at the roots of interpretation before exploring diverse approaches towards religious authority across space and time, especially in digital manifestations. There is a recognition that the term 'Sunni' has some fluidity and can infer multiple meanings across religious, cultural and political contexts. The term 'orthodoxy' suggests a rigid praxis, which may be how practitioners of specific 'Sunni' views see it. It may simply mean 'Islam' to many Muslims. It can also, however, incorporate a variety of spiritual, esoteric and political approaches to Islam. Conflicting ideas of the term's utility and relevance emerge when considering intra-Sunni perspectives. The intention here is not to suggest a rigid compartmental approach to Islam, with viewpoints confined to specific silos. However, this can be projected onto understandings of Islam and Muslims (by practitioners and observers – including academics). The influences discussed below may fit within various 'Sunni' models of Islam. However, they can also integrate into multiple other perspectives, crossing (primarily via the internet) barriers around knowledge and its transmission. Complex local influences and networks within various focal points underpin transnational and global generic understandings of 'Sunni' 'orthodoxy'. Audiences now go way beyond their original projected reach.

Introducing 'Islamic Law'

Any understanding of the dynamics of religious authority in cyber contexts require an understanding of Islamic law, which has four broad and connected divisions within Sunni contexts. These reflect different approaches towards the interpretation of religious knowledge, which now have a digital emphasis but are interpreted as being linked back to the time of Muḥammad. Those seeking answers to their religious questions online may be directed via algorithms to interpretations which are formulated towards developing ideas for ensuring (according to their advocates) proximity to the interpretations of the Qurʾān and other sources based on principles associated with the Prophet Muḥammad and captured within the corpus of *ḥādīth* sayings and Sunnah actions. Islamic legal information now presented in databases has a basis (in the eyes of advocates) in being part of a process subject to varying degrees of veracity-checking and knowledge of chains of transmission to establish their providence reliably back to the Prophet himself. Within this framework, Islam provides a system (or systems) of ethical and moral behaviour based on the Revelation from Allāh, received by Muḥammad via the Angel Jibrīl – and now available to all via CIE computer systems, algorithms, searchable interfaces and apps.

Theoretically, interpretation of all aspects and facets of human life can be according to an Islamic system collected in sources including the Qurʾān, *ḥādīth*, Sunnah, biographical sources of the Prophet (*sīra*), 'theology' (*kalām*), Islamic legal theory and jurisprudence (*ʾuṣūl al-fiḳh*, literally the 'roots of understanding') and knowledge of *fiḳh* and the essential tenets of faith (*sharīʿa*). Some aspects are clear and easy to understand; other knowledge requires specialist interpretation(s).

It can be filtered and augmented with other sources, including the frameworks associated with Shīʿa beliefs, Sufism and other branches of beliefs associated with specific regional and cultural interpretations over time. These are all represented online in different ways.

Contesting digital interpretations of Islam

As Islam developed, four primary schools (*madhāhib*) of Islamic law emerged. However, these elements can be subverted when non-traditionally trained individuals provide their interpretations online, offering their understandings and views. There are specific questions of legitimacy and whether knowledge in other fields 'qualifies' an individual to issue a religious opinion; technocrats, politicians and influences may feel they can do this. In my 2003 book *Islam in the Digital Age*, I noted how this brought these issues into sharp focus when any individuals (whatever their qualification) could proclaim themselves or be proclaimed online as 'authorities' on Islam and provide 'Islamic advice'. Family connections, political authority, religiosity and/or levels of education potentially contribute to the individual's power to interpret Islam. The debate on Islamic decision-making issues is long-standing and predates the emergence of the internet but has become amplified in cyberspace.[1]

Representatives of all the 'schools' of Islamic law feature in a combination of Q&A channels, publications, online courses and web pages. There is a contestation for religious authority influence in these zones, reflecting religious and, in some cases, commercial factors. They can demonstrate a range of influences which go beyond specific legalistic issues into the politicized religious discourse on issues such as multiple Islamic identities.

The principles articulated in these four schools (and others) have influenced generations of Muslim lives. Their interpretations of Qurʾān and Sunnah have been guides for people who have sought to understand Islam. They have affected all levels of society within different interpretations of 'Islamic law' across communities today. This is emphasized online, although the levels of 'user-friendly' content differ: many online resources contain substantial electronic materials that can be used in independent study, especially e-books and PDFs of manuscripts in multiple languages. This enabled some scrutiny at a distance which is not explicitly mediated by a scholar on-site, allowing for independent assessment of a particular school's viewpoint. Through such channels, exposure to ideas outside of zones of familiarity becomes increasingly viable, although this does not necessarily immediately enable understanding. Such materials may be placed online for the benefit of existing adherents rather than being an attempt to change the hearts and minds of those from other religious perspectives. Digital materials in CIEs can facilitate discussion and debate within specific world views. The legacy of various schools is reflected in part online, especially in question and answer and online *fatāwā* sites. However, it is less apparent in a developed way through online educational media.

Exposure still relies significantly on traditional approaches to knowledge transmission and absorption through educational frameworks, and this is less of a subject that could be studied easily online relative to other academic areas. Instead, it is augmented for some students or an opportunity for casual readers to acquire preliminary knowledge in these highly specialized fields, allowing observers and even detractors to acquire source material. To an extent, there is an opening up of source content online compared with this situation before the emergence of digital technologies. The immediacy of the internet and the proliferation of ways in which e-books are mediated make electronic media a natural place for disseminating and studying key texts.

Those individuals that we can classify as 'influences' have historical resonance, given that their works from many centuries ago continue to be the subject of detailed study offline and retain a presence and influence online, as well, however subtle or overt that might be. These authorities sought to collect significant sources associated with Muḥammad to ascertain the relative merit of each in the light of that provenance, reliability and authority as encapsulated in the traditional chains of transmission. These mark the journey from a statement or action made by Muḥammad to its observation, recording, cataloguing and distribution along traditional roots of knowledge associated with oral dissemination. The transmission networks and the process of attribution now incorporate distinctly digital conversations within contemporary contexts, such as chat and comments on specific sayings in terms of context and distribution channels. The routes and networks of religious authority are strongly associated with a continuity with the past. They are also locked into modernity, especially in the transmission, translation and dissemination through social media and the web.

Source codices: Islamic legal theory in cyberspace

Ḥanafī

The earliest recognized *maḏhab* is the Ḥanafī School, named after ʾAbū Ḥanīfa al-Nuʿmān (700–67). The Kufa (in modern-day Iraq) based scholar is presented as having interpreted Islam according to the day's requirements. He avoided interpretative extremes by presenting the ideals of the community of the Muslims as a 'middle road', established on the practice of the Prophet Muḥammad, in which authenticity of tradition was a dominant trope. The Ḥanafī school spread across the Muslim world as Islam extended in all directions from the Arabian Peninsula, favoured by Abbasid caliphs and later Seljuk and Ottoman empires.

One consequence of ʾAbū Ḥanīfa's influence is that he is discussed at length online in terms of the perceived exemplar of his own life, including his (possible) death in prison and his knowledge of Islamic sources. ʾAbū Ḥanīfa is also the subject of criticism, both contemporaneous to his period and in subsequent analyses and opinions. Followed internationally, his practices and interpretation precedents are reinforced in part by online output. ʾAbū Ḥanīfa's teaching was recorded by later authors, although there are questions of attribution for specific practices and statements projected onto ʾAbū Ḥanīfa from his successors.[2]

There are numerous hagiographic accounts of ʾAbū Ḥanīfa, focusing on his perceived qualities, jurisprudence knowledge, theological studies and even his success as a businessman.[3] ʾAbū Ḥanīfa's life features in YouTube narratives, some illustrated by stock images and graphics (featuring paintings drawn from orientalist sources), including biographical sermons.[4] ʾAbū Ḥanīfa's legacy is represented through his tomb complex in Baghdad, which is a tourist and religious destination, featuring on TripAdvisor and more spiritually included sites.[5] A 3-D digital rendering of a proposed extension of the mosque from its architects was enabled on social media, facilitating aerial views of the complex. However, while the work was proposed through a competition in 2012, it had not been implemented.[6] Eyewitness video shows the mosque and shrine from a tourist's perspective, noting that US forces had destroyed the shrine's original clock tower in 2003, and giving some interior views. Entry was permitted even during Covid-19, and the interior views (from a handheld camera) were spectacular. Permission to record the call to prayer was given, offering a digital degree of access and insight into ritual practice. Prayer was also recorded.[7] Separately it was also possible to view *mawlid* (*mīlād*) celebrations (of the Prophet Muḥammad's birthday) held at ʾAbū Ḥanīfa Mosque.[8]

The Hanafi Fiqh Channel reflects the work of the Deobandi Darul Uloom alongside video advice on religious rituals. Deoband Online maintains a blog discussing Hanafi issues in conjunction with their Q&A channels. Advice on Covid-19 on Deoband Online included restrictions on using generic search engines for religious issues unless individuals had engaged in their final year of undergraduate study.[9] In 2021, IslamQA.org offered a channel through locating different Sunni perspectives, indexing their contents according to specific schools: online, in its database of 83,000 responses to questions, in terms of the number of websites Ḥanafī approaches dominated, with thirty-four (out of forty) listed sites. This statistic may be because of the perspectives of the site compliers, but it offers some insight into influence issues across diverse contexts. They noted that they had 80,000 Ḥanafī answers, with only 1,900 from the other schools.[10]

Hanafi Madhhab is represented in its own Facebook channel, promoting interpretations and online sessions.[11] Ḥanafī concepts are also present on other social media channels, where they might engage more youthful audiences, such as Instagram. Hanafi Fiqh brought aspects of Ḥanafī practice, with a specific emphasis on ritual cleanliness, and also promoted specific fiḳh books and advice on prayer during the lockdown. There were links to Ḥanafī online events, podcasts and a photo of 'Spiderman' at prayer. Shaykh Muḥammad Awwamah al-Ḥanafī, a prominent Syrian religious scholar, is shown using a digital device (surrounded by other religious figures).[12]

Other Instagram Ḥanafī accounts promoted *fiḳh* books.[13] However, there was also integration of Ḥanafī beliefs and popular culture through memes, drawing on quotes from Ḥanafī sources and images drawn from cinema, television and comic book culture. Hanafi memes identified as 'Not your regular Haram-Halal meme page . . . Prerequisite: Strong fiḳh game.' Their content included memes featuring Omni-Man (a character from the Invincible comic and TV series) commenting on al-Ghazālī, the Joker (from Batman) 'rejecting the taqleed', the 'Life of Brian' appropriated as a comment on Salafis and Sufis, SpongeBob Squarepants celebrating breaking the fast and (negative) meme comments on other interpretations of Islam.[14] A widely circulated meme in 2021 concerning Ukraine and Taiwan indicated 'Types of Headaches' when living next to Russia and China, respectively, was adapted to defending religious practices (eight *raka ʿāt* of Taraweeh).[15]

While not typical, these are perhaps a radical departure from other approaches towards Ḥanafī fiḳh. There are specific issues and questions (raised elsewhere) as to whether such humour is permissible. Some scholarly opinions suggest that they go against religious principles, including an opinion based on Hanafi Fiqh from Darul UloomTT: 'These so called "Halal memes" amount to nothing but making fun, mockery and joke of Allah, His Messenger and His religion, which are all acts of Kufr.'[16]

Be that as it may, they potentially impact grassroots understanding of significant Ḥanafī issues and interpretations and contribute to levels of influence and dialogue (in conjunction with other discussions). This development emerges on channels such as Reddit, where memes are continually introduced, alongside links to related issues on religious authority and interpretation.[17]

Mālikī

When exploring diverse *maḏhab*, in terms of the sequence in which they emerged, chronologically, the Mālikī school is 'next'. It was established around the systematization of judicial codes established by Mālik ibn Anas (708–716–796 CE). One result was *Kitāb al-Muwaṭṭaʾ* ('book of the smoothed path'), with its focus on traditions and practices established by Muḥammad and his companions in Medina. This book is the earliest surviving judicial work and became the foundation of later recensions (*riwāyas*) commentaries and studies, with its emphasis on *ibādāt* (worship) and *mu ʿāmalāt* (law). It was a perspective bringing together materials from diverse locations with a focus on notions of consensus and going on to influence the (then) expanding Muslim world.[18]

Versions of *al-Muwaṭṭaʾ* are available online, although many are PDF or e-book versions of the collected texts.[19] One online resource introduced a level of searchability, allowing exploration of the narrators of specific ḥādīth sources. They take on a more dynamic online dimension in their transition into apps, where there is a level of searchability; Al-Muwatta Pro is one example for iPad and iPhone, containing sixty-one books translated into eighteen languages.[20] Azzure Labs' Al-Muwatta (Sahih Muwatta) allows for adjustable themes and rapid searchability.[21] The Right Way's version links *al-Muwaṭṭaʾ* to social media, enabling individual sections to be posted online, although its free version is advertising-supported (leading one user to complain about inappropriate advertising). The app does offer user-friendly interfaces in Arabic and English, with more customization than other offerings.[22] Shareability and variation of fonts can also assist in making interfaces more user-friendly for dense and complex texts, especially 'customisable' options such as Usman Pervez's app of Muwatta.[23] Mālik's collected ḥādīth are promoted on email lists and via Twitter.

Mālik sympathized with aspects of Sufism when their practitioners followed traditional religious practices and some state that he prayed towards the Prophet's tomb for intercession. One result of this is that there are various readings of Mālik represented online. Unlike ʾAbū Ḥanīfa, there is no mosque or shrine to Mālik. He was buried in Medina, where Saudi Arabian authorities razed many tombs.

Al-Shāfiʿī

There is a strong link between Mālik and the next prominent 'founder' of a school of Islamic law: Muḥammad ibn Idris al-Shāfiʿī (767–820) was born in Palestine or Yemen, depending on the biographical source, to a prominent tribal family. Raised in Mecca after the death of his father, he became a personal student of Mālik, although later became critical of aspects of Mālik's work. Al-Shāfiʿī travelled extensively in the Middle East and North Africa. This experience led al-Shāfiʿī to focus on the legalistic sciences of *ʾuṣūl al-fiḳh*, especially how every action of a Muslim can be linked to the Qurʾān and Sunnah, through legal statutes – and that this *sharīʿa* ('divinely revealed law') can be deduced through analytical processes.

This process was assembled and codified by al-Shāfiʿī in different versions of *al-Risāla* ('The Epistle') – with a specific focus on the prophetic practices, sayings and implicit acceptance of specific actions. There is a focus on forms of analogy (*qiyās*) and *ijtihād*, along with emphasis on the consensus of scholarly opinions (*ijmāʿ*). Al-Shāfiʿī's approaches went on to impact many zones of the Middle East, Africa and elsewhere across the 'Muslim world' over time. These influences resonate online.[24] Videos explain aspects of *al-Risāla* from different locations and perspectives, often in a 'lecture' format, and expounding on technical details from religious and academic perspectives (the two being mutually complementary at times).[25] This includes a lecture series by the Grand Mufti of al-Azhar, Sheikh Ali Gomaa.[26] Al-Shāfiʿī's Mausoleum is in Cairo, having been the subject of renovation work completed in 2021. A biographical video includes details from the restored interior of the mausoleum.[27]

The practices from *al-Risāla* become a driving force for establishing juristic opinions and religious practices, especially in ambiguous situations. One result is religious opinions or fatwas, as articulated across the internet on various Q&A sites. Those seeking to explore these issues from a personal perspective can explore various downloadable and e-book copies of *al-Risāla*. It may be easier to explore using a searchable app, such as Indonesian applications, which contain much of al-Shāfiʿī's works in a searchable and easy-to-navigate format.[28]

Ḥanbalī

There are claims that al-Shāfiʿī taught the Baghdad-based 'founder' of the Ḥanbalī 'school', Aḥmad ibn Muḥammad ibn Ḥanbal ʾAbū ʿAbdallāh al-Shaybānī al-Marwazī - shorted to Ibn Ḥanbal (780–855 CE). His focus was on the Qurʾān and *ḥādīth* as the principal sources of religious knowledge, rather than the application of forms of human reasoning. His emphasis on the transmission sources of ḥādīth is one focus of his teachings, which were collected and written down by his followers. They were the core of *al-Musnad*, an ḥādīth compilation classified according to the transmitter. A further compilation of Aḥmad ibn Ḥanbal's responses to specific questions formed the basis of versions of a*l-Masā ʾil*. Other works are attributed to him, associated with prayer, polemics and piety.[29] The principles associated with Ibn Ḥanbal influenced later interpretative frameworks, including those developed by Ibn Taymiyyah and Muḥammad ibn ʿAbd al-Wahhāb al-Tamīmī (both discussed below).

Aḥmad ibn Ḥanbal features extensively online, the subject of lectures and sermons, and a source of reference and citation associated with his collected compilations and teachings.[30] Pinterest has links promoting collections of his work (in print), alongside graphics highlighting key quotes – often as part of more comprehensive collections of 'inspirational' quote material. One of the most intriguing online aspects of Ibn Ḥanbal relates to the 2017 television series 'The Imam' produced by Qatar Media Foundation, shown on television over Ramadan. It was also posted on YouTube, achieving millions of hits.[31] This series introduces many dramatic biographical elements from Ibn Ḥanbal, which potentially brings new audiences for Ibn Ḥanbal's work, over and above the usual audiences that lectures and sermons receive. Specific apps incorporate his work, which offers searchability, diverse fonts and the ability to share specific links to *ḥādīth* sources.[32]

ALT.INTERPRETATIONS

It would be exhausting here to pursue all the digressions associated with interpreting Islam in diverse Sunni contexts and how they play out online. The intention is to explore critical figures and models which can act as digital reference points. There is substantial diversity of approaches and opinions in the legal and intellectual descendants of the four 'schools'. The complexities of how interpretation has 'evolved' over time include disputes as to whether the 'doors of *ijtihād*' were subject to closure.

Al-Ghazālī

The synthesis of disciplines intended to enhance understanding of Islam finds a specific focus in the work of Abu Hamid Muḥammad b. Muḥammad al-Tusi al-Ghazālī (1058–111), whose presence permeates CIEs and emerges with frequency across a range of subject areas. Al-Ghazālī also features in the Sufism section of this book, which demonstrated the interoperability of key figures in terms of influences and impact. Al-Ghazālī is perceived as a *mujaddid* (a 'renewer') who promoted the application of *ijtihād* by suitably qualified jurists while condemning *taqlīd*, defined as absolute adherence (without question) to the Qurʾān.[33] Al-Ghazālī emphasized the application of *sharīʿa* as a way of life and advocated the pragmatic interpretation of Islam, stressing the Qurʾān and ḥādīth rather than 'non-Muslim' sciences.[34]

Important factors connect al-Ghazālī to issues relevant to contemporary iMuslims seeking advice on a range of concerns, in particular, his responses to what he saw as 'threats' to Islam: al-Ghazālī constructed a model of the qualities he perceived a caliph or otherworldly ruler should possess, focusing on 'correct' religious practice.[35] The absence of central leadership is a central theme for many advocates of interpretation, up to the present day and had a bearing on readings of Muslim politics. The idea of a suitably qualified caliph continues to be seen by some groups as a panacea for the problems facing contemporary Muslims. Al-Ghazālī encourages Muslims to challenge and re-evaluate existing frameworks which steer away from the rigid teachings of Islam, for example, through the application of 'ignorant' interpretations of *ʾuṣūl al-fiḳh*. This formed a useful precedent for later generations, encountering sciences that certain scholars felt were a threat to Islam. Al-Ghazālī's online impact can be measured in the discussion on Sufism, where it has its most significant impact online (discussed later in this book). In terms of the political-religious demonstrations, there is an emphasis on books and essays rather than user-friendly apps. These pieces still retain an influence, however.

Ibn Taymiyyah

Algorithms will take iMuslims to complex and contrasting world views when encountering Ibn Taymiyyah online. In terms of advocating *ijtihād* and endorsing literal interpretations of the Qurʾān in the interests of reform, the role of Taqī al-Dīn ʾAḥmad ibn Taymiyyah (1263–328) retains an influence that has crossed political-religious interests and interpretations reflected in CIEs. Ibn Taymiyyah's personal experience and political environment informed his understanding. In 1258, five years before Ibn Taymiyyah was born, the Mughals had occupied Baghdad, a traditional centre of learning and the Abbasid capital. This event, the conclusion of six hundred years of the Abbasid caliphate, was seen as catastrophic by nearby Syria's inhabitants whom the Mughals threatened. The work of Ibn Taymiyyah stresses the need for a jihād against these alien forces.[36]

The influence of Ibn Taymiyyah permeates numerous advocations of 'reform' – especially within political contexts associated with Islam. One emphasis is on his stress on adapting Islam to the circumstances of any age through the application of Qurʾān and *ḥādīth* and the use of *ijtihād* and forms of analogy. Ibn Taymiyyah did not seek to produce a single source through which subsequent interpreters could refer to when faced with problems: instead, he encouraged the mechanisms of personal exegesis, if a person had the appropriate qualities, constantly stressing the communal interest of the Muslim community or *ummah*.[37] Ibn Taymiyyah draws together diverse sources and arguments that fit into his framework of understanding, avoiding the fractures based on political and religious differences that he saw as damaging. Within his work, there is some contradiction, though, as he opposed aspects of Shīʿa and Sufi beliefs as 'heretical', but also emphasized the Qurʾān's warning: 'When you go forth in the way of God, be discerning, and say not unto him who offers you peace, "You are not a believer," . . .'[38] Significantly, this argument was ignored (especially online) by influential parties who otherwise advocated much of Ibn Taymiyyah's world view, including some jihād-oriented groups such as 'Islamic State'.

Ibn Taymiyyah can be considered one of the influential paradigms for many subsequent 'reforms', whether by movements, individuals, renewers or reformers. Consequently, there is substantial information about Ibn Taymiyyah online as well. The strength of his learning presents a compulsive influence. Ibn Taymiyyah was a Muslim confronted by external dangers (invasion) and domestic dangers (threats to the orthodoxy of Islam). Many subsequent reformers could relate to this position: adverse political and religious conditions, coupled with deterioration in the ideals of Islam, stimulated the call for reform for many who followed him. Some see him as a dangerous influence, threatening the *status quo*. The concept of the reformer as a martyr also enters the equation. Like his many followers, Ibn Taymiyyah could not implement much of what he advocated personally, and was persecuted for his beliefs. As an influence, his thought has impacted subsequent generations in historical circumstances and influenced later generations of scholars, as well as online.

There are numerous texts associated with Ibn Taymiyyah freely available in CIEs, such as e-books and PDFs, and versions of his religious opinions.[39] Collections of interpretations of Ibn Taymiyyah's works by 'Salafi' entities project their specific 'pure' interpretations of Islam. Salafism comprises a spectrum of perspectives which are not mutually compatible. For example, Canadian dawah (propagation) organization TROID uses multimedia across various platforms to promote their worldviews, with electronic publications, online lectures and networking opportunities. This approach includes content delivered on the TROID app. Ibn Taymiyyah features extensively, with answers to specific questions analysed according to specific sources and interpretations.[40]

Apps are an accessible way of addressing the complexities of Ibn Taymiyyah, such as a collection of seventeen books (in Arabic) which are fully searchable and can be annotated.[41] Aphorisms and quotes attributed to Ibn Taymiyyah feature online in meme and poster form, including some that run counter to interpretations suggesting he was 'anti-Sufi'. Quotes talk about the permissibility of praying in languages other than Arabic, jihād, repentance, music being like 'alcohol for the soul', praying for the benefit of others and the volatility of male-female encounters: 'Men mixing with women is like fire mixing with wood.'[42] Ibn Taymiyyah is used to support and counter various arguments regarding religious authority, such as (some) Salafi inclinations that it was not permitted to follow more than one school of interpretation.[43]

Elsewhere, pro-Salafi online entities (representing a spectrum of understanding) utilize Ibn Taymiyyah in their output.[44] The term 'Salafi' itself is problematic, given its association with the earliest generation of Muḥammad's companions and followers, but now has an application in terms of an (idealized) affinity with the period, where contemporary individuals ascribe themselves as 'Salafi' while being themselves diverse and complex in their identities and affiliations. Piety, politics and militaristic jihād perspectives articulate opposition to others (e.g. against militaristic jihād). The Salafi are not a rigid organization but rather multiple different 'movements' in different locations and contexts, taking their inspiration from 'the "pious ancestors" representing the first three generations of Muslims (*al-salaf al-ṣāliḥ*)' and Muḥammad.[45] The persona of the Prophet, through actions and aphorisms, provides a template for interpreting the Qur'ān. However, there is a level of dissatisfaction, especially from those who seek the ideals of a 'golden age' without paying due attention to the modern realities. Muhammad Iqbal (1877–938) suggested that the lack of awareness about the history of Muslims played a crucial role. Indeed, there is the creation of a mythical space in interpretations, a desire to imitate ancestors rather than innovate. There is a variance in the preoccupation with Islamic values, dependent on whether it is on a personal interpretation or part of a community understanding. The desire to pacify peer pressure and become part of a collective voice with a religious motivation would seem to play an essential role in transferring theoretical ideals into some form of reality. Many of these themes play out online.

Ibn Taymiyyah's application as a reference point for some jihād-oriented platforms has been challenged, with claims that proponents have manipulated key jihād concepts to suit specific ideological concepts and ambitions, including so-called 'martyrdom missions'.[46] These claims emerged online through the outputs of al-Qaeda and 'the Islamic State'. Ibn Taymiyyah was a clear reference point for Abdu'llāh 'Azzām (1941–89), a key figure in developing interpretations of jihād that al-Qaeda and 'Islamic State' later utilized; 'Azzām 'self-described as a Salafi, quoted Ibn Taymiyyah, and expanded on terms associated with Salafism . . .'[47] Reductionist interpretations and readings of Ibn Taymiyyah are applied by analysts and jihād advocates alike to support understandings. These belie complexities of affiliations and influences on figures such as 'Azzām. There is also the telescoping of readings associated with (some of) those who cited 'Azzām as an influential figure, such as Abū Mus'ab al-Zarqāwī (1966–2006) and Osama bin Laden (1957–2011). Ibn Taymiyyah's anti-Shī'a perspectives were utilized by al-Qaeda in Iraq and – later on – by Daesh or 'Islamic State'.[48] This factor was particularly significant in Daesh's application of *takfīr*, the assertion of disbelief in others, which they based on a reading of Ibn Taymiyyah and articulated extensively through online channels.[49]

Although Ibn Taymiyyah was not the only voice seeking a re-evaluation of Islamic practice centred on Qur'ān and *ḥādīth*, his influence pervades many subsequent interpretations of Islam. It has impacted through online distribution of his work – and the distillation of interpretations of Ibn Taymiyyah. Thus, his digital footprint extends across many zones: Ibn Taymiyyah's thought permeates the Hijaz, the Maghreb, Egypt, South Asia, Southeast Asia and – especially – cyberspace. In contemporary Muslim societies, Ibn Taymiyyah is a focal point in the struggle for a pragmatic understanding of Islam in the face of purportedly hostile influences. Subsequent reformers and reform-centred movements have reappraised Ibn Taymiyyah's work, which has informed political processes ('positively' and 'negatively').

Ibn Qayyim

Ibn Taymiyyah's legacy is associated with his pupil and (partial) advocate Ibn Qayyim Al-Jawziyya (1292–1350), who holds substantial influence in Salafi, 'Wahhabi' and related zones. He was associated with the Ḥanbalī school and was imprisoned with Ibn Taymiyyah in 1326 for advocating against certain traditional practices. Ibn Qayyim's prolific output has been utilized by later generations of scholars and influences through to the present day. Attention is focused on criticism of practices such as worship at graves and attributing qualities to 'saints' – traits deemed innovative or outside of Islam. There is sympathy towards particular aspects of mystical practices (under the 'Sufism' umbrella); however, some of his writings explore mystic literature works.[50] His various volumes incorporate these perspectives and include commentaries on (commentaries of) the Qur᾽ān and ḥādīth.

Ibn Qayyim represents a significant online influence through his synthesis of Ibn Taymiyyah and Ḥanbalī scholarship, filtered through his scholarly interests. These works are available as e-books, downloadable PDFs and print media.[51] He also wrote polemical works against those he saw as challenging (his interpretation of) Islam. Quotations and aphorisms attributed to Ibn Qayyim are popular across social media, such as a 'Top 20' video slideshow of quotes (accompanied by guitar music) that may be machine-generated.[52] There are also several apps devoted to his quotes, offering quotes of the day and a Wikipedia-derived biography.[53] Ahmad Kutty of the Islamic Institute of Toronto presents Ibn Qayyim as one of the 'giants of Islamic civilization'. Kutty suggests that social media has negatively misinterpreted Ibn Taymiyyah and Ibn Qayyim and that they were being appropriated by 'scholars' who lacked appropriate qualifications for *fiḳh*.[54] Elsewhere Ibn Qayyim's poetic refutation of Christianity acquired a substantial online audience. Its YouTube recitation (juxtaposed with religious paintings and images from religious cinematic offerings) is one of several located online.[55] There is a discussion of these influences as follows.

*

Turning points in Islamic influence: Walīullāh and Al-Wahhāb

In the centuries following these figures, numerous others held influence across diverse contexts. They form part of the multiple conversations across generations on issues of religious interpretation and authority. To attain a granulated understanding of online Islamic influences, discussion now focuses on key figures from diverse cultural, historical and geographical contexts who have informed aspects of Sunni understanding. Figures are chosen to demonstrate continuing impact resonating online in contemporary contexts. Two share the same birth year of 1703, Shāh Walīullāh Dehlawī and Muḥammad ibn ʿAbd al-Wahhāb:

Shāh Walīullāh Dehlawī

The thoughts of Shāh Walīullāh Dehlawī (1703–62) from Delhi filter through many zones of cyberspace, seen as analogous to contemporary concerns by his readers. As a *hajji* who had studied in Mecca, he was initiated into a Sufi order and succeeded his father in heading a *madrassah*. Shāh Walīullāh lived during a time of radical change in India when movements emerged as reactions to the loss of Muslim political power and the encroaching English Imperialism.[56] Like Ibn Taymiyyah, Shāh Walīullāh feared foreign invaders and felt that Islamic life was threatened by 'unorthodox behaviour', such as particular aspects of Sufism and the influence of philosophy (*falsāfa*).[57] Shāh Walīullāh explains that once during prayer, he underwent a Sufi-style ritual in which he gave a vow of allegiance to Muḥammad and then felt united with the Prophet's spirit. He describes receiving Muḥammad's pen from the Prophet's grandsons, Ḥusayn and Ḥasan. Such experiences, indicative of his close links with the Naqshbandiyya Sufi order, were believed by Shāh Walīullāh to equip him for holding the function of a 'renewer' and 'reformer' of Islam.[58]

Shah Walīullāh's biography is cited across many websites and represented within a YouTube movie on the Ḥanafī Fiqh Channel. Essentially this is a lecture illustrated with a landscape photo, by Abdur Raheem Abu Nu'man, which emphasizes his 'nobility' (and that the British government translated his work in the past).[59] Walīullāh also includes PowerPoint presentations as an academic lecture subject (part of the Pakistan curriculum).[60] Naturally, he is also part of lectures and sermons recorded online, some more accessible than others. One of the most popular is a recording by Israr Ahmad (1932–2010), an influential Pakistani Islamic scholar whose film on Walīullāh attracted over 100,000 views.[61]

Shah Walīullāh's tomb in Delhi can be seen on YouTube, accompanied by an on-site commentary explaining his influence. There is an explanation of Shāh Walīullāh's impactful Qur'ān translation from Arabic to Persian and emphasis on his influence on later generations (Walīullāh's sons continued this Qur'ān translation trend, producing an Urdu version).[62] Another online tour takes the format of a walkthrough of the tomb complex (which includes Walīullāh's tomb) accompanied by a lecture and a (slightly incongruous) music track.[63] Walīullāh is cited extensively via Pinterest, utilizing key quotations.[64] Walīullāh's translation of the Qur'ān has been scanned and placed into the public domain and is also available as a download to install on Android phones.[65] Walīullāh's online influence permeates religious conversations, educational curricula and the dialogues associated with diverse approaches towards 'reform' and religious practices in the Indian subcontinent and within diaspora communities.

Muḥammad ibn 'Abd al-Wahhāb

Synonymous with so-called 'Wahhabism' and Saudi Arabian religious influence, Muḥammad ibn 'Abd al-Wahhāb al-Tamīmī's (1703–92) name has a resonance in cyberspace that transcends the borders of Saudi Arabia. His influence may be wrapped up in speculation and assumptions from followers and interpreters as much as external commentators. His digital footprint may encompass political-religious movements and ideologies, echoing through a myriad of interpretative matrices, reinforced by the financial muscle of Saudi Arabia in propagating an understanding of Islam associated with approaches developed and promoted by Ibn ʿAbd al-Wahhāb. There is continuity between al-Wahhāb's approaches and those of intellectual and religious predecessors (including some discussed earlier in this chapter).

In order to understand his role as a contemporary influence, one must first approach Muḥammad ibn ʿAbd al-Wahhāb through his historical and cultural context. He came from a family of jurists in Najd in central Arabia (then controlled by the Ottoman Empire) and spent time in al-Basra, Baghdad and Isfahan. He met *ḥādīth* experts on *hajj*, which developed his interest in the Islamic sciences of interpretation. Within the diverse and insecure tribal fractures of Arabia, Ibn ʿAbd al-Wahhāb believed that a shared understanding and application of orthodox Islam would promote political and religious unity. Particularly relevant was Ibn Taymiyyah's understanding of Ibn Ḥanbal, centred on rigid interpretations of the Qurʾān and ḥādīth. Unlike Ibn Taymiyyah, al-Wahhāb held less sympathy for Sufis – a factor that has a particular resonance in his supporters' contemporary articulations of their interpretations of Islam.

Unlike many interpreters and predecessors, the influence of Muḥammad ibn ʿAbd al-Wahhāb is amplified because he was able to experience in part the practical application of his theories through an alliance with Muḥammad ibn Saud (Ibn Suʿūd) (1710–65) of Diriyya which commenced in 1745. By Ibn ʿAbd al-Wahhāb's death, Ibn Saud's forces controlled the Najd region and threatened the Hijaz. In 1803, Saud's descendants and their supporters seized Mecca from the Ottomans, reducing the Ottoman Empire's status as a religious protector of Islam (as well as damaging the Ottomans strategically and financially). What followed was a significant but relatively short-lived period of controlling Mecca. Through the intervention of and five years later, the Sauds lost their last stronghold.[66]

Muḥammad ibn ʿAbd al-Wahhāb's influence was significant, not just in Arabia, but because of the transmission of his ideas via connection with the physical focus of Islam: the *Kaʿbah*. Exposure to Ibn ʿAbd al-Wahhāb's theories during a pilgrimage to Mecca led to their circulation, (re)interpretation and application throughout the Islamic world – a networking prototype that is now amplified through algorithms and digital influence. The presence of diverse communities in Mecca – centred on pilgrimage and scholarship for attaining *ijaza* (the certified learning from a scholar) – meant that influential individuals were affected by Ibn ʿAbd al-Wahhāb's interpretation of Islam. The wide-ranging effects impacted the Deoband School in India, al-Shawkani in Yemen, the Muhammadiyyah movement in Indonesia and the development of Syrian and Egyptian schools of 'reform'. These influences can be seen today across CIEs associated with these world views and also dominate conversations about contemporary understandings of Islam.

Most significantly, the thought of Ibn ʿAbd al-Wahhāb regenerated through the twentieth century re-emergence of the House of Saud. It formed the basis of consolidation and influence in (what became) Saudi Arabia emanating under the rule of ʿAbd al ʿAzīz bin ʿAbd ar Raḥman Āl Suʿūd (Ibn Saud) (1875–1953) and his descendants. This development was significant when the Saudis attained control of Mecca in 1925 and ultimately established Saudi Arabia as a kingdom in 1932. The prestige of Mecca in the Islamic world, and the Saud family as its custodians, has continued to promote Ibn ʿAbd al-Wahhāb to this day – even though the Saud family itself has come into criticism by other groups of 'reformers' of Islam, for example, through their spending programmes of 'petrodollars'.[67]

One consequence is Saudi Arabia's influence as a religious fulcrum, promoting a specific form of Sunni Islam associated with Ibn ʿAbd al-Wahhāb's framework of understanding and interpretation. Described by critics, if not its practitioners, as 'Wahhabism' (in English), the term acquired pejorative aspects in the eyes of some commentators. This issue presents specifically in cyberspace, through primary religious channels connected to religious authorities in Saudi Arabia and by networked affiliates endorsing these religious-political world views internationally. In short, Ibn ʿAbd al-Wahhāb filters through substantial online discussions about Islam, with an influence that permeates manifestations of 'global Islam' supported by Saudi Arabian agencies over time. This influence impacted generations of scholars, activists and interpreters of Islam who have been taught Islam based on his principles – along with government agencies who espouse views based on their understanding of Ibn ʿAbd al-Wahhāb.

Multiple agencies associated with Islam in Saudi Arabia have been associated with this development – especially those which are outward-facing in intentions to project global influence – such as pilgrimage organizations, scholarly bodies, Qurʾān printers and translators. Significant international Islamic organizations asserting global influence incorporated Ibn ʿAbd al-Wahhāb in their outlooks: this includes the Muslim World League and the publishers/promoters of religious propagation materials such as Qurʾān translations from the King Fahd Complex for the Printing of the Holy Quran. Even before the emergence of the internet, there was a sustained and intensive demand on public attention from various Saudi-led platforms and their detractors, which is now intensified online by parties seeking to present their definitions as 'authentic' and 'definitive' interpretations projecting legitimacy.[68]

It is helpful to see how some of these entities have integrated cyber activities into their profiles: the Muslim World League's web hub (in Arabic, English, French and Urdu) incorporates platforms for organizations such as the Islamic Fiqh Council, the Organization of Muslim Scholars and the World Supreme Council for Mosques. It projects these influences through regularly published PDF magazines, covering various topics, including responses to health crises, women and Islam and hajj traditions.[69] These themes are reinforced through social media, such as Twitter, which in 2023 had over 5 million followers.[70]

One key driver in Saudi Arabian strategies for promoting their understandings of Islam has been the King Fahd Complex for the Printing of the Holy Quran, which has had a long-term internet presence to promote its multilingual print translations of the Qurʾān, as well as the development of online resources in various formats over the years. In the past, this included outsourcing (and innovating) digital Qur'ān delivery in the 2000s, such as a package developed by an Egyptian company, Harf Information Technology, for the Saudi Arabian Ministry of Islamic Affairs, Endowments, Da'wah and Guidance. Harf delivered a separate Qur'ān site for the King Fahd Complex for the Printing of the Holy Qur'ān, which also had download options from various reciters and alternative language translations.[71] The Warsh application offered a navigable approach towards this specific recitation form in a multilingual approach across platforms.[72]

The site also offers analogue and virtual tours (TripAdvisor contains reviews).[73] Different digital copies of the Qur'ān are produced for download, with varied narrations, applied across multiple formats for printing and digital developments.[74] The King Fahd Complex continues to translate the Qur'ān into different languages, in print and digital versions, affording different reading rules and including sign language. This practice includes online copies of the print versions (rather than navigable internet-designed texts).[75] A thirteen-language app including interpretation books and various recitations and translations was launched in 2020.[76] The extent to which these tools represent 'Wahhabism' is open to exploration. However, there is a discourse to be explored regarding the intellectual, religious and interpretative effect of these and related tools emanating from the Qur'ān Complex and associated bodies.

Muḥammad ibn ʿAbd al-Wahhāb's world view filters the interpretations presented through these platforms, while it also impacts approaches towards significant ritual activities, especially the hajj. International educational establishments founded using Saudi Arabian finance have impacted across diverse contexts, such as the International Islamic universities in Malaysia and Pakistan. The funding also pervades higher education institutions teaching Islamic studies, in Muslim and other contexts, alongside funding and support for charities, religious foundations and mosques. To an extent, this influenced world events and developments associated with Islam and Muslims, through the emergence of 'Salafism', involvements in Egypt, Afghanistan and other zones, Sunni-Shīʿa relations, the Gulf War(s), the emergence of al-Qaeda (and other platforms) and political activism.

Consequently, Ibn ʿAbd al-Wahhāb is a significant influence across many contexts and understandings of Islam, which predate the emergence of the internet – but have become a subtext in many aspects and formulations of CIEs. While this influence may be globalized, it emerges from a context where there has been an emphasis on censorship, monitoring and filtering of cyber discourse, especially in religious discussion and interpretation areas. The umbrella term 'Wahhabism' is problematic and not one that its proponents necessarily apply in their discussions or understandings of their world view – which would fall under the banner of 'Islam'. It has negative connotations for advocates of its message, as well as from its critics.

The term 'horn of Satan' has been applied by opponents and supporters of Muḥammad ibn ʿAbd al-Wahhāb in their cyber discourse on his status as a religious figure.[77] There is a discussion on the theories and concepts surrounding al-Wahhāb and how he is made 'the bad guy' when fighting and killing Muslims.[78] There is also an association of 'Wahhabism' with 'terrorism' and how it can be made synonymous with Islam, without understanding how diverse interpretations and approaches towards Islam exist. The Shīʿa channel Imam Hussein TV3 focuses on this theme in one of its online videos, where it automatically connects 'Wahhabism' and terrorism (including bombing attacks and the emergence of ISIS). This connection reflects antagonism between aspects of Shīʿism and Saudi Arabia as well, part of a broader online conflict between 'Sunni' and Shīʿa' Islam, as evidenced in the comments section of the discussion's YouTube page. The discussion negatively notes the impact Ibn ʿAbd al-Wahhāb has purportedly had on political movements and terrorism – implicating him in contemporary crises.[79]

A search for 'Muḥammad Ibn 'Abd al-Wahhāb' online is as likely to result in a listing of detractors and opponents, as well as photographs of 'al-Wahhāb' clearly drawn from other sources (given his active dates were prior to the emergence of photography!). Discourse about Ibn ʿAbd al-Wahhāb also features the contestation of his work emanating from al-Wahhāb's brother Sulayman Ibn Abd al-Wahhāb (1699–1794), which resulted in conflict. Sulayman originated the term 'Wahhabi' in his writings on the subject, subsequently collected into different volumes. This treatise from Sulayman features in the dialogues of those contesting the veracity of his brother, circulated under various titles, famously as *al-Sawaʿiq al-Ilahiyya fi Madhhab al-Wahhābiyya* ('The Divine Thunderbolts Concerning the Wahhabi School').[80] Those works are available online in diverse formats, including PDF downloads and in e-book stores.[81]

Apps associated with al-Wahhāb encompass the spectrum from detractors to enthusiasts. One app containing a 'history' of Wahhabism resulted in supporters and opponents exchanging views in the reviews section of the app store, an unlikely location for religious polemics and discourse.[82] On the other side of the debate, Ibn ʿAbd al-Wahhāb's *Kitab al-Tawhid* features in several phone apps, which are searchable, and in an audiobook (one of several apps that fit this model).[83] A substantial library of complete works of al-Wahhāb, along with glossary explanations by other authors, is represented in an Arabic language app – whose content can be annotated (via 'likes'), copied and shared.[84] Muḥammad ibn ʿAbd al-Wahhāb's work features in numerous online libraries and collections. These present his work alongside other authors. Some are 'information dumps' of hundreds of books. Others provide user-friendly aspects of navigation, site design and thematic comprehension: one app focused on the concept of (an interpretation of) *tawḥīd*, in which it collected numerous works (including that of Ibn ʿAbd al-Wahhāb) to discuss the concept (translated and interpreted in this context as 'absolute monotheism').[85] Support for Ibn ʿAbd al-Wahhāb emanates from numerous online channels, including social media, often in the form of memes or graphics.[86]

'Wahhabi' movements have emerged in diverse Muslim contexts. At the same time, the term is also (not always accurately) equated with 'Salafism'. This issue is explored later within the manifestations of 'reform' centred movements.

Back to the Fatwa: Nineteenth- and twentieth-century Indian subcontinent Islamic influences in cyberspace

There are complex global interpretative influences to consider – although not all of them can be incorporated in this book. The focus here on the Indian subcontinent has particular relevance in the ways it impacted populations and movements, alongside the multiple migrations which have influenced the development of Muslim communities internationally. In CIEs there can be considerable connectivity between and within the subsequent generations of people with Indian subcontinent heritage living in diasporic contexts, with influences being transmitted in all directions. To understand the ways in which this operates, it is appropriate to briefly explore the foundations of these influences, which maintain a status across digital frameworks.

The quest to 'return' to principles contained in the Qur᾿ān and *ḥādīth* influenced reform-centred movements during the nineteenth century. Some suggested that the concept of a return to the seventh century of Medina was an unrealistic idealization. It required a form of compromise between contemporaneous conditions and the time of the Prophet Muḥammad. Similar influences informed messianic movements, for example, in Sudan, where they provided a militaristic reaction to external non-Islamic forces. Within the Indian subcontinent, the considerable diversity in movements and individuals provided differing reactions to the increasing influence of colonial Britain and the fear of an erosion of Islamic values. Communications between different portions of the Islamic world were improving, which meant that there could be more trips to Mecca and greater dispersal of ideas.

It is important to stress that every subsequent reform-centred movement or individual did not follow Shāh Walīullāh in India. For example, the prominent eighteenth-century Indian Farangi Mahali family of Ḥanafī theologians emphasized the study of jurisprudence and logic. They had a different agenda than Shah Walīullāh: 'The *Farangi Mahalis* fostered the skills designed to support Muslim states; the followers of Wali Allah were concerned to develop the resources to enable Muslims to cope with the loss of political power.'[87]

While maintaining an emphasis on the Qur᾿ān and *ḥādīth* and supporting Sufism, unlike Shah Walīullāh, the Farangi Mahali sought a dialogue with Shīʿa Muslims. In a reflection of al-Ghazālī, Farangi Mahali emphasized the concept of the caliphate. The Farangi Mahalis are also significant for maintaining their principles and support through different generations of the same family. The idea of passing the baton from generation to generation was not unprecedented but became more of a feature in later reform-centred movements, such as Syria and Egypt. This trend is shown through the presence of Farangi Mahali family members online, such as Maulana Khalid Rasheed Mahli, the chair of the Islamic Centre of India and Shahi Imam Eidgah, who utilized social media to present theological and religious messages, for example, on responses to Covid-19. His Facebook and Twitter feed included memes containing *ḥādīth*, images of charitable endeavours, Covid-19 Helpline advice and Sunnah practice reminders.[88] The Islamic Centre was advertised as a tourist attraction in Lucknow, featuring on several tourist websites. However, the comments pages emphasize that it is a place of religion rather than holiday 'fun'.[89] The Centre also drew on local media to present its religious information during Ramadan, including the news channel reporting from outside the centre, and interviewing Maulana Khalid Rasheed Mahli.[90] The Centre's Facebook also promoted religious practice advice while emphasizing aspects of Indian identity as integral to its world view. This page functioned better than its advertised URLs, which were down at the time of research.[91]

Other historical figures now present an influence online, such as Sayyid Ahmad Khan (1817–98), who explored the challenges of modernity and sought to protect interpretations of Islam from pejorative 'analyses' by Western detractors. Online, substantial writings and information on the foundation of the Aligarh movement, which was influential in developing educational systems in Muslim Indian societies, including the promotion of Urdu and the notion of separate Muslim and Hindu nations in India. Numerous works from his bibliography are online. As a subject for curricula in India in particular, several videos discuss his life and impact on society. His commentary on the Qurʾān is downloadable and discussed extensively online in lectures and sermons.[92]

Searches for key terms and issues are likely to result in the resonating influence of historical figures which manifest in different ways and contexts: Abul Aʿlā al-Mawdūdī (1903–79) founded the Jamaʿat-e-Islami in India in 1941, emphasizing the need for an Islamic State and a return to the ideals of seventh-century Medina as a means of combatting foreign influence, both before and after Indian independence and the foundation of Pakistan. Mawdūdī's significant corpus of publications echoes in cyberspace, demonstrating his attitudes in full, with reliance on returning to Qurʾān and *ḥādīth* and responses to what he saw as the erosion of orthodoxy in the face of syncretic practices.

According to followers, Mawdūdī sought to guide Muslims in asserting their Islamic identity and in their understanding of the Qurʾān. Mawdūdī reflects the influence of Ibn Taymiyyah and al-Wahhāb. As the product of South Asia, reformers such as Shāh Walīullāh and Siddiq Hasan Khan would have played a significant role in influencing Mawdūdī.[93] Jamaʿat-e-Islami differs from many of its reform-centred predecessors because of its direct political agenda, which in different forms has permeated several Muslim societies. For example, it has had significance in the UK context as providing a religious focus and source of ideological reference for organizations including the Islamic Foundation, Muslim Educational Trust and UK Islamic Mission.[94] The influential globalizing frameworks of these organizations and their affiliates led to the circulation of his translated works online and in print.

Jamaʿat-e-Islami maintains political resonance within and beyond its Indian subcontinent origins. Mawdūdī's legacy is promoted extensively online through websites and social media, including documentaries and biographical content.[95] This includes extensive sermons and lectures, archive footage of Mawdūdī speaking and an audio recording of an influential 1963 speech.[96] A video aimed at children shows historical images explaining his significance in the Indian subcontinent context (with a music soundtrack that seems out of context with the subject).[97]

Mawdūdī's posthumous role as an 'influence' was already significant prior to the broader adoption of the internet. It was significant that during the early phases of CIE development, his voice was prominent in chatrooms, message boards and early websites. This was not just in Pakistan but across communities with Indian subcontinent roots, especially among web-literate students studying in international contexts. The Pakistan government had been (at times) in conflict with Jamaʿat-e-Islami but has linked at various times to the writings of Mawdūdī and the related International Institute of Islamic Thought (IIIT) in Virginia (with reproductions of publications relating to jurisprudence).[98] Translations of Mawdūdī's Qurʾān commentaries and other materials in multiple languages have a sustained digital presence.

In the 1990s, Jamaʿat-e-Islami's online presence was substantial, utilizing it for fundraising, interpretations, activism and meetings. Their increased emphasis on multimedia and the internet indicated the party's middle-class, educated, English-speaking membership within the Pakistani social elite. It could also be associated with its support networks outside of Pakistan (where computer access was at the time much more expansive). During a fieldwork visit in 1995, I discussed the potential of the 'electronic superhighway' with their leaders in Mansoora, Pakistan. They had not considered this technology then – focusing on other media to propagate their interpretations. A few years later, their website became an effective medium for promoting (an interpretation of) Islam to a broad audience. It is more cost-effective than other media forms, especially for the propagation of Islam, often under the *daʿwah* banner.[99]

The official Jamaat page features Mawdūdī prominently on its pages.[100] Its social media showcases meetings, demonstrations and (at the time of viewing) a small child reciting. The online content had a greater focus on Urdu in its main pages, as opposed to the English content from the 1990s, showing the changing dynamics of internet literacy and usage, along with the development of online tools in specific languages and fonts, which accommodate non-Latin characters.[101] Given that he was a prolific author (and a former journalist) Mawdūdī wrote and published extensively, including works undertaken while imprisoned, which remain in print and online. A focal point is the searchable edition of Mawdūdī's Qurʾān commentary, along with apps containing his collected works.[102] This extension of Mawdūdī's influence continues across multi-language digital contexts, part of Jamaʿat-e-Islami's online activities, which extend into international social media with affiliated groups and organizations.

Digital tajdīd: 'Reform', 'Renewal' and 'Salafi' influences online

'Salafi' movements are a significant area of CIEs in which various platforms utilizing this identity have scoped out effective digital networks to facilitate dissemination of their world views. These play a role in seeking to define specific brand(s) of Islam and Muslim lifestyles, which are increasingly integrated into an online framework. In order to fully understand Salafi impact in digital contexts, the connections with formative movements and influences must be established. There is a focus on renewal (tajdīd) within this online discourse, establishing a continuity with historical discourse and movements.

The 'Salafiyya' movements that emerged in the late nineteenth century (particularly in the Indian subcontinent and Egypt) responded to the pressures of 'outside' non-Islamic influences, which played a critical role in stimulating a re-assessment of Islamic ways of life. The nature of the reform paradigm changed and adapted out of necessity, subtly readjusting to the new challenges facing Islamic societies. Clutching Islamic values, battered by invasion and with further intrusions on the horizon, the so-called reformers were conscious they were living in a critical period of change, articulated in the responsibility they felt for future generations and their own.[103] These factors form the basis of conversations generated by Salafi movements and individuals, especially online. There can be a continuity of themes between discourse from this period of 'reformers' and contemporary contexts, where their output has acquired further audiences and influence in CIEs.

These sources cite the example of Egypt, and the impact of increasing 'westernisation' in the nineteenth century, ranging from the introduction of military technology and education systems by Muḥammad ʿAlī (1769–1849) to the development of new legal codes to replace *sharīʿa* under Khedive Ismaʿil (1830–95). Through a process initiated by Jamāl al-Dīn al-Afghānī (1839–97) and passed onto Muḥammad ʿAbduh (1849–1905) and then Rashīd Riḍā (1865–1935), it is possible to document subtle changes in the aspirations of 'reform' during the nineteenth and twentieth century, specifically in the influential Indian subcontinent context. The figures in this have fascinating backstories, which may add to their online appeal:

Jamāl al-Dīn al-Afghānī

Jamāl al-Dīn al-Afghānī's ambiguous origins add to the air of mystery surrounding him, being (possibly) born in Afghanistan (hence 'al-Afghānī'). Widely travelled (for the period), he was evicted from Iran for opposing the Shah (1891) and ended up in Istanbul, under Ottoman Turkish Caliph Abdul Hamid II (1892).[104] Encouraged by the Ottomans, he promoted Islamic unity or 'pan-Islam' while recognizing the diversity of Muslim identities.[105]

Online, al-Afghānī remains a figure of contention and influence. There is considerable discussion as to whether he was of Shīʿa origin, given his heritage.[106] The extent of his writings can be seen online through libraries and journals, as well as numerous articles analysing his role as a 'renewer', 'reformer' and 'revitaliser' of Islam through notions of 'pan-Islam'. One prominent aspect of this online presence is the ubiquitous photograph portrait of al-Afghānī, now colourized, which crops up across the internet.[107] However, it is interesting to note that – outside of PDFs and e-books of tracts, letters and books in multiple languages – al-Afghānī apps and social media are relatively limited.

Muḥammad ʿAbduh online

Al-Afghānī's thoughts are integrated within principles passed onto Muḥammad ʿAbduh, who sought reform in education and social organization in Egyptian society, applying new concepts to strengthen Islam in the modern world. In this, the influence of Ibn Ḥanbal, Ibn Taymiyyah and their respective schools of thought is apparent. Sufi influences, however, permeated ʿAbduh's later life. ʿAbduh wanted Muslims to educate themselves in modern science, equip themselves for the changes their society was going through and take advantage of new technology and ideas from Western contexts.

ʿAbduh and Afghānī had first-hand experience of 'Western' life because, for a time, they were exiled by the British to Paris (1883), from where they published journals. While advocating Islamic unity, ʿAbduh associated with Egypt's British administration, including Lord Cromer (1841–1917).[108] ʿAbduh went on to become a senior religious figure, becoming Mufti of Egypt in 1899 and is a significant reference point within the contemporary discourse on Islam and Muslim societies whose influence has infused subsequent religious movements and approaches towards interpretation.[109] For example, versions of ʿAbduh's *Risālat al-Tawḥīd* are widely available online in different editions, formats and translations, including Kenneth Cragg's edition of this work.[110]

Abduh's exegesis on the Qurʾān was collected, based on notes and fragments, and edited by Rashīd Riḍā under the title *Tafsīr al-Manār* ('The Beacon' or 'The Lighthouse') as a vehicle of propagating ideas of 'reform'. This twelve-volume work is now available electronically in multiple languages and formats (including e-books alongside the traditional print version and translations).[111] ʿAbduh appears in other online contexts, with a narrated synthesis of archive film and photographs.[112] He is famous for his statement: 'I went to the West and saw Islam, but no Muslims; I got back to the East and saw Muslims, but not Islam.' This and other quotes appear as memes, accompanied by photos of ʿAbduh, where attention focused on his apparent membership of the Freemasons.[113] Particularly significant was *al-ʿUrwa al-Wuthqā*, published in 1884, and edited by ʿAbduh with al-Afghānī. This volume, banned by the British authorities, became an important reference point for 'reform' and 'awakening' movements in the Ottoman Empire. Versions are available online as PDFs.

Rashīd Riḍā

Rashīd Riḍā is very much part of the continuity of ideas and approaches towards 'renewal' from this period and consequently features as a key influence online. Born and educated as a religious scholar in Syria, Riḍā moved to Egypt and joined Muḥammad ʿAbduh in publishing *al-Manār*.[114] Ibn Taymiyyah's approach influenced Riḍā, especially its emphasis on supposed 'innovation', and the emphasis on the Qurʾān. Riḍā did not seek to implement prohibition of practices such as anti-saint worship with rigidity, perhaps because of a pragmatic fear of alienating the broader society for whom this was 'normal' religious practice. Riḍā supported the concept of a caliph, supported by qualified 'renewers' and 'reformers' who could offer advice and *ijtihād*.

Riḍā's work is also crucial for transmitting the ideas of al-Afghānī and ʿAbduh, filtered through his perspectives. The key issues have currency with earlier centuries: foreign oppression, perceived religious 'innovation' and a sense of 'stagnation' in Islamic society which 'failed' to accommodate contemporaneous circumstances fully, contributed to the feeling that the Revelation received by Muḥammad has been 'clouded', and the laws and actions of the Prophet and the early Medina community diluted. These themes influenced Egyptian and wider societies, with a resonance that continues into contemporary contexts, including online.

In Riḍā's eyes, the schools of interpretation had lost authority. Emphasis was on continuous *ijtihād* when faced with issues of uncertainty, based on traditions and consensus of authentic *ḥādīth*. This *ijtihād* included specific responses to aspects of modernity emerging in the early twentieth century, including technology (such as the gramophone) and changes in dress codes.

Al-Manār incorporated a fatwā section, where various opinions were published and subsequently circulated internationally in different formats and languages.[115] As such, Riḍā made an impact in the communication of religious ideas. *Al-Manār* attracted questions from global audiences and impacted communities far beyond the publication's geographical and cultural base. *Al-Manār* offered a format for later generations of online fatwā outlets and producers, based on classical models of interpretation but addressing contemporary issues of concern through the application of *ijtihād*, and its publication outlived Riḍā for many years.

As an influential work, *al-Manār* continues to have resonance, directly through the reproduction of its publications and indirectly through the various influences impacted by Riḍā (and others). *Al-Manār* is found across the internet in e-books and translated versions. A complete *al-Manār* set is on the Internet Archive, freely available to download.[116] Riḍā's life is captured in several documentaries, extolling his role in 'reform', primarily through the impact of *al-Manār* as a template for later fatwā outlets. The documentaries also highlight that Riḍā could be a controversial figure in his 'free thinking' reformist approach, by no means universally admired within Islamic contexts.[117] Consequently, he and his antecedents become the subject of significant levels of negativity online. Their roles as influences on later configurations of Muslim politics are significant.

Levels of criticism addressed towards Riḍā, al-Afghānī and ʿAbduh focus on how their ideas were to influence the later development of the Muslim Brotherhood and how their concept of 'Salafi' contradicts other interpretations.[118] This critique tends to homogenize outlooks rather than indicate a more nuanced, developmental interpretation (which includes differences of emphasis and understandings based on their historical context and other influences).

The reform paradigm

Within Egypt, Riḍā's work became one framework of reference for later 'reformers' and advocates of change, including the founder of *al-Ikhwān al-Muslimīn* (the Society of Muslim Brothers or Muslim Brotherhood) Ḥassan al-Bannāʾ (1906–

49). He also emphasized the need for *ijtihād* to counter the influence of the West and the erosion of 'Islamic values' – pressures similar to those described earlier relating to al-Afghānī, ʿAbduh, Riḍā and others.

The *Ikhwān* utilized many ideas and themes discussed earlier, and their views have had a significant impact throughout the Muslim world. Concepts of political reform have been shaped and focused within this highly organized movement. Al-Bannāʾ created a secret military element of the *Ikhwān* and endorsed interpretations of lesser jihād, factors impacting his later influence (including online). The *Ikhwān*'s emphasis on social welfare activities in business, health and education provided a later template for political activism. Al-Bannāʾ also has a role as a 'martyr', given that Egyptian authorities assassinated him. His son-in-law Said Ramadan (1926–95) continued promoting al-Bannāʾ's world view. Ramadan's son Tariq (1962–) became an important Islamic influence in European and other contexts, including on the internet.

Online, al-Bannāʾ is commemorated and discussed as a figure whose principles informed subsequent religious and ideological movements, with influence extending beyond Egypt. This representation can include hagiographic accounts and interpretations of his work, alongside biographies. On Islam21c, for example, he is presented as a martyr, commemorating his assassination anniversary.[119] Al-Bannāʾ wrote extensively, with writings preserved in different formats across the internet. There are also approaches to his guide to morning and evening prayers, with specific *duʿāʾ* and Qurʾān recitations, translated and in the original Arabic.[120] This content is at the less contentious end of al-Bannāʾ's writings. Supporters also cite memes drawing on al-Bannāʾ's quotations.[121]

Many internet zones are vehemently against al-Bannāʾ and what he stood for. The status of the Muslim Brotherhood as a banned organization following the 2013 coup led by Abdel Fatah al-Sisi (1954–) against the elected Muslim Brotherhood government of Mohamed Morsi (1951–2019) pushed its rhetoric online, in a zone where its members already had extended digital literacy and awareness. One consequence is the continued promotion of al-Bannāʾ and other *Ikhwān* figures (past and present).[122] This includes those later writers and advocates for change and 'reform' who developed al-Bannāʾ's ideas, especially Sayyid Quṭb (1906–66). Quṭb was a teacher and novelist whose education took him to the United States on a scholarship, and he subsequently published about his experiences (in a negative fashion).

Quṭb's output, often framed as 'anti-western' rhetoric, can be found extensively online. It includes his Qurʾān commentary and *Maʿālim fī aṭ Ṭarīq* – 'Signs along the Road' or 'Milestones'. In 1966, charges of planning President Nasser's assassination led to Quṭb's execution. His 'martyrdom' (and terms of imprisonment) resonated with followers and did little to reduce the impact of his writings, in which concepts of religious law were central – and political and religious identities were synchronous. Quṭb is a significant reference point in Egyptian and international Muslim political zones, translated, printed and emphatically distributed online. In the early phases of 1990s internet activity, Quṭb's *Fī Ẓilāl al-Qurʾān* ('*In the Shade of the Qurʾān*') appeared as massive text files on online message boards. This multivolume work is now available as a print book on eBay, Amazon and other outlets (with PDF and e-book copies).

Fī Ẓilāl al-Qur'ān also appears as an app, an ideal format for its thirty original volumes (in print format), offering searchability, bookmarking, sharing to social media and translation(s).[123] Links to Quṭb's work and associated memes feature on Pinterest, including the widely circulated image of him behind bars awaiting sentencing. Critiques of Quṭb also feature online: in a YouTube discussion, Assim al-Hakeem described *Fī Ẓilāl al-Qur'ān* as analogous to a 'blog' from a non-scholar (not seen as a *tafsīr* or legitimate commentary), who is more than a poet, but suggests that his intentions were good. However, only readers with 'necessary knowledge' should read it. It represented a 'no-go' for a layperson.[124]

Contentiously, the universal reach of works such as this provided new online audiences for Quṭb's work, especially those elements associated with interpretations of militaristic jihād, impacting across conflict zones.[125] While jihād and e-jihād have a separate chapter in this book, it is relevant to explore here the intersections into other zones, particularly relating to the work of Quṭb: *Ma'ālim fī aṭ Ṭarīq*, written in prison, provides a template for an idealized Islamic State. It has been widely cited and remains available in various translations across electronic formats and translated editions.[126]

Abdu'llāh 'Azzām (1941–89) – a major influence on al-Qaeda, 'Islamic State' and other platforms – was himself moved into action by Quṭb's publications.[127] Quṭb influenced Egyptian Islam Jihad, fronted by 'Ayman al-Ẓawāhirī (1951–2022). Al-Ẓawāhirī became a prominent ideologue impacting the development of al-Qaeda. Consequently, Osama bin Laden was influenced by Quṭb, a factor reinforced in the 9-11 Commission.[128] Inevitably, Quṭb's publications are circulated through jihād-oriented forums and platforms and selectively cited and utilized within conceptual frameworks such as the articulation of *takfir* or 'excommunication'.[129] For example, the work was reviewed online by Anwar al-Awlaki while in prison. Al-Awlaki was the Yemeni American scholar and imam who exerted ideological influence over al-Qaeda and was a significant online influence.[130] The impact of e-jihād features further later in this book.

There is scope for exploring a more detailed listing of influential figures across Sunni-oriented interpretations and histories within diverse contexts, including numerous critics of reform-oriented figures and those who have synthesized some aspects of their work and refuted others. It could incorporate figures such as Muḥammad Nāṣir ad-Dīn Nūh al-Albānī (1914–99), a prominent Sunni scholar for the advocacy of aspects of Salafi thought. 'Abduh and Riḍā influenced al-Albānī in his formative years. Al-Albānī became a significant figure in *ḥādīth* scholarship. He criticized the role of the four schools of law and disparaged figures in the Muslim Brotherhood such as Quṭb and al-Bannā'.[131]

This critique is utilized online in synthesized Salafi sources, including materials focused on specific individuals. Salafi Publications promoted a series entitled 'The Heresies of Sayyid Quṭb in Light of the Statements of the Ulamaa', which incorporated commendations of al-Albānī on other anti-Quṭb writers and works, including his handwritten notes.[132] Anti-Ikhwān (Muslim Brotherhood) sites have drawn on al-Albānī as a principal source.[133] There are also videos highly critical of Mawdūdī and Jamaʿat-e-Islami that apply al-Albānī's words, translated and put into a YouTube presentation (taken from a Q&A session), suggesting that Mawdūdī was 'not knowledgeable'.[134] However, there are memes and sites which note that al-Albānī said positive things about Quṭb's *Milestones*, including links to what became e-book editions.[135]

Al-Albānī has plenty of critics online, too, especially for his exposition of what he deemed 'weak' *ḥādīth*. The interpretation of these by critics as part of a 'Wahhabi' conspiracy is negated by al-Albānī's own departure from Saudi Arabia following differences between Ibn al-Wahhāb and his influence on Saudi religious authority. This formed is part of the complex dynamics of nuanced differences and 'scholarly' refutations, long a feature of message boards, online forums and social media. A specific Facebook community, 'The Deviation of Salafi/Wahabi' focused on this concern in a lengthy discussion of al-Albānī's 'errors'. The article included a graphic negatively equating al-Albānī and other authority figures with Jewish Rabbis, under the label 'Syaikh Wahabi' ('Wahhabi sheikhs'), and with scholars of Ahl as-Sunnah wa l-Jamāʿah ('People of tradition and community').[136]

The influence of these figures is particularly relevant online, with a continuity that can extend for (in some cases) centuries after their deaths. The 'martyrdom' of some ideologues extends and amplifies their currency as multifaceted figures with a spiritual, moral, political and paradigmatic impact in digital zones. This idea is stimulated through selective editing, reproduction and 'mediatisation' through the development of message articulation and reinforcement through apps and other online publications. A challenging and competitive information marketplace circulates ideas through creative strategies of presentation and articulation, drawing on innovative and cutting-edge developments and characterized through translation and hagiographic representations. There may be a separation between the realities of a figure and their online presentation, analogous to other historical representations and contexts in which critical perspectives are subsumed by propaganda and rewriting.

It is relevant to see that many of the Sunni 'influencers' emerge from non-traditional contexts, too, being writers, journalists and politicians: this may offer their audiences a 'fresh' perspective outside the bounds of traditional, time-bound narratives. This development locks into long-standing arguments about the 'closure' of the doors of *ijtihād* and who is qualified to provide religious opinions.[137] This issue was amplified through the increased opportunities to transmit religious knowledge and interpretations via digital interfaces since the 1990s.

Under contemporary digital influence

In aspects of contemporary authority within Sunni contexts, numerous figures now have websites and channels devoted to them. Various iterations through media and technology shifts emerged online, from basic websites of the 1990s to the multimedia enterprises utilized by online influencers in contemporary contexts. A critical development, influenced partly by information overload, is the rise of gatekeepers and aggregators who filter a complex and saturated information marketplace. They offer gateways to mediated content, filtered by their parameters and interests and heightened when combined with media innovation and cutting-edge developments. The exponential rise in the app market, associated with mobile phone development and a reduced digital divide for multimedia content, means that many of the apps that provide entry points to Islamic ideas and information may acquire their influence and currency in a market of digital natives. The next section explores the implications and impact of this content within diverse Sunni CIEs.

Gatekeeping of Islamic authority and knowledge takes many forms in apps and other interfaces. They can aid the search for information, but at the same time expose the app user to contrasting and conflicting Islamic perspectives. Aggregation could take the form of gateway apps such as *Islamic Audios Library*, offering vocal lessons, sermons and lectures from contemporary and other figures. Some of these derived from earlier formats and sources, such as cassette tapes, given that the individuals are deceased or were dominant in pre-digital contexts. At least 150 sources had material available. While this may also be publicly available elsewhere, the utility of a central point such as an Android app for such information offers easy access.

Figures listed in *Islamic Audios Library* include Salman al-Ouda (1956–), imprisoned by Saudi authorities in 2017 but retaining substantial influence online with 13 million Twitter followers even after his incarceration and the announcement of a death sentence (which remained in 2022).[138] The app also lists contrasting content from significant contemporary and historical figures: this includes Abd al ʿAzīz bin ʿAbdullāh bin Bāz (1912–99), the former Grand Mufti of Saudi Arabia. Egyptian media preacher Amr Khaled (1967–) is listed with 31 million followers on Facebook and 11.1 million followers on Twitter. Khaled is famous as a personality and multimedia influencer, including presenting with a chat show format, integrating interpretative materials with aphorisms, informal discussion and informed use of multimedia and graphics.[139] Yūsuf al-Qaraḍāwī (1926–2022) also featured; the Qatar-based Egyptian scholar and media personality was prominent online through channels such as IslamOnline, particularly relevant in the first decade of the twenty-first century, but some condemned him for alleged links to the Ikhwān al-Muslimin. His influence is a product of many figures discussed earlier in this chapter, from Ibn Taymiyya to Riḍā.[140]

The presence of these and other individuals with contrasting opinions is not necessarily consensual on these pathway apps and gateways. Copyright of recitations and sermons can be a grey area in online Islamic contexts. However, it offers an inroad into contemporary aspects of Sunni religious authority. It went beyond the remit of recitation apps into the complexities of individual perspectives and thought.[141] Many websites offer specific sermons, including in translation from Arabic, often focused on a specific institution, individual or

Islamic perspective. Some of these have been collected in searchable user-friendly interfaces, categorized by the author. Khutbah Bank is one example, organized by Royal Holloway University students in the UK, who collected sermons from several sources and placed them online (along with other writings by journalists and others).[142] Shaykh Abdal Hakim Murad (Tim Winter) (1960–) has several *khuṭbah* listed, including links to related videos, highlighting the perspective of an influential figure (and convert) in British Muslim societies.[143]

Another example of this was Nourishment of the Soul, which listed over one hundred khuṭbahs in Arabic and English, with full transcripts and audio, which could be downloaded and used.[144] It did not indicate the provenance of this content or the primary sources. Ibn Taymiyyah (discussed above) features in one section of short sayings designed for those who do not have time to explore the contents of a sermon.[145] The site featured options for *dhikr* (ritual invocation or remembrance of Allāh) and supplications in audio-visual formats with transliteration.

Other khuṭbah interfaces may be more extensive but lack user-friendly interfaces, such as the extensive listing of UAE sermons (in Arabic, English and Urdu) from YassaralQuran.[146] This site draws upon the better-organized, searchable interface of the General Authority of Islamic Affairs and Endowments in the United Arab Emirates (AWQAF), which contains audio versions in Urdu, English and Arabic downloadable transcripts.[147] The AWQAF app included extensive fatwā options, including the direct phone line to the authority, an archive of fatwas from 2008 on, electronic submission of questions and an SMS option guaranteeing an answer within five hours of submission.[148]

A Dubai artificial intelligence service sought to answer questions and issue fatwas, albeit in limited areas, adding new digital dimensions to concepts associated with Sunni influencers and religious authority. It contained access via WhatsApp.[149] The Grand Mufti (Fatwa section) of the Islamic Affairs and Charitable Activities Department in Dubai (IACAD), Mr Al Kubaisi, gave a rationale for the service:

'The virtual mufti is expected to take some of the load off the authority's 16 flesh-and-blood muftis, who issue about 130,000 fatwas a year.

'The previous methods required the presence of a mufti, but the virtual mufti analyses the questions and provides the answers itself.'[150]

The intention was to expand from an initial offering on basic religious practice towards more nuanced content. The IACAD app was available across platforms, integrating local information (such as prayer timings) with the fatwā service.[151] In its opinion, the virtual fatwā was only available when the AI determined a level of certainty of 85 per cent.[152] Elsewhere AWQAF were operating in Telegram, updating users on sermons (including live preaching), news, digital services, surveying users and presenting news. This service provided a continual data stream linked to (and often mirrored with) AWQAF's Instagram and Twitter feeds. The AWQAF Telegram channel only had several hundred subscribers, the Twitter feed had 150k and Instagram had 105k.[153]

Similar applications have emerged in other Muslim Sunni locations, indicating that notions of Sunni religious authority in digital contexts continue to develop further dimensions of service and interactivity. In this chapter, we have seen a shift from the traditional and textual forms of influence and authority to a myriad of digital approaches. This shift has included artificial intelligence – albeit underpinned with the Sunni 'Islamic Source Code' comprising the Qur'ān, *ḥādīth* and Sunnah (the latter to different degrees of integration and complexity). The integration of technologies and interfaces is a facilitator, rather than a replacement for conventional approaches, highlighted during the Covid-19 crisis, which impeded 'real world' approaches to knowledge. Under the pressure of circumstance, Islamic digital mediation of authority and information became in some cases more creative and flexible.

Conclusion

There is a direct relationship between aspects of contemporary digital discourse in CIEs and the work of figures discussed in this chapter, whose work is 'revived', translated, searched, inputted into databases, linked to metadata, cut and pasted and circulated across Muslim online networks. There are many other influential figures worthy of investigation, demonstrating attitudes within the myriad of Sunni-identified digital contexts. Several discussed above could be investigated further regarding their online impact. These authority nodes are as much a phenomenon within individual community sectors as across national and international networks. The impact on analogue activities includes differentials in communication styles and information absorption, requiring methodological adaptation to impart specific materials, which otherwise may not have seen a radical shift in delivery approaches for centuries.

The advantages of digital discussions on religious matters, and the acquisition of opinions on and from Sunni 'influences' across time and space, may form part of a blended approach towards religious knowledge acquisition, which also incorporates traditional analogue understandings. This approach may form part of further iterations of Sunni influences and authority issues, which will necessitate further *ijtihād*, fatwas and interpretation approaches to ensure continuity of values and themes with the roots of Sunni Islam outlined in this chapter.

Chapter 6

AHL AL-BAYT, SHĪʿĪSM AND IMAMATES IN CYBERSPACE

This chapter explores the manifestations of Shīʿa cyberspace which represents the rich religious, political and cultural diversity of Shīʿīsm throughout the Muslim world(s). These elements will play out in cyber contexts and inform Shīʿa metaverse constructs, established around historical and cultural influences which have interacted with core values of Islam. Algorithms lead towards varied interpretations of Shīʿa Islam and their online representation, including the key Shīʿa figures in history and traditional interpretations from Islam's formative phases through to contemporary times. Many significant Shīʿa figures discussed here (especially members of the Prophet's family) are significant in Sunni contexts, but the discussion here focuses on Shīʿa understandings and articulations of Islamic interpretation. This chapter looks at some 'main' influences. However, the reality is the osmosis of cross-religious networks, ideas, categories and ideas of the divine that inhabit a complexity of religious comprehension, which draws in diverse influences and historical pulses of knowledge.

There is a multiplicity of Shīʿa branches to investigate. The various lines of Shīʿa authority are well-represented online. Key figures have essential information in CIEs, often associated with their histories and shrines, but also representing specific, diverse approaches towards religious interpretation. Some influential figures are selected here to highlight approaches towards online representation from their supporters – especially those who may fall out of the remit of general studies of Islam. Traditionally quietist or low-key, respecting Shīʿīsm conventions of taqīyah (dissimilitude), they may apply online networks to facilitate cohesion, religious identities and networking. These contrast with politically oriented Shīʿa platforms, which also present their ideas online (such as Hezbollah in Lebanon and numerous Iran-backed religious organizations).

The chapter shows how diverse Shīʿa frameworks and beliefs network across diverse cyber media, linking disparate nodes of religious and cultural understanding, underpinning digitally connected Shīʿa Muslims.

Enter: Shīʿa Islam

The mainstream image of Shīʿa Islam in Western contexts was influenced by developments in Iran since the Islamic Revolution of 1979 – where the symbols of the Ayatollah (*āyatullāh*), veiled women and ideas of 'holy war' and 'holy law' proliferated in the media. This was reinforced during the 2022 protests in Iran. Such events stereotyped Shīʿa Islam as authoritarian and restrictive without acknowledging – as with other forms of Islamic expression – there is considerable diversity under the general banner of Shīʿa Islam that goes way beyond its political-religious presentation within the borders of the Islamic Republic of Iran. There can be disagreement between and within 'nodes' of Shīʿa networks, which might not recognize one another's interpretations of Islam. Throughout the Muslim world(s), at least 10–13 per cent of Muslims are Shīʿa in orientation.[1] In minority situations, where there is a Sunni majority, there can be oppression of Shīʿa communities (and vice versa). The position of Shīʿa Muslims as victims of oppression is highlighted in locations such as Iraq (during the era of Saddam Hussein in particular, despite being numerically in the majority) and in Saudi Arabia.

In order to understand the position of Shīʿa Muslims in CIEs, it is necessary to track back Shīʿa origins and determine what makes Shīʿa identities and perspectives different from other sectors in the Islamic spectrum: the term Shīʿa comes from 'Shīʿat ʿAlī' – 'the party of ʿAlī (bin Abī Ṭālib)', the group who (according to tradition) championed ʿAlī as Caliph after the death of the Prophet Muḥammad in 632 (ʾAbū Bakr was appointed). The reality of this paradigm is far more complex and open to interpretation. Distinguishing between historical and traditional readings of formative aspects of Islam raises several potentially contentious themes. What this establishes is the role of essential Shīʿa beliefs in determining the subsequent development of Shīʿa networks in historical and contemporary frameworks of understanding. These link to specific notions of religious authority and knowledge, which can distinguish them (in general terms) from the basic paradigms associated with 'Sunni' Islam.

In reality, there can be complex communications, networking and affiliations between and within these broad models of Islam – which can also draw in the paradigms of 'Sufi' Islam. Key figures in Shīʿa beliefs also receive respect in other Islamic contexts. The members of Muḥammad's family are venerated and respected in Sunni contexts. There is no specific 'ownership' of many of the figures discussed in this and other chapters. Esoteric dimensions of interpretation and ritual transcend the categorization models imposed upon them by academics and others. Compartmentalization may offer neat constructs, but these belie the realities of the natural world (and cyberspace). There are essential issues and problems when writing about these themes, especially given the fluid nature of cyberspace. The complexity intensifies further when exploring intra-Shīʿa networking and how diverse branches of religious affiliation have emerged from core beliefs. These are particularly significant when exploring the online dimensions of Shīʿa expression, specifically the key figures influencing its development and representation. The complexities play out in localized contexts, where figures from historical, cultural and religious pasts may have a status that is not commensurate across all contexts. They may be subject to ritual practices and veneration across a micro-zone of influence.

Interestingly, some of these figures are now attaining a wider audience and exposure through CIEs. The diversity of online expressions at macro- and micro-levels, all attributed to 'Islam' and seen as 'Muslim' practices, contests suggestions of a holistic and uniform Islam. There are specific aspects of Shīʿa beliefs with a highly visual and esoteric edge, which is represented online and might form significant elements of any future Muslim metaverse. Algorithms seeking an understanding of Shīʿa values and interpretations will be predicated on different influences, sources and notions of authority – especially relating to historically placed figures. Other influences and frameworks of knowledge are reflected, such as pre-Islamic figures and beliefs that predated the emergence of Islam in specific regions. This issue applies across this book, which applies broad categorization models to aid its organization.

Shīʿa origins and cyber representation

ʿAlī bin Abī Ṭālib

The events after Muḥammad's death in 632 CE impact these dynamics and complexities of online expression. What emerges is a contestation as to whom 'those charged with authority' over the Muslim community were to be. Some traditions state that Muḥammad had designated ʿAlī as his successor, as articulated in a ḥādīth known as 'al-Ghadīr'. This ḥādīth was part of Muḥammad's final sermon prior to his death (al-Ghadīr refers to a pond – and a Shīʿa specific ʿĪd celebrates the event itself). Diverse sources approach this event differently, which can challenge views about the first three caliphs. They had practices and precedents attributed to them, but while the process of Islam's expansion continued, certain flaws, administrative problems and defeats led to suggestions that the caliphs' status was unfounded. These are all 'live' issues within different CIE sectors, so some background is necessary to determine online representation concerns.

The episodes in ʿAlī's life are complex, frequently appearing in online narratives about Shīʿa beliefs, represented in multiple ways through digital media. The figures surrounding ʿAlī have significance. Such literature suggests that ʿAlī – as Muḥammad's cousin and son-in-law (married to daughter Fāṭimah) – was intended by Muḥammad as being his chosen successor. Through the 'scheming' of the appointment committee, ʿAlī could not become Caliph until 656 CE. There is a dispute as to whether ʿAlī was the second person to believe in the Revelation received by Muḥammad after Khadīja or whether ʾAbū Bakr was. ʿAlī participated in many battles alongside Muḥammad and was later to oppose aspects of the administration of the first three caliphs, suggesting that they were introducing innovations. There was an implication of complicity in the murder of the third Caliph 'Uthman in 656. During his brief Caliphate, ʿAlī conflicted with the governor of Syria and the Kharajite 'outsiders' who believed that any pious worthy Muslim could become caliph – not necessarily from the correct 'pedigree'.

Key events pivoting around Muʿāwiya ibn ʾAbī Sufyān (602–80) have a resonance when searching for information about Shīʿa Islam, in particular around conflicting narratives and traditions covering different perspectives: Muʿāwiya was the first ʾUmayyad Caliph, who sought revenge for his cousin ʿUthmān's murder. In a battle between two armies in 657 at Siffin, some sources suggest 70,000 died. Soldiers hoisted copies of the Qurʾān upon their lances to solve the impasse. Ultimately, the situation between Muʿāwiya and ʿAlī did not resolve itself. ʿAlī was struck by a poisoned sword at Kufa mosque by ʿAbd al-Raḥmān bin Muljam, dying on nineteenth Ramaḍān 661 CE. One belief is that ʿAlī's burial place is at Najaf, in modern-day Iraq.

The (idealized) life of ʿAlī bin Abī Ṭālib encapsulates the founding virtues of Shīʿa beliefs, which subsequent generations attempted to follow and are now articulated in CIEs. There is an emphasis on ʿAlī's poverty and humility. In these contexts, ʿAlī is called '*Imām*' in the sense of 'a knowledgeable leader' (it can also mean the person who leads others in prayers). ʿAlī's life story, combined with the guidance of the Qurʾān and the precedents associated with Muḥammad, was to form a basis for Shīʿīsm. Sunni and Shīʿa Muslims may exemplify him in different ways. His role in the development of Islam, as an early accepter of the Revelation and – later on – as the Prophet's son-in-law, alongside his proximity to the Prophet through critical events in Muḥammad's life, marks him out as a significant figure. There is divergence, too, in terms of his status as a 'caliph' and his role as a religious leader. There is a resonance with the conflicts associated with succession issues after Muḥammad's death. This status extends to 'Sufi' mystical zones, with interpretations of ʿAlī as 'the father' of Sufism.

Collected sermons, sayings, poems and commentaries on the Qurʾān attributed to ʿAlī's are contained in *Nahj al-Balāghah*, published online in different formats. This was compiled in the tenth-eleventh centuries by al-Sharīf al-Raḍī (ʾAbū l-Ḥasan Muḥammad b. al-Ḥusayn al-Mūsawī) (d.1015).[2] Its content filters into the many sites containing quotes from ʿAlī. However, interactive copies of the source (in digital format) were unavailable – suggesting a knowledge gap in this extensive field.

There is a representation of this complexity online: as with other critical figures, he is the subject of video lectures from many sources, including Yaqueen Institute and Mufti Menk.[3] When viewing the lectures, the public comments include condemnatory statements stating that those who killed ʿAlī were not Muslims. Others stress the unity between Shīʿa and Sunni Muslims, suggesting the separation belied the historical reality of close relations between ʿAlī and other companions. Alī's collected and codified sayings have different online representation forms, including a slideshow with guitar music.[4] ʿĪd Ghadeer is extensively represented in sermons and recorded online in YouTube videos. Imām Hussein TV 3 discusses how Shīʿa Muslims have not read the details of the Ghadeer Khumm, or the historical circumstances around it, suggesting a lack of education on the Prophet's family. The consideration is that the succession is a 'hidden narrative', despite the number of narratives associated with this event.[5]

There is considerable detail regarding the marking of the ʿĪd, including exploring its differences from other ʿĪds on the Islamic calendar. It reflects the diversity within Shīʿīsm, with different emphases on ʿĪd practices and meanings. Al-Maaref, based in Beirut, affiliated with Hezbollah and linked to Iran's Ayatollah ʿAlī Khamenei, has an information-rich website in Arabic, French and English. It includes an explanation of the ʿĪd al-Ghadir, explaining its recommended practices of ritual bathing and fasting alongside specific prayers, supplications and recitations. The sayings of the eighth Imām ʿAlī al-Riḍā reinforce these practices.[6]

Ismāʿīlī Muslims are highly networked, with the Ismaili website acting as a hub for international networks of religious authority. Their presentation of the ʿĪd demonstrates this: Ismaili Web Amaana.org resources include *qawwali* marking the ʿĪd, calligraphic artwork and detailed expositions on ritual and practice in text and performance. The 'package' includes Sufi chants, with a significant crossover between different iterations of mystical practices.[7] There is an academic treatise on the ʿĪd, featured as e-books on Ismāʿīlī websites, seeking to justify the practice in the light of condemnation from some Sunni perspectives. It is interesting to see this illustrated by artistic representations from a sixteenth-century manuscript held in the New York Metropolitan Museum, explaining and illustrating the 'ship of Shīʿīsm' as part of a fleet of religions launched by God.[8] These hyperlinks across diverse media forms create new information relationships from traditional, multimedia and artistic sources that can develop new understandings of conventional Islamic practices. The ʿĪd can also be represented in terms of its political interpretations and as a metaphor for broader campaigns.

Manqabat devotional poems performed to music celebrate essential figures with a Sufi perspective, including ʿAlī.[9] The youthful performer Sibtain Haider featured on Pakistan TNA records singing in commemoration of ʿEid e Ghadeer, with 'Ya Ali Moula' (part of a repertoire that also featured other Muslim 'saints', with a qaṣīda for Fāṭimah Zahrāʾ). Recordings are regularly released on multiple platforms under the *maqamat* genre by female and male performers, especially children. Shrines endorse recordings whose packaging features religious calligraphy and photographs.[10] Some videos achieve substantial online audiences. Syeda Waleha Batool and Hur Hussain Jaffri's 2019 'Tu Bari Sakhi Hai Fatima s.a' received nearly 3 million hits and thousands of appreciative comments for the 'cute' performers. The video had soft-focus camerawork and a wind machine accentuating the performance.[11] Adult musicians are prominent within this genre, racking up hits with videos and releases, such as songs commemorating the birthday of ʿAlī (thirteenth Rajab).[12] Others mourn his death.[13]

Iranian singer ʿAlī Ghelich adopts a rock sensibility with his band in 'Live Like Ali', performed in Urdu, Farsi, Arabic and English.[14] This case expresses Muslim popular culture in contemporary contexts using the internet as a primary channel for releasing content to international audiences. There is also a commercial underpinning to these releases, partially measured in the significant amount of internet traffic that YouTube channels can achieve along with sales of downloads and hard copies of media. The message about figures such as ʿAlī is a combination of, in some cases, spirituality and commerciality wrapped up in a digital package.

It is significant to consider the pictorial representation of ʿAlī and other members of his family as presented within Shīʿīsm. Within other Muslim contexts, this practice is often prohibited. Idealized portraits presented by contemporary artists can be found online alongside historical Persian miniature pictures from manuscripts and other sources. The range of portraits also goes into commercial areas through the sale of posters and other objects such as carpets with these idealized portraits. There are numerous pages online devoted to this specific genre of religious iconography and expression. Portraits feature within religious processions and rituals as part of the decor of religious buildings and family homes. Quotations from ʿAlī reproduced on Pinterest and Instagram sit alongside quotations from poets and philosophers, part of a specific genre of aphorisms in a digital format presented in calligraphic form.[15]

Members of the Prophet's family play a significant role in esoteric practices that fall under the banner of Sufism. It is important not to essentialize the term, which is not necessarily one utilized by practitioners of 'mystical Islam', which itself takes multiple forms and interpretations. Esoteric dimensions of Shīʿa beliefs are integral to ritual practices and mediation of the divine. It is interesting to consider the role of key members in articulating Sufi practices. ʿAlī is a prominent example of this with the devotional poetry associated with him receiving receptive audiences from Shīʿa Muslims and indeed from people have diverse religious backgrounds, as witnessed with the impact of material by Nusrat Fateh Ali Khan.[16] *Manqabat* in the Sufi context focus on specific religious figures from contemporary contexts.[17]

Naqshbandis trace their line of authority back to Muḥammad via the Caliph ʾAbū Bakr, but other Sufi orders have chains that go through the Prophet's family via ʿAlī. Many provide hagiographic accounts of ʿAlī.[18] Some sites emphasize the links between different forms of esoteric devotion associated with ʿAlī and cite sources such as the *Nahj al-Balāghah* while also observing Sufi practices and principles.[19] The emphasis on ʿAlī as an individual with proximity to Muḥammad is stressed in online sources as a key part of Islamic practice, especially in terms of his metaphysical significance.[20]

ʿAlī's death in Kufa (al-Kūfah) in 661 features in online hagiographic accounts, often linked to the deaths of his sons. There is an association with the political and religious fractures of the nascent Muslim society. The events surrounding the aftermath of ʿAlī's death play out online in diverse formats and contexts, pivotal to the beliefs of Shīʿīsm in terms of what makes it distinctive from other forms of Islamic expression.

Ḥusayn and Ḥasan bin ʿAlī bin Abī Ṭālib

ʿAlī's first son Ḥasan bin ʿAlī bin Abī Ṭālib resigned the right to succession. There is considerable disagreement as to why this occurred. There may have been a military treaty with Muʿāwiya ibn Abī Sufyān, financial compensation, or a promise of Ḥasan succeeding Muʿāwiya. The rationale for this departure may have been pragmatic and avoidance of conflict, although, in some interpretations, Ḥasan possesses an esoteric dimension and miraculous qualities. Ḥasan's death in

Medina in 670 CE was apparent due to poison (according to some sources) at his wife Jaʿda bint al-Ashʿat's hand in a plot associated with Muʿāwiya.

Ḥasan's brother Ḥusayn bin ʿAlī bin Abī Ṭālib sought the Caliphate after Muʿāwiya's death. In 680, Ḥusayn and his supporters fled Mecca and the Caliph Yazid bin Muʿāwiya (who had succeeded his father, Muʿāwiya). Stopping in Karbalāʾ en route to Kufa, Ḥusayn's small force was starved and denied water before a momentous battle. According to Shīʿa tradition, Ḥusayn's supporters showed great piety and courage. Outnumbered, they were defeated and there was a slaughter. Ḥusayn was decapitated, and tradition states there were seventy-two martyrs. Only Ḥusayn's son ʿAlī survived.

The stories of what occurred play a significant part in Shīʿa Islamic expression: the Battle of Karbalāʾ took place on ʿĀshūrā Muḥarram 680, the tenth day of the first month in the Islamic calendar. ʿĀshūrā became a day of mourning for Shīʿa Muslims. Ḥusayn has many attributes: Shīʿa interpretation of the Qurʾān interprets specific verses as referring to Ḥusayn. The high regard for martyrdom within Shīʿism is linked to Ḥusayn's death, annually 'recreated' in the *Taʿziyah* passion plays. Sunnis may also respect Ḥusayn as Muḥammad's grandson because of his martyrdom for a high religious ideal.

Sites associated with ʿAlī, Ḥasan and Ḥusayn became significant pilgrimage focal points, including online. Religious figures interacting with sacred spaces such as Karbalāʾ in 3-D animation: representation of Imām Ḥusayn shows him in Mecca as part of the animation of his journey to Karbalāʾ.[21] Mixed media represent the annual commemoration of Muḥarram across diverse Shīʿa contexts features, demonstrating the momentum of ritual performance, which includes emotional mourning practices in the streets, with self-flagellation in various forms featuring in some locations.

Exposure to these practices via YouTube videos opens these practices to observers, including critics, while facilitating networking within and between Shīʿa platforms commemorating the mourning across diverse locations. Mourning is also a feature outside of Shīʿa contexts, but the intensity of the bloody YouTube videos that appear online is challenging to match. In particular, the emotional lamentation for Ḥusayn is a further feature of the month of Muḥarram. Chest beating is also a feature in some contexts, with some mourners removing their shirts prior to the rhythmic procession.

Key questions emerge as to whether the online depiction of these rituals, in their diversity, has a role in reinforcing religious identities in their distinct forms. Associated with the martyrdom of Ḥasan and Ḥusayn, many videos showing the *Taʿziyah* –ritualistic performances depicting the martyrdom of Imām Ḥusayn, other imāms and heroes of conflict – demonstrate the diversity of Shīʿa religious expression.[22] This articulation includes a representation of the death of Ḥasan and Ḥusayn's half-brother ʿAbbās ibn ʿAlī ibn ʾAbī Ṭālib (through ʿAlī's marriage to ʾUmm al-Banin). According to tradition, ʿAbbas died while trying to save children by bringing water during the Battle of Karbalāʾ, when he was a bearer of Ḥusayn's flag standard (the *ʿalam*). Rituals, processions and events mark these events on different days during the month of Muḥarram. His mother, ʾUmm al-Banīn –

whose sons were 'martyred' – is a significant figure in Shīʿīsm as a model of piety and devotion, whose grave in al-Baqī cemetery in Medina became a site of *ziyāra* (pilgrimage).

Documentaries, often compiling clips from diverse other sources, bring together a narrative of the events of Karbalāʾ that combines traditional readings with cinematic special effects, using the events to encourage contemporary societies.[23] The commemoration of Karbalāʾ in Iraq is one of the most substantial annual global movements of people and features extensively on multimedia commemorations. The story of Karbalāʾ plays out in diverse formats, including sign language videos.[24] News agencies pick up clips of activities, inevitably focusing on the bloodier side of the rituals, often without commentary or explanation – and with the comments sections attracting distractors and opponents.[25] In 2020, during the Covid-19 pandemic, pilgrims were filmed wearing marks and observing social distancing measures in Karbalāʾ.[26] There are insights in lower-tech films, including one focusing on food, which shows footage of more mundane pilgrimage activities.[27] A documentary on Imām Ḥusayn Museum discussed religious rituals and the 'miraculous' (and televised) transformation of soil from Karbalāʾ from its normal colour to blood red. It also discusses exhibits such as the names of thieves of artefacts projected into a representation of hell.[28] Sunni interpretations link Mūsā to ʿĀshūrā. It is a traditional day of mourning in the Islamic calendar (as practised by Muḥammad). The videos suggest that Shīʿa practices are innovations or 'sins'.[29]

Commemorative images are posted on Pinterest, juxtaposed with commercial images that may be 'inappropriate' in Islamic contexts. Heroic airbrushed imagery resembles a video gaming cover, demonstrating shared armour, iconography, slogans and fonts. Different interpretations of Muḥarram jostle for position. On Instagram, high-quality images of shrines (especially their domes) nestle with idealized images of the Ahl al-Bayt. During the pandemic, images included masked visitors to shrines going through Shīʿa rituals.[30] The trend for short quotes and poems on Instagram is significant for Shīʿa expression in its application of traditional quotations for the Ahl al-Bayt. Again, there is a contestation of definitions and religious positions.[31] Some images are posted on (or taken from) artistic hubs such as Deviant Art, which has a section entitled Shia-ʿAlī.[32] The intersections between popular generic artistic representation and religiously inspired art, in terms of artistic techniques and themes, are intriguing online. The artwork of ʿAlī Bahreini features significant episodes associated with the Ahl al-Bayt, including a focus on martyrdom depicted in graphic detail.[33]

Digital Shīʿa influences

Ḥusayn's son ʿAlī survived to carry on the Shīʿa leadership of Imāms (*aʾimma).* Shīʿa beliefs indicated that a Mahdī – rightly guided one – had been prophesied to'. . . come at the end of time to 'fill the world with justice and equity as it is now filled with injustice and oppression'.[34] Until then, the Imāms were to maintain the traditions and line of ʿAlī and his descendants, make new judgements on legal and governmental matters and interpret previous Islamic thoughts. These networks (and micro-networks) form the basis of Shīʿa Islam as it is understood today in various theocratic, political, legal and/or spiritual models – all represented online. The persecution of Shīʿa led to 'underground' activities associated with *wikāla* networks, which established covert funding, facilitating the secret practice of Shīʿa rituals. The tradition of al-Ghayba – a concealed Imām or Mahdī – became prevalent. This Imām would rise to defeat the oppressive (ʿAbbāsid) Caliphate, linked to the ḥādīth in which Muḥammad had said there would be twelve Imāms after him. The fragmented line of Imāms resulted in the Shīʿa principles presented online and discussed as follows.

Fāṭimah al-Zahrā'

The Shīʿa reverence for Khadījah and Muḥammad's daughter Fāṭimah al-Zahrā' is apparent in CIEs (also retaining major significance in Sunni zones). Fāṭimah represents an exceptional individual whose human body hides an esoteric essence that goes back to a period before Creation. Shīʿa traditional sources attribute a sinless quality to Fāṭimah al-Zahrā'.[35] These include idealized images on Pinterest with associated quotations and lectures. Music performances and *maqamat* (stories) show audiences singing the praises of Fāṭimah, 'We are at your service, Oh Fattima [*sic*]'.[36] There are pictorial commemorations of Fāṭimah's birth.[37]

Fāṭimah's marriage to ʿAlī is well-represented in digitized biographical sources associated with Muḥammad and his family. These stress qualities of humility, forbearance, poverty and modesty – especially Fāṭimah's support of Muḥammad as he sought to understand and spread the Revelation. As a result of all of these important factors, and connections, Shīʿa imāms exemplify Fāṭimah's qualities through her honorific titles. Fāṭimah's marriage to ʿAlī was, according to tradition, sanctioned by God. The povertous context of the relationship, especially in its early days, is stressed in sources – making her an exemplar for others in similar positions. Her religiosity includes a specific *tasbīḥ* (remembrance of God) recited at the end of every prayer. Online khutbahs explain its significance.[38]

Within Shīʿīsm, Fāṭimah has the status of an infallible martyr. Some branches commemorate her death annually in Jumada al-Awwal – as she died on the fourteenth of this month (the fifth in the Islamic calendar), apparently from injuries acquired when protecting her property from the Caliph ʿUmar (Fāṭimah also miscarried a son named Muḥsin). Online sources and moon-sighting committees calculate the timings of Shīʿa commemorations.[39] In graphics and quotations, Instagram content demonstrates Fāṭimah as an exemplary figure who wanted to be buried in secret and foretold her death (doing housework in preparation).[40] In Shīʿīsm, all lines of authority emanate from Fāṭimah – as descendants of ʿAlī and Fāṭimah form the various branches of imāms and religious authority. Mourning rituals have strong links to Fāṭimah, mourning her sons Ḥusayn and Ḥasan even though she predeceased them and mourning her father just before her death.

Fāṭimah gives her name to the *ḥamsā* (Hand of Fāṭimah), the outstretched palm symbol said to ward off the evil eye. This symbol is explained online, alongside opportunities to purchase *ḥamsā* via commercial outlets. Commercial designs proliferate alongside tattoo outlines of the *ḥamsā*. As well as being relevant within diverse Islamic contexts, the symbolism stretches across to other religions, cultures and historical contexts.

One unique aspect of Shīʿa beliefs linked to Fāṭimah is *Muṣḥaf-e-Fāṭimah*, a book of 'revelations' Fāṭimah received from Jibrīl, which foretells future events – according to the *Uṣūl al-kāfī* source of *aḥādīth*. The *Muṣḥaf*, according to tradition, was passed down the lines of imāms to the hidden twelfth imām. Its hidden contents are said to contain prophecies of the imāmate and its future. There is no specific document representative of the book, but online books (derived from print sources), sermons and lectures speculate on the details.[41] Fāṭimah's sermon against the confiscation of her property at Fadak, interpreted as part of a conspiracy on the part of the Caliph ʾAbū Bakr, is represented online through texts, videos and multimedia.[42] There is also the iShia app containing Farsi and Arabic texts (with English promised) of the sermon, part of a suite of applications with Q&A, books, scholarly content and books.[43] There are inevitable polemical videos elsewhere discussing its 'deviancy'.[44]

Many traditions are associated with Fāṭimah, including prayers, supplications and visiting martyred followers' graves. The tradition of talking to angels is associated with Fāṭimah. The influence of Fāṭimah extends to her daughter Zaynab bint ʿAlī (626–82). The pronouncements after Husayn's death of the latter became a foundation point for later Karbalāʾ ritual practices, outlined extensively online.[45]

Fāṭimah represents a symbol against oppressive governments due to her stand against ʾAbū Bakr and ʿUmar. This representation can be seen online, with videos showing Ayatollah Khomeini's commemoration of Fāṭimah, emphasizing his comments against oppressive governments.[46] Ayatollah Khamenei's website contains a detailed discussion on Fāṭimah, emphasizing how Sunni Muslims also revere her.[47]

ʿAlī ibn Ḥusayn Zayn al-ʿĀbidīn

Other critical figures play important roles in CIEs: the fourth imām, ʿAlī ibn Ḥusayn Zayn al-ʿĀbidīn (659–713), was the son of Ḥusayn (who also had other sons called ʿAlī who predeceased this one). Known as Zayn al-ʿĀbidīn, he survived the Battle of Karbalāʾ and was a young prisoner before his release and residence in Medina. The role of the fourth imām was contested with questions as to legitimate inheritance, answered when ʿAlī prayed at the Kaʿbah – and the black stone shifted its position in response. In traditional sources, Zayn al-ʿĀbidīn's life focused on ḥādīth scholarship, secret charity and religious devotion rather than political intervention. However, his demise was not peaceful – poisoned on the initiative of the ʾUmayyad Caliphate. He had numerous children, which impacted subsequent succession issues. His death further emphasizes the significance of martyrdom within Shīʿism, especially as his title Sayyid al-Sajjad implies control over prayer and prostration.[48] This factor has represented Zayn al-ʿĀbidīn as a role model (retrospectively) for devotion and fidelity, especially in terms of his online representation. His characteristics appear in YouTube videos, biographies and animated interpretations based on Shī'a traditional sources.[49] The branches of Shī'īsm that emerged after the death of 'Alī ibn Ḥusayn Zayn al-'Ābidīn represent a significant split in concepts of the imamate, which fragment across cyber representations of Shī'īsm:

Zayd ibn 'Alī

What is interesting in terms of the development of CIEs is the ways in which intricate historical networks of affiliation are located online, reflecting long-standing developments of interpretation and culture. This development is particularly relevant in Shī'īsm contexts with the Zaydis (*al-Zaydiyyah*), a branch of Shī'a Islam established in 900 CE by the descendants of the fourth caliph Ḥusayn in Yemen. They revered the fifth caliph, Imām Zayd ibn 'Alī, whom his followers saw as the imām in his leadership of an uprising against the 'Umayyad Caliphate, in which he was killed (or martyred). This succession contrasted with those who saw Muḥammad al-Bāqir as the rightful successor. Zayd's followers follow teachings contained in *Majmu' al-Fiqh*, a law treatise similar to Ḥanafī sources, whose founder empathized with them. Zayd was sympathetic to earlier caliphs prior to 'Alī. Complex branches and communities of Zaydis were to emerge in diverse locations throughout Muslim contexts whose scholarship and interpretations led to specific theological and legalistic positions (or 'schools') that have continuity into contemporary times, especially in online contexts.

Conflicts and quarrels informed some of these splits and conflicts with other interpretations of Islam, such as Sufi orders. There have also been cases where sympathetic approaches towards Sunni interpretative concepts have informed world views. Cyberspace is a natural zone for these complexities from various branches of Shī'īsm linked to Zaydi Islam to play out.[50] Zaydis seek imāms to be descended from Fāṭimah (essentially Ḥasan or Ḥusayn ibn 'Alī) and hold a strong ethos against perceived injustices which has informed subsequent developments in the contemporary period.

Zaydi beliefs permeated regions near the Caspian Sea and Persia but were dominant in Yemen. In contemporary contexts, one branch of Zaydi beliefs with roots in the ninth century has prominence in Yemen, only concluding in 1962 with the emergence of the Republic of Yemen. Zaydis were linked to the development of the Houthi movement, which was part of the Yemen civil war. Zaydis represent 40 per cent of Yemen's population.[51] Houthis represented a Zaydi 'revival' initially under Hussein Badr Eddin al-Houthi in 2004 and then his son after the killing of al-Houthi.[52] The Houthi movement has a robust Zaydi identity (although not all members are Zaydi) and has sought to acquire control of Yemen while countering government forces and a Saudi-UAE coalition.

Zaydi ritual practices have also been captured online, such as a stadium commemoration of 'Āshūrā with thousands of participants in 2015.[53] The film of Zaydis praying alongside Sunnis perhaps provides one indicator of some theological and ideological similarities in specific contexts, while an interview on BBC News also discussed similarities.[54] Practices introduced from Iran relate to ʿĀshūrā and other commemorations, while the Houthis sought to counter a prevailing Sunni-centred narrative associated with Saudi Arabian influence.[55]

Muḥammad al-Bāqir

Cyberspace marks out the splits in religious beliefs and authority in Shīʿīsm, including the divide in the imāmate. This can be seen in the approaches towards the alternative fifth imām Muḥammad bin ʿAlī bin al-Ḥusayn bin ʿAlī bin Abī Ṭālib (677–733), commonly known as Muḥammad al-Bāqir, who was the grandson of both Ḥusayn (through his father) and Ḥasan (through his mother). Tradition states that he was present at the Battle of Karbalāʾ. The name 'al-Bāqir' suggests a 'splitter [of knowledge]', given that Muḥammad al-Bāqir had a reputation for ḥādīth scholarship and Qurʾān exegesis, cited in Sufi and Shīʿa contexts, and a legacy that continued under his son Imām Jaʿfar al-Sadiq.

Unlike the Zaydi branch, the legacy of genealogy is relevant for religious authority in Imām al-Bāqir's viewpoint, reinforcing the role of the Prophet's family (and consequently his heritage). He emphasized the collection of ḥādīth scholarship by students under his direction. Despite a scholarly disposition, he was adept with a bow and arrow and demonstrated this in front of Caliph Hishām ibn ʿAbd al-Malik. His death (through a poisoned saddle) was attributed to the ʾUmayyads' Caliph, who was, according to tradition, jealous of his religious influence and success.

In CIEs, commemorations, lectures, traditional accounts and imagery celebrate Muḥammad al-Bāqir's life. Studio recordings and mosque recitations are celebrating his birth, a practice also observed with other imāms' celebratory days.[56] Recordings also include unique versions for (and by) children, including participation by puppeteers.[57] A YouTube recording of a Zoom session marking Muḥammad al-Bāqir's birth contained Urdu and Arabic poetry and devotional discussions.[58] Biographical materials draw on specific traditions and anecdotes that reinforce his family status and activities.[59] These include an animated lecture showing his suffering during Karbalāʾ, his role in introducing Islamic currency and the breadth of his academic interests is also demonstrated, with focus points on philosophy and theology.[60] Al-Baqir's status as a descendant of Muḥammad is highlighted, where he is seen as possessing similar qualities (according to followers).[61]

Al-Bāqir's sayings are presented online, including with piano accompaniment (which might counter some interpretative approaches towards music).[62] Al-Baqir's sayings feature prominently on general sites associated with the sayings of other imāms, including (on Pinterest) matched with high-quality and emotive pictures of ritualistic practices.[63] The Iranian news agency Mehr marks the martyrdom of Al-Bāqir annually through online photo essays showing ceremonial rituals held at the Imām Reza Shrine, Mashhad, Iran.[64] Commemorative art is presented across multimedia platforms, marking his birth and death anniversaries.[65] He is buried in the earliest Islamic cemetery of al-Baqīʿ in Medina, the burial place of others from the Prophet Muḥammad's family. Many shrines in the cemetery were destroyed or damaged in 1925 when Wahhabi-Saudi authorities gained ascendancy (shrines being seen as innovative or against religious values).

Jaʿfar al-Ṣādiq

Investigating influence in online contexts opens up audiences to figures in Shīʿa contexts which have acquired audiences and influence across cultural and religious divisions with an impact which resonates in CIEs, such as Jaʿfar al-Ṣādiq (702–65 CE); the son of Muḥammad al-Bāqir (and descendant of both ʾAbū Bakr and ʿAlī), Jaʿfar has a particular reputation for learning across Islamic and other sciences which extended outside of Shīʿa spheres into wider Muslim contexts.[66]

As the sixth imām, Jaʿfar al-Ṣādiq is particularly influential in his collections of Shīʿa *aḥādīth* which inform the Shīʿa Twelver Ithnā ʿAsharī branches of Islam, leading to branches named after Jaʿfari because of his impact. He kept a lower profile from the Caliphate and other Shīʿa branches, including those who held that imāms had prophetic status. Jaʿfar al-Ṣādiq developed a network of *wikāla* deputies to act as proxies for his guidance and leadership, as well as being logistical nodes for collecting funds to support the imāmate. Some discussions he held with other scholars on religious issues were documented and can be downloaded online.[67]

The Sunni centre of Al-Azhar University presented Grand Mufti ʿAlī Gomaa giving a lecture on the scholarship and significance of Jaʿfar al-Ṣādiq, comparing his status to that of Sunni jurists, as he was particularly influential on Ḥanafī and Mālikī schools. Jaʿfar al-Ṣādiq was an important source of *aḥādīth* for scholars of the age, as highlighted in varied online lectures.[68] His scientific abilities are projected on YouTube, emphasizing knowledge that preceded that of Western scientists and drew on previous Greek scholars.[69] A children's cartoon predicts his emergence as a 'truthful Imām' generations before his birth, linked to statements from Muḥammad and Imām al-Sajjad.[70] There are also animated accounts of his life.[71] His sayings on platforms such as Pinterest are combined with contemporary imagery.[72] Jaʿfar al-Ṣādiq represents a pivotal figure and influence for Sunni and Shīʿa Muslims, represented online in diverse contexts, as an influential meeting point for online discussions on intra-Muslim issues.

Ismāʿīlī and Jaʿfari (Twelver) Shīʿism online

Sunni-Shīʿa conflict is a reality online, despite common threads which can draw scholars and authorities together over time. There can also be divergence and dispute between different branches of Shīʿism, reflected online, often as echoes of historical schisms and disagreements. The patterns of influence and transmission feature in cyberspace, especially at this juncture, where we see a substantive split of branches between Ismāʿīlī and Jaʿfari (Twelver) Shīʿism. They take separate routes, which play out in contemporary times, including online. The Jaʿfari branch(es) will be explored first, at least until the pivotal time of the occultation of the twelfth imām (according to Shīʿa tradition). We will then return to examine Ismāʿīlī branches and their contemporary online resonance.

Jaʿfari (Twelver) Shīʿīsm

Mūsā ibn Jaʿfar al-Kāẓim

Our search for influence whose historical and religious impact echoes across CIEs takes us to Mūsā ibn Jaʿfar al-Kāẓim (745–99 CE), the son of Jaʿfar and the seventh imām (according to Jaʿfari interpretation). Mūsā's influence is built around his scholarship of Islamic sources, such as the ḥadīth, and provides a further example of an imām held in high regard within Sunni contexts as well as in Shīʿa interpretative frameworks. He had considerable longevity for an imam, surviving for thirty-five years, the most prolonged period for any of the imāms associated with Jaʿfari traditions. Mūsā's grave became a pilgrimage site, and its site is an eponymous mosque and town north of Baghdad (Kadhimiya) which hosts a major annual pilgrimage – also the focus of online activity.

The many traditions associated with Mūsā al-Kāẓim are represented online, especially highlighting his continued religious teachings in Medina despite opposition and oppression from the Caliphate. Inevitably this is through text-heavy works reproducing significant books on his life.[73] Extended discussions on his virtues and their perceived contemporary resonance are online, linked to the pilgrimage to Khadimiya and to Mūsā's father (and ancestry).[74] A lecture by Mustafa Al-Modarresi explains that the shrine is significant to all religious perspectives, including Sunnis and Christians, emphasizing the miraculous nature of Mūsā's shine. Modarresi, from a prestigious line of Shīʿa scholars, states that Khadimiya is seen in this way even by those who are generally opposed to shrine attendance.[75]

Other lectures compare Mūsā and his predecessors, especially Ḥusayn, associated with an enforced departure from Medina. Mūsā's death in prison is a model of facing difficulties without complaint. At the same time, his body was left unburied for three days (contrary to Islamic practice), with his son ʿAlī miraculously visiting him to perform final rituals.[76] Another video marks his status as a gateway of prayer and requests (Bab al-Hawaji), an intermediary for those suffering illness, and constant prayer. The narrator is seated in front of a MacBook.[77]

Kadimiyya is the shrine for Mūsā and the later imām Muḥammad Taqi al-Jawād (discussed below), making it a significant site for pilgrimage activities. The concept that pilgrimage is simply associated with Mecca is negated when exploring forms of Shīʿa pilgrimage, especially in online expression and recording of activities. Essentially one can consider a complex typology of pilgrimages. In this case, the bodies of the imāms were buried elsewhere until the construction of the sixteenth-century mausoleum and shrine but had miracles attributed to them in previous locations.[78]

Al-Kadhimiya Mosque has been the object of pilgrimage for many Shīʿa Muslims, part of a week-long pilgrimage season; in 2018, according to official estimates, it received 5.6 million pilgrims.[79] The shrine receives substantial visitors outside of pilgrimage times: '5,000–10,000 people visit the shrine on a normal day, rising to 15,000–20,000 people on Wednesdays and Saturdays. On special religious days over 6,000,000 people visit the shrine in a 48 hour period'.[80] This frequency of traffic means that it features on travel websites such as TripAdvisor, where it received ratings, as well as official pilgrimage pages from religious authorities.[81] Numerous worship clips at the mosque are online, archiving unique aspects of religious activities and providing an insight into these specific Shīʿa practices.[82]

Professionally produced pieces are alongside video clips from more obviously handheld sources, giving a sense of a participant's perspective.[83] The internet also offers insights into representations of Al-Kadhimiya, including a remarkable 1930s travelogue (complete with orientalist connotations) showing the mosque.[84] This significance has led to its targeting by anti-Shīʿa factions. In 2005, a mortar attack instigated by Al-Qaeda in Iraq's Abu Musab al-Zarqawi led to a stampede across a bridge, resulting in at least 965 deaths.[85] In 2016, Al-Kadhimiya Mosque was targeted by 'Islamic State', which regards its pilgrimage activities as 'un-Islamic'; this led to at least thirty-eight deaths and multiple injuries. In 2021, further attacks led to injuries and heightened security, but this did not necessarily dissuade the pilgrims.[86] Iran's then-president Hassan Rouhani made a personal pilgrimage to Al-Kadhimiya (also captured online).[87] As a focal point for religious practice and linked to an influential imam, Al-Kadhimiya has a significant place in CIEs through associated virtual activities, alongside its continued real-world impact.

ʿAlī ibn Mūsā al-Riḍā

There is no intention to suggest specific imams have more impact than others, as that can be problematic to quantify, but in terms of the positioning of religious authority, financial power and political influence, the shrine associated with the eighth imām ʿAlī ibn Mūsā al-Riḍā (al-Reza) (766–818) in Mashhad (in modern-day Iran) has considerable international influence. ʿAlī ibn Mūsā al-Riḍā – according to tradition – was poisoned at Caliph Al-Maʾmūn's instigation. A collection of *aḥādīth* is attributed to al-Riḍā, while miracles link to tomb visits.[88]

This tomb is in a vast complex in Mashhad. According to its web sources, it hosts the second-largest pilgrimage in Islam.[89] It is responsible for activities that go beyond ritual practice into charitable, communications, commerce, education and strategic positioning of influence. The Astan Quds Razavi multilingual website is an international and regional hub for this foundation's specific interpretation of Shīʿism, directed by the Iranian governmental authorities.[90]

During the Covid-19 pandemic in 2020, the shrine was temporarily closed. It preserved its online activities and output, and the shrine could still be visited 'virtually' through online renditions, 3-D pictures and a webcam focused on the mausoleum.[91] Various camera angles post live and recorded images from the shrine, along with sermons and other broadcasts, although the bandwidth limited external access.[92] Uploaded recordings of the live webcam footage feature on YouTube, alongside musical clips of laments associated with ʿAlī al-Riḍā. These are technically sophisticated productions, but they receive low audiences on

YouTube (frequently banned by Iran's government). The domestic video channel and websites, such as the Aparat video-sharing site, also host them.[93] The site is a significant hub for the local economy as a destination for spiritual tourism. It appears as a TripAdvisor 'attraction', complete with reviews from visitors and lists of other local attractions and facilities; some reviews are critical of its security and lack of 'family-friendly' access.[94]

Representation of Imām Reza Shrine on Pinterest and other social media platforms combines 'official' photographs from religious and government authority agencies with personal pilgrim photos. This juxtaposition features on several boards, showing everyday ritual activities, shrine visits and the subtle details of the precincts, such as the volunteer workers, flowers and even pigeons.[95] The social media usage by the shrine demonstrated flexibility and creativity across platforms, even when those same platforms were subject to sporadic bans and filtering by the Iranian government. Their integration into the everyday religious life and activities of the shrine demonstrates awareness of user expectations, investment in resources and integrated ability to build digital frameworks into spiritual, religious and cultural activities associated with Imām Reza Shrine.

Muḥammad ibn Abī al-Jawād

The final phases of this imāmate line contain short-lived imams, whose impact is nevertheless not without influence, including across Shīʿa CIEs. They may not appear in top-level searches on Shīʿa beliefs but still maintain a resonance:

This can be seen online in depictions and descriptions of the ninth imām Muḥammad ibn Abī al-Jawād ('the Generous', also known as 'al-Taqi', 'the Pious') (811–35), who assumed the title in the eyes of his followers at the age of seven, having demonstrated his learning (according to tradition) at a precocious age to challengers. Al-Jawād's heritage, with a Nubian mother, suggested that his physical appearance has also fuelled distractors over time. He addressed concerns about his religious knowledge at an early age, which his father had paralleled with the Prophet ʿĪsā, also discussing religious issues at a young age.

Al-Jawād's imāmate concluded at an early age, as he died at the age of twenty-four – another victim of poisoning by a caliph, from al-Maʾmūn's successor Al-Muʿtaṣim al-ʿAbbasī (796–841) (who used al-Jawād's wife to plant the poison).[96] Traditions relate that he had previously survived an assassination attempt using a unique amulet in a climate where anti-Shīʿa sentiments were growing.[97] The challenges that al-Jawād confronted form part of contemporary dialogues on anti-Shīʿa sentiments. Sources and sayings exemplify al-Jawād's role. His tomb forms part of the Baghdad shrine complex alongside his predecessor Imām Mūsā al-Kāẓim at Kadhimiya (discussed above). Representations of al-Jawād's life focus on his youthful activities as an example to younger Shīʿa Muslims, especially his dialogues with scholars in which he proved his religious credentials and linkage with previous imāms. Content includes animated, cartoon versions of al-Jawād (with his face obscured).[98] His martyrdom is commemorated annually and marked online, including through a hashtag on Twitter which continues to curse his assassin. As such al-Jawād has been a symbol against political and religious oppression of all forms across Shīʿa Muslim history.[99]

ʿAlī al-Hādī

A further short-lived imām was Muḥammad al-Jawād's son ʿAlī al-Hādī (828–68 CE), the tenth imam, who nevertheless has an online influence through his spiritual virtues. He was born into a period of religious complexities and political intrigues focused on tensions between the ʿAbbāsid Caliphate and Shīʿa beliefs.[100] Traditions point to the depths of his religious knowledge, along with miraculous qualities demonstrated in foretelling events (such as storms). This insight did not prevent al-Hādī from becoming a further victim of poisoning at the hands of a caliph.

A significant work of *ziyāra* attributed to al-Hādī describes critical features of Shīʿism under the title *Al-Ziyāra al-Jāmiʿa al-Kabīra*. The text forms part of ritual practices in shrines and prayer, and is meant to be used when visiting shrines; its online presentation could have a ritual impact in its potential use. It discusses the attributes of al-Hādī's predecessors and the Ahl-al-Bayt, linking them to divine qualities. The text and translation of this work can be located online in full, but there are also commentaries and explanations in digital formats, including in apps. An app produced by Peaceforall contained English translations and audio presentations alongside the text.[101] Duas.org includes links to multiple versions, including YouTube videos featuring recitations and translations of *Al-Ziyara*.[102]

An animated YouTube version of Al-Hādī's life uses essentially static pictures with a child's voice narration and music.[103] Information on al-Hādī appears in some atypical online zones, including gaming fandom sites (supported by technology and other advertising).[104] Al-Hādī's shrine in Samarra features many pilgrimage and video sites, showing the rebuilding programme that followed bombings by al-Qaeda in 2006 and 2007.[105]

ʾAbū Muḥammad al-Ḥasan bin ʿAlī al-Askarī

The eleventh imām within the line was ʾAbū Muḥammad al-Ḥasan bin ʿAlī al-Askarī (846–74), ʿAlī al-Hādī's son, whose impact continues online. His short term in power was another example of an imām whose life concluded through poisoning (according to Shīʿa traditions), a point contested by ʿAbbāsid authorities.

Traditions still relate to how al-Askarī had an in-depth knowledge of religious issues and languages, precocious in knowledge through demonstrations of his piety and interpretations at a young age. Within traditional readings, his four-year-old son Muḥammad 'disappears' into concealment or 'occultation', where he would remain until the end of the days. The issue is represented on YouTube with narration in order for it to appeal to and instruct younger audiences.[106] Similar topics apply to lectures on the subject for older audiences.[107] More detailed lectures have been captioned and abstractly illustrated on YouTube, such as a presentation by Canada-based scholar Sayed Muḥammad Rizvi.[108] Sources on al-Askarī demonstrate the complexity and diversity of the Shīʿa networks, with materials emerging from East African sources, including a lengthy lecture by Sheikh Nuru Mohammed on al-Askarī.[109]

Muḥammad al-Mahdī

The twelfth imām Muḥammad al-Mahdī (868/70–) represents in many ways a culmination of the Ahl al-Bayt for adherents of this line of Shīʿīsm, providing a further focal point for online understanding and interpretations. These may refer to the various prophetic signs which were to herald the arrival of al-Mahdī. This notion is surrounded by a sense of mystery, given that at the end of time, according to tradition, the Mahdī would appear with Īsā to cleanse the world of bad influences and restore justice to humanity. This traditional reading is in various ḥādīth sources recognized in Sunni interpretations as well as within Shīʿīsm, where it has a greater emphasis.[110] There are different interpretations within Shīʿīsm as to the identity of the Mahdī. Muḥammad al-Mahdī was said to have gone into a minor occultation – where he communicated through four deputies – for sixty-nine years. Following this, he went into a major occultation, which continues to the end of time, where there is no communication and authority transmission emanates from scholarly sources.

In the absence of the Madhi – in occultation – the government had to continue. This development led to more disagreement. One line of thought was to follow the judgement of mujtahids: in the Shīʿa context, these are legal and theological authorities, trained in all aspects of Islamic (Shīʿa) thought, who offer opinions and decisions. These were not seen as 'divinely inspired' through Revelation or infallible. As will be seen, they do have a specific online presence in Shīʿa CIEs. Other Shīʿa approaches suggest any government on Islamic lines is adequate until the Mahdī arrives because all non-divine government is fallible. The consequences have been the presentation of a range of approaches and opinions associated with religious authority, which now play out online.

The Mahdī may not be present in the analogue world. However, he does have a digital presence, as represented in numerous devotional texts and interpretations (with continuity to earlier imāms and iterations). Explaining the Mahdī concept in Twelver-Shīʿīsm to followers may be less of a challenge than to external observers. Efforts are made through sermons breaking down key concepts alongside works designed for younger audiences, for whom the eschatological dimensions may represent a real challenge. Some sources seek to interpret challenges in the field from 'fake ḥādīth' materials and detractors to the concepts associated with the Mahdī. There is a reflection of traditional scholarship associated with Shīʿīsm.[111] This reflects a dry, textual approach – but others have invested in other media forms to present their interpretations of the Mahdī concepts: this includes basic multimedia introductions, drawing on animation and film clips (from external sources) to introduce the Mahdī.[112] Other options include various scholars presenting their video interpretations of the Mahdī in the form of recorded lectures with limited interactivity.[113] As with other imāms, the Mahdī is also represented in iconography, borrowing partly from stylized imagery in video games and airbrushed art, often used in multiple versions across Pinterest and other platforms.[114] There can be considerable online crossover between and within discussions about the merits of the various imāms in terms of discussions and approaches, reflecting the different audience expectations and the abilities of content creators. There is evidence of the respect and devotion surrounding the imams and their traditions online, maintaining continuity with traditional (pre-digital) sources while utilizing aspects of cyber technology to amplify and explain their messages and statuses as exemplary figures.

Branching out: Shīʿa digital networks

The complexities of Shīʿa networks and identities play out online, especially between and within the multiple branches discussed below. Their intricacies do not always emerge from top-level searches about Shīʿa Islam, where focus points may tend to be in Iranian contexts in particular, reflecting in part demographical emphases. Some have displayed high levels of cyber literacy, emphasizing their networking across continents and dispersals over time. Selected branches are discussed below as indicators of how smaller networks have embraced digital technologies to amplify their interpretative impacts, while bringing adherents closer together, including in minority contexts. The number of imāms and dāʿīs make a detailed discussion impossible here.[115] Some key features and examples of influential figures will be discussed, with the awareness that each imām on the various branches (and their families and followers) could be the subjects of detailed discussions relating to their online impacts and representation in contemporary contexts.

Ismāʿīlis

Branches emerging from the split in Shīʿīsm focus on the line of Ismāʿīl ibn Jaʿfar and Muḥammad bin Ismāʿīl through hereditary generations and further splits after the demise of the Fāṭimid Imām Caliph ʾAbū Tamīm Ma'ad al-Mustanṣir bi-llāh Billah (1029–94).[116] Results of this split included the Dawoodi Bohras (with concealed religious leaders or *dāʿīs* – based in India) and Nizāri Ismāʿīlīs (with hereditary *dāʿīs* – and globalized communities under the Aga Khan) through to the present day. The Dawoodis also produced the Sulaymānī communities in the Arabian Peninsula. The Alawites (also known as Anṣārīyya and Nuṣayrīyya) are a branch with a specific presence in Syria (with groups elsewhere), specifically in Syria through association with the ruling al-Assad family.

Ismāʿīl ibn Jaʿfar (719/2–765/75) was the son of Jaʿfar al-Ṣādiq but – according to some interpretations – predeceased his father and consequently did not inherit the role of imām. However, some sources suggest he survived, with his death staged to preserve his life. Others believed that his son Muḥammad bin Ismāʿīl (738?–796) was the legitimate hereditary imām – rather than the line of al-Kāẓim.[117]

These complexities play out in cyberspace, while their religious and intellectual origins have been discussed (and argued) through to contemporary times. This digital dialogue includes the presentation of 'proofs' justifying the existence and continuity of specific lines of religious authority – drawing on religious sources such as Shīʿa *aḥādīth* to present indicators and evidence.

The line of Ismāʿīl (represented as Ismāʿīlis) takes the name of Ismāʿīl ibn Jaʿfar and focuses on a tradition associated with a predicted line of eighteen imāms.[118] Medina and Salamiyah in Syria were both suggested as sites of his grave. The Medina location became a pilgrimage focal point during the period of the Fāṭimid Shīʿa Caliphate, before then being subject to destruction under the influence of 'Wahhabi' interpretations against the preservation of graves.

The 'disappearance' of Muḥammad bin Ismāʿīl raises specific issues of speculation and interest in cyberspace, given its significance in the development of Ismāʿīli-related branches of Shīʿa Islam and the subsequent low profiles of further generations of imāms. Attention is paid to the eighteenth imām ʾAbū Tamīm Ma'ad al-Mustanṣir Billāh (1029–94), who – according to some traditions – would be the designated and foretold leader of the community. His long reign was blighted by factionalism, with control of the Fāṭimid Caliphate in the hands of lieutenants and representatives. One branch of descendants followed his younger son al-Mustaʿlī (1074–1101), known as Ṭayyibī Ismāʿīlīs. The branch then split again into the Dawoodi Bohras (Dāʾūdī, Dāwūdī Bohras), Sulaymānī Bohras and ʿAlawī Bohras (Alavi).[119] It is significant in terms of Shīʿa influences online that the descendants of these factions provide a distinct function as a pivot for activism, coordination and circulation of information – as well as bring diverse digital elements of the branches together for events, rituals and networking.

Dawoodi Bohras have high levels of CIE networking, with the activities of the *dāʿī* Syedna (Sayyidnā) Mufaddal Saifuddin (b. 1946) and the Bohra network in the Indian subcontinent and international contexts widely represented.[120] Ideas of networking have a strong association with trade, on which the Bohras built foundations over the centuries (and from where their name in part derives). Social media on Instagram, Twitter, Facebook and other platforms regularly update global network concerns while branching into specific regional interests through localized groupings. Photos and biographies of Syedna Mufaddal Saifuddin, his father and his grandfather denote the succession line. It also emphasizes continuity from the Bohras' origins in Yemen to their presence in India.[121]

In the UK, a 'reformist' Dawoodi Bohra group emerged 'to challenge the authoritarian and un-Islamic system the current Bohra priesthood has put in place to control and fleece the Dawoodi Bohra community'. This established societies across the UK while promoting environmental concerns and – during Covid-19 – virtual Ramadan observance.[122] The complexities of Bohra sub-networks play out in cyberspace, with complex levels of 'official' sites and representation. Numerous branches and sub-branches are associated with the Bohras, presenting their own notions of religious authority and identity, including online. The Bohras are linked with Yemen and Arabia, with the Makārima branch numbering some 500,000 in Najran, Saudi Arabia (on the border with Yemen).[123]

Sulaymānī Bohras have been split too in line with disputes over leadership and succession. Claimants to the title of *dāʿī* have been promoted online, including Syedna Abu Taher Khuzaima Qutbuddin (1940–2016) whose supporters promote his statements under the Fatemi Dawat channel.[124] This channel promoted the videos and sermons of Syedna Taher Fakhruddin, which were regularly posted, especially during Ramadan 2021.[125] The Fatemi Dawat were proactive through their web channels, given the globalized nature of the branch's membership, with regularly updated audio-visual content and articles on all aspects of belief (in Arabic and English). The pages include opportunities to request an online audience with Syedna Taher Fakhruddin.[126]

Nizāri Ismāʿīlī Muslims followed al-Mustanṣir's older son Nizār ibn al-Mustanṣir (1045–95). He was a designated heir, forming another hereditary line led in contemporary contexts by Prince Shāh Karīm al-Ḥusaynī – Aga Khan IV – (1936–), the forty-ninth imām in this particular line of authority. The mobility of this branch has seen its presence across continents, reflected in its online networking. The Aga Khan is familiar in Western contexts, associated with wealth, philanthropy and horse racing. At the same time, his name and connected foundations have associations with hospitals, educational institutions and international networking. This phenomenon fits effectively into online discourse and networking, with a long-term internet presence indicating recognition of the effectiveness of online communication, which goes back to the formative period of the medium.[127] Several hubs and online networks continue to amplify these concerns, particularly the Ismaili – an official focal point for multimedia activities and networking. Content is regularly updated through this hub and across multiple social media channels.[128]

Ismaili TV offers a stream of on-demand programming, from game shows (between different branches of Ismailis) to more reflective offerings, lectures and lifestyle programmes. The Canadian Ismaili Volunteer Corps (IVC) Game Show Family Challenge saw Eastern Canada battle Western Canada in a TV trivia challenge. This show features audience noises, buzzers and questions based on Ismāʿīlī activities; when asked why people joined IVC, one of the answers was 'to meet cute people in uniform'.[129] Programming was offered to thirty-one countries (May 2021), with its digital archive going back to 1980. National programmes dominate the listings, but networking Ismaili TV originals for audiences from small children onwards also play a significant role, with content in nine languages. During Ramaḍān, presentations in several languages were observed at Laylat al-Qadr.[130]

Alavi Bohras have a focal point in Vadodara, Gujarat, under the forty-fifth Dāʿī Saiyedna Abu Saʿeed il-Khayr Haatim Zakiyuddin Saheb (1959–). Their official website is updated frequently, particularly during – detailing sermons, religious practice advice, interpretative information and a range of videos. The website explains the various splits within Shīʿa lines of authority.[131] Specific ritual practices throughout the religious calendar are recorded from diverse locations, providing insight into specific understandings and approaches to religious activities. The Alavi Bohra is proactive on YouTube, with sermons, recordings of ritual practices and discussions.[132] This channel includes advice on appropriate prayer and recordings of pilgrimage visits to Karbalāʾ and Najaf. During Laylat ul-Qadr, photos and video clips of religious observances in followers' homes were presented as a slideshow, with all family members participating (including online and following television broadcasts). During the Covid-19 pandemic, the commentary explains that 'Every home indeed got transformed into Masjid [mosque].'[133] The complexities of Alavi and related branches of belief play out in cyberspace, reflecting heterodox and syncretic identities and affiliations, including aspects of Sufism. Consequently, there is further discussion on their world views in the next chapter.

Building relationships in Shīʿīsm

Representation of Shīʿīsm can have a commercial edge, including matrimonial and dating websites, which have become increasingly important (and lucrative) elements of CIEs over the decades, either in conjunction with more traditional matrimonial agencies or as an alternative approach. Sites incorporate guardianship issues into their approaches to organized 'encounters' and the mediatization of contact through digital devices prior to 'analogue' face-to-face meetings. The Bohras are indicative of these approaches, with the specific branches and sub-branches being specifically part of the 'choices' that potential partners can make about one another.

Shaadi Online boasted 300,000 Dawoodi Bohra Singles in 2021; however, a search revealed thirty-three single female profiles between twenty and twenty-five from India, Pakistan, France and UAE – suggesting numbers may be less. Relatives may write profiles; photos may not always be provided immediately.[134] There are also specific Shaadi sites across India, United States, United Kingdom, UAE, Canada, Pakistan, Australia, Saudi Arabia, Malaysia and Singapore. This site enables region and language-specific searches, alongside other parameters – India Shaadi offers specific cities.[135] Another site offers specific services for those seeking remarriage, with profiles from (at the time of search) India and the United States; not all profiles seek another from the Bohra branch but may have other requirements based on qualifications and personal qualities.[136]

Bharat Matrimony has an app which facilitates live chat between prospective partners; it categorizes their professions, age, education levels, existing marital status and mother tongue – as well as locations (by Indian city, state and international location). The company offers this in conjunction with 'analogue' services across Indian locations and personal coordination.[137] This phenomenon represents an intersection between digital and analogue contexts across diverse religious perspectives (incorporating caste when relevant for prospective partners).

In the Ismāʿīli context, a number of competitive online platforms offer approaches towards matchmaking, dating and matrimony. Ismaili Love suggested it was 'quickly becoming the number one Ismaili dating site across the world', building its services across multiple platforms.[138] My Ismaili Life Partner offered similar services, with an LGBT option (not frequently found on Muslim dating sites) and free Apple and Android versions of its app.[139] IsmailiWorld's focus included 'chat and flirt' options, beyond some traditional approaches towards relationships, through online chat. It had connections with other forms of dating and meeting, such as 'How to meet International Beautiful Women Worldwide' (its focus was on males seeking females, according to the descriptor).[140] These are just a few of the many examples of a competitive online marketplace, linked in various degrees to ideas associated with Shī'ism and strands of Shī'a identities and lifestyles.

Conclusion

This section reflects the complexities of various Shī'a networks. Future Shī'a metaverses will be predicated on this rich diversity amidst the myriad of digital networks. The key figures associated with the Ahl-al-Bayt within Shī'a perspectives have a cyber presence. Sites contain numerous religious reference works alongside traditions of imparting scholarship across diverse media forms. These will form the frameworks of future iterations of CIEs, utilizing notions of immersive metaverses, as well as impacting on refining the parameters for seeking Shī'a religious knowledge.

It would be feasible to explore the Shī'a presence across locations to determine its specific cultural-religious representations and multiple networks associated with diasporas and migrant-origin communities, alongside the presence of Shī'a Muslims in many minority contexts. Transnational and globalized Shī'a networks are significant. Local networks also present their interpretative frames, influences and contemporary influencers – which would benefit from granulated studies across diverse Shī'a frameworks. Shī'a understandings also impact political influences and contexts when they form part of state articulations of religion, such as in the Islamic Republic of Iran (discussed in the next chapter).

Much of this religious articulation may be beyond the remit of cyber-exploration without a specific digital presence: it cannot be assumed that all elements within these contested areas of cyberspace have a formal or informal web presence. There may be voices representing these practices and understandings on social media platforms, not always available for external perusal by researchers, in a multitude of cultural-linguistic frameworks. Deliberate efforts may be made to maintain *taqiya* in cyberspace, to avoid unwanted attention, in a quest to avoid scrutiny by hostile observers. The secrets of religious practices remain guarded by gatekeepers, which may reveal limited information, but keep the inner practices safe from the uninitiated. This practice echoes the real-world manifestation at shrines and pilgrimage places and is a practice that goes beyond Shī'a interpretations.

The next section focuses on the representations of Shī'ism associated with contemporaneous religious leadership across several networks and zones under the auspices of Ayatollahs.

Chapter 7

SHĪʿĪSM – AYATOLLAHS IN DIGITAL ZONES

Exploring Shīʿa influences in cyberspace takes the reader down complex labyrinths of archives, treatises, religious interpretations, legalistic works and world views specific to diverse religious-cultural outlooks. The chapter focused on influences and figures across the Shīʿa political-religious milieu. To their advocates, these represent the 'successors' or maintainers of the principles associated with the imāmate. These are not universally recognized but reflect the outlooks in particular zones of Shīʿa influence. Iran has been a dominant player in projecting Shīʿīsm in general and its interpretations and influences as part of national and global strategies of power projection across borders – in line with other players on the world stage.

Grand Ayatollah Ruhollah Khomenei

The intersection of Grand Ayatollah Ruhollah Khomenei (1900–89) and media usage is a significant one. He dominated discourse about Islam in general and Shīʿa beliefs in particular after the 1979 Iranian Revolution and the subsequent 'fatwa' against Salman Rushdie. Khomenei became an important religious authority figure – albeit from a Shīʿa background which was not representative of most Muslims in the world. Khomeini's ascendance was partly due to the application of technology during the 'cassette tape revolution', where his speeches and sermons were recorded abroad and distributed effectively and cheaply through the 'new' cassette tape medium from the 1960s onwards.[1] His supporters applied diverse media forms during his lifetime to promote his message and interpretations of Islam, with iconographic posters and choreographed media speeches. For many outside of Iran, especially those unfamiliar with Islam, these images formed the basis for stereotypical understandings of Islam and Muslims in their entirety – an extension of the orientalism discussed by Edward Said that became the subject of his separate book on Islam and the media.[2]

Before the emergence of browsers, this included tracts appearing through FTP file distribution in chatrooms; these were heavy on text but had no imagery or media content. Even so, the files were searchable and easy to print and distribute. Those joining mailing lists received regular updates on these materials or accessed them through chatrooms, where they could communicate and discuss issues with other followers. In the early days of the World Wide Web, when it became easier to view, search and access online content via browsers, it was significant that Khomeini's supporters realized the importance of the 'new' medium. They placed assorted web content onto the internet to commemorate his life and activities – geared for international audiences. Arabic and Farsi content were more difficult to publish in early browsers (except as photographs of text). Content included photographs (with low file size compared to contemporary standards) and audio files. Such digital activities may have run counter to some of his other supporters' views on the internet in general at the time.

Now, Iran has developed its intranet for domestic consumption and control of the internet (Virtual Private Networks or VPNs can circumvent this). Iran also has proactive approaches to researching and developing its online presence. This development is represented by how Ayatollahs, past and present, are highly visible online. Abrenoor provides in-browser subscription interfaces with extensively detailed religious texts, drawing on Shīʿa sources and works from historical and contemporary perspectives. Content includes multivolume sets with the complete works of many Ayatollahs discussed in this chapter – such as Khomeini – and a zone for free-to-access books.[3]

'The Sun's House' was a web platform endorsing Khomenei's world view which emerged in the early phases of browser development.[4] Now, his life is exhaustively archived by the International Affairs Department in the Islamic Republic of Iran on a website, alongside other social media, in Farsi, Arabic, Urdu, French and English. It features a library of Khomeini's writings, statements, published books and biographical materials. It lists academic theses about Iran during the Revolution alongside a digital library of books and related materials. Materials include anecdotes taken from episodes in his life, often in responses to particular situations (from the mundane and everyday to responses to ritual and practice) reflecting religious, personal and behavioural qualities.[5]

The site's archives contain a collection of correspondence sent to his offices, including a letter from an American writer (addressed to Mr Ayatollah Khomeini, Head, Islamic Republic) congratulating him on the fatwa against Salman Rushdie in 1989.[6] Other preserved letters included requests for his autograph and picture, with the request 'please do not personalise'. One letter requested that Khomeini extract an apology from Britain for Salman Rushdie's 'Satanic Verses' before a Conservative party came into power. It is unclear how many of these preserved letters were responded to, as the replies are not published. Elsewhere, Khoemini's poems focus on religious concerns and the subject of the (esoteric and spiritual) 'Curative Wine'. Contents across the different language pages differed regarding resources, images and design. The investment in multi-language legacy resources indicates the continued influence of Khomeini and his message in the decades after his death.

The official site also links to locations associated with the Ayatollah: the Khomeini Mausoleum Complex website contains photographs of delegation visits, sermons and other religious activities associated with the memorialization of the

Ayatollah. This included information on the initiatives around the digitization of Khomeini's work.[7] The broader Behesht-e Zahra graveyard complex – containing Khomeini's mausoleum and the burial places of 'martyrs' – is well represented online with a virtual tour, histories and detailed advice on burial practices. A searchable archive for locating deceased individuals is available on Android devices.[8] Khomeini's Library is in the Apple App Store.[9] A 'Testament' focused on Khomeini's teachings and his 'recommendations'.[10] The various videos associated with tourism and other visits to the shrine were illuminating. This site includes political-religious leaders', pilgrims and tourists' visits to the mausoleum.[11]

When exploring online Khomeini materials, the Safir Eshgh International Symphony Ensemble boyband emerged singing a eulogy in front of Khomeini's tomb.[12] Khomeini also features posthumously on social media in different forms. Like many religious authorities from history, he has a place on Instagram, where his followers on several channels have placed images of him from different phases of his life alongside short media clips, accompanied by eulogies from followers. Posters highlight his status for some as a Grand Ayatollah and ultimate religious authority (for followers). Images incorporate stylized quotes taken from his writings and statements.[13] Some of the images on pro-Khomeini Instagram also related to contemporary issues, such as in support of Palestinian activism during Israeli attacks on Gaza and Palestine in May 2021.[14]

The trend for memorializing Khomeini extends to other media platforms, with Pinterest also containing a range of boards and galleries featuring his quotes and photos. Historical images from many phases in his life, from France and Tehran, feature alongside informal family photographs. These can break down the austere image presented in wider media. There are also images from his funeral, with the tearing of his shroud exposing his body to the elements.[15] 'Art' pictures include hagiographic airbrushed paintings of the young Khomeini released as a limited-edition print.[16]

The presence of Khomeini-related content online opens a window into a figure that marked a significant turning point in Iranian religious history, who died before many subjects of the Islamic Republic were born. As a digital exemplar, with a body of carefully curated photographs and film clips preserved and enhanced online, international and local audiences have access to a figure whose digital shadow continues to impact Iranian and wider societies today.

Grand Ayatollah Sayyid ʿAlī Hosseini Khamenei

Khomeini's successor Grand Ayatollah Sayyid ʿAlī Hosseini Khamenei (1939–) made pronouncements against aspects of the internet, but as supreme leader of Iran and president, his followers and governmental offices have placed Khamenei and Islam at the centre of their digital strategies. His official website Khamenei.ir is available in thirteen languages. The content includes a prominently displayed biography of Khomeini. Khamenei's statements and speeches feature in articles and videos on the website, featuring responses to contemporary issues impacting Islam and Iran. It sent messages of support to Palestinians during the May 2021 conflict between Israel and Palestine/Gaza, including congratulations to Palestinian Islamic Jihad (PIJ), Hamas and other 'jihad' groups. The paradox here is that these groups are not religiously oriented towards Shīʿa Islam but have received funding and logistical support; when Hamas and Iran found themselves on opposite sides during the Syrian conflict, support was suspended. PIJ and Hamas conflicted, but at the time of writing, funding went from Iran to both organizations.[17]

The Khamenei website also reflects on the role of Imām ʿAlī in a reflective op-ed. article, published during martyrdom commemorations. Parallels are drawn with the issues ʿAlī faced and contemporary situations seen as analogous, such as Palestine concerns and BlackLivesMatter campaigns. This includes a section on environmental concerns and animal rights based on ʿAlī's teaching and sayings.[18] Political-religious activism, in the forms of news and commentary, often holds a dominant position in the hierarchy of materials. Critics may see this as selective in scope, with issues closer to Iran's domestic agenda ignored. The site pays attention to Sunni-Shīʿa relations, showing Khamenei meeting and commemorating the families of Sunni 'martyrs' who died defending shrines in Sistan-Baluchistan province. The meeting is filmed as part of a video gallery and subtitled in English. At odds with the political speeches, perhaps, Khamenei is filmed cuddling the children of 'martyrs' and engaging in playful chat.[19]

At the start of the Covid-19 crisis, Khamenei stressed that medical experts should be always followed, criticizing those who did not wear masks – and his concern for the medical profession.[20] Regular statements from Khamenei appeared on social media, including his Twitter channels (in Arabic, English, Russian and Spanish), which offered immediate responses to significant ongoing events. While social media censorship is an issue within Iran, it does not prevent official channels from using the sources it censored to promote its causes and influence external audiences. There was censorship of some Iran channels over time, but primary outlets remain intact. Khamenei's Instagram account had 4.9 million followers in May 2023, with images and film clips showing his activities – alongside the occasional poster-style image.[21] Fan pages across Pinterest show Khamenei at various times during his life.[22]

In 2019, Khamenei's official Twitter channel confirmed that the 1989 fatwa against Salman Rushdie retained its validity: 'Imam Khomeini's verdict regarding Salman Rushdie is based on divine verses and just like divine verses, it is solid and irrevocable.'[23] The tweet was hidden by Twitter for violating its terms of service, and Khamenei's Twitter channel could not post further tweets afterwards (although this prohibition was withdrawn).[24] Rushdie was attacked while speaking at a New York event in August 2022. The individual accused of the attack allegedly had social media reflecting support for the Islamic Revolutionary Guard Corp. The pro-Khamenei newspaper *Kayhan* celebrated the attack (in pages reproduced on social media), although Khamenei's response was muted.[25]

Challenges to political-religious authority in Iran emerged during the 2022 protests, associated with issues of women's rights, following the death in custody of twenty-two-year-old Mahsa Amini and the targeting, imprisonment and (in some cases) executions of protesters challenging the regime. Authorities generated online responses justifying their approach while attempting censorship and control of online media. Khamenei ultimately claimed the vociferous protests in Iran were the result of United States and 'Zionist' intrigue. The Iranian government attempted to close internet access, to stop images and video from internal protests emerging outside of Iran (and vice versa), as well as prevent the logistical application of social media for organizational protests. Demonstrators were able to get around these restrictions through VPN use, while the authorities continued their projection of Khamenei's output through conventional social media channels.[26] The conscious usage of internet media by Ayatollah Khamenei's agents and affiliated governmental bodies such as the Islamic Revolutionary Guard Corps demonstrated its central role as a tool for projecting specific Shīʿa interpretative values. These agencies also maintained their own digital output, although many were blocked externally following the start of the 2022 protests, as part of wider embargos.

Other zones of Shīʿa online influence

There are many zones which have online influence in Shīʿīsm contexts, not necessarily in sync with each other. Classification on these factors led to the establishment of an official body in Iran for determining the legitimacy and status of Ayatollahs, the Jameʿeh-ye Modarresin-e Howzeh-ye Elmiyyeh Qom. Founded in 1961, it took on the role of advocating Ayatollah Khomeini as *marjiʿ taqlīd*, the highest authority and one for emulation.[27] The organization has a multilingual hub (in Farsi, Arabic and English) on the processes and authorities associated, particularly with Shīʿīsm in the Iranian axis of authorities. Ayatollahs and other authoritative representatives, along with news, authoritative statements and profiles, are presented on the site.[28] Many figures maintain (through their offices) increasing amounts of online content, which can form into typical patterns. The following discussion introduces snapshots from some significant figures to demonstrate the different approaches to projecting online influence.

Grand Ayatollah Wahid Khorasani

The influential head of the Howzeh-ye Elmiyyeh Qom (Qom Seminary), Grand Ayatollah Wahid Khorasani (1921–), projects influence, power and authority in the hub of Iranian Twelver Shīʿa beliefs. The city of Qom is dominated by religious activities, with its shrine of Fāṭimah bint Mūsā (ʿAlī ibn Mūsā al-Riḍā's sister) makes it a focal point for pilgrimage. Qom is a centre for Islamic interpretation and teaching activities, with multiple seminaries focused around the Hawzah al-Ilmiyya, although the city also contains other educational institutions.

Khorasani's *Risalah* is translated into English and adapted online.[29] Khorasani's official English Twitter stopped in 2013, due to a virus threat. However, an Arabic channel has been active since 2011.[30] His 'official' Instagram is frequently updated.

The Ayatollah is shown participating in ritual activities, including his mourning of Fāṭimah. He has focused on this practice since acquiring the *marji*ʿ title.[31]

During the pandemic, Khorasani advised that the rituals should continue 'with consideration of all the health issues and what the experts in this area suggest'.[32] Unlike the Arabic version of the leading site, the English site did not contain regular updates. The Arabic version directly streams all the Ayatollah's video pronouncements, categorized in terms of key figures associated with Shīʿīsm, with direct links to sermons on Muḥammad, ʿAlī, Fāṭimah and members of the Ahl al-Bayt. Two apps were available with fatwas and books from Khorasani; the Ahkam app (for iPhone and Android) includes direct text chat with official representatives of the Ayatollah, facilitating questions in English and Arabic; the book app focused on Arabic content.[33]

Grand Ayatollah Sayyid Muḥammad Taqi Ḥussaini Al-Modarresi

Grand Ayatollah Sayyid Muhammad Taqi Ḥussaini al-Modarresi (1945–) emanated from Iraq and descended from a prominent religious family background, which includes his brother Ayatollah Sayyed Hadi al-Modarresi and his nephew Sayed Mahdi al-Modaressi. He spent time in Iran – founding the al-Qaim Seminary in Tehran, which later closed on the orders of Ayatollah Khameini. He returned to Iraq in 2003 and later achieved prominence in Western contexts for his proclamations against the 'Islamic State' while achieving a global profile in a 2014 meeting with Pope Francis. An image from this meeting forms the header of the Ayatollah's Twitter page, which has captured the '@GrandAyatullah' tag from others. The Twitter feed explores questions sent to his office and responses to world issues and official statements. In April 2020, this included emphasizing the role of the internet as a means of disseminating Islamic knowledge, especially during the Covid-19 crisis. The Twitter feed also contained several responses to Covid-19-related questions on combatting the disease, travelling appropriately (and not avoiding security limits) and burial practices.[34] Al-Modaressi used Facebook to present a translated version of an environmentally oriented speech for international faith leaders participating in an online conference in Iceland.[35]

Al-Modaressi's regularly updated official Arabic and Farsi website contains a mixture of publications, responses to questions and statements on ongoing issues. In 2021, it featured responses to Israel's attacks on Gaza and Palestine.[36] A registration-only section allows site users to ask questions to al-Modaressi's offices, with archived responses frequently updated (in 2021 with Covid-19 associated questions). Responses to questions have a multimedia element, with YouTube being a dominant zone, frequently updated with statements on contemporary issues and interpretative discussions (with fifteen videos uploaded in one week in June 2021, although viewing numbers were in the low hundreds). Some films reflected on selections from the Qurʾān, with a discussion on the laws derived from the second *sūra* (*ʾal-Baqarah*) incorporating a recitation and discussion.[37]

For more detailed studies beyond the website's extensive archives of statements and interpretative materials, the complete works of the Ayatollah were available for download.[38]

Grand Ayatollah Lutfullah Saafi Golpaygani

The position of other religious leaders within Shīʿa traditions in contemporary contexts combines responses to ongoing events with reflections on religious interpretation, including understandings of the historical lines of imams (*a'immah*) over time – often in a biographical format. The website of Qom-based Grand Ayatollah Lutfullah Saafi Golpaygani (1919–2022), for example, brought these elements together in detailed scholarly discussion articles on the imāms and the qualities of Muḥammad, analysis of ritual practices and responses to attacks on Shīʿa communities in Kashmir and Afghanistan.[39] His posthumous reputation and legacy were maintained online in Arabic, Azeri, English, Farsi and Urdu. Content continued to be uploaded, such as details of institutional activities, and online services were maintained, including options for sending religious questions across diverse platforms. This represents a good example of how digital content can amplify religious influence and be searched after the death of a key figure such as Golpaygani.

Grand Ayatollah Makarem Shirazi

The globalizing nature of Shīʿa religious authority emerges on the website of Iran-based Grand Ayatollah Makarem Shirazi, with content available in seven languages, including Russian and Azerbaijani. The website highlights the organization of its online activities under a Council for Policy-making and Supervision of Modern Technologies. The Council is divided into other constituencies, representing Ideological Contents, Ethical Contents, Ideological and Jurisprudential Q&A, News and International Affairs. It recognized that 'the utilisation of modern technologies for the facilitation of one's work and other issues in life has become an inseparable part of people's lives'.[40] The strategy presents as 'defensive', in the sense that 'if the foundation of one's faith is laid on a sound basis of logics and rational reasoning, then no matter how overwhelming the negative propaganda is, it will never shake and will stand unharmed'.[41]

The Q&A form notes, 'Dream-interpretations, Istikhara and the likes will not be answered here'. *Istikhāra* represents the selection of an opinion from permissible options and can be associated with extra prayers to seek guidance. There are some limits to the time scholars have to answer questions, which are limited to three in an email, accompanied by a Captcha code. Questions are archived in a searchable database and organized thematically. Content can vary across languages, with more extensive archives in Arabic and Farsi.

This typology, in terms of website format, is becoming standard across different zones of religious authority, with levels of predictability associated with the types of content, levels of accessibility and Q&A archiving. The websites of other *marāji*ʿ reflect this to the extent that the potentially dynamic nature of online content in terms of design, use of tools and versatility is lost. Some sites present more dynamic content in audio-visual materials, while others remain in a time warp of web design that has not evolved for a decade. The sense of predictability and dry content levels might reflect the limits of technical ability in web design. The extent to which this might bring new audiences in for content is limited. For some, content maintenance can be minimal, with broken links impacting the surfer experience (for some languages more than others), suggesting investment focal points for specific cultural-religious zones.

Grand Ayatollah Mohammad-Taqi Bahjat Foumani

Images from Pinterest also represent other religious figures, including those who have died, whose reputations and legacies continue through digital media: such as Grand Ayatollah Mohammad-Taqi Bahjat Foumani (1916–2009), whose advice features extensively online in different formats. In particular, a website focuses on his sayings and writings alongside video materials. This content is frequently updated and organized into categories to locate answers to specific questions. It offers contemporary currency to Bahjat's work, emphasized through social media posts, with some attention to esoteric dimensions associated with Bahjat.[42]

Section conclusion

The offices of many other *marāji*ʿ maintain websites which detail all aspects of their religious authority projection, interpretation of current affairs and publication of critical texts. Iran-based Ayatollahs have specific audiences and affiliations locked into these materials while integrating multimedia content and social media ensures that these projections circulate widely and are updated. The complexities of information distribution are reduced, although content-overload issues also emerge. There are also Ayatollahs outside of the Iran-Iraq axis.

Global Ayatollahs

Ayatollahs, marājiʿ and religious authorities from other Shīʿa contexts also have prominence online. This section explores the impact of Ayatollahs outside of the immediate context of Iran while recognizing that many key marājiʿ have influences that extend far beyond national borders. This reflects the roles of other significant Shīʿa figures possessing a global influence, whose utilization of CIEs indicates the application of digital networking as part of long-term strategies to amplify interpretations and impact.

Ayatollah ʿal-Sāyyid ʿAlī Sistāni

Ayatollah ʿal-Sāyyid ʿAlī Sistāni (1930–) is based in Najaf, Iraq, with a support base which has generated sustained online content for decades. A multi-language interface responds to specific questions of interpretation. The official channel has always been strong on substance if lacking the stylistic touches of other religious authority websites with its textual emphasis.[43]

Religious opinions about Covid-19 appeared across his network: this included whether ritual washing of a corpse was still essential, changes in burial practice under Islamic requirements and ritual adaptation in the light of extreme medical crises.[44] In 2021, Sistāni's influence extended to a high-profile meeting with Pope Francis in Najaf, captured online in videos and official statements in local and global media, emphasizing the symbolism of the visit.[45]

The website is not afraid of addressing potentially controversial issues and questions. In 2019, it responded directly to a BBC reporter who had questions about alleged sexual impropriety and child abuse from people dressed as clerics. A complete religious opinion condemning 'abuses' in marriages of young girls, signed and dated by ʿAlī al-Sistāni (including the Arabic original), was reproduced on the website and prominently displayed on its front page.[46] An 'official' Sistāni Twitter account was inactive after 2013; an 'unofficial' site (linked to his Facebook) was active until 2020, prominently featuring visits to shrines in Iraq and Iran.[47] Al-Sistāni's responses to questions are located on other channels, such as Shafaqna; in 2020, he answered a question affirming cyberspace stock exchange dealings were allowed unless the items were haram.[48]

Statements and opinions from Sistāni also feature on Instagram, interspersed with images and film clips of the Ayatollah; some are in the forms of calligraphy, using a range of scripts.[49] An 'unofficial' Instagram page for Sistāni separated users by gender – with specific accounts for males and females (requiring a direct message for acceptance).[50] On Pinterest, images of al-Sistāni are more likely to be juxtaposed with advertisements, which may be incongruous next to images of the Ayatollah. Not all images are accompanied by complementary texts. There are also images of Khomeini and other clerics.[51] A page of images of al-Sistāni featured on a sequence of Pinterest pages, which also feature aspects of 'Islamic resistance'; this includes pages dedicated to Khamenei, the Islamic Revolution, other Shīʿa religious leaders and 'Resistance art'.[52] The latter includes graphics, drawings and photos of slain Iranian military leader Qasim Soleimani (1957–2020), who had been the head of the Revolutionary Guards' Quds Force until his assassination in a US airstrike in Baghdad. The breadth of Sistāni's online presence is demonstrated across numerous affiliated channels projecting his authority, emanating from Najaf, in a coordinated and effective approach to developing this specific understanding of Shīʿism.

Grand Ayatollah Abu al-Qāsim al-Khoei

Grand Ayatollah Abu al-Qāsim al-Khoei (1899–1992) was the precursor to al-Sistāni in terms of authority and influence in many sectors associated with Shīʿīsm, with al-Sistāni ultimately assuming his mantle and followers in the period after al-Khoei's death. Before becoming a Grand Ayatollah at the age of forty-two, al-Khoei worked as a scholar in Najaf focusing on law, Qurʾān interpretations and Islamic sources. His influence covered extensive zones but was not without contestation from other Shīʿa branches and leaders. Ultimately, during the 1992 Gulf War, he was threatened by Saddam Hussein and placed under house arrest before his death in 1992. His followers were persecuted in Iraq, influencing the development of 'diaspora' communities. The webspace offers a continued legacy of interpretation and knowledge three decades after al-Khoei's death.

The Al-Khoei Foundation has held a prominent space online in terms of 'early adoption' of internet technologies to network across different zones. In Jamaica, New York, its activities are live-streamed via YouTube, including sermons and other gatherings, such as a 'Ladies Majlis' broadcast live from the Imām Al-Khoei Islamic Center. Some of these broadcasts can be several hours long, and while the physical number of participants during lockdown was limited, gatherings were recorded for later viewing. The website reinforced the need for vaccines during the Covid-19 crisis and addressed other contemporary questions, such as the permissibility of Netflix. Sheikh Fadhel Al-Sahlani, al-Sistāni's North American representative, hosted a more comprehensive Q&A archive. This was limited to the extent to which this was viewed (averaging 50–60 views for one month). One feature of the New York site was an online Islamic store consisting primarily of Arabic language books, from children's religious tracts to more specialist religious tracts and Qurʾān commentaries.[53]

With multiple branches internationally, Al-Khoei Foundation's headquarters in London acts as a global hub. The main website URL held limited content with basic announcements (e.g. prayer times, ʿĪd moon sightings and charitable calls). Core activities focused on Facebook and Twitter.[54] However, alternative sites were richer in content, dedicated explicitly to al-Khoei, with archives of videos, writings and legacy materials. Interactive content included a substantial and regularly updated Q&A archive (including on Covid-19 health issues). Al-Khoei is cited frequently in the answers on ritual, interpretation and other matters.[55] The multivolume library – a 'bookshelf' of volumes – includes multi-format downloads of commentaries, religious interpretations and texts associated with al-Khoei and Shīʿīsm.[56] Al-Khoei Foundation produces apps bringing this content together with key writings, images and videos across platforms.[57]

The organization runs Dar al-ʿIlm in Najaf (near Imām ʿAlī ibn Abī Ṭālib's shrine), with regular content in Arabic, Farsi and English, which seeks to train later generations of leaders through a Hawza seminary system. Its site includes an interfaith academy, library, prayer hall and multimedia production.[58] The Institute's Twitter feed pays particular attention to 'interfaith' and 'intrafaith' activities, represented in various posts, including meetings with other Grand Ayatollahs and branches of Shīʿīsm. Key members of the Institute, such as Jawad al-Khoei, are seen visiting shrines in Mashhad and other locations – social media stressing the links between 'influencers' and authorities of previous generations.

So, what is the impact of this? Despite the investment of time, the video resources only have small numbers of hits (the highest was 2.7k).[59] The extent to which there is the capitalization of online materials appears relatively limited, compared with other channels, even though content mixes contemporary clips with archive media of al-Khoei. Translating the influence can be problematic for some Shīʿa platforms. Demand may focus on other media, including the hundreds of hours within the audio archive of sermons and discussions, which may be more portable and easier for those on mobile devices to listen to while undertaking other activities.[60]

Ayatollah Basheer Hussain Najafi

Pakistan-born Ayatollah Basheer Hussain Najafi (1942–) was based in Najaf but maintained strong links with Pakistan and other locations through regular visits and online activities. His website is in English, Arabic, Urdu and Farsi. He has worked extensively on interpretation issues, with Q&A sections on medical, interpretation and ritualistic issues. Statements, sermons and discussions are all captured on video. This integration into the daily life of religious pronouncements offers a broader audience for matters of interpretation and belief. However, it changes some of the reflective dynamics traditionally associated with clerical activities. Pronouncements on critical religious issues feature on the website. In 2020, one statement suggested that the pandemic was the result of humanity's 'sins': 'The pandemic outbreak nowadays (Coronavirus) is a result of accumulated sins and oppression by mankind in not obeying Allah Almighty. This is to bring mankind to Him so that they return to His mercy and kindness . . . It is not permissible to quit the idea that the mercy of Allah will not return and remove this pandemic from us with His mercy.'[61]

The statement indicates that prayer and the medical advice of competent authorities were essential. There is a fusion of the spiritual, the legalistic and the practical within this approach. Ayatollah Basheer Hussain's religious credentials, including where he derived his teachings, are exhaustively chronicled on his website – reflecting traditional approaches to religious learning 'at the feet of scholars'. There is also a discussion about the 'threat' of Wahhabi scholars to learning. Pedagogy associated with the study of Islam within the seminary context is explored, including challenges of language and behaviour. This discussion links the scholarship with the traditions of the imāmate over time.[62] Ayatollah Basheer Hussain's opinions are also circulated widely via social media, with Twitter and Facebook as the primary channels for fatwas, as well as updates on the Ayatollah's religious activities, available in English and Arabic.[63]

Gulf Shīʿa

The absence – at the time of writing – of a senior Ayatollah or *marjiʿ* in the Gulf states places a dependence on external authority, which is problematic for those states politically and religiously in terms of influence and authority. Shīʿa in these states could become dependent on authority emanating from Qom or Najaf. The internet has opened people in these zones to increases in Iran-backed Shīʿa religious influence, which is problematic especially given that a majority of Shīʿa live outside of Iran. There is also the sense that some potential religious leaders are deferential to the authority of Ayatollah al-Sistāni or other authorities and are playing a 'waiting game'.[64]

The religious authority situation in Shīʿa majority Bahrain was impacted by the exile of its primary cleric, Grand Ayatollah Sheikh Isa Ahmed Qassim (1937–). The leader of the al-Wefaq opposition group, his political activism placed him at odds with Bahrain's Sunni leadership. Al-Wefaq maintained an active Twitter feed showing campaigns, protests and meetings. Its Instagram focused on human rights issues in Bahrain and the needs of reconciliation in the state. This included statements and videos of its leadership, with direct links to reels on Ayatollah Qassim, and galleries illustrated by drawings of the 'martyrs'.[65] Its Instagram consisted of a gallery of its members and activists, including prisoners of the Bahrain government and those 'martyred' in al-Wefaq's cause.[66] Al-Wefaq's Facebook pages paid attention to human rights conditions in Bahrain, including the imprisonment of journalists and issues of media control and censorship.[67] Videos of other religious leaders delivering sermons also featured on al-Wefaq's pages and the London-based LuaLua TV channel, which maintained its own proactive digital presence, including an English-language Twitter feed.[68] Centred around Ayatollah Qassim, Bahrain's Shīʿa opposition amplified the religious and human rights messages across social media platforms.

Lebanon Shīʿa

Ayatollah Muḥammad Husayn Fadlallah

In Lebanon, Ayatollah Muḥammad Husayn Fadlallah (1935–2010) was the most senior cleric until his death. A substantial online site continues his mission with an archive of religious opinions, political statements and campaigns – particularly those relating to Israel. He had a significant role in influencing the ideological approaches of Hezbollah (although he did not lead it and had disputed some of its principles), in part through the wide distribution of his sermons on cassette tapes in the 1980s and 1990s.[69] He had been targeted by different parties over time, with a failed assassination attempt in 1985 killing eighty people within a Beirut suburb.[70]

Fadlallah's religious legacy features on the website, which also shows religious opinions on family and marriage, Qurʾān interpretation, gender and contemporary concerns.[71] Articles reproduce Fadlallah's opinions. His son al-Sayid Ali Fadlallah continues in his path, with a website of sermons, statements and interpretations, along with associating social media content. Sermons are live-streamed, with opportunities for live Q&A responses to questions.[72] In Lebanon, as with other locations, Shīʿa Muslims follow Ayatollahs from elsewhere, such as al-Sistani and from Iranian spheres of influence. Consequently, the online output from these authorities plays a role in Islamic understanding in Lebanon, alongside the influence of local religious leaders, clerics and scholarly bodies.

Conclusion

These practices are typical of many other Ayatollahs, in terms of websites and social media being central to their activities. Other Shīʿa authorities in majority and minority contexts – for example, in Central Asia, sub-Saharan Africa and India – make pronouncements online in diverse media, applied to engender support, finance, networking and a spiritual connection with their believers through a sense of online identity.[73] People also observe the authority of marājiʿ from elsewhere, as part of the networking associated with Shīʿa authority, which requires further analysis and discussion beyond the scope of a chapter.

There is a sense of dialogue between contemporary and past scholars, emphasizing their opinions being easily accessible and comparable through internet media. This links with the earlier chapter on the Ahl ul-Bayt, the sense of continuity between generations and linkages between ideas and scholarship. The application of social media as a means to protest and protect religious values from other influences is particularly significant in Shīʿa contents, with echoes of the legacies of the formative influences on the development of Shīʿa beliefs.

Scholars and authorities' intellectual and religious descendants can develop further legitimacy and influence by connecting themselves to online systems of knowledge distribution. In contrast, deceased scholars' reputations are embellished and circulated to wider audiences nationally and internationally through translations and networking. These embrace not just the internet in the form of web pages, but apps and other multimedia approaches integrated into a joined-up strategy demonstrating Shīʿa authority, power, knowledge, integrity and heritage. This forms a legacy of religious understanding and the transmission of knowledge, whose roots lay in tradition but whose contemporary manifestation integrates within digital interfaces.

Fields of knowledge and influences go beyond previously conventional boundaries of scholarship and qualifications, a development with the potential to challenge and disrupt the established order and infuse it with new approaches and strategies for Shīʿa beliefs in the twenty-first century. This development contains political ramifications, especially in the context of the Islamic Republic of Iran and its efforts to extend its areas of influence internationally. This practice is parallel with controlling its population and internal networks – through censorship programmes and the development of an intranet. Both phenomena are open to subversion. The next generations of Ayatollahs will likely have a firmer grasp and understanding of digital influence, especially within CIEs, facilitating new approaches to the digital extension of religious knowledge and soft power and the further control of online activities and representation within the republic's population.

Chapter 8

SUFI PATHWAYS IN MUSLIM METAVERSES

Sufism is a dynamic force within contemporary Islam, with orders and adherents worldwide. These take advantage of communications media to network effectively. Their presence can be in many 'minority' contexts too, with a message that also resonates with those (potential) converts seeking to explore dimensions of personal spirituality on an Islamic pathway of knowledge. This factor significantly affects our understanding of Muslim networks, providing perspectives on Islam beyond the stereotypes presented in much of the popular media. This chapter explores key figures and influences in Sufi contexts, outlining their resonance across CIEs. This is particularly important in relation to historical figures who have a formative impact on the development of the multiple identities and interpretations associated with Sufism and the ways they manifest within digital frameworks.

Meta Sufi

With increased online and digital content integration within virtual environments, the projected metaverses seem like an appropriate context for the physically intangible, metaphysical elements of 'Sufism'. The concept of 'influencers' may, however, seem particularly inappropriate within mystical traditions where eradication of the 'self' and a quest for spiritual annihilation are key themes. Specific individuals and organizations play significant roles within societies regarding contemporary figures and people from Muslim history. Aspects of esoteric Islam associated with 'Sufism' (*Ṣūfism*) or *taṣawwuf* reflect broad concepts (acting as an umbrella term for a myriad of primarily esoteric approaches towards interpreting Islam) and numerous Sufi movements or orders (pl. *ṭuruq*, sing. *ṭarīqah*).

Algorithms seeking out 'Sufism' may lead the searcher towards diffuse understandings and conceptual frameworks.[1] Labelling the term 'Sufism' can be problematic. It represents so many diverse understandings and approaches, which are not necessarily mutually compatible – but it can be applied here as a label to help facilitate the exploration of diverse themes associated with selected esoteric interpretations of Islam. Paradoxically the label may not be used by those seen as practising 'Sufism', for which it is simply 'Islam'.

There are numerous complex fusions of Sufi identities worthy of exploration. The spectrum ranges from classical Islamic figures to 'New Age' ideologues – and many points in between. Not all will recognize the other. Links and identities associated with 'Sufism' are diffuse. They can blend, for example, when people choose to follow several orders and their founders (and make a pledge of affiliation to them). This ambiguity of identity and affiliation is easy for online individuals to observe across traditions and continents while also establishing the commonalities of beliefs and principles. It is also possible to visit many shrines, in their various online definitions and forms – whose importance reflects cultural and regional influences as religious factors. They may only have an immediate impact geographically in a specific area. However, influence now extends through internet interfaces, as shrines are destinations for online pilgrimage and visitation. Individuals connect with these significant places through digital *ziyārah*, a concept associated with 'pilgrimage' but with numerous possible definitions.[2]

In this discussion, key themes underpinning Sufism reflect on how concepts have been articulated and have progressed online while also identifying what is new and innovative concerning influences and social media. Sufism can integrate into the content of general 'Islam' sites, rather than 'exceptionalising' Sufism or distilling it from 'mainstream' Islam. It is impossible to generalize, given the diversity of opinion, religious expression, cultural outlooks and linguistic differences on numerous online platforms. Aspects of a particular Islamic outlook can be represented in multiple formats and languages with immediacy and presented to different levels of site users within a competitive and diverse internet knowledge marketplace.

Drawing on a technological edge, esoteric dimensions of Islam connect with long-standing Muslim traditions, historical knowledge frameworks and diverse ideas of the sacred. Sermons and religious meetings are streamed and archived. These form part of a complex media process, with links to other media forms, such as radio, television, print and multi-format recordings, part of the development described as '*al-ʾIslām al-ṣawti*' or 'voiced Islam'.[3]

The mystical quest forms an integral part of the Islamic internet landscape. The central focus around an individual or an order can provide a different – but no less valid – emphasis to other sectors of CIEs. The distribution of texts and propagation material 'digitally' can be effective and comprehensive, and organizations have taken advantage (either 'officially' or 'unofficially') of the internet's networking potential. Like other shades of the Islamic spectrum, Sufis attempt to represent their online perspectives to other Muslims and non-Muslims.

According to many Sufi traditions, the *ṭarīqah* path is not 'human-made' but created by Allāh. It is not a 'physical' but a spiritual reality beyond the senses. It now has a digital element, mediated through devices and interfaces. CIEs impact how Sufism is understood and transmitted to others. It can be a contentious area: Sufis may also claim to be 'orthodox' Muslims, following 'non-mystical' obligations within Islam, a perspective contested by others. Additional *sunnah* ways of the Prophet and other Qurʾānic practices (not necessarily incumbent upon non-Sufis) are practised.[4] Sufism is described as 'a body of teachings and methods having love and knowledge of God as their goal . . .' and considers itself 'the very essence of Islam – and even its spiritual heart'.[5]

Sufism's Islamic identity heightens through the symbols applied as theophanies, a means through which humans might encounter the Divine; the use of the Qur'ān; the regard for Muḥammad as an exemplary model; its use of Arabic; the fact that Sufis (theoretically) retain all Islamic practices and precepts. These elements play out online and form part of the cyber-Islamic experiences for Sufis in digital contexts. Sufi religious expression may 'augment' universal Islamic values with specific elements, such as extra prayers, meditation, music and textual sources. There is no denial of Islam by Sufis, although elements in so-called 'orthodoxy' may suggest that the Sufis' actions alone are a sufficient 'statement' of withdrawal. These complex theophanies and symbols are represented online and expressed digitally. Cyberspace is full of arguments presenting 'definitive' interpretations and concepts of Islam, especially around aspects of Sufism, with conspiracy theories making its interpretation complicit with 'un-Islamic' forces or association with other sects.

The broad networks of interpretations under the Sufism banner contain elements of secrecy in some contexts, hiding knowledge from non-adherents. This contemporary framing has a historical resonance. In Sufi histories, the knowledge possessed 'dangerous' (in the wrong hands) 'mystical qualities'. There was fear of being persecuted as 'unbelievers' straying from 'conventional' Islam. To an extent, these fears are also present today within contemporary Sufi understandings and practices: elements of the esoteric are located within so-called 'orthodoxy' and with aspects of Shī'ism, and some commentators (and critics) would suggest that there is a thin line (or common ground) between these practices and Sufism. There is no mutual agreement between *ṭarīqah* orders regarding what is acceptable in Sufi practices. Discussions on issues of 'acceptability' surface in CIEs. While some Sufi orders may adhere to their practice of dissimulation, others display extensive information relating to allegiances and instructions for believers.

The challenge of Sufism is that it offers a different 'non-orthodox' interpretation(s) of (elements of) the Qur'ān, which 'conservative' scholars and interpreters had interpreted as being immutable and inviolable: commentaries were not open to significant challenges on pertinent issues in the Qur'ān. While esoteric dimensions were not denied, for example, in the discussions of the life of Muḥammad, certain lines are drawn regarding the extent to which proximity towards (or unity with) Allāh could be engendered through 'extra' religious activities. There are reflections of the diversity of interpretation across Muslim networks. These are long-standing discussions within Muslim circles, which now have a place in cyberspace, and can include antagonism, 'flaming' and accusations of unbelief and apostasy.

For some, there was no contradiction between having an 'orthodox' background and an interest in forms of mysticism (which itself could be categorized depending on how 'esoteric' the practices might be). Sufis have practised openly in many cultural and religious contexts. The orders encouraged members to continue in trades and professions so that Sufism might permeate society. This permeation features within CIEs in contemporary contexts, where aspects of Sufism have had a long-term digital presence.

Aspects of Sufism entered 'mainstream' Islamic culture and became forms of Islamic expression (e.g. in art and music) or part of religious practices (especially in Shīʿīsm), transcending multiple boundaries and linking into wider conversations with other esoteric religious perspectives and influences.[6] The history of Sufis shows many travelling and being welcomed in some places and endangered (or martyred) in others. Some Muslims believe that Sufi practices and ideas have invigorated Islam throughout diverse networks, providing fresh approaches and generating widespread enthusiasm. While some practices retain a low profile out of the public gaze, others have generated new audiences (including online) as part of popularizing aspects of Sufism, especially in some non-Muslim contexts. 'Sufi' interpretations of Islam formed a significant element of the early networking process for Islam, which now has continuity in CIEs.

The 'filtering' of Sufism – with the removal of specific Islamic elements and language – has led to the emergence of forms of 'Sufism' divested of religious content, with a focus instead on certain practices as part of lifestyle choices (including in association with 'New Age' and 'Wellbeing' activities). Highly edited Sufi works have become bestsellers, translated for 'western' markets, in some cases with little regard to their Islamic origins. For example, the works of Rūmī, the poet and 'mystic' (discussed later), have acquired popularity in 'western' contexts.

What follows is a snapshot of Sufi CIEs and influences: many influential figures have played a role in the development of Sufism, so it is not the intention here to refer to them all. Instead, the online manifestations of influential figures will be discussed and explored, including through their descendants. The chains of authority and transmission are significant in developing multiple networks associated with the branches and orders associated with Sufism across cultural and religious contexts, especially as these networks play out in digital zones.

Digital manifestations of Sufi figures

The following figures represent a selection of key figures associated with Sufism, across diverse historical and religious contexts. They comprise part of contemporary online discourse about Sufism, while also being influential figures, representative of a plethora of seminal Sufis. The online content surrounding these figures also demonstrates the creative and (in some cases) innovative digital approaches to disseminating information about their lives, beliefs and practices – while also recognizing that there are aspects of Sufi practices that can also be shrouded in secrecy. As will be seen below, some of these figures were also relevant within orientalist discourse, attracting attention from scholars studying, interpreting and translating their works. They influenced perceptions of Islam and Muslims within Western discourse, not only positively.

Rābiʿa al-Baṣrī

Sufism is not an exclusively male domain in terms of its practitioners and influences. Female Sufis held high status in their societies, responsible for poetry and exemplary behaviour, marking them as significant, influential figures. The most famous of these is Rābiʿa al-Baṣrī (714–801). Accounts of her life present legendary and saintly qualities, with a narrative that includes her captivity after being stolen from her povertous home. Released due to inherent devotional qualities, Rābiʿa pursued a secluded life in the desert, before building a following in Basra based on qualities of asceticism and mystical interactions with the divine through 'Pure Love', with miracles attributed to her.[7]

Rābiʿa's online manifestation fuses popularity with (female) spirituality and the quest for poetry with an audience of people who are not Muslim. She personifies the qualities of independence, feminism, spirituality and poverty – an exemplar who was not universally endorsed by contemporaneous (male) Sufi masters. The religious quest for prayer and withdrawal from the pressures of life positions Rābiʿa on some Muslim lifestyle websites as a key figure. Hashtags of #equality, #Muslim Woman and #Gender draw in interested viewers.[8] The 'feminist' angle places her in a central position on websites that explore identities and campaigns, which might not have spirituality at their centre.[9] Reproduced poems from external sources appear on websites within the 'Sacred Poetry' category.[10] Her poems feature on Pinterest and Instagram.[11] As with others in the Sufi zone, the Rābiʿa quotes are accompanied by background photos, not necessarily in the immediate context. Orientalist images of a romanticized version of the 'east' are shown (including paintings used across other contexts).[12]

There are different opinions as to Rābiʿa's burial place, indicative of other religious figures: tradition states her burial place is near Basra, but there is also a tomb in Jerusalem; the latter features as part of an online tour, including prayers over her tomb by visitors and the guide, Shaykh Burhaan Khandia.[13] Other pilgrims feature in an Urdu film featuring a sermon soundtrack.[14] Her story features in an online talk, which picked up over 2 million views, by Allama Mukhtar Shah Naeemi Ashrafi – one of a series on saints. Ashrafi was based in Barkaat ul Quraan Center, Irving, Texas, and the sermon is in Urdu. The centre emphasizes Sufism while also promoting itself as Hanafi in terms of jurisprudence.[15] Other female-led talks are online, picking up positive responses and audiences for YouTube narratives.[16]

The works of other female Sufis permeate elements of cyberspace, but Rābiʿa dominates the conversations. She is enshrouded in legend and speculation, with perceptions filtered by the content of the several feature films produced about her, clips of which are available online on YouTube. The full-length Egyptian 1963 film 'Rabaa al-Adawiyya' is included, featuring music performances by the legendary singer Umm Kulthum (1898–1975).[17] Rābiʿa's influence as a figure extends through digital means, although the technical qualities of some of the film clips may not meet contemporary standards of quality in sound and vision.

Manṣūr Al-Ḥallāj

The presence in CIEs of the Persian Manṣūr al-Ḥallāj (858–922) is an example of a pivotal Sufi figure whose influence resonates across the centuries, impacting 'western' academic approaches towards Islam as well as Sufi Muslims. Al-Ḥallāj's wide travels impacted his approach towards Islam; he visited India and Central Asia, becoming familiar with and influenced by other world views, including Hinduism, Buddhism and Christianity. These travels influenced al-Ḥallāj's poetry and his approach towards esoteric understandings of Islam, which he taught to others. Al-Ḥallāj is a controversial figure, as he believed that he conversed with God, and became 'one' with him, pronouncing '*Ana 'l-Ḥaqq*' ('I am God'/'truth'/'reality').[18] Despite efforts to make him repent, al-Ḥallāj was 'martyred' in Baghdad for his 'blasphemy'. One result was that he became the epitome of self-sacrifice, an exemplar for followers but a dangerous figure for those who do not endorse his controversial perspective. Al-Ḥallāj was as much a controversial figure among groups of Sufis as among others, forcing him to travel and preach before returning to Baghdad.[19]

Al-Ḥallāj also has a place in cyberspace, especially in representations of his sayings (*ḥādīth qudsī*) which form part of more comprehensive online collections of 'spiritual quotations'. Some of these are fused with orientalist paintings, such as the work of American artist Frederick Arthur Bridgman (1847–1928), whose oil painting *The Prayer* is used in conjunction with a quotation from al-Ḥallāj on Pinterest.[20] Bridgman's painting is contextually not necessarily immediately connected in period or location with al-Ḥallāj. However, it may reflect the meaning of the quotation in the eye of the person posting the image. Jean-Léon Gérôme's (1824–1904) *Le Muezzin*, a painting showing a call to prayer from a minaret against the backdrop of nineteenth-century Cairo, is similarly applied to illustrate a further quotation from al-Ḥallāj.[21] This is a common phenomenon online concerning Islam, Sufism and quotations – opening their thoughts to wider audiences through such easy-to-digest memes and bytes of wisdom. The extent to which it projects the influence of al-Ḥallāj to further audiences is worthy of consideration.

Al-Ḥallāj's poetry also intersects with the popularity of Rūmī and other 'mystical' poets, consequently transcending specifically religious online content and fusing with wider poetry outlets in cyberspace. Adjacent to such diverse poets as William Shakespeare, Alfred Lord Tennyson, Emily Dickinson and Philip Larkin, al-Ḥallāj's work projects new audiences as part of an online poetic oeuvre.[22] This features a short biographical note, but much religiously oriented content is removed from the page's content. Material attributed to Al-Ḥallāj is translated and reproduced by commercial publishers and in PDFs and web pages published by followers and enthusiasts, including as part of more exhaustive collections of 'Holy Books'.[23] This includes extensive commentaries on specific aspects of mystical 'Truths' and 'Reality', associated with Qur'ānic commentary and speculation.

These translated works have also impacted the interpretation of Islam and Sufism in Muslim contexts rather than the original works in Arabic. Al-Ḥallāj is a central figure for mysticism in Southeast Asia.[24] His online presence in Indonesian reflects this, where many works are translated and studied in depth, along with additional quotes and memes. Al-Ḥallāj's impact, in the eye of a 'seeker' on a Sufi Path in the United States, is discussed in detail. This is a further entry point online for his work and is part of the perceptions of Sufism within 'western' contexts that have seen the rise of its poetry and thought (if not 'religious' content).[25]

Abū Ḥāmida al-Ghazālī

Abū Ḥāmid al-Ghazālī (1058–111) features in the 'Sunni influences' section of this book: there is a substantial crossover between that section and his contribution to Sufism. Al-Ghazālī crosses many zones within CIEs and represents a significant figure in philosophical contexts way beyond his Muslim roots. The focus here is his impact on Sufism. Al-Ghazālī's reputation was for bringing disparate strands of understanding together. He was (possibly) the first to establish a 'brotherhood' – *zāwiya* in Arabic – requiring strong allegiances between shaykh and disciple. Several orders formed from this, which spread internationally, to influence the development of modern Islam. Founders and descendants were revered, with their lives celebrated as 'saints'. There was an emphasis on the 'inner struggle', a form of jihād as part of an approach towards knowledge. Al-Ghazālī influenced many saints and scholars after him (not all of whom agreed with him!), whose esoteric approaches towards Islam resonate in cyberspace. Many Sufi scholars and philosophers are well-represented online, particularly on academic-related sites. Al-Ghazālī wrote primarily in Arabic; these sources are online alongside translations.[26] Al-Ghazālī is the focus of academic treatises and papers, which explore his impact on ethics, theology and mystical contexts.[27]

Many apps feature the writings and quotations of al-Ghazālī across languages and cultural contexts. A teaching app to calculate *dhikr* and *wirid* using digital *tasbīḥ* forms part of his online presence as a means of remembrance of Allāh (and God's names) and praise towards the Prophet Muḥammad. '*Wirid*' is a term of Malay language origin, synonymous with the Arabic term *dhikr*, while *tasbīḥ* represents prayer beads used as a means of remembrance. The focus is on the repetition of specific prayers or quotes from the Qur᾿ān, whose multiple readings enhance the religious status and spirituality of the reciter with specific benefits. This app's digital interface helps in that process.[28]

Complete libraries of al-Ghazālī's works are accessible through websites: some are jump pages towards other sources or extensive data gateways to PDFs and other materials, including from traditional sources and 'orientalist' perspectives.[29] Muslim academic approaches on al-Ghazālī (and others) explore his life and work in depth, with videos and e-books (free and for sale), along with the delivery of courses and seminars.[30] More detailed and complex information about al-Ghazālī also features on apps, including biographical and reference works, made more searchable and accessible on digital devices.

Some al-Ghazālī content focused on younger audiences, including materials for children via a parent-children website.[31] This echoes al-Ghazālī's own emphasis on holistic education based on Islamic principles. In their online manifestation, these materials can acquire 100,000+ downloads for Android alone (more for Apple), including a source developed by JS-Soft, incorporating quotes and graphics from al-Ghazālī.[32] These explore systematic approaches towards Sufism, as articulated in al-Ghazālī's writings. Other works provide a framework for daily living based on al-Ghazālī's principles, with everyday actions, prayers for all parts of the day and ritual practice advice. Titles reflecting these ideas have been translated into multiple languages online and produced on apps, which indicate al-Ghazālī as a prominent, influential figure online. The complexities of al-Ghazālī's critical positions on aspects of Shīʿīsm, particularly Ismaili beliefs, can be found online on multiple Reddit and other discussion channels.[33] While influential, he remains (for some) a controversial figure too.

Key quotes from al-Ghazālī inevitably appear accompanied by stock images on Pinterest and aphorisms which would not be out of place in lifestyle magazines or self-help websites. These utilize diverse fonts – linked to other 'wisdom' and 'Sufi' quotes or grouped with other jurists and scholars (complete with artistic impressions).[34] Videos explain aspects of al-Ghazālī's life and times, exploring complex philosophical and religious issues. Some of these are generic educational videos.[35]

Many scholarly perspectives on al-Ghazālī, taken from talks and discussions recorded in mosques, achieved extensive audiences: Hamza Yusuf's talk on al-Ghazālī acquired over 418,000 views.[36] By contrast, an animated discussion under the Spiritual Psychologist label on al-Ghazālī incorporates quotations and drawings to explain his principal conceptual frameworks. It is an effective generic discussion of his philosophy, which had over 356,000 views (complete with computer-generated narration). It is an idiosyncratic and visually engaging approach to a complex religious subject, produced as part of a series by RainDrop Academy.[37]

Shorter combinations of quotes and images achieve substantial audiences on TikTok, where tens of thousands of likes are generated for simple appreciations of al-Ghazālī.[38] It is interesting to see how al-Ghazālī remains an influential figure, where approaches towards disseminating his messages to diffuse audiences apply a range of technological approaches. While some content is specifically 'religious' and 'Sufi' in orientation, as with others in this zone, there is more generic content and does not have the emphatic Islamic perspective. Themes include self-help, general philosophy and lifestyle choices. Approaches range from detailed tomes to apps aimed at younger audiences. Al-Ghazālī retains a position as an influential reference point within contemporary Islamic discourse online for multiple audiences.

Abd al-Qādir al-Jīlānī [39]

Abd al-Qādir al-Jīlānī (1078–166) has become a high-profile influence online, whose publications and thoughts permeate diverse social media and online sources. Al-Jīlānī was a teacher and preacher whose sermons were written down by students, becoming the foundation of the subsequent orders that emerged after his death.

The contemporary influence of al-Jīlānī is represented online: the Qadiriyya Sufi Order is a prominent example of an order presenting its activities online. This is part of a variety of networks and movements based on the principles established by al-Jīlānī, which have spread worldwide. Sermons and quotations established a legacy, now promoted online. His position is not universally endorsed, so there is also content that contests his Sufi perspectives and characterization as a 'saint' (while acknowledging his role as a scholar and religious figure).[40]

An important representation of al-Jīlānī's digital influence can be found at his mausoleum, the Mazar Ghous in Baghdad, a feature of online zones associated with the Qadiriyya order. It was bombed and damaged in 2007, resulting in twenty-four deaths: the resulting reconstruction was charted online. Drone technology provided views of reconstruction work, allowing a view of the site from unique angles.[41] As one of the most significant Sufi shrines, it has been the subject of many online videos, from official perspectives to those generated by individual visitors. This is a great opportunity for online surfers to develop knowledge about Al-Jīlānī.

Content includes clips of Sufi activities and a complete virtual tour/pilgrimage (*ziyāra*) of the shrine, library and mausoleum.[42] The qualities feature across various online sources, such as anecdotes in 'Miracles of Huzoor Ghaus Paak' (an alternative title for al-Jīlānī), highlighting his saintly qualities and anecdotes which point to his special status. Other Islamic perspectives would not necessarily endorse such qualities.[43] Al-Jīlānī's tomb complex is the subject of pilgrimage and associated ritual practices – including the prayers when unlocking the shrine doors. Online video shows participants capturing the event on cell phones.[44] Associated Sufi practices marking al-Jīlānī's status, including a *dhikr* ceremony, are recorded on YouTube (again, showing devotees capturing the proceedings on their phones).[45] A virtual tour features the tomb and the mosque in detail, linking it to other mosques associated with the Qadiri order, the film was accompanied by poetry recitation.[46]

The annual commemoration of *Gyarvi Sharīf* marks the death of al-Jīlānī.[47] Given the global nature of the Qadariyya order, Al-Jīlānī is commemorated internationally, including online. The *Gyarvi Sharīf* marks the eleventh month and the eleventh day in the Islamic calendar when processions and ritual festivals mark al-Jīlānī's death with different traditions and practices.[48] Devotional music associated with al-Jīlānī also features in various versions on YouTube, accompanied by pictures of the saint.[49] *Gyarvi Sharīf* can be a monthly ritual event, also captured online.[50]

These and other ritual practices act as indicators of al-Jīlānī's influential role and provide an entry point to other works, including commentaries on the Qur'ān. The miraculous qualities form a theme in other works, such as a video series showing episodes of al-Jīlānī's life, presented with basic animation and images of the shrine. In line with his status as a saintly figure, a bright light obscures al-Jīlānī's face.[51]

Sermons by influential contemporary figures can include discussion of the works of al-Jīlānī, such as a sermon from Shaykh Hisham Kabbani on SufiLive about the station (*maqāmāt*) of al-Jīlānī.[52] Many videos discuss approaches towards al-Jīlānī's work, some critical of the Qadiriyya (even if not specifically critical of al-Jīlānī himself).[53] Other materials can range from devotionally oriented sermons to children's videos, with hagiographic accounts of al-Jīlānī, including about his childhood.[54] Books relating to al-Jīlānī are available extensively in e-bookstores, along with PDFs of key works freely available online, transcending copyright requirements. These include works outlining al-Jīlānī's life.[55]

Pinterest contains key quotes from al-Jīlānī, extracts from his biography and an image of al-Jīlānī from a painting auctioned by Bonhams.[56] The Madani Channel on YouTube, with 2.4 million followers, has scholarly discussions on al-Jīlānī's life and times, alongside opportunities to purchase related merchandise.[57] This is one of many channels offering content relating to al-Jīlānī, from audio files to lectures and illustrated materials emphasizing aspects of his life and spirituality.[58]

Some orders integrate online knowledge into their approaches, such as the Qadiri Rifai Order. It discusses dervish training through introductory Guidance to the Path, encouraging followers to pursue religious knowledge online. This easy-to-navigate resource links to further reading (from the order's historical founders al-Jīlānī and Ahmed Al-Rifāʿī) and links to various branches in the United States and elsewhere.[59] The Qadari Order posted a range of multimedia materials online. In terms of spirituality and religious experience, the *dhikr* ritual invocation of the names of Allāh, Qurʾān verses and other recitations has a performance element. One *dhikr* recorded in Cape Town obtained 928,000 views on a Shaykh Dr Abdalqadir as Sufi channel. A diverse group of ṭarīqah followers participate in the *Haḍra*, ritualized invocation and movement.[60]

The founders' 'influence' spreads through to others through the generations, establishing essential connections of spirituality and *barakah*, which are important in maintaining the integrity of specific religious orders and their ideals. Within CIEs, the endorsement issue is important. Sites produced by individual members of orders or sects are not necessarily 'endorsed' by *ṭarīqah shaykh*. However, endorsement may not be essential, especially given the esoteric nature of various Sufi hierarchies.

Suhrawardīyya

Key founding figures of orders are commemorated online, where digital media are significant hubs of influence. The Suhrawardīyya order links to Abu ʿl-Najīb Suhrawardī (1097–168), responsible for the *Kitāb ʾAdab al-Murīdīn*, a rule book for Sufi novices. His nephew Shihāb al-Dīn ʿUmar Suhrawardī (1145–234) was the founder of the order in Baghdad. His *Awārif al-maʿārif* teaching manual impacted the dissemination of Sufi concepts.[61] The Suhrawardīyya is important across the Indian subcontinent. Through Muʿīn al-Dīn Chishtī, the writings of the *Awārif* became central to the foundation of the Chishtīyya order (see below). There was an emphasis on *dhikr* rather than the emphasis on poetry and music presented by other orders. The online output reflects this. The *Kitāb ʾAdab Al-Murīdīn* and the *Awārif* are widely available commercially and in various translated and downloadable versions. Shrines associated with the order can be 'visited' online, including the distinctive mausoleum of ʿUmar Suhrawardī in Baghdad, with its distinctive conical dome – and a complex which contained a higher education institution founded under the ʿAbbāsids. There are several site videos, from religiously oriented materials to tourist and architectural guides.[62]

Subsequent influential members of the Suhrawardīyya order are commemorated through mausoleums and shrines, such as the *dargar* in Multan, Pakistan, belonging to Baha-ud-Din Zakariya (1170–268), pivotal in helping establish the order in North Western India. Baha-ud-Din is attributed with proximity to 'Umar Suhrawardī spiritually, having studied with him. He was recognized for exceptional 'mystical' qualities before being sent back to India to propagate the order's message. Various miracles are associated with him, and he founded a branch of the order that greatly impacted the region, along with its disciples and his descendants. He features in a biography presented on YouTube, drawing on episodes taken from Baha-ud-Din 's life; the film is partially recorded inside the shrine, accompanied by an English language *nāshīd*.[63] The tomb can be visited online, including through a film with special effects and zone photography, to highlight the site from different angles.[64] It is also the subject of a documentary, indicating shrine practices and the influential role of the saint within the modern ritual.[65]

Dātā Ganj Bakhsh

Significant figures within regional contexts have important shrines that act as focal points for physical pilgrimage and wider online networks. It is impossible to explore all of them here, but some examples of specific influential figures indicate how their roles transmute into digital contexts. The eleventh-century Shaykh Syed ʿAlī al-Hujwīrī (1009–72) – also known as Dātā Ganj Bakhsh – has a prominent mausoleum (Data Darbar) in Lahore, Pakistan.

ʿAlī al-Hujwīrī's heritage was linked, according to tradition, all the way back to the Prophet Muḥammad. His ancestors and relatives were highly regarded for important Sufi qualities, including key figures in the Ahl ul-Bayt and the imamate. The importance of following orthodox Sunni law is integral to his identity. This is paradigmatic of other Sufi figures claiming the imams as Sufis, declaring they were 'anti- Shīʿa'. ʿAlī al-Hujwīrī is responsible for writing the Persian language *Kashf al-maḥjūb* or 'Revelation of the Veil', which describes approaches towards Sufism and explores the heritage of Sufi saints.[66] It is available in multiple online versions and translations – some simple PDF versions of print editions. Online mediations make the work more accessible, as it has been discussed in depth in lectures and broadcasts – alongside other explanations.

The Dātā Darbar's *khateeb* (the person who delivers a sermon) Mufti Muḥammad Ramzan Sialvi hosted a *Kashf al-maḥjūb* chat show. This formed part of extensive social media and online activities focused on the *darbar*, including the celebration of Prophet Muḥammad's birthday at the shrine and live-streamed *jummah* prayers.[67] ʿAlī al-Hujwīrī's *darbar* became a state-managed shrine in Pakistan in the 1960s, as much for his role as a key figure in regional Islam as for his ('sober') Sufi activities, marking it out as a political symbol in Pakistan. Bomb attacks in 2010 and 2019 targeted it. The annual *ʿurs* celebration features online and broadcast news coverage of luminaries attending Dātā Darbar, highlighting the logistical demands and celebratory 'dancing', recitation and prayers.[68] A tour around the *darbah* site achieved over 1.3 million views, despite technical limitations in the recording.[69] Another tour featured a narrative, photos drawn from Google and embedded YouTube clips.[70] The Dātā Darbar shows how digitally infused Sufi traditions transmit through online content, whose reach extends beyond traditional frameworks into global networking contexts.

Chishtīyya

As an example of the ways in which Sufi networks and influences have developed digitally, content linked to Khwājah Muʿīn al-Dīn Chishtī (1141–236) can be explored. It is significant as he was the founder of the eponymous Chishtīyya order in India, influential in the conceptualization and networking associated with Sufism internationally. His *ṭarīqah* became significant beyond the Indian subcontinent. It based its perspective on his preaching and attributed miracles, a lineage going back to Muḥammad and inherent flexibility in approaches to ritual, which incorporated music within its *dhikr*. Several accounts of his life feature legends and hagiographic materials, written centuries after his death.

Emphasis is on his miraculous qualities, enshrined in textual narratives (based on traditional sources) alongside YouTube video explanations. Content includes accounts of Chishtī's annual 'trip' to hajj, where he was 'seen' in Mecca despite remaining in Ajmer, Rajastan – and his appearance after death to intervene in a dispute.[71] His tomb in Ajmar became a significant shrine – popular among some Hindus and Muslims (including some Shīʿa Muslims). Its importance can be gauged by the number of photos and related paintings available online, across Pinterest and Instagram, capturing the perspectives of devotees and observers to the shrine – especially on commemorative days.[72] Content includes virtual tours, shot in the immediate proximity of the tomb, showing ritual practices and invocations over the tomb, where visitors are covered over their heads by the shroud connected with the tomb, and blessed by an incumbent imam. The hashtag '#fulldua' marks the film.[73]

Other clips show 'live' streaming from Khwaja Garib Nawaz Dargah, with mixed groups of pilgrims in the shrine precincts and procession (with many participants recording activities on their cell phones). Devotional *qawwali* music accompanies the film. The live streaming features numerous related links.[74] The shrine's keepers, known as Khadim, also have web pages explaining their activities and responsibilities – along with a link for donations as payment for devotional activities (by proxy).[75] Individuals chart their *dargah* visits to the shrine online, for example, on Twitter.[76] The Chishtīyya extends to many other locations represented online, illustrating the networking effect of this Sufi movement.[77] It enters zones of popular culture through music applications, while social media and other outlets mark local events.

The multiple lines of contemporaries, descendants and other saints associated with the order have online representation – indicating the history of its spiritual lineage (*silsila*) and the multiple dervishes and spiritual successors. Their influence continues into modernity. Qutubuddin Bakhtiyar Kaki (1173–235) is a further significant successor of Chishtī, who influenced the spread of Islam (specifically Sufi interpretations) across the Indian subcontinent. There is stress on his poverty, miraculous interventions and intense devotional practices; tradition states that he died when participating in *sama*' (devotional poetry and dance), bringing him closer to God.

Qutubuddin's burial place in Delhi became a significant *dargah* site, represented online in numerous videos exploring its precincts and the practices undertaken within, showing people praying in the precincts and covering the tomb with rose petals.[78] This includes a governmental heritage site, highlighting the *dargah*'s role as a sacred place for pilgrims across traditions. Particularly significant are the *ʿurs* (annual commemoration of a saint's death) and a specific festival featuring sticks, in which pilgrims proceed in the *dargah* and make a wish by tying a string to Qutbuddin's grave.[79] The attendance of devotees at this festival was marked by local news, recording a packed crowd at the shrine, many filming proceedings on their cell phones.[80] Phone clips offering grassroots perspectives and commentaries also made it onto YouTube, showing the *dargah* and *ʿurs* from a pilgrim's perspective.[81]

'Official clips' from the *dargah* also appear on Facebook, presenting shrine activities and *qawwali* recordings.[82] Some pilgrims' experiences are captured in more secular surroundings through travel sites such as TripAdvisor, which provides detail, advice and a sense of the experience – although women are not permitted to enter the main *dargah*, only observe it from a specially designated portal. The personal photographs on TripAdvisor offer that sense of detail and experience.[83] A generic site was used to construct a family tree around Qutbuddin and his *silsila* spiritual line of descendants, noting 10,000 blood relatives as part of this profile. Genealogical trees are often part of Sufi literature and listings are online.[84]

Muḥyī ad-Dīn Ibn ʿArabī

The internet opens aspects of Sufism to wider audiences, including its intellectual and philosophical influences. Muḥyī ad-Dīn Ibn ʿArabī (1165–240), as interpreted by stepson Ṣadr al-Dīn Qūnawī (1210–74), was influential in his approach towards speculative theology and ideas surrounding 'divine unification', articulated in his work *Fuṣūṣ al-Ḥikam* ('Bezels of Wisdom' or 'unity of perception').[85] Ibn ʿArabī is a fundamentally influential figure in philosophy and interpretations of Islam across generations and cultures. This influence plays out online, from popular culture to academic works. The Muhyiddin Ibn ʿArabī Society is a key 'western' reference point, with a Facebook group (11,700 members) and a YouTube channel. It offers online courses of Ibn ʿArabī, part of education programmes which go back to the society's foundation in 1977. The Facebook pages act as a hub for events and information on Ibn ʿArabī.[86]

The society noted that attention increased through the representation of Ibn ʿArabī in the *Ertuğrul* series, streamed on Netflix. This series has impacted how Ibn ʿArabī is represented and understood while opening his life to an entirely new audience. The phenomenon amplified during the coronavirus pandemic, where the series (with 478 episodes) became the subject of 'binge viewing' during lockdown across many contexts. As a key figure and subject of consultation by Ertuğrul, specific extracts featuring Ibn ʿArabī also became popular across social media, from official and other channels, with the work dubbed and translated into many languages. The Ertuğrul channel had 9.5 million views on YouTube for season 1 and 2.55 million subscribers.[87] The presence of Ibn ʿArabī as a figure in this series has intensified interest in a figure with a high profile and has been the subject of scholarship and widespread religious interest.

One of Ibn ʿArabī's critical popularizers was Idries Shah (1924–96), whose work now has an online life, especially through readings of his book on Ibn ʿArabī, although Shah's work has come under critical scrutiny.[88] At the other end of the scale, Ibn ʿArabī has a presence on social media such as Instagram, where collections of his quotes under the hashtag #ibnalarabi have 36,000 entries. Some were devoted to *Ertuğrul*, but others had a more scholarly disposition, fused with images of Whirling Dervishes (discussed as follows) and cross fertilized with quotes from Rūmī and other influential figures. Book covers showing works on Ibn ʿArabī from orientalist scholars such as Henry Corbin and A. J. Arberry were interspersed with aphorisms and contemplative images. Whether this is by intention or design is difficult to determine.[89]

Ertuğrul dominated videos of Ibn ʿArabī on TikTok, with clips receiving hundreds of thousands of views.[90] The multilingual appreciation of Ibn ʿArabī represented in these short video clips indicates the widespread cultural impact of this significant intellectual figure by those whose only exposure may be through a digitally streaming source. Lurking in the TikTok feeds are some performative clips from *Ertuğrul*, too, showing Sufi ritual activities, such as the *dhikr* in Jerusalem – which features Ozman Sirgood (the actor playing Ibn ʿArabī) in a recreation of Al-Aqṣā Mosque in Jerusalem.[91]

There was some negative feedback for this representation, with an online pronouncement from Scholars of Ahlus Sunnah wal Jamaah Standing Committee stating that this was in an 'innovative' fashion. Ibn ʿArabī was a 'disbeliever', according to this Committee, suggesting that he is not a universally respected figure and that there can be hostility or antipathy towards (forms of) Sufism in general and Ibn ʿArabī in particular. This came up at the top of a search on Twitter for Ibn ʿArabī.[92] Generally, the hashtag is used on Twitter to circulate quotations from traditional sources of Ibn ʿArabī and associated poetry. Ibn ʿArabī is a unique figure in digital influence and popularity: the extent to which *Ertuğrul* acted as a gateway to further investigation of Sufism is open to question. However, it is certainly one to track in the future. The intersection of popular culture and Sufism is not unique to Ibn ʿArabī, as will be seen below.

Jalāl al-Dīn Rūmī

Jalāl al-Dīn Muḥammad Rūmī's (1207–273) high-profile influence on contemporary perceptions of Sufism permeates digital discourse. Born in Afghanistan and the son of a theologian, Rūmī composed epic collections of (mainly) Persian language poetry and laid the foundations for the Mawlawi (Mevlevī) order, famous for its 'dervishes'. His encounters with his spiritual guide, Shams-i Tabrīzī (1185–248), seen as 'divine beloved', form the basis of some of his most famous works. Rūmī's work has gone through multiple translations and interpretations. It influenced Western poetry and approaches towards mysticism in general and Sufism in particular.

Rūmī's poetry is a feature of 'orientalist' scrutiny in works by A. J. Arberry, R. A. Nicholson and many others.[93] The popularity of Rūmī's poetry and (part of) his spiritual message has seen it on contemporaneous bestseller lists, albeit with controversial reinterpretations, as well as other works which have taken the specifically religious elements out of the poetry in terms of interpretation and meaning.[94] The 26,000 rhyming couplets in his *Mathnawī* lend themselves well to internet searches to navigate its volume and complexity. They have taken on new life on the internet, with quotations and works utilizing Rūmī as a key source for lifestyle posts, 'mindfulness', meditation and other sectors of contemporary contemplation – often by influencers lacking specific regard for the Islamic roots of the source materials, more focused on the 'best-selling' qualities of his work.[95] One critical issue has been the emergence of 'quotations' purportedly from Rūmī, which come from other sources.[96]

Quotes can feature across genres. Instagram and Pinterest provide extensive collections, often categorized, drawn from Rūmī's work, often presenting Rūmī as a 'lifestyle' choice and influence(r), although the accompanying advertising can dilute their impact.[97] A collection of poems (lacking specific commentaries or explanations) features on several sites, categorized thematically and searchable.[98] Rumi.org.uk heavily relies on external works; for example, it draws on Arberry's 1949 collection of quatrains for its 'Persian with Rūmī' page, which opens up the work as a means of learning Persian.[99]

Rūmī's popularity – and that of the Mevlevī Order he influenced – is predicated in part on the importance of the performative aspects of spirituality and religious expression, as exemplified (to its followers) within the loud *dhikr*, music and dance that marks the 'performances' of the so-called Whirling Dervishes. There is a scale for Sufism, from very sober and quiet contemplation to this dynamic and expressive mode of practice. In reality, seekers on the path of knowledge in Sufism may pledge allegiance to several spiritual leaders and orders – which may have different sources, perspectives and even approaches towards politics. This development impacted the Mevlevī Order during the emergence of Kemal Atatürk, whose secularizing approach suppressed the Mevlevī Order and its rituals in Turkey, ultimately resulting in performance becoming part of tourism and the status of the tomb of Rūmī in Konya being relegated from shrine to museum. Online tours reflect the touristic potential of the space, including ritual performances by the Whirling Dervishes as part of a sound and light show, potentially devoid of specific religious value or interpretation.[100]

Opposition to Sufism in general, and particularly Rūmī, is apparent in many online Islamic contexts, where associated ritual performances such as shrine veneration and *dhikr* are outside the accepted boundaries of religious understanding and practices. Rūmī is one particular focus, partly because of his posthumous legacy and (edited) work, which continues to be widely circulated across cultures and languages, facilitated by the wide availability of online content.

Naqshbandiyya

Other perspectives hold online significance as part of the digital Sufi expression and at grassroots levels: the Naqshbandiyya *ṭarīqah* holds prominence within contemporary Sufism. Muḥammad Bahā' al-Dīn Naqshband Bukhārī (1318–89) laid the order's foundations, whose subsequent spiritual chains and significant Sufi lines of authority retain influence today.[101] The focus on his spiritual training and *dhikr* practices included visions when he was 'initiated' through a vision by previous Sufis – in a chain that went back to the Prophet Muḥammad, all of whom can be deemed influential with varying degrees of an online presence.[102] Some of this appears in Naqshbandiyya activities, networked globally across different branches and orders, whose digital media cite his sayings and deeds. This is part of the hagiography surrounding Bukhārī but also blends with the sayings and images associated with other Naqshbandiyya influences and sources.[103]

Bukhārī's tomb in Uzbekistan is a pilgrimage site with numerous digital approaches, including what is described as a 'virtual ziarat' (*ziyāra*) in Bukhara, from the airport to the shrine to the craft gift shop, which takes the viewer through all stages of a visit. Other videos show dimensions of travel, from tourism trips to visits by politicians, with Pakistan's then prime minister Imran Khan filmed at the shrine in 2021 as part of an election campaign.[104]

Hashtags such as #bahauddinnaqsbandibukhari represent ziyarat visits.[105] *Ziyāra* tourism is a big business in Uzbekistan, with a fusion of travel and religious obligation on several sites and pages. *ʿUrs* celebrations are marked online not just in Bukhara but across Sufi contexts internationally, featured on news broadcasts and recorded for posterity and for those unable to attend in person. A video from Birmingham, UK, shows a sermon in English discussing the role of being in a *silsila* and being a *mujtahid* on the Sufi path. The *ṭarīqah*'s Shaykh Sufi Arshad Mahmood is on the stage listening.[106] A news broadcast from Pakistan notes the rituals associated with *ʿurs* locally and the presence of military personnel guarding the shrine from attack.[107] Online discussions regarding Naqshband Bukhārī's qualities are across the internet, from detailed biographies, collections of sayings and YouTube discussions.[108]

The Naqshbandiyya *ṭarīqah* has branches in many different forms. For example, the Naqshbandiyya *ṭarīqah* in Anatolia owes its foundations to the life and works of Shaykh Aḥmad-i Bukhārī (d.1516), who was influenced by Ibn 'Arabī and Rūmī and focused on the practices of *dhikr* as central to his *tekke* (Sufi lodge).[109] The order has impacted several 'western' contexts, including branches and mosques that are part of international networks. Some of these have proactively disseminated their message online.

The Naqshbandi Sufi Way presents *taṣawwuf* online, with elements combining specific practices with net technology: a *bay'a* or 'pledge of allegiance' to the *ṭarīqah* can be heard through the clicking of the cursor on the 'hands' of *ṭarīqah* followers represented within a photograph.[110] Shaykh Hisham Kabbani (1945–) described the order as Naqshbandi-Haqqani and focused on its Grand Shaykh Muḥammad Nazim al-Haqqani (1922–2014). Al-Haqqani's authority and spiritual line of descent came from previous Grand Shaykhs, chronicled on the site.[111] Kabbani's website is a hub for diverse online content and activities associated with the order, explored below.[112]

The Naqshbandi Sufi Way includes transliterated transcripts of various prayers and *dhikr*: these can be followed in real time through downloading audio files. Thus, the surfer can 'experience' aspects of these Sufi practices – also explained and justified. The digital objects have specific religious values. An online invocation by Kabbani protects homes against evil influences.[113]

This page goes through to a YouTube video of Kabbani invoking this *du'ā'*. A series of PDFs provide information on different ritualistic recitations and aspects of belief. This includes practices associated with using a talisman (*taweez*) and other invocations used for healing and the ethics of whether there should be a charge for these elements (derived from the Qur'ān).[114] In terms of 'influence', this aspect of spirituality, which links into *ruqya* and other practices, is most pertinent within Sufi contexts – but might be deemed as 'innovation' outside these zones for going outside of the perceived 'boundaries' of acceptable practice.

For example, Dhikr in Congregation or *Khatm-ul-Khwajagan*, a weekly ritual central to the *ṭarīqah*'s practices, can be followed and downloaded: part of this practice is 'silent' but involves repetition. Another aspect is congregational and participative. The number of phrase repetitions is provided, together with guidelines on pronunciation. They can be followed on the audio file download. Shaykh Hisham Kabbani participates directly in the recordings and is on video practising *dhikr*. Questions emerge as to whether this could constitute a 'religious experience' for members of the *ṭarīqah* unable to attend a *Khatm-ul-Khwajagan*.[115] It might also contribute to the sense of 'community' or suggest a 'digital *umma*', at least for adherents of the Order. Alternatively, it may simply be a 'performance' with no immediate direct religious value.

SufiLive, organized by followers of the Naqshbandi-Haqqani Sufi Order, reflects the globalization of an Islamic movement, with centres and followers worldwide.[116] The main SufiLive page linked to the complete multimedia libraries of Al-Haqqani and Kabbani.[117] Followers of Mawlana Shaykh Nazim Adil Al-Haqqani and the Naqshbandi-Haqqani Sufi Order established eShaykh as part of their extensive international internet presence. Although Al-Haqqani was based in Northern Cyprus, the hub website SufiLive is hosted in the United States, and its primary religious opinions outlet is eShaykh.

SufiLive is on Twitter and Facebook and pages are regularly updated; donations to the Sufi order (which can form part of religiously obligated charity) can be made electronically through PayPal. Categories include building a mosque and donating a car, although other (cheaper) donation possibilities are also available. Transcripts of (some) videos are in sixteen languages; these are searchable archives, allowing exploration of key terms. A live broadcast calendar indicates times for live streaming of sermons. SufiLive TV broadcasts live '24/7'.

An annotated Google map shows the order's numerous global locations, demonstrating its networking capacity and potential influence across platforms, especially given the intensity, frequency and open availability of digital output. SufiLive provides links to online shopping channels (themselves offering e-books and sound files for download). The materials are continually updated, especially videos of sermons, invocations, prayers and discussions. Videos are categorized: for example, the Mawlid an-Nabi 1443 (2021) features different stages of ritual practice, with participation in English. There is reading of religious texts associated with *mawlid* practices and a high-definition view of a sermon from the mosque floor. The material is in Arabic and English.[118] These are extensive recordings in their own right. They offer insight into the order's perspective and practices and opportunities for those unable to attend events in person to 'participate' or observe virtually. In time, these materials become an archive for the order's activities, especially when key figures die, so they can be referred to posthumously and retain 'influence' among those seeking knowledge. The statements of al-Haqqani remain available years after his death; presumably, the order has a strategy for maintaining and preserving archived materials for educational, spiritual and historical purposes.

SufiLive connects to eShaykh.com, an advice site that responds to readers' questions by email and requests for prayers and dream interpretation. Using question-and-answer pages such as eShaykh has been a significant development within CIEs across the Muslim spectrum of diverse interpretations and understandings. It has a significant role in religious, political and spiritual influences.[119] The development of Q&A pages empowered Muslims to search for an opinion that suits their circumstances (a phenomenon which predated the net). In some contexts, it has introduced a practice that has subverted the traditional roles of local religious scholars in analogue contexts. The extent to which these impact or influence individuals is difficult to measure: the site presented data with 6,000+ visits in a calendar month (October–November 2021), which is relatively low-level traffic, and there is no indication of how these online responses were utilized (if at all). Questions are anonymous; answers are concise and reference specific Islamic concepts and sources. They can relate specifically to current issues and events; in 2021, this led to questions on Covid-19. A search for 'COVID' brought up a hundred links to various Q&A discussions, looking at aspects of vaccines, permissibility, health, safety and obligation.[120]

Some dreams relate specifically to religious experiences, with the presence of the shaykh within them (seen in a very positive light). Dreams provide advice concerning relationships, rituals and religious obligations. Symbolism is attached to these dreams in different forms. Some general questions elsewhere on the site concerning beliefs and practices also link to the interpretation of dreams. eShaykh

.com goes into substantial detail on many aspects of religious practices, especially the requirements of this Naqshbandi-Haqqani branch of Sufism. Among the thousands of opinions and responses, advice is given on approaching allegiance to the Sufi order, including the benefits of religious practice and understanding, focusing on this order. Divine intercession is also available online through submitting a prayer request via an online form (this requires logging in to the site). There were 580 pages of dream interpretations, with visions of jinn, animals, shrines, religious figures and family members in the posts. Responses referred to the Qur᾿ān, ḥādīth sources and significant Sufi texts.[121] This online dream service, drawing on the responses and interpretations of religious figures, is not unique to eShaykh. There were also precursors in print journalism, as the phenomenon of Q&A services predated the internet.

The activities of Naqshbandiyya Sufis in the Midlands of the UK were under Pir Abdul Wahab Siddiqi (1942–94); Coventry Islamic Study Centre and Hijaz College, Nuneaton, were established – the latter to train Muslim scholars. After Siddiqi's death, his shrine became the first Sufi Western European *dargah*, while his line continued through his son. This site has a significant online presence, where it is possible to visit the shrine through a virtual tour.[122] Siddiqi's sermons and speeches were recorded on video and remain accessible across YouTube and other social media. For example, his final speech – recorded in Holland – was captured and remained online.[123]

Such sites do not necessarily represent a mainstream of Islamic religious opinion in their fusion of traditional Sufi values and outlook with integrated approaches to online activities. Online activities in both global and local contexts promote their interpretations and understandings of Islam. In a competitive Islamic internet knowledge economy, there will be different levels of readership interest, where attention spans (as with other content) can be limited. Drawing site users in through multimedia, offering podcasts, videos and a sense of affiliation represents a classic marketing strategy and a contemporary approach to religious propagation.

In Turkey, there were stylistic challenges to the concept of listening to a sermon or speech from a religious leader, which may differ between and within Naqshbandiyya branches. Cübbeli Ahmet Hoca, known as 'Ahmed in Cassocks', achieved millions of views for his *sohbet* or 'conversation(s)', described by one observer as 'free-spirited, experimental rants'.[124] With 1.09 million subscribers on YouTube, he achieved substantial audiences for regularly posted conversations and films of other activities. Content included a funeral speech, a ḥādīth and *tafsīr* discussion, 'letters of faith' and 'healing lessons'. A discussion about the religious permissibility of oral sex attained over 5 million views in six years.[125] He had a presence across social media channels, while the Cübbeli Ahmet Hoca website promoted more detailed publications, such as commentary on a portion of the Qur᾿ān. Kaya Kenç noted that social media had been a specific focal point of Ahmet's organizational strategy: 'The hours-long format of the traditional sohbet has given way to snippets that can go viral on Twitter or on Instagram, and like all savvy modern-day preachers, he tailors his speeches to better fit those platforms.'[126]

This integration of online media into Sufi activity represents a cutting-edge awareness of the potential impact of digital content, albeit with continuity linking it to the formative influences on Sufism from across the centuries.

Other Sufi zones

The presence of diaspora communities and networks led to the development of specific branches of Sufism. These evolved in terms of influences and interpretations, which operate extensively online, developing articulations of world views, creating new audience affiliations and ideas of connectivity. Other zones resonate with forms of esoteric interpretations of Islam, which increasingly draw on their presence within CIEs and the Sufi metaverses. Many would benefit from detailed studies (this present work offers snapshots). The next section explores how these understandings present themselves across CIEs, indicating diverse approaches towards religious interpretations and understandings online.

Al-Tijāniyyah

One dynamic strand of online Sufism is represented through Al-Ṭarīqah al-Tijāniyyah, the Tijāniyyah order, which has networks with links in the North and West Africa (and affiliates elsewhere). These connect to diaspora communities and networks through digital materials: the central focus is Sidī Aḥmad al-Tijāniyy (1737–1815), whose vision of the Prophet Muḥammad in 1782 led to development of a 'sober' Sufi order. It had a specific focus and identity, combining observation of *sharīʿa* with selected ritual practices. Al-Tijāniyy abandoned allegiance to other orders, having met significant Sufi figures on his travels, including the pilgrimage to Mecca. Details of these encounters, and the complexities of his affiliations, feature in several online biographies.[127]

The *Zāwiyah* of Sidī Aḥmad al-Tijāniyy in Fez, Morocco, is a focal point in numerous videos when searching for Sufi rituals online. These clips show the role of *dhikr*, with phone footage indicating different aspects of ritual practice at an intimate 'grassroots' level.[128] The collective recitation of *suwar* from the Qurʾān and prayers and invocations grouped as a *wazifa* (collected practices of recitations, prayers and *duʿāʾ* within a *ḥalaqah* (circle) reaches wide audiences online. Whether the observation and online recitation would offer the same qualities of spiritual benefit as being at the zāwiyah is open to question. However, the materials are put onto social media by an 'official' Tidjania.com platform, where it received tens of thousands of views. Other orders link to it in different international contexts.[129] A 2007 documentary showed a conference in Morocco, which brought together key Tijāniyyah members – some of whom have now passed away – making it an artefact of historical and religious interest.[130] With a focus on the religious leaders of earlier generations, legacy recordings such as this can have specific connotations in Sufi contexts,

Tidjaniya.com acts as a hub, focusing on al-Tijāniyy, his descendants and spiritual authorities since his death. Arabic, English and French website version content varies according to the level of detail and amounts of material. Specific episodes and locations associated with al-Tijāni's life are highlighted, including clips showing al-Tijāni's village and house. The site offers advice on the spiritual pathways which individuals can follow based on his example. It indicates the specific requirements of following this specific Tijāniyyah path. The site offers a Q&A service, which in 2020 explored the question of information technology used to observe ritual activities during the coronavirus period. The authorities 'strongly warned against the practice of performing the blessed wazifa and haylala in a group via video conferencing applications, stating that this is a deviation that has no basis other than excess ignorance'.[131] This opinion was counter that in other Islamic zones on this issue. However, it offers advice on teaching recitations via YouTube videos.[132]

The online presence of Tijāniyyah regional branches demonstrates allegiance to core founder values, along with specific cultural-regional differences: these highlight the life of the order's founder through a biography accompanied by an audio reading. They also demonstrate the integral role of Shaykh Ibrahima Niasse (1900–75) in developing the order in Senegambia (where it is the predominant *ṭarīqah*) and broader contexts.[133] Practices of the Tijāniyyah order were captured in a detailed documentary, connecting practices in Sweden with those of Senegal, showing ritual practices and pilgrimages, and *dhikr* (showing participants recording their activities on cell phones).[134] Senegal-specific practices featured group *dhikr* (*Ḥaḍrah*) invocations in a *Zāwiyah* of Sidi Abdel Moutalib Tijāni in Dakar.[135]

This influence extended to Shaykh Hassan Cisse (1945–2008), with followers in the United States and West Africa. The *ṭarīqah*'s outreach focused on Nasrul Ilm America, emphasizing its humanitarian work in Senegal and the United States. It includes the African American Islamic Institute Schools Project, funding a Senegal school where American students undertake Islamic Studies. The influence of Cisse is pervasive in this endeavour and the Nasrul Ilm American's activities. Online, they present their interpretation of Islam through promoting Cisse's humanitarian activities and including United Nations recognition.[136] Videos of Cisse maintain his influence online.[137]

Hassan Cisse's brother Sheikh Ahmad Tijani Ali Cisse (1955–) succeeded him. Ahmad Cisse's activities have been captured for internet consumption: the film crew recorded his 2012 visit to Ghana and Nigeria, showing his Ghana motorcade (and Oyo State motorbike accompaniment), crowd reception (themselves capturing the event on social media) and ritual practices.[138] Ahmad Cisse's followers archived his activities. In a series of portraits via an Instagram channel, several images showed him checking or holding his iPhone, suggesting connectivity to his digital followers and perhaps awareness of the significance of online media in his *ṭarīqah*.[139] Interestingly, the Tijāniyyah were also linking up with the Western university sector through an online database development exploring authorities and sources associated with Northwestern University in Qatar. This resource promised sources from the order, scholarly information and research outputs.[140]

Bauchi

Other African branches are proactive online. Those associated with Sheikh Dahiru Usman Bauchi (1927–) of Nigeria developed a YouTube channel claiming 9.5 million views in 2021; this captures him and his followers with weekly updates of ritual activities, including celebrating specific rituals and meetings with other leaders.[141] The digital capture of the sheikh and his followers' everyday activities includes a daily Qur'ān Instagram commentary.[142]

Murīdiyya

West African 'Sufi' practices are reflected in dynamic online spaces, utilizing networking capacities across various nodes of influence regionally and internationally. Extended digital access and literacy play an essential role in this context, as shown by the Murīdiyya (Mouride) *ṭarīqah*, which networks branches worldwide from its base in Senegal and provides spiritual advice through the Ṭarīqaht-ul-Muridiyya website.[143] It traces its origins to Amadou Bamba (Aḥmad ibn Muḥammad ibn Ḥabīb Allāh, 1850–1927). Bamba combined religious teachings, the status of *mujaddid* ('renewer'), and an anti-colonial non-violent ideologue who led a spiritual jihad against French colonial powers in West Africa.[144] Bamba was imprisoned and exiled by the French, and during exile in Mauritania he claimed a miraculous vision of Muḥammad. Several other miracles were attributed to Bamba.[145]

Bamba's legacy is in the millions of followers in West Africa and in international communities of migrant descent, focusing on pilgrimage to Bamba's spiritual hub and burial place in Touba, Senegal. This focal point on Bamba led to specific rituals dedicated to him, rather than the traditional emphases in 'mainstream' Islam, leading some critics to suggest it has become its own religious framework.[146] The Grand Magal pilgrimage to Touba is based on commemorating Bamba's exile by the French in 1895. It is marked by recitation of the Qur'ān and Bamba's *khassaīd* poetry, alongside visits to the tombs of Bamba and his descendants.[147] The Grand Magal has been videoed by followers, picked up by news channels and was the subject of a 2013 documentary (with trailers online).[148]

The story of Bamba's exile features in sermons and videos, often using the singular image as a reference point, superimposed with other background content.[149] The Jâlibatoul Mazîyah YouTube channel attracted millions of views among Murīdiyya followers for its videos of Qur'ān recitations, Bamba's (and his descendants') poems, sermons and documentaries – often subtitled in French.[150] Khass TV shows documentary and information films about Bamba and Touba, with access to shrines and pilgrimage points, as well as discussions with significant religious figures; these give insights into the religious activities and the pervasive influence of Bamba in contemporary contexts.[151] An animated biography, clearly designed for very young audiences, describes Bamba's life.[152] TikTok, Instagram and Pinterest have associated content.[153]

With his face covered and wearing an enveloping robe, Bamba's distinctive image pervades the Murīdiyya movement. The movement's members also focus on an ethos of hard work as part of its spiritual and religious identity.[154] Some of this is articulated in charitable endeavours and community networking, for example, in the United States, where Foncab is proactive in promoting projects, highlighting the Murīdiyya's activities and using multimedia to spread its ethos through its TV channel (online). It supports and fundraises for various projects, including community help during the Covid-19 crisis.[155] Bamba's grandson, Serigne Mountakha Mbacké (1930–) is the current caliph of the Murīdiyya. Assuming the title in 2018, he and Bamba's other descendants have a unique spiritual status in the Murīdiyya *ṭarīqah* and an extensive online presence, which builds on their reputations while also placing Bamba as a significant contemporary influence in CIEs.[156]

Barēlwī

The presence of the Barēlwī in cyber contexts echoes its historical past, resulting in a variety of networks emerging in diverse contexts: Ahmed Riza Khan (1856–1921) is a key figure in Barelwī (*Barēlwī*) *Ahle Sunnat Wal Jamaat* ('people/followers of the Sunnah and community') development. The movement is represented as 'defending' Sufi interpretations in nineteenth-century north India. It has particular significance in Mirpur, the source of many migrants to the UK. Over time, Barēlwīs established their network of mosques under *pīr*s (spiritual guides), some of whom claim descent from Sufi masters. There is specific attention on the qualities of the Prophet Muḥammad, whose birthday is the focus of *mīlād (mawlid)* celebrations conducted by Barēlwī Muslims, including through qawwali singing praises of Muḥammad (and significant Barēlwī religious figures). As with other branches of Sufism, *pīr*s are deemed as having properties that give them proximity to God, and remain 'alive' in their tomb, with spiritual powers. This is contrary to many other religious opinions and practices. The Barēlwī have linkages with other Sufi movements discussed above.

An influential figure within contemporary Barēlwī contexts is the founder of Minhaj ul-Quran, Muḥammad Tahir ul-Qadri (1951-). Established in 1980 in Pakistan, Minhaj ul-Quran has branches across the UK. Tahir ul-Qadri draws on digital media forms as an effective channel to promote ideas of mission and interpretation, with focal points on explaining fundamental concepts and issues impacting Muslim communities – especially at crisis points such as in the aftermath of 9-11 and 7/7 attacks. Tahir ul-Qadri has been promoted internationally at various events, and his Qur᾽ān translation amplified his profile.

Minhaj ul-Quran draws on video content through its online channels to explore concepts associated with Sufism and mystical teachings.[157] There is investment in presenting specific programming online, demonstrated on a Minhaj YouTube channel, although audience figures were relatively low.[158] Specific apps are utilized, including a Minhaj TV app, as well as generic apps where WhatsApp and other platforms present live-streaming content. The Ghosha-e-durood app contains material specific to Sufi ritual practices, such as the recitation of Allāh's Ninety-Nine Names, a *tasbīḥ* counter to record *dhikr* activities (using a digital *misbaḥa* or prayer bead counter) and clips of Tahir-ul-Qadri.[159] Tahir-ul-Qadri's Qur'ān translation has an app with an eclectic selection of languages (English, Urdu and Norwegian). It applies a specific script style associated with India and Pakistan, along with prayers.[160] Minhaj ul-Quran provides a *fatāwā* app, answering questions according to the organizational ethos.[161]

Deoband movements

Tensions exist between Deobandi and Barelwī perspectives, which can emerge online across diverse platforms and perspectives. The roots of these conflicts can be found in the historical foundations of the Deobandi in India. The establishment of a Darul Uloom (Dār al-ʿUlūm) in Deoband, a 'House of Knowledge', sought to 'protect' Islam against external influences and perceived threats, especially colonial powers. Their focus on religious practices and identities was partly because of their founders' failed rebellion against the British in 1857, which led them towards a quietist, religion-centred approach and a 'sober' form of Sufism. The high levels of diversity within the Deobandi frameworks are influenced by geopolitical factors, with some strands espousing elements of mystical practices. The impact of ḥādīth scholarship and the focus on legal interpretations meant a denial of Sufism, while others integrated practices and affiliations into their world views.

The impact of 'Wahhabism' in Deobandi teachings diminished the Sufi influences, especially towards how Muḥammad is perceived and celebrated through *mīlād* practices, condemned as 'innovative'. However, there is an emphasis on *taṣawwuf* (Sufism) as a form of spirituality. These factors were explored by Shaykh Mohammad Yasir al-Hanafi, in a video series. This was a response to a Salafi-oriented video, 'Reality of Deobandi Aqeedah', by Abu Ibraheem Husnayn, seen as influential among Muslim youth. It includes a discussion of Sufi texts and commentaries, alongside crucial influences such as al-Shāfiʿī and Ibn Ḥanbal. They have had a central role in the movement's development in promoting the role of *tasawwuf*. There were accusations that they were 'pseudo-Salafis'. It suggests that Muḥammad ibn ʿAbd al-Wahhāb did not state anything negative about Sufism within his writings, which runs counter to 'Wahhabi' perceptions, suggesting that *ʾuṣūl al-fiḳh* and Sufi-focused perceptions of Islam are both 'acceptable'.[162] The impact of this type of discussion online is featured on the MuftiSays forum. Suggestions that the work needed refutation were made but not over-publicized.[163]

The branching out of the Deobandi movements includes the Tablighi Jamaat (Jamāʿat), the *daʿwa* 'mission'-oriented movement, which eschews many aspects of Sufism. However, it originates in Sufi practices from earlier generations of Naqshbandi shaykhs and religious leaders. The movement was established by Maulana Muḥammad Ilyas Kandhalawi (1885–1944), using a cell preaching process and ensuring that members practice *dhikr*. Tablighi Jamaat, as a movement, emphasized personal piety and preaching to deal with issues facing Muslim society.[164] Tablighi Jamaat is described as 'a free floating religious movement',[165] with a minimum dependency on hierarchy and a traditional base – endeavouring to provide basic teachings of Islam through a 'pyramid' networking system.

The movement spread internationally and – as with the Deobandis – has taken the ritual practices of *mīlād*, *ʿurs* and grave worship out of the religious equation. Ilyas was a member of the Chishtīyya order and established its headquarters adjacent to significant shrines associated with Nizamuddin Awliya (1238–1325) in Delhi. There is some contention about whether it is a 'Sufi' entity. Some suggest that its language, literary references, practices and lineage mark it as a form of Sufism, while others indicate that the absence of ecstatic initiation processes means it could not be considered as having a role within Sufism. Tablighi Jamaat has been the subject of online abuse for its (alleged or ambiguous) connections to Sufism.[166]

Whatever the case may be, especially about the tensions between Tablighi Jamaat and the Deobandis (beyond the scope of this chapter), Tablighi Jamaat has a proactive online presence. Its *ijtema* is a collective annual gathering in many Tablighi locations internationally, representing one of the most significant collective events within Muslim contexts. *Ijtema* in India, Bangladesh and Pakistan are documented extensively online.[167] Tablighi Jamaat organizations' video channels regularly update on activities and content. In the past, there was more resistance from the Tablighi Jamaat to online activities. However, it is now integrated into all ritual practices (such as reciting *naat* devotional poetry) while recording sermons and collective events.[168] This trend is evidenced in its 'diaspora' networks and communities: the Dewsbury Markazi Masjid is the focal point for the Tablighi Jamaat in Western Europe: many *ijtema* events are recorded and placed online.[169] The death of its UK instigator Hafiz Patel in 2016 attracted tens of thousands of mourners to Dewsbury and substantial online coverage for videos capturing the funeral proceedings.[170]

The digital literacy of its followers continues to amplify the movement's online presence and activities, embedding them into activities and boosting Tablighi Jamaat as a significant player in CIEs, whose followers now track its interpretative perspective and ritual practices from across the globe.

Inayati order and related movements

Many Western 'Sufi' orders – associated in some cases with 'New Age' religion(s) – also have a presence on the internet. Sufi Order International is one example of this, associated with Pir-O-Murshid Inayat Khan and the Sufi Order of the West. The International Association of Sufism derived from the teachings of Hazrat Inayat Khan (1882–1927), presenting Sufism as a mystical universal religion that may be pursued through dancing and chanting without requiring the practice of ritual prayer or other duties of Islamic law.[171] The Inayati Order utilizes social media to promote its interpretation of Sufism, influenced by its founder and now led by his grandson Pir Zia Inayat Khan (1971–).[172] Their YouTube output includes explanations of significant ritual practices and seasonal mediations.

The Sufi Order International has linkages or lineages to other movements, presenting online content in various Western contexts. The Sufi Ruhaniat International, established by Samuel Lewis (or 'Sufi Sam') (1896–1971), continues with its Sufi-Zen influences. Online study and practice circles were meeting on Zoom in 2021, while video classes and talks were available for download in video and audio format. Their content included a detailed archive of Lewis' papers. The website linked to recordings by the Sufi Choir(s), a combination of popular, classical, medieval and Christian music alongside tracks based on Inayat Khan's poetry and the Qur᾽ān. The Ruhaniat's teachers or murshids all present their websites and activities as part of a circle encouraging online engagement.[173] Lewis identified with the Dances of Universal Peace, seen as esoteric practices within a circle, digitally captured. These activities fall into the complexities of New Age movements. Some Sufi practitioners may not see them as part of the 'mainstream' in terms of ritual, practice, sources and Islamic identities.[174]

Within the Inayat Khan lineage, reference is made to Sufism Reoriented, founded by Avatar Meher Baba (1894–1969), not espousing specific religious identification. Baba's programmes continued under Murshida Carol Weyland Conner (1942–2023). The website links to clips of Conner. It emphasizes its links to Inayat Khan and links to 'the east' through multiple videos while emphasizing its ethos of extending the line and its leadership (through a 'dramatised' account of its history).[175]

Bektashi and Alevi

The spectrum of identities directly or obliquely associated with Sufism's history in Turkey includes the various branches associated with Bektashi and Alevi Islam, which can also link Shīʿa beliefs' concepts with Sufism principles. There is a blurring of interests and identities associated with these branches of understanding, given the heterodox and ambiguous nature of Alevi beliefs and their roots.

This complex linkage includes the Bektashi *ṭarīqah*, primarily based in Albania, with an Ottoman Turkish heritage. Their focus is on Ḥājī Baktāš Walī (1209–71) who claimed ancestry from the Ahl ul-Bayt line (going back to Muḥammad), which he preached about alongside 'fourteen innocents' who shared martyrdom with Ḥusayn. There is an integration of a 'trinity' focused on ʿAlī with Allāh and Muḥammad.[176] Bektashi identities can be synonymous with Alevi Islam, which itself divides into different groupings with diverse approaches towards (and relationships with) religiosity, Sufism and Shīʿa beliefs, different emphases in urban and rural contexts and syncretic and heterodox concepts associated with religion which can draw criticism from all sides. The reach of Bektashi constructs goes beyond its Anatolian, Turkish and Kurdish heartlands, given the migration of people into Western Europe, and the presence of Besktashi movements in Syria, Iraq, Albania and other Balkan contexts.

The Bektāshi Shīʿa Alevi incorporates a tradition which includes influences from 'Sufi' mysticism alongside Shīʿa teachings, filtered by a Turkic perspective originating in Central Asia, focused on the teachings created by generations of religious leaders and travelling with the migrations of Turkish peoples into Anatolia. A combination of practices is incorporated into their world view, adapting core Shīʿa beliefs within esoteric dimensions associated with Sufi conceptual frameworks. Several branches and sub-branches are associated with Bektāshi beliefs, which constitute at least a third of Turkey's population, resulting in different orientations and understandings of sources and concepts.[177] The Bektāshi world view would impact the Janissaries in the Ottoman period. Some specific festivals and commemorations occur in Bektāshi contexts, including a fast focused on al-Khiḍr, a repertoire of sacred music and poetry and ritual *ziyarat* to the tombs of saints.

Ḥājjī Bektāsh Walī wrote the *Maḳālāt* in the thirteenth century; it is widely available in different translations and versions online, marking a specific presence of ideas and spirituality. Readings and videos devoted to Bektāsh – going beyond Turkey into other zones of influence. Websites also focus on his lineage and religious values, exploring the global elements of his order (e.g. in the United States).[178] This order crosses over from Shīʿīsm and Sufism (with points in between). Specific Bektāshi practices feature online, with channels devoted to Alevi-Bektāshi beliefs and representation from Albania, the United States and Turkey. Secret of Ilya regularly updates content, including sermons, rituals and episodes associated with Shīʿa beliefs, across YouTube, Facebook and Instagram.[179] Bektāshi understandings demonstrate that the imposition of neat categorization models for interpreting different religious frameworks is not always appropriate or functional, but that – for their practitioners – this represents an authentic and coherent articulation of 'Islam'.

Some Alevi branches are surrounded by secrecy and project contrasting approaches towards religious authority which are atypical of other Sufi zones. However, efforts have also been made to explain Alevism in its different aspects, focusing on the spiritual pathway and its cultural, ritual and historical elements. The School of Alevism produced short YouTube tutorials in a user-friendly manner, explaining practical and theoretical aspects, including various Cem ceremonial and musical elements. It explained the rationale for secret practices on the basis of seeking to avoid persecution; the YouTube channel's comments indicate that there are strong feelings against Alevi practices from some other Muslim perspectives.

This complexity of Bektashi identities plays out in cyberspace and would be worthy of a detailed investigation. One focal point is the World Bektashi Headquarters in Tirana, Albania, under the auspices of Hajji Dede Edmond Brahimaj (referred to as 'Baba Mondi'). The official website networks with its international followers, with details of its archives, library and news of activities.[180] Baba Mondi features on Instagram, combining historical images, photos of ongoing activities and an image of him receiving his Covid-19 vaccination.[181] Alevi Islam has a substantial online presence: on Instagram, there are galleries demonstrating the fusion of Sufi and Shīʿa values in depictions of prominent figures from the Ahl ul-Bayt.[182] Alevi Bektaşi Federasyonu (ABF) networks across Turkey, with a web hub updating on religious, political and cultural activities. It highlighted the

December 2022 Great Alevi Congress, which brought together disparate branches to discuss local and international issues.[183]

In terms of wider communities, high levels of internet connectivity in Germany combine with the presence of long-standing Alevi communities to produce a dynamic online milieu. A good example of this comes from Alevi Islam Deutschland, whose use of TikTok indicates high levels of audience engagement across a range of religious and other topics. This includes short clips showing visits to shrines, along with details of online Islamic courses.[184] The networks of Alevis in Germany are represented by the Almanya Alevi Birlikleri Federasyonu (AABF), an umbrella organization for 160 different Alevi organizations with a web hub and social media outlets, focused on cultural activities. A key aspect of networking and identity is the use of social media to project religious rituals and ideas. This includes the importance of dance for Alevi identity and mystical religious practices such as Semah, indicating its Sufi, Shīʿa and other religious influences.[185] Social media is a significant element of networking in other Alevi contexts: in the UK, the British Alevi Federation draws on Instagram to show cultural-religious activities, alongside campaigning on political and disaster relief agendas.[186] The expansion of online explanations of Alevi beliefs and explanations may offer clarity on this academically under-represented element of Islam, especially when it can emerge from practices of dissimilitude and secrecy.

Conclusion

The metaphysical pathways of Islam are digital in scope, with many stations and retreats along the way, where an influential, *pīr*, *shaykh* or *murshid* (and synonymous terms) may connect to digital devices to disseminate guidance, interpretations and approaches towards *taṣawwuf* for the online *murīd* or 'novice'. In many ways, the notion of a digital metaverse is an appropriate vehicle for esoteric branches and routes towards divine knowledge, evoking the personal and profoundly spiritual (in the eyes of beholders) perspectives on their interpretations of Islam. These meta-constructs contain significant historical figures and contemporary ideologues. They bring perspective to ideas about Islam which may go outside of 'mainstream' opinions in some contexts but represent popular manifestations of everyday religious expression for others.

Increasingly they are mediated or witnessed online and facilitated in some cases by specific programming, apps and media pathways. These may not 'match' being in the physical proximity of a saint's tomb or a *pīr*'s sermon. However, they can connect followers whose access can be limited or inhibited in some cases because authorities may locally restrict this form of religious understanding. In other ways, forms of Islam defined (if only by outsiders) as 'Sufism' can exert political or military influence and power. The concept of it being a purely quietist and pacific form of Islamic understanding is contradicted by the actions of some of the influential figures discussed above.

Sufis, who may simply see themselves as 'Muslims' rather than advocating an alternative label, come in many shades and interpretative frameworks. Not all of these are complementary – followers of a *ṭarīqah* can face opposition based on practices and ideals. This negativity is online, although exploring the litany of anti-Sufi rhetoric online is beyond the scope of this present chapter. In many ways, the esoteric dimensions of Islam can also be seen as binding Muslims from disparate locations, cultures and contexts together, especially when there is an online comparison and discussion of experiences. The presence of *ṭarīqah* orders with historical and religious connections, which have become intellectually, geographically and religiously dispersed over time, may now find opportunities for networking and knowledge exchange enhanced through internet media.

In the future, this may even include virtual participation options online through Web3 tools offering new dimensions of virtual reality and experience within a metaphysical metaverse. This can contradict concepts of 'orthodoxy' from other quarters in terms of 'essential' or 'official' practice, which sees forms of mystical Islam as being outside of the pale of Islam. Notions of control and cohesion under a singular interpretation and identity seem an unrealistic and impossible ideal when the nodes of the internet present multiple forms of mystical practice outside of censorship or closure. While commonality exists on other levels, the complex range of expressions and affiliations falling under the ambiguous banner of 'Sufism' demonstrates for those involved in intra-Muslim dialogues and exploration complexities unreceptive to 'reform' or change, even when challenged as 'innovation'.

Some Sufi perspectives with secretive and private interpretation values prefer not to be publicly online. Notions of dissimilitude have been a long-term factor of Sufi practices in history and now manifest online. It may be that these still operate in private, membership-only online groups – much like analogue counterparts. As we edge towards metaphysical metaverses, Sufism remains a significant driver in the ongoing development of Islam, reinforced and networked in new ways as complements to traditional religious networks of communication, knowledge dissemination and control.

Chapter 9

MEDIA OFFENSIVE

DOOMSCROLLERS, DIGITAL CONTENT, INFLUENCERS AND E-JIHĀD

This chapter looks at the ways in which electronic-jihād (e-jihād) has impacted CIEs across the decades in diverse conflicts and contexts, focusing on key influencers and influencers specifically associated with militaristic interpretations of e-jihād. Notions of jihād traverse very different causes, whose engagement and campaigns present disparate agendas, rather than singular aims and objectives. This can stretch from causes associated with asserting national identities with political elements (such as Palestine) to globally reaching groups (such as al-Qaeda). Many form part of the algorithmic results of searches by prospective advocates and supporters seeking to engage in jihād activities. The intention here is to reflect how influential militaristic e-jihād campaigns have drawn up on internet technologies within contemporary contexts, on the periphery of the Muslim metaverse. The focus here is on the Taliban, al-Qaeda and 'Islamic State'.[1]

E-jihād encounters

The term e-jihād has encompassed a variety of online activism forms, from social protest and activism to militaristic campaigns (and points in between). This might also include digital disruption in the form of hacking and cracking, which has formed undercurrents in some jihād-oriented campaigning. These reflected the different approaches towards the word jihād. Not all these elements are mutually compatible. Advocates of militaristic jihād may be campaigning against others who are also applying jihād as a term to reinforce their campaigns. Its sense of 'striving' in its greater definition is associated with spirituality and the religious quest, while its minor (wider publicized) definitions relate to militaristic activities. Jihād has entered the English language with this latter emphasis, although its religious and historical roots from the time of Muḥammad are often ignored.

These different perceptions of militaristic jihād and its aims have permeated CIEs from the 1990s, shifting format and approach in line with shifts in campaigns and digital technologies. This was seen in chat rooms and email lists, for example, about campaigns associated with different platforms in Algeria in the early 1990s.

An extension of activities using other media such as fax machines, much of this content was in English and written in western capital cities such as London. Activists undertook high-intensity campaigning without much scrutiny from authorities, which lacked awareness of these activities.

The development of the World Wide Web and early web browsers was significant in areas associated with militaristic activism of various shades, projected as 'jihād' by proponents. The internet offered a means to promote militaristic campaigns, circulate ideological manifestos and provide embedded activity in the form of photographic records initially and later with audio-visual content. It became a natural conduit for fundraising activities too.

After 9-11, these online activities received greater attention, especially those in the name of al-Qaeda and the Taliban. Supporters were able to draw on to online media as a cost-effective, anonymous and rapid distribution medium to recruit, fundraise and publicize activities and interpretations to local, regional and global audiences. Over time, content became more nuanced in different languages, focused on specific agendas and campaigns, and benefitting from shifting technological platforms and innovations. While in the early days, much of this content was in English or Romanized languages, the emergence of browsers in the 2000s accommodating non-Latin characters led to an exponential rise in content in Arabic, Persian and other languages. No longer did their representation have to be through photographs of texts. Here was a more interactive and accessible opportunity to place content online.

Digital natives increasingly embedded online content into their campaigning in the 2000s. The emergence of social media such as Facebook and Twitter provided further opportunities to disseminate campaigning information, which, coupled with the reduction in the digital divide and the opening up of internet access, resulted in efficient and calculating online propagation programmes. The production of online magazines was one example of this, with glossy images, editorial content and standards comparable with other forms of media content. Multiple platforms and organizations produced these materials in different languages. It became a high-profile and effective means of information distribution for affiliates of al-Qaeda and other platforms.

The sense of embeddedness culminated in the online strategies associated with the so-called 'Islamic State', which took digital media activity to a more technologically sophisticated level through real-time propagation and publicity to promote its territorial and ideological ambitions. Jihād-oriented platforms and individuals learned from their peers, equivalents and even competitors in terms of the best ways in which to disseminate digital messages to back up offline activities, post-operational material and through the weaponization of digital media and immediacy of reporting and analysis in the proximity of effective campaigns and events, such as attacks in Europe.

The jihād banner featured on campaigns, agendas and groups not necessarily mutually compatible with each other. Definitions of 'jihād' varied too, focused on the lesser jihād (with its militaristic connotations) but with numerous attached nuances and commentaries. Rival groups were targeted explicitly through these online channels, with accusations of 'heresy' and calls for ex-communication (*takfīr*). Multiple entities expressed notions of jihād online, including the different affiliates of al-Qaeda, Islamic State, Palestinian militaristic advocates of jihād, Hezbollah and numerous other groups. The extent to which intended audiences received these opinions was linked to digital literacy and access issues. Some platforms had substantial audience figures and forms of allegiance online, as well as being observed by regional and world media in different ways, becoming news conduits and channels that could offer perspectives that 'competed' with national and international media. They were also monitored by security and intelligence governmental organizations in regional and global contexts, becoming a useful gauge of militaristic activities conducted under the jihād banner. Jihād content providers were very aware that their readers included opponents and 'enemies' as well as supporters and designed materials accordingly.

Production standards and technological facilities improved, with streaming, podcasts, high definition and advanced production values found in television studios applied. Enhanced editing and graphics were used by those with the resources and skills to embed them into their output. At times, this output became competitive as different channels sought to acquire audiences, while also playing games of cat and mouse with governmental and technological authorities who sought to shut them down. This was ironic, given that the internet was not intended to be censored or shut down effectively. Various advocates of these platforms and organizations were able to exploit these vulnerabilities to present the content through their technical expertise.

Voices did not have to be 'official' either; individuals and 'unofficial' supporters or advocates had a role in distributing content to global audiences. Translation became a significant adjunct to activities, with suggestions that such materials could play a role in influencing people to participate in militaristic jihād activities (along with other 'analogue' factors such as radicalization networks and influential authorities). Combinations of these elements were influential, as represented in several prosecutions. As governments became more aware of the impact of jihād entities' digital content in radicalization, recruitment and funding, efforts increased to censor or shut down content. This was a problematic task, given the decentralized nature of jihād material and the frequent copying and reproducing of content on mirror pages and free sites globally. Some sites would remain open as a means of monitoring jihād associated activities.

Production and ownership of this material became criminalized in several western contexts, but this did not stop the flow of material radicalizing individuals. Closed areas of the internet and the so-called 'Dark Web' were difficult for authorities to police. The development of secure apps and peer-to-peer networks encrypted at a high level made it problematic for authorities to track down the content providers and close the outlets producing it. Highly encrypted apps such as WhatsApp, Signal and Telegram became channels of choice for those seeking secure communication outside the authorities' gaze. Those wanting to publicize their campaigns and activities could easily circumnavigate the controls of technology companies, as seen in the discussion below. Influential individuals had profiles even when deceased or incarcerated, especially when there were recordings of speeches or other activities available online.

These factors are not necessarily universal across e-jihād contexts, but are evident when examining the online activities of the Taliban:

The Taliban[2]

The 2021 Taliban re-emergence in Afghanistan and its takeover of the country was not only a significant event in terms of its religious and cultural implications and the political impact it would have on the countries in the region. It was also relevant because of how social media and the internet were applied during different aspects of the Taliban's campaigning. This was not an immediate capitulation, as there had been campaigning since the fall of the Taliban in 2001. In the intervening period, the Taliban in its various forms did not hold specific political power but was still present in Afghanistan and Pakistan in different ways. During this time, there was intensified application of the internet as a means of propagation, logistical support, fundraising and general publicity. Some outside observers might see this as contradictory to the Taliban's general approaches to modernity. In truth, however, even in the 1990s, their supporters promoted the Taliban online. They developed news outlets and other pre-social media forms of digital expression and used secure internet tools to facilitate their activities.

In 2000, *Taliban Online*, produced in Pakistan, claimed over 146,000 'hits' in one year from its inception in November 1997. The site included details on Taliban policies and its ideas of Islamic interpretation, focused on 'jihād'. News stories in 1998 included defences of Osama bin Laden, who had been implicated in the bombing of the US Embassies in Kenya and Tanzania – and local news taken from the Dharb-i-Muʾmin service. News announcements detailed implementation of the Taliban's interpretation of *sharīʿa*, including capital punishments, using 'Islamic Emirate' banners. The site encouraged donations to an address in Pakistan, advertised as funding medicine and education for the Afghani population – and essential equipment for Taliban military forces, with a price list of equipment and encouragement for donations in the form of quotes from the Qurʾān and ḥādīth.[3]

'Taliban' sites continued after 9-11 and the fall of the Taliban in Afghanistan in 2001: while Taliban Online did not function, several 'mirrors' existed to reflect the Taliban's changed circumstances. The media content had also 'improved', with a multimedia Flash banner featuring the Qurʾān, a map of Afghanistan, gunfire and recitation. Pages incorporated apologetics associated with the movement and its relationship with al-Qaeda. Other sites supported the Taliban, including some in the UK. A New York-registered Taliban News site continued online after 9-11, linking to Azzam Publications (named after the assassinated advocate of jihād Sheikh Abdullah Azzam) and other jihād pages.[4] A pattern of mirrored content meant that when pages were shut down, their content appeared elsewhere, often with similar domain names.[5]

On occasions, Taliban online activities appeared on hubs which joined together aspects of so-called jihād online: consequently, campaigning from Chechnya, al-Qaeda affiliates in diverse international zones and Taliban activities were presented in a single jump page.[6] This content would offer an entry point into diverse forms of interpretations and activities. This digital connectivity was engineered by supporters as part of a perceived global jihād movement that at least could be ideologically represented in a virtual format, whatever the realities at ground level. With a ready audience among supporters, aficionados and external observers, sharing of ideological documents and media clips increased in the 2000s. Chatrooms were significant too as ideological connexion points. In the 2000s, pages and websites associated with al-Qaeda included Taliban-related links and content. These pages only had a relatively short existence before being shut down by service providers and moved by content developers to other online locations, frequently linked to free web space. In the early phases of such jihād activities online, there was little regulation or censorship control. Supporters were able to present bank details with physical addresses for people to send money to the Taliban, with a post office box number in north London advertised as an address for contact to receive additional publicity materials and as a potential contact point for other activities.

After 9-11, greater attention was paid to this online discourse. However, it did not prevent its presentation in diverse digital formats, usually associated with chat rooms or web pages. The increased multimedia content, as digital technology improved and became cheaper and more accessible, saw increased integration of these materials into publicity; the emergence of online magazines was part of an escalation in diffuse jihād-focused content online, including Taliban materials, with magazines specifically on Afghanistan developed in multiple languages. Forms of expression were significant: early pro-Taliban online pages were usually in English as local languages' fonts were unavailable, meaning that local language materials had to be photographed and put online as images rather than pure hypertext markup language (HTML).

New opportunities for expression emerged with the introduction of Arabic fonts for browsers and related fonts. While levels of digital access were low in Afghanistan, even within urban contexts, the consciousness that production of online publicity remained, especially for acquisition of international support. There is a dichotomy between the need to produce publicity and promote the cause and an underlying view that forms of information technology could be detrimental to religious values. Supporters made efforts to keep online audiences updated with the latest campaign information, often in granular detail, including location and other logistical factors. Leaders' statements were presented through various channels able to circumnavigate censorship, primarily hosted externally and outside the range of any local control.

The phenomena of embedded reports were seen in different jihād operations throughout Afghanistan in the 2000s, from short film clips to audio statements and magazines. The shift in attitude and recognition of the importance of forms of information technology as a relevant attribute to profile campaigns and promote agendas was influenced by the activities of other organizations for whom the internet was integrated into activities, especially al-Qaeda.

Throughout the 2000s, there was a continuity of internet media supportive of the Taliban, including the use of Telegram and WhatsApp to seek secure donations. Twitter and Facebook were promoted by supporters in multiple languages, while affiliate platforms announced strategic aims and operations news. A Taliban app in 2016 became a marker of their supporters' informed use of online media. A range of news channels became conduits for news and official statements and logistic support. Much of this focused on international audiences, especially given Afghanistan's continued relatively low internet access levels. However, reductions in the digital divide (encouraged by international development) saw an increasing relevance for content aimed at local audiences.[7] The Islamic Emirate banner was utilized in magazines and videos in the 2000s, alongside increasing production values and intensity, highlighting educational activities, military training, recruitment and regional campaigning.

The Taliban's media consciousness was demonstrated when they took control of Kabul in August 2021. Aljazeera showed the Taliban commander in government headquarters, sitting behind the presidential desk with a group of his close supporters.[8] Two Taliban members recorded pronouncements on their phones. At other times during the campaigning in Kabul, fighters were seen capturing the moments on phones as they drove down the streets in armoured vehicles, recording their procession. Smartphones were used at every turn. Leaders were taking selfies. A 'softer' image was on social media. Taliban members were also seen in less official contexts, using a presidential gym, riding bumper cars in a fairground and eating ice cream. Taliban fighters posed inside grounded Black Hawk helicopters for photographs. Taliban statements emerged on social media, with leaders and representatives presenting official content and statements for local audiences and international viewers, including governments and media.

A self-consciousness projected itself on social media that would not have been present in the original incarnation of the Taliban, at least in urban centres under the gaze of media cell phones. Taliban members posed for photographs, and in contrast with the earlier generation of the Taliban in 1996, carried smartphones and took selfies.[9] The use of social media by the Taliban led to service providers blocking access to WhatsApp and Facebook for Taliban content.[10] Websites went offline.[11] WhatsApp had become a significant channel for private communication among different Taliban units.[12] This was problematic for social media companies, whose products were applied as a means of coercion and control by the Taliban.[13] It was essential to make announcements to followers on Twitter, as well as to journalists and external bodies.[14]

Taliban social media tracked the appearance of ideologues and followers as they returned to Afghanistan, such as Abdul Ghani Baradar, a founder of the Taliban – filmed flying into Kandahar. He had previously announced that 'we have reached a victory that wasn't expected . . . we should show humility in front of Allah . . . now it's time of test – now it's about how we serve and secure our people, and ensure their future/good life to best of ability.'[15]

It also presented its own 'legitimacy' through interviews with news outlets, which were reposted on Taliban social media, such as Baradar speaking to NBC

News and Abdul Qahar Balkhi's (of the Taliban Cultural Commission) interview on Al Jazeera.[16] Balkhi's interview, conducted in (Australian-accented) English, discussed the 'surprise' at Kabul's capitulation by the government, when the Taliban had been expecting negotiation and how the Taliban would follow (its interpretation of the) principles of Islam closely.

The Taliban used Twitter to officially declare the 'Islamic Emirate of Afghanistan' via the Official Twitter Account of the spokesman of the Islamic Emirate of Afghanistan, Zabihullah Mujahid. This channel announced the interim government and other Taliban actions, including official statements and video clips, often via temporary file-sharing sites.[17] This was part of the longer-term Taliban media strategy rather than an ad hoc arrangement. A voluntary unit worked on getting hashtags trending and promoting Taliban messages online, such as #westandwithTaliban and #kabulregimewarcrimes.[18]

Zabihullah's Twitter had 391,000 followers (September 2021), working alongside the emirate social media director Qari Saeed Khosty, with 180,000 followers.[19] Their Twitter feeds remained open, although other social media and websites were closed. Khosty's feed showed him distributing money to orphans from families associated with the Taliban and the Afghanistan army, claiming both as the Taliban's responsibility.[20]

The public relations offensive included Taliban officials visiting Shīʿa mosques to commemorate Muḥarram. This was a counter to perceptions of anti-Shīʿa sentiments traditionally associated with the Taliban in a community that had feared the implications of the Taliban taking over Afghanistan; the extent to which this attitude would be maintained was open to question.[21] There may be correlation with logistical support offered by Iran for the Taliban – despite religious differences. The Taliban additionally dealt with more technical issues, such as national infrastructure concerns, at least in terms of the power system. They visited the National Power Utility with a photo opportunity in front of technical equipment, emphasizing that they would protect the system.[22] The Taliban shared their activities at the street level. In urban Kabul, photos of advertising billboards (showing women) were painted over.[23]

World media channels were invited to press conferences to outline policy. These events were live-tweeted through Taliban channels. This included the declaration of an 'amnesty' to former opponents and opportunities for women to (continue) work in the public sector.[24] The reality of how this would play out was met with scepticism at the time. The Taliban escalated Twitter activities after retaking Kabul, it being the most immediate and effective means of rapidly communicating with its followers across languages and cultures. In some ways, this superseded the traditional magazine format presented in *Al-Sumud* ('Resilience') magazine by the Taliban over the years, with its format of official proclamations, analysis of international events, ideological tracts and 'educational' resources. Generic international media reinforced the Taliban's agenda and image and gave informal insights into Taliban behaviours. Clips from a Vice documentary on the Taliban circulated on social media, including one where members broke down laughing when faced with the question of female political participation.[25]

Taliban News channels provided information on specific units and military activities, including the Badri 313 Special Forces unit, named after the Battle of Badr (Prophet Muḥammad's first major military victory after establishing the community in Medina – the number 313 is associated with the number of 'martyrs' at that battle). The #badri313 hashtag featured on numerous posts throughout campaigns, showing the unit's forces in American uniforms and using acquired equipment in strategic areas. It produced 'media friendly' images as it geared up for conflict in Panjshir. The Northern Alliance held out against the Taliban, generating its embedded social media to acquire support for its stand under Ahmad Massoud.[26]

Social media channels became zones where supporters expressed appreciation for the 'victory' in Afghanistan: al-Qaeda in the Arabian Peninsula used social media to do this.[27] Critics of the Afghanistan Army and its government applied social media to suggest that they had capitulated too quickly to the Taliban and handed over provinces; the army was shown sending surrendered soldiers back to their homes.[28] The events were used to project grievances on other issues, such as alleged Pakistan involvement in Taliban activities (criticized, for example, by some Indian social media activists). The reality, in all cases, was more nuanced.

Social media showed how media organizations within Afghanistan sought to adapt to the changed situation, where notions of freedom of expression and the types of content presented were very different. This included media broadcasters such as the TOLO News network: it resumed its broadcasts with a female anchor, presented on social media. It also interviewed key Taliban figures and at the time had female journalists active in the field.[29]

The problem in any general closure of access to global media channels is that they also had a role in aiding those who were opposed to the Taliban or wanted to escape Afghanistan. They offered a secure channel for the presentation of sensitive materials. The presence of the Taliban on Twitter benefited its many supporters and fighters in Afghanistan. In Kabul, some apparently attempted to present a different form of religious authority and law in Afghanistan, dubbed 'Taliban 2.0' by some.[30] The presentation of this 'softer' image in Kabul was not reflected elsewhere in Afghanistan. The level of control the central leadership might have within different regions among fighters from diverse cultural and ethnic backgrounds, speaking in different languages and with varied approaches towards Islam, meant that such pronouncements would have a limited impact, especially outside the urban centres.[31] The Taliban encompassed diversity if not cohesion: 'It seems the Taliban now has three faces: The Rahbari Shura leaders who are the custodians of the Taliban ideology; the political Shura leaders who are trying to gain legitimacy by improving the Taliban's public image; and the mass of fighters forged in war.'[32] The male-only meeting of religious leaders in the Loya Jirga ('grand council') hall also made it into social media, where it would have an impact on establishing educational policies and other developments before the emergence of a Taliban government.[33]

In September 2021, the announcement of the first Taliban government featured on social media, including the lists of various ministers.[34] Attention focused on the presence of individuals in the cabinet wanted on criminal charges by the FBI, notably Interior Minister Sirajuddin Haqqani. He featured in a *New York Times* op-ed in February 2020 outlining his vision for the Taliban. This piece was subsequently widely circulated on Taliban (and other) social media to project legitimacy.[35] Haqqani had a 10-million-dollar reward for his capture as the figurehead of the Haqqani network, founded by Jalaluddin Haqqani (1939–2018) in the 1980s. Supported by the United States, Jaluluddin Haqqani initially fought against the Soviet forces before leading forces affiliated with the Taliban against NATO forces post-9/11. As Jaluluddin's successor, Sirajuddin Haqqani was deemed responsible for numerous attacks against coalition and American forces.[36]

The historical relationship between the Taliban and al-Qaeda suggested that the capitulation of Afghanistan might lead to a repositioning of al-Qaeda in Afghanistan (again). At the same time, there was also the consideration that this 'victory' would appeal to global 'jihād' audiences supportive of al-Qaeda (if not the 'Islamic State'). Viewed in real time, with the sense of connectivity and interaction available through social media, it might encourage or reinforce the principles of others: 'There is no doubt that the astonishing rapidity of the Taliban's victory will deliver a tremendous boost to Islamist extremists everywhere – whether al-Qaida, Islamic State, fighters in Mozambique or Syria, or jihādi fanboys in bedsits in Birmingham or Manila.'[37]

Awareness of information technology had the potential to become a tool for intensified control of the population, especially with the acquisition of biometric core details.[38] Concerns that digital histories could become 'incriminating' were expressed, leading to many people trying to erase their digital histories.[39] Advocacy groups and social media providers offered tools in this area for such removal of inappropriate content.[40] Others provided secure locations where sensitive materials could be safely stored and protected from Taliban acquisition. Some social media users also posted about their efforts to delete digital histories and profiles.[41]

The efforts of individuals and families to leave Afghanistan, primarily through Kabul International Airport, were influenced by social media rumours and different forms of advice. The thousands of people who tried to leave used digital means to try and present their credentials, with varying degrees of success, to the authorities at the airport's gates, having to go through various boundaries controlled by the Taliban.

Social media captured the crowds at the airport who – having entered the precincts – could not get flights (who were also recording their activities on the tarmac). This culminated in some desperate people hanging onto a C17 transport plane as it taxi-ed and eventually took off. Social media caught the journeys of those on the fuselage and, ultimately, the deaths of at least two people who fell from the undercarriage. The original video of this was viewed 2.3 million times in the month following the incident.[42]

The refugee situation led families to queue standing in airport sewers while trying to get through checkpoints. Security became a major issue on the airport site, culminating in a suicide bomb attack linked to the 'Islamic State', in which over 170 people were killed. Online materials associated with the instigator were posted online shortly after this attack. The aftermath of this featured in graphic social media content.[43] The social media dimension included Islamic State Khorasan Province (ISKP) claiming responsibility, via their AMAQ News Agency, for the bombing via its Telegram channel, subsequently circulated on Twitter.

When the US and other forces evacuated Afghanistan on 31 August 2021, Taliban members were filmed the next day in the airport, parading with newly acquired armaments, uniforms and military technology, presenting actuality through social media. A range of interviews emerged online with different leadership members, some filmed returning from exile. Again, these events circulated through Twitter and other channels. News organizations within Afghanistan had to follow the Taliban's specific line or face the consequences. Journalists had been a target for the Taliban and many felt threatened.

Broadcasters such as TOLO continue to operate under new restrictions, interviewing Taliban leaders and bringing in new presenters from the organization; some presenters had to adjust their dress code to continue on the channel. TOLO and others presented output in English and local languages such as Pashto, Dari, Arabic and Urdu, associated with the takeover of Afghanistan, charting an uneasy journey between editorial credibility and potential consequences of not following the Taliban line. In one interview broadcast through social media, a TOLO presenter in a western suit interviewed a Taliban leader in traditional dress. In the background, several Taliban fighters lined up, brandishing their guns. This type of action placed pressure on the presenter to do the job efficiently.

The Taliban demonstrate that there are multiple forms of e-jihād influencers online who consider information technologies appropriate in presenting their world views to global audiences while otherwise often restricting access to social media channels to domestic users. Integrated Taliban e-jihād strategies continued to be refined, as they transitioned towards governmental state roles whose 'legitimacy' was underpinned by digital media. Whether this will enhance their role as 'influencers' remains to be seen.

9-11 and al-Qaeda online

al-Qaeda embedded the internet into its activities from its early days, with figures distributing operational and logistical information through its multiple channels, often file-sharing sites with a very short existence whose presence was publicized through emailing lists. This content projected influence in terms of being a conduit for radicalization, fundraising and publicity. In line with technological developments such as improved graphics and multimedia, they could present a glossy image for the campaigns in different contexts. As franchises expanded in different zones, other followers adopted these principles. Digital content became a critical adjunct to other forms of activity and as part of training programmes, with figures holding responsible roles in the propagation of religious and ideological content. This was coordinated at high levels within the different organizations and continues to this day.

Osama bin Laden recognized the importance of this media through the presentation of various campaigning videos and the issuing of official statements, preserved after his death on other websites and channels. His successors in terms of authority (if not profile or charisma), such as Ayman al-Zawahiri (1951–2022), continued this practice. It was maintained even when the production of videos became less regular due to health issues and the need to hide from attacks. The rhetoric linked back to bin Laden, whose oratory skills brought his interpretative world views to a wider audience.[44] As an influence, he remains a significant figure. The success of al-Qaeda's media strategy was linked to Anwar al-Awlaki. Before his drone targeted death by US forces, al-Awlaki presented videos and other content in English and Arabic, including magazines directly linked to recruiting fighters and publicizing agendas.[45] Both bin Laden's and al-Awlaki's related messages retain their influence online.

Al-Qaeda supporters marked the twentieth anniversary of 9-11 in 2021 online, amplified as it coincided with US forces departing Afghanistan. Interpreted as a 'defeat' for the United States, Ayman al-Zawahiri contributed to a video, allegedly to mark the anniversary. However, there were no direct indicators it was recorded specifically.[46] Under the headline 'Jerusalem will not be Judaized', it had the *Ḥarām al-Sharīf* backdrop (including the Dome of the Rock Mosque) – but was not specific in commemorating 9-11. There was speculation that al-Zawahiri had died or was incapacitated and that this (and other) video material was from an archive source.[47] Experts calculated its references to determine the date. Zawahiri's publications continued to be published by as-Sahab Media in PDF and other forms. Some of his videos had a more professional gloss, with him sitting behind a desk with a black background of graphics and quotations. However, they were often indeterminate in establishing specific dates and times of production.[48]

The re-emergence of another al-Qaeda leader, Amin ul-Haq, following the Taliban's conquest of Afghanistan, was marked online with a video showing him and his entourage arriving in Nangahar (and photographed by al-Qaeda soldiers and supporters on their cell phones).[49] Al-Qaeda and its affiliates issued congratulatory statements on the re-emergence of the Taliban and its 'success' in Afghanistan.

Al-Qaeda continued to issue magazines online, such as multiple editions of *One Ummah* (available in Arabic and English). Edition One explained the objectives of *One Ummah*, based on a foreword by Ayman al-Zawahiri. A quote from Osama bin Laden was attributed to a letter to 'Shaykh Attiya', presumably a reference to Atiyah Abd al-Rahman (d.2011). In it he focused on how trust between mujahideen and the ummah had broken down due to 'errors' committed by al-Qaeda. The aims of the magazine explained how *One Ummah* held significance to al-Qaeda as an awareness-raising intellectual and cultural output.

Reference to the Islamic Emirate of Afghanistan's support and 'sound leadership' was made. Later in the magazine, there was a focus on Saudi Arabia and the Gulf, particularly the presence of churches in the latter and the signing of accords between Prince Muḥammad bin Salman and the Roman Catholic and Orthodox churches. *One Ummah* reflected on key figures, such as Osama bin Laden, Anwar al-Awlaki, Abdullah Azzam and Umar Abdul Rahman (instigator of the first attack on the World Trade Center in 1993). With regards to Azzam and bin Laden, it offered a comparative discussion on their methodologies, complex given that the former was a trained juristic scholar.

Elsewhere in the first edition of *One Ummah*, an article on more prosaic matters associated with mobile phone and data security noted the dangers of the 'enemy' monitoring systems as part of intelligence systems and how this can lead to targeted assassinations. *One Ummah* was not afraid of drawing on 'western' media sources, using (and paraphrasing) a CNN report on stock market performance under different US presidents.[50]

One Ummah's commentary notes the 'deep' impact of the 9-11 attacks on many levels, accompanied by a photo of United Airlines Flight 175 about to hit the South Tower of the World Trade Center. It focuses on the economic impact, especially as an attack on the interest-centred economies, which were seen to go against Islamic principles and fund attacks against the Mujahideen. It suggests this was important to bin Laden (over and above the casualties). A 'memoir' on 'crimes' reinforced *One Ummah*'s Afghan connection: America had committed attacks 'against Muslims'. In this, Ayman al-Zawahiri's wife, Umaymah Hasan Ahmad, discusses a missile strike in which she and other 'pious exemplars' were caught up and buried under rubble.[51]

One Ummah's initial publication was significant in continuing the trend for online magazines, in this case with a personal connection to the leadership, use of external 'western' sources and a close affinity to the Taliban – suggesting a continual level of influence and proximity in 2019. The format was 'glossy' and effectively designed, illustrated in colour and with the typical poster-style pages of earlier magazines. The combination of analysis and rhetoric would suggest a market for an 'informed' online reader/supporter interested in the continuity between earlier iterations of al-Qaeda and its (at the time diminished) contemporary manifestation. The magazine continued utilizing Qurʾān quotations alongside (deceased) leadership quotes and longer religiously oriented tracts combining commentary and 'analysis' based on religious themes and justifications.[52]

By June 2020, *One Ummah*'s fifth edition contained an extensive response to Black Lives Matter, following the death of George Floyd at the hands of Minnesota police officers. The article cited Malcolm X, through a voice bubble of a young child on an adult's shoulders facing a riot police officer pointing a gun: '"The price of freedom is death" if your ancestors had taken this advice seriously, you would have been free today. So do not do injustice to your grandchildren by choosing slavery over freedom.'[53] It was perhaps disingenuous of *One Ummah* – which itself projects divisive policies – to indicate a form of unity in this way online. The extent to which it would have reached its target audience is also open to question.

Jaysh Al-Malahim Al-Electronic, one of al-Qaeda's distribution channels (with links to affiliates in AQIM) – produced other publications focused on the issues in January 2021 facing the United States. After right-wing protesters invaded the Capitol building in Washington DC, the *Manhattan Wolves Magazine* predicted dire warnings of civil war and strife in the United States, suggesting that it was an 'opportunity' for its supporters to project further unrest in the country.[54] In a digital twist on its activities, Bitcoin rewards for assassinating people were promised.[55] The first *Manhattan Wolves Magazine* in 2020 also recommended utilizing Covid-19 restrictions as a means to avoid being detected when conducting operations or as a barrier when implementing poison attacks. The magazine – hosted on file-sharing sites – maintained a format of responses to contemporary issues, logistical information and religious commentaries. Al-Qaeda publications also responded to Covid-19, suggesting that it was due to humanity's sinful behaviour (a theme which also emerged in non-jihād contexts), including the occupation of the holy sites of Jerusalem, Medina and Mecca.

An intermittent stream of al-Qaeda videos continued to surface (and disappear rapidly) on social media and other outlets. Some videos appeared to show al-Zawahiri recorded in the same session and then edited into separate videos. Some content was nuanced towards specific audiences, such as a series of advice for jihādi wives (emphasizing patience).[56] There was also evidence that they continued using third-party generic storage for strategic and propagation materials, including Dropbox and Google Drive.[57]

Bin Laden maintains currency as a form of 'influencer' for al-Qaeda, even after his demise, with continued reproduction of photos, quotes and media content on supporters' sites. This pattern is familiar elsewhere, such as in Anwar al-Awlaki's example. Ayman al-Zawahiri's impact seemed muted by comparison, but websites and new outputs promoting al-Qaeda's positions are published and distributed through secure web channels and social media sites.[58] Many regional affiliates and networks operate and produce their own materials. As such, al-Qaeda remains an influential 'brand' online, albeit in competition with other players. Its influence includes the archive of digital recordings and tracts, including the reality of its activities and pronouncements; there is also a methodological influence, associated with the ways in which its supporters pioneered integration of iterations of digital media into notions of jihād.

'ISLAMIC STATE'

'Islamic State' capitalized on effective digital media strategies at many stages of its campaigns, including principles initiated by predecessors and rival perspectives. The relative downturn of activities in the early 2020s of *al-Dawlah al-Islāmīyah fī al-ʿIrāq wa al-Shām*, 'Islamic State in Iraq and Syria' or ISIS, pejoratively described as '*Dāʿish*' or '*Daesh*', saw a significant decline in the number of online materials associated with the platform. It relied on the medium to proactively assert its interpretative framework, promote its requests for logistical and material support and publicize various activities in the name of its interpretations of jihād. During its ascendancy, there was a demonstration of how integrated web literacy could impact specific campaigns and high-profile reinforcing events, notoriously including executions and bombing campaigns.[59]

After the decline of its 'caliphate' in Iraq and Syria, the Islamic State utilized secure platforms to share its materials, including Telegram and Rocket Chat. Strategic, political and religious differences meant that some of its ire was focused on the Taliban through the *Nashir* multilingual news channels. The *al-Naba* newsletter provided a glossy exposition of its international affiliates: for example, issue 304, from September 2021, focused on campaigns in sub-Saharan Africa while also touching on activities in Syria and Iraq.[60]

Key members of the Islamic State had been killed, imprisoned or prosecuted; the Canadian-Saudi narrator of their video output, Mohammed Khalifa, faced charges in 2021 of translating and commentating on a series of Islamic State video output, alongside production of online magazines.[61] This included narration of ISIS videos, encouraging attacks and recruitment.[62] In 2022 Khalifa received a life sentence for his online activities.[63] As well as developing digital content, he had also participated in the killing of Syrian soldiers on behalf of Islamic State, featuring in (as well as producing and narrating content for) the two 'Flames of War' videos.

This and other prosecutions have highlighted the specific impact of social media in driving the Islamic State's narrative across diverse contexts, rather than focused on Iraq and Syria. The prosecution of key figures is a salutary reminder of how the internet drove recruitment, logistics and campaigns. In 2021, the prosecution of surviving Paris November 2015 attacker Salah Abdeslam brought further attention to how these events manifested themselves online, along with traumatic digital memories, as the sequence of attacks appeared as a timeline in court and through news media. Abdeslam received a life sentence, while accomplices received substantial sentences.[64]

Several influences were removed from the Islamic State equation, although their digital legacy remained: most prominent was ʾAbū Bakr al-Baghdādī (1971–2019), the 'caliph' whose sermon in July 2014 presented his manifesto in an event designed for digital consumption, with a clarity of purpose (and Arabic) that quickly circulated through online channels. His death in 2019 in an air strike did not prevent the continued circulation of videos, images and speeches.[65] Other key figures were also 'neutralised': Turki Bin ʿAli was a significant ideological influence on the development of the Islamic State. His statements and sermons substantially influenced digital and analogue contexts for their clarification of the Islamic State's positions on diverse issues.[66]

These statements' translators and producers of online digital materials in various languages could not continue due to prosecution and persecution. For example, the Australian (then) jihād advocate Musa Cerantonio promoted the Islamic State from a distance via social networks and digital publications until being arrested for terrorist activities in 2016.[67] Yahya ʾAbū Ḥassan ibn Sharaf (known as 'Yahya the American') (1983–2017) became a prolific and influential contributor to *Dabiq*, Islamic State's magazine, applying social media and highly tuned knowledge of Islam and Arabic to make his arguments for the caliphate – until he died in 2017.[68]

Since the relative decline of the Islamic State in analogue contexts, a digital footprint was maintained, enhanced by utilizing the Islamic State *nom de guerre* in other cultural and geographical contexts as a 'franchise'. This included Khorasan (Afghanistan, also known as ISIS-K and ISKP), West Africa, the Democratic Republic of Congo (DRC) and Mozambique entities that pledged allegiance (sometimes tentatively) and developed online presences as an operational adjustment to on-the-ground campaigning. Channels were used for recruitment, logistics and publicity. It is important not to generalize, so the activities of franchises are outlined as follows:

Islamic State of Khorasan Province

ISKP drew on the membership of disaffected Taliban, al-Qaeda and Tehrik-e-Taliban members.[69] ISKP applied the internet as part of their strategy, including a video of their (now-deceased) leader Hafiz Saeed. ISKP's targets are as much the Taliban as any foreign influences, such as Pakistan and the United States. Their digital media focused on this after the Taliban negotiated with the United States in 2021, but this was part of a long-term strategy railing against perceived weaknesses and concessions made by the Taliban.[70] Consequently, the Taliban targeted ISKP online and on the ground in contestation for power and influence in Afghanistan.

ISKP maintained a social media presence, including text and images. This included them pledging a new emir in March 2022, which showed masked fighters (complete with weapons) around an Islamic State flag and facing the camera. Other images on Twitter showed ISKP fighters marking Ramadan with an *ifṭār* meal (albeit continuing to wear masks for the photos).[71] ISKP were proactive in producing other online content, including an English language *Voice of Khurasan* (VoK) magazine via its al-Azaim Foundation for Media Production, as well as magazines in Urdu and other languages, focusing on Uzbek, Tajik and Kyrgyz speakers.[72] VoK paid particular attention to the Taliban, especially its relations with the United States and Shīʿa communities in Afghanistan and other perceived 'enemies' of Islam.[73]

In 2022 ISKP's twenty-minute video focused on alleged violations by the Pakistan state while encouraging Pakistan nationals and movements to join ISKP in its campaigns against the Taliban.[74] ISKP's utilization of social media and online publications integrated multi-language discourse and campaigning transcending borders while also agitating against domestically rooted issues associated with the Taliban. Their international networking and affiliation with 'Islamic State' reflects the latter's media strategies and policies as a means of generating influence in jihād spheres, with an integration of digital content collection with their campaigning, a trend also found in other zones.

Islamic State Central Africa Province (ISCAP)

There are two significant elements to ISCAP, its central African branch (focused on DRC) and its Mozambique branch.[75] Despite their use of the name al-Shabaab, the group used the ISCAP title and claimed allegiance with 'Islamic State', confirmed in 2019. It is linked with branches in Somalia and the DRC, with its media content being networked by the central Islamic State media department (*dīwān al-iʿlam al-markāzī*).[76] Also known as Ansar al-Sunnah, there was discussion that it might only be a faction within the organization that identified as 'Islamic State'.[77] They have used online media to publicize their campaigns and have connected with other groups elsewhere in Africa.[78] These activities could impact access to significant gas reserves and attendant investment in the region.

The Allied Democratic Forces (ADF) represents ISCAP's affiliate, operating in Uganda and the DRC, a context where Muslims remain in the minority (10 per cent). ADF has expanded its operations and implemented propagation activities in eastern Congo, which were the subject of online allegiance videos. These outreach activities are atypical compared to other 'Islamic State' branches.[79] ADP leader Seka Musa Baluku pledged allegiance to IS in 2016. He was designated a 'global terrorist', alongside his organization, by the Department of State in the United States in 2021.[80] ADF featured in *al-Naba*, including an infographic explaining ADF activities. However, it focused its media activities, such as videos and photographs, through central channels rather than generating substantial unique content.[81] The channel announced its first 'martyrdom' operations in the DRC, which were claimed online in June 2021.[82]

ISCAP have a role in drug trafficking, seemingly not in contradiction with their religious values: 'Cabo Delgado is also a huge heroin hub, with 25 to 30% of Afghanistan's production transiting through there, translating to up to $800 million/year. With IS increasing presence in Afghanistan, it is possibly that in the medium term the jihād group could control part of the chain of the heroin distribution.'[83] ISCAP made extensive use of embedded media to highlight their operational activities, including their pledge of allegiance to IS and their attack on the city of Palma in March 2021, which led to it coming under their control, impacting local gas production.[84] In 2022, ISCAP were attacking Christians in the DRC, Mozambique and Cameroon – and publicizing these activities online with posters.[85] The different branches of ISCAP strategically utilized graphic digital media to emphasize their agenda and boost their influence, with an extensive social media presence drawing on precedents from ISIS practice, which enabled ISCAP to link into wider online jihād discourse.

Other platforms

It is recognized that there are numerous other jihād platforms and organizations in diverse global contexts which warrant in-depth investigation. The focus here is on entities which have developed sustained online influence, embedding digital materials into their strategic approaches towards networking, propagation, logistics and funding.

Al-Shabāb

Al-Qaeda affiliate Ḥarakat al-Shabāb al-Mujāhidīn (al-Shabaab) drew on social media to publicize their campaigns in East Africa and Yemen. It used Al Kataib

Foundation for Media Productions channel to publicize and stream footage from the high-casualty attacks at the Nairobi Westgate shopping centre in 2013, the Garissa University massacre in 2015 and the 2019 attack on a Nairobi hotel complex.[86] Not only did this add impetus to their operations, but it also alerted other organizations to the further potential of embedded reporting as part of attacks on infrastructures and societies. Social media also had potency in logistics, funding and recruitment – even drawing combatants from abroad: a 2021 trial of two men from the UK and Malaysia highlighted how they were using the internet to bring in others to bolster the ranks of al-Shabaab.[87] Officials in Kenya and Somalia struggled to stop al-Shabaab from using social media platforms to recruit to its cause, focusing on socially disenfranchised young people, including refugees and migrants.[88] This output is part of a multimedia effort that incorporates radio broadcasting.[89] The impact of al-Shabaab's leadership as influential within this process is significant. It also had to counter the growing influence of the Islamic State in Somalia, which was attempting to recruit members from al-Shabaab.[90]

Former leader Ahmad Abdi Aw Muhammad Godane (1977–2014) appeared on video with Ayman al-Zawahiri and in videos marking the shopping mall attack in 2013. He also attacked other al-Shabaab members, such as Omar Hammami (Abu Mansoor al-Amriki) (1984–2012), an online critic from the United States.[91] Godane's death in a US-targeted assassination led to a leadership vacuum, filled by Sheikh Ahmed Umar (Ahmed Diriye) and announced online. In 2021 Ahmed Umar was calling online for attacks in Dijbouti against 'western' interests and foreigners, and more generally, to attack foreign forces across Africa.[92]

Online campaigning has continued across social media, including magazines in local languages, focusing not just on Somalia but on Kenya and Uganda – to encourage support and recruitment.[93] In terms of 'influencers' outside of the leadership, the figure of the so-called 'white widow' Samantha Lewthwaite dominated narratives about al-Shabaab. The convert wife of a 2005 London bomber, Jermaine Lindsay, Lewthwaite had blogged her perspectives on jihād, attracting media headlines in the UK (including an interview with the Sun newspaper where she claimed ignorance of Lindsay's activities). Lewthwaite was alleged to have been a figure in the Westgate attacks – an allegation that al-Shabaab later denied online.[94] Whether Lewthwaite is a 'jihād influencer' is open to question. Whatever the reality, her role as an 'influence' was perpetuated by continued media interest, including a 2020 Netflix documentary widely available online, although her own social media activities went quiet.[95]

Boko Haram

Islamic State in West Africa Province faced off against Boko Haram, resulting in the Boko Haram leader Abubakar Shekau (1965?–2021) committing suicide after being targeted for kidnap. This influential figure (if not an 'influencer') had a complex approach to media: Boko Haram (*Jamā'at Ahl as-Sunnah lid-Da'wāh wa'l-Jihād*) has sought to distance itself from 'western' influences, including forms of technology and education, although they utilized broadcast and print media to spread their message, including a video recorded by Shekau in support of Islamic State, the Taliban and al-Qaeda – despite these elements not necessarily being compatible with each other. The complexities of Boko Haram are beyond the scope of this section.[96] However, there is considerable evidence that they have drawn upon digital media as a recruitment tool and means of propagating their specific interpretation of 'jihād'.[97]

There is synchronicity between the expansion of social media and internet usage in Nigeria, and the intensified focus of Boko Haram on their digital output, marked by relative 'improvements' in technical quality and coordinated brand consistency on social media including the *al-Urwah al-Wuthqa* Twitter channel. These are comparable with the earlier online pronouncements of other Boko Haram channels, with fragmentation and identity levels focused against the Nigerian government and its Christian population.[98]

Drawing on the 'Islamic State' influence in different territories, *al-Urwah al-Wuthqa*'s content included videos and images of executions.[99] Boko Haram sees no contradiction in using technology to disseminate its message, using technology taken from Nigerian military forces.[100] The relatively poor production values were part of its strategy:

> the crudity of the production is itself part of its messaging technique: the rawness is intended to instil fear and dread of the terrorist organization in the Nigerian viewers. Boko Haram's social media messaging is not directed specifically at potential recruits. In fact, members of the Nigerian armed forces are the target audience, the aim being to convince them of the futility of fighting against a superior force.[101]

However, in 2020 it was suggested that they use high-specification technology to record and edit their videos, using Telegram and WhatsApp (across numerous channels) to avoid shutting down online. One researcher noted that they used up to fifty WhatsApp pages and moved across to Telegram when WhatsApp shut them down. When they were away from a viable internet network, they would record content and then physically transport it to a town to upload it to an internet network, but this was also the reason for the lack of immediacy in some output.[102]

Conclusion

Discussions on Muslim metaverses cannot ignore the pervasive themes associated with militaristic (lesser) jihād and its articulations in cyberspace. Influences and influencers have a role within aspects of militaristic jihād which traverse campaigns and religious-cultural boundaries, especially in CIEs. Even organizations previously reluctant or sceptical of the 'benefits' of online activity placed the content online in increasingly diffuse and nuanced ways to reach various audiences, considering technical and production requirements where appropriate, using a combination of live-action material from smartphones combined with the slicker studio-based recordings.

At the same time, actuality can have a violent and persuasive tone, attracting audiences, including world media. Even when organizations have been suppressed or defeated, the online content continues, generated by supporters, affiliates and those who aspire to the ranks of action, described in some contexts as keyboard warriors. Influence comes from the deceased, whether significant figures from more recent history or historical precedents drawing on interpretations of sources. Figures such as Osama bin Laden and Anwar al-Awlaki continue to have an audience with the legacy of digital content, despite the efforts of content platforms and authorities to close them down. Integrating digital media is no longer an option but a necessity within e-jihād contexts. Their advocates have always taken care to utilize the latest technological developments to spread their content, and there is no reason to suggest that future iterations of the internet and metaverses will be immune from e-jihād.

Chapter 10

Processing Islam

Contemporary influences and influencers in evolving Muslim metaverses

Different approaches towards influence and influencers within contemporary Muslim contexts are explored in this chapter. These transcend networks and locations but have a commonality in that their impact is from online activities, specifically within forms of social media. Influence cannot be quantified, as even click numbers and 'likes' can be fabricated or bought. Some choices may be speculative and provide a sense of the foundations of future Muslim digital worlds and metaverses, which could build on the types of influences and influencers discussed below within diverse contexts. Choices are based on themes that resonated during the book's development. The focus is on platforms and individuals who have generated authority through their roles as 'influencers' whose capital is based directly around online activities and pronouncements, rather than 'influences' whose output and resonance may have been placed online (e.g. posthumously). There can be ambiguity between these two concepts, depending on context, rather than clearly defined parameters.

These aspects are challenging to quantify scientifically; they can be measured through the application of snapshots and anecdotal understandings to get a sense of the zeitgeists associated with specific themes and approaches. The presence of Islam and Muslims on diverse social media channels is represented differently, and the examples show responses regarding gender, age and teams under discussion. Algorithms – especially surrounding influencers with high levels of traffic to their content – have a symbiotic relationship with aspects of the influence projected by individuals and organizations: traffic begets further traffic. Content from influencers which is regularly posted and updated (or streamed) generates audience loyalty and momentum. In turn, links within influencer content to external sources have value in engendering new markets and affiliated loyalties. For example, an influencer's link to a specific translation or commentary on the Qur᾽ān could build an audience towards that specific world view; an influencer's link to associated content, such as a female reciter of the Qur᾽ān linking to another, creates support for the concept surrounding female recitation and a synergy between like-minded content providers. Links in turn can impact on aspects of searchability, underpinning algorithms within some search engine constructs (although parameters constantly shift), including through voice search in phones and smart speakers. The ways in which the digital Qur'ān is mediated shifts in line with technological developments, consequently impacting understanding.

This chapter discusses how influence and influencers impact disparate contemporary Islamic themes and contextual frameworks within continually developing and evolving zones. It commences with an overview of Muslim women, gender and influence in Muslim digital frameworks, which links in part to the second section on the Qur'ān, which looks at the different ways it is interpreted and recited online, specifically by female reciters. The chapter then explores how influence frameworks and religious authority were impacted during the Covid-19 pandemic (2020–3), in which specific attention was placed on the use of digital content to mediate social distancing restrictions. Two brief case studies follow on the contrasting ways influence and influencers operate in Muslim contexts: first, there is discussion on Muslim influence in Palestine and Gaza, specifically how influencers have operated under the pressures of conflict and discrimination. Second, a case study of Indonesia explores the impact of its relatively high levels of digital connectivity (especially in urban centres) and the ways in which an emphasis on social media use by Islamic platforms and organizations changes dynamics of religious authority and identity. The chapter concludes with a lighter but no less influential theme, that of how Islamic memes present in effective and concise ways complex ideas about religion and society.

Muslim women, gender issues and influencers

Gender issues are significant in terms of CIEs, with manifestations of female religious authority and the presence of female voices, including activists. The study of these activities forms part of a wider academic discussion on gender and women's online activities.[1] Digital literacy has been a key driver across complex and diverse identities, associated with educated, urban and technologically aware women with access to technology. This does not negate sensitive issues impacting Muslim women online, including 'flaming' and other forms of abuse, and the continuity of gendered online spaces.[2] These may form foundations for future iterations of Muslim metaverses, which raises questions as to whether these separations will be maintained. Online spaces have provided opportunities for exploration of female identities and self-expression, including in zones where dress codes may create (self-imposed or involuntary) barriers to access. The internet became a zone where those seeking forms of parity and religious expression, especially in under-represented contexts, can find a voice (subject to access, forms of censorship and digital literacy).[3] This has included opening up the opportunities to discuss and interpret interpretative issues and to acquire knowledge from alternative sources, especially female interpreters.[4] 'Female only' zones outside of the range of male voices may have some benefits for their participants if there is an element of choice. This should not necessarily be seen through idealistic lenses. In some contexts, however, in the MENA region, according to a 2017 survey, female access to the internet was seen as unacceptable by 75 per cent of male respondents.[5]

Girls and young women face additional barriers to access digital content.[6] There will be a diversity of experiences, so the intention here is not to generalize but to show how there can be an impact in terms of influencers and forms of activism. It was highlighted in responses to the Taliban from female activists in and outside Afghanistan when Taliban officials commented on how they intended to treat women in the revived 2021 version of the Emirate.[7] Attention inevitably focused on dress codes, but other significant concerns such as education, employment and interpretation of Islam appeared on social media. For example, a Taliban official discussed the merits of the hijab in a way that attracted international attention: 'A Taliban official in an interview in Kabul on the importance of Hijab: "Do you buy a sliced melon or an intact melon. Of course the intact one. A woman without Hijab is like a sliced melon."'[8] The video attracted over a million views. Many protests in Kabul organized by women drew on social media for publicity, showing demonstrations in the presence of Taliban fighters, some of whom just observed while others proactively sought to prevent the activities.

Male clerical interventions on gender-associated issues might seek to impact forms of advice and influence behaviour. However, it can negatively bounce back at religious authorities: in 2021, following the victorious Turkish women's volleyball activities in the Tokyo Olympics, clerical influencer İhsan Şenocak tweeted opposition to the team's behaviour: '"Daughter of Islam! You are the sultan of faith, chastity, morality and modesty . . . not of sports fields," he tweeted. "You are the child of mothers who refrain from showing their nose [out of modesty]. Don't be . . . the victim of popular culture. You are our hope and our prayer."'[9] Şenocak has a substantial profile on Twitter, with 953,600 followers (October 2021), but received a great deal of criticism for his comments on the players' dress (although he stated that he had no opposition to them playing sports).

In Egypt, social media formed part of a #MeToo movement against sexual harassment, which is seen as endemic in public spaces and online. The movement emerged in 2018, a response to the sustained sexual harassment experienced in Egypt, where 'according to a 2017 survey by UN Women and Promundo, nearly 60% of Egyptian women have been sexually harassed. In a 2017 Thomson Reuters poll that surveyed experts in women's issues, Cairo was named the most dangerous city in the world for women.'[10] A campaign by a group using the Instagram and Twitter handle 'Assault Police' against an American University of Cairo student led to his prosecution and imprisonment for sexual harassment, assault and cybercrimes.[11] The issue of 'sextortion' in Egypt, which might include blackmail using digital photos of women taken by former partners, resulted in the Qawem ('resist') online campaign organized by Mohammed Elyamani, which profiles and proactively responds to such physical and digital threats, offering advice and collecting data.[12] The #MosqueMeToo hashtag initiated by author and activist Mona Eltahawy emerged as a response to her being subject to sexual assault while on hajj at the age of fifteen. This campaign generated many shared stories and experiences of sexual violence. It was presented in conjunction with a parallel #IBeatMyAssaulter campaign which was the result of an assault in a secular space.[13]

One social media activist noted that in her posting of articles about Islam on a Facebook page, she started to receive substantial online harassment from (mainly) Muslim men, including a case of stalking. One site administrator received unsolicited messages seeking marriage and conversations from men posting as females wanting conversations about intimacy. Another received pornographic videos 'sent by a man in Egypt, whose FB profile picture had words from the Qurʾān!'[14] Such alarming and atypical posts would be condemned by many (Muslim) males and are part of a broader picture of online harassment but are still a subtext within online activities in Muslim contexts.

One response to such trends is the development of female-only platforms, where users can feel safer and not be exposed to these pressures. The UK platform Amaliah.com claimed 5.2 million users and over 300 contributors in 2021 as a way of 'amplifying the voices of Muslim women'.[15] Content includes a blend of lifestyle, relationship and identity categories – many underpinned by religiously oriented discussion. When discussing 'influencers', it seems relevant not just to consider individuals but also collective hubs such as Amaliah, which can also make an impact, blending with its commercial endeavours, such as a brand agency.[16]

Female-friendly content certainly has an influential impact and crosses genres. Among the many examples, Salam Girl! offered lifestyle advice, interpretation of aspects of the Prophet Muḥammad's life and fashion from the perspectives of two hijab-wearing American converts. The podcast series ran for eighty-four episodes (as of June 2020); during the Covid-19 pandemic, they discussed approaches towards Ramaḍān in the unusual situation and had an interview with an infectious diseases' specialist (also a Muslim woman). One primary focus was profiles of other converts and lifestyle issues associated with gender equity, living as Muslims in the United States and relationship concerns.[17]

Another significant offering in this zone is The Digital Sisterhood, a podcast which engaged with significant personal and religious issues and had a substantial presence on Instagram. It explores issues of sexual violence, sexual health, grief, mentorship and advice on 'becoming a better Muslim'. Its TikTok showed extracts from episode themes. The website focused on blog posts, which included discussions on Islamic sources. The multiple entry points for The Digital Sisterhood include the podcast, a merchandizing channel, a sponsorship Patreon page and an online chat forum via Discord. These reflect the potential audiences for this influential output, which had over a million downloads in 2022.[18] Listeners form strong bonds with the podcast, especially on the reflections from survivors of sexual assault, such as 'Sabryna': 'What was most powerful about Sabryna's story was that she told listeners that what happened to them wasn't their fault and reminded them of their worth – a message that is not always spoken about loudly in Muslim communities.' 'Sabryna' temporarily established an Instagram channel to respond to listeners but had to suspend it due to the powerful and 'overwhelming' response.[19]

The internet has offered opportunities for the articulation of specific and nuanced female online identities to present their world views and generate a following. A good example of this is the self-styled Salafi Feminist, Zainab bint Younus, whose blog and online output discussed lifestyle choices, Islamic interpretation, issues impacting Muslim women and the relationship between understandings of feminism and Islam. Zainab bin Younus's blog banner had shown her in her niqab astride a motorcycle and holding a goth-style sword.[20] Zainab bin Younus wrote and talked further on her understanding of 'Salafi feminism', output which received (along with her online output) substantial positive and negative publicity online.[21] She contributed to online channels such as Muslim Matters, where she provided an Eid podcast in 2023.[22] While it is beyond the scope of this section to enter discussions on 'Salafi feminism', what is significant is the way in which Zainab bin Younus applies digital media as an influential voice in discussions and representations of complex Muslim female identities, which became particularly relevant given other developments in cyberspace.

In 2023, increasing discussions on toxic 'manospheres' generated online by convert and influencer Andrew Tate placed further emphasis on gender issues and representation online. Former kickboxer Tate was accused of a misogynistic approach towards women, had a business background in adult webcams and was seen as highly influential among young Muslim men:[23] 'Tate has mastered the science of manipulating social media algorithms to broadcast his message, which is often countered by users who respond or "stitch" the videos with their disapproving reactions.'[24] In 2022, he was arrested on human trafficking and rape charges in Romania and imprisoned for four months prior to being placed under house arrest. In 2023, he was facing trial on multiple charges in Romania.[25]

The perception of Tate having negative approaches towards women was discussed extensively online, especially the 'red pill misogyny' associated with the view that men were disenfranchised through increased female rights and power and had become 'incels' or involuntarily celibate. The term 'Mincel', a conflation of 'incel' and 'Muslim', started appearing online. These views contradicted egalitarian and female-friendly interpretations of the Qur'ān.[26] The negative impact Tate and his supporters were having on Muslim women was being 'justified' through a specific and distorted understanding of Islam allied with a secular ideology circulated on Reddit and other forums online.[27]

Mariyah bint Rehan suggested that 'The binary nature of the internet, and the divisive social architecture it creates means the contrived male vs. female dynamic was always the most vulnerable to manipulation on digital terrain.'[28] Religious platforms have also engaged in these issues. Mariyah bint Rehan discussed this in Islam21C, indicating that poor religious education and relationship education was also having an impact, especially in 'Mincel' attitudes towards relationships, in line with the concept of temporary marriages and relationships without commitment: 'While Islam was sent to free society (and women in particular) from this pernicious and exploitative promiscuity, some in the modern-day Muslim manosphere call for a return to pre-Islamic regressive relationships, paradoxically, in a claim to harking back to traditional Islamic masculinity.'[29]

There were attempts on Reddit and other forums to counter 'red pill' perceptions even before the emergence of Tate as a Muslim.[30] Rasha Al Aqeedi notes that Tate's pre-conversion profile made him one of the most Googled people internationally and that other Muslim influencers with similar world views, high profiles and audiences have 'adopted' him to benefit from this global reach and expand their own impact.[31] The ways in which Muslim women influencers can counter 'red pill' associated understandings of female roles in Islam. The full impact of the 'red pill' and 'Mincel' movement has yet to be seen.

The internet can clearly influence approaches to relationships and intimacy. There was a Zoom seminar (for females only) in 2020 on this topic, hosted by a female scholar.[32] There are also female-led Q&As, such as Muska Jahan's video on intimacy and marriage questions.[33] MuslimMatters launched an online video series on sex and marriage.[34]

General Q&A sites also tackle individual questions on these issues. Blogs and magazine sites unpacked related issues in a non-sensationalist way, such as Ayqa Khan's discussion with Fariha Róisín on 'growing up without intimacy, losing their virginity before marriage, and navigating faith and a sex life in the Western world'.[35] Guidance from Umm Muladhat's 'The Muslimah Sex Manual: A Halal Guide To Mind Blowing Sex' was available as an e-Book on Kindle and also received substantial publicity elsewhere. It received positive feedback from Muslim women's organizations.[36]

It is possible to extend this discussion out to those who identify as Muslim women, non-binary or gender fluid in LGBTQ+ contexts, whose voices can be heard across diverse social media and online channels, often utilizing anonymity given that an LGBTQ+ identity potentially raises difficulties in traditionally oriented Muslim contexts. There are websites and social media channels which are emphatic that identities which are 'Muslim' and 'LGBTQ+' are complementary, organizing communities and networks at local, national and international levels.

An example of this is Hidayah, which operates in US and UK contexts, seeking to develop Muslim-friendly spaces online and offline for people with LGBTQ+ identities, alongside educational and information resources. This utilizes a range of social media to facilitate its networking opportunities, such as opportunities to join religious discussions and events, Gay Pride demonstrations and attend book readings.[37] Imaan, which had a twenty-year record as an LGBTQ+ charity, facilitated Ramaḍān and Eid events, online meetings and a Trans workshop.[38] The UK Muslim Women's Helpline offered affirming advice for LGBTQ+ people.[39] The Inclusive Mosque Initiative presented as a feminist mosque, which sought to: 'train imams to support Muslim communities with an intersectional feminist understanding of social justice. We work primarily with imams who are women, nonbinary or genderqueer'. They offered marriage services for LGBTQ+ people.[40]

One significant online focused LGBTQ+ channel was Daar ul-Gharib, based in St Louis, Missouri, which identified as 'a Queer, femme and non-binary focused mosque with an emphasis on disabled and other marginalized persons'.[41] In 2022, it provided a series of Qur'ān readings through Ramaḍān, drawing in part from an English language translation by M. A. S. Abdel Haleem.[42] Daar ul-Gharib also offers sermons on YouTube, in which the *adhān* is also called.[43] Under the Queer Masjid moniker, they announced a thirty-day podcast series for Ramaḍān in 2023, using Spotify.[44] It is significant that hijab is worn in delivering sermons, but its presenter Rikva Sajida did not wear niqab (face covering) as this would impede the understanding of their deaf viewers (who are lip-reading). Daar ul-Gharib is a good example of how social media and other channels can be utilized by LGBTQ+ people for networking purposes, reinforcing identities and developing activism programmes.

Coincidentally Rivka Sajida – who contributes to Daar ul-Gharib's output – is also present on YouTube, where she offers advice on dress code and fashion issues, including how to create hijabs and niqabs using scarves in different international styles.[45] Dress code issues inevitably draw the ire of some scholars, with clerics expressing anger when people on social media take off their hijabs and post about it. Fashion 'influencers' can make an impact, as seen in the discussion below on Indonesia, where lifestyle, business and religious interpretations fused into a digital milieu.[46] Equally significant are ideas about performative religion, such as Qurʾān recitation, which features in the next section.

Qurʾān reciters and influence

Influence takes many forms. It can be embodied in an individual, an organization or a set of principles. The Qurʾān represents the ultimate 'influence' in Islam, being God's Revelation received by Prophet Muḥammad via the angel Jibrīl. In a reflection of Muslim analogue societies, the Qurʾān's integral embedded position in digital media extends across and permeates formats and applications, on occasion mediated by online influencers via recitation, interpretation and analysis. As such the Qurʾān will underpin future Muslim metaverses (in whatever form), while access to it is impacted by the variations of searchable interfaces and algorithms (Islamic and other). These have built on earlier iterations and approaches towards mediating the Qurʾān online.

Early recordings of the Qurʾān have featured across technological innovations, with early versions on cylinder and acetate (now available to hear online!).[47] The cassette tape popularized recitations to the masses, with specific shops devoted to the genre. MP3s took the phenomena online, even in the early phases of the World Wide Web; many websites now present a similar breadth of choice to the more traditional Qurʾān cassette tape shops of the past, even including some of the 'classic' recordings from exponents of the art of recitation. These jostled on the shop shelves with cassettes of sermons, part of an influential media form which impacted political-religious discourse across the Middle East, which has now been transcended by an online equivalent.[48]

Recitation recordings and broadcasts, especially by proficient and highly trained *qāriʾūn* (exponents of the science of *tajwīd*), generate substantial audiences and fan bases online. Traditionally, these *qāriʾūn* public figures have usually been male, and there is a plethora of choices, some drawn from classic recordings (including cassettes) from previous decades, as well as more recent additions to the recitation online marketplace. The complexity of choice is demonstrated on Assabile.com, which by 2023 included over 530 reciters, searchable by nation and popularity.[49] One notable feature of this and many other Qur᾽ān resources was that its listing was entirely male. This might suggest to a casual observer that women do not recite the Qur᾽ān, especially within a public context. However, the internet has opened opportunities for increased presentation and popularity of recitations by women.

Before the World Wide Web, there were many important female reciters, especially in some cultural contexts – with a few recorded on vinyl. Some have appeared on social media, such as a rare recording of Sheikha Mabrouka from 1905, remastered and circulated on Twitter.[50] In Egypt in the first half of the twentieth century, female 'Sheikhas' recited the Qur᾽ān, including Sheikha Munira Abdou, who achieved fame when she became the first Qur᾽ān reciter for Egyptian Radio in 1934.[51] Munira Abdou's recordings are rare, but some are online, acquiring a new and appreciative audience.[52] Female reciters have featured in national and international Qur'ān recitation competitions, whose performances increasingly appeared to wider audiences through broadcast media and the internet.[53] However, the mediation online of the Qur᾽ān by female reciters continues to challenge some normative approaches towards *tajwid*, with various religious opinions on the permissibility (or not) of women reciting the Qur'ān.[54] An example of this challenge of convention was a 2010 recitation by Tahera Ahmed, the first by a woman at the national Islamic Society of North America (ISNA) convention, which was itself ultimately uploaded onto YouTube.[55]

The internet is facilitating an expansion in female recitation, offering 'safer' spaces and improved opportunities for reciters' recordings to reach wider audiences, to the extent that the online breadth of recitation enters influencer territory in terms of audience capture: child reciters include (the then) two-year-old Fatima reciting Sūra al-Fātiḥah (not without some persuasion), under the label 'Cutest Video'.[56] Her older sister Maryam Masud hosted her own YouTube recitation channel, along with lifestyle clips (and interviews with her sister) which had 1.3 million subscribers in 2020. Masud's YouTube channel featured other online influencer characteristics familiar from the religious milieu: a clip of an 'unboxing' of toys, visiting dolphins, baking cupcakes and the sisters interacting and reciting portions from the Qur'ān. A video of her receiving a family gift on becoming Ḥāfeẓa (having memorized the Qur'ān) received over 4 million visits.[57]

Masud also had an Instagram channel, with other clips and recitations, alongside information about her activities as a judge on various Qur'ān recitation competitions.[58] The sisters were used to promote a line of Muslimah Stickers on a different website, reflecting their lifestyle (and highlighting their memorization of the Qur'ān).[59] A 2018 question-and-answer video of Fatima and Maryam with Sheikh Yusuf Estes acquired nearly 2 million views.[60] She also briefly met Mufti Menk, where they exchanged views on reaching online audiences.[61] Clips of Maryam surfaced on TikTok, such as a tutorial on wearing the hijab (using her sister Fatima as a 'model', with some humorous interludes where Fatima is 'naughty').[62] During a pandemic lockdown Maryam Masud video-blogged from her New Jersey home, discussing her Qur'ān studies and responding to questions (alongside more lifestyle-oriented clips).[63]

Nusaiba Mohammad Timol combines Qur'ān recitation with an 'influencer' lifestyle, promoting a creative Muslim channel and fashion photos on Instagram. Her YouTube channel focuses on recitation clips dating back to 2006 when she was winning recitation competitions, but after a long gap, a further clip appeared in 2020.[64] She is one of several reciters promoting the concept of Qur'ān recitation as appropriate for women. There have been cultural and religious barriers over time which – in some contexts – restricted the participation of Muslim women in general in public recitation. The internet opened opportunities for women to develop a profile to showcase their skills in this field, emanating from many backgrounds and with different levels of experience. They demonstrate diverse styles of recitation as well as recordings at different times in their careers. Some developed substantial profiles online for these recitations.

American convert Jennifer Grout won an 'Arabs Got Talent' competition as a singer before developing a profile in Qur'ān recitation. This performance led to several online videos, alongside posts of Tarab music, which also feature on her Instagram and TikTok channels. One key issue was her status as a convert, and the surprise at this was evident in reactions from listeners. She also recited on news channels and other broadcasters. Her YouTube content has received millions of visits, including a recording of part of Sūra al-Baqarah received over 3 million views in less than a year.[65] A recording she made in a concert for prisoners performing 'Ya Mohammad' received 1.2 million views on YouTube.[66] It is interesting to see this mixture of genres presented online.

From Scotland, Madinah Javed built an online profile as a reciter of the Qur'ān and promoted other female reciters through social media. She has used Twitter and the #FemaleReciters hashtag to promote the cause of recitation. Content includes recitation by Javed presented at the Scottish Parliament.[67] It is significant how the internet has enabled women who recite the Qur'ān based in 'minority' contexts to reach out to other majority zones. Approaches to recitation vary in different contexts. When there is resistance in mosques or local contexts, and long-standing cultural barriers may seem insurmountable, the ways women used the internet to promote female Qur'ān recitation is a significant way to overcome these barriers. Those who see recitation by women as a 'distraction' for men or of 'lesser quality' than that performed by men, contested this content.

American Maryam Amir developed a YouTube channel to present her thoughts on Islam, over eight episodes recorded in 2019.[68] The channel included religious advice and discussion. She also presented recitation. On Facebook, Amir encouraged women to send their recitations, which she would post out (with their permission) on social media: she added the proviso: 'You can include a note before your recitation begins that says something like, 'I will be reciting. Men, please turn off your volume.' And leave it to them to be responsible if you're concerned.'[69] She discussed the barriers facing Muslim women in some contexts in presenting their recitations in the public sphere.

Not all cultural-religious contexts are necessarily resistant to female recitation, with examples such as Maria Ulfah having had a significant profile in Southeast Asia and beyond prior to the broader emergence of the internet.[70] Her work is now available online, notably in a complete set of Qur'ān recitations freely available on Soundcloud.[71] The evolution of online media sees Ulfah's material featured on YouTube (with recordings of broadcasts) and copied onto TikTok.[72]

Placing women's online recitations on YouTube alongside more traditional male reciters has had some interesting consequences. Some female reciters acquire more substantial audiences/clicks than their male equivalents. The Adh-Dhikr Channel focused on female reciters, collecting significant recordings together, with a recording by Zahraa Helmy receiving many more views than male reciters.[73] A recitation of Sūra al-Raḥmān received nearly 6 million views in four years.[74] A recording by Sharifah Khazif Fadzilah recorded at a Malaysian recitation competition (outdoors, in a noisy environment) received over 37 million views from its publication in 2009.[75] Egyptian Hafiz Sümeyye Eddeb's recording of recitation had over 8 million hits in two years.[76] Beyond recitation, the presentation of *anāshīd* (Islamic songs) could also receive substantial audiences: a recording by a female choir of a 'Ramaḍān Nasheed' had over 73 million views.[77] There are significant other areas of online recitation which impact redressing the gender balance of online activities – which shift into other areas of online religious authority and the projection of online influence.

This development extended into apps: the Qariah app, launched in 2022, featured more than sixty female reciters (including some discussed in this chapter). These reciters range from contemporary to historical figures across diverse Muslim contexts. Sakina Hassan is featured in a recording from the 1920s of three *suwar* (complete with recording scratches) alongside modern Qur'ān recitation competition winners. The app's organization allowed recitation styles of specific *suwar* to be compared.[78] The app provides a justification for its content and approach, incorporating detailed discussions on the different approaches towards permissibility (or not) of women reciting. Much depends on the context in which a woman is heard, and whether there might be susceptible men likely to face '*fitnah*' (defined as 'tribulation') 'having unholy thoughts to the point that he is turned on by a woman who is reciting Quran.' The app developers note that it is a greater *fitnah* for women not to know that they can become reciters.[79] Qariah points out that female recitation is accepted and approved by authorities within many Muslim contents and that the app will facilitate an opening up of recitation online to encourage the development of recitation among women, along with a broader appreciation of the reciters' skills.

This latest iteration of online influence and the presentation of Muslim values across formats and genres is significant, especially in terms of the opening of recitation by women to wider audiences. This trend has operated in TikTok and other channels beyond censorship and, with general levels of access, draws recitation into zones of widespread cultural transmission where the language and attitudes of the internet combined with traditional religious framing. The Qur'ān is an integral influence in its own right; influencers recite and project it across diverse digital contexts, including female reciters – adding new audiences and dimensions towards their understandings. Future female-friendly Muslim metaverses may resonate with these recordings, while Islamic algorithms will increasingly point towards female Qurʾān reciters as they build in influence and reputation.

Covid-19, Islam and influence

The Covid-19 pandemic is included in this discussion on influence because it represented (within some contexts) a turning point in the ways in which social media in particular would be used as a means of facilitating religious practices and enhancing continuity of authority and understanding during periods of social distancing. This included the raising of influencer profiles as audiences sought to fill the vacuum left by not being able to visit mosques, hear sermons in congregations and interact face-to-face with peers and authorities. The increasing digitized mediatization of Islam during the Covid-19 pandemic built on existing practices within CIES, hacking and adapting them to suit the crisis. Key events in the Islamic calendar, such as Ramaḍān, acquired an increased online dimension through the enhanced facilitation of online *ifṭār*.[80] Religious authorities generated religious opinions to answer the unique questions associated with the outbreak. Approaches continued to evolve, given that the virus and its variants continued to impact on societies after the initially recognized outbreak. There were also concerns regarding forms of information and misinformation circulating about Covid-19, vaccines and health responses, bolstered by the generation of fabricated traditions and sources.[81] Government and religious authority influence on strategies associated with Covid-19 could be challenged, especially in relation to limits on religious practices; in Indonesia, this extended to official public health warnings regarding attendance at public prayers, which did not initially stop gatherings from continuing.[82]

One interesting indicator of the role of social media was the promotion of apps presenting streaming content broadcasting specific ritual practices associated with the primary *ḥajj* pilgrimage and secondary *ʿumrah* pilgrimage, projecting ideas of religious influence and 'appropriate' practice during the Covid-19 outbreak where social distancing became a norm, and access to Mecca and Medina was limited. Images and clips showed social distancing during prayer and wearing masks in the precincts of the *Kaʿbah*. Social media showed cleaners praying towards the empty precincts surrounding the *Kaʿbah*. Religious and other functionaries (from imams to security personnel) wore masks, maintained social distancing and tested for Covid-19 in front of the social media cameras. The 2020 *ḥajj*, open to limited numbers of Saudi Arabia-based pilgrims, focused on the approaches religious authorities provided to mitigate the impact of social distancing.

The socially distanced 2020 *ḥajj* generated innovative imagery such as time-lapse photography of the *ṭawāf*.[83] These practices continued for the second socially distanced *ḥajj* and *ʿumrah* in 2021. Typical were clips showing technological innovation in the ritual hearts of Islam, such as special aerial sterilization devices to disinfect pilgrims after their performance of *ṭawāf* and the use of robots to distribute refreshments to pilgrims.[84] Even as the *ʿumrah* reactivated for non-Saudis in July 2021, digital measures were promoted and pilgrimage activities were publicized online. These required a digital underpinning to function effectively, with digital wristbands used to monitor pilgrims and advise them on appropriate ritual timings. The Holy Mosques Twitter feed for the 2021 *ḥajj* (1442 AH) introduced infographics on specific Covid-19-related practices while promoting the efforts of Saudi agencies in offering medical and logistical support across the Meccan precincts – showing male and female voluntary support.[85] The site drew on diverse local media sources to show pilgrims at different stages of ritual practices, with clips on its Twitter feed.[86] Using an online 'lottery' for international allocation of places for the 2022 non-socially distanced *ḥajj* generated complaints for it taking travel agencies out of the equation for *ḥajj* preparation, while the system received criticism for making *ḥajj* simultaneously more expensive and access-restrictive.[87] It was also problematic for (potential) pilgrims when the Motawif system had technical problems, causing significant booking problems. The Saudi Arabian authorities apologized as many could not take their scheduled and paid trips, although prospective pilgrims were still awaiting refunds in 2023, generating further furore online.[88]

Elsewhere, the Sunni centre of learning at Al-Azhar in Egypt applied Twitter to present its views on Covid-19 measures, with its photos of sermons emphasizing social distancing measures, and speeches and conference activities embedded into numerous digital outlets.[89] These updated as the pandemic situation changed, especially when mosque access became more restricted. It demonstrated 'good practice' of key figures in the light of shifting conditions, with real-time events being recorded and transmitted as live feeds.

Responses to Covid-19 also impacted other areas of religious practice. In the UAE, a survey suggested that Īd gifts were increasingly being conveyed electronically in response to the pandemic.[90] This development reflected a general shift in shopping and commercial transaction habits towards online shopping among consumers since the pandemic.[91] Platforms in other locations also advocated the use of electronic finance to convey Īd gifts, with the Muslim Council of Britain (MCB) suggesting that the *zakāh* for *Īd al-Fiṭr* could also be given electronically. In 2021, the MCB promoted the use of home virus detection tests before people met with family and friends.[92]

Social media were applied to show the endorsement of vaccinations by religious authorities. In Saudi Arabia, photos were widely distributed online of Abdulrahman al-Sudais (grand president for the Grand Mosque) receiving the vaccination.[93] In the UK, local authorities and health agencies used Muslim medical doctors on social media to promote good practices during the pandemic, particularly during *Īd al-Fiṭr* 2021, when socialization potentially would increase and safeguards diminish.[94] Internet channels circulated adverse claims about vaccines and their permissibility within Islamic contexts, impacting take-up. UK National Health Service officials sought to find Muslim influencers and activists to spread a positive message about vaccines in the face of rumours and resistance.[95]

Counter-campaigns from religious leaders and medical professionals sought to change negative responses towards vaccination, including through online sermons. Senior imams from across the Muslim spectrum promoted vaccine safety on YouTube.[96] This content included justification from the Qur'ān regarding vaccination.[97] Imam Qari Asim from Leeds Mosque, a prominent social media user, noted that 'questions about the vaccine should be answered by religiously and culturally competent individuals not by the keyboard warriors'.[98] In East London, Imam Mohammad Ammar from Masjd Ibrahim sought to discourage vaccine misinformation by being videoed having the vaccine.[99]

In the same part of London, other centres got on board with vaccine advice and information. This initiative reflected a diversity of approaches, but commonalities of interest associated with the vaccine and interpretations of vaccine permissibility. East London Mosque and London Mosque Centre is a significant and influential hub of Muslim activity in Tower Hamlets. Its Senior Imam (their term), Sheikh Mohammed Mahmoud, released a video encouraging vaccine uptake. This content was in line with the interpretation of *sharīʿa* and notions of consensus of knowledge and religious opinions in the obligation of preserving life – citing scholars requiring people by recommendation or obligation to take the vaccine. Mahmoud noted the preponderance of 'half-baked' conspiracy theories associated with the vaccine, ignoring scientific evidence from people of knowledge, including medical professionals.[100] In some cases, mosques became vaccine centres where imams and elders were seen on social media having jabs.[101] In the United States, religious authorities' concerns that taking up the vaccine would somehow break the requirements of the Ramaḍān fast were countered by social media, countering the online rumour mill and disinformation – not just within Muslim contexts but in broader American society.[102]

The al-Abbas Islamic Centre in Birmingham became the first UK mosque to act as a vaccination hub in conjunction with the National Health Service. Its imam Sheikh Nuru Mohammed saw this to counter vaccine scepticism and concerns regarding the halal nature of the jab.[103] Sheikh Nuru was later featured on a social media campaign by UK Government Department for Digital, Culture, Media and Sport, advising people not to share vaccine rumours.[104] It was significant, perhaps, that Al-Abbas Islamic Centre is a Khoja Shīʿa ʾIthnā ʿAsharī hub associated with this specific branch of Shīʿīsm.[105] Shīʿa institutions also responded to the Covid-19 situation through official religious online outlets associated with Ayatollahs and other religious luminaries.

Ayatollah Ali Hosseini Khamenei received the locally produced COVIran Barekat vaccine on Twitter. The advocation of a 'local-only' policy was reversed just over a month later in the face of increasing infections in Iran.[106] Different branches of Shīʿīsm responded digitally to Covid-19: the Dawoodi Bohra community in Mumbai, for example, conducted rituals and festivals associated with the conclusion of Īd online – decorating their homes to create 'a mosque-like atmosphere'. Prayer recitation was virtual: 'It has been a unique experience for all of us as we are making optimum use of modern technology and virtual platforms to participate in live-stream discourses, recitation of the Holy Quran and other religious and educational activities.'[107]

Other Islamic portals offer advice on responses to Covid-19, such as 'Holding Virtual *Jumu'ahs*' and a *fatwā* or religious opinion on a virtual congregational prayer. The online mediation of Islam had been a phenomenon prior to the pandemic. However, caution was exercised in its application in some quarters. In contrast, in the extraordinary context of the pandemic, it became a 'new normal' across institutions and cultural-religious zones, with potential to retain this level of interaction in post-Covid-19 contexts.[108] International Muslim religious organizations drew on online video streaming channels such as Zoom to present *ifṭār* celebrations to broad audiences during lockdowns. Outreach activities to wider communities became virtual events, with the MCB's annual Visit My Mosque event hosted digitally. Webcams and social media were used in different ways to bring guests to mosques' precincts. Cambridge Central Mosque, for example, had a virtual tour of its eco-mosque hosted by community members. It enabled the writer to 'visit' three mosques across the UK in one day, highlighting diverse approaches to tours, with a mosque in east London's Old Kent Road emphasizing its community's unique heritage and identity.[109]

As with previous years, content providers and platforms provided content aimed at Ramaḍān, always a lucrative commercial period of gift-giving and high levels of social media use, with an emphasis on adapting this for the Covid-19 context. The presentation of specific apps reflects Ramaḍān's principles of charity and contemplation and the promotion of hashtags and community-centred content. Infographics were developed to promote ideals and distributed on Facebook's Instagram platform, with Ramaḍān stickers for use on cameras and in apps – including for children.[110]

The Covid-19 issue became a dominant theme within online Question & Answer *fatāwā* sites. IslamQA dealt with enquiries about ritual practices such as *ghusl* (the ritual bathing prior to prayer) and whether a Covid-19 death was the equivalent to martyrdom. More 'practical' questions were presented as to whether the traditional approach towards the deceased regarding ritual washing and funeral prayer could be performed in absentia. A question was whether someone could wear Personal Protective Equipment (PPE) during prayers.[111] Discussions were associated with socially distanced prayers, ritual purity and mask-dominated online forums.[112] Questions emerged in other formats: Deenspiration's 'chatshow' format discussed aspects of spirituality during the pandemic (and promoted an online course on Islam which was a response to Covid-19).[113]

Mediating religious authority during the pandemic situation reflected diverse cultural-religious paradigms and practices. These transcended close networks of family and localized religious authorities which could not offer this level of engagement in mosques and family homes due to social distancing. This presented new options for digital authorities to present an alternative form of mediation, religious interaction and influence – including forms of recitation and religious education.[114] The shifting digital models of interpretation, understanding and knowledge transmission were embedded and intertwined into Islamic contexts in a way that – post-pandemic – would be difficult or unnecessary to unpick.

'Protecting Islam' in Palestine and Gaza

Not all platforms associated with Palestine and Gaza are motivated by religious values or interests. They may present diffuse agendas linked to territorial rights, assertions of political power and notions of statehood.[115] They may articulate notions of 'jihād' sharing complex political, ideological and/or religious roots with other platforms, but also have distinct emphasis on regional concerns and issues. Many jihād-oriented organizations promote themselves across social media, continuing long-standing media engagement. Cyber issues were a focal point of Israeli Defence Force (IDF) activities: in 2019, this included bombing an alleged 'cyber headquarters' in Gaza.[116]

Over two decades, disparate campaigns utilized the internet to promote their agendas, including early versions of so-called martyrs' galleries and live updates on campaigns. Social media became a touchstone for many Palestinian campaigns and causes, of which 'jihād' is a small element. Activism should not be conflated with militaristic jihād causes or elements. However, these causes can form a subtext, especially when they endorse a demonstration (including retrospectively) or talk about the victims of Israel's campaigns in Palestine and Gaza.[117]

The IDF was proactive in the precincts of al-Aqsa Mosque in 2021 and 2022, with the demonstrations being captured and posted online by activists, and images from the Sheikh Jarrah district of Jerusalem trending on social media. The potency of these emotive images came from their creation by eyewitnesses using smartphones, including inside mosques and precincts surrounding the Dome of the Rock – the third most holy site in Islam due to its association with Muḥammad's Night Journey. These images were circulated across various Twitter feeds, including those associated with campaigns their instigators may define as 'jihād'.

The concept of defending Islam or aspects of symbols and practice is a significant one, that has links with concepts of jihād within Islamic sources, but also is a relevant element when discussing contemporary influencers. It manifests itself in many forms of social-religious activism across causes, from political frameworks through to responses to specific events. Such activism can cross into numerous zones involving organizations and individuals, whose campaigns manifest in diverse social media areas. Activism and influencers associated with diverse campaigns, which can have a religious subtext, feeds into the scope of CIEs in many ways, especially at regional and local levels.

One significant example of this relates to the conflict in Palestine and Gaza, especially individual activists, rather than the political-religious-militaristic platforms (although some campaigns and values may be shared). The impact of IDFs' bombing campaigns in Gaza in May-June 2021 was recorded and broadcast via social media to international audiences. Content included live-streamed footage of attacks on Palestinians and the aftermath of bombings, with visually striking and graphic images. One critical part of this was the launch of attacks in Jerusalem (Al-Quds) against protesters in the vicinity of the Dome of the Rock Mosque and precincts of al-Aqsa, focused on preventing East Jerusalem's Sheikh Jarrah neighbourhood from being occupied by Israeli settlers. This footage included attacks during the conclusion of Ramaḍān, which prevented people from praying on the third most significant site in Islam. The defence of East Jerusalem, and especially access to significant holy places in Islam, galvanized further international attention. Real-time social media coverage was integrated into mainstream broadcasts, using live features across Facebook, Twitter and other platforms. This provocative trampling of the religious sanctuary, in terms of ritual cleanliness, the presence of violence in a place of worship and insensitive actions was a dynamic combination of factors. This attack was taken on by many activists, not just overtly religious platforms, as an attack on identity and values. Condemnation also emerged from Netanyahu's opponents in Israel and international Jewish communities and organizations. The incursions into al-Aqsa were repeated in 2022, with social media coverage showing IDF members inside the Dome of the Rock Mosque.

Campaigns drew attention to social activist influencers (who did not operate in the 'jihād zone'), such as twins Mohammed and Muna El-Kurd (1998-), whose online activities drew the ire of Israeli authorities – but also placed them in a *Time Magazine* listing of 100 Most Influential People of 2021.[118] Influencers confronted the Israeli narrative, especially significant given some pro-Israeli social media activists used hate speech.[119] There were serious concerns that social media platforms were censoring social media content amidst claims from platforms that technical issues were causing posts to be blocked.[120] The bombing of civilian targets in Gaza caused high casualties, part of efforts of (then prime minister) Benjamin Netanyahu's administration to distract from a crumbling power base and domestic agenda.

Many Muslim influencers outside of Palestine and Gaza, including those with Palestinian heritage, comment on the situation there. Influencers and commentators from other Muslim contexts were proactive too. Paradoxically, perhaps, there was criticism that some influencers from the United Arab Emirates, which in 2021 signed agreements with Israel known as the Abraham Accords, were endorsing and praising the role of the IDF [*sic*] and its police, suggesting that it was thwarting the protests of Hamas and protecting al-Aqsa.[121]

Influencers and opinions are complex and nuanced in zones where external expectations might suggest the opposite. The suggestion that the al-Aqsa demonstrations were connected to Hamas belied the specific issue of the Sheikh Jarrah neighbourhood, associated with a media strategy employed by some pro-Israel voices in a propaganda campaign incorporating stereotypical tropes of Arabs and Muslims. The more significant concern for the UAE was that political-religious parties might challenge their status quo if they were to confront Israeli actions in Palestine and Gaza. Ironically, there were voices within Israel and wider Jewish communities articulating their opposition to the attacks.

Online voices in Muslim contexts presented more predictable outpourings of Muslim anger against Israel's actions. Many were vocal during the 2021 attacks on Gaza. Influencers could take many forms: a 2018 meme series using the hashtag 'WeAreAllMary!' showed Palestinian women facing up to aggression from Israeli forces and citizens, often in conjunction with the hashtag #MotherPalestine, and a 2009 image of an elderly woman waving her walking stick in defiance at a refugee camp.[122]

By contact, video blogger Naseir Yassin published a blog a day for 1,000 days, in which he attempted to present a fresh perspective on Palestinian-Israeli relations from his position as an Israeli Arab, who (atypically) went through a privileged education in Harvard: 'Yassin's critics highlight that while he has aired his personal grievances about being restricted travel to Kuwait simply because he was born in Israel, he makes little mention in his videos of the millions of Palestinian refugees who do not hold a passport, nor those living in what has been described as the world's largest open air prison – the Gaza strip.'[123] Yassin built on the profile his blogging acquired to develop a social media production studio with international branches.[124] While he received criticism for allegedly downplaying the Palestinian conflict and religious issues in general, he identified as a Muslim Arab who happens to be an entrepreneur. In 2017 he was barred from travelling on Kuwaiti airlines because he held an Israeli passport. He saw himself as an intermediary between Israel and Arabs, motivated by inequities in his country of birth: 'I think that being a Palestinian in Israel opened my eyes to the other side and fostered a sense of empathy.'[125]

In typical fashion, Yassin produced a one-minute video in which he countered criticism that he was a 'bad Muslim', which received over a million views, but also substantial criticism in the 15,000+ comments for his implicit acceptance of alcohol, dating and homosexuality.[126] He talked about religion in a 2017 video, his 'Muslim' identity in a more 'humanistic' fashion and relations with and between other religions. He stressed his belief that religion should not be a 'sensitive' topic.[127] This is an interesting example of a religiously fluid identity manifest in an influencer with a Muslim background.

Engagement with the internet and computer industry has been significant for those in Palestine and Gaza, facilitating access to a wider world when travel and opportunities may be limited. The challenging situation for Israeli Arabs in general, and Muslims in particular, is relevant within discussions too. The use of social media has offered an outlet. Coding opportunities have, in some cases, also provided forms of industry and employment: when there was a mass Facebook outage in 2021, Palestinian computer entrepreneurs complained that this impacted dramatically on their businesses. Coding education programmes such as Gaza Sky Geeks enabled graduates to study technology and develop projects. It sought to create start-ups and self-employment opportunities. In many ways, this greatly influences attitudes and approaches towards social media and technology.[128]

The sector of civil voices, whose output may have a subtle religious underpinning, is relevant in terms of activism and influence in the Gaza and Palestine context – as shown in 2021. This is a part of a long-term media engagement associated with related issues but at times dependent on internet access and reductions of the digital divide.[129]

Contemporary Islamic influencers – Indonesia

Indonesia was chosen here as a case study for its relatively high levels of internet connectivity. Indonesian cyberspace offers insight into how digital Islamic influencers go through different levels of society, from 'top-down' official influence from religious bodies and authorities to less formal (but no less influential) platforms and style influencers presenting ideas about Islam and interpretation in the Indonesian context.[130] Shared issues may be interpreted very differently across the spectrum of understandings. Intricate lattice networks draw together diverse platforms of influencers, authorities, preachers and others online. Online authorities play multiple roles, building relationships with their audiences, as part of a 'preacher economy': 'Preaching today consists not only of talking to a religious crowd, whether directly or via electronic media, but also of personal exchanges between the preacher and his followers.'[131] The relatively high levels of net access in urban contexts through the ubiquitous cell phone are particularly relevant when exploring these networks of understanding.[132] There was also a discussion with Indonesian President Joko Widodo about the possibility of reciting the Qurʾān and daʿwah activities through a projected metaverse.[133]

Indonesia's population of 277,000,000 (2021) has an increasing urbanized population (56 per cent, 2000) with an increasing median age (29.7 years, 2000).[134] Indonesia's estimated population in 2015 at 87.1 per cent Muslim.[135] A 2019 survey noted that 64.8 per cent of the population were internet users (171.17 million).[136] Projected smartphone penetration of 70 per cent in 2020 did not imply internet penetration, as economic and network boundaries impacted on smartphone acquisition, along with the phenomena of multiple SIM card ownership not reflecting individual smartphone ownership.[137] Projections of digital access and smartphone ownership suggested substantial rises in an increasingly digitally literate demographic context. Inevitably, among the diverse online content available, there is a substratum of digital Islamic content available and, to an extent, embedded in the outputs and actions of various religious players.

Indonesian Islamic influencers conduct themselves in various zones, from commerce to fashion, fusing religious ideals and political activism with commercial considerations, demonstrating a fluid area between and within these areas. The traction is significant in terms of site traffic and impact, especially (but not exclusively) within Indonesian urban contexts. It is a competitive information marketplace for influence and ideas alongside internet zones with a less religious edge. Again, it cannot be assumed that all online activity in Indonesia is religiously based – especially given the diverse cultural-religious identities throughout the republic.

Gender plays a significant role, too, especially among audiences for influencers, where younger women follow diverse social media platforms to facilitate and engender forms of religiosity through digital and offline interaction.[138] A number of individuals could be classified within the religious influencer category in Indonesia, representing complex ideas and identities online. This includes female scholars presenting interpretative notions of authority, especially during the Covid-19 context in 2020–1.[139] Influence also transcends generations, among digitally fixated youth (or younger), even in relatively restricted contexts such as Islamic boarding schools, where media-literate children are exposed to influences beyond their traditional and cultural-religious frameworks.[140]

Influencers combine financial and religious elements in their output, such as the prominent example of stock-picker and *ustadz* Jam'an Nurchotib Mansur – otherwise known as Yusuf Mansur, whose 13 million followers pick up on his advice within the more 'halal' zones of trading.[141] Mansur's primary website combines diverse online and analogue modules on Islamic principles.[142] There are several Instagram pages (official and otherwise) and hashtags associated with Mansur.[143] Profiles of his activities included news of a blood transfusion he had received; he had a choice of donors but selected people who had memorized the Qur᾽ān.[144]

The Majelis Ulama Indonesia (MUI, Indonesian Ulema Council) is Indonesia's main Muslim clerical body. It comprises numerous Muslim platforms; this includes those with prominent roles in Indonesian society, such as Nahdlatul Ulama and Muhammadiyah, closely linked to Indonesian political-religious spheres of influence. The council contains smaller groups representing specific religious-political interests.[145] The MUI website is a hub for access to diverse strands of religious authority, delineated through subject-specific *ʿulamāʾ* sections, including faith, politics and economics. Several regional MUI offices are represented in this hub, focused on significant Muslim population areas in Indonesia. The impact of social media on moral values, such as honesty in digital economic issues and the distribution of rumours, was seen as a significant issue to be addressed by MUI through the distribution of an official statement.[146]

The impact of diverse social media in Indonesian contexts was reflected in the presence on Instagram of the MUI at national and regional levels. This channel included photos of key events, numerous award ceremonies, photos of the leadership 'in action' and notices of lectures and conferences promoting MUI agendas. Posts highlight the integration of technology in these contexts. While there is an emphasis on these easy-access visual materials throughout its social media, more serious agendas are found in the archives of religious opinions via the MUI webpages, through a searchable index of downloadable fatwas. The Dewan Syariah Nasional-Majelis Ulama Indonesia also provides detailed *fatāwā* associated with approaches to law and business in the Indonesian context – including PDFs of specific opinions. It can issue certification of *sharī*ʿa status on different transactions in financial and other contexts.[147]

MUI confronted issues associated with vaccines in 2018 through a fatwa issued against a measles vaccine because it allegedly contained cells from pork and human beings. This fatwa did not prevent the vaccine's use, given the significance of child immunization and a perceived lack of alternative options available.[148]

The MUI social media highlighted a 2021 webinar offering alternative herbal treatments for Covid-19, whose practitioners claimed would 'neutralise' Covid-19 – although they emphasized that they would require clinical trials.[149] Elsewhere, MUI provided an online version of their religious opinion on the permissibility of swabbing for Covid-19 during Ramaḍān. Separately, an opinion appeared on whether the Astra Zeneca vaccine was allowed following allegations that it contained pork-derived ingredients; the opinion was that it could be used, given the specific circumstances of Covid-19, but remained 'haram'. Its distribution was primarily to zones in Indonesia where most populations were not Muslim.[150]

The government was conscious of online influence during the initial utilization of vaccines, with high-profile influencers across Indonesian society prioritizing vaccination under the glare of the cameras. One influencer decided that the vaccination provided a licence to party afterwards, which might have been counterproductive for the campaign.[151]

MUI responded online to the Covid-19 situation by producing several opinions on religious practices, including participation in ḥajj, prayers for victims of the pandemic and the provision of fatwa guidelines for those medical staff wearing Personal Protection Equipment while praying. Some fatwas appeared as infographics, including a series relating to practices during ʿĪd ul-Fiṭr and adjustments for Covid-19, including integrating digital media into ritual activities.[152]

MUI has had close connections with Indonesian administrations. In 2019, the former MUI chair Maʿruf Amin (1943–) became Indonesia's vice president (to President Joko Widodo). In fact, in 2020, he sought MUI and other platforms to develop their religious responses in the form of fatwas associated with the Covid-19 situation.[153] Amin had also previously been the leader of Nahdlatul Ulama (NU), a Sunni organization associated with Shāfiʿī interpretations of Islam, which has sought to counter perceived 'Wahhabi' influences in Indonesia.[154] While Amin is an elder statesman in Indonesian political-religious circles, his supporters ensured that he had a social media impact with pages showing his profile and activities. His profile on Facebook suggests a 'man of the people', in a drawing showing him surrounded by generations of ethnically diverse Indonesians.[155] His Instagram page was particularly active: one post showed him (in animated form, with a mosque background) using a smartphone to promote mask-wearing in the population.[156] Elsewhere he was photographed having a vaccine, celebrating *ʿĪd* (on his phone, with his wife) and promoting education in the Covid-19 context. He kept a relatively low profile in Indonesian political contexts, focusing on religious issues.

NU, or 'awakening of the Islamic scholars', emerged in 1926 as a reaction to the events in Turkey, including the abolition of the caliphate, along with concerns about other influences emerging from Arabian contexts. NU presented a specific Indonesian identity and interpretation of Islam, with practices emphasizing outward religious practices.[157] NU sought to reconcile its origins as scholarly (*ʿulamāʾ*) defenders of traditional religious practices linked to Sufism with contemporary requirements of operating in 'democratic' systems. They contested different forms of 'radical' agendas, which presented themselves in Indonesia through violent events such as the 2002 Bali bombings, as well as responding to the international stage (as the nation with the highest Muslim population) to the events of 9/11.

NU's official page projected onto national and regional agendas, with sections on Islamic finance, commentaries on the Qur'ān, sermons, 'wisdom', traditional religious practices and news. It presents a modern image with a strong emphasis on social media and visual materials. There is considerable discussion about aspects of Sufi identity and 'Sufism', utilizing influential sources (such as al-Ghazālī) to provide accessible information. A 2021 search of the provincial page for Jawa Tengah (Central Java) showed nineteen articles in nine months about al-Ghazālī. This includes advice on how al-Ghazālī's thoughts could be integrated into everyday Islamic practices (such as how employers treat employees); al-Ghazālī's attitude towards those seeking to 'excommunicate' others through *takfīr* (suggesting people are infidels); and a discussion on how al-Ghazālī would memorize texts to preserve and protect their content.[158]

Sermons from NU draw together specific agendas and themes. In September 2019, this included approaches to ḥajj and 'appropriate' practices and a sermon focused on combatting racism. The central NU hub divides up into other provincial zones with their regional interests, which is demonstrated through diffuse content and approaches to news and events while maintaining core values and content: for example, the Banten pages focus on the province in Java (120 kilometres from Jakarta), with its own regional agenda, news and interests associated with religious practices and interpretations.[159]

In 2021 NU were promoting their 'Super App' for Android and iOS, to make this web content more accessible and user-friendly to mobile phone users (presumably focused on the younger demographic). It included links for news, sermons, ritual tutorials, prayer times and Sufi practices.[160] NU also promote the Dana Syariah 'Shariah Funds' app via its website, which offers people opportunities to invest in halal projects; these observe traditional prohibitions on *riba* (interest) in Islam by providing a chance to support a project and share in its returns financially. The app claims a 15–20 per cent return on project investments listed.[161]

Other interests also maintain firm internet profiles: Persyarikatan Muhammadiyah, founded by Ahmad Dahlan (1868–1923) in 1912, presents as a significant reformist religious organization with a specific education infrastructure, healthcare and religious provision that crosses Indonesia. Dahlan returned from ḥajj to promote interpretations focused on *tawḥīd* or the oneness of God. The Muhammadiyah's focus on education influences online activities, projecting concerns across educational, medical and business sectors.[162]

Key leadership associated with Muhammadiyah features on their main page, with a chain of authority linking back to Dahlan. The main website has featured internet radio streaming for several years while acting as a significant hub of news, religious advice, infrastructural information and networking. This includes promoting various educational and other endeavours and influencing the status and funding of its work across Indonesian provinces.[163] By 2021, an increasing amount of content was being produced in English and Arabic, emphasizing social media and multimedia and projecting specific Muhammadiyah worldviews to a broader audience.

The figure of Dahlan still permeates the site, with hagiographic essays detailing episodes of his life and feature works projecting Dahlan as an international figure with impact across Muslim contexts. There is a discussion of his interactions with ʿAbduh and Afghānī when living in Mecca, figures who influenced Dahlan's international outlook. According to the website, this is now projected in Muhammadiyah activities globally, including using the Tapak Suci martial art as a soft influence in Germany and Egypt.[164]

Muhammadiyah utilizes YouTube channels with animations and clips of activities (31k subscribers, although view numbers were relatively low in the hundreds at the time of writing). One clip in 2021 discussed approaches towards mask-wearing in mosques, using a dramatized encounter between two congregants in a mosque. It showed worshippers consulting their cell phones for Muhammadiyah's opinions.[165] Muhammadiyah initiated an online 'Command Centre' channel focused on Covid-19, updating infection numbers from their 'Aisyiyah' Hospital, providing detailed medical advice, saluting medical workers and suggesting in one video with infographics that breaking the chain of transmission was a religious duty.[166]

Muhammadiyah's president Haedar Nasir focused on traditional sources such as the Qurʾān and Sunnah to combat Covid-19 but also emphasized that a perceived lack of knowledge and distrust had influenced the spread. Muhammadiyah Chair Dadang Kahmad also countered the suggestion that Covid-19 represented a 'conspiracy' via the online resource: 'I think Muhammadiyah people don't use their mind if they say the COVID-19 is conspiracy. It's real. Many people have fallen sick, suffered from the virus, and passed away . . . People should be aware that we have to be cautious about the coronavirus and believe Allah also creates a tiny creature such as this virus'[167] Muhammadiyah draws on Instagram to present interpretations via sermons, with recordings and prayer times available and infographics highlighting key issues and agendas for the organization. Content includes photos and statements from regional and national leaders, reminders of practices, sayings and updates on events.[168]

Other figures utilize online media to project influence and authority: Rizieq Shihab (1965–) is styled as the 'Grand Imam' from Front Pembela Islam (FPI), the 'Islamic Defenders Front', which has had a prominent voice online in its campaigning and protests, including the application of social media to make threats. It led to FPI's banning from Twitter in 2017. Shihab had, in the past, pledged allegiance to Islamic State. FPI draws on ethnic conflict and conflicts with other religious perspectives in Indonesia. Its definition of *sharīʿa is* driven by an exclusionary approach towards the republic, conspiring through bombings and other attacks against the state and attacking Christian communities and leaders in Indonesia (including Jakarta's major Basuki Tjahaja Purnama Ahok in 2017).[169] In 2021, Shihab received a four-year sentence for making a YouTube video stating that he was healthy, although he had Covid-19. This was in addition to an earlier eight-month sentence for breaching Covid-19 regulations. Shihab had been in exile in Saudi Arabia, having fled Indonesia in 2017 following pornography and anti-state charges (later dropped) before he returned in 2020: 'In a streamed broadcast, Judge Khadwanto said Rizieq was guilty of "announcing false information and purposefully causing confusion for the public."'[170]

It led to supporters protesting in mass demonstrations on Jakarta's streets, coordinating protests through social media and presenting images and clips in real time.

Elsewhere, Al-Azhar and Morocco-trained scholar Abdul Somad Batubara (1977–) made an influential impact online through lectures on various religious issues, including hadith studies and Islamic jurisprudence, alongside significant contemporary issues impacting Muslims in Indonesia. As a university lecturer described as a 'digital scholar', he gained publicity for online lectures and comments, including controversial opinions associated with diversity issues.[171] The use of Instagram heightened his profile, alongside engagement in news-associated themes. With 1.85 million subscribers to his YouTube channel in 2021 and much higher audiences for his lectures, this marks Abdul Somad as a key Indonesian player in online opinions and interpretations. Content included a 'chatshow' format discussing Palestine issues, Qur'ān commentaries and special programming for Ramaḍān.[172]

Numerous other scholars vie for influence in Indonesian CIEs: Adi Hidayat (1984–) is a traditionally oriented scholar who founded Quantum Akhyar Institute and embedded social media into every element of his programming activities. Content included personable lectures and discussions on principles of faith, some recorded in front of substantial live audiences or part of streamed activities. Images on the Instagram page reflect more intimate discussions on Islam.[173] During the pandemic context, where restrictions on live events were restricted, imagery focused on specific campaigns and issues – such as Palestine and responses to Covid-19. One lecture series asked, 'Who are the Jews?', exploring Jews in the context of the Muḥammad, regarding hadith sources, before bringing the issue of Israel into the contemporary context.[174] There is product placement on these pages, too, with books and other reference works available for download onto phones via the Quantum Akhyar Store. Such placement is not unique to Hidayat and suggests one way to make the platforms more sustainable through offline integrated (paid and free) content.

Qur'ān reciter Muzammil Hasballah's social media promotes his own Qur'ān app of specially recorded material, available offline as MP3 content.[175] Hasballah built a reputation for recitation recordings, which feature across his social media channels, with (in July 2021) approaching 4 million followers on Instagram. His channel included endorsements for various clothing ('MoslemWear'), Islamic books, watches, sunscreen, toiletries and other products. Family members are also brought into the pictures.[176] The core of Hasballah's influential social media impact is high-quality audio-visual recordings of recitations; the YouTube channel shows videos reaching 21 million views for some *suwar* recitations, across a subscription base of over 2 million subscribers (July 2021). Within three days, one three-hour recording reached 50,000 views.[177] Hasballah reflects his lifestyle on Islamic lines, endorsing Islamic products and family values along with way, in sync with his social media and recitation output.

There is a substantial market for online 'Islamic' products: Quran Best Indonesia & Waktu Sholat is officially certified by the Indonesian Ministry of Religion, with specific elements showcasing recitation and translation, enabling individuals to develop their own recitation through daily recording, reaching personal recitation targets to increase worship. Audio recitation includes reciters familiar from other apps, with high profiles throughout Muslim contexts, such as Abdul Rahman al-Sudais and Saad al-Ghamidi. The standard Mushaf Arabic font used in Indonesia is presented on this app, which gives the online product similarity to the printed version, along with its use of the universal Rasm Al-'Uthmani font found in many editions of the Qurʾān (in Arabic).[178]

Influencers from the entertainment and arts project Islamic lifestyles and values, integrating these into social media output. For example, soap actress and singer Shireen Sungkar's 23 million Instagram followers are exposed to Islamic aphorisms, hijab fashion shoots and product placements, such as halal toothpaste, clothes-washing technology and medical apps for chatting with doctors.[179]

Wardah Maulana and Natta Reza represent an influencer couple showing Islamic lifestyle choices across social media: Wardah (who is fully veiled) is represented as a 'brand ambassador' and 'entrepreneur', especially in terms of hijab, veils and other fashions – with a special channel dedicated to clothing, including individual designers. Her Instagram channel – with 2.2 million followers in 2023 – shows 'everyday' activities and product placements alongside her husband, Natta Reza, whose own trajectory includes a singing career. Images and products are interspersed with quotations from the Qur'ān and hadith. This can include promotions for food items, toothpaste and slimming drinks.[180]

In 2021, Wardah was embroiled in controversy by (allegedly) stating that her husband could take another wife, as she had been unable to conceive, a statement later suggested as a misinterpretation. Wardah shows Natta Reza indulging in his hobby of riding motorbikes (wearing designer trainers), praying prior to riding off.[181] Natta Reza promotes a range of goods too and uses a video blog to chart motorbike excursions and other digressions. His music videos attract tens of millions of views, such as 'Kekasih Impian' ('Dream Lover'), which features Reza in prayer, in the quest for a (veiled) woman (who provides him with a phone number after a café encounter), alongside a religiously themed soundtrack. This tenuous association with music video culture and religious values concludes with Reza in front of an imam, getting married. This is reflected in a caption, noting his 2017 official marriage to Wardah, and promoting a related book on the subject.[182] By 2023, Wardah and Reza's channels were dominated by baby photographs (a new 'influencer'?), which may indicate a recalibration of their influencer status – but also new market opportunities for lifestyle choices, travel photos and products.

The complexities of influencers in Islamic contexts can be extended to Hijrah Fest, which draws upon the 'hijrah' as it relates to Muḥammad's journey from Mecca to Medina and the establishment of the first Muslim community-state, but now has a transformative or transitive connotation. The term's uses reflect in this context new customs, ideas of ritual and appearance which go beyond conventional approaches in Indonesia. The use of informal language targets young people in urban contexts, relating through cultural themes as a way of attracting audiences. Hijrah Fest, with associated Hijrah Squad (male) and Hijrah Squad (female) promoted religious gatherings through the use of social media, projecting a contemporary identity to Indonesian Muslim youth.[183]

Hanan Attaki (1981–) attracted audiences via Pemuda Hijrah from 'alternative' cultures in Indonesia, associated with urban sports such as skateboarding and parkour, while generating counter-music culture interest from punks and other communities.[184] This is represented in the online output associated with its associated campaigns and events, including an anti-alcohol drive and youth-friendly alternatives. A 2015 poster for a lecture featured a mock-up of a vodka bottle, with the label changed to advertise the speaker of a study event (Ustadz Evie).[185]

This movement of hijrah (in its contemporary sense) includes aspects of dress code, with a Punk Hijrah shop presenting religious messages with a punk ethos. This links into the ethos of Taqwa Core presented in the work of Michael Muhammad Knight and developments in American Muslim punk music. Strikingly, images used by Punk Hijrah showed youth in Converse trainers praying and a muezzin with a Mohican haircut.[186] Punk Hijrah showed graphics of tattooed hands in supplication for prayer and a Marshall amp retitled 'Marishalat'.[187] A further hashtag for #punkhijrah on Instagram showed similar images, coupled with religious quotes, such as hadith suggesting that anyone can pray to God (implying this could include a punk).[188]

Section conclusion

The role of influencers in the Indonesian contexts demonstrates diversity, albeit with the underlying affiliation with (aspects of) Indonesian religious identities. There is complexity and the sense that digital frameworks are embedded in many of the projections of knowledge and understanding located online. This is represented in broad religious structures of interpretation and authority, to significant political-religious players and to those projecting lifestyles (and products) within the more conventional framework of influencers in the wider social media context. This is not necessarily a 'top-down' model of projection, especially where audiences for content from individuals might surpass that of the more traditional organizations and platforms, even if the latter can invest time and resources into digital output and activities.

Engineered photo opportunities and staged selfies reflect more on the legacy of print media than the conventions of contemporary social media. The output of influencers can fall under the umbrella of 'entertainment' or 'edu-tainment', competing with other media forms and online outputs, in contexts where religiously oriented memes and tropes mean more than the sermons and statements of scholars. The digital religious marketplace has opened to new and hybrid forms of presenting an Islamic message, integrating (in some cases) music, comedy, cooking, product placement and travelogues. The importance of the 'personality' and their digital literacy may have a greater impact than any formal religious credentials.

Notions of spirituality and religiosity exist under the surface of these outputs and expose audiences to new forms of religious messages and understandings. Unpacking the code (digital and religious) provides insights into the dynamics of online influence. Given the tens of thousands of possible sites and streams, which change on a daily (or hourly) basis, the individual researcher is faced with the challenge of how to approach this content. Snapshots of trends and key issues can give introductory insights into mapping a digital territory, which can then be further developed in more detailed research. There is a body of researchers working in Indonesia undertaking such activities. It is significant to try to record the landscape and diary the developments, for current and future readers, especially as much of the internet (especially the World Wide Web) is not archived and instead presents a transitory and ethereal space of ever-changing conversations, trends, news and content. This forms the basis for any future Indonesian Islamic metaverses, given the popularity of digital content and levels of online development in the area, especially as different platforms and products seek to assert their dominance in shifting technological frameworks. Whether these metaverses move beyond the rhetoric and hype of political-religious statements into reality is open to question.

Islamgram: Memes and religious influence

There are also different ways of accessing information, especially on social media. For younger demographics, the importance of memes as a means of quickly transmitting religious ideas is significant, giving them a particular influence. It is not without irony in the context of this discussion that we discover that Richard Dawkins – not noted for his appreciation of Islam – devised the term 'memeplexes': 'Memes are multimodal artifacts that combine image with text, usually have an uncertain and popular origin, no attributed authorship and are perfect examples of participatory media since readers are free to reproduce, appropriate and modify them.'[189]

The memes follow the format and patterns from other memes generated by apps such as Mematic, in which text can be added to a set of images that often appear on other meme pages and contexts.[190] Memes have already been referred to earlier in this volume about approaches towards Islamic law. AI offers alternative methods of generating memes and avatars. They feature across platforms, especially TikTok, Instagram and Reddit.

Rahat Ahmed explored diverse memes on varied themes in 2016, including differences in faith perspectives and 'Islamophobia'. He noted that there was no specific contradiction between humour and religious values. 'One thing to note is that none of these are making fun of Islam or its rules. The juxtaposition may be the core of the humor but underneath it is a sincere belief in the values expressed.'[191]

Memes raised differential Muslim perspectives between and within specific interpretations of religious practice, such as differing prayer rituals or timings.[192] Memes emerged from diverse Islamic perspectives to encapsulate complex points (in some cases) with familiar images aimed at a specific demographic. Their level of influence may be substantial in this sector too. They appeared in numerous locations, focusing on religious issues combined with humour. They offer an alternative perspective on long-standing themes and arguments; a futuristic meme noted that – in 2077 – it would be possible to pray everywhere and 'Air Jordans have security when u go to the Mosque', but it was still not clear when Ramaḍān commences (a long-standing issue of dispute, depending on the school of interpretation and location of an individual).[193]

There can be an integration of cinematic themes, such as a praying Spiderman or a 'Fasting and Furious' poster based on the *Fast and Furious* franchise.[194] Characters from Marvel films and comics feature as a sub-genre in social media, for example, with the spectacular 'Avengers: Ramadhan Infinity' poster, which placed Marvel characters in Islamic contexts and costumes.[195] Another image showed Muslim women dressed as Marvel superheroes, adapted for hijab dress codes.[196] Some memes have specific focal points on gender and Islam, such as highlighting dress code issues or the 'rationale' for preventing women from receiving a university education.[197]

Marvel and DC Comic characters both featured marking the death of Marvel founder Stan Lee at a 'funeral' featured on a meme. Some comments on Facebook asked why this was observed when Stan Lee was not a Muslim. Others discussed whether the Hulk was observing the appropriate dress code.[198] Some memes focus on gender and Islam, highlighting dress code issues or the 'rationale' for preventing women from receiving a university education. These can explore dress code issues, relationships and comments on the pressures of being a Muslim in non-Muslim contexts.[199] In the interest of balance, DC characters also feature in memes, such as a comic of a Muslim Superman produced by Justbrozz, who regularly produces four-frame comics on Islamic themes through Instagram, which circulated elsewhere; in this comic, the Muslim Superman is unable to wake up for Fajr prayer.[200] Some memes did not emphasize reproducing the human form, keeping their memes textual, partly in conformity with their interpretation of religious values.[201]

Memes can also be applied to attack Islam and Muslims. An image of a woman in a burqah captioned 'Dear atheists, You'll be First' indicated the tone of some meme areas.[202] Star Wars-associated memes were applied in negative depictions of Muslims; an image of Luke Skywalker, Obi-Wan Kenobi and R2D2 looking over Mecca, with the caption 'You'll never find a more wretched hive of scum and villainy' is one of many examples.[203] The presence of Muslim actor Rizwan Ahmed in the Star Wars film 'Rogue One' also generated negative memes.[204]

Memes were associated with anti-Muslim sentiments and 'Islamophobia' in various zones, especially in responses to specific world events associated (however obliquely) with Muslims. Memes became part of jihād-oriented discourse associated with the 'Islamic State' and against it and other militaristic jihād entities.[205] The term '*taqiyya*' or dissimilitude became the subject of anti-Muslim memes when used to suggest secret 'third column' Muslim conspiracies against other societies.[206]

Memes were also applied to counter negativity; an example is Ordinary Muslim Man. This is based on a stock image of a male Muslim, with a provocative headline (usually a stereotype) then countered by a strapline in the lower third of the photograph. It achieved prominence in 2011, with headlines such as 'I am Da Bomb' and the strapline 'at making falafels'.[207]

In 2019, a meme series featuring American Muslim politician Ilhan Oman (1982–) adjacent to quotations purportedly from 'the Qur'ān' gained traction online, which were, in fact, from misrepresentations and distortions of the text that had their origins in an anti-Islam website from 2005. These quotations were compared with the language from the Qur'ān, demonstrating that materials had been mistranslated, misappropriated and selectively edited. They had been applied in a negative way for Ilhan Oman, to suggest that she shared the negative values of this 'Qur'ān', and in a way that was also impactful on broader Muslim constituencies in terms of perpetuating long-standing tropes and stereotypes.[208] There were echoes with the case of the SuraLikeIt website, which emerged in 1998, and became a much-circulated online 'source' for fabricated 'translations' from 'the Qur'ān', presenting sources which did not exist.[209] Stylistically they bore little relation to the Qur'ān, but for susceptible readers, they became a focal point for the manifestation or formulation of prejudice. Attempts were made to remove the pages from the internet by Muslim platforms, which only heightened their profile and publicity, while Al-Azhar University responded by launching a complaint and establishing its counter webpage (which was largely ineffective at the time). The site's closure on one platform only led to its reproduction on others. Over twenty years after the controversy, it remains relatively straightforward to locate the verses online.

Memes became a significant adjunct to other forms of expression about Islam and Muslims. They effectively convey substantial amounts of information in a compact and memorable way, whether a discussion on aspects of Islamic law or a means to counter negativity about Islam. Simple images, such as a woman in a hijab on a skateboard, may resonate across diverse audiences.[210] Anime is applied to generate memes and other images, part of popular culture trends and synthesis across diverse cultural contexts while recognizing that not all interpretations accept the representation of facial features in pictures (so leave these elements blank).[211] A series of images drawing on and adapting Disney figures (and adding hijabs) is part of the meme-verse, alongside adaptations of the Mona Lisa.[212] Religious messages in a single frame have been presented across religious traditions and interpretations through different influencer channels, on Pinterest, Instagram and other platforms.

They are simply the latest in a long chain of communication forms which have articulated messages about the religion and its believers over the centuries. The earliest fragments of the Qur'ān were recorded on rocks and animal skins; now, they are digital artefacts. It is only a matter of time before the imagery is further developed: non-fungible tokens (NFTs) may become a way of capturing ideas about religious expressions – such as artistic calligraphic rendering of the Qurʾān – and projecting them into the metaverse.

Influence and influencers: Concluding point

The internet and digital lifestyle concerns are pervasive within religious and cultural contexts and integrated into broader conversations about Islam, identity, authority and interpretation within contemporary contexts. Many influencers who identify as Muslim have content which is not specifically focused on religious issues. These may reflect specific religious values and tropes as part of the cultural contexts they emerged from. Contemporary influencers and issues represent continuity with earlier generations discussed in this book but also push innovative patterns of digital utilization and integration within CIEs. These inform future online developments, as technology edges towards concepts surrounding any projected metaverse. They demonstrate a fluidity of approaches and identities associated with being Islam and Muslim online, in some cases reflecting ideas of cosmopolitanism and multiple identities, rather than binary understandings and interpretations of religion and spirituality. Influencers also play a role in their potential to appear high up in search hierarchies, generated by generic search algorithms as well as site-specific internal search engines and mechanisms. These go beyond browsers, into diverse online platforms, where Instagram and TikTok increasingly dominate digital activities. These interfaces are shaping the ways in which Islam is articulated, through activities of influencers whose embedded digital literacy is shaping and constantly evolving within CIEs.

Chapter 11

ISLAMIC ALGORITHMS AND META MUSLIM FUTURES

This book investigated influences on Islam and Muslim communities to determine how they are presented in digital contexts, to understand whether legacies have been maintained online and how digital media have shaped the articulation of diverse religious influences across space and time. It has also looked at how contemporary influences and influencers present their ideas about Islam in digital formats and the connections between influential sources and these modern frameworks of dissemination and transmission of religious knowledge and ideals. These influence notions of Islamic algorithms, informing discourse, searchability and digital networking. They also underpin future CIEs, including projected metaverses (or equivalent concepts) which may transmit specific Muslim identities as well as fluid ideas of how Islamic lifestyles can be projected.

These CIEs may be 'filtered' by traditional forms of religious authority, or 'unfiltered' voices unendorsed by conventional frameworks of interpretation and power. This extends questions of the qualifications deemed necessary (by some authorities) to interpret aspects of Islam and movements which have sought to promote pragmatic personal interpretations through *ijtihād*, especially on those issues not directly mentioned in the Qur'ān and other Islamic sources. The veracity of opinions, interpretations and information is challenged in online environments, especially in an era where disinformation circulates rapidly (potentially generated by bots and AI). Of course, this can work both ways with counter information grounded in content from CIEs, potentially including those discussed in this book. The methods through which AI 'scrapes' information continue to evolve, with more depth and breadth of sites being integrated into massive databases. While the Islam-related content is a small component of the overall data, it will have an impact and influence on those seeking to use AI to inform themselves about different aspects of Islam and Muslim societies.

The multitude of online voices, influences and influencers presented in the book reflects a snapshot of these contemporary Islamic diversities. These will form the foundation of future iterations of CIEs, as part of Muslim metaverses (or simply the next versions of 'cyberspace') which will project complexities of Islamic discourse across diverse formats and virtual worlds. The concepts associated with metaverses may be ambiguous, but whatever form they take, they will be informed by Islamic algorithms of search and influence and created with the roles of influencers in mind. The rationale, as questioned in relation to generic metaverses in general, is linked to the ongoing search for Islam, religious knowledge, identities and authority.[1] The technological interfaces become a means towards these objectives within projected metaverses, a small part of wider digital innovation and activity positioned around future iterations of the World Wide Web.

The essence of religious encounters and experiences may permeate future Muslim metaverses, in a way that would be recognized in non-digital contexts. On one level, readers can ask whether there is continuity with previous generations and understandings in transmitting religious ideas, or does the digital development suggest an epoch-shifting period (depending on context)? In some cases, digital influences are impinging on Islamic development, understanding, faith and propagation. Determining how these influences work within future digital contexts can be problematic: networks do not conform to the neat geometric patterns in Islamic science, mathematics and architecture – as found in art and mosque design. Key figures can act as pivotal figures or points within the latticework pattern of influences which are not neat but distorted.

This complexity may not have been so prevalent when Habermas constructed his ideas about information flow and influence. Still, the concepts retain relevance regarding the impact on the public sphere and the potential for passive consumption.[2] Lawrence's emphasis on studying the 'messy' interconnectivity at various societal levels has proven relevant within this book's discussion, as has the de-centring from MENA contexts of studies of Islam and Muslims.[3] The fluid and non-binary elements of religious identities and complexities explored by Lawrence (and Hodgson) as part of 'Islamicate' frameworks have also been relevant, especially as many of the CIEs under investigation present these in overt or subtle ways.[4] Complexity and diversity are significant elements within any discourse on CIEs. Patel's consideration of the importance of 'authenticity' and audience expectations within these zones are relevant and worthy of further investigation in other focused work, especially focused on disinformation issues and legitimacy concerns.[5] This fits with Echchaibi's exploration of the idea of 'celebrity' religious figures, which is an issue when looking at influence and influencer issues and can be extended across space and time in consideration of significant historical figures.[6] These elements may be more significant than any focus on e-jihād, even though that remains a focal point for much academic, political and media discourse about Islam and Muslims. In this work, e-jihād is a small but relevant pixel within a high-resolution picture whose exclusion might impact a more comprehensive vision of religion, identities and practices. Agendas shift: influence and influencers clearly play a significant role, as demonstrated by the emergence of the 'red pill' movement heralded by Andrew Tate and impacting some younger Muslim males' perspectives on gender roles and relationships.

Not all the influence points connect, recognize or identify with each other. There are intellectual links, with Allāh as the ultimate influence. There might be more scope for a neater pattern within specific networks and micro-networks where there can be potential to bring continuity between all these points. There is also a continuity between influences, reflected in narratives, imagery and shared interpretations back to specific sources and figures, albeit with different emphasis. This goes back before Muḥammad to many prophets and figures, along with non-human entities such as angels and jinn. The relationship between these sources and internet developments is one now discussed in scholarly circles, on occasion with controversial results. In 2022 al-Azhar scholar Mabrook Atiyah suggested that the Qur'ān refers to Facebook and the internet and provided a textual analysis to 'prove' it.[7] This was a fringe opinion unrepresentative of nor shared by others across Islamic contexts.

However, the Qur'ān as the Revelation from God received by Muḥammad via the Angel Jibrīl could be analogous to Islam's source code which filters through CIEs, including Facebook and the internet and will continue to be articulated through diverse Islamic metaverses. The extent to which this could contribute to religious 'experience', for example, through the use of virtual reality glasses, is open to question. The evocative sounds of recitations heard within virtual mosques, alongside multiple digital congregations, may have a greater impact than earlier attempts (e.g. through Second Life) at creating virtual mosques and religious activities online. In part this will be in line with technological advancements and increased access, as well as new forms of immersive multi-sensory experiences promised in future iterations of the metaverse. Artificial Intelligence offers potential construction of new forms of 'Islamic' environments, such as artistic renderings of futuristic mosques in science fiction inspired landscapes.

By 2023, AI chatbots such as OpenAI's ChatGPT offered potential to answer questions on any subject – including Islamic issues – and receive an instant informed response. Answers were generated through system access to generic databases, predicated by the input question (and, of course, who put the content into the generic database). Responses to questions asked on Islamic issues indicated a reliance on standard encyclopaedias and wikis, but this may change over time as the tool develops.[8] There is also considerable potential for fake news and disinformation (including about Islam and Muslim issues) to be generated by AI as a reinforcement of anti-Muslim prejudice and stereotyping online.[9] There were concerns that Chat AI apps contain, in some cases, inherent anti-Muslim prejudices which were problematic to remove – being contained in the AI's 'training'.[10] This is concerning as search engines compete to integrate AI interfaces into their platforms.[11]

So, can we talk about 'Islamic algorithms', in which multiple interfaces connect with Islam in general and the essence of Islam in particular? Why should digital devices be different to other forms of mediation? The word of God is filtered by algorithmic elements impacting how the Qur'ān is processed and experienced across multimedia, echoing *Sūrah al-Qāf* in the Qur'ān, in which Allāh indicates greater proximity to humanity than the jugular vein.[12] This could be linked to the sense that the divine essence is contained in all things, even digital devices and electronics, and across cyber networks.

Inevitably, whether this is an appropriate analogy in this context depends on world views and approaches. Does the question emerge of the extent to which digital artefacts and objects possess an intrinsic sacred value, such as filmed sermons, Qur'ān apps, Sufi ritual clips, Shī'a religious imagery and religious activities in general? Arjuna's consideration that these might have a commercial edge is also relevant.[13] Within these contexts, an undercurrent should reflect diversity in practices described by observers and (at times) practitioners as 'Islam', which may also incorporate aspects of religious charisma, charm and inspiration that seek to transmit their qualities across digital interfaces. This may counter assumptions that focus on legalistic and doctrinal positions associated with religious practices that consider aspects of esoteric ritual understandings as 'innovations' or 'un-Islamic'.

Notions of online and offline have blurred in contexts where digitally literate individuals (and their devices) are always on. The extent to which this impacts ideas of the sacred and articulating religion requires the extension of theoretical approaches to religion in cyberspace in general and CIEs in particular. The concept of a compartmentalized 'cyberspace' seems dated within articulations of a (forthcoming) metaverse environment.

The suggestion that (Web3+) 'meta' internet will form the technological transition towards a more decentralized digital context, promising online identities and digital integration within metaverses, goes beyond the control of the primary tech industry players and may also emerge in Islamic contexts. The blending may be more profound and integrated, reducing the separation between analogue and virtual contexts. This would suggest a richer experience within virtual worlds, where Muslims may observe sermons and prayers through Web3 interfaces and pay charity through Bitcoin or Blockchain could be taken up several levels in terms of digital experience. However, this is speculative at the time of writing, a form of religious sci-fi, but something that may evolve rapidly in line with the understanding that technological interfaces and internet applications are not going to plateau or stagnate.

One approach is to consider a breakdown of CIEs within granulated studies so that these patterns can become more 'ordered' than 'messy' (if, indeed, that is desirable). Over time, Islamic networks and affiliations will be the subject of more nuanced approaches and meaningful studies – a process that is already commencing.[14] This is not to suggest that the sites, organizations and networks are not themselves intrinsically 'messy', neither is the intention to project an order that is not there onto these CIEs. There is a need to explore further the dissemination strategies and processes among organizations and platforms, where digital materials are fully integrated into discourse about profound and mundane religious concerns. This factor was amplified during the Covid-19 crisis but was undoubtedly a phenomenon before then. One should not generalize, but some parties emphasized digital connectivity with greater intensity after the pandemic. And now the audiences are aware of these various outputs, it might be difficult or impossible to put the digital jinn back in the bottle.

The extent to which there are shifts within core interpretations and values is important, especially where there is decentralization in authority models. Key players hold onto authority by amplifying the digital output in many cases and integrating it into organizations where, in terms of their users and demographics, an increasing proportion are, in many cases, digital natives. Those seeking forms of influence and control will increasingly seek to mediate aspects of CIEs, including algorithmic search (directing the seeker to specific knowledge strands) and the spiritual architecture and ownership of metaverses.

Attempts to mediate or provide gatekeeping options that reflect specific cultural and religious outlooks within communities are not necessarily successful. There can be intergenerational disconnects based on differences in ideas and approaches to knowledge and more prosaic factors such as digital literacy limitations. The competitive nature of online content, the need to ensure the design is fresh and navigable and the constant demands for immediacy and identity/affiliation with networks and causes have meant that opportunities for reading about alternative world views and interpretations have extended exponentially with the reduced digital divide and increases in digital literacy.

Exploring influences and influencers enables consideration of new network shaping and how this is reflected in analogue contexts, especially how pre-digital networks have responded to and adapted their messages to suit digital outputs. This is increasingly a factor, with the impact of the changing digital divide opening broader and better access to online content in multiple forms. There is an equation here in terms of access and technology shifts predicated on wealth and early adoption of newer forms of digital interfaces, including those technologies associated with the promised (if not heralded) metaverse of wearable tech and integrated devices, offering integrated access to Islamic (and other) metaverses. The extent to which these will alter approaches to CIEs will be significant to observe in future research, especially across diverse zones and cultural-linguistic frameworks.

Individual Muslim metaverses may offer integrated interfaces and experiential dimensions, but as with other areas of CIEs, there are issues of control of content and perspectives. The internet can be a means to control and promote state mechanisms of specific interpretations of the Qurʾān and ideas. Some might say this stops the spread of 'subversive', 'radicalisation' and/or 'un-Islamic' perspectives. The mechanisms are in the eyes of the beholder regarding whether such limitations are desirable within societies. The presence of state actors in these zones extends to academic investigations encouraged by governmental agencies to develop 'understandings' and (in some cases) mechanisms of control, censorship and submission. This may be in Muslim-majority contexts but can equally apply elsewhere. Islamic religious authorities can utilize online content to mobilize and reinforce agendas to synergize 'approved' forms of practices and discourse. As the digital divide reduces, this increasingly becomes an issue across diverse Muslim contexts. Along with other digital sectors, Muslim metaverses will compete with each other, but also with wider platforms and content (way beyond the parameters of Islam) as part of complex infotainment marketplaces.

There are also issues regarding crypto-digital-ḥalāl contexts and how online payments are made for religious transactions while avoiding interest. There are examples of the use of digital transactions, for instance, in ʿĪd al-ʾAḍḥā as a means of financing sacrifices of animals and the use of digital transactions in *zakāh* and other forms of donation. There are some critical concerns regarding the production of cryptocurrencies, Islamic fintech and the use of blockchain in Islamic contexts, reaching back to conventional financial principles and *sharīʿa* compliance, as well as consideration of the environmental impacts of crypto production.

Muslim financial behaviours, from individual to corporate level, became increasingly bound into digital constructs. Cryptocurrencies had become a major market in the Middle East and North Africa by 2022, while economically depressed Muslim-majority zones increasingly became proactive in the use of cryptocurrencies, such as in Afghanistan, Palestine, Lebanon and Turkey. A 'halal' crypto coin was also being touted on a blockchain exchange.[15] However, cryptocurrency and related technologies were proving to be volatile and unpredictable, so it is difficult to determine what their medium to long-term impact might be in CIE context.

These products point towards broader issues regarding the ethics of technology products, including disposability of devices, ecological implications, server environmental impact, data security concerns, personal security and identity, Virtual Private Networks (VPNs), hacking and cracking and surveillance issues across digital interfaces. It is essential to consider how digital influences will inform strategy and apply new approaches to CIEs. Other technologies will be used. These might impact ritual, networking, organization, symbolism, practice, interpretation, propagation and control.

In many ways, this is continuity with pre-digital contexts in terms of exploring ideas about Islam and Muslims in society. One cannot be reductive and compartmentalized across such diversity. However, what can be done is to analyse and observe how influencers, whose impact can be predicated by Islamic algorithms, apply digital communication and dissemination methods to promote specific Islamic world views within CIEs. This will continue to require an intensity of analysis and scholarship so that its mediation can be comprehended, catalogued and understood within shifting technological and religious contexts. The methodologies for doing this vary, and this field will benefit from a range of perspectives from academia and observers with diverse skill sets, religious outlooks and world views. There is potential for conversations on these phenomena, which potentially engender greater understanding and mutual respect between and within different Muslim groups and affiliations, as well as between Muslims and those with other identities. In an era of disinformation, fake news and instant digital reactions to what are, in many cases, unsubstantiated social media rumours, such consideration can only be seen as a small but positive development, especially if filtered up to wider audiences.

CIEs remain an element for understanding and interpreting Islamic developments across diverse zones. Influences, both historical and contemporary, have continuity within these CIEs. Voices from the past play a role here, where the heroes and ghosts of interpretation and authority play, in some cases, a revived role in discourse through how digital content presents them to new audiences and captures attention through different forms of multimedia. At a personal level, notions of spirituality and religious expression may be profoundly impacted and influenced by digital interfaces and content. Those searching for Allāh and Islam will be influenced by the algorithms that underpin the internet, which have digital and human factors behind the functions. This constantly shifting context does not fit into neat boxes for analysis. CIEs will transform, develop and continue to mutate over the coming decades, probably in unanticipated directions. Continuity of monitoring and analysis is an integral part of the development of responses and approaches towards understanding Islam, Muslims and contemporary societies. In increasingly digital worlds and metaverses, Islamic algorithms will continue to impact and influence Muslim discourse and understanding for generations to come.

NOTES

Introduction

1 Gary R. Bunt, *Virtually Islamic: Computer-Mediated Communication and Cyber Islamic environments* (Cardiff: University of Wales Press, 2000).
2 Gary R. Bunt, *iMuslims: Rewiring the House of Islam* (Chapel Hill: University of North Carolina Press, 2009), 1.
3 Benj Edwards, 'Remember BBSes? Here's How You Can Visit One Today', *How-To Geek*, 24 August 2021, https://www.howtogeek.com/686600/remember-bbses-heres-how-you-can-visit-one-today/, Christopher Helland, 'Popular Religion and the World Wide Web', in *Religion Online: Finding Faith on the Internet*, edited by Douglas E. Cowan and Lorne L. Dawson (New York: Routledge, 2004), 24–5. Howard Rheingold, *The Virtual Community: Homesteading on the Electronic Frontier* (Reading: Addison-Wesley Pub. Co., 1993).
4 IslamiCity, 'Islam and the Global Muslim eCommunity', http://www.islamicity.com (accessed 13 October 2004). Note: I have transliterated and Romanized key terms and historical individuals, but generally avoided romanization of contemporary figures, using instead the spellings from their online content (while acknowledging variations).
5 Dale F. Eickelman and James Piscatori, *Muslim Politics* (Princeton: Princeton University Press, 1996). Peter G. Mandaville, *Transnational Muslim Politics: Reimagining the Umma* (London and New York: Routledge, 2001). Gary R. Bunt, 'Surfing Islam: Ayatollahs, Shayks and Hajjis on the Superhighway', in *Religion on the Internet: Research Prospects and Promises*, edited by Jeffrey K. Hadden and Douglas E. Cowan (New York: Elsevier Science, 2000).
6 Gary R. Bunt, 'Islamic Studies Pathways (archived site, 24 April 2000)', https://web.archive.org/web/20000816224231/http://www.lamp.ac.uk/cis/pathways/pathways.html.
7 Gary R. Bunt, 'Cyber Islam (Keynote paper)', in *British Society for Middle Eastern Studies 1998 Confererence, 'Religion and Pluralism'*, Selly Oak Colleges, University of Birmingham
8 Eric Ravenscraft, 'What Is the Metaverse, Exactly?' *Wired*, 25 April 2022, https://www.wired.com/story/what-is-the-metaverse/.
9 Nina Xiang, *Parallel Metaverses: How the US, China and the Rest of the World are Shaping Different Virtual Worlds* (Amazon Digital Services LLC: Independently Published, 2022).
10 Kari Paul, 'Facebook Announces Name Change to Meta in Rebranding Effort', *The Guardian*, 28 October 2021, https://www.theguardian.com/technology/2021/oct/28/facebook-name-change-rebrand-meta.
11 Herman Narula, *Virtual Society: The Metaverse and the New Frontiers of Human Experience* (London: Penguin Business, 2022), xviii.

Chapter 1

1 See the discussion here: Islamweb, 'Seek Knowledge Even if it was in China (Fatwa 92268)', https://www.islamweb.net/en/fatwa/92268/seek-knowledge-even-if-it-was-in-china. Also see Islam Stack Exchange, 'What did Prophet Muhammad mean by "Seek Knowledge Even as far as China"?', 2 January 2018, https://islam.stackexchange.com/questions/22909/what-did-prophet-muhammad-mean-by-seek-knowledge-even-as-far-as-china. This suggests that this ḥādīth is fabricated, and that its true version was: 'Seeking Knowledge is Obligatory upon Every Muslim' (220. Classed as saheeh by al-Albaani in Saheeh Sunan Ibn Maajah).

2 Bahman Mehri, 'From Al-Khwarizmi to Algorithm', *Olympiads in Informatics*, no. Special Issue (2017): 71–4, https://doi.org/10.15388/ioi.2017.special.11.

3 Kate Crawford, *Atlas of AI: Power, Politics, and the Planetary Costs of Artificial Intelligence* (New Haven and London: Yale University Press, 2021), 78. This refers to image capture issues but raises similar concerns on data's integrity and 'objectivity' (if desired).

4 Stephen Lucci and Danny Kopec, *Artificial Intelligence in the 21st Century. A Living Introduction* (Dulles: Mercury Learning and Information, 2016), 298–309.

5 Jaron Lanier, 'There is no AI', *The New Yorker*, 20 April 2023, https://www.newyorker.com/science/annals-of-artificial-intelligence/there-is-no-ai. Lanier is a computer scientist and musician, described in the article as 'Prime Unifying Scientist' at Microsoft.

6 Eli Pariser, *The Filter Bubble: What The Internet Is Hiding From You* (London: Penguin, 2012), 135.

7 Alexander Campolo and Kate Crawford, 'Enchanted Determinism: Power without Responsibility in Artificial Intelligence', *Engaging Science, Technology, and Society* 6 (2020): 1–19, 1, https://doi.org/10.17351/ests2020.277.

8 Ted Chiang, "ChatGPT is a Blurry jpeg of the Web', *The New Yorker*, 9 February 2023, https://www.newyorker.com/tech/annals-of-technology/chatgpt-is-a-blurry-jpeg-of-the-web.

9 Hayden Field, 'OpenAI is Pursuing a New Way to Fight A.I. "Hallucinations"', *CNBC*, 31 May 2023, https://www.cnbc.com/2023/05/31/openai-is-pursuing-a-new-way-to-fight-ai-hallucinations.html.

10 M. Khadduri, 'Maṣlaḥa', in *Encyclopaedia of Islam, Second Edition*, edited by P. Bearman et al., 2 February 2023, http://dx.doi.org.ezproxy.uwtsd.ac.uk 10.1163/1573-3912_islam_SIM_5019.

11 Sparsh Ahuja, 'Muslim Scholars Are Working to Reconcile Islam and AI', *Wired*, 2023, https://www.wired.co.uk/article/islamic-ai.

12 B. Popova, 'Islamic Philosophy and Artificial Intelligence: Epistemological Arguments', *Zygon* 55 (2020): 977–95, https://doi.org/10.1111/zygo.12651.

13 T. Bettina Cornwell and Helen Katz, *Influencer: The Science Behind Swaying Others* (New York and London: Routledge, 2021), 15–16.

14 Abdellah Iftahy et al., 'Digital Consumers in the Middle East: Rising Adoption and Opportunity', *McKinsey & Company*, 9 January 2023, https://www.mckinsey.com/capabilities/mckinsey-digital/our-insights/digital-consumers-in-the-middle-east-rising-adoption-and-opportunity.

15 International Telecommunication Union, 'Measuring Digital Development: Facts and Figures: International Bandwidth per Internet User, kbit/s, 2021', https://www.itu.int/itu-d/reports/statistics/2021/11/15/international-bandwidth-usage/.

16 There are substantial differences in terms of age groups, gender, rural-urban locations and types of devices being used. See Anne Delaporte and Kalvin Bahia, 'The State of Mobile Internet Connectivity 2022', *GSMA Connectivity*, October 2022, https://www.gsma.com/r/wp-content/uploads/2022/12/The-State-of-Mobile-Internet-Connectivity-Report-2022.pdf.

17 Coconuts Jakarta, 'Indonesians Spend the 5th Longest Amount of Time on the Internet Per Day: Survey', 1 February 2019, https://coconuts.co/jakarta/news/indonesians-spend-5th-longest-amount-time-internet-per-day-survey/, Datareportal, 'Digital 2022: Indonesia', 15 February 2022, https://datareportal.com/reports/digital-2022-indonesia, Hootsuite, 'Time Per Day Using the Internet', *We are Social*, 26 January 2022, https://www.hootsuite.com/resources/digital-trends.

18 Office for National Statistics, 'Muslim and Non-Muslim Internet Users and Internet Non-users by Sex, Age Group and Economic Activity, UK, 2015 Q1 (Reference: 005297)', 1 February 2016, https://www.ons.gov.uk/peoplepopulationandcommunity/culturalidentity/religion/adhocs/005297muslimandnonmusliminternetusersandinternetnonusersbysexgroupandeconomicactivityukquarter12015.

19 Marshall McLuhan, *Understanding Media: The Extensions of Man*, 2013 edn (Berkeley: Ginko Press, 1964). Preface to the Second Edition. 13. Marshal McLuhan et al., *The Medium is the Massage* (Harmondsworth: Penguin, 1967), Marshall McLuhan et al., *War and Peace in the Global Village* (New York and Toronto: McGraw-Hill Book Co., 1968).

20 Alexander Stille, 'Marshall McLuhan Is Back From the Dustbin of History; With the Internet, His Ideas Again Seem Ahead of Their Time', *New York Times*, 14 October 2000, http://alexanderstille.net/marshall-mcluhan-is-back-from-the-dustbin-of-history-with-the-internet-his-ideas-again-seem-ahead-of-their-time/ (accessed 24 April 2023).

21 Jean Baudrillard, *Simulations* (New York: Semiotext(e), 1983). Michel Foucault and Alan Sheridan, *Discipline and Punish: The Birth of the Prison* (London: Allen Lane, 1977). Roland Barthes, *Mythologies*, translated by Annette Lavers (London: Cape, 1972).

22 Jürgen Habermas, *The Structural Transformation of the Public Sphere: An Inquiry into a Category of Bourgeois Society* (Cambridge, MA: MIT Press, 1989). Also see Nicholas Garnham, *Emancipation, the Media, and Modernity: Arguments about the Media and Social Theory* (Oxford: Oxford University Press, Oxford Scholarship Online, 2000, 2011). James Bohman and William Rehg, 'Jürgen Habermas', *The Stanford Encyclopedia of Philosophy*, edited by Edward N. Zalta, 2014, http://plato.stanford.edu/archives/fall2014/entries/habermas/. William Outhwaite, *Habermas: A Critical Introduction* (Cambridge: Polity Press, 2009).

23 Manuel Castells, *The Rise of the Network Society*, 2nd edn (Oxford: Blackwell, 2000).
Manuel Castells, *The Internet Galaxy: Reflections on Internet, Business, and Society* (Oxford: Oxford University Press, Oxford Scholarship Online, 2001, 2011).

24 Stewart M. Hoover, *Mass Media Religion: The Social Sources of the Electronic Church* (London: Sage, 1988), Stewart M. Hoover, *Religion in the Media Age* (London: Routledge, 2006), Stewart M. Hoover, *Religion in the News: Faith and Journalism in American Public Discourse* (Thousand Oaks and London: Sage, 1998), Stewart M. Hoover and Knut Lundby, *Rethinking Media, Religion, and Culture* (London: Sage, 1997), Stewart M. Hoover and Lynn Schofield Clark, eds, *Practicing Religion in the Age of the Media: Explorations in Media, Religion, and Culture* (New York: Columbia University Press, 2002).

25 Jeffrey K. Hadden and Douglas E. Cowan, eds, *Religion on the Internet: Research Prospects and Promises* (New York: Elsevier Science, 2000). Douglas E. Cowan and Lorne L. Dawson, eds, *Religion Online: Finding Faith on the Internet* (New York: Routledge, 2004). Morten T. Højsgaard and Margit Warburg, eds, *Religion and Cyberspace* (London: Routledge, 2005).

26 Bruce B. Lawrence, *The Complete Idiot's Guide to Online Religion* (Indianapolis: Alpha Books, 1999). Gary R. Bunt, *The Good Web Guide to World Religions* (London: Good Web Guide, 2001).

27 Johanna Sumiala, 'Digital Religion: A Methodological Approach', in *The Oxford Handbook of Digital Religion*, edited by Heidi A. Campbell and Pauline Hope Cheong, Online Edition edn (Oxford: Oxford Academic, 2022), C24.S1–C24.S12.

28 Heidi Campbell, 'The Digital Religion Yearbook 2021', *Oak Trust*, https://hdl.handle.net/1969.1/195024. Heidi Campbell, *Digital Creatives and the Rethinking of Religious Authority* (Oxford: Routledge, 2020). Institute for Religious Studies, *Online – Heidelberg Journal of Religions on the Internet*. 2005-, http://journals.ub.uni-heidelberg/index.php/religions/. Douglas E. Cowan, *Cyberhenge: Modern Pagans on the Internet* (New York: Routledge, 2005), Christopher Helland, 'Virtual Tibet: Maintaining Identity through Internet Networks', In *The Pixel in the Lotus: Buddhism, the Internet, and Digital Media*, edited by Gregory Grieve (New York: Routledge, 2014), 155–72. Heidi A. Campbell, *When Religion Meets New Media* (London and New York: Routledge, 2010). Heidi Campbell, *Exploring Religious Community Online: We are One in the Network* (New York: Peter Lang, 2005). Tim Hutchings, ed., *Journal of Religion, Media and Digital Culture* (Leiden: Brill, 2012–).

29 Giula Evolvi, 'Theoretical Approaches in Digital Religious Studies', in *The Oxford Handbook of Digital Religion*, edited by Heidi A. Campbell and Pauline Hope Cheong, Online Edition edn (Oxford: Oxford Academic, 2022), C25.S1–C25.S15. Giulia Evolvi and Maria Chiara Giorda, 'Introduction: Islam, Space, and the Internet', *Journal of Religion, Media and Digital Culture* 10 (2021): 1–12, https://doi.org/10.1163/21659214-bja10047.

30 Heidi A. Campbell and Ruth Tsuria, 'Introduction to the Study of Digital Religion', in *Digital Religion: Understanding Religious Practice in Digital Media*, edited by Heidi A. Campbell and Ruth Tsuria, Second edn (New York and London: Routledge, 2022), 7.

31 Jon W. Anderson, 'The Internet and Islam's New Interpreters', in *New Media in the Muslim World: the Emerging Public Sphere*, edited by Dale F. Eickelman and Jon W. Anderson (Bloomington and Indianapolis: Indiana University Press, 2003), 45–60. especially 54–5 Jon W. Anderson, 'Arabizing the Internet', *The Emirates Occasional Papers* 30 (1998), Jon W. Anderson 'Globalizing Politics and Religion in the Muslim World', *The Journal of Electronic Publishing* (1997), http://www.press.umich.edu/jep/archive/Anderson.html.

32 Ali Altaf Mian, 'Introduction', in *The Bruce B. Lawrence Reader: Islam beyond Borders*, edited by Ali Altaf Mian (Durham and London: Duke University Press, 2021), 1–28, 8.

33 Bruce B. Lawrence, 'Muslim Cosmopolitanism', *Critical Muslim* 2 (2012): 19–39.

34 Mian, 'Introduction', 1–28. Bruce B. Lawrence, 'Allah On-Line: The Practice of Global Islam in the Information Age', in *Practicing Religion in the Age of the Media: Explorations in Media, Religion, and Culture*, edited by Stewart M. Hoover and Lynn Schofield Clark (New York: Columbia University Press, 2002), 237–53, Bruce B.

Lawrence, *Defenders of God: The Fundamentalist Revolt against the Modern Age* (San Francisco: Harper & Row, 1989).

35 Bruce B. Lawrence, *Who is Allah?* (Chapel Hill: The University of North Carolina Press, 2015), 149–62.

36 miriam cooke and Bruce B. Lawrence, eds, *Muslim Networks from Hajj to Hip-Hop*, (Chapel Hill: University of North Carolina Press, 2005).

37 Taieb Belghazi, 'Afterword', in *Muslim Networks from Hajj to Hip-Hop*, edited by miriam cooke and Bruce B. Lawrence (Chapel Hill: University of North Carolina Press, 2005), 281.

38 Bruce B. Lawrence, *Islamicate Cosmopolitan Spirit* (Hoboken: Wiley Blackwell, 2021), xxi. The discussion on 'Islamicate' vocabulary and labels features in xii–xxxv. While beyond the parameters of this book, there is potential to explore 'Cyber Islamicate Environments' in future research. This would include approaches towards the term *barzakh* logic and fuzzy logic as a way to avoid binary categorizations (xxx). Lawrence reflects on Hodgson extensively. See Marshall Hodgson, *The Venture of Islam: Conscience and History in a World Civilisation* (Chicago and London: University of Chicago Press, 1974). Hodgson's work extended into multiple volumes of this series.

39 Dale F. Eickelman and Jon W. Anderson, eds., *New Media in the Muslim World: The Emerging Public Sphere* (Bloomington and Indianapolis: Indiana University Press, 2003), Peter G. Mandaville, 'Information Technology and the Changing Boundaries of European Islam', in *Paroles d'islam: Individus, sociétés et discours dans l'islam européen contemporain*, edited by Felice Dassetto (Paris: Maisonneuve et Larose, 2000), 281–97. Mandaville, *Transnational Muslim Politics*. Eickelman and Piscatori, *Muslim Politics*. Noha Mellor and Khalil Rinnawi, eds., *Political Islam and Global Media: The Boundaries of Religious Identity* (London: Routledge, 2016). Mohamed A. El-Nawawy and Sahar Khamis, *Islam Dot Com: Contemporary Islamic Discourse in Cyberspace* (New York: Palgrave Macmillan, 2009).

40 Jon B. Alterman, *New Media, New Politics?: From Satellite Television to the Internet in the Arab World* (Washington, DC: Washington Institute for Near East Policy, 1998). Mellor and Rinnawi, eds, *Political Islam and Global Media*.

41 In particular, see Albrecht Hofheinz, 'The Internet in the Arab World: Playground for Political Liberalisation', *Internationale Politik und Gesellschaft /International Politics and Society* 3 (2005): 78–96. Deborah L. Wheeler, *Digital Resistance in the Middle East: New Media Activism in Everyday Life* (Edinburgh: Edinburgh University Press, 2017), Deborah L. Wheeler, *The Internet in the Middle East: Global Expectations and Local Imaginations in Kuwait* (New York: State University of New York Press, 2005).

42 Anna Grasso, 'Les imâms dans la cité: Politisation et syndicalisation des imâms dans la Tunisie contemporain' (PhD, L'Institut d'études politiques d'Aix-en-Provence Aix-Marseille Université, 2018).

43 Roxanne D. Marcotte, 'The New Virtual Frontiers: Religion and Spirituality in Cyberspace', *Australian Religion Studies Review* 23, no. 3 (2010): 247–54, http://www.equinoxjournals.com/ARSR/article/view/10060/pdf. El-Sayed El-Aswad, *Muslim Worldviews and Everyday Lives* (Lanham: AltaMira Press, 2012). Sariya Cheruvallil-Contractor, '"Online Sufism" – Young British Muslims, Their Virtual "Selves" and Virtual Reality', in *Sufism in Britain*, edited by Ron Geaves and Theodore Gabriel (A. & C. Black, 2013), 161–76. Thomas Hoffmann and Göran Larsson, eds., *Muslims and the New Information and Communication Technologies: Notes from an Emerging*

and Infinite Field (Amsterdam: Springer, 2013), Smeeta Mishraab and Gaby Semaan, 'Islam in Cyberspace: South Asian Muslims in America Log In', *Journal of Broadcasting and Electronic Media* 54, no. 1 (2010): 87–101.

44 Mona Abdel-Fadil, 'Islam Online Guides Spouses Towards Marital Bliss: Arabic vs. English Counselling Perspectives on Marital Communication'. *Muslims and the New Information and Communication Technologies: Notes from an Emerging and Infinite Field*, edited by Thomas Hoffmann and Goran Larsson, vol. 7 edn (Dordrecht, Heidelberg, New York and London: Springer, 2013), 49–71. *Muslims in Global Societies,* Gabriele Marrianci and Bryan S. Turner.

45 CyberOrient, 'CyberOrient: Online Journal of the Virtual Middle East', http://www.cyberorient.net.

46 Andrea L. Stanton, 'Islamic Emoticons: Pious Sociability and Community Building in Online Muslim Communities', in *Internet and Emotions*, edited by Tova Benski and Eran Fisher (London: Routledge, 2013), 80–98.

47 Jonas Svensson, 'TZ BIDAH BRO!!!!! GT ME?? – YouTube Mawlid and Voices of Praise and Blame', in *Muslims and the New Information and Communication Technologies: Notes from an Emerging and Infinite Field*, edited by Thomas Hoffmann and Goran Larsson, vol. 7 edn (Dordrecht, Heidelberg, New York and London: Springer, 2013), 89–112. *Muslims in Global Societies,* Gabriele Marrianci and Bryan S. Turner.

48 Ayesha Khan, 'Sufisticated: Exploring Contemporary Sufism among Young British Muslims' (PhD, Cardiff University, 2020).

49 Rosemary Pennington, 'Seeing a Global Islam?: *Eid al-Adha* on Instagram', in *Cyber Muslims: Mapping Islamic Digital Media in the Internet Age*, edited by Robert Rozehnal (London and New York: Bloomsbury Academic, 2022), 176–88. Andrea L. Stanton, 'From Mecca with Love: Muslim Religious Apps and the Centering of Sacred Geography', in *Cyber Muslims: Mapping Islamic Digital Media in the Internet Age*, edited by Robert Rozehnal (London and New York: Bloomsbury Academic, 2022), 161–75.

50 Sophia Rose Arjana, *Buying Buddha, Selling Rumi: Orientalism and the Mystical Marketplace* (London: Oneworld Publications, 2020), Sophia Rose Arjana, *Pilgrimage in Islam: Traditional and Modern Practices* (London: Oneworld Publications, 2017).

51 Robert Rozehnal, *Cyber Sufis: Virtual Expressions of the American Muslim Experience* (London: Bloomsbury, 2020).

52 Wendi Bellar, 'Prayer App Rituals How Islamic Participants Engage with Technological and Religious Affordances in Muslim Pro', in *Digital Religion: Understanding Religious Practice in Digital Media*, edited by Heidi A. Campbell and Ruth Tsuria, Second edn (New York and London: Routledge, 2022), 157.

53 Nabil Echchaibi, 'From Audio Tapes to Video Blogs: The Delocalisation of Authority in Islam', *Nations and Nationalism* 17, no. 1 (2011): 25–44, https://doi.org/10.1111/j.1469-8129.2010.00468.x.

54 Sana Patel, 'Hybrid Imams: Young Muslims and Religious Authority on Social Media', in *Cyber Muslims: Mapping Islamic Digital Media in the Internet Age*, edited by Robert Rozehnal (London and New York: Bloomsbury Academic, 2022), 34–50. This picks up an important point about understanding the grassroots usage of online media, which I am exploring in ongoing collaborative projects in the UK and European contexts.

55 Yvonne Howard-Bunt, 'Ambassadors and Influencers: The Digital-Analogue Pendulum of Community Communication in the Age of the COVID-19

Pandemic', in *Islamic Responses to COVID-19: Authority and Religiosity in #Muslim Communities and Digital Worlds*, University of Wales Trinity Saint David, 1 July 2021, https://youtu.be/mJd0Whqq7_U.

56 Moch. Syarif Hidayatullah et al., 'The Cyber Islam Contestation In Indonesia', *International Journal of Advanced Science and Technology* 29 (2020): 34–44. An unofficial Indonesian translation of *Virtually Islamic* appeared in 2005. Gary R. Bunt, *Islam Virtual. Menjelajah Islam di Jagad Maya* (Yogyakarta: Suluh Press, 2005).

57 AICIS, 'Proceedings of the 19th Annual International Conference on Islamic Studies', in *Annual International Conference on Islamic Studies*, edited by Noorhaidi Hasan et al. (Jakarta: European Union Digital Library, 2019). I provided a paper. Gary R. Bunt, 'The Fatwa Machine: Influencers & Authority in Cyber Islamic Environments', in *'Digital Islam, Education and Youth: Changing Landscape of Indonesian Islam'. 19th Annual International Conference on Islamic Studies, 2019*, Jakarta.

58 Hussein Kesvani, *Follow Me, Akhi: The Online World of British Muslims* (London: C. Hurst & Co., 2019).

59 Sadek Hamid, *Sufis, Salafis and Islamists: The Contested Ground of British Islamic Activism* (London: Routledge, 2017).

60 Ibrahim N. Abusharif, 'Cyber-Islamic Environments and Salafī-Ṣūfī Contestations: Appropriating Digital Media and Challenges to Religious Authority' (PhD, Humanities, University of Wales Trinity Saint David, 2019). Director of Studies: Gary R. Bunt, https://repository.uwtsd.ac.uk/id/eprint/1196/.

61 Shaheen Amid Whyte, 'Islamic Religious Authority in Cyberspace: A Qualitative Study of Muslim Religious Actors in Australia', *Religions* 13, no. 69 (2022), https://doi.org/10.3390/rel13010069.

62 Farrah Sheikh, 'Korean Muslims: Shaping Islamic Discourse and Identities Online', *European Journal of Korean Studies* 19 (2020): 129–47.

63 Canadian Muslims Online, 'New Muslim Public Spheres in the Digital Age', Université du Québec à Montréal, https://musulmanscanadiensenligne.uqam.ca/en.

64 ITN-MIDA, 'Mediating Islam in the Digital Age', https://www.itn-mida.org/.

65 Digital British Islam, https://digitalbritishislam.com (accessed 30 October 2023), University of Wales Trinity Saint David et al.

66 Digital Islam Across Europe, https://blogs.ed.ac.uk/digitalislameurope/ (accessed 30 October 2023), University of Edinburgh et al.

67 Office of Islamic Studies on Cyberspace, 'Home', https://oisc-virtual.com/ (accessed 15 February 2022).

68 Robert J. Riggs, 'Global Networks, Local Concerns: Investigating the Impact of Emerging Technologies on Shi'a Religious Leaders and Constituencies', in *Shi'a Minorities in The Contemporary World: Migration, Transnationalism and Multilocality*, edited by Oliver Scharbrodt and Yafa Shanneik (Edinburgh: Edinburgh University Press, 2020), 123–41. This was explored in Gary R. Bunt, *Hashtag Islam: How Cyber-Islamic Environments Are Transforming Religious Authority* (Chapel Hill: The University of North Carolina Press, 2018), 55–60.

69 Heather Marie Akou, 'Interpreting Islam through the Internet: Making Sense of Hijab', *Contemporary Islam* 4, no. 3 (2010), 331–46.

70 Anna Piela, *Muslim Women Online: Faith and Identity in Virtual Space* (New York: Routledge, 2012). Anna Piela, '"The Niqab Is a Beautiful Extension of My Face": Niqab Adoption as Meta-conversion in YouTube Lifestreaming Videos', in *Digital*

Religion: Understanding Religious Practice in Digital Media*, edited by Heidi A. Campbell and Ruth Tsuria, Second edn (New York and London: Routledge, 2022), 167–75.

71 Vahideh Golzard and Cristina Miguel, 'Negotiating Intimacy through Social Media: Challenges and Opportunities for Muslim Women in Iran', *Middle East Journal of Culture and Communication* 9, (2016): 216–33. Chiara Bernardi, 'Saudi Bloggers, Women's Issues and NGOs', *Arab Media & Society*, 11, http://www.arabmediasociety.com/?article=757.

72 Eva F. Nisa, 'Indonesian Women ʿUlamāʾ Go Online amid COVID-19', in *Islamic Responses to COVID-19 Online Conference*, YouTube, 1 July 2021, https://youtu.be/V9VcUf07c-g.

73 Eva F. Nisa, 'Muslims Enacting Identity: Gender through Digital Media', in *The Oxford Handbook of Digital Religion*, edited by Heidi A. Campbell and Pauline Hope Cheong (Oxford Academic, 2022), C.33.51–C33.59, https://doi.org/10.1093/oxfordhb/9780197549803.013.33.

74 Farah Hasan, 'Keep It Halal! A Smartphone Ethnography of Muslim Dating', *Journal of Religion, Media and Digital Culture* 10 (2021): 135–54, https://doi.org/10.1163/21659214-bja10042.

75 Ruqaiyyah Kauser, 'Exploring the Self-presentation of Female Muslims, Who Wear the Hijab, on the Social Networking Site "Instagram"' (Undergraduate Project, Manchester Metropolitan University, 2019), https://e-space.mmu.ac.uk/623943/. Alila Pramiyanti, 'Self-Presentation of Indonesian Hijabers on Instagram', in *2nd International Conference on Advanced Research in Social Sciences & Humanities*, Munich, 6–8 December 2019, https://www.dpublication.com/wp-content/uploads/2019/11/45-194.pdf.

76 Robert Rozehnal, ed., *Cyber Muslims: Mapping Islamic Digital Media in the Internet Age* (London: Bloomsbury, 2022).

77 Madelina Nuñez and Harold D. Morales, 'Latinz Muslim Digital Landscapes: Locating Networks and Cultural Factors', in *Cyber Muslims: Mapping Islamic Digital Media in the Internet Age*, edited by Robert Rozehnal (London and New York: Bloomsbury Academic, 2022), 84–99.

78 Rozehnal, ed., *Cyber Muslims*, 9. Campbell and Tsuria, 'Introduction to the Study of Digital Religion'.

79 Evgeny Morozov, *The Net Delusion: How Not to Liberate The World* (London: Allen Lane, 2011).

80 Arab Media Society, http://www.arabmediasociety.org, CyberOrient, 'CyberOrient: Online Journal of the Virtual Middle East'. Andrew Helms, *Politics of Information, The Internet and Islamist Politics in Jordan, Morocco and Egypt*. Center for Contemporary Arab Studies (Georgetown University, 2010). Marc Owen Jones, *Digital Authoritarianism in the Middle East: Deception, Disinformation and Social Media* (London: Hurst Publishers, 2022). Also see Marc Owen Jones, 'Saudi Arabia's Bot Army Flourishes as Twitter Fails to Tame the Beast', *Middle East Eye*, 20 January 2020, https://www.middleeasteye.net/opinion/despite-twitter-culls-riyadhs-disinformation-network-still-going-strong.

81 Wissam S. Yafi, *Inevitable Democracy in the Arab World* (Palgrave Macmillan, 2012).

82 David Faris, *Dissent and Revolution in a Digital Age: Social Media, Blogging and Activism in Egypt* (London: I.B.Tauris, 2012), Philip N. Howard, *The Digital Origins of Dictatorship and Democracy: Information Technology and Political Islam* (Oxford: Oxford University Press, 2010). Sean Aday et al., 'Blogs and Bullets II: New Media

and Conflict after the Arab Spring' (United States Institute of Peace, 2012), http://www.usip.org/publications/blogs-and-bullets-ii-new-media-and-conflict-after-the-arab-spring, Gary R. Bunt, 'Mediterranean Islamic Expression and Web 2.0', in *Arab Society in Revolt: The West's Mediterranean Challenge*, edited by Olivier Roy and Cesare Melini (New York: Brookings Institution Press, 2012), Sahar Khamis et al., 'Beyond Egypt's "Facebook Revolution" and Syria's "YouTube Uprising:" Comparing Political Contexts, Actors and Communication Strategies', *Arab Media & Society*, https://www.arabmediasociety.com/beyond-egypts-facebook-revolution-and-syrias-youtube-uprising-comparing-political-contexts-actors-and-communication-strategies/. Laila Shereen Sakr, 'A Digital Humanities Approach: Text, the Internet, and the Egyptian Uprising', *Middle East Critique* 22, no. 3 (2013): 247–63, http://www.tandfonline.com/doi/abs/10.1080/19436149.2013.822241.

83 Nada Alwadi and Sahar Khamis, 'Voices Shouting for Reform: The Remaining Battles for Bahraini Women', in *Arab Women's Activism and Socio-Political Transformation: Unfinished Gendered Revolutions*, edited by Sahar Khamis and Amel Mili (New York and London: Palgrave Macmillan, 2018), 53–72.

84 While complexities of Muslim identities are represented in this book, for reasons of space, Ahmadiyya and other communities are not included here in detail.

85 Philip Seib and Dana M. Janbek, *Global Terrorism and New Media: The Post-Al Qaeda Generation* (New York: Routledge, 2010). Aaron Y. Zelin, 'Jihadology', http://jihadology.net. Christopher Anzalone, 'Ibn Siqilli', http://twitter.com/ibnsiqilli.

86 Abdel Bari Atwan, *Islamic State: The Digital Caliphate* (London: Saqi Books, 2015), Hassan Hassan and Michael Weiss, *Isis: Inside the Army of Terror* (London: Regan Arts, 2015), Aaron Y. Zelin, *Your Sons are at Your Service: Tunisia's Missionaries of Jihad* (New York and Chicester: Columbia University Press, 2020). Charlie Winter, 'Is Islamic State Losing Control of its Virtual Caliphate?', *BBC News*, 9 November 2017, https://www.bbc.co.uk/news/world-middle-east-41845285.

87 Gary R. Bunt, 'islam@britain.net: British Muslim Identities in Cyberspace', *Islam and Christian-Muslim Relations* 10, no. 3 (1999): 353–62.

88 My approach is discussed in more detail in: Gary R. Bunt, 'Studying Muslims and Cyberspace', in *Studying Islam in Practice*, edited by Gabriele Marranci (London and New York: Routledge, 2014), 190–203.

89 Gary R. Bunt, 'Decoding the Hajj in Cyberspace', in *The Hajj: Pilgrimage in Islam*, edited by Eric Tagliacozzo and Shawkat M. Toorawa (Cambridge: Cambridge University Press, 2015), 231–49, Gary R. Bunt, 'From Mosque to YouTube: Cyber Islamic Networks in the UK', in *Postcolonial Media Cultures*, edited by Ros Brunt and Rinella Cere (London: Palgrave Macmillan, 2011), Gary R. Bunt, '#Islam, Social Networking and the Cloud', in *Islam in the Modern World*, edited by Jeffrey T. Kenney and Ebrahim Moosa (New York: Routledge, 2014), 177–208, Gary R. Bunt, 'The Qur'an and the Internet', in *The Routledge Companion to the Qur'an*, edited by Daniel A. Madigan et al. (New York: Routledge, 2021), 384–93. Gary R. Bunt, 'Studying Muslims and Cyberspace', 190–203, Göran Larsson, 'The Ultimate Test: The Qur'an and Information and Communication Technologies', in *Muslims and the New Media: Historical and Contemporary Debates*, edited by Göran Larsson (Farnham: Ashgate, 2011), 167–92. Andrew Rippin, 'The Qur'ān on the Internet: Implications and Future Possibilities', in *Muslims and the New Information and Communication Technologies*, edited by Thomas Hoffmann and Göran Larsson, vol. 7 (Dordrecht: Springer Netherlands, 2013), 113–26, https://link.springer.com/chapter/10.1007/978-94-007-7247-2_7.

90 Gary R. Bunt, 'Virtually Islamic', https://www.virtuallyislamic.com.
91 Chris Anderson, 'The Long Tail', *Wired* 12, no. 10 (2004), http://www.wired.com/wired/archive/12.10/tail.html.
92 Kemal A. Faruki, *Islamic Jurisprudence* (Karachi: Pakistan Publishing House, 1962), 288.
93 The transliterated plural of fatwa is *fatāwā*. Given that the term has been anglicized, 'fatwa' will be applied in the remainder of this book in the singular and 'fatwas' in the plural when appropriate.
94 Muhammad Khalid Masud et al., eds., *Islamic Legal Interpretation: Muftis and Their Fatwas* (Harvard: Harvard University Press, 1996).
95 Max Weber, *Weber, Max [1904] (1958), The Protestant Ethic and The Spirit of Capitalism*, translated by Talcott Parsons (London: Allen & Unwin, 1958, 1904).
96 Ernest Gellner, 'Muslim Society', in *Cambridge Studies in Social Anthropology 32* (Cambridge and New York: Cambridge University Press, 1981), 134.
97 Neal Robinson, *Discovering the Qur'an* (London: SCM Press, 1996). Bruce B. Lawrence, *The Qur'an: A Biography* (London: Atlantic Books, 2006). Andrew Rippin, *Muslims: Their Religious Beliefs and Practices* (London and New York: Routledge, 2012), John L. Esposito, *Islam: The Straight Path,* 3rd edn (New York: Oxford University Press, 1998).
98 Bunt, 'The Qur'an and the Internet', 384–93. Rippin, 'The Qur'ān on the Internet: Implications and Future Possibilities', 113–26.
99 Aziz al-Azmeh, *Islam and Modernities* (London and New York: Verso, 1993), 70–1.
100 Jon W. Anderson, 'Muslim Networks, Muslim Selves in Cyberspace: Islam in the Post-Modern Public Sphere', in *Working Papers on New Media and Information Technology in the Middle East* (Georgetown University, 2001), Jon W. Anderson, 'Wiring Up: The Internet Difference for Muslim Networks', in *Muslim Networks: From Hajj to Hip Hop*, edited by miriam cooke and Bruce B. Lawrence (Chapel Hill: University of North Carolina Press, 2005), 252–63.
101 Gary R. Bunt, *Islam in the Digital Age: E-jihad, Online Fatwas and Cyber Islamic Environments* (London and Michigan: Pluto Press, 2003).
102 Andrew Hutchinson, 'TikTok is Fast Becoming a Key Search and Discovery Platform for Younger Audiences', *Social Media Today*, 25 August 2022, https://www.socialmediatoday.com/news/tiktok-is-fast-becoming-a-key-search-and-discovery-platform-for-younger-aud/629718/, Sarah Perez, 'Google Exec Suggests Instagram and TikTok Are Eating into Google's Core Products, Search and Maps', *TechCrunch*, 12 July 2022, https://techcrunch.com/2022/07/12/google-exec-suggests-instagram-and-tiktok-are-eating-into-googles-core-products-search-and-maps/.
103 R. C. Licata, 'The Truth About Google, Gen Z, and the TikTok Search Eng', *Terakeet*, 4 October 2022, https://terakeet.com/blog/tiktok-vs-google/.
104 I had not searched for Nigel Farage, his politics nor his affiliates.
105 Crawford, *Atlas of AI*, 149.
106 For an introduction to Shīʿīsm, see Andrew Newman, *Twelver Shiism : Unity and Diversity in the Life of Islam, 632 to 1722* (Edinburgh: Edinburgh University Press, 2013).
107 Howard-Bunt, 'Ambassadors and Influencers'.
108 Charles Hirschkind, *The Ethical Soundscape: Cassette Sermons and Islamic Counterpublics* (New York: Columbia University Press, 2006).

109 Tor Project, https://www.torproject.org (accessed 7 February 2022). A 2015 study indicated that direct religious content (from any perspective) forms only a small (and difficult to determine) proportion of Tor content compared with sectors such as drugs, market, fraud and bitcoin. Gareth Owen, 'Tor: Hidden Services and Deanonymisation', media.ccc.de, 1 January 2015, https://youtu.be/-oTEoLB-ses (accessed 7 February 2022).

110 Bellar, 'Prayer App Rituals How Islamic Participants Engage with Technological and Religious Affordances in Muslim Pro', 157.

Chapter 2

1 Qur᾿ān, Sūra *al-Ḥijr* 15:26-7; Sūra *Raḥmān,* 55:14-15; Sūra*Aḥqāf* 46:29-32. This book uses the following translated edition unless otherwise stated: Seyyed Hossein Nasr et al., eds, *The Study Quran: A New Translation and Commentary* (New York: Harper One, 2015).

2 The Muhammadan Way Sufi Realities, 'Jinn / Unseen Beings Feed off of your Anger? Excited about Qiyamah? End Times Islamic Eschatology', YouTube, 10 February 2021, https://youtu.be/3RfgQn2oToc.

3 Brother Rahman, 'A Simple Yet Effective Method for Removal of Stubborn Jinn from Your Home', 6 February 2014, https://www.brotherrahman.net/topic/a-simple-yet-effective-method-for-removal-of-stubborn-jinn-from-your-home/, Islamweb, 'How to Get Rid of Jinns, Fatwa No. 86197', 9 November 2023, https://www.islamweb.net/en/fatwa/86197/how-to-get-rid-of-jinns.

4 Gordon Newby, 'Satan', in *The Oxford Encyclopedia of the Islamic World*, edited by John Esposito (2009), 14 October 2014, https://www.oxfordislamicstudies.com/article/opr/t236/e0706.

5 Qur᾿ān, Sūra al-Baqarah, 2:30-34, Sūra al-Ḥijr, 15:30-34, Sūra al-Isrā᾿, 17:61.

6 For example, see the Qur᾿ān, 17: 61-65.

7 Huda TV, 'Powerful Ruqyah DUA Against Bad Evil Eye, Black Magic Sihir, Jinns, & Jealousy HD Cover Changed', YouTube, 25 September 2019, https://youtu.be/CWTQbDB97oE. Yahya Ibrahim, 'Out of Sight: Belief in Angels, Jinn and Qadr', Al Kauthar, https://online.alkauthar.org/courses/out-of-sight/ (accessed 10 March 2021).

8 One Islam Productions, 'These Jinns Come in Your Body Everyday', YouTube, 15 June 2020, https://youtu.be/i3GHtq-dcYI. Merciful Servant, 'Jinn & Magic Explained (Never Fear Jinn Again) – Lecture by Shaykh Yasir Qahdi', YouTube, 13 February 2020, https://youtu.be/oLPooLHkbT8.

9 Naseeha Sessions, 'A Jinn Rapes Her Every Night!', 25 January 2018, https://youtu.be/OSWFu4XdOjk. Muhammad Tim Humble, 'Jinn Attacks and Assault at Night', 12 August 2015, https://muhammadtim.com/posts/jinn-attacks-and-assault-at-night. Also see Freshly Grounded, '#85 Tim Humble: Jinn, Shaytan, Magic & Movies', 2 January 2019, https://youtu.be/cfXJlTb5SzU.

10 OnePath Network, 'Exposing Fake Jinn Healers abusing Muslims (Full Documentary) | Malaz Majanni', YouTube, 2 November 2018, https://youtu.be/TudkLIwV5z0. See my discussion in Gary R. Bunt, 'Is it Possible to have a "Religious Experience" in Cyberspace?' in *The Study of Religious Experience*, edited by Bettina E. Schmidt (Sheffield: Equinox Publishing, 2016), 160–8.

11 Etsy, 'Jinn Talisman', https://www.etsy.com/market/jinn_talisman (accessed 28 March 2022), Picclick.com, 'Taweez Amulet Jinn Protection Talisman Pendant Evil Eye

Business Success', https://picclick.com/Taweez-Amulet-Jinn-Protection-Talisman-Pendant-Evil-Eye-251767093728.html (accessed 28 March 2022).

12 ArabicSpells, 'Arabic Talismans, Amulets, Taweez and Rituals', Etsy, https://www.etsy.com/shop/ArabicSpells (accessed 9 March 2021), E-Bay, 'Handmade Arabic Luck Amulet/Talisman/Taweez', https://www.ebay.co.uk/itm/Handmade-arabic-luck-amulet-talisman-taweez-/283723357176 (accessed 9 March 2021), IslamTaweez, 'Taweez for All Problems, Arab Magic Rituals, Islamic Talismans, Amulets', Pinterest, https://www.pinterest.co.uk/pin/812196114031310454/.

13 Gary R. Bunt, 'Jinn in the Machine', *Summer School,* University of Wales Trinity Saint David, Lampeter. 2015, https://www.uwtsd.ac.uk/media/uwtsd-website/content-assets/documents/library-and-learning-resources/ahrerc/Gary-Bunt_moodleversion.pdf, Alizeh Kohari, 'Jinnfluencers: Inside the World of Internet Exorcisms', *The Juggernaut*, Pulitzer Center, 21 February 2021, https://pulitzercenter.org/stories/jinnfluencers-inside-world-internet-exorcisms.

14 Ar-Ruqya Ash-Shariyah, 'Shaytaan', http://www.ruqyashariyah.org/shaytaan-description-deceptions-destruction-by-murtaza-khan (accessed 26 June 2015). Online Exorcism, 'Ruqyah Sharia', http://www.islamicexorcism.com/ruqyah-sharia/ (accessed 26 June 2015). Ruqyah Services, https://www/ruqyahservices4u.org (accessed 25 June 2015). Ruqyah Centre, Twitter, https://twitter.com/ruqyahcentre?lang=en (accessed 9 March 2021).

15 About Islam, 'Give the Angel on Your Left Shoulder Time Off and have the Angel on the Right Work Overtime', Pinterest, https://www.pinterest.co.uk/pin/277957226829766662/ (accessed 11 March 2021). The Muslimah Network, 'Maalik', Pinterest, https://fi.pinterest.com/pin/106890191137277677/. Instagram, 'Why Don't You Give Your Angels a Break?' Pinterest (accessed 11 March 2021).

16 One Islam Productions, '[Emotional] The Birth & Death Of Angel Jibreel', YouTube, https://youtu.be/HMLwO_BCeJY (accessed 11 March 2021).

17 Omar Suleiman, 'Episode 19: Have You Ever Seen an Angel in Human Form? | Angels in Your Presence with Omar Suleiman', *Yaqeen Publications*, 2020, https://youtu.be/tMcmq1YAhD4 (accessed 12 May 2020).

18 Mevlana Jalaluddin Rumi/Balkhi, 'RumiQuotesOfficial', Instagram, 11 March 2021, https://www.instagram.com/rumiquotesofficial/?hl=en. Rumi Quotes, 'rumi_poetry', Instagram, https://www.instagram.com/rumi_poetry/?hl=en (accessed 11 March 2021). Kulibah, 'Rumi Poem', Instagram, https://www.pinterest.co.uk/amp/pin/143270831869577636/ (accessed 11 March 2021). Rumi Quotes, 'Rumi Quotes Official', https://www.facebook.com/rumiquotesofficial/ (accessed 11 March 2021), StrengthAwakened, 'Top 25 Mystical Rumi Quotes on Love III', https://www.pinterest.co.uk/pin/376402481350922322/ (accessed 11 March 2021). Rūmī' is discussed in Chapter 8.

19 Karen G. Ruffle, 'An Even Better Creation: The Role of Adam and Eve in Shiʿi Narratives about Fatimah al-Zahra', *Journal of the American Academy of Religion* 81 (September 2013): 791–819, https://doi.org/10.1093/jaarel/lft047.

20 Shabir Ally and Safiyah Ally, 'Q&A: Original Sin? Shia Hadith?' Let the Quran Speak, 2013, https://youtu.be/9VrQSQx5ARs (accessed 9 May 2013).

21 Aalulbayt Global Information Center, 'The Infallibility of the Prophets of Allah and The Imams (2) Did Adam and Eve (PBUTH) Commit a Sin?' http://en.al-shia.org/content/infallibility-prophets-allah-and-imams-2-did-adam-and-eve-pbuth-commit-sin.

22 Stories of the Prophets – Quran Stories, 'Prophet Stories In English | Prophet Adam (AS) | Stories Of The Prophets | Quran Stories', 11 March 2017, https://youtu.be/xxnZuAHCAjY.

23 Abu Bakr Zoud, 'The Amazing Story of Adam & Hawa', One Islam Productions, 10 May 2020, https://youtu.be/TrowTCbUAS4.
24 Sheikh Shady Alsuleiman, 'The Death of Adam (AS)', Islamic Media, 7 March 2019, https://youtu.be/KraFoxLGWHU.
25 Sayed Ammar Nakshawani, 'Prophet Adam (as) E2 – E2 S4', *Imam Hussein TV 3*, 10 May 2019, https://youtu.be/rNl2j3vrajw.
26 Ibn Kathir, 'The Story of Nuh (Noah)', Sunnah Online, https://sunnahonline.com/library/stories-of-the-prophets/290-story-of-nuh-noah-the (accessed 8 March 2021). Islamic House of Wisdom, 'Nuh (S)', 27 January 2013, http://www.islamichouseofwisdom.com/prophets-in-islam-/2013/1/27/nuh-s- (accessed 8 March 2021).
27 Muhammad Baqir Majlisi, 'Hayat al-Qulub, Vol. 1, Stories of the Prophets', Al-Islam, https://www.al-islam.org/node/45149.
28 Hamza Karamali, 'Was Noah's Flood Global or Local?' Basira Education (accessed 8 March 2021).
29 Islamic Landmarks, 'Resting Place of the Ark of Prophet Nuh', https://www.islamiclandmarks.com/turkey/resting-place-of-the-ark-of-nuh-as (accessed 8 March 2021).
30 Azerbaijan Travel, 'Visit Noah's Tomb', https://azerbaijan.travel/ancient-noahs-ark-place-at-nakhchivan-city (accessed 8 March 2021). 360Degree, 'Cizre Noah Tomb', http://www.360degree.org/?panorama=cizre-noah-tomb (accessed 8 March 2021), Love ALI, 'Adam, Noah and Ali all Buried in Same Place – WHY?' YouTube, 8 January 2017, https://youtu.be/V7R25kyxDVc (accessed 8 March 2021). Mazar Mubarak - Imran Ghazi, 'Hazrat Nooh | The Most Prominent Prophet of God', 1 November 2018, https://youtu.be/6a_QSlEvumo (accessed 8 March 2021).
31 Bunt, 'Decoding the Hajj in Cyberspace', 231–49.
32 Muslim Aid, 'Ibrahim's Sacrifice', https://www.muslimaid.org/what-we-do/religious-dues/qurbani/story-of-ibrahim/ (accessed 6 March 2021).
33 Asma Abdulaziz Abdullah Abdakhail and Sumiah Mashraf Abdullah Al Amri, 'Saudi Arabia's Management of the Hajj Season through Artificial Intelligence and Sustainability', *Sustainability* 14, no. 14142 (2022), https://doi.org/10.3390/su142114142, Saudi Press Agency, 'AI Algorithms to Help Crowd Management at Holy Sites, Lt. Gen. Bassami Says at Global AI Summit', 15 September 2022, https://www.spa.gov.sa/viewfullstory.php?lang=en&newsid=2384122, Maisah, 'The Islamic Information, Robots Will Be Serving Hajj Pilgrims, The Use Will Be Increased, Says Grand Mosque', 2 June 2022, https://theislamicinformation.com/news/robots-serving-hajj-pilgrims/.
34 Alhaq Travel, 'Station of Abraham', Pintrest, https://www.pinterest.co.uk/pin/290200769738986758/ (accessed 6 March 2021).
35 Islamic Finder, 'Story of Prophet Abraham (Hazrat Ibrahim)', https://www.islamicfinder.org/knowledge/biography/story-of-prophet-ibrahim/ (accessed 6 March 2021).
36 Let the Quran Speak, 'Abraham in the Bible & Quran. Dr. Shabir Ally', https://youtu.be/GzVy1BsQPGY (accessed 25 December 2019). The series is available on the same page as the Ibrāhīm discussion.
37 Nouman Ali Khan, 'Prophet Ibrahim – Quran Weekly', 1 July 2014, YouTube, https://youtu.be/sm1netwj0q8?si=7eKS3o7tH83YbfMy (accessed 6 March 2021).
38 Imam Hussein TV 3, 'Prophet Ismail and Ishaq (as) E9 – Dr. Sayed Ammar Nakshawani – E9 S4', 16 May 2019, https://youtu.be/f1G01oethiE.
39 Teona Sukhiashvili, 'Moses in the Qur'an', *Journal of Religious & Theological Information* 20, no. 1 (2021): 1–9.

40 Abu Khadeejah Abdul-Wahid, 'The Story of Mūsā ('alaihis-salām): His Birth, Struggles, Miracles and Victory over Pharaoh on the Day of "Āshūrā"', SalafiBookstore .com, 17 September 2018, https://www.abukhadeejah.com/story-of-musa-birth -struggles-miracles-victory-pharaoh-ashura/.
41 IslamChannel.tv, 'The Chronicles of Musa, Season 2', https://islamchannel.tv/video -category/the-chronicles-of-musa/ (accessed 4 March 2021), Stories of the Prophets – Quran Stories, 'Prophet Stories In English | Prophet Musa (AS) | Part 4 | Stories of the Prophets | Quran Stories', YouTube, https://youtu.be/E40QshQOyc8.
42 'Sahih al-Bukhari 4416, Book 64, Hadith 438, Vol. 5, Book 59, Hadith 700', https:// sunnah.com/bukhari:4416.
43 Shaykh Muhammad Jawad Chirri, 'The Brother of the Prophet Muhammad: Imam 'Ali', Al-Islam, https://www.al-islam.org/brother-prophet-muhammad-imam-ali-mohamad -jawad-chirri/35-hadith-analogy-you-are-me-aaron-moses (accessed 5 March 2021).
44 Answering-Ansar Unveiled, 'Is there only one difference between Aaron and Ali?' 23 June 2012, https://aaunveiled.wordpress.com/2012/06/23/is-there-only-one -difference-between-aaron-and-ali/.
45 Shia Pen, https://shiapen.com (accessed 5 March 2021).
46 Mariam Fatimah, 'Ali is to me as Aaron to Moses', ShiaSunniInfo, 19 June 2013, https://shiasunniinfo.wordpress.com/2013/06/19/ali-is-to-me-as-aaron-to-moses/ (accessed 19 June 2013).
47 Community, 'Exposing the Lies, Myths and Misunderstanding about Shia Islam', Facebook, https://www.facebook.com/Exposing-the-lies-myths-and -misunderstanding-about-Shia-Islam-142245479260824/?ref=page_internal (accessed 5 March 2021).
48 Arjana, *Pilgrimage in Islam*, 117.
49 Chisti, 'Sufi Concept: Thursday – Prophet Moses', Sufi Tavern, 18 March 2018, https:// sufi-tavern.com/sufi-doctrine/sufi-concept-thursday-prophet-moses/.
50 Shaykh Abdulkerim el Kibrisi, 'Who is Hazrat Khidr? What was Prophet Moses Encounter with Hazrat Khidr about?' Osmanlı Dergahı, https://youtu.be/zc_1jnK -44w (accessed 5 March 2021).
51 Shaykh Sayed Nurjan Mirahmadi, 'Musa & Khidr -Three Tests that Reflected the Life of Musa Sufi Meditation Center', Muhammadan Ways Sufi Realities, https://youtu.be /hBEIG335zjE (accessed 5 March 2021). Pepper and Pine, 'Letter N Story | Al-Khidr and Prophet Musa (AS)', https://youtu.be/-h1Pvy1oT-U (accessed 6 March 2021). Shaykh Sayed Nurjan Mirahmadi, 'Reality of Mirrors and Musa (as) Accompanying the Unseen Khidr', Muhammadan Way Sufi Realities, 11 May 2020, https://youtu.be/ p9f6qVC1nhU.
52 G. C. Anawati, 'Īsā', in *Encyclopaedia of Islam, Second Edition, Online*, edited by P. Bearman et al. (Leiden: Brill, 2012), http://dx.doi.org/10.1163/1573-3912_islam _COM_0378.
53 Qur'an (4:171, 5:116).
54 David Thomas, 'Christian Religion (Premodern Muslim Positions)', in *Encyclopaedia of Islam, THREE*, edited by Kate Fleet, Gudrun Krämer, Denis Matringe, John Nawas and Everett Rowson (Leiden: Brill, 2017), http://dx.doi.org/10.1163/1573-3912_ei3 _COM_25503.
55 Abu Khadeejah Abdul-Wahid, 'Jesus the Messiah in Islam, in Christianity and in Reality: 10 Points Every Christian Really must Know', SalafiBookstore.com, 14 June 2016, https://www.abukhadeejah.com/jesus-the-messiah-in-islam-in-christianity-and -in-reality/. There are many other perspectives on Jesus and Islam online.

56 Beran1979, 'Minaret of Jesus in Damascus', YouTube, https://youtu.be/TvY3mSNT6Zo. Islamic Landmarks, 'Minaret of Prop', https://www.islamiclandmarks.com/syria/minaret-of-isa-as.
57 Prophet Stories – Quran Stories, 'The Story of Prophet Isa', https://youtu.be/0vJVbWh56GE.
58 Nader Talebzadeh, 'The Messiah', 2007, https://youtu.be/9f7yqAucoHQ.
59 Al-Islam, 'An Account of 'Isa ibn Maryam (from Muhammad Baqir Majlisi, "Hayat Al-Qulub")', https://www.al-islam.org/hayat-al-qulub-vol-1-allamah-muhammad-baqir-al-majlisi/account-isa-ibn-maryam. Khalil Andani, 'The Crucifixion in Shi'a Isma'ili Islam', Ismaili Gnosis, Muhammad Legenhausen, 'Jesus Christ (as) through Shia Narrations', Aalulbayt Global Information Center, http://en.al-shia.org/content/jesus-christ-through-shia-narrations-2, The Ismaili, 'The Significance of Jesus (Nabi Isa) in Islamic Traditions', 22 December 2020, https://iicanada.org/community/significance-jesus-nabi-isa-islamic-traditions.
60 Sayyid Shouhadaa (AS) Center for Islamic Researches, 'Jesus in Shia Beliefs', Facebook, https://www.facebook.com/Jesus.Shia/photos/ (accessed 2 March 2021).
61 Rabbani Way, 'Sufism of Jesus Christ', 22 December 2014, https://rabbaniway.wordpress.com/2014/12/22/sufism-of-jesus-christ-peace-be-upon-him-and-his-successor/.
62 Rabbani Way, 'Celebrating the Birthday of Prophet Jesus Christ (AS)', 25 December 2014, https://rabbaniway.wordpress.com/2014/12/25/celebrating-the-birthday-of-prophet-jesus-christ-a-s/.
63 Mawlana Shaykh Nazim Adil Sultanul Awliya, 'Heed the Words of Jesus in Holy Qur'an', SufiLive, 19 January 2010, https://sufilive.com/Heed-the-Words-of-Jesus-in-Holy-Qur-an-2154.html.
64 Mawlana Shaykh Hisham Kabbani, 'Allah Made Jesus Speak in the Cradle', 22 January 2010, https://sufilive.com/Allah-Made-Jesus-as-Speak-in-the-Cradle-2159.html.

Chapter 3

1 The term ḥādīth is singular, but frequently denotes (especially in English) the plural *aḥādīth*, so is used here in the singular where appropriate. In its Islamic context, ḥādīth links to the words and actions of Muḥammad.
2 Hammad Safi, 'A Complete Search Engine of Quran And Hadith / Islam 360 App' (accessed 7 March 2020). Nouman Ali Khan, 'Why Do We Need Hadith If the Quran is Enough?', https://www.youtube.com/watch?v=bB4cARWalY4 (accessed 7 March 2020). Shabir Ally, 'Should We Follow All Hadith?', 16 January 2017, https://www.youtube.com/watch?v=JdFyd0HHkAE (accessed 7 March 2020). Omar Suleiman, 'Hadith #2 – God Is More Capable Than You | 40 Hadiths On Social Justice', https://www.youtube.com/watch?v=e2V1c0ABSL0.
3 Google UK Search, 'hadith', 7 March 2020, 2:56.
4 Jonathan A.C. Brown, 'Hadith: Muhammad's Legacy in the Medieval and Modern World', (Oxford: OneWorld Publications, 2009), 14.
5 The original page is available through Internet Archive. See Islamic Server of MSA-UNC, Internet Archive, 29 February 2000, https://web.archive.org/web/20000815230042/http://www.usc.edu/dept/MSA/ (accessed 7 April 2022).
6 Sunnah.com, 7 March 2020, https://sunnah.com/.

7 Daily Hadith Online, https://www.facebook.com/DailyHadithOnline/ (accessed 7 March 2020). There is a discussion on Hadith apps in chapter 6.
8 Saqib Hakak et al., 'Digital Hadith Authentication: Recent Advances, Open Challenges, and Future Directions', *Transactions on Emerging Telecommunications Technologies* 33, no. 6, https://doi.org/10.1002/ett.3977.
9 For example, see: Greentech Apps Foundation, 'Hadith Collection (All in one)', Google Play, https://play.google.com/store/apps/details?id=com.greentech.hadith&hl=en_AU (accessed 31 May 2023). This was for Android only. There were no metrics on the Apple iOS equivalent, which also had Mac and iPad versions. Greentech Apps Foundation, 'Hadith', Apple Store. https://gtaf.org/apps/hadith/ (accessed 31 May 2023). The app held 41,000 hadith sources in Arabic and English.
10 Imamia Education Center Inc, 'Hadith Database', Apple Store, https://apps.apple.com/us/app/hadith-database/id1474416214?platform=iphone (accessed 31 May 2023). This was available in different versions.
11 AlphaApps, 'The Seerah of Prophet Muhammad', https://apps.apple.com/us/app/sira-story-prophet-muhammad/id998179353 (accessed 7 March 2020), Ummah Wide, 'Teach the Life of the Prophet Muhammad to Children with the Seerah App', https://ummahwide.com/teach-the-life-of-the-prophet-muhammad-to-children-with-the-seerah-app-1fba9b150ffb (accessed 17 April 2017).
12 Taimiyyah Zubair, 'Seerah: Life of Prophet Muhammad PBUH Audio Mp3', MasterpieceApps, https://play.google.com/store/apps/details?id=net.andromo.dev653868.app655587 (accessed 7 March 2020).
13 Mufti Ismail Menk, 'Life of Muhammad PBUH', https://open.spotify.com/album/4iZNvJ4qM2oRXFPm6pKqN7?si=YuRx0UimSUO5IlhlO_Y2lQ (accessed 7 March 2020).
14 KareemTKB, 'Life of Prophet Muhammad Audio', https://play.google.com/store/apps/details?id=com.andromo.dev391844.app565436 (accessed 7 March 2020).
15 Pulu Mukharji, 'Buraq', Pinterest, https://www.pinterest.co.uk/pulumukharji/buraq/ (accessed 30 March 2022). Instagram, '#Buraq', https://www.instagram.com/explore/tags/buraq/?hl=en-gb (accessed 30 March 2022). Pinterest, 'Miraj – Ascension of the Prophet', https://www.pinterest.co.uk/pin/486177722267938348/ (accessed 31 March 2022). Pinterest, 'Isra and Mi'raj', https://www.pinterest.co.uk/americacelebrates/isra-and-miraj/ (accessed 31 March 2022).
16 Haniya Hassan, 'Scientists Proved Muhammad PBUH's Night Journey Scientifically', 28 February 2022, https://theislamicinformation.com/blogs/muhammad-night-journey-scientists/.
17 Safa Faruqui, 'Al-Isra' wal-Mi'raj: The Story of the Miraculous Night Journey', Muslim Hands, https://muslimhands.org.uk/latest/2019/04/al-isra-wal-mi-raj-the-story-of-the-miraculous-night-journey (accessed 31 March 2022).
18 Iqra Cartoon, 'Miraj & Isra', YouTube, 3 April 2019, https://youtu.be/ZafClZ7W4mc (accessed 31 March 2022).
19 Yasir Qadhi, 'The Night Journey (Al Isra Wal Miraj) – Story of Muhammad', The Daily Reminder, 24 November 2019 (accessed 31 March 2022). Yahya Ibrahim, 'The Night Journey – Al-Isra Wal-Mi'raj', *Islamic Guidance*, 2 June 2018, https://youtu.be/Gi0dbmI2CyY (accessed 31 March 2022). Mufti Ismail Menk, 'Isra-Wal-Miraj', 2 December 2020, https://youtu.be/zzT4nfgmB3w.
20 Abdal Hakim Murad, 'Messages from the Miraj', Cambridge Central Mosque, 25 February 2022, https://youtu.be/IfHhYqNPHcs.
21 Sayed Ammar Nakshawani, '2 Reasons Behind Prophet Muhammad Meraj', Thaqlain, https://youtu.be/Ov9rVxOT5zs (accessed 31 March 2022).

22 Sayed Saleh Qazwini, 'Life of the Prophet: The Isra & The Miraj', 4ilmNet, 23 May 2018, https://youtu.be/DxzlLfoa-kQ (accessed 31 March 2022). Maulana Nusrat Abbas Bukhari, 'Safar E Meraj', Message of Hidayat, 3 April 2019, https://youtu.be/LH4BPYBG83w.
23 The Ahl ul-Bayt 'people of the house (of the prophet)' feature in Chapter Six.
24 Shaykh Sayed Nurjan Mirahmadi, 'Intergalactic Gateway to Heaven via Jacob's Ladder Isra Miraj', Sufi Meditation Center, 26 March 2020, https://www.nurmuhammad.com/intergalactic-gateway-to-heaven-via-jacobs-ladder-isra-miraj-sufi-meditation-center/.
25 Shaykh Hisham Kabbani, 'The Wisdom Behind Isra' and Mi'raj (The Night Journey)', SufiLive, 24 April 2013, https://youtu.be/vUhoKR6GqlU.
26 Angga Arifka, 'Isra Miraj of Muhammad According to Sufism', Perrenial Wisdom, 27 February 2022, https://youtu.be/KS-JzeR9wfU (accessed 31 March 2022).
27 More detail on jihad features in chapter 10.
28 Onepath Network, 'Five Major Lessons from the Battle of Badr', YouTube, 29 June 2017, https://youtu.be/kQ_qcw05BHI (accessed 4 April 2022).
29 Sheikh Shady Alsuleiman, 'The Epic Battle of Badr – 313 Vs. 1000', The Daily Reminder, 11 June 2017, https://youtu.be/HHJKkP7AfVw.
30 HistoryMarche, 'Battle of Badr, 624, Islam's First Arrow', YouTube, 25 July 2021, https://youtu.be/zioVlE8Vt_s (accessed 4 April 2022).
31 Moustapha Akkad, 'The Message', Film, 1976. Mushtaque Munshi, 'Islamic War – Battle of Badr also known as Gazwa-e-Badr', YouTube, 12 July 2013, https://youtu.be/JStUv1lnFxU.
32 Iqra Cartoon, 'Battle of Badr', https://youtu.be/3Tfnt-DafPM (accessed 4 April 2022).
33 Abu Huzaifa, 'Site of the Battle of Badr', https://www.islamiclandmarks.com/saudiarabia-additional-places/site-of-the-battle-of-badr (accessed 4 April 2022), Tripadvisor, 'Mosque of Badr', https://www.tripadvisor.co.uk/Attraction_Review-g298551-d319512-Reviews-Mosque_of_Badr-Medina_Al_Madinah_Province.html (accessed 4 April 2022).
34 A3 Creations, 'Badr, A Battlefield in Islamic History- Saudi Arabia-Vlog', 8 March 2021, https://youtu.be/8Fh3zw-DHrM (accessed 4 April 2022), Shaykh Amer Jamil, 'The Battle of Badr Recorded at the Site of Badr (Short Reminder)', 4 July 2015, https://youtu.be/Sg38E80f4S4 (accessed 4 April 2022), Travel & Food Show, 'Road Trip/Tour of Badr, Saudi Arabia', https://youtu.be/zy6YD1B9eu8 (accessed 4 April 2022).

Chapter 4

1 Yaqeen Institute, 'Khadijah: His First Love, Our First Mother | The Firsts with Sh. Omar Suleiman', 12 December 2019, https://www.youtube.com/watch?v=gRBTQKlfC78.
2 Quran Weekly, 'The Superstars: Women of Paradise! Khadijah bint Khuwaylid (#Loyalty) – Omar Suleiman', https://youtu.be/IKASMwUWV9c (accessed 25 May 2013).
3 Stories of the Prophets – Quran Stories, 'Family of Prophet Muhammad (SAW) Stories | Khadija (RA) Wife of Prophet | Part 1 | Quran Stories', 3 April 2018, https://youtu.be/LqcavQ2AlQM.
4 Ahlulbayt, 'Khadijah: The Lady of Quraish', 25 November 2018, https://www.youtube.com/watch?v=_HBfm71Y_4I.

5 Yasin T. Al-Jibouri, 'Khadijah, Daughter of Khuwaylid, Wife of the Prophet Muhammad', Ahlul Bayt Digital Islamic Library Project, 1 February 2021, https://www.al-islam.org/articles/khadijah-daughter-khuwaylid-wife-prophet-muhammad-yasin-t-al-jibouri.

6 Ghuraba, 'Khadija, R.A.', https://www.pinterest.co.uk/dicuento/khadijah-ra/ (accessed 1 February 2021).

7 The Islamic Quotes, '50 Best Islamic Quotes About Hijab with Images', Pinterest, https://www.pinterest.co.uk/pin/281897257912919952/ (accessed 4 March 2021).

8 Sahih Al-Bukhari – Book 58 Hadith 164. Hadith of the Day, 'Khadijah Bint Khuwaylid RA: Umm-Al-Mu'minīn (Mother of Believers)', https://hadithoftheday.com/khadija-ra/ (accessed 1 February 2021).

9 Muzmatch, 'Khadijah & Muhammad: The Story of Love & Faith (Zainab bint Younus)', https://muzmatch.com/en-GB/blog/community/khadijah-muhammad-the-story-of-love-faith (accessed 1 February 2021).

10 Dar ul-Ifta al Missriyya, 'Why did Prophet Muhammad Marry Lady 'Aisha When She was only 9 Years Old?', https://www.dar-alifta.org/Foreign/ViewArticle.aspx?ID=144 (accessed 2 February 2021).

11 Hatem Aly, 'Moments of Romantic Love Between Prophet Muhammad & Aisha', About Islam, https://aboutislam.net/family-life/husbands-wives/moments-of-romantic-love-between-prophet-muhammad-aisha/ (accessed 2 February 2021).

12 Muslim Central, 'Married At Nine – Aisha RA – Prophet Muhammad', https://youtu.be/rTIlm1JFyt8 (accessed 2 February 2021).

13 Abû Imân 'Abd ar-Rahmân Robert Squires, 'Muslim Answers: The Young Marriage of cAishah', Islamic Awareness, https://www.islamic-awareness.org/polemics/aishah.html (accessed 2 February 2021).

14 Al Islam, 'Did Muhammad Marry Aisha When She was only Six Years Old?', https://www.alislam.org/question/muhammad-marry-aisha-six-years/ (accessed 2 February 2021).

15 Nuriddeen Knight, 'The Woman Behind the Number: The Irrelevance of the Age of 'Aisha (ra)', https://yaqeeninstitute.org/nuriddeen-knight/the-woman-behind-the-number-the-irrelevance-of-the-age-of-aisha-ra (accessed 3 February 2021).

16 See, for example, the discussion on *Sūra al-N*ūr (24) in Nasr et al., eds., *The Study Quran*, 865–76.

17 For one account of this episode, see Martin Lings, *Muhammad: His Life based on the Earliest Sources* (London: George Allen & Unwin, 1983), 240–6.

18 Islam Hashtag, 'Ayat about Hazrat Aisha in Quran: "The Story of ifk-Slander of Aisha ra"', https://islamhashtag.com/ayat-about-hazrat-aisha-in-quran-the-story-of-slander-of-aisha/.

19 al Missriyya, 'Why did Prophet Muhammad Marry Lady 'Aisha When She was only 9 Years Old?'

20 Abdul Hakeem Oranu, 'The Devil's Deception of the Salafi-Deobandi Partnership', http://www.shiapen.com/nasibi/salafi-deobandi/preface.html.

21 Gawaher, 'Refuting Shia Allegations Against Wives of the Prophet (S)', https://www.gawaher.com/topic/740956-refuting-shia-allegations-against-wives-of-the-prophet-s/.

22 Shia Pen, 'Chapter Nine – Objections to the Shia criticisms Leveled at Ayesha' (accessed 17 February 2021).

23 V. Vacca and Ruth Roded, 'Ṣafiyya', in *Encyclopaedia of Islam: Second Edition*, edited by P. Bearman et al. vol. Online (Leiden: Brill, 2012), http://dx.doi.org/10.1163/1573-3912_islam_SIM_6451.

24 Laura (Muhajabah), 'Potentially Asexual Women in Early Muslim History', https://www.asexualityandislam.com/2015/07/potentially-asexual-women-in-early-muslim-history.html.
25 Islamic Guidance, 'Sawdah Bint Al-Zam'ah [RA]', https://youtu.be/1isH6Zemit0 (accessed 17 February 2021). This was based on Islamic Media, 'Mothers of the Believers – Sawda bint Zamʿa', https://youtu.be/-eKwz5gVJXM. Also see Memphis Islamic Center, 'Mothers of the Believers pt.6 | Sawda Bint Zam'a | Sh. Dr. Yasir Qadhi', https://youtu.be/OcPOZd1edec.
26 Questions and Answers in Islam, 'Is It True that Our Prophet Offered Divorce to His Wife Hazrath Sawda?' https://questionsonislam.com/question/it-true-our-prophet-offered-divorce-his-wife-hazrath-sawda (accessed 16 February 2021).
27 Discussed on the Ahmadiyya site Al Hakam, 'Hazrat Hafsa bint Umar ibn al-Khattab', https://www.alhakam.org/hazrat-hafsa-bint-umar-ibn-al-khattab/ (accessed 17 February 2021).
28 TwelverShia.net, 'Hafsa in the Eyes of Sunnis and Shias', https://www.twelvershia.net/ (accessed 17 February 2021).
29 Theresa Corbin, 'Discovering the Personality of Hafsa bint Umar', 25 May 2023, https://aboutislam.net/family-life/husbands-wives/discovering-the-personality-of-hafsa-bint-umar/.
30 Let the Quran Speak, 'A Woman (Hafsa bint Umar) Compiled the Quran? (discussion with Dr Shabir Ally)', https://youtu.be/pn_aboEvXt8. Ruqayyah Y. Khan, 'Did a Woman Edit the Qur'ān? Hafṣa and her Famed "Codex"', *Journal of the American Academy of Religion* 82 (March 2014): 174–216, https://www.jstor.org/stable/24488028.
31 Mansoor Alam, 'The Quran: History of its Compilation', https://www.islamicity.org/17075/the-quran-history-of-its-compilation/ (accessed 17 February 2021).
32 al-Islam, 'Exemplary Women: Lady Umm Salamah – Fahimeh Fahiminejad (trans.)', https://www.al-islam.org/message-thaqalayn/vol-12-no-4-winter-2012/exemplary-women-lady-umm-salamah-fahimeh-fahiminejad/exemplary.
33 Al-Sirraj, 'Mother of the Believers Umm Salama', http://www.alsiraj.net/English/albayt/html/page05.html (accessed 22 February 2021). Islam Wikia, 'Umm Salama Hind bint Abi Umayya: Biography by Ibn Kathir', *Wives of Muhammad*, https://islam.wikia.org/wiki/Umm_Salama_Hind_bint_Abi_Umayya.
34 Netanel Miles-Yépez, 'Risala: The Chain of Transmission', http://inayatisufism.org/risala-blog/tag/Umm+Salama (accessed 22 February 2021.)
35 Islamweb, 'Search: Umm Salamah', https://www.islamweb.net/en/index.php?page=result&q=umm+salamah (accessed 22 February 2021).
36 Wiki Islam, 'The Massacre of the Banu Qurayza', https://wikiislam.net/wiki/The_Massacre_of_the_Banu_Qurayza (accessed 22 March 2021). Prophet of Mercy, 'Was Prophet Muhammad Anti-Semitic, and did He Slaughter the Men, Women, and Children of the Jewish Tribe of Banu Qurayza? Did He Plan an Ethnic Cleansing of the Jewish People from the Arabian Peninsula?' Muslim World League – Global Commission for Introducing the Messenger, https://mercyprophet.org/mul/node/3319 (accessed 22 February 2021).
37 Vacca and Roded, 'Ṣafiyya'.
38 WikiIslam, 'Safiyah', https://wikiislam.net/wiki/Safiyah#Analysis (accessed 23 February 2021).
39 Mohd Elfie Nieshaem Juferi, 'Ansar Al-'Adl: Umm ul-Mukminin Safiyyah: The Jewish Wife of Muhammad(P) (Thread)', IslamicBoard.

40 Tamana Kahn, *Untold: A History of the Wives of Prophet Muhammad* (Rhinebeck: Monkfish, 2010).
41 *Sūra al-Kawthar* (108).
42 Sayyed Mohammad al-Musawi, 'Can You Please Explain the Incident Involving Mariya al-Qibtiya. Did it have a Connection with the Revelation of any Quranic verses?' https://www.al-islam.org/ask/can-you-please-explain-the-incident-involving-mariya-al-qibtiya-did-it-have-a-connection-with-the-revelation-of-any-quranic-verses/sayyed-mohammad-al-musawi (accessed 30 October 2023). Abdullah Anik Misra, 'Was Mariya al-Qibtiyya Ever a Wife of the Prophet Muhammad?' IslamQA, https://islamqa.org/hanafi/seekersguidance-hanafi/32841 (accessed 30 October 2023).
43 IslamWeb, 'Fatwa No: 90298: Being Married to a Christian Wife', 12 July 2005, https://www.islamweb.net/en/fatwa/90298/.
44 Yasir Qadhi, Muslim Central, 'Seerah – 97 Maria the Copt & Death of Ibrahim', 7 December 2014, https://muslimcentral.com/yasir-qadhi-seerah-97-maria-the-copt-death-of-ibrahim/.
45 Sam Shamoun, 'Mary, Muhammad's Concubine', Answering Islam, https://www.answeringislam.info/Shamoun/mary_concubine.htm (accessed 27 February 2021). Muslim Responses, 'On Mary, The Holy Prophet (S) Wife (Round Five)', http://muslim-responses.com/Round_5/Round_5/.
46 Qur᾽ān, *Sūraal-Ahzab,* 33:37.
47 QuestionsOnIslam, 'The Prophet Marries Hazrat Zaynab Bint Jahsh', https://questionsonislam.com/article/prophet-marries-hazrat-zaynab-bint-jahsh.
48 IslamWeb, 'Fatwa No: 139996: The Year when Adoption was Forbidden', 17 August 2015, https://www.islamweb.org/en/fatwa/139996/the-year-when-adoption-was-forbidden.
49 IslamQA, 'Question 96464: Detailed Discussion about the verse "But You Did Hide in Yourself (i.e. what Allaah has Already made Known to You that He will Give Her to You in Marriage) that which Allaah will make Manifest" [al-Ahzaab 33:37]', https://islamqa.info/en/answers/96464/detailed-discussion-about-the-verse-but-you-did-hide-in-yourself-ie-what-allaah-has-already-made-known-to-you-that-he-will-give-her-to-you-in-marriage-that-which-allaah-will-make-manifest-al-ahzaab-3337 (accessed 23 February 2021). Dar-alifta.org, 'Closer Look at Prophet Muhammad's Marriages', https://www.dar-alifta.org/Foreign/ViewArticle.aspx?ID=17&CategoryID=5 (accessed 23 February 2021).
50 Ideal Muslimah, 'Zaynab bint Jahsh Al-Asadiyah', https://idealmuslimah.com/personalities/sahaabiyaat/196-zaynab-bint-jahsh-al-asadiyah.html (accessed 23 February 2021).
51 Islamic Guidance, 'Zaynab Bint Al-Jahsh [RA]', 15 November 2018, https://youtu.be/vEYkgHi6yQM.
52 This theme forms part of an extensive selection of Shīʿa lectures available on Nudba.com; Al Qazwini lived and studied in the United States from a long-standing family of scholars who returned to Karbala when Saddam Hussein's regime fell. Sayed Hossein Al Qazwini, 'The Controversial Marriage of the Prophet to Zainab bint Jahsh', https://youtu.be/JbxFCqrLNRQ (accessed 23 February 2021).
53 Iqraa, 'The Best Women on Earth Um Habiba (with Dr Abla Kahlawi)', 28 February 2014, https://youtu.be/jcX-T4R5IpM.
54 Abu Tariq Hijazi, 'Bilal ibn Rabah: The Symbol of Human Equality', *Arab News*, 15 January 2015, https://www.arabnews.com/islam-perspective/news/689996. Stories of the Prophets – Quran Stories, 'Sahaba Stories – Companions of the Prophet | Hazrat Bilal Ibn Rabah (RA) | Part 1 | Quran Stories', https://youtu.be/bBAy81MwxLY.

55 Pashew Nuri, 'From Slave to Master: The Story of Bilal the Unbreakable', *Medium*, 27 June 2020, https://medium.com/know-thyself-heal-thyself/from-slave-to-master-the-story-of-bilal-the-unbreakable-9b2754f0ec0c (accessed 1 March 2021).

56 Questions on Islam, 'Abdullah bin Zayd (r.a.)', https://questionsonislam.com/article/abdullah-bin-zayd-ra (accessed 1 March 2021).

57 Tri-D, 'Bilal', App. Google Play, 2019, https://play.google.com/store/apps/details?id=trid.bilal&hl=en&gl=US. 360 ADN, 'Bilal Muezzin – Islam – Sunna – Coran – Duas', Google Play, 2021, https://play.google.com/store/apps/details?id=com.bilalmeuzzin.bilalmuezzinapp, Arabia For Information & Technology, 'Bilal', Google Play, 2020, https://play.google.com/store/apps/details?id=com.arabiait.belal.

58 JACOAPPS, 'Bilal Ibn Rabah Biography', Google Play, 2020.

59 Berhan Apps, 'Bilal: Ethiopian Muslim Neshida', Google Play, 2020, https://play.google.com/store/apps/details?id=com.berhanapps.ethiopian_muslim_neshida.

60 YouTube, 'The Message – Bilal Giving the 1st Call to Prayer', https://youtu.be/IwoM64-a4rg, (accessed 30 October 2023).

61 For example, see Kanal 7, 'Hazreti Bilal-i Habesi', 7 February 2018, https://youtu.be/sSQHWyr03yU. Çetin Inanç, 'Hazreti Bilal-i Habesi', Film, Turkey, 1973.

62 Reviews are on IMDb, 'Bilal: A New Breed of Hero', https://www.imdb.com/title/tt3576728/ (accessed 1 March 2021), Umm Muhammad, 'Why I Walked Out of the Film, Bilal', Muslim Matters, 5 February 2019, https://muslimmatters.org/2018/02/05/why-i-walked-out-of-the-film-bilal/. Khurram H. Alavi and Ayman Jamal, 'Bilal: A New Breed of Hero', Film, 2015.

63 Appsinnovate, 'Bilal: A New Breed of Hero', 2016, https://play.google.com/store/apps/details?id=com.appsinnovate.bilal.

64 Islamicity, 'Omar Ibn Khattab Series: Episode 1 – Omar Ibn Khattab', https://www.islamicity.org/series/omar-ibn-khattab-series-episode-1-english-subtitles/. Egypt Independent, 'Omar ibn al-Khattab TV Series Raises Controversy', *Al-Masry al-Youm*, https://egyptindependent.com/omar-ibn-al-khattab-tv-series-raises-controversy/. Huda TV, 'Huda, Is it Allowed to Watch Series about Umar (RA)', https://youtu.be/1hiMwxek0Nw.

65 Prophetic Journey, 'Omar Series-English Subtitles-Episode-1', 3 May 2023, https://youtu.be/OSxqoWdwdNA?si=b5B37LTSk-dpkdK1.

66 Oregon Islamic Chaplains Organization, 11 February 2013, https://www.facebook.com/oico1reentry/posts/umar-ibn-al-khattab-was-once-a-tyrant-before-he-entered-islam-he-committed-many-/142121592615180/.

67 Sufia Khann, 'Death Of Second Caliph- Umar Ibn Al-Khattab', https://www.wattpad.com/766791896-inspirational-islamic-stories-death-of-second (accessed 15 February 2021).

68 Islamic Guidance, 'Uthman Ibn Affan RA', 1 March 2018, https://youtu.be/P1aOV-fd3eA.

69 Zulfiqaar Media, 'The Story Of Uthman Ibn Affan ~ Mufti Ismail Menk ~ Ramadan 2014', 3 July 2014, https://youtu.be/oXie-AAPqtc.

70 My Favorite Islamic Videos, 'Uthman bin Affan', 7 December 2020, https://www.facebook.com/watch/?v=783768765687855.

71 Stories of the Prophets – Quran Stories, 'Sahaba Stories – Companions of the Prophet | Uthman Bin Affan (RA) | Quran Stories in English', 13 July 2018, https://youtu.be/mme8KpLdf_0.

72 Questions on Islam, 'What Are the Reasons for the Wars among Ashara al-Mubashshara (Companions)?' 9 January 2017, https://questionsonislam.com/question/what-are-reasons-wars-among-ashara-al-mubashshara-companions (accessed 8 April 2022).

73 For example, a series of audio lectures features each of the ten. Yasir Qadhi, 'Lives of Sahaba 38 – Talha Ibn Ubaydullah (Ashara Mubashara)', n.d., https://soundcloud.com/zikr/lives-of-sahaba-38-talha-ibn. Also see Elif Eryarsoy Aydın, 'Companions Promised Paradise (Ashara Mubashara)', 20 June 2013, https://www.lastprophet.info/companions-promised-paradise-ashara-mubashara.

74 ZamZam Academy, 'Abu Ubaidah ibn al-Jarrah | Mufti Abdur-Rahman ibn Yusuf', 3 November 2016, https://www.zamzamacademy.com/2016/11/abu-ubaidah-ibn-al-jarrah-mufti-abdur-rahman-ibn-yusuf/.

Chapter 5

1 Bunt, *Islam in the Digital Age*, 124–204.

2 Hiroyuki Yanagihashi, 'Abū Ḥanīfa', in *Encyclopaedia of Islam, THREE*,, edited by Kate Fleet et al., Online edn (Leiden: Brill, 2007).

3 Miftaah Institute, 'Imam Abu Hanifa: The Juggernaut of Jurisprudence', 21 January 2019, https://miftaah.org/articles/2019/1/21/imam-abu-hanifa-the-juggernaut-of-jurisprudence (accessed 1 December 2021).

4 Islamic Guidance, 'Imam Abu Hanifa (RA)', YouTube, 11 January 2018, https://youtu.be/CRc1b0ogVx4 (accessed 1 December 2021). Light of the Ummah, 'Who Was: Imam Abu Hanifa | His Early Life', 3 February 2017, https://youtu.be/LptH5xXA4rM (accessed 1 December 2021). Shaykh Saqib Iqbal Shaami, 'Mind Blowing Intellect of Imam Abu Hanifa', YouTube, 30 March 2020, https://youtu.be/lEhfkazR7iw (accessed 1 December 2021).

5 Tripadvisor, 'Abu Hanifa Mosque', https://www.tripadvisor.co.uk/Attraction_Review-g294001-d5999963-Reviews-Abu_Hanifa_Mosque-Baghdad_Baghdad_Province.html (accessed 1 December 2021).

6 Makan Consulting Engineers, 'Abu Hanifa Mosque', 2 June 2020, https://www.facebook.com/watch/?v=334944570820234.

7 Korean Traveler, 'Abu Hanifa Call to Prayer', 7 August 2021, https://youtu.be/T-6cxSwTvIM (accessed 1 December 2021). Also see Mazar Mubarak - Imran Ghazi, 'IMAM ABU HANIFA: Hazrat Noman Bin Sabit | Founder of Hanafi School of Islamic Law', YouTube, 28 February 2018 (accessed 1 December 2021).

8 The National, 'Watch Prophet Muhammad's Birthday Celebrations in Baghdad', 18 October 2021, https://www.thenationalnews.com/mena/iraq/2021/10/18/watch-prophet-mohammeds-birthday-celebrations-in-baghdad/.

9 Deoband Online, 'Online Islamic Primacy Source Search Facility during COVID-19 Pandemic – Mar 2020', http://www.deoband.net/blogs/online-islamic-primacy-source-search-facility-during-covid-19-pandemic-mar-2020.

10 IslamQA.org, 'About', https://islamqa.org/about/ (accessed 8 December 2021).

11 Hanafi Madhhab, Facebook, https://www.facebook.com/hanafimadhhab/ (accessed 8 December 2021).

12 Hanafifiqh, https://www.instagram.com/explore/tags/hanafifiqh/?hl=en (accessed 8 December 2021).

13 Essentialislamicknowledge, https://www.instagram.com/essentialislamicknowledge/ (accessed 8 December 2021).

14 Hanafi Memes, https://www.instagram.com/hanafimemes/ (accessed 8 December 2021).

15 Hanafi Memes, 'Types of Headaches', 15 May 2020, https://www.instagram.com/p/CAM9gJBAA-M/.
16 Mufti Waseem Khan, 'Halal Memes', DarulUloomTT.net, 13 June 2018, https://islamqa.org/?p=149102.
17 Reddit, '/r/Izlam', https://www.reddit.com/r/Izlam/ (accessed 10 December 2021).
18 N. Cottart, 'Mālikiyya', in *Encyclopaedia of Islam, Second Edition*, edited by P. Bearman et al., vol. Online (Leiden: Brill, 2012). J. Schacht, 'Mālik b. Anas', in *Encyclopaedia of Islam, Second Edition*, edited by P. Bearman et al., vol. Online (Leiden: Brill, 2012).
19 `A'isha `Abdarahman at-Tarjumana and Ya`qub Johnson, trans., 'Translation of Malik's Muwatta', International Islamic University Malaysia, https://www.iium.edu.my/deed/hadith/malik/index.html (accessed 3 December 2021). Hadith Collection, 'Malik's Muwatta', http://hadithcollection.com/maliksmuwatta.html (accessed 3 December 2021).
20 Islamobile, 'Al-Muwatta Pro', App Store, https://apps.apple.com/us/app/al-muwatta-pro-english-arabic/id1535874914#?platform=iphone (accessed 3 December 2021).
21 Azzure Labs, 'Al Muwatta (Sahih Muwatta)', https://apps.apple.com/gb/app/al-muwatta-sahih-muwatta/id572829585#?platform=ipad (accessed 3 December 2021).
22 The Right Way, 'Muwatta Imam Malik Arabic & English', https://play.google.com/store/apps/details?id=com.islam.asta.muwatta_malik&hl=en_US&gl=US (accessed 3 December 2021).
23 Usman Pervez, 'Muwatta Imam Malik – Urdu and English Translation', https://play.google.com/store/apps/details?id=com.quranemajeedapp.org.Muwatta&hl=en&gl=US (accessed 3 December 2021).
24 E. Chaumont, 'al-S̲h̲āfiʿī', in *Encyclopaedia of Islam, Second Edition*, edited by P. Bearman et al., vol. Online (Leiden: Brill, 2012), http://dx.doi.org/10.1163/1573-3912_islam_COM_1020>.
25 Louay Safi, 'Shafi'i's Risala', Education City, 25 September 2019, https://www.educationcity.qa/index.php/en/Shafi_Risala. Abdal Hakim Murad, 'Imam al-Shafi'i: The Worshipping Saint', 4 March 2013, https://youtu.be/bUxc-g4rP4g. Joseph E. Lowry, 'Translating al-Shafi`i's Risala', NYUAD Institute, 1 April 2016, https://youtu.be/0uYlJJgV0yI.
26 Sheikh Ali Gomaa, 'Imam al-Shafi'i Part 1', 20 November 2012, https://www.youtube.com/watch?v=fHVR20D3gH8.
27 EgySwag | Aya Ebrahim, 'Imam al-Shafi'i dome', 24 September 2021, https://youtu.be/WXQlMTE057s.
28 At the time of writing, a complete English version was unavailable. Several people had petitioned the app developers of this Indonesian version for an English equivalent. TKZ Apps, 'Fiqih Islam Imam Syafi'i Lengkap', 21 January 2019, https://play.google.com/store/apps/details?id=com.kitab.fiqihimamsyafiilengkap&hl=en&gl=US. Mumtaz Innovation, 'Ar-Risalah As-Syafie', 6 March 2020, https://play.google.com/store/apps/details?id=com.andromo.dev887750.app1027894. There were collections of different schools, with extracts of Shafi'i, such as Sayyid Saabiq, 'Fiqh-us-Sunnah', WIN Solutions, https://apps.apple.com/us/app/fiqh-us-sunnah/id448143877.
29 Livnat Holtzman, 'Aḥmad b. Ḥanbal', in *Encyclopaedia of Islam, THREE*, edited by Kate Fleet et al., vol. Online (Leiden: Brill, 2009).
30 Abdal Hakim Murad, 'Imam Ahmad ibn Hanbal: Victor Over Tribulation', Qanit Takmeel, 12 March 2013, https://youtu.be/kLP4azotzrA.

31 Abdul Bari Abu al-Khair, 'The Imam', Online ed., YouTube, (Qater, 2017). General editor, Qatar Media Foundation, https://youtu.be/JRSEuQdi3yU.

32 Akhzar Nazir, 'Musnad Imam Ahmad | Hadith', App Store, https://apps.apple.com/us/app/musnad-imam-ahmad-hadith/id1491532099 (accessed 7 December 2021). Also see a compilation of several hadith sources by the same developer: Akhzar Nazir, 'Hadith Collection English', App Store, https://apps.apple.com/us/app/hadith-collection-english/id1549214067 (accessed 7 December 2021).

33 Wael B. Hallaq, 'The Gate of Ijtihad: A Study in Islamic Legal History' (University of Washington, 1983.), 45–6.

34 F. R. C. Bagley, 'Introduction', in *Ghazali's Book of Counsel for Kings (Nasihat al-muluk), al-Ghazali, Abu Hamid Muhammad b. Muhammad al-Tusi, Translated by F R C Bagley* (London: Oxford University Press/University of Durham Publications, 1964), xxxiv.

35 Ibid., lv. Albert Hourani, *A History of the Arab Peoples* (London: Faber & Faber, 1991), 143.

36 For a detailed analysis, see Jon Hoover, *Ibn Taymiyya* (London: OneWorld, 2019). Also see Henri Laoust, *La Profession de Foi d'ibn Taymiyya: Texte, traduction et commentaire de la Wasitiyya,* vol. 10 (Librairie Orientaliste Paul Geuthner, Bibliotheque d'etudes Islamiques, 1986). Yahya Michot, *Muslims under non-Muslim Rule. Ibn Taymiyya* (Oxford: Interface Publications, 2006).

37 Henri Laoust, *Essai sur les doctrines sociales et politiques de Taki-d-Din Ahmad b. Taimiya* (Cairo: Imprimerie de l'Institute Francais d'Archeologie Orientale, 1939), 578–9.

38 The Qur᾽ān, al-Nisā᾽, Women. 4:94. Nasr et al., eds, *The Study Quran*, 235.

39 Noor Book, 'Ibn Taymiyyah Expounds on Islam', https://www.noor-book.com/en/ebook-Ibn-Taymiyyah-Expounds-on-Islam--pdf (accessed 16 December 2021). Kamamullah, 'Ibn Taymiyyah', https://www.kalamullah.com/ibn-taymiyyah.html (accessed 16 December 2021).

40 TROID, 'Ibn Taymiyyah', https://www.troid.org/authors/the-salaf-scholars-of-the-salaf/97-ibn-taymiyyah (accessed 16 December 2021). See the discussion on Salafi publications online: Abusharif, 'Cyber-Islamic Environments and Salafī-Ṣūfī Contestations'.

41 So Smart Apps, 'مكتبة ابن تيمية - 17 كتاب بدون نت', 21 August 2020, https://play.google.com/store/apps/details?id=so.ateya.ahmed.tymain_3books (accessed 16 December 2021).

42 Akhil Varghese, 'Ibn Taymiyyah', Pinterest, https://in.pinterest.com/akhilbabuvarghese/ibn-taymiyyah/ (accessed 16 December 2021), Mohammad Nawaz, 'Ibn Taymiyyah', Pinterest, https://www.pinterest.co.uk/monawaz11/ibn-taymiyyah/ (accessed 16 December 2021).

43 Shaykh Mohammad Yasir Al-Hanafi, 'Ibn Taymiyyah's Opinion on The 4 Madhāhib', Hanafi Fiqh Channel, 14 June 2015, https://youtu.be/oAqvKZIlKOg.

44 Salafi Ahlus Sunnah, 'The Salafi Hero Shaykh Al-Islam Ibn Taymiyyah (RA)', YouTube, 18 July 2012, https://youtu.be/mUiCUILgQKE. Henri Lauzière, *The Making of Salafism: Islamic Reform in the Twentieth Century* (New York: Columbia University Press, 2015).

45 Hourani, *A History of the Arab Peoples*, 308.

46 Annabelle Böttcher, 'Ibn Taymiyya and Ibn Qayyim al-Jawziyya as Changing Salafi Icons', in *Islamic Theology, Philosophy and Law: Debating Ibn Taymiyya and Ibn Qayyim Al-Jawziyya*, edited by Birgit Krawietz and Georges Tamer (Berlin: de

Gruyter, 2013), 461–92, Rebecca Molloy, 'Deconstructing Ibn Taymiyya's Views on Suicidal Missions', *CTC Sentinel* 2, no. 3 (2009), https://ctc.usma.edu/deconstructing-ibn-taymiyyas-views-on-suicidal-missions/.

47 Thomas Hegghammer, *The Caravan: Abdallah Azzam and the Rise of Global Jihad*, Ebook edn (Cambridge: Cambridge University Press, 2020), 290.

48 N. Kazimi, 'Zarqawi's anti-Shi'a Legacy: Original or Borrowed?' Hudson Institute, 1 November 2006, https://www.hudson.org/research/9908-zarqawi-s-anti-shi-a-legacy-original-or-borrowed (accessed 20 December 2021). See the discussion on Zarqāwī in Bunt, *iMuslims*, Chapter 5.

49 Jamileh Kadivar, 'Exploring Takfir, Its Origins and Contemporary Use: The Case of Takfiri Approach in Daesh's Media', *Contemporary Review of the Middle East* 7, no. 3 (2020): 259–85, https://doi.org/10.1177/2347798920921706. Bunt, *Hashtag Islam*, 123–40.

50 Henri Laoust, 'Ibn Ḳayyim al-Djawziyya', in *Encyclopaedia of Islam, Second Edition*, edited by P. Bearman et al., vol. Online (Leiden: Brill, 2012), http://dx.doi.org/10.1163/1573-3912_islam_SIM_3242.

51 Islampdfs, 'Provisions of the Afterlife Which Lie Within Prophetic Guidance – Ibn Qayyim', https://islampdfs.wordpress.com/category/authors/ibn-qayyim-al-jawziyyah/ (accessed 21 December 2021), Kalamullah, 'Ibn Qayyim', https://www.kalamullah.com/ibn-qayyim.html (accessed 21 December 2021).

52 Quotefancy, 'TOP 20 Ibn Qayyim Al-Jawziyya Quotes', YouTube, 26 January 2018, https://youtu.be/YOnRDxGOD6c.

53 APKPure, 'Ibn Qayyim Al-Jaqziyya Quotes', https://m.apkpure.com/ibn-qayyim-al-jawziyya-quotes/com.quotesgarden.ibnqayyimaljawziyyaquotesapp (accessed 21 December 2021). Also see So Smart Apps, 'مكتبة كتب ابن القيم - 21 كتاب بدون نت', Google Play, 20 December 2020, https://play.google.com/store/apps/details?id=so.ateya.ahmed.ibnElqaim_Lib_BT (accessed 21 December 2021). This was also subject to 'inappropriate advertising' according to reviewers.

54 Ahmad Kutty, 'Giants of Islamic Civilization – Ibn Qayyim al-Jawziyya', YouTube, 16 January 2017, https://youtu.be/0ruj5ZV5VBs.

55 Simply Seerah Studios, 'Ibn Al-Qayyim's Poem to Christians', 19 February 2018, https://youtu.be/FNGGaY50ey8.

56 C. A. Bayley, *Indian Society and the Making of the British Empire* (Cambridge: Cambridge University Press, 1988). *The New Cambridge History of India II:1*, 165–7.

57 J. M. S. Baljon, *Religion and Thought of Shah Wali Allah Dihlawi 1703-1762* (Leiden: E.J. Brill, 1986), 1–17.

58 Ibid., 18–19.

59 Abdur Raheem Abu Nu'man, 'Life of Shah Waliullah Muhaddith Dehlawi', Hanafi Fiqh Channel, 16 January 2011, https://youtu.be/nOi_pPjEsnY.

60 Services Academy, 'Pakistan Affairs', 19 April 2020, https://www.youtube.com/watch?v=UA_2S4PHyTw (accessed 29 December 2021). Ali Shah Jindani, 'Shah Waliullah Dehlawi', Jindani Academy, 28 May 2021, https://youtu.be/AtiS7AaGRCo (accessed 29 December 2021).

61 Israr Ahmad, 'Shah Waliullah Dehlawi (R.A) – (1/2) Dr.Israr', 16 September 2012, https://youtu.be/hl1OxboxleY. Also, see: Yahya Momla, 'Life of Shah Waliullah Dehalwi', Masjid al-Salaam and Education Centre, 13 November 2017, https://youtu.be/NOqYpulDu8Q (accessed 29 December 2021). Zakariyya Masjid, 'SHAH WALIULLAH DEHLAWI (R.A) -Scholars of the Subcontinent series- Part 3', 20 November 2020, https://www.youtube.com/watch?v=TpNk1K4R_7U (accessed 29

December 2021). I interviewed Israr Ahmad during PhD research in the mid-1990s.

62 Kashif-ul-Huda, 'Shah Waliullah', TwoCirclesTV, 10 February 2012, https://youtu.be/Uzr9kpeSO1U (accessed 29 December 2021).

63 Mazar Mubarak - Imran Ghazi, 'Famous Mohaddish: Hazrat Shah Waliullah Muhaddith E Dehlvi (lecturer: Allama Sayyed Muhammed Mukhtar Shah Naeemi Ashrafi)', 10 April 2018, https://youtu.be/CfzAtKvnyyc.

64 Pinterest, '"Shah Waliullah" Search', https://www.pinterest.co.uk (accessed 29 December 2021).

65 Internet Archive, 'Quran e Kareem Va Tarjuma e Ma'ani e An Ba Zaban e Farsi – Translator: Shah Waliullah Dehlavi (Farsi)', 23 February 2016, https://archive.org/details/QuranEKareemVaTarjumaEMaaniEAnBaZabanEFarsi-ShahWaliullahDehlaviFarsi. apk.cafe, 'Quran Persian 2.5 for Gooweel M7', https://quran-persian.apk.cafe/gionee/m7 (accessed 29 December 2021).

66 Henri Laoust, 'Ibn ʿAbd al-Wahhāb', in *Encyclopaedia of Islam, Second Edition*, edited by P. Bearman et al., vol. Online (Leiden: Brill, 2012).

67 For a detailed discussion of Saudi Arabia, see Peter G. Mandaville, *Islam and Politics (Second Edition).* (London and New York: Routledge, 2014), 207–25. Also see Peter G. Mandaville, ed., *Wahhabism and the World Understanding Saudi Arabia's Global Influence on Islam* (New York: Oxford University Press, 2022).

68 Eickelman and Piscatori, *Muslim Politics*, 157–8.

69 Muslim World League, 'Muslim World League Journal', https://www.themwl.org/en/mwl-joural-english (accessed 10 January 2021).

70 Muslim World League, Twitter, 4 May 2023, https://twitter.com/MWLOrg_en (accessed 10 January 2022).

71 Endowments Saudi Arabian Ministry of Islamic Affairs, Da'wah and Guidance, 'Islam – Resources and Information', http://www.al-islam.com/eng/. King Fahd Complex for the Printing of the Holy Qur'an, http://www.qurancomplex.org (accessed 26 July 2004). Harf Information Technology, 'The Holy Qur'an', http://www.harf.com. Discussed in Bunt, *iMuslims*, Chapter 3.

72 Arab News, 'King Fahd Complex Launches Warsh Qur'an App', 15 December 2021, https://arab.news/pk3v3.

73 Tripadvisor, 'King Fahd Glorious Quran Printing Complex', https://www.tripadvisor.co.uk/Attraction_Review-g298551-d9714512-Reviews-King_Fahd_Glorious_Quran_Printing_Complex-Medina_Al_Madinah_Province.html (accessed 10 January 2022).

74 Quran Complex, 'Digital Mushaf of Madinah', https://dm.qurancomplex.gov.sa/en/projectabstract/ (accessed 10 January 2022).

75 Quran Complex, 'Publications', https://publications-img.qurancomplex.gov.sa/ (accessed 10 January 2022).

76 Endowments Ministry of Islamic Affairs, Dawah, and Guidance, 'iPhone Mushaf Version', App Store, https://apps.apple.com. An iPhone/iPad version is also available.

77 The title of this video is deceptive, given it is supportive of al-Wahhāb: Abu Mussab Wajdi Akkari, 'The Horn of Satan (Wahhabism/Wahabi)', 22 May 2020, https://youtu.be/cxQZwbzXwxg. A negative representation of al-Wahhāb is here: Sunni Encyclopedia, 'THE WAHHABI TREE: Part 5: The Crown (Horn of Satan)', 22 February 2019, https://www.sunni-encyclopedia.com/2019/02/the-wahhabi-tree-part-5-crown-horn-of.html?m=0 (accessed 4 January 2022). Also see Islam

Treasure, 'Refutation of Wahabism (Lord of shirk)', https://islamtreasure.wordpress.com/page/5/?app-download=ios (accessed 4 January 2022).

78 Ustadh Wasim Ismail, 'Muhammad Ibn Abd al-Wahhab Killed & Fought Muslims – Mufti Muhammad Ibn Muneer', 30 June 2021, https://youtu.be/AiBgzlBnBhA.

79 Imam Hussein TV 3, 'Dr. Sayed Ammar Nakshawani – Wahhabism I Ramadan 1438-2017', 6 June 2017, https://youtu.be/eNjwN2P0nwk.

80 Esther Peskes and W. Ende, 'Wahhābiyya', in *Encyclopaedia of Islam, Second Edition*, edited by P. Bearman et al., vol. Online (Brill, 2012). For a discussion on this brotherly rivalry, see Shahajada Md. Musa, 'The Emergence of a Scholar from a Garrison Society: A contextual analysis of Muhammad Ibn Abd al-Wahhāb's doctrine in the light of the Qur'ān and Hadīth', *MRes*, University of Wales Trinity Saint David, 2022. Director of Studies: Gary R. Bunt, https://repository.uwtsd.ac.uk/id/eprint/2096/.

81 A free version is here: Noor Book, 'Suleiman Bin Abdul Wahab [sic], Divine Lightning in Response to Wahhabism', Noor, 1 January 2019, https://www.noor-book.com/.

82 HistoryoftheWorld, 'History of Wahhabism', Google Play, 24 August 2021, https://play.google.com/store/apps/details?id=com.historyisfun.wahhabism.

83 mobitech.tn, 'Kitab al-Tawhid', Google Play, 4 April 2020, https://play.google.com/store/apps/details?id=com.mobitech.matntawhid (accessed 6 January 2022).

84 So Smart Apps, 'Library of Muhammad Ibn Wahhab', Google Play, 23 July 2021.

85 Andromax Studio, 'Islamic Monotheism', Google Play, 24 April 2021, https://play.google.com/store/apps/details?id=com.islamicmonotheism.app (accessed 6 January 2022).

86 Tawheed and Sunnah, 'Lamp Spreading Light', Instagram, https://www.instagram.com/tawheed_and_sunnah/?hl=en-gb (accessed 6 January 2022).

87 F R C Robinson, 'Farangi Mahall', in *The New Encyclopedia of Islam, Supplement Fascicules 5-6* (Leiden: Brill, 1982), 292.

88 Khalid Rasheed Farangi Mahli, 'Facebook (Public Figure) Page', https://www.facebook.com/profile.php?id=100045111312887&sk=photos (accessed 12 January 2022). Khalid Rasheed Farangi Mahli, Twitter, https://twitter.com/khalidrasheed (accessed 12 January 2022).

89 Inspirock, 'Farangi Mahal Islamic Centre of India, Lucknow', https://www.inspirock.com/india/lucknow/farangi-mahal-islamic-centre-of-india-a1121138491 (accessed 12 January 2022).

90 News 18, 'Lucknow: Islamic Center Of India Guidelines For Ramzan', https://youtu.be/YjYQLps8G1E (accessed 9 April 2021).

91 Islamic Centre of India, '2021', Facebook, https://www.facebook.com/islamiccentreofIndia/ (accessed 12 January 2022).

92 Israr Ahmed, 'Properties of matter: Naturalism', 24 March 2020, https://www.youtube.com/watch?v=HsBNDKf2Pb0, Drishti IAS, 'Important Personalities of India – Sir Syed Ahmed Khan', https://www.youtube.com/watch?v=y8wNZ65CWEU, Javed Ahmed Ghamidi, 'Principles of Tafsir', YouTube, 15 April 2021, https://www.youtube.com/watch?v=L9xcBBjD_84 (accessed 28 April 2022), Javed Ahmed Ghamidi, 'Sir Syed Ahmad Khan kay Usool e Tafseer', YouTube, 12 April 2021, https://www.youtube.com/watch?v=3pirduBc-gM, Pinterest, 'Syed Ahmad Khan', https://nl.pinterest.com/pin/612559986798320144/ (accessed 28 April 2022). Internet Archive, 'Search: "Sir Syed Ahmed Khan"', https://archive.org/search.php?query=sir%20syed%20ahmed%20khan (accessed 28 April 2022).

93 Ronald Geaves, 'Sectarianism in Sunnī Islam', in *Brill Handbooks on Contemporary Religion*, edited by Muhammad Afzal Upal and Carole M. Cusack (Leiden: Brill, 2021). *Brill Handbooks on Contemporary Religion*, Terhi Utriainen and Benjamin E. Zeller. 43
94 Islamic Foundation, 'Index', 6 June 2023, http://www.islamic-foundation.org.uk. Muslim Education Trust, 'Index', https://muslimeducationtrust.org/ (accessed 6 June 2023). UK Islamic Mission, 6 June 2023, https://www.ukim.org/.
95 Ameen Amanullah, 'The Maulana for the Millions | Abul A'la Maududi', Islam21c, 3 March 2021, https://www.islam21c.com/islamic-thought/history/the-maulana-for-the-millions-abul-ala-maududi/. PassFCPS E-Learning Official, 'Abul A'la Maududi', Pinterest, https://www.pinterest.co.uk/PassFCPS/abul-ala-maududi/ (accessed 12 January 2022). The latter page is linked to e-learning and course provision, as Maududi is also a subject for study. He used to have a dedicated website, but maududi.org is not function (although an archived version is available). WebArchive, 'maududi.org (2001-2018)', 12 January 2022, https://web.archive.org/web/20140517214521/http://maududi.org/. A typical biography is Ilm Film, 'Maulana Abul Alaa Syed Maududi – Biography Documentary', 7 August 2020, https://youtu.be/jbuFXOj9gZc.
96 Hammad ur Rehman, 'Historic Speech of Maulana Maududi ra in Lahore, Pakistan (1963)', 24 March 2012, https://youtu.be/U0nUh4IDZWE, jamaatjpj, 'Interview of Maulana Maududi', YouTube, 23 June 2012, https://youtu.be/oZgkQjFnjws (accessed 12 January 2021).
97 KJ Reports, 'Who was Mawlana SAYYID Abu Al-`ala MAWDUDI?', 23 April 2018, https://youtu.be/4McyLO5qOAE.
98 International Institute of Islamic Thought, https://iiit.org (accessed 6 June 2023).
99 Bunt. *Virtually Islamic*, 93–7.
100 Jamaat-e-Islami, https://jamaat.org (accessed 17 January 2022).
101 Jamaat-e-Islami Official, Twitter, https://twitter.com/JIPOfficial (accessed 17 January 2022).
102 EnglishTafsir, 'Sayyid Abul Ala Maududi – Tafhim al-Qur'an – The Meaning of the Qur'an', http://www.englishtafsir.com/ (accessed 12 January 2022). Other versions are available. See islamicstudies.info, 'Towards Understanding the Quran', http://www.islamicstudies.info/tafheem.php (accessed 12 January 2022). Akhzar Nazir, 'Tafheem ul Quran – Tafseer', App Store, https://apps.apple.com/tr/app/tafheem-ul-quran-tafseer/id1448485462, Evergreen Islamic Center, 'Tafheemul-Quran', App Store, https://apps.apple.com/tr/app/tafheemul-quran/id1296134230, Usman Pervez, 'Tafheem ul Quran – Tafseer – Syed Abul Ala Maududi', Google Play, https://play.google.com/store/apps/details?id=com.atq.quranemajeedapp.org.tfq&hl=en_GB&gl=US.
103 Lauzière, *The Making of Salafism*.
104 Nikki R. Keddie, 'Afgani, Jamal-al-Din', *Encyclopædia Iranica* I, no. 5 (1983): 481–48, http://www.iranicaonline.org/articles/afgani-jamal-al-din.
105 A. Albert Kudsi-Zadeh, 'Afghānī and Freemasonry in Egypt', *Journal of the American Oriental Societ* 92, no. 1 (1972): 25–35, https://doi.org/10.2307/599645.
106 WikiShia, 'Sayyid Jamal al-Din al-Asad Abadi', https://en.wikishia.net/view/Sayyid_Jamal_al-Din_al-Asad_Abadi (accessed 18 January 2022).
107 QuotePark, 'Jamal-al-Din Afghani Quotes', https://quotepark.com/authors/jamal-al-din-afghani/ (accessed 18 January 2022).
108 Anthony R. Byrd and Richard C. Martin, 'From Isfahan to the Internet: Islamic Theology in the Global Village', in *Islam in the Modern World*, edited by Jeffrey T. Kenney and Ebrahim Moosa (New York: Routledge, 2014), 79–106.

109 David Dean Commins, *Islamic Reform: Politics and Social Change in Late Ottoman Syria* (Oxford: Oxford University Press, 1990). This book contains a description of Syrian Salafi visits to Cairo, 60–1.

110 This book includes scanned copies of Muhammad 'Abduh, *The Theology of Unity*, translated by Isḥāq Masa'ad and Kenneth Cragg (London: George Allen & Unwin, 1966). For a detailed exploration of 'Abduh's intellectual, political and religious activities, see Oliver Scharbrodt, *Muhammad 'Abduh: Modern Islam and the Culture of Ambiguity* (London: I.B. Tauris, 2022).

111 For example, see Muhammad 'Abduh, 'Tafsir al-Manar', Shamela, https://shamela.ws/index.php/book/12304.

112 Ilm Films, 'Sheikh Muhammad Abduh & Islamic Revivalism', YouTube, 3 October 2016, https://youtu.be/J6CUowQUEx4.

113 Oxfordshire Masons, 'Bro Muhammad Abduh Died Today in 1905', Twitter, 11 July 2017, https://twitter.com/oxonmasons/status/884643639858745344. StoreMyPic, 'Muhammad Abduh Quotes', https://www.storemypic.com/album/muhammad-abduh-quotes.PaT (accessed 19 January 2022).

114 W. Ende, 'Rashīd Riḍā', in *Encyclopaedia of Islam, Second Edition*, edited by P. Bearman et al., vol. Electronic (Leiden: E.J. Brill, 2012).

115 Leor Halevi, *Modern Things on Trial: Islam's Global and Material Reformation in the Age of Rida, 1865–1935* (New York: Columbia University Press, 2019).

116 Rashid Ridha, 'Al-Manar', Internet Archive, https://archive.org/details/Almanar/almanar00/ (accessed 25 January 2022).

117 Ilm Film, 'Sheikh Muhammad Rashid Rida (Al-Manar Magazine)', YouTube, 5 December 2016, https://youtu.be/I8ggKochEzE.

118 Abu Khadeejah Abdul-Wahid, 'Jamal al-Din al-Afghani, Muhammad Abduh, Rashid Rida, Hasan al-Banna: Modernism, Revolution and the Muslim Brotherhood', 23 March 2017, https://abukhadeejah.com/jamal-aldin-afghani-muhammad-abduh-rashid-rida-hasan-albanna-radicals-modernists/.

119 Hamad Momin, '72 years since the Assassination of Hasan al-Banna', Islam21c, 12 February 2020, https://www.islam21c.com/news-views/72-years-since-assassination-hasan-al-banna/ (accessed 26 January 2022).

120 Achel developer, 'Prayer Al-Ma'tsurat Hasan Al-Banna', Google Play, 29 May 2021, https://play.google.com/store/apps/details?id=com.Acheldeveloper.DoaAlMatsuratHasanAlBanna. An Indonesian version is here: Waluku Studio, 'Al Ma'tsurat – Dzikir Pagi dan Petang', 6 October 2020, https://play.google.com/store/apps/details?id=com.walukustudio.almatsurat. An English edition is here: 99images, 'Al Matsurat Hasan Al Banna', https://www.99images.com/apps/books-reference/com.bulu7labs.almatsurathasanalbanna (accessed 26 January 2022). Eidetic Limited, 'Al-Ma'thurat', 18 May 2014, https://play.google.com/store/apps/details?id=ng.eidetic.almathurat&hl=en_GB&gl=US.

121 Ajeng Pipit, 'Hasan al-Banna', *Islamic Quotes*, Pinterest, https://www.pinterest.co.uk/pin/548735535817455906/ (accessed 26 January 2022). Islamicartdb.com, 'Imam Hasan al-Banna Quotes', http://islamicartdb.com/quotes/imam-hasan-al-banna-quotes/ (accessed 26 January 2022). An indication of the breadth of quotation material can be found through a basic search: Google Search, 'Hasan Al Banna Quotes', https://www.google.com (accessed 26 January 2022).

122 IkhwanWeb, 'Erian: Imam Hassan Al-Banna Died; But His Idea Lives On', 12 February 2013, https://www.ikhwanweb.com/article.php?id=30649 (accessed 26 January 2022). This links to related articles. Also see Ikhwan Online, https://www.ikhwanonline.com/ (accessed 25 January 2022).

123 APKTume, 'Fi Zilalil Quran English – The Shade of the Quran – Sayyid Qutb', Islamic Books, 15 April 2020, https://apktume.com/android/us/app/islamicbooks.fizilalilquran/. Akhzar Nazir, 'Fi Zilalal Quran – Tafseer by Sayyid Qutb Shaheed', App Store, https://apps.apple.com/us/app/fi-zilalal-quran-tafseer/id1448913919#?platform=iphone.

124 Assim al-Hakeem, 'Sayyid Qutb- Dhilal al-Quran (In the Shade of the Qur'an)', 19 November 2014, https://youtu.be/5aRBRMU0Snc.

125 Paul Berman, 'The Philosopher of Islamic Terror', *New York Times Magazine*, New York, https://www.nytimes.com/2003/03/23/magazine/the-philosopher-of-islamic-terror.html.

126 APK, 'Milestones – Sayyid Qutb', 11 December 2016, https://apkgk.com/com.kitab.maalimfitarik.sayidkotbe. Internet Archive, 'Special Edition – Milestones', Maktabah Booksellers and Publishers, https://archive.org/stream/SayyidQutb/Milestones%20Special%20Edition_djvu.txt.

127 Hegghammer, *The Caravan*, 40–5.

128 9-11 Commission. *The 9-11 Commission Report, Final Report of the National Commission on Terrorist Attacks Upon the United States, Official Government Edition* (Washington, 2004). Also see Bruce B. Lawrence, ed., *Messages to the World: The Statements of Osama Bin Laden*, translated by James Howarth (London and New York: Verso, 2005).

129 Kadivar, 'Exploring Takfir, Its Origins and Contemporary Use', 259–85, 7.

130 Anwar al-Awlaki, 'Book Review From Prison: Fi Dhilal Al Qur'an – Sayyid Qutb (18 Volumes)', Kalamullah, https://www.kalamullah.com/shade-of-the-quran.html (accessed 27 January 2022). Multiple versions of *In the Shade of the Qur'an* are available, including copies of a translated version published by the UK-based Islamic Foundation. AdviceforParadise, 'In the Shade of the Qur'an', https://adviceforparadise.com/books/bookseries/10/.

131 Emad Hamdeh, 'al-Albānī, Nāṣir al-Dīn', in *Encyclopaedia of Islam, THREE*, edited by Kate Fleet et al. (Leiden: Brill, 2019).

132 Salafi Publications, 'The Heresies of Sayyid Qutb in Light of the Statements of the Ulamaa', http://www.salafipublications.com/sps/sp.cfm?subsecID=ndv01&articleID=NDV010011&articlePages=1 (accessed 31 January 2022).

133 One of the numerous examples is here: themadkhalis.com, 'Imaam al-Albani to Shaykh Rabee: Everything with Which You Refuted Qutb for is Correct and True and May Allaah Reward You for Fulfilling the Obligation of Exposing His Ignorance and Deviance', 7 January 2010, http://www.themadkhalis.com/md/articles/iosjk-imaam-al-albani-to-shaykh-rabee-everything-with-which-you-refuted-qutb-for-is-correct-and-true.cfm (accessed 31 January 2022).

134 Ultimate Islam, 'Nasir Uddin Albani warns about Abu Ala Maududi and Jamaat e Islami', YouTube, 11 September 2019, https://youtu.be/rkECJwRwMBA (accessed 31 January 2022).

135 Umm Ibrahim, 'Clarifying the Role of Sayyid Qutb', Book of 'Ilm, 27 August 2015, https://thebookofilm.wordpress.com/2015/08/27/clarifying-the-role-of-sayyid-qutb.

136 The Deviation of Salafi/Wahabi, 'Al-Albani Unveiled: An Exposition of his Errors and Weakening of Some of Imam Bukhari and Muslim's Ahadith', Facebook, 22 October 2013, https://www.facebook.com/Salafi.Wahabi/photos/al-albani-unveiled-an-exposition-of-his-errors-and-weakening-of-some-of-imam-buk/602508819795649/ (accessed 31 January 2022).

137 Hallaq, 'The Gate of Ijtihad: A Study in Islamic Legal History'.
138 Salman al-Odah, 'Twitter Feed', 10 September 2020, https://twitter.com/salman_alodah (accessed 1 February 2022).
139 Amr Khaled, 'Amr Khaled: Facebook', https://www.facebook.com/AmrKhaled (accessed 1 February 2022) Amr Khaled, 'Twitter Feed', https://twitter.com/amrkhaled/status/1488482263620894720 (accessed 1 February 2022).
140 See the al-Qaradawi and Islam Online discussion in chapter 8, Bunt. *Islam in the Digital Age*, 147–59. Also see Jakob Skovgaard-Petersen and Bettina Gräf, eds, *The Global Mufti: The Phenomenon of Yusuf Al-Qaradawi* (London: C. Hurst & Co., 2008). Bettina Gräf, 'Qaradawi and the Struggle for Modern Islam', *New Lines Magazine*, 25 October 2022, https://newlinesmag.com/first-person/qaradawi-and-the-struggle-for-modern-islam/.
141 Some of the app was paywalled. Islamic Ency, 'Islamic Audios Library', 28 January 2022 (accessed 1 February 2022).
142 Khutbah Bank, 'Home', https://khutbahbank.org.uk/ (accessed 1 February 2022).
143 Khutbah Bank, 'Abdal Hakim Murad', https://khutbahbank.org.uk/v2/tag/abdal-hakim-murad/ (accessed 1 February 2022).
144 Nourishment of the Soul, 'Khutbah', https://www.khutbah.info/khutbahs/ (accessed 1 February 2022).
145 Nourishment of the Soul, 'Gems', https://www.khutbah.info/gems/ (accessed 1 February 2022).
146 YassaralQuran, 'Sermons', 9 July 2021, https://yassarnalquran.wordpress.com/sermons/ (accessed 1 February 2022).
147 General Authority of Islamic Affairs and Endowments in the United Arab Emirates, 'Friday Sermons Archive (Arabic)', https://www.awqaf.gov.ae/ar/Pages/FridaySermonArchive.aspx (accessed 1 February 2022), General Authority of Islamic Affairs and Endowments in the United Arab Emirates, 'Friday Sermons Archive (English and Urdu)', https://www.awqaf.gov.ae/en/Pages/FridaySermonArchive.aspx (accessed 1 February 2022). Also see Awkaf UAE, Facebook, https://www.facebook.com/AwqafUAE (accessed 1 February 2022).
148 General Authority of Islamic Affairs and Endowments in the United Arab Emirates, 'Services', 8 November 2017, https://www.awqaf.gov.ae/ar/Pages/MobileServices.aspx (accessed 3 February 2022).
149 Ibid., Islamic Affairs and Charitable Activities Department in Dubai, 'Fatwa Archive', https://services.iacad.gov.ae/SmartPortal/en/fatwa/PublishedFatwa/Index (accessed 1 November 2019).
150 Haneen Dajani, 'Virtual Fatwas Delivered in Dubai to Better Guide the Faithful', *The National*, 30 October 2019, https://www.thenationalnews.com/uae/government/virtual-fatwas-delivered-in-dubai-to-better-guide-the-faithful-1.930365.
151 Islamic Affairs and Charitable Activities Department in Dubai, 'IACAD (Android)', Google Play, https://play.google.com/store/apps/details?id=com.iacad.apps&hl=en&gl=US&showAllReviews=true (accessed 3 February 2022), Islamic Affairs and Charitable Activities Department in Dubai, 'IACAD (iPhone)', App Store, https://apps.apple.com/gb/app/iacad/id986318300#?platform=iphone (accessed 3 February 2022).
152 Discussion with project manager Abdullah Al Awadhi in Saman Haziq, 'Now, "Virtual Mufti" to Issue Quick Fatwas in Dubai', *Khaleej Times*, 29 October 2019, https://www.khaleejtimes.com/technology/now-virtual-mufti-to-issue-quick-fatwas-in-dubai.

153 General Authority of Islamic Affairs and Endowments in the United Arab Emirates, '@AwqafUAE', https://twitter.com/AwqafUAE (accessed 3 February 2022), General Authority of Islamic Affairs and Endowments in the United Arab Emirates, 'Instagram', https://www.instagram.com/awqafuae/?igshid=1xdw9zl9zyoav%E2%80%AC&fbclid=IwAR3xuC9rHBSz4RH2N9ei1iD2pDp4k2JjkJJ9L8BW5BGFaHXK5VU3cmtDF-Q (accessed 3 February 2022), General Authority of Islamic Affairs and Endowments in the United Arab Emirates, 'Telegram', Telegram, https://t.me/Awqafuae (accessed 3 February 2022).

Chapter 6

1 This figure comes from 2009 research, which suggested that 10–13 per cent of the global Muslim population is Shīʿa. These figures will have changed in the intervening years but represent a detailed analysis (albeit one subject to critique). Pew Research Center, 'Mapping the Global Muslim Population' (Washington, DC: Pew Research Center's Forum on Religion & Public Life, 2009), https://www.pewresearch.org/religion/wp-content/uploads/sites/7/2009/10/Muslimpopulation-1.pdf.

2 al-Islam, 'Nahjul Balagha Part 1, The Sermons', https://www.al-islam.org/nahjul-balagha-part-1-sermons (accessed 4 February 2021).

3 Yaqeen Institute, 'Ali ibn Abi Talib (ra): Courageous & Steadfast | The Firsts with Sh. Omar Suleiman', https://youtu.be/In91yLh_WFU (accessed 4 February 2021). Mufti Ismail Menk, 'Getting to Know the Companions – Ali ibn Abi Talib (RA) by Mufti Menk', https://youtu.be/yA1FJiAQJ5I (accessed 4 February 2021).

4 QuoteFancy, 'TOP 20 Ali ibn Abi Talib Quotes', https://youtu.be/272eTpzGcmc (accessed 4 February 2021).

5 Imam Hussein TV 3, 'Dr. Sayed Ammar Nakshawani | Eid Al Ghadeer | Live In London – Season One', https://youtu.be/2VZlolbHyeQ.

6 Al-Maaref, 'The Rituals of Eid al-Ghadir', https://english.almaaref.org/essaydetails.php?eid=4368&cid=385 (accessed 8 February 2021).

7 Ismaili Web Amaana, 'Eid-e Ghadir – Declaration at Ghadir e Khumm, Prophet Muhammad Appoints Imam Ali as His Successor', http://www.amaana.org/ISWEB/wilayat1.htm (accessed 8 February 2021).

8 Allama Sayyid Abdul Hussayn Sharafuddin, *Ghadir Khum*, Peermohamed Ebrahim Trust, 1988, https://ismailimail.blog/2017/09/08/the-most-extensive-account-of-ghadir-khum/. Metropolitan Museum of New York, '"Firdausi's Parable of the Ship of Shi'ism", Folio 18v from the Shahnama (Book of Kings) of Shah Tahmasp', https://www.metmuseum.org/art/collection/search/452110 (accessed 8 February 2021).

9 Azadari Chitora, 'Eid E Ghadeer Manqabat 2020 | Hasan Jafar Manqabat | New Manqabat 2020 | Ghadeer Manqabat | Ali Ali', https://youtu.be/t4nhZ-9gmKg.

10 TNA Records, 'New Bibi Fatima Manqabat 2021 || Azmat E Fatima (sa) || Waleha Batool & Hur Hussain', https://youtu.be/haKHYputSQQ (accessed 8 February 2021). Imam Reza Shrine, 'Syeda Waleha Batool | Ya Fatima | Manqabat 2020 | Bibi Fatima Manqabat | Tu Bari Sakhi Hai Fatima', https://youtu.be/uZcdisxQxhA.

11 Focus Studio, 'Tu Bari Sakhi Hai Fatima s.a || Syeda Waleha Batool – Hur Hussain Jaffri || New Manqabat 2019' (accessed 8 February 2021).

12 Syed Raza Abbas Zaidi, 'Ali Ibne Abi Talib | | 13 Rajab | Mola Ali Manqabat'.

13 Shahid Baltistani, 'Naad e Ali AS | Manqabat | 2020', https://youtu.be/zrXy8xI-sH8.
14 TNA Records, 'Ghadeer Song – Ali Ghelich || Live Like Ali (As)', 7 August 2020, https://youtu.be/isAOhIcI3Pw.
15 alibinabitalib2021, 'Amir al-mu'minin Ali', https://www.instagram.com/alibinabitalib2021/ (accessed 9 February 2021).
16 Real World Records, 'Nusrat Fateh Ali Khan', https://realworldrecords.com/artists/nusratfatehalikhan/ (accessed 10 February 2023), theofficialnusrat, 'Nusrat Fateh Ali Khan', https://www.instagram.com/theofficialnusrat/ (accessed 10 February 2023).
17 Shaikh Nazim Peer Sohna, 'Younis Ghulam Nabi', https://youtu.be/y_gzfi-r11w.
18 Hazrat Khawaja Moinuddin Chisti, 'Hazrat Ali -The Father of Sufism', https://khawajamoinuddin.wordpress.com/hazrat-ali-the-father-of-sufism/.
19 A Sufi Metamorphosis, 'Hazrat Ali, the Father of Sufism', 7 May 2017, http://zoya-thewayofasufi.blogspot.com/2017/05/hazrat-ali-father-of-sufism.html.
20 Waltham Forest Islamic Association, 'Sayyiduna Ali Ibn Abi Talib – The Gate to the City of Knowledge – Syed Muhammad Hussaini Miah Ashraf', 2019, https://youtu.be/YgDwQ23wnFw. Shaykh Abdal Hakim Murad, 'Why is Imam Ali Connected to All the Sufi Tariqas?' 16 January 2013, https://youtu.be/RCoHHjQeM4g.
21 hasanabbas.com, 'Imam Husayn', http://hasanabbas.com (accessed 10 November 2021).
22 Alexander Kolbitsch, 'The Reciprocal Relationship between the Ritualistic ta'zie Role-Play and Twelver Shi'ite Collective Identity in Iranian History' (PhD, University of Wales Trinity Saint David, Lampeter, 2016). Director of Studies: Gary R. Bunt, 2012.
23 Who is Hussain? 'The Story of Hussain | Battle of Karbala | FULL DOCUMENTARY', https://youtu.be/emfT8syx7R0.
24 ISH News, 'Muharram – The Story of Karbala', 10 February 2021, https://youtu.be/C9XLG2zEI1w.
25 Al Jazeera English, 'Day of Ashoura Marked in Karbala', 7 December 2011, https://youtu.be/DNqUd13m3EQ, Ruptly, 'Iraq: Shia Muslims Mark Ashura with Bloody Ritual in Baghdad', 2020, https://youtu.be/2ucBp-w7VBM.
26 WION, 'Muharram 2020 | Pilgrims mark Ashura in Iraq's Kerbala with Masks & Gloves | World News', 30 August 2020, https://youtu.be/P7q2Bp3Xx_4.
27 Tarar Support, 'Karbala City Tour Streets Walk Shops Foods In Iraq', 9 February 2020, https://youtu.be/oA94_Jfv6Fg.
28 Ahlulbayt, 'Imam Hussain Museum – Karbala, Iraq', 22 October 2015, https://youtu.be/kEYA-rYQpXo.
29 Eman, 'What is ASHURA all about? | The 10th of Muharram – TODAY – Saturday 29th August 2020', https://youtu.be/C9XLG2zEI1w.
30 karbalamerijaan, 'Dua e kumayl', https://www.instagram.com/p/CLKEACejn5I/ (accessed 11 February 2021_. This link points to a more extensive Karbala resource of photos, blogs and resources. Karbalamerijaan, https://karbalamerijaan.org/index.html (accessed 11 February 2021).
31 Instagram, '#Hussain', https://www.instagram.com/explore/tags/husayn/ (accessed 11 February 2021).
32 Deviant Art, 'Shia-Ali', https://www.deviantart.com/shia-ali/gallery (accessed 11 February 2021).
33 Ali Bahreini, https://www.instagram.com/alibahreini.art/ (accessed 12 February 2021).

34 Nikki Keddie, *Roots of Revolution: An Interpretive History of Modern Iran* (New Haven and London: Yale University Press, 1981), 7.
35 Ruffle, 'An Even Better Creation: The Role of Adam and Eve in Shiʿi Narratives about Fatimah al-Zahra'.
36 Husaini Islamic Library, 'O Fatima Zahra (S)', 30 January 2019, https://youtu.be/7Kn0xPK9qHM. Ali Abbas, 'Manqbat Bibi Fatima Zahra s.a – Janab e Zahra s.a', 18 November 2018, https://youtu.be/3GoNPdZrb0Q.
37 Shi'a Calendar, 'Birth of Lady Fatimah al-Zahra", 2 February 2021, https://www.instagram.com/p/CKyu4lQjE6F/.
38 Jaffer H. Jaffer, 'Friday Khutba – 20th Jumada al-Thani 1436/2015', https://www.al-islam.org/media/friday-khutba-20th-jumada-al-thani-14362015.
39 The Council of Shia Muslim Scholars of North America, 'The Crescent Moon of the Month of Jumada al-Awwal, 1440 A.H', 6 January 2019, https://imam-us.org/crescent-moon-jumada-al-awwal-1440.
40 Shia Calendar, '14th Night of the Jumada al-awwal', 29 December 2020, https://www.instagram.com/p/CJY3HkcjJ_d/.
41 There are various editions and formats available, including e-books and web pages. Ayatullah Lutfullah Safi Gulpaygani, *Fatimiyyah is ʿAshuraʾ*, www.islam.org, 2021, http://alhassanain.org/english/?com=book&id=708; https://www.al-islam.org/fatimiyyah-%CA%BFashura%CA%BE-lutfullah-safi-golpaygani/historic-fadak-sermon-fatima.
42 Aalulbayt Global Information Center, 'The Historic Fadak Sermon of Fatima (1)', http://en.al-shia.org/content/historic-fadak-sermon-fatima-1. shiakhairulbaria, 'Fidak Sermon of Fatima SA', https://shiakhairulbaria.blogspot.com/2019/01/fidak-sermon-of-fatima-sa.html (accessed 12 February 2021). Sheikh M. S. Bahmanpour, 'Fatima's Sermon (Fadakiya) in Madinah – Part 1 (Sheikh M.S Bahmanpour)', 2015, https://youtu.be/6WORDjqeGlI. Masumeen Islamic Centre, '[1/4] Nurturing The Qualities of Lady Fatima (as) – 29th Jumada al-Awwal 1439 – Sh. Murtaza Bachoo', https://youtu.be/2PZuoSq52u8. houmam03, 'The Fadakiya Sermon- Sermon of Lady Fatima Part 1', https://youtu.be/_cIzSgtslCs (accessed 12 February 2021). Shabnam Dewji, 'The Prophet's (p) Daughter Fatimah: A Model for All Times', YouTube, 20 November 2015, https://www.youtube.com/watch?v=wBMbnf95bIQ.
43 iShia Foundation, 'iShia', http://ishia.org/ (accessed 12 February 2021).
44 Sheikh Assim Al Hakeem, 'Quran of the Shia, The Mushaf of Fatima and the Deviant Shia Aqeedah', https://youtu.be/VGzbTH4qpMc (accessed 12 February 2021).
45 Arjana, *Pilgrimage in Islam*, 66–7.
46 Pure Stream Media, 'An Introduction to the House of Sayyida Fatima Zahra (A) by Imam Khomeini', https://youtu.be/Mwc35u5z7lE (accessed 12 February 2021).
47 khameimi.ir, 'Four Lessons by Lady Fatima Zahra for Humanity', https://english.khamenei.ir/news/5439/Four-lessons-by-Lady-Fatima-Zahra-for-humanity (accessed 12 February 2021), khameimi.ir, 'Sunnis Too Attribute Numerous Hadiths to Prophet Praising Fatima Zahra (pbuh)', https://english.khamenei.ir/news/5483/Sunnis-too-attribute-numerous-hadiths-to-Prophet-praising-Fatima (accessed 12 February 2021).
48 E. Kohlbert, 'Zayn al-ʿĀbidīn', in *Encyclopaedia of Islam, Second Edition*, edited by P. Bearman et al. (Leiden: Brill, 2012), http://dx.doi.org/10.1163/1573-3912_islam_SIM_8144.
49 Baqir Sharif al-Qurashi, 'The Life of Imam Zayn al-'Abidin', Al-Islam, https://www.al-islam.org/life-imam-zayn-al-abidin-baqir-shareef-al-qurashi/chapter-2-great-baby.

Thaqlain, '07 – Biography of Imam Zayn al-Abidin (Imam Sajjad) – Sayed Ammar Nakshawani', YouTube, 7 April 2018, https://youtu.be/IYMz2ZfPIVY (accessed 14 March 2021), Imam al-Khoei Islamic Center New York, 'Imam Ali ibn al-Hussain (p)', https://imam-us.org/islamic-awareness/islam-101/beliefs/ahl-al-bayt/imam-zayn-al-abidin (accessed 14 March 2021).

50 Wilfred Madelung, 'Zaydiyya', in *Encyclopaedia of Islam: Second Edition*, edited by P. Bearman et al., vol. XI (Leiden: E.J. Brill, 2012), 477–81, http://dx.doi.org.ezproxy.uwtsd.ac.uk/10.1163/1573-3912_islam_COM_1385.

51 Minority Rights, 'Zaydi Shi'a', January 2018, https://minorityrights.org/minorities/zaydi-shias/.

52 Juan Cole, 'Why you Need to Understand Yemen's Houthi Rebels', Informed Comment, 15 December 2018, https://www.juancole.com/2018/12/understand-yemens-houthi.html. Charles Schmitz, 'The Rise of Yemen's Houthi Rebels', BBC News, 28 February 2015, https://www.bbc.co.uk/news/world-middle-east-31645145.

53 Associated Press, 'Zaydi Muslims Pack Sanaa Stadium to Mark Ashoura', YouTube, 3 August 2015, https://youtu.be/dIgTZdn9wQU.

54 ImamZaid, 'Performance of Prayers in Sana'a Grand Mosque', 7 July 2009, https://youtu.be/cxOJ1LhrOao (accessed 15 March 2021), BBC News, 'What Zaidi Sect do most Houthi Belong To?' 16 March 2015, https://youtu.be/P5Mpw65BLP0.

55 Eleonora Ardemagni, 'Framing Yemen's Zaydi Shi'a', OASIS, 28 July 2019, https://www.oasiscenter.eu/en/framing-yemen-s-zaydi-shi-a.

56 Mehdi Quran Center, 'Birth Anniversary of Imam Muhammad Baqir', 26 February 2020, https://www.facebook.com/MehdiQuranCenter/videos/201161237631491. The KSIMC of London – Stanmore, 'Qasida – Wiladat Eve of Imam Muhammad Baqir (AS) – 18/03/2018', YouTube, https://youtu.be/5uCTMwX31Ms. Qurban Jafri Official, 'Munqbat Imam Muhammad Baqir As |First Time Live From Karbala Studio | Zawar Qurban Jafri', YouTube, 15 February 2021, https://youtu.be/CyQJuCM-4M0. IMAM, 'Imam Muhammad al-Baqir (p)', https://imam-us.org/islamic-awareness/islam-101/beliefs/ahl-al-bayt/imambaqir.

57 Hadi TV, 'Jashan-e-Wiladat Imam Muhammad Baqir (A.S.) – Kids Mania-', 15 February 2021.

58 Saba IGC, 'Birthday of Imam Muhammad al-Baqir | Moulana Nabi Raza Abidi | 1st of Rajab', 13 February 2021, https://youtu.be/EDXkVST48Po.

59 Wali ul Asr, 'Birthday of Imam Muhammad al-Baqir (A) (According to Some Traditions)', 3 October 2020, https://waliulasr.ca/event/birthday-of-imam-muhammad-al-baqir-a-according-to-some-traditions/.

60 Islamic Lessons Made Easy, 'Imam Muhammad al Baqir (as)- The 5th Imam', 10 April 2018, https://youtu.be/T2713WqHVQM.

61 IMAM, 'Birth Anniversary of Imam Muhammad al-Baqir (p). Citing Shaykh al-Kulayni, Kitab al-Kafi, vol. 1, p. 469', https://imam-us.org/birthday-of-imam-muhammad-al-baqir (accessed 17 March 2021).

62 QMI, 'Sayings of Muhammad Baqir', YouTube, 28 April 2015, https://youtu.be/bHXiV2yRC6I.

63 Shia-The Followers of Ahlulbayt A.S, 'Sayings of Imam Muhammad Al Baqir (as)', https://www.pinterest.co.uk/FollowAhlulbayt/sayings-of-imam-muhammad-al-baqir-as/ (accessed 17 March 2021).

64 Mehr, 'Imam Muhammad Baqir (AS)', https://en.mehrnews.com/tag/Imam+Muhammad+Baqir+%28AS%29.

65 Iayf, 'Wiladat of Imam Baqir (a.s.)', Deviant Art, 26 May 2012, https://www.deviantart.com/iayf/art/Wiladat-of-Imam-Baqir-a-s-304417076.
66 Kohlbert, 'Zayn al-ʿĀbidīn'.
67 Ahmad b. Ali b. Abi Talib al-Tabrisi, *Al-Iḥtijāj ʿalā ahl al-lijāj*, Aalulbayt Global Information Center, https://en.al-shia.org/the-book-of-al-ihtijaj/. The text is in online bookstores. Al-Iḥtijāj refers to 'argumentation'.
68 Sheikh Ali Gomaa, 'Imam Ja'far al Sadiq', YouTube, 7 February 2013, https://youtu.be/C26hUODHJzg (accessed 18 March 2021).
69 Imam Hussein TV 3, 'Imam Ja'far Sadiq (as): The Great Muslim Scientist', 28 June 2019, https://youtu.be/VzpYD4Jkrc8.
70 KAZ School, 'Imam Jafar Al-Sadiq || Masoomeen || The Truthful One', 15 November 2019, https://youtu.be/6oWi7GNEbXw (accessed 18 March 2021).
71 Islamic Lessons Made Easy, 'Imam Ja'far as-Sadiq (as)- The 6th Imam', 13 April 2018, https://youtu.be/9PPVqbHBP2A (accessed 18 March 2021).
72 Shafiqul Islam, 'Imam Jafar Al-Sadiq', Pinterest, https://www.pinterest.co.uk/shafiq010167/imam-jafar-al-sadiq/ (accessed 18 March 2021).
73 S. M. H. Shabbar, 'Story of Holy Ka'aba and Its People: Seventh Imam Musa Ibn Ja'far Al-Kazim (as)', Al-Islam, https://www.al-islam.org/story-of-the-holy-kaaba-and-its-people-shabbar/seventh-imam-musa-ibn-jafar-al-kazim. Ali Azhar Arastu, 'Imam Musa al-Kadhim ibn Jafar (A.S.)', Imam Reza Network, https://www.imamreza.net/old/eng/imamreza.php?id=13288 (accessed 19 March 2021), Ali Teymoori, 'A Brief Biography of Imam Musa Ibn Jafar al-Kadim (as)', 9 August 2020, http://ijtihadnet.com/a-brief-biography-of-imam-musa-ibn-jafar-al-kadim-as/.
74 MYC Media, 'Who is Musa al-Kadhim [a]? – Imam Hassan Qazwini', 30 April 2016, https://youtu.be/aztJLgOQPc4.
75 Sayed Mustafa Al-Modarresi, 'Virtues of Imam Musa Al-Kadhim (as)', *Ahlulbayt TV*, 20 March 2020.
76 Thaqlain, 'Remembering Imam Musa Kazim (al-Kadhim) alaihis salaam | Shaykh Dr. Usama Al-Atar', 7 March 2021, https://youtu.be/LAefoht_r-U.
77 Imam Hussein TV 3, 'The Door To Needs – A Short Biography of Imam Musa ibn Ja'far al-Kadhim (as)', YouTube, 21 May 2020, https://youtu.be/DZoNuwaAdMU.
78 Al-Islam, 'History of Shrines: History of the Shrine of Imam Musa Al-Kadhim & Imam Muhammad Al-Jawad', https://www.al-islam.org/history-shrines/history-shrine-imam-musa-al-kadhim-imam-muhammad-al-jawad.
79 xinhuanet.com, 'Iraqi Shiite Pilgrims End Major Ritual under Tightened Security', 12 April 2018, http://www.xinhuanet.com/english/2018-04/12/c_137106866.htm.
80 HNNA, 'Holy City Masterplan', http://www.hnna.co/holy-city-masterplan (accessed 22 March 2021).
81 Tripadvisor, 'Al-Kadhimiya Mosque', https://www.tripadvisor.co.uk/Attraction_Review-g294001-d8733478-Reviews-Al_Kadhimiya_Mosque-Baghdad_Baghdad_Province.html (accessed 22 March 2021).
82 Ruptly, 'Iraq: Shiite Worshippers Commemorate Imam Moussa al-Kadhim in Baghdad', 23 April 2017, https://youtu.be/3F_ZIxyqhsA.
83 Hassnain Ali TV, 'Taboot-e-Imam Musa Kazim a.s | Live Kazimain | Al-Kadhimiya Mosque |', 18 April 2018, https://youtu.be/soVBexgOJew.
84 Arthur Tode and Kate Tode, 'Circumnavigating the Earth [Circumnavigation #3]', Penn Museum, 1930, https://www.penn.museum/collections/videos/video/204.

85 Al Jazeera English, 'Hundreds Killed in Baghdad Stampede', 1 September 2005, https://www.aljazeera.com/news/2005/9/1/hundreds-killed-in-baghdad-stampede.

86 Natalie Muller, 'Shiite Pilgrims Targeted in Deadly Baghdad Car Bombing', Deutsche Welle, 30 April 2016, https://www.dw.com/en/shiite-pilgrims-targeted-in-deadly-baghdad-car-bombing/a-19226399. The AA, 'Bomb Attack Injures 10 Shia Pilgrims in Baghdad', https://www.aa.com.tr/en/middle-east/bomb-attack-injures-10-shia-pilgrims-in-baghdad/2169370 (accessed 22 March 2021).

87 Official website of the President of the Islamic Republic of Iran, 'President Makes Pilgrimage to Al-Kadhimiya Shrines', 11 March 2019, http://www.president.ir/en/108576.

88 S. M. R. Shabbar, 'The Eighth Imam, "Ali Ibn Musa, Al-Ridha" (as)', in *Story of the Holy Ka'aba and Its People*, Al-Islam, https://www.al-islam.org/story-of-the-holy-kaaba-and-its-people-shabbar/eighth-imam-ali-ibn-musa-al-ridha. Imam-US, 'Imam Ali ibn Musa al-Rida (p)', https://imam-us.org/islamic-awareness/islam-101/beliefs/ahl-al-bayt/imamrida (accessed 26 March 2021).

89 It is also known as Mashhad al-Riḍā/Reza. The Reza spelling is used here in line with the shrine's own English language output.

90 Astan Quds Razavi, 'Index', https://globe.razavi.ir/ (accessed 25 March 2021). See the discussion in Bunt, *Hashtag Islam*, 93–4.

91 BalticLiveCam, 'Imam Reza Shrine', https://balticlivecam.com/cameras/iran/mashhad/imam-reza-shrine/ (accessed 24 March 2021).

92 Ibid., Razavi.tv, 'Farsi Programming', https://tv.razavi.ir/fa (accessed 26 March 2021).

93 Razavi.tv, 'YouTube Channel (RazaviFillm)', https://www.youtube.com/c/RazaviFilm/videos. Aparat, https://www.aparat.com/ (accessed 24 March 2021).

94 Tripadvisor, 'Imam Reza Holy Shrine', https://www.tripadvisor.co.uk/Attraction_Review-g2189612-d320818-Reviews-Imam_Reza_Holy_Shrine-Mashhad_Razavi_Khorasan_Province.html (accessed 24 March 2021).

95 Shia Multimedia Team, 'Ya Imam Raza / Reza (A.S)', https://www.pinterest.co.uk/shiamultimediaa/ya-imam-raza-reza-as/ (accessed 13 April 2021). Fulla Kareen, 'Eman Reza', https://www.pinterest.de/Fullakreen/emam-reza/ (accessed 13 April 2021).

96 IMAM, 'Imam Muhammad al-Jawad (p)', https://imam-us.org/islamic-awareness/islam-101/beliefs/ahl-al-bayt/imamjawad (accessed 13 April 2021). Majlis-e-Ulama-e-Shia (Europe), '10th Rajab: Birthday Anniversary of Imam Muhammad Taqi al-Jawad (A.S.) / Biography', https://majlis.org.uk/rajab/10th-rajab-birthday-anniversary-of-imam-muhammad-taqi-al-jawad-a-s-biography/ (accessed 13 April 2021).

97 Al-Islam, 'Imam Muhammad Al-Taqi (as)', https://www.al-islam.org/articles/infallibles-imam-muhammad-al-taqi (accessed 13 April 2021).

98 Islamic Lessons Made Easy, 'Imam Muhammad al Jawad (as) – The 9th Imam', 22 April 2018, https://youtu.be/Q_dMJmNQ-ZM (accessed 13 April 2021).

99 Twitter, '#شہادت_امام_جوادؑ', Twitter, https://twitter.com/hashtag/ (accessed 13 April 2021). India Shia News Agency, 'Shahadat of 9th Imam Muhammad at-Taqi (A.S.)', 2 August 2018, https://india.shafaqna.com/EN/shahadat-of-9th-imam-muhammad-at-taqi-a-s/ (accessed 13 April 2021).

100 S. M. H. Shabbar, 'Story of Holy Ka'aba and Its People: The Tenth Imam, 'Ali Ibn Muhammad (Al-Naqi, Al-Hadi) (as)', Al-Islam, https://www.al-islam.org/story-of-the-holy-kaaba-and-its-people-shabbar/tenth-imam-ali-ibn-muhammad-al-naqi-al-hadi.

101 Peaceforall, 'Al-Ziyara Jamia Kabira 7.0', https://apkcombo.com/al-ziyara-jamia-kabira/org.meraaj.jame/ (accessed 9 May 2023).

102 WikiShia, 'Al-Ziyara al-Jami'a al-Kabira', https://en.wikishia.net/view/Al-Ziyara_al-Jami%27a_al-Kabira (accessed 14 April 2021). Duas.org, 'Common Ziarats: The Major Comprehensive Form of Ziyarah (al-Ziyarah al-Jamiah al-Kabirah)', http://www.duas.org/commonziarats.htm#JAMIAKABIRA (accessed 14 April 2021). Zainab Organization, 'Ziyarat e Jamia Kabeer – Haaj Mahdi Samavati – الزيارة الجامعة الكبيرة', YouTube, 2011, https://youtu.be/e7cy0boXGHc.

103 KazSchool, 'Imam Al-Hadi A.S – The Talking Quran | The Tenth Imam, Ali Ibn Muhammad | Animated Story | KAZSchool', YouTube, 2021, https://youtu.be/Bs8CgYMSUbg (accessed 14 April 2021).

104 Ahletashe Wiki, *Fandom*, https://ahletashe.fandom.com/wiki/Hazrat_Imam_Ali_Naqi(as) (accessed 14 April 2021).

105 Mazar Mubarak - Imran Ghazi, 'THE 10th(Ninth) IMAM: Imam Ali Naqi Al Hadi | Samarra the City of Imams | Samarra, Iraq', YouTube, 2019, https://youtu.be/bMhWo1iI6Zc.

106 KazSchool, 'Imam Hassan Askari (as) || Masoomeen || Imam Mahdi 2020', YouTube, 6 December 2019, https://youtu.be/9grW3_df88I (accessed 15 April 2021).

107 Islamic Lessons Made Easy, 'Imam Hasan al Askari (as) – The 11th Imam', YouTube, 28 April 2018, https://youtu.be/s6sqHwyGVLE.

108 Ahlulbayt TV, 'Wisdom and Lessons from the Life of Imam Hasan Al-Askari', YouTube, 25 November 2020, https://youtu.be/dDYqtFOX0IY.

109 SAAJ Nairobi, '11th Imam (AS) and The Qualities of a True Shia Community"-8th RABI'UL AWWAL 1437 A.H/2015', YouTube, 19 December 2015, https://youtu.be/uc4hXdU3UbQ.

110 Wilfred Madelung, 'al-Mahdi', in *Encyclopaedia of Islam, Second Edition*, edited by P. Bearman et al. (Brill, 2012), V:1230b. *Encyclopaedia of Islam*, https://referenceworks.brillonline.com:443/entries/encyclopaedia-of-islam-2/al-mahdi-COM_0618. Amanat Abbas et al., 'Islam in Iran i – iv', in *Encyclopaedia Iranica Online* (Brill), 130–72, https://referenceworks.brillonline.com:443/entries/encyclopaedia-iranica-online/islam-in-iran-i-iv-COM_3687.

111 Islamicweb, 'Who Is Imam al-Mahdi?' http://www.islamicweb.com/history/mahdi.htm (accessed 22 April 2021). Shi'a.org, 'The Twelfth Imam', http://www.shia.org/mehdi.html (accessed 22 April 2021).

112 Ahlulbayt TV, '5 Facts About Imam al-Mahdi', Youtube, 30 March 2021, https://youtu.be/LcNL-ASx2-8 (accessed 22 April 2021).

113 Ahlulbayt, 'Shia Belief in Imam Mahdi – Sayed Moustafa Al-Qazwini', YouTube, 29 July 2021, https://youtu.be/wBHmcUC9sPQ. Al-Rasoul Islamic Society, 'What will Happen after the Re-Appearance of Imam al-Mahdi? – Sayed Mohammed Baqer Al-Qazwini', YouTube, 9 April 2020, https://youtu.be/109JyJ--RPA.

114 'Google Search: Imam al-Mahdi Pinterest', Pinterest, https://tinyurl.com/2n4azmw3 (accessed 22 April 2021).

115 Paul E. Walker, 'Dāʿī (in Ismāʿīlī Islam)', in *Encyclopaedia of Islam, THREE*, edited by Kate Fleet et al. (Leiden: Brill), http://dx.doi.org/10.1163/1573-3912_ei3_COM_25781.

116 H. A. R. Gibb and P. Kraus, 'al-Mustanṣir Bi'llāh', in *Encyclopaedia of Islam, First Edition*, edited by M. Th. Houtsma et al. (Leiden: Brill, 1913–36), http://dx.doi.org/10.1163/2214-871X_ei1_SIM_4923.

117 Paul E. Walker, 'Muḥammad b. Ismāʿīl', in *Encyclopaedia of Islam, THREE*, edited by Kate Fleet et al. (2014-), http://dx.doi.org/10.1163/1573-3912_ei3_COM_36626.

118 Ismaili Gnosis, 'Who Succeeded Imam Jafar al-Sadiq? Seven Proofs for the Imamat of Imam Ismail ibn Jafar', https://ismailignosis.com/2014/10/02/who-succeeded-imam-jafar-al-sadiq-seven-proofs-for-the-imamat-of-imam-ismail-ibn-jafar/ (accessed 26 April 2021).

119 Tahera Qutbuddin, 'Bohras', in *Encyclopaedia of Islam, THREE*, edited by Kate Fleet et al., http://dx.doi.org/10.1163/1573-3912_ei3_COM_24020.

120 Jonah Blank, *Mullahs on the Mainframe: Islam and Modernity among the Daudi Bohras* (Chicago and London: University of Chicago Press, 2001).

121 Dawoodi Bohras, 'About the Bohras', https://www.thedawoodibohras.com/about-the-bohras/#dai (accessed 27 April 2021).

122 Dawoodi Bohras UK, http://www.dawoodi-bohras.org.uk (accessed 27 April 2022).

123 Institute of Ismaili Studies, 'Taxonomy: Sulaymani Bohras', https://www.iis.ac.uk/taxonomy/term/25626 (accessed 4 May 2021). ecoi.net, '2018 Report on International Religious Freedom: Saudi Arabia', https://www.ecoi.net/en/document/2011068.html (accessed 4 May 2021).

124 Fatemi Dawat, 'Official Statement Syedna Khuzaima Qutbuddin', YouTube, 19 January 2014, https://youtu.be/rTkp2_RLJUM.

125 Fatemi Dawat, 'Fatemi Dawat YouTube Channel', https://www.youtube.com/channel/UCLAxSC9eJHJKzeV-tEsykjw.

126 Fatemi Dawat, 'Dawat-e-Hadiyah', https://www.fatemidawat.com/ (accessed 4 May 2021).

127 See Bunt, *Virtually Islamic*, 47–58.

128 The Ismaili, https://the.ismaili/ (accessed 4 May 2021).

129 Ismaili TV, 'Canada - IVC Game Show - Family Challenge', n.d., https://tv.ismaili/watch/canada-ivc-game-show-family-challence (accessed 5 May 2021).

130 ibid.

131 Alavi Bohras, 'The Official Website of the 45th ad-Da'i al-Mutlaq al-Haqq Haatim ul-Khayraat, Rabee' ul-Barakaat Saiyedna Abu Sa'eed il-Khayr Haatim Zakiyuddin saheb (tus)', http://alavibohra.org/index.php (accessed 5 May 2021).

132 Alavi Bohras, 'YouTube Channel', https://www.youtube.com/channel/UC1xkdIC-lTTmWKrJmhJRWyQ (accessed 5 May 2021).

133 Alavi Bohras, 'Alavi Bohras – Laylat ul Qadr 1442 in the Homes of Mumineen', YouTube, 2021, https://youtu.be/6KVh5Smhz7Y.

134 Shaadi.com, 'Search: Dawood Bohra 20-25 Female', https://www.shaadi.com/search/matrimonial/result (accessed 10 May 2021).

135 Gujurati Shaadi, 'Dawoodi Bohra Canada Brides', https://www.gujaratishaadi.com/matrimony/dawoodi-bohra-canada-brides.

136 Re-marriage.com, 'Search: Dawoodi Bohra Females 30-45', https://www.re-marriage.com/matrimonial_search/quicksearch.php (accessed 10 May 2021).

137 Bharat Matrimony, 'Muslim Bohra Brides', 10 May 2021, https://www.bharatmatrimony.com/muslim-bohra-service-ias-ips-irs-ies-ifs-brides.

138 Ismaili Love, http://ismaililove.com/ (accessed 10 May 2023).

139 My Ismaili Life Partner, https://myismaililifepartner.com/ (accessed 10 May 2023).

140 Ismaili World, https://ismailiworld.com/ (accessed 10 May 2023).

Chapter 7

1 Eickelman and Piscatori, *Muslim Politics*, 121–2.
2 Edward W. Said, *Covering Islam: How the Media and the Experts Determine How We See the Rest of the World*, 2nd edn (New York: Vintage, 1997).
3 Astan Virtual Network, https://astaan.ir (accessed 12 May 2023).
4 Bunt, *Virtually Islamic*, 51–2.
5 The Institute for Compilation and Publication of Imam Khomeini's Works, 'Who is Imam Khomeini?' International Affairs Department, http://en.imam-khomeini.ir/en/s345/Memoirs (accessed 21 May 2021).
6 The Institute for Compilation and Publication of Imam Khomeini's Works, 'A Congratulatory Message for Denouncing Rushdie's "Satanic Verses"', International Affairs Department, http://en.imam-khomeini.ir/en/p1_13796/heart-letters/Letters_Sent_to_Imam/A_congratulatory_message_for_denouncing_Rushdie_s_Satanic_Verses_ (accessed 21 May 2021).
7 Astan Virtual Network, https://astaan.ir (accessed 12 May 2023).
8 Beheshte Zahra Organization, https://beheshtezahra.tehran.ir/ (accessed 20 May 2021).
9 'Imam Khomeini's Library', Apple App Store, https://apps.apple.com/ug/app/imam-khomeinis-library/id1117387576 (accessed 20 May 2021).
10 Kamal Yeganeh, 'Imam Khomeini Testament', https://appadvice.com/app/imam-khomeinis-testament-s/1139765248 (accessed 20 May 2021).
11 Ivan Teng, 'Imam Khomeini Tomb Iran in 4K', 11 December 2016, https://youtu.be/-ONd2t-Pkhc. Mehr News, 'Leader's visit to Imam Khomeini Mausoleum', 1 February 2020, https://en.mehrnews.com/news/155141/VDIEO-Leader-s-visit-to-Imam-Khomeini-mausoleum, Nurettin Odunya, 'Iran/Tehran (Mausoleum of Ayatollah Khomeini1) Part 18', https://youtu.be/X32RhixfaGw (accessed 3 November 2015).
12 Al Arabiyya, 'Iranian Boyband Video Clip Eulogizing Khomeini Goes Viral', 20 June 2020, https://english.alarabiya.net/News/middle-east/2020/06/10/Iranian-boyband-video-clip-eulogizing-Khomeini-goes-viral. Lisa Daftari, 'Iranian Boy Band Praises Khomeini in English Propaganda Music Video – The Foreign Desk', YouTube, 10 June 2020, https://youtu.be/illW0IyfU80 (accessed 20 May 2021).
13 Instagram, 'rouhalla_khomeini', https://www.instagram.com/rouhalla_khomeini/ (accessed 21 May 2021). Instagram, 'Ruhollah Khomeini', https://www.instagram.com/ruhollahkhomeini/ (accessed 21 May 2021). Instagram, 'Ruhollah.Khomeini', https://www.instagram.com/ruhollah.khomeini/ (accessed 21 May 2021).
14 Instagram, 'khomeini.imam', https://www.instagram.com/khomeini.imam/ (accessed 21 May 2021).
15 A Pinterest example is: Honar e Defa, 'Imam Khomeini', https://www.pinterest.co.uk/sazmanehonari/imam-khomeini- (accessed 21 May 2021).
16 SaatchiArt, 'What if they were Unicorns – Ruhollah Khomeini – Limited Edition 1 of 6 Photograph', https://www.pinterest.co.uk/pin/578994095844992419/ (accessed 21 May 2021).
17 Daniel Levin, 'Iran, Hamas and Palestinian Islamic Jihad', US Institute for Peace, 21 May 2021, https://iranprimer.usip.org/blog/2018/jul/09/iran-hamas-and-palestinian-islamic-jihad.
18 Khamenei.ir, 'Who was Imam Ali (pbuh)?' 4 May 2021, https://english.khamenei.ir/news/8473/Who-was-Imam-Ali-pbuh.

19 Khamenei.ir, 'Imam Khamenei Meets with Family of Sunni Martyr', 22 April 2021, https://english.khamenei.ir/news/8460/Imam-Khamenei-meets-with-family-of-Sunni-martyr.
20 Khamenei.ir, 'When Some People Don't Wear Masks, I Feel Ashamed before the Devoted Nurses', 20 July 2020, https://english.khamenei.ir/news/7771/When-some-people-don-t-wear-masks-I-feel-ashamed-before-the.
21 Instagram, 'Khamenei.ir', https://www.instagram.com/khamenei_ir/?hl=en (accessed 12 May 2023).
22 Pinterest, 'Sayed Ali Khamenei', https://www.pinterest.co.uk/t4m4n4/sayed-ali-khamenei/ (Accessed 21 May 2021).
23 Khamenei.ir, 'Ayatollah Khomenei's Verdict', Twitter, 14 February 2019, https://twitter.com/khamenei_ir.
24 Ellen Ioanes, 'Twitter Hid Post from an Account Linked to Iran's Supreme Leader', Daily Dot, 20 May 2021, https://www.dailydot.com/layer8/twitter-supreme-leader-ayatollah-khamenei-fatwa/.
25 Oliver Milman, 'Salman Rushdie Attack: Details Emerge about New Jersey Suspect', *The Guardian*, 2022, https://www.theguardian.com/books/2022/aug/13/salman-rushdie-attack-suspect-new-jersey. The extent to which social media directly influenced the attack could not be determined at the time of writing.
26 Gary R. Bunt, 'Iran Protests 2022', *Virtually Islamic Blog*, https://virtuallyislamic.com/vi2023/category/iran-protests-2022/ (accessed 6 June 2023).
27 Iran Data Portal, 'Society of the Lecturers of Qom Seminary (JMHEQ)', Princeton University, 5 November 2012, https://web.archive.org/web/20121105063859/http://www.princeton.edu/irandataportal/parties/modaressineqom/ (accessed 2 June 2021).
28 Society of Seminary Teachers of Qom, https://www.jameehmodarresin.org/.
29 Ali Teymoori, 'Islamic Laws by Ayatollah Wahid Khorasani', Ijtihadnet.co m, 10 December 2018, http://ijtihadnet.com/islamic-laws-by-ayatollah-wahid-khorasani/.
30 Ayatullah Khurasani, https://twitter.com/akhurasani?lang=en (accessed 2 June 2021). Ayatullah Khorasani, '@Al5orasani', https://twitter.com/Al5orasani.
31 Ayatullah Khurasani, Pinterest, https://www.instagram.com/wahidkhorasani/?hl=en (accessed 2 June 2021). also see The Office of Grand Ayatollah al-Uzma Shaykh Husayn Vahid Khorasani, 'The Greatness of the Tragedy of Hazrat Zahra's Martyrdom, The Position of Her Progeny, and their Responsibility on the Day of Her Martyrdom', 27 April 2010, http://wahidkhorasani.com/English/. Hadi TV, 'Shahadat Hazrat Fatima SA (Ayatullah Waheed Khorasani) with Urdu Subtitle', YouTube, https://youtu.be/st8NwnSWgJE. See the earlier discussion on Fāṭimah in Chapter 4.
32 The Office of Grand Ayatollah al-Uzma Shaykh Husayn Vahid Khorasani, 'Fatimiyyah Ought to be Held and Conducted in the Best Manner', 21 December 2020, http://wahidkhorasani.com/English/News/Content/438_Fatimiyyah-ought-to-be-held-and-conducted-in-the-best-manner.
33 The Office of Grand Ayatollah al-Uzma Shaykh Husayn Vahid Khorasani, 'Applications', 2 June 2021, http://wahidkhorasani.com/English/Appliations.
34 Ayatullah Modarresi, 'Grand Ayatollah Modarresi Urges the Dissemination of Islamic Knowledge Theough the Internet', Twitter, 20 April 2020, https://twitter.com/grandayatullah?lang=en.
35 Grand Ayatullah al-Modaressi, 'The (English Audio Translation of the) Speech of Grand Ayatollah Syed Mohammed Taqi al-Modarresi at the Opening of the Faith for

Nature: Multi-Faith Action Conference (5/10/2020), Hosted by the Prime Minister of Iceland', Facebook, 5 October 2020, https://www.facebook.com/GrandAyatollahAlModarresi/videos/656430961959398 (accessed 3 June 2021).
36 Grand Ayatullah al-Modaressi, 28 May 2021, https://almodarresi.com/ar/contact.
37 Grand Ayatullah al-Modaressi, YouTube, 3 June 2021, https://youtu.be/LK6oolhY3lQ.
38 Abrenoor, 'Complete Works of Ayatollah Mohammad Taqi Modarresi', https://abrenoor.ir/en/app/abrenoor_modarresi.
39 The Official Website of Grand Ayatollah Saafi Golpaygani, https://saafi.com/en# (accessed 29 May 2021).
40 The Official Website of Grand Ayatollah Makarem Shirazi, 'The Website of the Office of Grand Ayatollah Makarem Shirazi', https://makarem.ir/main.aspx?lid=1&typeinfo=36&catid=0&pageindex=0&mid=394295 (accessed 29 May 2021).
41 Ibid.
42 bahjat.ir, 'The Centre for Compilation and Publication of the Works of Grand Ayatollah Bahjat', https://bahjat.ir/en (accessed 27 May 2021), The Centre for Compilation and Publication of the works of Grand Ayatollah Bahjat, 'Grand Ayatollah Bahjat', https://www.instagram.com/en.bahjat.ir/ (accessed 27 May 2021).
43 See Bunt, *Hashtag Islam*, 91–2.
44 The Office of Al-Sayyid Al-Sistani, 'Questions about Preparing the Bodies of those Deceased from CoronaVirus (COVID-19)', 27 March 2020, https://www.sistani.org/english/archive/26412/, The Office of Al-Sayyid Al-Sistani, 'Rulings Regarding the Efforts of Medical Professionals Caring for Coronavirus Patients (COVID 19)', 16 March 2020, https://www.sistani.org/english/archive/26398/.
45 Al Jazeera English, 'Pope Francis Meets Iraq's Shia Leader al-Sistani', 7 March 2021, https://youtu.be/Ud7BLYVB-D0, The Office of Al-Sayyid Al-Sistani, 'Statement » A Statement Issued by the Office of the Supreme Religious Authority of World's Shia Muslims, Grand Ayatollah Sistani, Regarding His Meeting with the Grand Pontiff, the Pope', 6 March 2021, https://www.sistani.org/english/statement/26508/.
46 The Office of Al-Sayyid Al-Sistani, 'Questions from BBC about Some Inappropriate Practices, and the Responses to Them', 26 September 2019, https://www.sistani.org/english/archive/26348/.
47 Sistani.org, https://twitter.com/orgsistani?lang=en (accessed 26 July 2021).
48 Shia News Association, 'What is the Ruling on Taking Part in Stock Exchange Dealings? The Grand Ayatollah Sistani's Answer', 14 July 2020, https://en.shafaqna.com/154062/what-is-the-ruling-on-taking-part-in-stock-exchange-dealings-the-grand-ayatollah-sistanis-answer/ (accessed 27 May 2021).
49 sistani_org, Instagram, https://www.instagram.com/sistani_org/?hl=en (accessed 27 May 2021).
50 sistani.english, 'Ayatollah Sistani FAQ', Instagram, https://www.instagram.com/sistani.english/ (accessed 27 May 2021).
51 honar e defa, 'al-Sayid 'Ali al-Sistani', Pinterest, https://www.pinterest.co.uk/pin/733594226780761979/ (accessed 27 May 2021).
52 sazmanehonari, 'Islamic Resistance: Ayatollah Sistani', Pinterest, https://www.pinterest.co.uk/sazmanehonari/islamic-resistance (accessed 27 May 2021)–, sazmanehonari, 'Resistance Art: Painting', https://www.pinterest.co.uk/sazmanehonari/ (accessed 27 May 2021).

53 Imam Al-Khoei Foundation, 'Last Fatwas', https://www.al-khoei.org/latest-fatwas/.
54 Al-Khoei Foundation, Facebook, https://www.facebook.com/alkhoei.org (accessed 1 June 2021).
55 Al-Khoei Institute, 'Questions', http://alkhoei.net/ar/Question (accessed 1 June 2021).
56 Al-Khoei Institute, 'Library', http://alkhoei.net/ar/khlib/index.php (accessed 1 June 2021).
57 For example, see Al Khoei Islamic Institute, 'iPad App', https://apps.apple.com/us/app/alkhwyy/id810110885 (accessed 1 June 2021).
58 Dar al-'Ilm, 'About Daralilm', http://daralilm.net/en#About (accessed 1 June 2021).
59 Al-Khoei Institute, https://www.youtube.com/channel/UCOztr4Cu3r9OAeNOyvFXMkA/videos (accessed 1 June 2021).
60 Al-Khoei Institute, 'Sound', https://www.alkhoei.com/ar/Sound (accessed 1 June 2021).
61 The Central Office of His Eminence Grand Ayatullah Sheikh Bashir Al-Najafi, 11 March 2020, https://www.alnajafy.com/list/mainnews-2-444-6852.html.
62 The Central Office of His Eminence Grand Ayatullah Sheikh Bashir Al-Najafi, 'Biography', https://www.alnajafy.com/list/mainnews-2-444-594.html (accessed 28 May 2021).
63 The Grand Ayatullah Al Sheikh Hafiz Bashir Hussain Al Najafi Dama Zillahu, Facebook, https://www.facebook.com/ayatullahnajafi/. Ayatollah Al-Najafy, Twitter, https://twitter.com/AytollaALNajafi?lang=ar (accessed 28 May 2021).
64 Abbas Kadhim and Abdullah F. Alrebh, 'A Shift among the Shi'a. Will A Marj'a Emerge from the Arabian Peninsula?' *Middle East Institute Policy Paper*, Middle East Institute, January 2021, https://www.mei.edu/.
65 Alwefaq, Instagram, https://www.instagram.com/alwefaqenglish/ https://www.instagram.com/alwefaq/ (accessed 13 May 2023).
66 Alwefaq Society, Facebook, https://www.facebook.com/profile.php?id=100090809156559 (accessed 13 May 2023), Alwefaq Tawasul, Instagram, https://www.instagram.com/alwefaq_tawasul/ (accessed 13 May 2023).
67 Alwefaq Society, Facebook.
68 LuaLua TV, https://lualuatv.net/ (accessed 13 May 2023), LuaLua TV English, Twitter, https://twitter.com/LuaLuaEnglish (accessed 13 May 2023).
69 Martin Kramer, 'The Oracle of Hizbullah: Sayyid Muhammad Husayn Fadlallah', in *Spokesmen for the Despised: Fundamentalist Leaders in the Middle East*, edited by R. Scott Appleby (Chicago: University of Chicago Press, 1997), 83–181, https://scholar.harvard.edu/files/martinkramer/files/martinkramer.org-the_oracle_of_hizbullah_sayyid_muhammad_husayn_fadlallah_1.pdf.
70 David Kenner, 'The Sheikh Who Got Away', *Foreign Policy*, 2010, https://foreignpolicy.com/2010/07/06/the-sheikh-who-got-away-2/.
71 Bayynat, http://arabic.bayynat.org.lb; http://english.bayynat.org.lb (accessed 29 May 2021).
72 Sayyed Ali Fadlallah Official Website, http://www.alifadlallah.net/home/ (accessed 29 May 2021). Sayyed Ali Fadlallah, Facebook, https://www.facebook.com/Sayyed.Ali.Fadlallah/ (Accessed 24 May 2021).
73 Islamic Movement of Nigeria, https://www.islamicmovement.org/ (accessed 10 February 2023). Bohras, 'About the Bohras', Bunt, *Hashtag Islam*, 58–60.

Chapter 8

1 Carl W. Ernst, 'Tariqa', in *Encyclopedia of Islam and the Muslim World*, edited by Richard C. Martin, vol. 2 (New York: Macmillan Reference, 2004), 680–4.
2 Arjana, *Pilgrimage in Islam*, 6–16.
3 Eickelman and Piscatori, *Muslim Politics*, 125.
4 Jalāl al-Dīn Rūmī and William C. Chittick, *The Sufi Path of Love: The Spiritual Teachings of Rumi* (Albany: State University of New York Press, 1983).
5 Ahmed ibn Muhammad Ibn 'Ata'Allah et al., *The Book of Wisdom: Ibn 'Ata'illah; Intimate Conversations*, edited by Ahmad ibn Muhammad et al., 1979 edn (London: SPCK, 1969).
6 As discussed in Lawrence, *Islamicate Cosmopolitan Spirit*, 75–8.
7 Margaret Smith, 'Rābiʿa al-ʿAdawiyya al-Ḳaysiyya', in *Encyclopaedia of Islam, Second Edition, Online*, edited by P. Bearman et al. (Leiden: Brill, 2012), http://dx.doi.org/10.1163/1573-3912_islam_SIM_6160. Also see Margaret Smith, *Rabi'a the Mystic & Her Fellow-Saints in Islam: Being the Life and Teachings of Rabi'a al-'Adawiyya Al-Qaysiyya of Basra, together with Some Account of the Place of the Women Saints in Islam* (Cambridge: Cambridge University Press, 1928).
8 Batoul Mesdaghi, 'She's the Most Famous Sufi Woman in the World: Meet Rabia al-Adawiyya', mvslim.com, 18 January 2019, https://mvslim.com/shes-the-most-famous-sufi-woman-in-the-world-meet-rabia-al-adawiyya/.
9 Nabeela Jamil, 'Was Rabi'a Basri – The Single Most Influential Sufi Woman – A Feminist?' Feminism in India, 10 October 2019, https://feminisminindia.com/2018/10/10/rabia-basri-sufi-woman-feminist/.
10 Poetry Chaikhana, 'Rabia al-Basri', https://www.poetry-chaikhana.com/Poets/R/RabiaalBasri/index.html (accessed 26 October 2021).
11 Naz Munir, 'Rabia Basri', Pinterest, https://www.pinterest.co.uk/ikeepyourheart/rabia-basri/ (accessed 26 October 2021).
12 Sunder Singh, 'Narayani', https://in.pinterest.com/pin/754845587541964912/ (accessed 26 October 2021). The same painting appears in Ballandalus, 'The Destruction of Hispano-Islamic Civilization: Recollections, Reflections, and Significance', 1 January 2014, https://ballandalus.wordpress.com/2014/01/01/the-destruction-of-hispano-islamic-civilization-recollections-reflections-and-significance-2/.
13 Ziyara Tours, 'Tomb of Sayyida Rabia Al-Basri – Great Muslim Saint & Sufi Mystic – Mount of Olives, Jerusalem', 28 October 2020, https://youtu.be/aAFFJGfVtJI (accessed 26 October 2021).
14 Mazar Mubarak - Imran Ghazi, 'RABIA BASRI: Hazrat Bibi Qalandaria | Makam Rabi'atul Adawiyah | Shrine in Palestine', https://youtu.be/xGcS4cqPtHU (accessed 26 October 2021).
15 Allama Mukhtar Shah Naeemi Ashrafi (Whitestone 786), '(36) Story of Hazrat Rabia Basri (I visited her grave in Jerusalem)', YouTube, https://youtu.be/PStBPSzsffQ.
16 Yaqeen Institute, 'Episode 4: Rabiah Al-Adawiyya | Inspirational Muslim Women', 30 July 2017, https://youtu.be/aGqoz2m0ecI (accessed 26 October 2021). Tamana Daqiq, 'Great Figures of Islam – Rabi'a al-'Adawiyyah – Lecture Series (Session 6)', YouTube, 14 April 2016, https://youtu.be/f03zN_66HxU (accessed 26 October 2021).
17 Niazi Mostafa, *Rabaa Al-Adawiya, 1963*. There were also Turkish films about her, including Osman F. Seden, *Rabia*, 1973.

18 For a detailed discussion on al-Ḥallāj and his work, see Husayn ibn Mansur Hallaj, *Hallaj: Poems of a Sufi Martyr*, translated by Carl W. Ernst (Chicago: Northwestern University Press, 2018).

19 L. Gardet Louis Massignon, 'al-Halladj', in *Encyclopaedia of Islam, Second Edition, Online Edition*, edited by P. Bearman et al. (Leiden: Brill, 2012), III:99b. *Encyclopaedia of Islam*, https://referenceworks.brillonline.com:443/entries/encyclopaedia-of-islam-2/al-halladj-COM_0256 (also see Robert Irwin, 'Al-Hallaj's Truth, Massignon's Fiction', *Critical Muslim*, no. 12.1, https://www.criticalmuslim.io/al-hallajs-truth-massignons-fiction/.

20 Sadeeque, 'You Drew Me so Close To You – Until I thought, "You Are Me"', *Rumi Love Quotes*, Pinterest, https://in.pinterest.com/pin/474707616971531489/?d=t&mt=login (accessed 13 October 2021).

21 Sadeeque, 'Rumi Love Quotes: "Your Spirit is Mingled with Mine"', Pinterest, https://in.pinterest.com/pin/474707616971536747/ (accessed 13 October 2021).

22 All Poetry, 'Mansur Al Hallaj', https://allpoetry.com/Mansur-Al-Hallaj (accessed 13 October 2021).

23 Mansur al-Hallaj, 'The Tawasin of Mansur Al-Hallaj', HolyBooks.com, reproducing Diwan Press book, 1974, https://holybooks.com/tawasin-mansur-al-hallaj/.

24 R. Feener, 'A Re-examination of the Place of al-Hallaj in the Development of Southeast Asian Islam', *Bijdragen tot de Taal-, Land- en Volkenkunde* 154, no. 4 (1998): 571–92, https://brill.com/downloadpdf/journals/bki/154/4/article-p571_2.xml.

25 The Threshold Society, '2 Poems by Hussein Ibn Mansur Al Hallaj', https://sufism.org/library/articles/2-poems-by-hussein-ibn-mansur-al-hallaj (accessed 15 October 2021).

26 Muslim Philosophy, 'Index', https://muslimphilosophy.org/ (accessed 5 May 2022). Ghazali.org, 'A Virtual Online Library', https://www.ghazali.org/ (accessed 15 October 2021). W. Montgomery Watt, 'al-Ghazālī', in *Encyclopaedia of Islam, Second Edition*, edited by P. Bearman et al. (Leiden: Brill, 1954–2005), http://dx.doi.org/10.1163/1573-3912_islam_COM_0233.

27 Justin Parrott, 'Al-Ghazali and the Golden Rule: Ethics of Reciprocity in the Works of a Muslim Sage', *Journal of Religious & Theological Information* 16, no. 2 (2017): 68–78, https://doi.org/10.1080/10477845.2017.1281067.

28 Yahya GP, 'Wirid Imam Al-Ghazali', Google Play, https://play.google.com/store/apps/details?id=id.yahyagp.wiridimamalghazali (accessed 15 October 2021). F. M. Denny, 'Wird', in *Encyclopaedia of Islam, Second Edition*, edited by P. Bearman et al. (Leiden: Brill, 1954–2005), http://dx.doi.org/10.1163/1573-3912_islam_SIM_7914.

29 Ghazali.org, 'A Virtual Online Library'.

30 Imam Ghazali Institute, https://www.imamghazali.org (accessed 15 October 2021). Al Ghazali Institute, Instagram, 16 October 2021, https://www.instagram.com/imamghazaliinstitute/?hl=en.

31 Ghazali Children, https://ghazalichildren.org/ (accessed 15 October 2021).

32 JS-soft, 'Life of the Scholar of Religion Imam Al-Ghazali', https://play.google.com/store/apps/details?id=naitsoft.android.ihya2 (accessed 15 October 2021).

33 Reddit, r/islam, https://www.reddit.com/r/islam/ (accessed 30 September 2023). In contrast, an academic approach can be found in Frank Griffel, 'al-Ghazali', in *The Stanford Encyclopedia of Philosophy*, Online, edited by Edward N. Zalta (2020), https://plato.stanford.edu/archives/sum2020/entries/al-ghazali/.

34 Zubair, 'Imam Ghazali', Pinterest, https://www.pinterest.co.uk/zi_idah/imam-ghazali/ (accessed 16 October 2021). The Meaning of Islam, 'Imam Al Ghazali', *Islamic Scholars*, Pinterest, https://www.pinterest.co.uk/meaningofislam/ (accessed 16 October 2021).
35 KJ Vids, 'The Proof of Islam: Imam Ghazali', https://youtu.be/bbeqhxAH9gc (accessed 16 October 2021). Let's Talk Religion, 'Al-Ghazali – The Reviver of Religious Sciences', 8 November 2020, https://youtu.be/ZL-ZxXQ6HCU (accessed 16 October 2021).
36 Hamza Yusuf, 'The Critical Importance of Al Ghazali in Our Time', YouTube, 23 March 2015, https://youtu.be/PoRRoqVXeGw.
37 Raindrop Academy, 'Imam Al Ghazali Advice on Knowing Yourself – #Spiritual Psychologist', 18 January 2015, https://youtu.be/rbyH0GbwAMc.
38 Habaib, 'Ahlussuffah', TikTok, https://www.tiktok.com/foryou?lang=en&is_copy_url=1&is_from_webapp=v1&item_id=6993397014130134298#/@_ahlussuffah/video/6993397014130134298.
39 This section reflects the influence of my former tutor at the University of Kent, John Bousfield (1948–2004), who spoke eloquently about al-Jīlānī and Sufism.
40 The term 'saint' can be problematic here, with limited equivalence to other religious contexts. Assimalhakeem, 'Who was Abdul Qadir Al Jilani Are His Followers these Days on the Right Path (Qadaris) Assimalhakeem', YouTube, 7 January 2021, https://youtu.be/mPo_OEvOt38.
41 Mazar Mubarak - Imran Ghazi, 'Baghdad Sharif Drone View | Under Construction Shrine of Sheikh Abdul Qadir Jilani', YouTube, 20 February 2019, https://youtu.be/4b6SPH3eomc (accessed 18 October 2021).
42 Dramas Central, 'Hazrat Sheikh Abdul Qadir Jillani Kay Mazar Mubarik Ki Ziarat', YouTube, 23 June 2017, https://youtu.be/whsmbrTN0Fk (accessed 18 October 2021). Mazar Mubarak - Imran Ghazi, 'Complete Ziyarat of Baghdad Sharif | Tomb of Hazrat Shaikh Abdul Qadir Jilani | Baghdad Sharif 2021', 17 August 2021, https://youtu.be/I79wsNmp-s0 (accessed 18 October 2021).
43 Musjidul Haq Research Department, 'Miracles of Huzoor Ghaus Paak', https://musjidulhaq.com/2016/01/31/miracles-of-huzoor-ghaus-paak/.
44 Kashif Khatri, 'Sheikh Abdul Qadir Jilani Tomb (Inside view) – Baghdad City', 23 May 2020, https://youtu.be/ip-TS7ybEa4. Astana Qadiri France Dergah Baba Shejh Dzafer, 'Shaykh Sayyid Hashim Al Gaylani Opening the Door of Maqaam Hz Abdul Qadir Gaylani with Shejh Dzafer', 30 April 2021, https://www.youtube.com/watch?v=1TJ83gASUjw.
45 Mujtaba Tahir, 'Zikr-Allah in Aastana of Shaikh Abdul Qadir Al-Gaylani', 13 June 2020, https://youtu.be/KvbyRvqhtuU.
46 Mazar Mubarak - Imran Ghazi, 'Complete Ziyarat of Baghdad Sharif | Tomb of Hazrat Shaikh Abdul Qadir Jilani | Baghdad Sharif 2021.
47 Ameer Hamza, 'Jilani Shrine: The Sufi Heart of Baghdad', *Express Tribune*, 22 March 2015, https://tribune.com.pk/story/855261/jilani-shrine-the-sufi-heart-of-baghdad (accessed 26 October 2021).
48 Qadri Shattari Silsila's Online Platform, 'Gyarvi Sharif', https://www.qadrishattari.xyz/p/gyarvi-sharif.html (accessed 18 October 2021).
49 Niyazi Sufi Mehfil-e-Sama, 'Mere Peer Hain Jilani, Ismail Azad Qawwal', 2 December 2019, https://youtu.be/G6mEeKl9zuc.
50 Sufi Post, 'Monthly Gyarvi Sharif Celebration at Darbar of Ghous e Azam Abdul Qadir Jilani (Vijaypur)', 24 December 2010, https://youtu.be/92OkLiafQqw.

51 Xmart Explorer, 'Karamat e Ghous e Azam Abdul Qadir Jilani | Murda Zinda Ho Gaya Gausal Azam Dastagir R.A', 8 December 2019, https://youtu.be/7Hw3z3L2KRU.

52 Shaykh Hisham Kabbani, 'The Maqaam of Shaykh `Abdul Qadir al-Jilani (q)', SufiLive, 4 February 2016, https://youtu.be/COkLoeR8KvM.

53 Assimalhakeem, 'Who was Abdul Qadir Al Jilani Are His Followers these Days on the Right Path (Qadaris)'

54 Ink of Knowledge, 'Amazing Story of Shaykh Abdul Qadir Jilani (R.A) as a Child', 7 April 2013, https://youtu.be/a5ar8HgD2xA. Sacred Knowledge, 'Shaykh 'Abdul Qadir al-Jilani | Sh Muhammad Yaseen', 20 May 2012, https://youtu.be/uIhxFV8tjTQ.

55 Quran wa Hadith, 'Seerat Sheikh Abdul Qadir Jilani', Pinterest, https://no.pinterest.com/pin/590886413588007316/ (accessed 18 October 2021).

56 Nadia Ross, 'Abd Qadir Al Jilani', Pinterest, https://www.pinterest.co.uk/nadross256/abd-qadir-al-jilani/ (accessed 18 October 2021).

57 Madani Channel, 'Ghous e Pak Ki Mubarak Seerat', 21 November 2020, https://youtu.be/zIpDF1Hp654.

58 YouTube, 'Searech: #sheikhabdulqadirjilani', https://www.youtube.com/hashtag/sheikhabdulqadirjilani (accessed 18 October 2021).

59 Ansari Qadiri Rifai Tariqa Sufi Order, https://www.aqrtsufi.org (accessed 18 October 2021).

60 Shaykh Dr. Abdalqadir as-Sufi, 'Qadiriyya Dhikr', YouTube, 27 April 2012, https://youtu.be/9BaQunfXPpE.

61 F. Sobierroj, 'Suhrawardiyya', in *Encyclopaedia of Islam, Second Edition, Onlne* (Leiden: Brill, 2012), IX:784b. *Encyclopaedia of Islam*, P. Bearman et al., https://referenceworks.brillonline.com:443/entries/encyclopaedia-of-islam-2/suhrawardiyya-COM_1108.

62 Mazar Mubarak - Imran Ghazi, 'Hazrat Shaikh Shahabuddin Umar Soharwardi: Suharwardi Sufi Order | Awarif ul-Maarif: Tasawwuf', YouTube, 10 October 2018, https://youtu.be/UE_rFlATpLc.

63 News Leaks Mux, 'Hazarat Shah Rukn E Alam Shrine Documentary 2020 In Urdu', YouTube, 27 December 2019, https://youtu.be/qiK-Lrdrx0U.

64 Ahmed Amini, 'Shah Rukn-e-Alam | Bahauddin Zakariya Tomb – Multan – Pakistan', 6 February 2019, https://youtu.be/AQ9-1j5kn3U (accessed 1 November 2021), Naeem Shah Bukhari, 'Tomb of Bahauddin Zakariya Multan', YouTube, 12 March 2016, https://youtu.be/lBquXMwJPUU (accessed 1 November 2021).

65 News Leaks Mux, 'Hazarat Shah Rukn E Alam Shrine Documentary 2020 In Urdu'.

66 Linus Strothmann, 'Dātā Ganj Bakhsh, Shrine Of', in *Encyclopaedia of Islam, THREE*, Online, edited by Kate Fleet et al. (Leiden: Brill, 2014), http://dx.doi.org/10.1163/1573-3912_ei3_COM_27729.

67 ARY Qtv, 'Kashaf-ul-Mahjoob', YouTube, 13 November 2019, https://youtu.be/vBLuGeP5dGM (accessed 2 November 2021). Mufti Muhammad Ramzan Sialvi, Facebook, https://www.facebook.com/muftiramzansialviofficial (accessed 2 November 2021). Sialvi attracted controversy in 2016 for supporting Mumtaz Qadri, responsible for assassinating a politician who was supportive of Asia Bibi (who was accused of blasphemy); Sialivi's support included online photos of him kissing Qadri's corpse after execution.

68 Lahore News HD, 'Hazrat Data Ganj Baksh Urs 2020', 8 October 2020, https://youtu.be/Z8b9fEDsm8M (accessed 2 November 2020). City 42, 'Hazrat Data Ganj

Bakhsh Urs Celebrations Begin', 26 September 2021, https://youtu.be/RIR4rCCSf4k (accessed 2 November 2021). City 42, 'Hazrat Data Ganj Bakhsh Ali Hajveri (R.A) 978th Urs Ceremony | 27 Sep 2021', 27 September 2021, https://youtu.be/efMPiUS0_L4 (accessed 2 November 2021).

69 abuhafsa2008, 'Dargah Hazrat Data Ganj Baksh Ali Hajveri', 22 March 2012, https://youtu.be/yx63ZrTTHL4 (accessed 2 November 2021).

70 Musaf Hanif, 'My Visit to the Famous Shrine of Hazrat Data Ganj Baksh (DATA DARBAR)', Bitlanders, 13 February 2018, https://www.bitlanders.com/blogs/my-visit-to-the-famous-shrine-of-hazrat-data-ganj-baksh-data-darbar/5671293.

71 Sufism15, 'Miracles Of Khwaja Moinuddin Chisti', 30 April 2017, https://sufism15.wordpress.com/2017/04/30/miracles-of-khwaja-moinuddin-chisti/ (accessed 28 October 2021).

72 Mohammed Firozshah, 'Khwaja Garib Nawaz', Pinterest, https://in.pinterest.com/mfirozshah/khwaja-garib-nawaz/ (accessed 28 October 2021).

73 Street Food Zaika, 'Inside the Video of Khwaja Moinuddin Chisti | Khwaja Garib Nawaz Dargah Video |', 13 Octover 2020, https://youtu.be/PWlJ6ODDmgQ.

74 Chistiya Darbar, 'Jumerat Live Qawwali |Khwaja Garib Nawaz Qawwali | Super Hit Qawwaliya | Best Qawwali 2021', https://youtu.be/YxPZ2AdVdfE (accessed 28 October 2021).

75 Gulum-E-Garib Nawaz (R.A.), 'Mission of Khawaja Garib Nawaz (R.A.)', http://chishtiyasilsila.weebly.com/ (accessed 18 October 2021).

76 Tahir Qadiry, 11 January 2021, https://twitter.com/sufimusafir/status/1348627479078948867. Haji Syed Salman Chishty, Twitter, https://twitter.com/sufimusafir (accessed 28 October 2021). Khwaja e Ajmer, Twitter, https://twitter.com/DivineSufi (accessed 28 October 2021).

77 Carl W. Ernst and Bruce B. Lawrence, *Sufi Martyrs of Love: Chishti Order in South Asia and Beyond* (New York and Basingstoke: Palgrave Macmillan, 2002).

78 abuhafsa2008, 'Dargah Khwaja Qutbuddin Bakhtiar Kaaki', YouTube, 23 July 2011, https://youtu.be/8-4w8F4S5iI (accessed 4 November 2021). Shemaroo Ibaadat, 'Urs Mubarak 2019 – Dargah Khwaja Qutubuddin Bakhtiyar Kaki (RH) - Delhi', YouTube, 17 September 2019, https://youtu.be/Cu0nXMsvi2g (accessed 4 November 2019).

79 National Mission on Monuments and Antiquities, 'Tomb of Khwaja Qutubuddin Bakhtiar Kaki', http://nmma.nic.in/nmma/builtDetail.do?refId=11698&dynasty=11 (accessed 4 November 2021).

80 ANI News, 'Urs of Qutbuddin Bakhtiyar Kaki Symbolises Religious Harmony', 1 November 2021, https://youtu.be/6vLz0f38ehc.

81 Ibaadat, 'Urs Mubarak 2019 – Dargah Khwaja Qutubuddin Bakhtiyar Kaki (RH) – Delhi'. Mukhtar Ashraf, 'Urs Mubarak 2021 | Khwaja Qutbuddin Bakhtiyar Kaki | Mehrauli Sharif | Mukhtar Ashraf', 22 October 2021, https://www.youtube.com/watch?v=TgjUxewVeeA.

82 Hazrat Syed Khwaja Qutbuddin bakhtiyar kaki R.A, Facebook, https://www.facebook.com/Hazrat-Syed-Khwaja-Qutbuddin-bakhtiyar-kaki-RA-249201865511240/ (accessed 4 November 2021).

83 TripAdvisor, 'Qutbuddin Bakhtiar Kaki', https://www.tripadvisor.co.uk/ShowUserReviews-g304551-d11998678-r623954342-Qutbuddin_Bakhtiar_Kaki-New_Delhi_National_Capital_Territory_of_Delhi.html (accessed 4 November 2021).

84 Geni, 'Hazrat Khawaja Syed Qutubuddin Bakhtiyar Kaki', https://www.geni.com/family-tree/index/6000000107656169969.

85 Ibn al-ʿArabī, *The Bezels of Wisdom*, translated by Ralph Austin (Mahwah: Paulist Press, 1980), 290.
86 Muhyiddin Ibn ʿArabi Society, Facebook, https://www.facebook.com/groups/ibnarabi.society/ (accessed 19 October 2021).
87 TRT, 'Resurrection Ertugrul', YouTube, https://www.youtube.com/channel/UCSCHrDLjlO9sZk6iLEAuE0w (accessed 19 October 2021).
88 Idries Shah, 'The Sufis: Ibn el Arabi, The Greatest Sheikh', Idries Shah Foundation, 2 August 2016, https://youtu.be/PZbZN_oSDmI (accessed 18 October 2021).
89 Instagram, '#ibnalarabi', https://www.instagram.com/explore/tags/ibnarabi/ (accessed 18 October 2021).
90 For example, see kingkash787, 'Entry of Ibn Al Arabi', TikTok, https://www.tiktok.com/@kingkash787/video/6852433668133178629 (accessed 18 October 2021).
91 TRT Resurrection Ertugrul, 'Ibn Arabi's Dhikr in Jerusalem – Season 1', YouTube, 6 June 2019, https://youtu.be/TlnXuEJTZRc.
92 MomineenTeam, 'The Dancing of Ibn Arabi', Twitter, 5 June 2020, https://mobile.twitter.com/momineenteam/status/1268868407463604224?lang=ar (accessed 18 October 2021).
93 Rūmī Jalāl al-Dīn et al., *The Mathnawí of Jalálu'ddín Rúmí* (London: Printed by Messrs. E.J. Brill, Leiden, for the Trustees of the "E. J.W. Gibb memorial" and published by Messrs. Luzac & Co., 1925), '*E J W Gibb memorial" series New series*, vol. 4. A. J. Arberry, *The Life and thought of Rumi* (Lahore, 1956). See Richard O. Watkin, 'Arthur John Arberry (1905-1969): A Critical Evaluation of an Orientalist' (PhD, Institute of Humanities and Education, University of Wales Trinity Saint David, 2021). Director of Studies: Gary R. Bunt, https://repository.uwtsd.ac.uk/id/eprint/1692.
94 Rozina Ali, 'The Erasure of Islam from the Poetry of Rumi', *The New Yorker*, 2017, https://www.newyorker.com/books/page-turner/the-erasure-of-islam-from-the-poetry-of-rumi.
95 See Arjana, *Buying Buddha, Selling Rumi*, 218–21.
96 Ibid., 200–1. Discussing Omid Safi, 'Personal Page', Facebook, https://www.facebook.com/ostadjaan/ (accessed 17 August 2018).
97 Pinterest, 'Search: "Rumi"', https://www.pinterest.co.uk/search/pins/?q=rumi&rs=typed&term_meta[]=rumi%7Ctyped (accessed 21 October 2021). Rumi Quotes & Poetry, Instagram, https://www.instagram.com/rumi.quotes/?hl=en (accessed 21 October 2021), rumiquotesfficial, Instagram, https://www.instagram.com/rumiquotesofficial/?hl=en (accessed 21 October 2021).
98 Rumi Quotes, 'Rumi Quotes and Rumi Poems', https://www.rumi.org.uk/ (accessed 21 October 2021).
99 A. J. Arberry, *The Ruba'iyat of Jalal al-Din Rumi – Select Translation into English verse* (London: Emery Walker, 1949). Rumi Quotes, 'Persian with Rumi', https://www.rumi.org.uk/persian/ (accessed 21 October 2021).
100 Safa Ceylan, 'Kale Pazarlama – Konya – Mevlana Sema Gösterisi', 4 October 2007, https://youtu.be/OpymloKMSJk (accessed 21 October 2021). In my 1990s travels to Konya, I saw devotees praying towards and inside the 'museum' complex. At the same time, visitors still performed *ziyārah* visitations or 'pilgrimages', some travelling on the back of tractors from adjacent villages.
101 He is not to be confused with the ḥādīth scholar Imām Bukhārī (810–70), whose tomb is also in Bukhara.
102 Hamid Algar, 'Naḳshband', in *Encyclopaedia of Islam, Second Edition*, edited by P. Bearman et al., vol. Online (Leiden: Brill, 2012). SufiWiki, 'Bahauddin

Naqshband', https://sufiwiki.com/Bahauddin_Naqshband (accessed 9 November 2021).

103 Seeker of the Sacred Knowledge, 'Some Sayings of Hazrat Khwaja Bahauddin Naqshband', Pinterest, https://www.pinterest.co.uk/pin/579275570819295406/ (accessed 9 November 2021).

104 Muhammad Yaqub, 'Virtual Ziarat Shah Naqshband, Baha-ud-Din Naqshband', YouTube, 23 March 2020, https://youtu.be/_GY-lFMkcoM (accessed 9 November 2021). Also see Dar-ul-Uloom Taleem-ul-Quran, 'Ziarat Hazrat Khwaja Bahauddin Naqshbandi (R.A) (4)', YouTube, 7 November 2019, https://youtu.be/vuriNBys8j4. ARY News, 'PM Khan visits Tomb of Baha' al-Din Naqshband in Uzbekistan', YouTube, 17 July 2021, https://youtu.be/_CcdCF4f3wM (accessed 9 November 2021). myVideoMedia, 'Bahauddin Naqshband Bokhari Memorial Complex – Uzbekistan 4K Travel Channel', 30 March 2018, https://youtu.be/BcBvVIl2ozE (accessed 9 November 2021).

105 Gramhir, '#bahauddinnaqsbandibukhari', 12 October 2021, https://gramhir.com/explore-hashtag/bahauddinnaqshband (accessed 9 November 2021).

106 Naqshbandi Sufi, 'Urs of the Imam of Tariqat, Sayyiduna Shah Muhammad Baha'uddin Naqshband Rahmatullah 'Alayh', YouTube, 10 February 2019, https://youtu.be/cYtRu-1ZNjs.

107 Rohi, 'Hazrat Bahauddin Zakariya Urs Started from Tommorow', 22 September 2020, https://youtu.be/kee1UC3cem4 (accessed 9 November 2021.

108 Aal-e-Qutub, 'Hazrat Khawaja Bahauddin Naqshbandi Rehmatullah alaih aur Ishq-e-Rasool', 9 October 2021, https://aalequtub.com/2021/10/09/hazrat-khawaja-bahauddin-naqshbandi-rehmatullah-alaih-aur-ishq-e-rasool-ﷺ/ (accessed 9 November 2021). Love Meditation Naqshbandi, 'URS Imam Tariqah Sheikh Khwaja Muhammad Bahauddin Shah Naqshband Uwaysi al-Bukhari QS – 3rd Rabi ul-Awwal', 19 October 2020, https://www.lovemeditation-naqshbandi.com/urs-imam-tariqah-sheikh-khwaja-muhammad-bahauddin-shah-naqshband-uwaysi-al-bukhari-qs-3rd-rabi-ul-awwal-2020/.

109 Dina Le Gall, 'Aḥmad-i Bukhārī', in *Encyclopaedia of Islam, THREE*, edited by Kate Fleet et al., vol. Online (Leiden: Brill, 2013).

110 Naqshbandi Sufi Way, 'Initiation', https://naqshbandi.org/the-tariqa/initiation/ (accessed 5 May 2022), Sufi Live, 'Bay'a into the Naqshbandi Tariqa', 7 November 2014, https://youtu.be/cAQnkwgFI5c (accessed 5 May 2022).

111 Naqshbandi Sufi Way, 'Shaykh Muhammad Hisham Kabbani, "History and Guidebook of the Saints of the Golden Chain"', https://naqshbandi.org/the-golden-chain/the-chain/ (accessed 5 May 2022).

112 Hisham Kabbani, http://hishamkabbani.com/ (accessed 11 November 2021). This discussion synthesizes previous work on the Naqshbandi-Haqqani Order. Bunt, *Hashtag Islam*, 94–6.

113 Mawlana Shaykh Hisham Kabbani, 'Invoking the Masters of the Naqshbandi Golden Chain for Protection', SufiLive, 31 December 2015, https://sufilive.com/media/index.cfm?id=6111 (accessed 11 November 2021).

114 Shaykh Muhammad Hisham Kabbani, 'Taweez – Talisman', https://naqshbandi.org/resources/taweez/ (accessed 11 November 2021).

115 Naqshbandi Sufi Way, 'Khatm-ul-Khwajagan', https://naqshbandi.org/khatm-ul-khwajagan/ (accessed 11 November 2021).

116 Stefano Allievi and Jørgen S. Nielsen, *Muslim Networks and Transnational Communities in and across Europe* (Leiden: Brill, 2003). *Muslim Minorities*; vol.

1, Mustafa Draper et al., 'Transnational Sufism: The Haqqaniyya', in *Sufism in the West*, edited by Jamal Malik and John Hinnells (London: Routledge, 2006), 103–14.

117 SufiLive, https://sufilive.com/ (accessed 11 November 2021).

118 Nour Kabbani, 'Mawlid An-Nabi', SufiLive, 15 October 2021, https://sufilive.com/Mawlid-An-Nabi-pbuh--7579.html. Mawlana Shaykh Hisham Kabbani, 'Eid Khutbah: "Take This Holy Book Off the Shelf!"', SufiLive, 30 October 2021, https://sufilive.com/Take-This-Holy-Book-Off-the-Shelf--7587.html (accessed 11 November 2021).

119 AskImam, Islamicity, IslamOnline, Islam Q&A and OnIslam are prominent examples of the developments of such services from different Muslim perspectives, drawing on traditional approaches to decision-making and knowledge acquisition, and providing searchable databases (AskImam, 2012, Islamicity, 2012, IslamOnline, 2012, Islam Q&A, 2012, OnIslam, 2012).

120 Some of these search results were advertisements and duplicates. SufiLive, 'Search: "Covid"', https://eshaykh.com/search/?q=covid (accessed 11 November 2021).

121 eShaykh, 'Dream Interpretation', https://eshaykh.com/category/dreams/ (accessed 15 November 2021).

122 Zahir Khan, 'Visiting the Mazar of Hazrat Allama Pir Abdul Wahab Siddiqui', https://fallingintomystery.com (accessed 11 November 2021). See Naomi de Souza, 'Inside Hijaz College, Nuneaton', *Coventry Telegraph*, 5 January 2021, https://www.coventrytelegraph.net/news/coventry-news/gallery/inside-hijaz-college-nuneaton-19565731.

123 Shaikh Tauqir Ishaq, 'Hazrat Allama Peer Abdul Wahab Siddiqi (r.a.)', 7 December 2013, https://youtu.be/o6sUVg8JCbw.

124 Kaya Kenç, 'The Cleric has Uploaded a New Video', Rest of World, 2 February 2021, https://restofworld.org/2021/the-cleric-has-uploaded-a-new-video/.

125 Cübbeli Ahmet Hoca, 'Cübbeli Ahmet Hoca YouTube Channel', Youtube, https://www.youtube.com/cubbeliahmethoca Accessed 29 November 2021.

126 Kenç, 'The Cleric has Uploaded a New Video'.

127 Aal-e-Qutub, 'Hazrat Ahmad al Tijani', https://aalequtub.com/hazrat-ahmad-al-tijani (accessed 15 November 2021).

128 blitzzzmode, 'Dhikr at the Zawiya of Sidi Ahmed Tijaani (RA) Fez Morocco 2/3', YouTube, 25 December 2011, https://youtu.be/5rLaX4PCKuw (accessed 15 November 2021).

129 Suhail Khairy, 'Tijani Wadhifa in Grand Zawiya Fez -Tidjaniya.com', YouTube, https://youtu.be/SVkcVyG7G-8 (accessed 15 November 2021).

130 Suhail Khairy, 'Tariqah Tijaniya Documentary', 16 March 2011, https://youtu.be/MOmxmXKJVfE (accessed 15 November 2021).

131 Tidjaniya.com, 'Question: Is it okay to join the Wazifa or the Friday Hadhra via Video Conferencing Applications e.g. Zoom, WhatsApp, Skype etc. because of the Lockdown Restrictions due to the Coronavirus?' 9 June 2020, http://www.tidjaniya.com/en/faq-tidjaniya (accessed 15 November 2021).

132 Tidjaniya.com, 'Teaching of Recitations', 14 August 2018, http://www.tidjaniya.com/en/tariqa-tidjaniya/teachings-of-recitations (accessed 15 November 2021).

133 La Tariqa Tidjaniya au Senegal, 'Tidjaniya Senegal', 23 October 2013, http://tidjaniya.populus.org (accessed 16 November 2021).

134 Filip Holm, 'Tijaniyya & the Ziyara Bogal – A Modern Pilgrimage', Let's Talk Religion, 19 August 2018, https://youtu.be/SZqGRYqw9V0.

135 wwwtidjaniyacom, 'Hadra du Vendredi Sidi Abdelmoutaleb Tidjani – Zaouia Tijaniya Pekine Sénégal', YouTube, 13 November 2011, https://youtu.be/ES3ZDDRQnUE.
136 Nasrul Ilm America, 'Home', https://www.nasrulilmamerica.org (accessed 16 November 2021).
137 Alhousseynou Ba, 'Shaykh Hassan Cisse', YouTube, 9 September 2009, https://youtu.be/dDsfBtoOQYI (accessed 16 November 2021).
138 Sheikh Dahiru Usman Bauchi YouTube Channel, 'Imam Shaykh Tijani Aliyu Cisse Visit Ghana 01_1', YouTube, 30 May 2012, https://youtu.be/5v3SZU128WA. Sheikh Dahiru Usman Bauchi YouTube Channel, 'Imam Shaykh Tijani Aliyu Cisse Visit Oyo State, Nigeria 3/3', YouTube, https://youtu.be/3mUt_cPIaKk (accessed 16 November 2021).
139 For example, see cheikhtijanicisse, Instagram, 8 March 2021, https://www.instagram.com/p/CMLCEpNn8gM/ (accessed 16 November 2021).
140 Tijani.org, 'Tijani Literature Online', https://tijani.org (accessed 16 November 2021).
141 Sheikh Dahiru Usman Bauchi YouTube Channel, 'YouTube Channel', YouTube, https://www.youtube.com/user/fatawugado/videos (accessed 16 November 2021).
142 Sheikh Dahiru Usman Bauchi, 'shekhdahirubauch', Instagram, https://www.instagram.com/shekhdahirubauchi/?hl=en (accessed 16 November 2021).
143 Bunt, 'Surfing Islam', 144–5.
144 Cheikh Babou, *Fighting the Greater Jihad: Amadu Bamba and the Founding of the Muridiyya of Senegal, 1853-1913* (Athens: Ohio University Press, 2007).
145 Kamran Haikal, 'Freedom-Fighter and Saint of Senegal: Cheikh Aḥmadou Bamba Mbacke', 10 September 2015, https://medium.com/ummah-wide/freedom-fighter-and-saint-of-senegal-cheikh-aḥmadou-bamba-mbacke-3bfdacc7986f.
146 J.-L. Triaud, 'Murīdiyya', in *Encyclopaedia of Islam, Second Edition, Online*, edited by P. Bearman et al. (Leiden: Brill, 2012), http://dx.doi.org/10.1163/1573-3912_islam_SIM_5543.
147 Thomas Delattre and Marie-Caroline Trichet, trans., 'The Grand Magal, Senegal's Greatest Pilgrimage', *Le Journal International*, 28 January 2015, https://www.lejournalinternational.fr/The-Grand-Magal-Senegal-s-greatest-pilgrimage_a2323.html.
148 AfricaNews, 'Senegal Marks Grand Magal Touba Anniversary', 18 October 2019, https://youtu.be/65eRtVvfXTE. Elizabeth Chai Vasarhelyi, *Touba*, 2013.
149 Jâlibatoul Mazîyah, 'The Exile of Sheikh Ahmadou Bamba Khadimou Rassoull', YouTube, 30 December 2011, https://youtu.be/4I0ZT766m70 (accessed 17 November 2021).
150 Jâlibatoul Mazîyah, 'Jâlibatoul Mazîyah YouTube Channel', YouTube, https://www.youtube.com/c/JâlibatoulMazîyah/featured (accessed 17 November 2021).
151 Khass TV, 'L'histoire de Cheikh Ahmadou Bamba à Khourou Mbacké', YouTube, https://youtu.be/yDk6qvibZsE, Khass TV, 'L'histoire de Serigne Touba a Diourbel Incroyable', YouTube, 26 September 2021, https://youtu.be/2xijh4nAqd0.
152 Afrika Toon, 'Cheikh Ahmadou Bamba', 2 September 2020, https://youtu.be/8aOAQWczGuI.
153 peace_maker_28, 'Sheikh Ahmadou Bamba Mbacke', Instagram, https://www.instagram.com/peace_maker_28/?hl=en (accessed 17 November 2021). Rahmi, 'Cheikh Ahmadou Bamba Mbacké', Pinterest, https://www.pinterest.es/pin/150307706283212649/ (accessed 17 November 2021). As_Salih, TikTok, #touba #mosque (accessed 12 October 2022).

154 Ephrat Livni, 'The Senegalese Sufi Saint Who Inspired a Banking System based on Generosity', Quartz, 27 July 2018, https://qz.com/1336596/the-senegalese-sufi-saint-who-inspired-a-banking-system-based-on-generosity/.
155 Foncab (Foundation Cheikh Amamdou Bamba), 'Welcome', https://foncab.org/# (accessed 17 November 2021).
156 Daaray Serigne Bassirou Mbacké Khelcom, 'Daaray Serigne Bassirou Mbacké Khelcom YouTube Channel', YouTube, https://www.youtube.com/c/DaaraySerigneBassirouMbackéKhelcom/featured (accessed 17 November 2021).
157 Minhaj TV, 'Introduction to Series | Sufism & Teachings of Sufis | in the Light of Qur'an & Sunna | Episode: 01', https://www.minhaj.tv/english/video/3155/Introduction-to-Series-Sufism-Teachings-of-Sufis-in-the-Light-of-Qur-an-Sunna-Episode-1-by-Shaykh-ul-Islam-Dr-Muhammad-Tahir-ul-Qadri.html.
158 Minhaj TV, 'Minhaj TV Official', YouTube, https://www.youtube.com/user/minhajtvofficial/videos (accessed 24 November 2021).
159 Minhaj-ul-Quran International, 'Gosha-e-Durood', https://get.gosha-e-durood.com (accessed 24 November 2021).
160 Minhaj ul-Quran, 'Irfan-ul-Quran Mobile App', https://get.irfan-ul-quran.com (accessed 24 November 2021).
161 Minhaj Publications, 'The Fatwa', Google Play, https://play.google.com/store/apps/details?id=com.thefatwa&hl=en&gl=US (accessed 24 November 2021).
162 Shaykh Mohammad Yasir al-Hanafi, 'Response to "Reality of Deobandi Aqeedah"- Ep 1: Intro/Aqidah and Tasawwuf', Hanafi Fiqh Channel, 9 September 2015, https://youtu.be/vVWc8lh-F9E. Shaykh Mohammad Yasir al-Hanafi, 'Response to "Reality of Deobandi Aqeedah"- Ep 2: The Salafi & Imams On Sufism', Hanafi Fiqh Channel. 1 October 2015, https://youtu.be/q1y3sJkCOFM.This was contesting: Abu Ibraheem Husnayn, 'Reality of Deobandi Aqeedah –', YouTube, 11 February 2014, https://youtu.be/XWxy-gO94LI.
163 MuftiSays, 'Reality of Deobandi Aqeedah by Brother Husnayn', 16 July 2014, https://www.muftisays.com/forums/14-peoples-say/9221-reality-of-deobandi-aqeedah-by-brother-husnayn-.html.
164 Jorgen Nielsen, *Muslims in Western Europe*, 3rd edn (Edinburgh: Edinburgh University Press, 2004), 133.
165 Mumtaz Ahmad, 'Islamic Fundamentalism in South Asia: The Jamaat-i-Islami and the Tablighi Jamaat of South Asia', in *Fundamentalisms Observed*, edited by Martin E. Marty and R. Scott Appleby (Chicago: University of Chicago Press, 1991), 459.
166 Marc Gaborieau, 'What is Left of Sufism in Tablîghî Jamâ'at?', *Archives de sciences sociales des religions [En ligne]* 135, no. Juillet–Septembre (2006), https://doi.org/10.4000/assr.3731, Riyaz Timol, 'Structures of Organisation and Loci of Authority in a Glocal Islamic Movement: The Tablighi Jama'at in Britain', *Religions* 10 (2019), https://doi.org/10.3390/rel10100573.
167 Darsequran.com, 'Karachi Tablighi Ijtema 2020 Molana Faheem – Second Day, Bayan After Jumma – 31 January 2020', 31 January 2020, https://youtu.be/UVRNW27My_E, News18 Urdu, 'Bhopal: Last Day of Aalami Tablighi Ijtema', YouTube, 25 November 2018, https://youtu.be/U9rgFIaDdnw. Hafiz Aziz Ahmed, 'Raiwind Tablighi Ijtema 2021 | Maulana Nazrul Rahman Sahab Bayan | World Tablighi Ijtema 2021', 4 November 2021, https://youtu.be/n2t-7aIS_Yc.
168 Hafiz Aziz Ahmed, 'YouTube Channel', YouTube, https://www.youtube.com/channel/UCG_DbjIKMaA0tgX7p-AiNPQ/featured (accessed 25 November 2021). This channel had 1.5 million subscribers in November 2021. Also, see Darsequran.co

m, 'YouTube Channel', YouTube, https://www.youtube.com/c/darsequran1/videos (accessed 25 November 2021).

169 Anas Tamil, 'Markazi Masjid, Dewsbury – ijithima 2018.10.20-21', 22 October 2018, https://youtu.be/M_saQlJlt00.

170 Biny Amin, 'Hazrat Hafez Patel Saheb funeral in Savile Town, Dewsbury...(Part 2)', YouTube, 19 February 2016, https://youtu.be/SifMuBmU65A. Uthmaan Sadik, 'Beautiful Naat on the Demise of Hafiz Patel Sb RA', 20 February 2016, https://youtu.be/J9IsUNjN0JM.

171 Rozehnal, *Cyber Sufis*. This book includes discussions on other 'western' Sufi movements. Also, see Robert Rozehnal, 'Virtual Community in the Time of Covid: An American Sufi Order's Expanding Digital Footprint', *Islamic Responses to COVID-19 Conference*, University of Wales Trinity Saint David, 1 July 2021, https://youtu.be/Cbud1HIbuFM.

172 Inayatiyya, 'YouTube Channel', https://www.youtube.com/channel/UCiOe1WaP3UQkJx2G-j2Po_A (accessed 25 November 2021). Inayatiyya, https://inayatiyya.org/ (accessed 25 November 2021).

173 Sufi Ruhaniat International, https://www.ruhaniat.org/ (accessed 29 November 2021).

174 Dances of Universal Peace, 'About The Dances of Universal Peace', https://www.dancesofuniversalpeace.org/about.shtm (accessed 29 November 2021).

175 Sufism Reoriented, 'The Lineage of Meher Baba's Sufism Reoriented', https://www.sufismreoriented.org/sufism-reoriented-lineage (accessed 29 November 2021).

176 R. Tschudi, 'Bektāsh', in *Encyclopaedia of Islam, First Edition (1913-1936)*, edited by M. Th. Houtsma et al., R. Tschudi, 'Bektāshiyya', in *Encyclopaedia of Islam, Second Edition (Online)*, edited by P. Bearman et al., http://dx.doi.org/10.1163/1573-3912_islam_SIM_1359.

177 Tschudi, 'Bektāshiyya'.

178 AaleQutub.com, 'Hazrat Syed Haji Bektash Veli', Aal-e-Qutub Aal-e-Syed Abdullah Shah Ghazi, https://aalequtub.com/hazrat-syed-haji-bektash-veli (accessed 17 May 2021).

179 Ali Sirri Ari Sirri, 'Ali Sırrı Arı Sırrı – Alevilik, Bektaşilik Nedir', YouTube, https://www.youtube.com/channel/UCRP0ZJEYwoS_rvRI7q-ASYg (accessed 17 May 2021).

180 Kryegjyshata Boterore Bektashiane, 'Home', https://kryegjyshataboterorebektashiane.org/en/home-2/ (accessed 3 July 2023).

181 Haxhi Dede Edmond Brahimaj, Instagram, https://www.instagram.com/haxhi_dede_edmond_brahimaj/ (accessed 3 July 2023).

182 Alevi Islam, Instagram, https://www.instagram.com/alevi_islam/ (accessed 3 July 2023).

183 Alevi Bektaşi Federasyonu, http://www.alevifederasyonu.org.tr/ (accessed 3 July 2023).

184 Alevi Islam Deutschland, TikTok, https://www.tiktok.com/@alevi.islam.de?lang=en (accessed 3 July 2023).

185 Dance Journals, 'Semah in Alevis: "Moving to be with God"', YouTube, 9 March 2020, https://youtu.be/CBnSql7bgMM.

186 British Alevi Federation, 'Home', http://www.alevinet.org/ (accessed 3 July 2023). British Alevi Federation, Instagram, https://www.instagram.com/baf_alevi/?hl=en (accessed 3 July 2023). British Alevi Federation, 'Twitter', https://twitter.com/BAFederation (accessed 3 July 2023).

Chapter 9

1 Readers are advised to take care when searching, surfing, sharing and downloading content associated with e-jihād. In some contexts, downloading and sharing such context can be illegal. It can also be dangerous to travel with this content on digital devices. Consequently, direct links to *jihād* web-platforms are not provided here.
2 I am grateful to Kane Howard-Bunt for providing some background research on Taliban social media for this section.
3 Bunt, *Virtually Islamic*, 68–9.
4 Azzam had for a time been operating in London (hosted on a US server) and run by Babar Ahmad, extradited to the United States in 2013 after several years of incarceration without trial in the UK and charged with conspiracy and supporting terrorism. Ahmad was released in 2015 and returned to the United Kingdom.
5 Bunt, *Islam in the Digital Age*, 67–71.
6 Emerson T. Brooking, 'Before the Taliban took Afghanistan, it took the Internet', New Atlanticist, 26 August 2021, https://www.atlanticcouncil.org/blogs/new-atlanticist/before-the-taliban-took-afghanistan-it-took-the-internet/.
7 Bunt, *Hashtag Islam*, 104–5.
8 Al Jazeera English, 'Exclusive: Taliban Enters Afghan Presidential Palace | Al Jazeera Newsfeed', YouTube, https://youtu.be/JkI8JSLforo (accessed 16 August 2021).
9 Ali M. Latifi, 'Kabul Near Standstill on Day One of the Taliban's "Emirate"', Al Jazeera, 16 August 2021, https://www.aljazeera.com/news/2021/8/16/kabul-near-standstill-on-day-one-the-talibans-emirate.
10 Oscar Gonzalez, 'Facebook Reportedly Shuts Down Taliban Accounts on WhatsApp', CNET, 17 August 2021, https://www.cnet.com/tech/facebook-reportedly-shuts-down-taliban-accounts-on-whatsapp/. CNN, 'Facebook Reiterates Ban on Taliban Content on Its Platforms, Including WhatsApp and Instagram', https://edition.cnn.com/world/live-news/afghanistan-taliban-us-news-08-17-21/ (accessed 17 August 2021).
11 Craig Timberg, 'Taliban Websites Operating in Five Languages go Dark', *Washington Post*, 20 August 2021, https://www.washingtonpost.com/technology/2021/08/20/taliban-internet-websites-twitter-facebook/.
12 Bhaskar Chakravorti, 'Facebook's Taliban Ban Will Prove Costly for Afghans', Foreign Policy, 26 August 2021, https://foreignpolicy.com/2021/08/26/taliban-facebook-ban-social-media-afghanistan/.
13 Taylor Hatmaker, 'Social Platforms Wrestle with What to do about the Taliban', TechCrunch, 20 August 2021, https://techcrunch.com/2021/08/20/taliban-social-media-facebook-youtube-twitter/.
14 Katie Collins, 'The Taliban Thrive on Social Media, Despite Sites' Bans', CNET, 18 August 2021, https://www.cnet.com/news/the-taliban-thrive-on-social-media-despite-sites-bans/.
15 Muhammad Jalal, 'Congratulatory Message from Mullah Baradar Akhund', https://twitter.com/MJalal700/status/1426988659409047554 (accessed 15 August 2021).
16 Today Show, 'Interview of Abdul Ghani Baradar by Richard Engel', https://twitter.com/TODAYshow/status/1430852304039710726 (accessed 26 August 2021) (al Jazeera English, 'Interview: Abdul Qahar Balkhi', https://twitter.com/AJEnglish/status/1429373972924276736 (accessed 22 August 2021).
17 Zabihullah Mujahid, 'Zabihullah M33' (accessed 6 September 2021).

18 Sarah Atiq, 'The Taliban Embrace Social Media: "We too want to Change Perceptions"', BBC News, 6 September 2021, https://www.bbc.co.uk/news/world-asia-58466939.
19 Qari Saeed Khosty, 'Saeed Khosty', https://twitter.com/saeedkhosty?lang=en (accessed 6 September 2021).
20 Qari Saeed Khosty, 'Saeed Khosty', 3 September 2021, https://twitter.com/SaeedKhosty/status/1433789567098920961.
21 SAMRI, 'Thread on Shi'a', https://twitter.com/SAMRIReports/status/1427274806311931904 (accessed 18 August 2021).
22 Mohsin Amin, 'Taliban Visited the National Load Control Center of @DABS_Official', https://twitter.com/MohsinAmin_/status/1427609794546966533/photo/1 (accessed 17 August 2021).
23 Lotfullah Najafizada, 'Kabul', Twitter, https://twitter.com/LNajafizada/status/1426852794175270915 (accessed 15 August 2021).
24 Eltaf Najafizada, 'Taliban Vow No Haven for Terrorists, Breaking with Own Past', 17 August 2021, https://www.bloomberg.com/news/articles/2021-08-17/taliban-say-women-can-work-shifting-from-stance-before-9-11. BBC News (World), 'Afghanistan: Taliban Takeover', Twitter, https://twitter.com/BBCWorld/status/1427651928880607241 (accessed 17 August 2021).
25 APN News, 'Taliban Fighters Laugh over Women Politicians', YouTube, https://youtu.be/apN-em9k0mw (accessed 18 August 2021).
26 Panjshir Province, @PanjshirProvin1 (accessed 6 September 2021), TOLO News, 'Ahmad Massoud', https://twitter.com/TOLOnews/status/1434821023141138432 (accessed 6 September 2021).
27 Elisabeth Kendall, 'New 2-Page Statement from #AlQaeda in #Yemen Congratulates #Taliban on Victory in #Afghanistan', 19 August 2021, https://twitter.com/Dr_E_Kendall/status/1428295094449446913.
28 Chaudhary Parvez, 'Afghan People Throwing Shoes and Stones to #Afghan Army', https://twitter.com/ChaudharyParvez/status/1426873021940199431. Tariq Ghazniwal, 'In #Jalalabad, #Kabul Administrative Governor @ZiaulhaqAmarkhi Officially Handed over the Province to Shikh Nida Muhammad, Governor of the Islamic Emirate for #Nangarhar', https://twitter.com/TGhazniwal/status/1426730960834469890 (accessed 15 August 2021).
29 Miraqa Popal, 'We Resumed Our Broadcast with Female Anchors Today', https://twitter.com/MiraqaPopal/status/1427497536219123712 (accessed 17 August 2021). Abdul Farid Ahmad, 'Hasiba Atakpal Our Brave Female Journalist is Reporting Live from #Kabul City', Twitter, https://twitter.com/FaridAhmad1919/status/1427537973046874112 (accessed 17 August 2021).
30 Graeme Wood, 'This Is Not the Taliban 2.0', *The Atlantic*, 18 August 2021, https://www.theatlantic.com/ideas/archive/2021/08/dont-trust-taliban/619790/.
31 AFP/Arab News, '"Zombie Apocalypse": Fear Grips Afghans under Taliban Rule', 25 August 2021, https://www.arabnews.com/node/1917036/world.
32 Owais Tohid, 'From Motorcycle Warriors to Knife and Fork Wielding Diplomats: How the Afghan Taliban Insurgency Evolved', *Arab News*, https://arab.news/4u6xp (accessed 14 August 2021).
33 Tajuden Sorouch, 'Loya Jirga hall', https://twitter.com/TajudenSoroush/status/1431879043864047623 (accessed 29 August 2021).
34 TOLO News, 'Thread on Interim Government', 7 September 2021, https://twitter.com/TOLOnews/status/1435252708680810496.

35 Sirajuddin Haqqani, 'What We, the Taliban, Want', *New York Times*, 20 February 2020, https://www.nytimes.com/2020/02/20/opinion/taliban-afghanistan-war-haqqani.html.

36 FBI, 'Sirajuddin Haqqani', https://www.fbi.gov/wanted/terrorinfo/sirajuddin-haqqani (accessed 8 September 2021). Mina Aldroubi, 'Who is Sirajuddin Haqqani, Afghanistan's New Interior Minister?' *The National*, 8 September 2021, https://www.thenationalnews.com/world/asia/2021/09/08/who-is-sirajuddin-haqqani-the-new-afghanistan-interior-minister/. Zia Shahreyar, 'طالبان حکومت جدید خود را به ریاست حسن آخوند اعلام کرد', BBC Persian, 8 September 2021, https://www.bbc.com/persian/afghanistan-58477769.

37 Jason Burke, 'What does the Taliban's Return mean for al-Qaida in Afghanistan?' *The Guardian*, https://www.theguardian.com/world/2021/aug/15/what-does-the-talibans-return-mean-for-al-qaida-in-afghanistan (accessed 15 August 2021).

38 Sam Sabin and Heidi Vogt, '"An Enormously Valuable Trove": America's Race against Afghan Data', Politico, 24 August 2021, https://www.politico.com/news/2021/08/24/taliban-afghan-data-target-allies-506638. Paul Mozur and Zia ur-Rehman, 'How the Taliban Turned Social Media into a Tool for Control', *New York Times*, 20 August 2021, https://www.nytimes.com/2021/08/20/technology/afghanistan-taliban-social-media.html.

39 Chris Stokel-Walker, 'Afghans Are Racing to Erase their Online Lives', *Wired*, 17 August 2021, https://www.wired.co.uk/article/afghanistan-social-media-delete.

40 Human Rights First, 'How to Delete Your Digital History', https://www.humanrightsfirst.org/sites/default/files/How to delete your history_updated.pdf (accessed 15 August 2021).

41 Fatimah Hossaini, '"The Last Days in Kabul …"', https://twitter.com/HossainiFatimah/status/1429694199784480771 (accessed 23 August 2021).

42 Aśvaka News Agency, 'Exclusive- A Clear Video (from other Angle) of Men Falling from C-17', Twitter, https://twitter.com/AsvakaNews/status/1427206845706379266 (accessed 16 August 2021).

43 Ivana Kottasová et al., 'US Troops and Afghans Killed in Suicide Attacks Outside Kabul Airport', CNN, 27 August 2021, https://edition.cnn.com/2021/08/26/asia/afghanistan-kabul-airport-blast-intl/index.html.

44 Associated Press, 'Bin Laden was Logged Off, but not al-Qaida', http://www.npr.org/templates/story/story.php?storyId=136334743 (accessed 15 May 2011), Bin Laden and Lawrence, *Messages to the World*, J. M. Berger, 'New Osama Bin Laden Videos: More Questions than Answers', intelwire.com, http://news.intelwire.com/2011/05/new-osama-bin-laden-videos-more.html. Nelly Laoud, *The Bin Laden Papers: How the Abbottabad Raid Revealed the Truth about al-Qaeda, Its Leader and His Family* (London: Yale University Press, 2022).

45 Gary R. Bunt, '#Islam, Social Networking and the Cloud', in *Islam in the Modern World*, edited by Jeffrey Kenney and Ebrahim Moosa (New York: Routledge, 2013), 193–5.

46 Asianet Newsable, 'Al Qaeda leader Ayman al-Zawahiri, Rumoured Dead, Surfaces in Clip on 9/11 Anniversary: Report', https://newsable.asianetnews.com/world/al-qaeda-leader-ayman-al-zawahiri-surfaces-in-clip-on-9-11-anniversary-gcw-qzbh8v (accessed 12 September 2021).

47 Tore Refslund Hamming, 'Al-Qaeda After Ayman al-Zawahiri', *Lawfare*, 11 April 2021, https://www.lawfareblog.com/al-qaeda-after-ayman-al-zawahiri.

48 Mina al-Lami, BBC Monitoring, https://twitter.com/Minalami/status/1092859179549765632 (accessed 19 April 2019).
49 MelvinB, 'Amin ul-Haq's Return', Twitter, https://twitter.com/MelvinBGlobal/status/1432085917297225728 (accessed 29 August 2021).
50 The original article is Matt Egan et al., 'From Reagan to Trump: Here's How Stocks Performed under Each President', CNN Business, 19 January 2021, https://edition.cnn.com/interactive/2019/business/stock-market-by-president/index.html.
51 Women and jihād are discussed in Tuty Raihanah Mostarom and Nur Azlin Mohamed Yasin, 'The Internet: Avenue for Women Jihadi "Participation"', Rajaratnam School of International Studies, 3 August 2010, https://www.rsis.edu.sg/rsis-publication/rsis/1378-the-internet-avenue-for-women/.
52 Al-Qaeda Organization, 'One Ummah (Majalla Ummah Wahida)', Link Deleted (accessed 11 September 2019). An Arabic language edition was published online in April 2019.
53 Elisabeth Kendall, '#AlQaeda Seizes the Moment to Release New 83-page Issue of "One Ummah" Magazine – in English', Twitter, 8 June 2020, https://twitter.com/Dr_E_Kendall/status/1270103339712249857.
54 Aymenn Jawad Al-Tamimi, '"The Wolves of Manhattan Magazine": Interview', 5 March 2021, http://www.aymennjawad.org/2021/03/the-wolves-of-manhattan-magazine-interview.
55 Arab Weekly, 'Jihadist Magazine Offered $60,000 Bounty for the Killing of Western Police Officer', 5 June 2021, https://thearabweekly.com/jihadist-magazine-offered-60000-bounty-killing-western-police-officer.
56 Elisabeth Kendall, 'Advice for Jihadist Wives', https://twitter.com/Dr_E_Kendall/status/1135165864410537984 (accessed 19 June 2019).
57 Bloomberg/My Broadband, 'Terrorists Prefer Google Drive and Dropbox to YouTube', https://mybroadband.co.za/news/internet/279721-terrorists-prefer-google-drive-and-dropbox-to-youtube.html (accessed 12 October 2018).
58 For a detailed archive which includes 'safe' copies for download, see Zelin, 'Jihadology'.
59 Bunt, *Hashtag Islam*, 123–40.
60 Islamic State, 'al-Naba' (accessed 27 September 2021).
61 BBC News, 'Islamic State: Canadian Accused of being "Voice Behind the Violence"', 3 October 2021, https://www.bbc.co.uk/news/world-us-canada-58777274.
62 United States Attorney's Office: Eastern District of Virginia, 'Leading ISIS Media Figure and Foreign Fighter Charged with Conspiring to Provide Material Support to a Terrorist Organization, Resulting in Death', 2 October 2021, https://www.justice.gov/usao-edva/pr/leading-isis-media-figure-and-foreign-fighter-charged-conspiring-provide-material. Also see Department of Justice, 'Press Release 22-818, Leading ISIS Media Figure and Foreign Fighter Sentenced to Life Imprisonment', 29 July 2022, https://www.justice.gov/opa/pr/leading-isis-media-figure-and-foreign-fighter-sentenced-life-imprisonment.
63 Salvador Rizzo, 'Washington Post, Life Sentence for Canadian Man Who Joined ISIS, Narrated Propaganda Videos', 29 July 2022, https://www.washingtonpost.com/dc-md-va/2022/07/29/khalifa-life-sentence-isis-propaganda/.
64 Angelique Chrisafis, 'Paris Attacker Salah Abdeslam Found Guilty of Murder and Jailed for Life', *The Guardian*, https://www.theguardian.com/world/2022/jun/29/

paris-attacker-salah-abdeslam-found-guilty-of-and-terrorism, Benjamin Dodman and Aude Mazoue, 'Salah Abdeslam Sentenced to Life in Prison as Paris Attacks Trial Winds Up', France24, 29 June 2022, https://www.france24.com/en/france/20220629-live-french-court-to-issue-verdicts-in-landmark-2015-paris-attacks-trial

65 Graeme Wood, *The Way of the Strangers: Encounters with the Islamic State* (London: Penguin, 2018), 51–5.

66 Cole Bunzel, 'The Kingdom and the Caliphate: Duel of the Islamic States', 16 February 2016, https://carnegieendowment.org/2016/02/18/kingdom-and-caliphate-duel-of-islamic-states-pub-62810.

67 Wood, *The Way of the Strangers*, 88–139. By 2022, Cerantonio had apparently abandoned Islam. Graeme Wood, 'Why an ISIS Propagandist Abandoned Islam', *The Atlantic*, 31 March 2022, https://www.theatlantic.com/ideas/archive/2022/03/deprogramming-isis-supporters-jihadi-extremism/629433/.

68 Wood, *The Way of the Strangers*, 140–76. Bunt, *Hashtag Islam*, 133–6.

69 Catrina Doxsee, 'Examining Extremism: Islamic State Khorasan Province (ISKP)', Center for Strategic International Studies, 8 September 2021, https://www.csis.org/blogs/examining-extremism/examining-extremism-islamic-state-khorasan-province-iskp. Also see Frank Gardner, 'Afghanistan: Who are Islamic State Khorasan Province Militants?' 11 October 2021, https://www.bbc.co.uk/news/world-asia-58333533.

70 Kabir Taneja, 'Afghanistan: A Strategic and Tactical Battle between the Taliban and Islamic State Khorasan Province', Observer Research Foundation, 31 August 2021, https://www.orfonline.org/expert-speak/strategic-and-tactical-battle-between-the-taliban-and-islamic-state-khorasan-province/.

71 M. Shabir Ahmadi, 'ISKP Branch during Ramadan', Twitter, https://twitter.com/Shabir__Ahmadi/status/1519724601730899972 (accessed 28 April 2022), War Noir, 'Militants Pledged Bayah to New IS #Emir', Twitter, 12 March 2022, https://twitter.com/war_noir/status/1502747373126270979.

72 Lucas Webber and Riccardo Valle, 'Perspectives | Islamic State in Afghanistan Seeks to Recruit Uzbeks, Tajiks, Kyrgyz', Eurasianet, 17 March 2022, https://eurasianet.org/perspectives-islamic-state-in-afghanistan-seeks-to-recruit-uzbeks-tajiks-kyrgyz.

73 Lucas Webber, 'Voice of Khorasan Magazine and the Internationalization of Islamic State's Anti-Taliban Propaganda', *Terrorism Monitor*, Jamestown Foundation, 6 May 2022, https://jamestown.org/program/voice-of-khorasan-magazine-and-the-internationalization-of-islamic-states-anti-taliban-propaganda/. Also see Bridget Johnson, 'Inaugural Magazine from ISIS Khorasan Declares Taliban Can "Become Our Brother"', Homeland Security Today, 7 February 2022, https://www.hstoday.us/featured/inaugural-magazine-from-isis-khorasan-declares-taliban-can-become-our-brother/.

74 Riccardo Valle, 'Islamic State Khorasan Province Releases First Video of 2022: "O Lions of the Tribes!"', Militant Wire, 13 January 2022, https://www.militantwire.com/p/islamic-state-khorasan-province-releases?s=r.

75 For a detailed analysis of these branches, see: Jason Warner et al., *The Islamic State in Africa: The Emergence, Evolution, and Future of the Next Jihadist Battlefront* (Oxford: Oxford University Press, 2022), 452–533.

76 Tore Refslund Hamming, 'The Islamic State in Mozambique', *Lawfare*, 24 January 2021, https://www.lawfareblog.com/islamic-state-mozambique.

77 Caleb Weiss, 'Islamic State Claims Capture of Coastal City in Mozambique', FDD's Long War Journal, 29 March 2021, https://www.longwarjournal.org/archives/2021/03/islamic-state-claims-capture-of-coastal-city-in-mozambique.php.
78 Frank Gardner, 'Mozambique: Why IS is so Hard to Defeat in Mozambique', BBC News, 31 September 2021, https://www.bbc.co.uk/news/world-africa-56597861.
79 Caleb Weiss and Ryan O'Farrell, 'Analysis: The Islamic State's Expansion into Congo's Ituri Province', FDD's Long War Journal, 9 September 2021, https://www.longwarjournal.org/archives/2021/09/analysis-the-islamic-states-expansion-into-congos-ituri-province.php.
80 U.S. Department of State, 'State Department Terrorist Designations of ISIS Affiliates and Leaders in the Democratic Republic of the Congo and Mozambique', 10 March 2021, https://www.state.gov/state-department-terrorist-designations-of-isis-affiliates-and-leaders-in-the-democratic-republic-of-the-congo-and-mozambique/.
81 Linnete Bahati and Driss El-Bay, 'Allied Democratic Forces: The Ugandan Rebels Working with IS in DR Congo', BBC News, 14 June 2021, https://www.bbc.co.uk/news/world-africa-57246001.
82 AFP, 'Islamic State Claims Its First Suicide Blast In DRC: Monitor', 30 June 2021, https://www.barrons.com/news/islamic-state-claims-its-first-suicide-blast-in-drc-monitor-01625052907.
83 Olivier Guitta, 'A New Caliphate in Africa? Akhbar al-Aan TV, 13 Apr 2021', LinkedIn, 13 April 2021, https://www.linkedin.com/pulse/new-caliphate-africa-akhbar-al-aan-tv-13-apr-2021-olivier-guitta/.
84 Weiss, 'Islamic State Claims Capture of Coastal City in Mozambique'.
85 MEMRI/Anglican Ink, 'ISIS kills about 190 African Christians over Two Months', 9 August 2022, https://anglican.ink/2022/08/09/isis-kills-about-190-african-christians-over-two-months/.
86 Victoria Fassrainer, 'Tweeting Terror Live: Al-Shabaab's Use of Twitter during the Westgate Attack and Implications for Counterterrorism Communications', Army University Press, https://www.armyupress.army.mil/Journals/Military-Review/English-Edition-Archives/March-April-2020/Fassrainer-Tweet-Terror/.
87 Gardner, 'Mozambique: Why IS is so Hard to Defeat in Mozambique'.
88 Halima Gikandi, 'The Group behind Nairobi's Recent Terror Attack Recruits Young People from Many Faiths. Officials can't Stop It', PRI/GlobalPost, 25 January 2019, https://www.pri.org/stories/2019-01-25/group-behind-nairobi-s-recent-terror-attack-recruits-young-people-many-faiths.
89 Oscar Gakuo Mwangi, 'State Collapse, Al-Shabaab, Islamism, and Legitimacy in Somalia', *Politics, Religion & Ideology* 13, no. 4 (2012): 513–27, https://doi.org/10.1080/21567689.2012.725659.
90 Warner et al., *The Islamic State in Africa*, 408–9.
91 Bunt, *Hashtag Islam*, 107.
92 Australian National Security, 'Terrorist Organisations: Al-Shabaab', https://www.nationalsecurity.gov.au/Listedterroristorganisations/Pages/Al-Shabaab.aspx (accessed 6 October 2021).
93 Alexander Meleagrou-Hitchens, Shiraz Maher and James Sheehan, 'Lights, Camera, Jihad: Al-Shabaab's Western Media Strategy' (London: International Centre for the Study of Radicalisation and Political Violence (ICSR), King's College London, 2012).
94 Bunt, *Hashtag Islam*, 106. The Sun, 'Married to a 7/7 Suicide Bomber', 23 September 2005. BBC News, 'Profile: Samantha Lewthwaite', 26 September 2013, https://www.bbc.co.uk/news/uk-24204517.

95 Hugo van Offel, 'World's Most Wanted', *Samantha Lewthwaite: The White Widow*, Netflix, 2020.

96 See Abdulbasit Kassim and Michael Nwankpa, eds., *The Boko Haram Reader: From Nigerian Preachers to the Islamic State* (Oxford: Oxford University Press, 2018), particularly 717–966.

97 Soufan Center, 'IntelBrief: Jihadist Groups Continue to Consolidate Territory Throughout West Africa', *Intel Brief*, Soufan Center, 4 October 2021, https://thesoufancenter.org/intelbrief-2021-october-4/.

98 See the discussion on earlier tweets in Innocent Chiluwa and Esther Ajiboye, '"We Are after Ideals": A Critical Analysis of Ideology in the Tweets by Boko Haram', *Global Media Journal: African Edition* 8, no. 2 (2014): 318–46, http://globalmedia.journals.ac.za/.

99 Kate Cox et al, 'Social Media in Africa: A Double-Edged Sword for Security and Development', UNDP-Rand, https://www.rand.org/pubs/external_publications/EP67728.html (accessed 4 October 2021).

100 Benjamin Maiangwa, 'Killing in the Name of God? Explaining the Boko Haram Phenomenon in Nigeria', *Journal of Social, Political and Economic Studies* 38, no. 1 (2013): 55–79, https://citeseerx.ist.psu.edu/viewdoc/download?doi=10.1.1.687.6966&rep=rep1&type=pdf#page=55.

101 Chris Wolumati Ogbondah and Pita Ogaba Agbese, 'Terrorists and Social Media Messages: A Critical Analysis of Boko Haram's Messages and Messaging Techniques', in *The Palgrave Handbook of Media and Communication Research in Africa* edited by Bruce Mutsvairo (Cham: Springer International Publishing, Palgrave Macmillan, 2018), 313–45.

102 Security analyst Bulama Bukarti, discussing Boko Haram in BBC Pidgin, 'Boko Haram: How di Insurgents Dey get Internet to Post Videos, Make Calls from Inside Bush?', 7 December 2020, https://www.bbc.com/pidgin/tori-55212200.

Chapter 10

1 See the discussion on gender and digital religion in: Mia Lövheim, 'Gender and Agency in Digital Religion', in *The Oxford Handbook of Digital Religion*, edited by Heidi A. Campbell and Pauline Hope Cheong (Oxford: Oxford Academic, 2022), C12.P1–C12.N1.

2 Nisa, 'Muslims Enacting Identity: Gender through Digital Media', C.33.51–C33.59.

3 Piela, '"The Niqab Is a Beautiful Extension of My Face"', 167–75.

4 Anna Piela, 'Claiming Religious Authority: Muslim Women and New Media', in *Media, Religion and Gender: Key Issues and New Challenges*, edited by Mia Lövheim (London and New York Routledge, 2013), 125–40. Also see Piela, *Muslim Women Online*.

5 UN Women and Promundo-US, 'Understanding Masculinities: Results from the International Men and Gender Equality Survey (IMAGES) – Middle East and North Africa', 16 May 2017, 46, https://promundoglobal.org/wp-content/uploads/2017/05/IMAGES-MENA-Multi-Country-Report-EN-16May2017-web.pdf.

6 Plan International, 'The Truth Gap: How Misinformation and Disinformation Online Affect the Lives, Learning and Leadership of Girls and Young Women', *The*

State of the World's Girls, Plan International, https://www.plan.org.au/wp-content/uploads/2021/10/SOTWGR2021.pdf (accessed 7 October 2021).

7 Ruchi Kumar, 'Afghan Women's Worst Fears Realised as Taliban Returns', *The National*, 11 July 2021, https://www.thenationalnews.com/world/2021/07/12/afghan-womens-worst-fears-realised-as-taliban-returns/.

8 Laila Mohammadi, Twitter, 6 September 2021, https://twitter.com/laila_mohammadi/status/1434888260661170178.

9 Nazlan Ertan, 'Controversial Cleric's 'Modesty Call' to Turkish Volleyball Team Bounces Back at Him', Al-Monitor, 27 July 2021, https://www.al-monitor.com/originals/2021/07/controversial-clerics-modesty-call-turkish-volleyball-team-bounces-back-him#. Article cites and translates İhsan Şenocak, Twitter, 25 July 2021, https://twitter.com/ihsansenocak/status/1419296320267997187?s=20.

10 Heba Afify, 'Egypt's #MeToo Moment Targets Street Harassment', 19 January 2019, https://edition.cnn.com/2019/01/04/health/egypt-sexual-harassment-intl/index.html. Citing UN Women and Promundo-US, 'Understanding Masculinities'. Thomson Reuters, 'Cairo Named most Dangerous Megacity for Women; London Best - Poll', 16 October 2017, https://www.reuters.com/article/women-poll-megacities-idAFL8N1L74J3.

11 Middle East Eye, 'Egypt Jails Man for Harassment Spree that Sparked #MeToo Movement', 12 April 2021, https://www.middleeasteye.net/news/egypt-jails-man-metoo-movement-eight-years.

12 Qawem, 'Qawem', Facebook, 7 October 2021, https://www.facebook.com/qawem.community. Ihab Zidan, 'In Egypt, Online Group Qawem Saving Hundreds of Women from Sextortion', DW.com, 20 June 2021, https://www.dw.com/en/in-egypt-online-group-qawem-saving-hundreds-of-women-from-sextortion/a-57950634.

13 Mona Eltahawy, Twitter, 11 February 2018, https://twitter.com/monaeltahawy/status/962747859878719488 Also see Laignee Barron, Time, 'A Revolutionary Moment,' Activist Mona Eltahawy Talks Sexual Assault, Self-Defense and #MosqueMeToo, 7 March 2018, https://time.com/5170236/mona-eltahawy-mosquemetoo/.

14 'Ameera', cited in Lauda El Alam, 'Unsolicited: Online Sexual Harassment Poisons Social Media For Sisters In Faith', 2 October 2019, https://muslimmatters.org/2019/10/02/unsolicited-online-sexual-harassment-poisons-social-media-for-sisters-in-faith/.

15 Amaliah.com, 'About', https://www.amaliah.com/about (accessed 11 October 2021).

16 Nafisa Bakkar, 'How I Created a Platform to Amplify the Voices of Muslim Women', The Stylist, https://www.stylist.co.uk/opinion/how-i-created-a-platform-to-amplify-the-voices-of-muslim-women/25260 (accessed 18 July 2019).

17 Monica Traverzo and Nicole Queen, 'Salam, Girl!' https://www.salamgirl.com/podcast (accessed 11 October 2021). At the time of writing, it was unclear why the podcast suspended activities.

18 The Digital Sisterhood, https://linktr.ee/digitalsisterhood (accessed 10 June 2022).

19 There is a discussion of the Digital Sisterhood podcast in detail in Ikran Dahir, 'A Muslim Podcast became a Weekly Comfort for Women around the World', Buzzfeed, 10 June 2022, https://www.buzzfeednews.com/article/ikrd/digital-sisterhood-podcast-brings-muslim-women-together.

20 The Salafi Feminist, http://thesalafifeminist.blogspot.com/ (link deleted). An archived version of the blog is here: Internet Archive, 'Salafi Feminist', https://web

.archive.org/web/20140706143122/http://thesalafifeminist.blogspot.com/ (accessed 30 May 2023). See the profile and interview of Zainab bint Younus in Kristin M. Petersen, 'The Salafi Feminist Fights Stereotypes of Niqabi Women', 17 January 2017, https://kristinmpeterson.com/2017/01/17/the-salafi-feminist-fights-stereotypes-of-niqabi-women/. Also see Kristin M. Petersen, 'Hybrid Styles, Interstitial Spaces, and the Digital Advocacy of the Salafi Feminist', *Critical Studies in Media Communication* 37, no. 3 (2020): 254–66, https://doi.org/10.1080/15295036.2020.1786142.

21 Rasha Al Aqeedi, 'Andrew Tate and the Moral Bankruptcy of Muslim Proselytization', New Lines Magazine, 26 January 2023, https://newlinesmag.com/argument/andrew-tate-and-the-moral-bankruptcy-of-muslim-proselytization/.

22 Zainab bint Younus and Irtiza Hasan, 'The Eid Mubarak Episode', Muslim Matters, 19 April 2023, https://muslimmatters.org/2023/04/19/podcast-the-eid-mubarak-episode/.

23 Rahmah Ghazali, 'Andrew Tate: "Misogynist" Influencer Converts to Islam after Video of Him Praying in UAE Mosque Goes Viral', *The Scotsman*, 25 October 2023, https://www.scotsman.com/read-this/andrew-tate-misogynist-influencer-converts-to-islam-after-video-of-him-praying-in-uae-mosque-goes-viral-3892455.

24 Al Aqeedi, 'Andrew Tate and the Moral Bankruptcy of Muslim Proselytization'.

25 Emine Sinmaz, 'Andrew Tate and His Brother to Face Trial in Romania', *The Guardian*, 20 June 2023, https://www.theguardian.com/news/2023/jun/20/andrew-tate-romanian-prosecutors-trial.

26 Nadeine Asbali, '"Red-Pill" Misogyny is Thriving – Here's How Muslim Women Are Challenging it in their Communities', *Glamour Magazine*, 16 January 2023, https://www.glamourmagazine.co.uk/article/red-pill-misogyny-opinion-muslim-women. The red-pill is linked to *The Matrix* film, as one of the protagonists' choices on whether to acquire understanding of the Matrix's illusions, as opposed to a blue-pill which maintained the vision generated by the virtual reality generated by its AI system. The initial film spawned three sequels. Lana Wachowski and Lilly Wachowski, *The Matrix*, Film, 1999.

27 Sana Noor Haq, 'Andrew Tate's Muslim Fanbase Is Growing. Some Say He's Exploiting Islam for Internet Popularity', CNN, 16 February 2023, https://edition.cnn.com/2023/02/16/world/andrew-tate-muslim-men-manosphere-intl-cmd/index.html.

28 Mariyah bint Rehan, 'The Rise of the Muslim Incel: Ideological Victim Blaming and Its Harm to Muslim Women and Men', 24 October 2022, https://www.amaliah.com/post/66016/muslim-incel-mincel-red-pill-ideology-islam.

29 Mariyah bint Rehan, 'No-Strings-Attached Nikah, Mincel, Red Pill: The Case for Islamic RSE', 20 August 2022, https://www.islam21c.com/culture/no-strings-attached-nikah-mincel-red-pill-the-case-for-islamic-rse /.

30 r/Muslim, 'There is a New Group of Muslims called "Muslim Red Pill" or "Muslim Incels". Please be Aware!' Reddit, n.d., 2020, https://www.reddit.com/r/Muslim/comments/gik1yt/there_is_a_new_group_of_muslims_called_muslim_red/.

31 Al Aqeedi, 'Andrew Tate and the Moral Bankruptcy of Muslim Proselytization'.

32 Imams Online, 'Intimacy in Marriage Webinar', 7 August 2020, https://rb.gy/lg72kg.

33 Muska Jahan, ' Marriage and Intimacy Q&A', YouTube, 20 March 2021, https://youtu.be/Log-bkiyvL8.

34 Saba Syed (Umm Reem), 'Loving Muslim Marriage Episode #1: Is it Haraam to Talk About Sex?' Muslim Matters, 10 August 2019, https://muslimmatters.org/2019/10/08/loving-muslim-marriage-episode-1/.

35 Ayqa Khan, 'The Real Sex Lives of Muslim Women', 30 August 2016, https://medium.com/muslim-women-speak/the-real-sex-lives-of-muslim-women-6e8d58ca3c0e.
36 Umm Muladhat, *The Muslimah Sex Manual: A Halal Guide To Mind Blowing Sex*, Kindle Unlimited, https://www.amazon.co.uk/Muslimah-Sex-Manual-halal-Blowing-ebook/dp/B0BK9MVTYK. Also see Alia Waheed, 'Taboo-busting Sex Guide Offers Advice to Muslim Women Seeking Fulfilling Love Lives', 16 July 2017, https://www.theguardian.com/lifeandstyle/2017/jul/16/muslimah-sex-manual--halal-sex-guide-muslim-women-seeking-fulfilling-love-lives.
37 Hidayah, https://hidayahlgbt.com/
https://www.instagram.com/hidayahlgbtqi/?hl=en (accessed 22 May 2023).
38 Imaan LGBTQ+, Twitter, https://twitter.com/ImaanLGBTQ (accessed 22 May 2023).
39 Muslim Women's Helpline, https://www.mwnhelpline.co.uk/issuesstep2.php?id=23 (accessed 25 May 2023).
40 The Inclusive Mosque, 'What We Do', https://inclusivemosque.org/services/ (accessed 25 May 2023).
41 Daar ul-Gharib, 22 May 2023, https://www.daar-ul-gharib.org/.
42 For example, see Daar ul-Gharib, 'Juz' 5 - Wa'l-muhsanatu - "And Prohibited Are the Ones Who Are Married" Suratan Nisa 24 to 147 Quran, translation by M. A. S. Abdel Haleem. Reading by Sheikha Sajida', Facebook, https://www.facebook.com/100079060278678/videos/2615325325267664?
43 Rikva Sajida, 'Daar ul-Gharib - Ramadan Khutbah - 29 Ramadan 1441', YouTube, 13 May 2020, https://youtu.be/e8q7KDY78aY.
44 Queer Masjid, Twitter, 22 May 2023, https://twitter.com/Daar_ul_Gharib.
45 Rikva Sajida, 'Tutorials', YouTube, 12 April 2019, https://www.youtube.com/playlist?list=PL-XSVKFDxcV5sc085aaHhI3CEmDJawHV4. See her profiled in Modestish, 'Meet Rivka Sajida: The Muslim Revert Whose Wardrobe Contains Pride T-Shirts And Lace Niqabs', https://modestish.com/rivka-saji/ (accessed n.d.).
46 Karina Sharma, '15 Muslim Influencers with Modern Modest Fashion', 27 March 2021, https://en.vogue.me/fashion/muslim-influencers-modest-fashion/.
Haute Hijab, '10 Hijabi Influencers to Follow on Instagram', The Muslim Vibe, 15 November 2022, https://themuslimvibe.com/muslim-lifestyle-matters/women/10-hijabi-influencers-to-follow-on-instagram.
47 The Dutch scholar Christiaan Snouck Hurgronje used an Edison wax cylinder recording device in Mecca in 1885. Ilm Feed, 'Surah al-Dhuha, "The OLDEST Quran Recitation Recording in the World!" (recorded by Christiaan Snouck Hurgronje in 1885)', 10 August 2019, https://youtu.be/b4nQEjpQBOU.
48 Hirschkind, *The Ethical Soundscape*, 1–31.
49 assabile.com, 22 May 2023, http://www.assabile.com (accessed 1 September 2021).
50 Rania Awad, 'Shaykhah Mabrouka of Cairo', Twitter, 25 April 2020, https://twitter.com/DrRaniaAwaad/status/1254044535505645570.
51 Scene Arabia, 'Her Voice Wasn't 'Awrah: Meet Sheikha Munira Abdou, Egypt's First Radio Quran Reciter', 14 June 2020, https://scenearabia.com/Life/Meet-Sheikha-Munira-Abdou-Egypt-s-First-Radio-Quran-Reciter.
52 عالم الطرب, 'Recitation of 'Ya Rasool Allah' by Sheikha Minira Abdou', YouTube, 20 September 2018, https://youtu.be/8FBIdZXizK8.
53 Al Haqyar TV, 'Top 10 Winner Women Quran Competition Dubai 2022', YouTube, 23 October 2022, https://youtu.be/AV4m7cmJ4zk, Al Jazeera, 'Woman Wins Nigerian Quran Contest', 17 May 2010, https://youtu.be/UviTvih-g0c.

54 For example, see Darul Iftaa Jordan, ' Fatwa 3482, Ruling when a Woman Recites Quran in the Presence of Non-Mahram Men', 25 March 2019, https://www.aliftaa.jo/Question2En.aspx?QuestionId=3482. Shaykh 'Abd al-'Aziz ibn Baz, '*Fatawa Nur 'ala ad-Darb, Reproduced and Translated in Islam Question and Answer, 97276,* What is the ruling on listening to women's recitation in Qur'an contests that are held in some Muslim countries?' 30 November 2022, https://islamqa.info/en/answers/97276/listening-to-women-recite-the-holy-quran. Islamweb, 'Is it Allowed for a Woman to make a Public Recitation or to be a Reciter?' 28 January 2003, https://www.islamweb.net/en/fatwa/85517/female-reciters.

55 This recitation is discussed in Lauren E. Osborne, 'Qur'an Recital', *Routledge Handbook of Islamic Ritual and Practice*, edited by Oliver Leaman (Oxford and New York: Routledge, 2022), 234–45. Also see Tahera Ahmed, 'First Female to Recite Quran at ISNA Convention', 18 January 2021, https://youtu.be/2D7AuYNHAEs.

56 Maryam Masud, 'Cutest Video: Fatima is Reciting Surah Al-Fatiha with Maryam Masud', YouTube, https://youtu.be/LSuN7ZktrXw (accessed 9 November 2020).

57 Maryam Masud, 'Maryam is Honored by Her Parents for Becoming Hafiza (حافظة)', YouTube, https://youtu.be/ynw4ZaR3ETA (accessed 9 November 2020).

58 Maryam Masud, 'Maryam Masud Official', Instagram, https://www.instagram.com/maryammasudofficial/?hl=en (accessed 9 November 2020).

59 Muslimah Sticker Studio, 'Maryam & Fatima', https://muslimahstickerstudio.com/products/maryam-fatima-collab (accessed 9 November 2020).

60 Maryam Masud, 'Sheikh Yusuf Estes Interviews Fatima Masud [3 yrs]', YouTube, 6 December 2018, https://youtu.be/2Nfllkf2U_g (accessed 13 November 2020).

61 Maryam Masud, 'A Great Advice [sic] from Mufti Menk to Maryam Masud', YouTube, 16 November 2019, https://youtu.be/nExG1OcVW7c (accessed 9 November 2020).

62 Jaynal4875, 'Maryam Masud', TikTok, https://www.tiktok.com/@jaynal4875/video/6638811607658925317?lang=en.

63 Maryam Masud, 'Quarantine vLog (Part 1): Maryam is in Quarantine at Her Home in New Jersey', https://youtu.be/C2HcKdpvzQo (accessed 9 November 2020).

64 Nusaiba Mohammad, 'Nusaiba Mohammad', YouTube (accessed 10 November 2020).

65 Jennifer Grout, 'Qur'an, Al-Kursi', YouTube, https://youtu.be/phFSXlGCwq4, Jennifer Grout, 'Verses 285-286 of Surat-ul Baqarah', YouTube, https://youtu.be/y8PcGK5eE-s (accessed 9 November 2019).

66 Mohamed Lotfi, 'Jennifer Grout chante en prison - Yaa Mohammed - Émission Souverains Anonymes (Lire ci-bas) (from Original Broadcast, Souverains Anonymes, https://www.souverains.qc.ca/jennifer-grout)', YouTube, https://youtu.be/oYkTyfR7uew.

67 Madinah Javed, 8 November 2020, https://twitter.com/MadinahJaved.

68 Maryam Amir, 'The Maryam Amir Show', https://www.youtube.com/watch?v=c8zVZMEbyDo (accessed 29 October 2020).

69 Maryam Amir, Facebook, 21 April 2020, https://www.facebook.com/100001526008868/posts/3107209022673267/?d=n.

70 I recall purchasing cassettes of her recitation from roadside stalls in rural Malaysia in the 1990s and later seeing her featured in a significant collection of recitations by Michael Sells (distributed in his book). Michael Sells, *Approaching the Qur'an: The Early Revelations* (Ashland: White Cloud Press, 1999).

71 Hj. Maria Ulfah, 'Quran Complete', Soundcloud, https://soundcloud.com/quran-30ajza-female/sets/maria-ulfah-recitation-complete-quran (accessed 16 November 2020).

72 YouTube, 'Search: "Maria Ulfa"', YouTube Search, https://www.youtube.com/results?search_query=maria+ulfa (accessed 29 October 2020). Hj. Maria Ulfah, 'Al Israa - 23-31', TikTok, https://www.tiktok.com/music/Al-Israa-23-31-6703086704087009282?lang=en (accessed 29 October 2020).

73 Maria Ulfah, 'Quran Complete'.

74 Kuran Sofrasi, 'Women Beautiful Quran Recitation Surah ar-Rahman', https://www.youtube.com/watch?v=5lhrBijmmbE (accessed 28 October 2020).

75 Samsudin Abdjalil, 'Sharifah Khazif Fadzilah-International Quran Reciter, 11 October 2009', YouTube, https://www.youtube.com/watch?v=prYJM6SBz24 (accessed 30 October 2020).

76 Kur'an Tilaveti, 'Mısırlı Hafız Sümeyye Eddeb'ten Harika Bir Kur'an Ziyafeti', YouTube, https://youtu.be/Xrkap-v8EEE (accessed 29 October 2020).

77 Music Upscale, 'Ramadan Nasheed', https://youtu.be/u7rsJ420PVE (accessed 28 October 2020).

78 Qariah, https://www.qariah.app/ (accessed 19 May 2022).

79 Qariah, 'FAQ', 27 May 2023, https://www.qariah.app/faq/.

80 The term *iftār* relates to breaking the (Ramaḍān) fast. Practices can vary in diverse religious and cultural contexts. 'Lailat ul-Qadr', the 'Night of Power', is associated with marking the day of the initial Revelation received by Muhammad. It is marked by additional prayers and readings of the Qur'ān, often over several nights, as there is no precise contemporaneous date. The use of online space in Ramaḍān is discussed in: Laura Jones, 'Ramadan in the UK: A Month of Ambiguity' (PhD, Cardiff University, 2022). Director of. 76–7.

81 Mahsa Alimardani and Mona Elswah, 'Online Temptations: COVID-19 and Religious Misinformation in the MENA Region', *Social Media and Society* 6, no. 3 (2020), https://doi.org/10.1177/2056305120948251. Yusra Habib Khan et al., 'Threat of COVID-19 Vaccine Hesitancy in Pakistan: The Need for Measures to Neutralize Misleading Narratives', *American Journal of Tropical Medicine and Hygiene* 103, no. 2 (2020): 603–4, https://doi.org/10.4269/ajtmh.20-0654. A. Z. Sarnoto and L. Hayatina, 'Polarization of the Muslim Community towards Government Policies in Overcoming the COVID-19 Pandemic in Indonesia', *Linguistics and Culture Review* 5 (2021): 642–52, https://doi.org/10.21744/lingcure.v5nS1.1449. Most. Zannatul Ferdous et al., 'Knowledge, Attitude, and Practice Regarding COVID-19 Outbreak in Bangladesh: An Online-Based Cross-Sectional Study', *PLoS ONE* 15 (2020), https://doi.org/10.1371/journal.pone.023925.

82 N. Kuipers et al., 'Encouraging Indonesians to Pray From Home During the COVID-19 Pandemic', *Journal of Experimental Political Science* 8 (2021): 211–22, https://doi.org/10.1017/XPS.2020.26. Yan Mardian et al., 'Sharia (Islamic Law) Perspectives of COVID-19 Vaccines', *Frontiers in Tropical Diseases* 2 (2021), https://doi.org/10.3389/fitd.2021.788188. Aldona Maria Piwko, 'Islam and the COVID-19 Pandemic: Between Religious Practice and Health Protection', *Journal of Religion and Health* 60 (2021): 3291–08, https://doi.org/10.1007/s10943-021-01346-y.

83 The term *ṭawāf* refers to the ritual of walking around the *Ka ʿbah* at the commencement and conclusion of the hajj. See an online summary of this hajj: Gary R. Bunt, 'Hajj 2020/1441', *Virtually Islamic Blog*, 2 August 2020, https://virtuallyislamic.com/blog/files/hajj2020.php.

84 Haramain Sharifain, 'The Aerial Sterilisation of the Mataaf', Twitter, 4 May 2021, https://twitter.com/hsharifain/status/1389699327375851527.
85 The Holy Mosques, Twitter, 16 July 2021, https://twitter.com/theholymosques/status/1416142549614477312.
86 For detailed discussions on pilgrimage and COVID-19, see: Sophia Rose Arjana, 'Pilgrimage, Technology, and Ritual in the Age of COVID', *Islamic Responses to COVID-19: Authority and Religiosity in #Muslim Communities & Digital Worlds' Conference*, University of Wales Trinity Saint David, 1 July 2021, https://virtuallyislamic.com/irc19/ircpanel2videos.php. Andrea Stanton, 'Hajj and Umrah in the COVID Era: Digital and Government Responses', *Islamic Responses to COVID-19: Authority and Religiosity in #Muslim Communities and Digital Worlds*, University of Wales Trinity Saint David, 1 July 2021, https://virtuallyislamic.com/irc19/ircpanel3videos.php. Also see Gary R. Bunt, 'The Net Imam Effect: Digital Contestations of #Islam and Religious Authority', in *Cyber Muslims: Mapping Islamic Digital Media in the Internet Age*, edited by Robert Rozehnal (London and New York: Bloomsbury Academic, 2022), 19–32.
87 Ryma Tchier, 'Australian Muslims 'Devastated' by Saudi Arabia's New Hajj Pilgrimage Lottery', ABC News, 22 June 2022, https://www.abc.net.au/news/2022-06-22/hajj-lottery-saudi-arabia-upsets-muslim-australians-pilgrimage/101169798.
88 Seán McLoughlin, 'Hajj: How a New Saudi-Run Travel Agency Failed Western "Guests of God"', Middle East Eye, 27 June 2022, https://www.middleeasteye.net/opinion/hajj-saudi-arabia-new-online-portal-fails-western-pilgrims. Mohammad Jibran Khan, 'Hajj 2022: The Failed launch of Motawif', Haramain Sharifain, 27 June 2022, https://www.haramainsharifain.com/hajj-2022-the-failed-launch-of-motawif/. Samir Jeraj, 'Pilgrims Are Still Fighting for Compensation from Ill-Fated Hajj Platform Motawif', Hyphen, 18 March 2023, https://hyphenonline.com/2023/03/17/pilgrims-are-still-fighting-for-compensation-from-ill-fated-hajj-platform-motawif/.
89 Al-Azhar, 'Tweet Emphasising Precautionary Measures', 4 September 2020, https://twitter.com/AlAzhar/status/1264409252505911297.
90 The National, 'Eid during Covid-19: Could the Pandemic Push Eideyya Online?' 12 May 2021, https://www.thenationalnews.com/mena/eid-during-covid-19-could-the-pandemic-push-eideyya-online-1.1221384.
91 The National, 'Online Shopping Soars in UAE as Pandemic Transforms Consumer Attitudes', 28 March 2021, https://www.thenationalnews.com/uae/online-shopping-soars-in-uae-as-pandemic-transforms-consumer-attitudes-1.1192577.
92 Healthy Brum, 'Safe Eid 2021', 11 May 2021, https://twitter.com/healthybrum/status/1392044328755859456. The response of the MCB and other UK organizations is discussed in Amin Al-Astewani, 'To Open or Close? COVID-19, Mosques and the Role of Religious Authority within the British Muslim Community: A Socio-Legal Analysis', *Religions* 12, no. 11 (2021), https://doi.org/10.3390/rel12010011.
93 Haramain Sharifain, ' Sheikh Sudais Receives Covid Vaccine Jab', 22 March 2021, https://www.haramainsharifain.com/2021/03/sheikh-sudais-receives-covid-vaccine-jab.html.
94 For example, see Newham London, '#KeepNewhamSafe: "Dr @fhussain73 has Some Advice on Celebrating Eid Safely this Year"', https://twitter.com/NewhamLondon/status/1392114607121108999. Muslim Doctors Cymru, 'We will be Celebrating #Eid on Thursday', 11 May 2021, https://twitter.com/muslimdoccymru/status/1392166534462726151.

95 BBC News, 'Covid: Fake News "Causing UK South Asians to Reject Jab"', 15 January 2021, https://www.bbc.co.uk/news/uk-55666407.

96 Shaykh Umar Hayat Qadri, 'Safety of Covid19 Vaccine', Suffah Foundation, 9 February 2021, https://youtu.be/cvSEuKJia4Y. ITV News, 'Bradford Central Mosque Latest Mosque in Yorkshire to become Vaccination Centre', 17 February 2021, https://www.itv.com/news/calendar/2021-02-17/bradford-central-mosque-latest-mosque-in-yorkshire-to-become-vaccination-centre, Mufti Mohammed Zubaria Butt, '"I Took the Vaccine"', Imams Online, 10 February 2021, https://twitter.com/ImamsOnline/status/1359583323509710852.

97 Qur'ān, 5:32 Farzana Hussain, '#getthejab', Twitter, 17 February 2021, https://twitter.com/fhussain73/status/1362032505063374852.

98 Qari Asim, '#Vaccines SaveLives', 2 February 2021, https://twitter.com/QariAsim/status/1356584211281571840.

99 BBC News, 'Covid: Side-by-side in a London Mosque - Funerals and a Food Bank', BBC News, 22 January 2021, https://www.bbc.co.uk/news/uk-55735630. Also see Michael Buchanan, 'Thread on COVID-19 in East London', Twitter, 22 January 2021, https://twitter.com/BBCMBuchanan/status/1352720545159249923.

100 East London Mosque & London Muslim Centre, 'ELM Update: Take the Vaccine, Save Lives', 22 January 2021, https://twitter.com/elondonmosque/status/1352696152773242881.

101 Frank Langfitt, 'How A U.K. Imam Countered Vaccine Hesitancy and Helped Thousands Get the "Jab"', NPR, 26 April 2021, https://www.npr.org/2021/04/26/988165812/how-a-u-k-imam-countered-vaccine-hesitancy-and-helped-thousands-get-the-jab. Muslim Doctors Cymru, 'Make Sure You Spread the Word', 23 March 2021, https://twitter.com/muslimdoccymru/status/1374325452936994816.

102 Associated Press, 'Islamic Leaders Battle Misconception about Vaccines, Fasting', US News & World Report, 9 April 2021, https://www.usnews.com/news/best-states/maine/articles/2021-04-09/islamic-leaders-battle-misconception-about-vaccines-fasting.

103 Arab News, 'UK Mosque becomes COVID-19 Vaccination Center', 21 January 2021, https://arab.news/4pxf8.

104 Culture UK Government Department for Digital, Media and Sport,, 'Sheikh Nuru Mohammed', 30 April 2021, https://twitter.com/dcms/status/1388127779955396608.

105 KSIMC of Birmingham Al-Abbas Islamic Centre, 'Index', https://www.ksmnet.org (accessed 13 August 2021).

106 Al Jazeera, 'Iran's Supreme Leader Khamenei Receives Local COVID Vaccine', Twitter, 25 June 2021, https://t.co/r2yCcAiinl?amp=1.

107 Narsi Benwal, 'Eid-al-Adha 2020: Dawoodi Bohra Community Hold Virtual Prayers to Stay Connected with Religion by Maintaining Social Distance', *Free Press Journal*, 2 August 2020, https://www.freepressjournal.in/mumbai/our-homes-are-mini-mosques.

108 Kutty is the director of the Islamic Center of Toronto and a resident scholar at the Islamic Institute of Toronto. His religious opinions have been widely circulated online on prominent Islamic websites. His opinions also feature on his personal Ask the Scholar website, which links to About Islam. Sheikh Ahmad Kutty, 'Ask the Scholar', https://askthescholar.com/ (accessed 7 January 2021). About Islam, https://aboutislam.net (accessed 7 January 2021).

109 Old Kent Road Mosque, 'Visit My Mosque', Muslim Council of Britain, https://t.co/1uHUpT5sI0 (accessed 21 June 2020). Cambridge Central Mosque,

'Virtual Open Day', Twitter, https://twitter.com/CambCentMosque/status/1274814909340094464 (accessed 21 June 2020). Muslim Council of Britain, 'Visit My Mosque', https://www.visitmymosque.org/ (accessed 20 June 2021).

110 Facebook, 'Celebrating the #MonthofGood', 6 April 2021, https://about.fb.com/news/2021/04/celebrating-ramadan-monthofgood/.

111 IslamQA, 'How can Someone Who is Wearing PPE (personal protective equipment) to Guard against Viruses do Wudoo' and Pray?', 8 May 2020, https://islamqa.info.

112 Islamic Portal, 'Covid-19: Status of Performing Salah in the Masjids and Restrictions', 9 July 2020, https://islamicportal.co.uk/covid-19-status-of-performing-salah-in-the-masjids-and-restrictions/.

113 Deenspiration, 'Episode 44: Covid-19 through the Lens of Spirituality – Shaykh Ruzwan Mohammed', 22 October 2020, https://deenspiration.com/covid-19-through-the-lens-of-spirituality-shaykh-ruzwan-mohammed/.

114 Subkhani Kusuma Dewi and M. Johan Nasrul Huda, 'Indonesian Muslims' Reception toward Wirid, Zikr and Shalawat during Covid-19 Outbreak; A Mediated Living Hadith', *DINIKA: Academic Journal of Islamic Studies* 5, no. 2 (2020): 34, https://doi.org/10.22515/dinika.v5i2.2769. Muhammad Mansur Ali, 'E-Majlis: Nikah, Tarawih and Hadith Audition during Covid-19 Lockdown', *Islamic Responses to COVID-19: Authority and Religiosity in #Islamic Communities and Digital Worlds' Conference*, University of Wales Trinity Saint David, 1 July 2021, https://virtuallyislamic.com/irc19/irc19-videos.php.

115 There are no implications that they are necessarily directly associated or affiliated with any or all the entities discussed in the jihād chapter. The intention here is to focus on 'civil' voices. Hamas and other players featured in Bunt, *Hashtag Islam*, 112–13. Bunt, *iMuslims*, 263–74.

116 Lorenzo Franceschi-Bicchierai and Ben Makuch, 'Israel Bombing "Cyber Operatives" Isn't Cyber War, It's Just War', Motherboard, https://www.vice.com/en/article/gy4vn3/israel-bombing-cyber-operatives-gaza-palestine (accessed 6 May 2019).

117 My collection of blog posts from 2021 covers this issue extensively: Gary R. Bunt, 'Palestine and Gaza - Live Updates', 21 May 2021, https://virtuallyislamic.com/virtuallyislamicblog/?id=al-aqsa-sheikh-jarrah-live.

118 Sanya Mansoor, 'Muna El-Kurd and Mohammed El-Kurd', *The 100 Most Influential People of 2021*, Time, 15 September 2021, https://time.com/collection/100-most-influential-people-2021/6096098/muna-mohammed-el-kurd/.

119 7amleh, 'The Attacks on Palestinian Digital Rights', 21 May 2021, https://7amleh.org/2021/05/21/7amleh-issues-report-documenting-the-attacks-on-palestinian-digital-rights.

120 Layla Mashkoor, 'Sheikh Jarrah Content Takedowns Reveal Pattern of Online Restrictions in Palestine', *The National*, 10 May 2021, https://www.thenationalnews.com/mena/sheikh-jarrah-content-takedowns-reveal-pattern-of-online-restrictions-in-palestine-1.1220037.

121 Andreas Kreig, 'Opinion: Al-Aqsa attacks: UAE Social Media Influencers Jump on Israel's Hasbara Bandwagon', Middle East Eye, 12 May 2021, https://www.middleeasteye.net/opinion/israel-palestine-aqsa-attacks-uae-influencers-hasbara. The article references several UAE influencers.

122 albawaba.com, 'They Are Beating Her! "We are all Mary" Exposes Treatment of Palestinian Women in Jerusalem', 29 January 2019, https://www.albawaba.com/loop

/they-are-beating-her-'we-are-all-mary'-exposes-treatment-palestinian-women-jerusalem-1245270, Carlos Latuff, '#WeAreAllMary', Twitter, 28 January 2019 https://twitter.com/LatuffCartoons, Twitter, '#WeAreAllMary', https://twitter.com/hashtag/WeAreAllMary?src=hash&ref_src=twsrc%5Etfw (accessed 6 October 2021).

123 Naomi Joseph, 'Nas Daily: Palestinian Blogger Delivers Upbeat Message to Millions – But He can Afford To', *The Conversation*, 4 January 2019, https://theconversation.com/nas-daily-palestinian-blogger-delivers-upbeat-message-to-millions-but-he-can-afford-to-106828. Also see this critique in Jade Saab, 'We Need to Talk about Nas Daily: The Normalizing Face of Privilege', 11 June 2018, https://jadesaab.com/we-need-to-talk-about-nas-daily-37ad93f47351.

124 NasDaily, https://www.nasdaily.com (accessed 6 October 2021).

125 Danny Zaken, 'Arab-Israeli Vlogger Nas Daily Wins over Viewers', Al-Monitor, 26 April 2021, https://www.al-monitor.com/originals/2021/04/arab-israeli-vlogger-nas-daily-wins-over-viewers.

126 Nas Daily, 'Am I Bad Muslim?!' YouTube, 21 June 2020, https://youtu.be/c62fi6B11rI.

127 Nas Daily, 'Let's Talk About Religon', Facebook, 14 October 2017, https://fb.watch/8twNo94Z2g/.

128 Gaza Sky Geeks, 'Index', https://gazaskygeeks.com (accessed 6 October 2021). Discussed in detail in Fedaa al-Qedra, 'Palestinian "Geeks" Code their Way to a Better Future in Gaza', Al Jazeera, 17 November 2018, https://www.aljazeera.com/features/2018/11/17/palestinian-geeks-code-their-way-to-a-better-future-in-gaza/.

129 Miriyam Aouragh, *Palestine Online: Transnationalism, the Internet and the Construction of Identity* (London: I.B. Tauris, 2011). Albana S. Dwonch, *Palestinian Youth Activism in the Internet Age: Online and Offline Social Networks after the Arab Spring* (London: I.B. Tauris, 2021). *SOAS Palestine Studies*. See Bunt, *iMuslims*, 263–74.

130 Nico J. G. Kaptein, 'The Voice of the `Ulamâ': Fatwas and Religious Authority in Indonesia', *Archives de sciences sociales des religions, Authorités Religieuses en Islam* 49, no. 125 (2004): 115–30.

131 Martin Slama, 'A Subtle Economy of Time: Social Media and the Transformation of Indonesia's Islamic Preacher Economy', *Economic Anthropology* 4 (2017): 94–106, 99, https://doi.org/10.1002/sea2.12075.

132 This snapshot comes from a 2019 conference presentation in Jakarta, focusing on 'influencers' in various forms. Bunt, 'The Fatwa Machine'.

133 Kompas.tv, 'Menkominfo Sebut Indonesia Berpeluang Kembangkan Metaverse Dunia karena Punya Kearifan Lokal', 22 January 2022, https://www.kompas.tv/article/251650/menkominfo-sebut-indonesia-berpeluang-kembangkan-metaverse-dunia-karena-punya-kearifan-lokal. Tim Redaksi, 'Metaverse di Kepala Jokowi adalah Mengaji Virtual, Bagaimana Visi Metaverse di Kepala Banyak Futuris?' VOI, 23 December 2022, https://voi.id/bernas/116817/metaverse-di-kepala-jokowi-adalah-mengaji-virtual-bagaimana-visi-metaverse-di-kepala-banyak-futuris.

134 Worldometer, 'Indonesia Population (Live)', https://www.worldometers.info/world-population/indonesia-population/ (accessed 27 July 2021). Based on Worldometer's RTS algorithm estimated population, interpreting United Nations Population Division data.

135 Pew Research Center, 'The Future of World Religions: Population Growth Projections, 2010-2050', Pew Research Center, 2 April 2015, https://www.pewforum.org/2015/04/02/religious-projections-2010-2050/.

136 Indonesia-Investments.com, 'Association of Internet Service Providers in Indonesia (APJII) Survey', https://www.indonesia-investments.com/news/todays-headlines/number-of-internet-users-in-indonesia-rises-to-171-million/item9144? (accessed 30 September 2019).

137 Hanadian Nurhayati-Wolff, 'Smartphone Market in Indonesia - Statistics and Facts', Statista, 12 March 2021, https://www.statista.com/topics/5020/smartphones-in-indonesia/.

138 Annisa R. Beta, 'Commerce, Piety and Politics: Indonesian Young Muslim Women's Groups as Religious Influencers', *New Media & Society* 21, no. 10 (2019): 2140–59, https://doi.org/10.1177/1461444819838774.

139 Nisa, 'Indonesian Women ʿUlamāʾ Go Online amid COVID-19'.

140 Claire-Marie Hefner, 'Morality on the Digital Edge: Social Media Usage among Indonesian Muslim School Girls', CRCS UGM, https://youtu.be/Mcm_VTaYZHY.

141 Fatihiya Dahrul and Soraya Permatasari, 'A Meme-Stock-Recommending Cleric Moves Indonesia's Market', Bloomberg, 16 July 2021, https://www.bloomberg.com/news/articles/2021-07-16/how-yusuf-mansur-pushes-meme-stocks-and-moves-indonesia-s-markets-on-instagram.

142 Kuliah Wisatahati, https://www.kuliahwisatahati.com/ (accessed 26 July 2021).

143 Yusuf Mansur, Instagram, https://www.instagram.com/yusufmansurnew/ (accessed 26 July 2021). The page had 2.9 million followers on the date of access. Also see Instagram, '#yusufmansur', https://www.instagram.com/explore/tags/yusufmansur/ (accessed 26 July 2021).

144 The article itself had a negative headline. RanaNews.id, 'Dicap Sombong Karena Pilih Darah Pendonor yang penghafal AlQuran Ketika Sakid, Ini Kata Ustaz Yusuf Mansur ("Branded Arrogant for Choosing Blood Donors who memorized the Koran, said Ustaz Yusuf Mansur")', 24 July 2021, https://www.instagram.com/p/CRskBQJsweZ/.

145 This includes entities that played a role in Indonesia's historical-religious development, including the precursors to the MUI and political parties. Members include Al Ittihadiyyah, Syarikat Islam, Al Washliyah, Math'laul Anwar and Pergerakan Tarbijah Islamijah.

146 H. Abdul Muiz Ali, 'Pentingnya Kejujuran dalam Bermuamalah di Media Sosial', MUI, 11 June 2021, https://mui.or.id/opini/30282/pentingnya-kejujuran-dalam-bermuamalah-di-media-sosial/.

147 Dewan Syariah Nasional-Majelis Ulama Indonesia, 'Fatwa', https://dsnmui.or.id/kategori/fatwa/ (accessed 14 June 2021).

148 Tasha Wibawa, 'Indonesia's Top Islamic Body Issues Fatwa against Measles Vaccine, Calling It "Religiously Forbidden"', ABC News, 21 August 2018, https://www.abc.net.au/news/2018-08-21/indonesia-vaccines-measles-fatwa-issued-by-mui/10147040.

149 Berita, 'Di Webinar MUI, Pakar: Herbal Berpotensi Jadi Obat Alternatif Covid-19', 8 June 2021, https://mui.or.id/berita/30241/di-webinar-mui-pakar-herbal-berpotensi-jadi-obat-alternatif-covid-19/.

150 Ardila Syakriah, 'After MUI Fatwa, AstraZeneca Vaccine Sent to East Java', Jakarta Post, 25 March 2021, https://www.thejakartapost.com/academia/2021/03/23/vaccines-save-lives.html, Majelis Ulama Indonesia, 'Fatwa MUI : Hukum Penggunaan Vaksin Covid-19 Produk AstraZeneca', Majelis Ulama Indonesia, 19 March 2021, https://mui.or.id/produk/fatwa/29883/fatwa-mui-hukum-penggunaan-vaksin-covid-19-produk-astrazeneca/ (accessed 15 June 2021). VOI,

'MUI: AstraZeneca Vaccine Is Haram, But Can Be Used', 19 March 2021, https://voi.id/en/news/39888/mui-astrazeneca-vaccine-is-haram-but-can-be-used.

151 Stanley Widianto and Kate Lamb, 'Instagram Influencers Are a Vaccine Priority in Wary Indonesia', Reuters, 14 January 2021, https://www.reuters.com/business/media-telecom/instagram-influencers-are-vaccine-priority-wary-indonesia-2021-01-14/.

152 Majelis Ulama Indonesia, 'Infografis Fatwa Panduan Kaifiat Shalat Idul Fitri saat Pandemi Covid-19', 18 May 2020, https://mui.or.id/produk/infografis/28064/fatwa-panduan-kaifiat-shalat-idul-fitri-saat-pandemi-covid-19/.

153 Wahyudi Akmaliah and Ahmad Najib Burhan, 'Digital Islam in Indonesia: The Shift of Ritual and Religiosity during Covid-19', *ISEAS Perspectives* 107 (2021), https://www.iseas.edu.sg/articles-commentaries/iseas-perspective/2021-107-digital-islam-in-indonesia-the-shift-of-ritual-and-religiosity-during-covid-19-by-wahyudi-akmaliah-and-ahmad-najib-burhani/.

154 Andrée Feillard, 'Nahdlatul Ulama in Indonesia', in *The Oxford Handbook of Islam and Politics*, edited by John L. Esposito and Emad El-Din Shahin (Oxford: Oxford University Press, 2013), https://www.oxfordhandbooks.com/.

155 K. H. Ma'ruf Amin, 'Public Page', Facebook, https://www.facebook.com/Kiyai.MarufAmin/ (accessed 29 October 2019).

156 K. H. Ma'ruf Amin, 'Memakai Masker Saat Pandemi Itu Wajib', Instagram, 10 May 2021, https://www.instagram.com/p/COrhxl9g7qz/.

157 Muhamad Ali, 'Far from Mecca: Modern Islam in Indonesia and Malaysia', in *Islam in the Modern World*, edited by Jeffrey Kenney and Ebrahim Moosa (New York: Routledge, 2013), 411.

158 NU Online, '"Jateng" – Search: "Ghazali"', https://jateng.nu.or.id/search?q=ghazali (accessed 16 June 2021).

159 NU Online, 'Banten', https://banten.nu.or.id/.

160 NU Online, 'NU Online - Super App', Google Play, https://play.google.com/store/apps/details?id=id.or.nu.app.

161 Dana Syariah, Google Play, https://play.google.com/store/apps/details?id=com.danasyariah.mobiledanasyariah (accessed 16 June 2021).

162 Ali, 'Far from Mecca: Modern Islam in Indonesia and Malaysia', 409–15.

163 Persyarikatan Muhammadiyah, 25 November 2015, https://muhammadiyah.or.id.2015.

164 Persyarikatan Muhammadiyah, 'Haedar Nashir: Kiai Dahlan's the Cosmopolitan', 21 June 2021, https://muhammadiyah.or.id/en/haedar-nashir-kiai-dahlans-the-cosmopolitan/.

165 Muhammadiyah Channel, 'Salat Kok Pakai Masker?' YouTube, 4 March 2021, https://youtu.be/fk7E7wB5jr8.

166 Muhammadiyah Channel, 'Kitalah Garda Terdepan Mengakhiri Pandemi - Covid19', 30 March 2020, https://youtu.be/_uniJ_dOYYI. Persyarikatan Muhammadiyah, 'Muhammadiyah Covid-19 Command Center', https://covid19.muhammadiyah.id/tentang-kami/ (accessed 21 June 2021). For a discussion on Muhammadiyah's approach to Covid-19, including their role in countering influencers whose opinions about vaccines were negative, see Suyadi et al., 'The Fiqh of Disaster: The Mitigation of Covid-19 in the Perspective of Islamic Education-Neuroscience', *International Journal of Disaster Risk Reduction* 51 (2020), https://doi.org/10.1016/j.ijdrr.2020.101848.

167 Persyarikatan Muhammadiyah, 'Haedar: COVID-19 Cases Surge Probably Because of Public Ignorance and Arrogance (citing Dadang Kahmad)', https://

muhammadiyah.or.id/en/haedar-covid-19-cases-surge-probably-because-of-public -ignorance-and-arrogance/.

168 Persyarikatan Muhammadiyah, 'Lensamu', Instagram, https://www.instagram.com/lensamu/ (accessed 21 June 2021).

169 BBC News, 'Indonesian Muslim Preacher Named as Porn Case Suspect', 30 May 2017, https://www.bbc.co.uk/news/world-asia-40089410.

170 Reuters, 'Indonesia Jails Cleric for Four Years over Spread of False COVID-19 Information', 24 June 2021, https://www.reuters.com/world/asia-pacific/indonesia-jails-cleric-four-years-over-spread-false-covid-19-information-2021-06-24/.

171 Muhammad Sufyan Abdurrahman, 'Mengenal Dakwah Digital Ustadz Abdul Somad Pekanbaru', DetikNews, 18 July 2017, https://news.detik.com/opini/d-3563958/mengenal-dakwah-digital-ustadz-abdul-somad-pekanbaru.

172 Tafaqquh Online, YouTube, 19 July 2021, https://www.youtube.com/c/TAFAQQUHVIDEO/featured.

173 Adi Hiyat, 'AdiHiyatOfficial', Instagram, https://instagram.com/adihiyatofficial.

174 Adi Hiyat, 'AdiHiyatOfficial', *Sejarah Lengkap Yahudi (Geniologi Bani Israil)*, Instagram, 3 June 2021, https://www.instagram.com/p/CPpfxkin34f/.

175 Muzammil Hasballah, 'Murottal Muzammil Hasballah MP3 Offline', https://play.google.com/store/apps/details?id=com.arfdev.MurottalMuzammilHasballah&hl=en&gl=US (accessed 20 July 2021).

176 Muzammil Hasballah, Instagram, https://www.instagram.com/muzammilhb/?hl=en (accessed 20 July 2021).

177 Muzammil Hasballah, 'Surah Yasin, Surah Yusuf, Surah Al-Kahfi, Surah Maryam, Surah al-Mulk, Surah Al-Waqiah, Surah ar-Rahman', YouTube, 15 July 2021, https://youtu.be/LFXSBfBggVQ (accessed 20 July 2021).

178 QuranBest, 'Al Quran Digital #1', https://www.quranbest.com/ (accessed 20 July 2021).

179 Shireen Sungkar, Instagram, https://www.instagram.com/shireensungkar/?hl=en (accessed 20 July 2021).

180 Wardahmaulina_, Instagram, https://www.instagram.com/wardahmaulina_/ (accessed 24 May 2023).

181 Natta Wardah, 'Hobi Motor Gak Lupa Istri - Istri Auto Cemburu. Siapa itu?' 26 July 2019, https://youtu.be/YWPMZxMt-sU.

182 Natta Reza, 'Kekasih Impian/Offical Music Video', YouTube, 23 November 2018, https://youtu.be/hPYTYgTYOzc.

183 Hijrah Fest, https://hijrahfest.com/ (accessed 19 May 2022).

184 Pemudah Hijrah, https://pemudahijrah.id/ (accessed 20 June 2021). Quinton Temby, 'Shariah, Dakwah, and Rock 'n' Roll: Pemuda Hijrah in Bandung', 30 June 2019, https://www.newmandala.org/shariah-dakwah-rock-n-roll-pemuda-hijrah-bandung/ Juke Carolina, 'Indonesia's Muslim Youth Find New Heroes in Instagram preachers', GlobalPost, 29 March 2019, https://theworld.org/stories/2019-03-29/indonesia-s-muslim-youth-find-new-heroes-instagram-preachers.

185 Pemudah Hijrah, 'Raod Tapi Dosa', https://pemudahijrah.id/assets/shift_porto_bpsmb/Raos_Tapi_Dosa.jpg (accessed 20 June 2021).

186 Michael Muhammad Knight, *The Taqwacores*, 2nd edn (Williamsburg, Brooklyn: Autonomedia, 2004). Punk Hijrah Shop, Instagram, https://instagram.com/punkhijrah.shop (accessed 19 September 2019).

187 Punk Hijrah, https://www.instagram.com/punkhijrah/?hl=en (accessed 22 July 2021).

188 Instagram, '#punkislam', 22 July 2021, https://www.instagram.com/explore/tags/punkhijrah/.
189 Carmen Aguilera-Carnerero, 'Memes of Hate: Countering Cyber Islamophobia', Fair Observer, 17 April 2019, https://www.fairobserver.com/world-news/cyber-islamophobia-memes-hate-speech-muslims-news-19112/ (accessed 11 December 2021).
190 Mematic, https://www.mematic.net/ (accessed 9 December 2021).
191 Rahat Ahmed, 'The Uncanny World of Muslim Memes', *Wired*, 16 May 2016, https://www.wired.com/2016/05/the-uncanny-world-of-muslim-memes/, 10 December 2021.
192 Leyla Khalife, '14 Muslim Memes that Will Make You Laugh Till You Cry', StepFeed, 25 February 2017, https://stepfeed.com/14-muslim-memes-that-will-make-you-laugh-till-you-cry-0787.
193 Justbrozz, 'Ramadan 2077', American Muslim Memes, 17 December 2020, https://www.facebook.com/MuslimMemes/photos/a.194559027316710/3239373209501928/.
194 Ahmed Ali Akbar, '20 Times The Internet Hilariously Summed Up Your Ramadan', buzzfeed.com/Pinterest, https://www.pinterest.co.uk/pin/798896421390798173/. Memes Monkey, 'Halal Memes', https://www.memesmonkey.com/topic/halal (accessed 10 December 2021). Reddit, '/r/Izlam'.
195 Reproduced on Pinterest, 'If the Avengers were Getting for Ramadan. (Done by Johan Liebert on fb)', https://www.pinterest.co.uk/pin/682436149765741844/ (accessed 10 December 2021). Also, see Muslim Matters, 'If Superheroes were Muslims / Dua' Request l Sunday Open Thread 6/13/2010', https://www.pinterest.co.uk/pin/744642119609454224/ (accessed 10 December 2021). Zaid Hamid Official Blog, 'A Glimpse in to the Future of United States of Islam', 19 August 2012, https://zaidzamanhamid.wordpress.com/2012/08/19/a-glimpse-in-to-the-future-of-united-states-of-islam/.
196 buzzfeed.com, 'Avengers: Hijab Heroes', 10 October 2018, https://www.pinterest.co.uk/pin/826762444070161124/. Also see: Ikran Dahir, 'These Muslim Girls Entered and Won a Marvel Cosplayer Competition and People Love Them', Buzzfeed News, 13 October 2018, https://www.buzzfeed.com/ikrd/these-muslim-girls-cosplayed-as-the-avengers-and-people.
197 halal.me.mes, 'Muslim Women Aren't Allowed to have an Education', 5 December 2021, https://www.instagram.com/p/CXGkvVkN_AP/.
198 American Muslim Memes, 'Janaza of Stan Lee', 13 November 2018, https://www.facebook.com/MuslimMemes/photos/well-miss-stanmuslim-muslimmemes-muslims-memes-stanlee-stan-stanleecameo-stanlee/1710196859086245/ (accessed 10 December 2021).
199 halal.me.mes, 'Muslim Women Aren't Allowed to have an Education'. Also see Zaaiinnaaabbb, 'Halal Memes', https://in.pinterest.com/szainab808/halal-memes/ (accessed 10 December 2021).
200 Justbrozz, 'Muslim Superman', https://www.instagram.com/p/CIx1UXJgtPb/ (accessed 10 December 2021).
201 Halal Memes, Facebook, https://www.facebook.com/Thehalalmemes/ (accessed 10 December 2021).
202 jeff13151, 'Dear Atheists', imgur.com, 9 January 2015, https://imgur.com/gallery/DAuYrw1.

203 It also used the term 'sandpeople' in a derogatory analogy to Muslims. Brassidio, 'Star Wars Meets Islam: "You'll Never Find a More Wretched Hive of Scum and Villainy"', imgur.com, 12 April 2015, https://imgur.com/gallery/LBftAOk/comment/396120153.
204 StrykeBackAU, 'I Think I'm Out of Rogue One Memes. Help', *Star Wars Memes*, Reddit, https://www.reddit.com/r/starwarsmemes/comments/d6awuy/i_think_im_out_of_rogue_one_memes_help/.
205 Bunt, *Hashtag Islam*, 123–40. A. McCrow-Young and M. Mortensen, 'Countering Spectacles of Fear: Anonymous' Meme "War" against ISIS', *European Journal of Cultural Studies* 24 (2021): 832–49, https://doi.org/10.1177/13675494211005060. Get the Trolls Out, 'Memes and Shareables', https://getthetrollsout.org/memes-and-shareables (accessed 11 December 2021).
206 Ismael N. Daro, '"Taqiyya": How An Obscure Islamic Concept Became An Obsession of Anti-Muslim Activists', Buzzfeed, 12 April 2018, https://www.buzzfeednews.com/article/ishmaeldaro/taqiyya-explained (accessed 1 December 2021).
207 Know Your Meme, 'Ordinary Muslim Man - Image #196,448', https://knowyourmeme.com/photos/196448-ordinary-muslim-man. The original image is said to be: u/hi7en, 'Introducing ordinary Muslim man', Reddit, https://www.reddit.com/r/pics/comments/ew7zf/introducing_ordinary_muslim_man/ (accessed 11 December 2021).
208 Saranac Hale Spencer, 'Meme Distorts Quran Verses', Factcheck, 18 March 2019, https://www.factcheck.org/2019/03/meme-distorts-quran-verses/. The source for the fabricated quotations was Abul Kasem, 'Whither the Islamic Infidels?', 23 June 2005, https://web.archive.org/web/20080516225541/http://www.islam-watch.org/AbulKasem/whither_the_islamic_infidels.htm (accessed 13 December 2021).
209 Bunt, *Virtually Islamic*, Chapter 5.
210 me.me, 'Ooops I Forgot to be Oppressed, Too Busy being Awesome!', https://me.me/i/ooops-i-forgot-to-be-oppressed-too-busy-being-awesome-11867215 (accessed 13 December 2021). This phrase has been utilized elsewhere, including with a roller-skating hijab wearer. superseagems, 'Ooops, I Forgot to be Oppressed, Too Busy being Awesome!', Facebook, https://www.facebook.com/watch/?v=939681430095193.
211 Pinterest, 'Anime Muslim', https://www.pinterest.co.uk/search/pins/?q=Anime%20muslim (accessed 13 December 2021).
212 For example, see Naadiya Mohammed, 'Muslim Disney Princess', Pinterest, https://www.pinterest.co.uk/naadiyamohmmed/muslim-disney-princess/ (accessed 3 December 2021).

Chapter 11

1 Narula, *Virtual Society*, ix–xx.
2 Habermas, *The Structural Transformation of the Public Sphere*. Also, see arnham, *Emancipation, the Media, and Modernity*. Bohman and Rehg, 'Jürgen Habermas'. Outhwaite, *Habermas*.
3 Lawrence, 'Muslim Cosmopolitanism', 19–39.
4 Lawrence, *Islamicate Cosmopolitan Spirit*. Hodgson, *The Venture of Islam*.
5 Patel, 'Hybrid Imams', 34–50.
6 Echchaibi, 'From Audio Tapes to Video Blogs'.

7 The New Arab, ‘Quran Predicted Facebook, Internet Says Egyptian Preacher’, 23 May 2022, https://english.alaraby.co.uk/news/quran-predicted-facebook-internet-says-egyptian-preacher.
8 OpenAI, ‘ChatGPT’, https://chat.openai.com (accessed 24 January 2023).
9 David Klepper, ‘Learning to Lie: AI Tools Adept at Creating Disinformation,” Associated Press, 26 January 2023, https://apnews.com.
10 Sigal Samuel, ‘AI’s Islamophobia Problem’, *Vox*, 2021, https://www.vox.com/future-perfect/22672414/ai-artificial-intelligence-gpt-3-bias-muslim. This discussion was based around Open-AI’s GPT-3. The article reflects the research contained in Tom Brown et al., ‘Language Models Are Few-Shot Learners’, *Advances in Neural Information Processing Systems* 33 (2020): 1877–901, https://arxiv.org/abs/2005.14165.
11 David Armano, ‘Conversational Computing Changes Everything: Bing vs. Bard is Just the Beginning’, Forbes, 8 February 2023, https://www.forbes.com/sites/davidarmano/2023/02/08/conversational-computing-will-change-everything-it-starts-with-search/?sh=70c7600965f1, James Vincent, ‘7 Problems Facing Bing, Bard, and the Future of AI Search’, The Verge, 9 February 2023, https://www.theverge.com/2023/2/9/23592647/ai-search-bing-bard-chatgpt-microsoft-google-problems-challenges.
12 *Sūrah al-Qāf*, Qur᾽ān. 50:16. Nasr et al., eds, *The Study Quran*.
13 Arjana, *Buying Buddha, Selling Rumi*, Arjana, *Pilgrimage in Islam*.
14 Rozehnal, *Cyber Sufis*.
15 Benzinga, ‘Islamicoin (Islami) Is Now Available for Trading on LBank Exchange’, Benzinga, 22 August 2022, https://www.benzinga.com/pressreleases/22/08/28696238/islamicoin-islami-is-now-available-for-trading-on-lbank-exchange, Deepthi Nair, ‘Mena Region is “World’s Fastest-Growing Cryptocurrency Market”’, *The National*, 5 October 2022, https://www.thenationalnews.com/business/money/2022/10/05/mena-region-is-fastest-growing-crypto-market-in-the-world-report-says/, Harry Clynch, ‘Cryptocurrencies and Bitcoin Surge Help Mitigate Floundering Turkish Economy’, The New Arab, 5 September 2022, https://www.newarab.com/features/cryptocurrencies-help-mitigate-floundering-turkish-economy, Jeffrey Gogo and Ryan James, ‘Islamic Coin Claims it Will Scale Like Bitcoin and Hit $1 Trillion in Value’, Beincrypto.com, 26 October 2022, https://beincrypto.com/islamic-coin-claims-it-will-scale-like-bitcoin-and-hit-1-trillion-in-value/, Mohammed R. Mhawish, ‘Bitcoin Offers a Digital Lifeline for Palestinians in Blockaded Gaza Strip’, *The National*, 28 November 2022, https://www.thenationalnews.com/mena/2022/11/28/bitcoin-offers-a-digital-lifeline-for-palestinians-in-blockaded-gaza-strip/, Paula Aceves, ‘Afghanistan’s Crypto Lifeline’, *New Yorker, Intelligencer*, 2022, https://nymag.com/intelligencer/2022/09/afghanistans-crypto-lifeline.html.

INDEX

Abdeslam, Salah 186
Abdou, Munira 200
ʿAbduh, Muḥammad 95–6, 214
ʾAbū Bakr 60, 62, 69–70, 107, 114
ʾAbū Ḥamid Muḥammad b. Muḥammad al-Ṭūsī al-Ghazālī 82–3, 149–50
ʾAbū Ḥanīfa al-Nuʿmān 78–80, *see also* Ḥanafī school
ʾAbu ʿl-Najīb Suhrawardī 152–3
ʾAbū Muḥammad al-Ḥasan bin ʿAlī al-Askarī 121–2
ʾAbū Tamīm Maʿad al-Mustanṣir Billāh 124
Abul Aʿlā al-Mawdūdī 93–4, 100
Abyssinia, *see* Ethiopia
ʾĀdam 37, 39, 40
adhān, see prayer
Adh-Dhikr Channel 202
Advanced Research Projects Agency Network (ARPANET) 3
al-Afghānī, Jamāl al-Dīn 95–6, 214
Afghanistan 71, 90, 135, 157, 176–83, 187, 188, 195
Aga Khan IV (Prince Shāh Karīm al-Ḥusaynī) 125, *see also* Nizāri Ismāʿīlī
aḥādīth, see ḥādīth
Ahl al-Bayt 62, 71, 73, 105–27
Aḥmad al-Tijāniyy 162–4
Aḥmad ibn Ḥanbal (Aḥmad b. Muḥammad b. Ḥanbal ʾAbū ʿAbdallāh al-Shaybānī al-Marwazī) 81–2, 96, 166, *see also* Ḥanbalī school
ʿĀʾishah bint Abī Bakr 60–3, 65–6
Akkad, Moustapha 54, 67–8, *see also The Message, under cinema*
Al-Islam (Ahlul Bayt Digital Islamic Library Project) 59
ʿAlawī Bohras (Alavi) 124, 125–6, *see also* Ismāʿīlī; Shīʿism
al-Albānī, Muḥammad Nāṣir ad-Dīn Nūḥ 99
Albania 168, 169
Alevi 169
Alevi-Bektashi 168–9
Algeria 173
algorithms 3, 9–12, 26, 29–31, 35, 38, 45, 51, 63, 75, 76, 143, 193, 223–9
  definition 9–10
Ali, Nouman 43, 50
ʿAlī al-Hādī 121
ʿAlī al-Hujwīrī (Dātā Ganj Bakhsh) 153–4
ʿAlī al-Riḍā 109
ʿAlī ibn Abī Ṭālib 32, 40, 42, 43, 59, 63, 68–72, 106–14, 132, 168
ʿAlī ibn Ḥusayn Zayn al-ʿĀbidīn 114–15
ʿAlī ibn Mūsā al-Riḍā (al-Reza) 119–20, 133
Allāh 37, 69, 76, 145, 152, 168, 217, 224, 225
Allied Democratic Forces 188, *see also* Islamic State, Islamic State Central Africa Province
Ally, Shabir 41, 50
Alsuleiman, Sheikh Shady 39, 54
Alwadi, Nada 23
Amazon 37, 99
Amin, Maʿruf 212
Amina, Mahsa 132–3
Amir, Maryam 201
angels 35, 37–40, 45, 54, 225
  Isrāfīl 38
  Jibrīl (Gabriel) 38, 48, 54, 76, 114
  Mīkhāʾīl 38
  Munkar 38
  Nakīr 38
animation 52, 58, 117, 120–1, 164–5

Antichrist 43, 44
Apple 3
apps 19–20, 34, 35, 48, 50, 59, 67, 80, 81, 83, 84, 91, 94, 99–101, 121, 131, 134, 149, 150, 166, 178, 213, 216, 218, 226
 matrimonial apps and websites 126–7
 Qariah App 202
'Arab Spring' 22–3
Arabic 70, 80, 87, 101, 109, 116, 130, 134, 135, 137, 139, 149, 182
Arberry, A.J. 156, 157
Arjuna, Sophia Rose 19, 226
ARPANET, *see* Advanced Research Projects Agency Network
artificial intelligence (AI) 9–12, 26, 30, 32, 41, 51, 102, 103, 218, 225
 AI art 37, 39
 ChatBots 10–11
 ChatGPT (OpenAI) 10–11, 26, 225
al-ʿAshara al-Mubashshara 68–72
Asim, Qari 205
Astan Quds Razavi 119–20
Attaki, Hanan 217
Australia 21, 186
al-Awlaki, Anwar 51, 99, 183–5, 191
Azeri 135
Al-Azhar 30, 70, 81, 117, 204, 215, 220, 225
 Grand Mufti Sheikh Ali Gomaa 81, 117
Azzam, Abdallah 85, 99, 176, 184

Baba, Avatar Meher 168
Badr, Battle of 53–4, 71, 180
Baghdad 79, 137, 148
al-Baghdādī, ʾAbū Bakr 186, *see also* 'Islamic State'
Baha-ud-Din Zakariya 153
Bahrain 23, 140
Bali 213
Balkhi, Abdul Qadir 179
Baluku, Seka Musa 188, *see also* Allied Democratic Forces
Bamba, Amadou (Aḥmad ibn Muḥammad ibn Ḥabīb Allāh) 164–5
al-Bannāʾ, Ḥassan 97–8
Baradar, Abdul Ghani 178–9
Barelwī 165–6
Barthes, Roland 15
Batubara, Abdul Somad 215
Bauchi, Dahiru Usman 164
Baudrillard, Jean 15
Bektash 168
Belghazi, Taieb 18
Bilāl ibn Rabāḥ 67–8
bin Bāz, Abd al ʿAzīz bin ʿAbdullāh 101
bin Laden, Osama 85, 182–5, 191
bint Rehan, Mariyah 197
#BlackLivesMatter 67, 132, 184
Boko Haram (Jamāʿat Ahl as-Sunnah lid-Daʿwāh waʾl-Jihād) 189–90
Brahimaj, Hajji Dede Edmond (Baba Mondi) 169
Bridgman, Frederick Arthur 148
browsers 4, 33, 129–30, 174, 199, 221
Buddhism 148
Bukhārī, Aḥmad-i 158

caliphate(s) 68–72, 83, 107–27, *see also* ʾAbū Bakr; ʿAlī ibn Abī Ṭālib; Imamate; ʿUmar ibn al-Khaṭṭāb; ʿUthmān
Campbell, Heidi 16–17, 22
Canada 20, 21, 125, 186
cartoons, *see* animation
Castells, Manuel 15
censorship 31, 90
ChatGPT, *see under* artificial intelligence
Chechnya 176
Chiang, Ted 11
China 9
Chishtīyya Order 64, 154–5, 167, *see also* Muʿīn al-Dīn Chishtī; Sufism
Christianity 43–5, 65, 148, 183–4, *see also* ʿĪsā
 Bible 40, 44
 Christian-Muslim relations 66
cinema 36, 54, 59, 67–8, 79–80, 219
 DC 219
 Disney 220
 Marvel 36, 219
 The Message 54, 67–8 (*see also* Akkad, Moustapha)
 Star Wars 219
Cisse, Ahmad Tijani Ali 263

Cisse, Hassan 163
coding 209, 218
comic books 79–80, 219, *see also* cinema
Conner, Carol Weyland 168
cooke, miriam 18
Corbin, Henry 156
Cornwell, T. Bettina 12–13
Covid-19 7, 22, 79, 92, 103, 119, 124, 126, 132, 134, 137, 139, 156, 160, 165, 170, 185, 196, 201, 203–7, 211–12, 214, 226

Daar ul-Gharib 198–9
Daesh, *see* 'Islamic State'
Dahlan, Ahmad 213–14, *see also* Muhammadiyyah
Dar ul-Ifta (Egypt) 61, 62
Dawkins, Richard 218
Dawoodi Bohras 123, 124–5, 126, 205–6, *see also* Ismāʿīlī; Shīʿism
Day of Judgement 38, 43, 44
Deenspiration 206
Democratic Republic of Congo 187, 188
Deoband Online 79
Deobandi 62, 79, 88, 166–7
Dewsbury, West Yorkshire 167
digital divide, *see* internet access
Digital Sisterhood 196
disinformation 26, 30, 228
  'fake news' 11, 225
divorce 64, 66
dream interpretation 135, 160–1
dress code 195, 199, 200, 220

eBay 37, 70
Echchaibi, Nabil 20, 224
education 77
Egypt 14, 28, 33, 60, 65, 71, 85, 90, 95–100, 195–6, 200, 214
e-jihād 23–4, 54, 99, 219–20, 224
Eltahawy, Mona 195
English language 130, 135, 139, 166
Environmental issues 24, 53, 124, 132, 228
Ertuğrul 156
eShaykh 159, *see* Naqshbandiyya
Estes, Yusuf 200
Ethiopia 43, 66–7
exorcism 37

Facebook 6, 79, 92, 93, 100, 101, 124, 134, 137–40, 155, 156, 159, 169, 174, 178, 196, 201, 206, 208, 209, 212, 219, 225
Fadlallah, al-Sayid Ali 141, *see also* Hezbollah
Fadlallah, Muḥammad Husayn 140–1, *see also* Hezbollah
Fakhruddin, Syedna Taher 125, *see also* Sulaymānī Bohras
Farangi Mahali 92
Fāṭimah bint Muḥammad (Fāṭimah Zahrāʾ) 58, 64, 71, 109
Fāṭimah bint Mūsā 133
Fāṭimid Caliphate 124, *see also* caliphate
fatwas (*fatāwā*) 19, 26, 27, 31, 81, 97, 102, 103, 129, 130, 139, 166, 206, 212
finance
  Bitcoin 226
  Blockchain 226, 228
  Crypto 227–8
  Islamic finance 20
Foucault, Michel 15
Foumani, Mohammad-Taqi Bahjat 136
Front Pembela Islam (FPI) 214–15

gaming 6, 54, 112, 121, 123
Gellner, Ernest 28
gender issues 21–2, 57–67, 132, 193–9, 210–11
Germany 214
Ghana 163
al-Ghazālī, *see* Abū Ḥamid Muḥammad b. Muḥammad al-Ṭūsī al-Ghazālī
God, *see* Allāh
Godane, Ahmad Abdi Aw Muhammad 189, *see also* al-Shabāb
Golpaygani, Lutfullah Saafi 135
Google 29–30, 160
Grout, Jennifer 201

Habermas, Jürgen 15, 224
ḥādīth (*aḥādīth*) 8, 12, 38, 39, 42, 47–55, 60, 63, 75, 77, 80, 81, 85, 88, 92, 99, 103, 113, 117, 124, 161, 166, 215

Ḥafṣah bint ʿUmar 63, 64
ḥajj 19, 37, 41, 69, 87, 90, 154, 195, 203–4, 212, 213, *see also* Mecca
  Minā 37
al-Ḥallāj, Manṣūr 148
Hamas 132, 208
al-Ḥanafī, Shaykh Muḥammad Awwamah 79
Ḥanafī school 78–80, 92, 115
Ḥanbalī school 81–2, 86, 117
ul-Haq, Amin 183
Haqqani, Jaluluddin 181
al-Haqqani, Muḥammad Nazim 159–60
al-Haqqani, Sirajuddin 181
Hārūn 42
Ḥasan bin ʿAlī bin Abī Ṭālib 32, 43, 71, 87, 110–12
Hasballah, Muzammil 215–16
Hawwāʾ 39
heaven 36, 40, 42, 44, 52, 53, 66
Hezbollah 105, 108, 140–1, 175
Hidayat, Adi 215
hijab, *see* dress code
hijrah 28, 41, 216–17
Hijrah Fest 216–17
Hinduism 148, 154
Hoca, Cübbeli Ahmet 161
Hodgson, Marshall 18, 224
Holy Mosques 204
Houthi 115
Howard-Bunt, Yvonne 20, 32
Humble, Tim 37
Ḥusayn bin ʿAlī bin Abī Ṭālib 32, 43, 71, 87, 110–12

Iblīs 36–7, 39
Ibn ʿArabi, *see* Muḥyī ad-Dīn Ibn ʿArabī
Ibn Kathīr 52
Ibn Qayyim Al-Jawziyya 86
ibn Sharaf, Yahya ʾAbū Ḥassan 186
Ibn Taymiyyah, *see* Taqī al-Dīn ʾAḥmad ibn Taymiyyah
Ibrāhim 38, 40–1
Ibrāhīm ibn Muḥammad 65
identities 17–18, 28, 77, 221
ijtihād 27, 62, 75, 81, 82, 100, 103, 223
al-Ikhwān al-Muslimīn, *see* Muslim Brotherhood
Ilyās (Elijah) 43
Imaan 198
Imamate 107–27
iMuslims 2, 9, 12
Inayat Sufi Order 167, 168
Inclusive Mosque Initiative 198
India 92, 95, 141, 153, 165–7
Indonesia 1, 14, 20, 88, 149, 199, 210–18
influencers 1–2, 18–20, 26, 31, 33, 157, 193, 210–18, 223–9
  definitions 12–13
  Indonesia 210–21
  Palestine and Gaza 208–18
influences 13, 18, 19, 29, 33, 34, 77, 193, 223–9
Instagram 22, 39, 79, 102, 110, 112, 113, 124, 131, 132, 137, 154, 157, 163–5, 196, 200, 201, 206, 211, 212, 214–21
internet access 13–14, 31, 32, 210
Internet Archive 23, 97
Iqbal, Muhammad 85
Iran 27, 31, 105–6, 116, 119, 127, 129–36, 179, *see also* Khamenei; Khomenei
  Iranian Office of Islamic Studies in Cyberspace 21
Iraq 31, 78–80, 137–9, 185–7
ʿĪsā (Jesus) 38, 43–5
Isḥāq 41
Islam Online 19, 101
Islamic Audios Library 101
Islamic Awareness 61
Islamic Emirate of Afghanistan, *see* Taliban
Islamic Society of North America (ISNA) 200
'Islamic State' (al-Dawlah al-Islāmīyah fī al-ʿIrāq wa al-Shām) 31, 49, 72, 85, 173, 174, 181, 189, 190, 219
  Islamic State Central Africa Province (ISCAP) 187
  Islamic State Khorasan Province (ISKP) 182, 187
  Islamic State in West Africa Province 189
'Islamophobia' 218, 219
IslamQA 79, 206
Ismāʿīl 41

Ismāʿīl ibn Jaʿfar 123–4
Ismāʿīlī 117, 123–7, 150, *see also* Aga Khan; Dawoodi Bohras; Nizāri Ismāʿīlī; Shīʿism; Sulaymānī Bohras
Ismaili TV 125
Israel 134, 207–10
Israel Defence Force (IDF) 207–10

Jaʿfar al-Ṣādiq 117
Jamaʿat-e-Islami 93–4, 100
Javed, Madinah 201
Jerusalem (al-Quds) 42, 52, 156, 183, 207–10
Jesus, *see* ʿĪsā
Jibrīl, *see* angels
Jihād (Lesser) 23–4, 26, 42, 53–4, 83, 84, 98, 99, 149, 173–91
al-Jīlānī, Abd al-Qādir 150–2
  Mazar Ghous 151
Jinn 35–6, 40, 45, 161, 225, 226
Judaism 41, 45, 65, 215

Kaʿbah 40, 203–4, *see also* ḥajj; Mecca; pilgrimage
Kabbani, Shaykh Hisham 53, 159, *see also* Naqshbandi
kalām 76
Karbalāʾ 31, 111, 116, 120, 126
Kashmir 135
Katz, Helen 12–13
Kenya 176, 189
Khadīja bint Khuwaylid 58–60, 107
Khaled, Amr 101
Khalifa, Mohammed 186
Khamenei, ʿAlī Hosseini 109, 131–3, 137, 205
Khamis, Sahar 23
Khan, Ahmed Riza 165
Khan, Inayat 167
Khan, Nusrat Fateh Ali 110
Khan, Sayyid Ahmad 93
Khan, Zia Inayat 167
al-Khiḍr 49, 169
al-Khoei, Abu al-Qāsim 138–9
Khomenei, Ruhollah 129–31
  Khomeini Mausoleum Complex 130–1
  The Sun's House 130
Khorasani, Wahid 133–4
al-Khwarizmi, Muḥammad ibn Mūsā 9–10
el-Kurd, Mohammed 208
el-Kurd, Muna 208
Kurds 168
Kuwait 209
Kyrgyz language 187

Lanier, Jaron 10
Latinx Muslims 22
law 75–103, 218
Lawrence, Bruce B. 17–18, 224, 235n.38
Lebanon 140–1
Lewis, Samual ('Sufi Sam') 168
Lewthwaite, Samantha 189, *see also* al-Shabāb
LGBTQ+ 126, 198–9

Maghreb 85
Majelis Ulama Indonesia (MUI, Indonesian Ulema Council) 211–12
Malaysia 14, 202
Mālik ibn Anas 80–1
Mālikī school 80–1, 117
Mansur, Ja'man Nurchotib (Yusuf Mansur) 211
Mariyāh al-Qibtiyya 65
marriage 59, 60–2, 63, 65, *see also* matrimonial apps
  distance marriage 67
  polygamy 63
Maryam (Mary) 38, 44
Mashhad 116, 119, 139
al-maslaha 12
Masud, Fatima and Maryam 200–1
Maulanda, Wardah 216
Mawlawi (Mevlevi) Order 157
Mbacké, Serigne Mountakha 165
McLuhan, Marshall 14–15
#MeToo 195–6
Mecca 19, 37, 41, 42, 52, 89, 174, 185, 203, 214, *see also* ḥajj; pilgrimage
  Mount Hirāʾ 58
medical ethics 211–12
Medina 28, 52, 65, 69, 81, 116, 118, 185, 203

memes 24, 38, 79, 80, 99, 100, 148, 149, 194, 217–21
Menk, Ismail bin Musa 51, 71–2, 108, 200
mental health 37
The Message, see under cinema
metadata 50, 51, 103
metaverses 26, 45, 47, 72, 105, 127, 143, 193, 199, 210, 218, 223–9
  definition 5–6
  Virtual Reality devices 6, 225
Minhaj ul-Quran 165
Mirpur 165
al-Modarresi, Muḥammad Taqi Ḥussaini 118, 134
Morocco 162, 215
Morsi, Mohamed 98
mosques 1, 26, 31, 32, 79, 204, *see also* Mecca; Medina; pilgrimage
  ʾAbū Ḥanīfa Mosque 79
  Al-Aqṣā 156, 207–10
  Cambridge Central Mosque 53, 206
  Dome of the Rock 183, 207–10
  Damascus Mosque 44
  Al-Kadimiyya Mosque 118–19
  minbar 1
Mozambique 181
Muʿāwiya Abī Sufyān 62, 71, 108, 110
Muḥammad al-Bāqir 115–17
Muḥammad Bahāʾ al-Dīn Naqshband Bukhārī 158–9, *see also* Naqshbandiyya
Muḥammad bin Ismāʿīl 123–4
Muḥammad ibn ʿAbd Allāh 28–9, 31, 35, 39, 43, 45, 43–73, 76, 78, 97, 106, 107, 145, 165, 168, 173, 196, 207, *see also* Qurʾān
  family 32, 43–73, 105–27, 153
  mawlid 19, 79, 153, 160, 165
  Night Journey 38, 42, 44, 52–3
  Sīra (biographical sources) 51, 76
Muḥammad ibn ʿAbd al-Wahhāb al-Tamīmī 72, 86, 100, 166
Muḥammad ibn Abī al-Jawād 120–1
Muḥammad ibn Idrīs al-Shāfiʿī 81, 167, *see also* al-al-Shāfiʿī school
Muḥammad ibn Saud (Ibn Suʿūd) 88
Muhammadiyyah 88, 213–14
Muḥyī ad-Dīn Ibn ʿArabī 39, 43, 155–7
Muʿīn al-Dīn Chishtī 153, 154–5, *see also* Chishtīyya
Mujahid, Zabihullah 179, *see also* Taliban
Murad, Abdal Hakim 52–3, 102
Murīdiyya (Mouride) Sufi Order 164–5
Mūsā ibn ʿImrān (Moses) 41–3, 52
Mūsā ibn Jaʿfar al-Kāẓim al-Kadhimiya 118–20
music 30, 37, 51, 58, 66, 84, 86, 87, 93, 108, 109, 113, 116, 119, 121, 145, 151, 152, 154, 155, 157, 168, 169, 202, 216, 218, 227, 270
  nashīd 67
Muslim Brotherhood (*al-Ikhwān al-Muslimīn*) 97–101
Muslim Council of Britain 204, 206
Muslim World League 89

Nahdlatul Ulama (NU) 212–13
Najaf 137–8
Najafi, Basheer Hussain 139
Nakshawani, Syed Ammar 39, 53
Naqshbandi-Haqqani 159–60
Naqshbandiyya 43, 53, 87, 158–61, *see also* Muḥammad Bahāʾ al-Dīn Naqshband Bukhārī; Naqshbandi-Haqqani; Sufism
Narula, Herman 11
networks 18, 19, 31
'New Age' 146, 167–8
Nicholson, R.A. 157
Nigeria 163, 164, 190
9-11 174, 176–7, 182–3
Nizamuddin Awliya 167
Nizār ibn al-Mustanṣir 125, *see also* Nizāri Ismāʿīlī
Nizāri Ismāʿīlī 124–5, *see also* Aga Khan IV; Ismāʿīlī; Shīʿīsm
Non-Fungible Tokens (NFTs) 221
Nūḥ (Noah) 40

Ordinary Muslim Man 220
Orientalism 60, 72, 146, 156
al-Ouda, Salman 101

Pakistan 32, 93–4, 153, 176, 187
Palestine and Gaza 81, 132, 134, 175, 207–10, 215

Palestinian Islamic Jihad 132
Papacy 134, 137
Paris attacks 2015 186
Pashto 182
Patel, Sana 20, 224
Pemuda Hijrah 217
Persia 71, 87
Persian 38, 130, 134, 157
  Dari 182
Piela Anna 21–2
pilgrimage 113, 121, 126, 144, 155, 158, *see also* ḥajj, Karbalāʾ; Mashhad; Meccal; Medina; *zāwiyah*
  Imam Reza Shrine 10
  Konya 279n.100
  Mazar Ghous 151
  Touba 164
Pinterest 39, 43, 59, 123, 131, 132, 148, 150, 154, 157, 165, 220
prayer 1, 3, 19–20, 34, 43, 98, 114, 118, 145, 149, 206, 212, 219
  Call to Prayer (*adhān*) 67, 79
  Personal Protective Equipment (PPE) and prayer 206, 212
  rakaʿāt 80
Punk Hijrah 217

al-Qadhi, Yusuf 52
Qadiriyya Sufi Order 151–2
ul-Qadri, Muḥammad Tahir 165
al-Qaeda 49, 85, 90, 111, 173–7, 180–5, 190, *see also* al-Awlaki, Anwar; al-Ẓawāhirī, ʾAyman; bin Laden, Osama; 9-11
  al-Qaeda in Iraq 119 (*see also* Al-Zarqawi, Abu Musab)
  Jaysh Al-Malahim Al-Electronic 184–5
  One Ummah magazine 184
al-Qaraḍāwī, Yūsuf 101
Qassim, Isa Ahmed 140
Qatar 70, 82, 101, 164
Qazwini, Sayed Hossein Al 66
Qom 21, 133–5, 140
Queer Masjid 199
Question and Answer (Q&A) Websites 3, 64, 66, 77, 81, 135–6, 138, 139, 160, 163, 198, 206
Qurʾān 4, 25, 27, 29, 34–6, 38–43, 45, 64, 66, 70, 76, 77, 81–3, 87, 88, 98, 103, 121, 134, 145, 151, 161, 164, 165, 168, 176, 193, 194, 198, 220, 223, 226
  Harf Information Technology 89–90
  King Fahd Complex for the Printing of the Holy Qurʾān 89–90
  Muḥammad and the Qurʾān 47–55 (*see also* Muḥammad)
  Recitation of the Qurʾān 199–203, 210, 215–16
  Sūra al-Baqarah 40, 134, 201
  Sūra al-Fātiḥah 200
  Sūra al-Ḥijr 36
  Sūra al-Nūr 61
  Sūra al-Raḥmān 202
  Sūra Isrāʾ 36
  University of Southern California-Muslim Students Association (USC-MSA) 50
Quraysh 60, 66
Quṭb, Sayyid 98–9
Qutbuddin, Syedna Abu Taher Khuzaima 125, *see also* Sulaymānī Bohras
Qutubuddin Bakhtiyar Kaki 155

Rahman, Umar Abdul 184
Ramadan (Ramaḍān) 36, 93, 125, 187, 198, 202, 203, 206, 212, 219
Ramadan, Said 98
Ramadan, Tariq 98
Ravenscraft, Eric 4
Rayhāna bint Zayd 65
'red pill' movement, *see* Tate, Andrew
Reddit 80, 150, 197, 198, 218
Reza, Natta 216
Riḍā, Rashīd 95–7
Rouhani, Hassan 119
Rozehnal, Robert 22
Rūmī, Jalāl al-Dīn Muḥammad 38–9, 53, 146, 148, 157–8
Ruqayyah bint Muḥammad 71
Rushdie, Salman 129, 130, 132
Russia 80

al-Ṣādiq, Imam Jaʿfar 40
Ṣadr al-Dīn Qūnawī 155–6

Ṣafiyya bint Ḥuyayy 65
Said, Edward W. 129
Sajida, Rikva 198–9
Salafi 20, 42, 62, 79, 84, 90, 94, 97, 99, 100
Salafi Feminist 197
Salafi Publications 99
Salam Girl 196
Saudi Arabia 14, 27, 70, 81, 87–91, 183, 204–5, 212, 215
Sawda bint Zamʿa 64
search engines 4, 10, 11, 29–30, 35, 37, 48–50, 79, 194, 225
Second Life 225
Senegal 163–5
Senegambia 163, *see also* Senegal
sermons 43, 48, 101, 102, 108, 125, 141, 144, 150, 158, 194, 221, 224
sexual violence 195–6
al-Shabāb (al-Shabāb al-Mujāhidīn/al-Shabaab) 188–9
al-Shāfiʿī school 81, 212
Shah, Idris 156
Shāh Walīullāh Dehlawī 86–7, 92
sharīʿa 27, 75–103, 162, 176, 205, 214, 228
shayṭān 35–7, 39, 45
Shekau, Abubakar 189, *see also* Boko Haram
Shihāb al-Dīn ʿUmar Suhrawardī 152–3
Shihab, Rizieq 214–15
Shīʿism 21, 31, 32, 40, 41, 42, 51, 53, 59, 64, 66, 71, 77, 83, 85, 91, 105–42, 150, 154, 168, 169, 187, 205–6, *see also* Ahl al-Bayt; ʿAlī ibn Abī Ṭālib; Ḥasan bin ʿAlī bin Abī Ṭālib; Ḥusayn bin ʿAlī bin Abī Ṭālib; Imamate
  Ismāʿīlī 117, 123–7
  Jaʿfari Ithnā ʿAsharī (Twelver) 117–23
  Khoja Shīʿa ʾIthnā ʿAsharī 205
  Zaydi 115
Shirazi, Makarem 135–6
Siddiqi, Abdul Wahab 161
Signal 175
al-Sisi, Abdel Fatah 98
Sistāni, ʿal-Sāyyid ʿAlī 137–40
Snapchat 30
Soleimani, Qasim 137
Somalia 187–9
South Africa 152
South Korea 21
As-Sudais, Abdulrahman 204
Sufi Order International 167
Sufi Ruhaniat International 168
SufiLive 160, *see also* eShaykh; Naqshbandi-Haqqani
Sufism 19, 20, 26, 32, 36, 38, 39, 42, 43, 44, 45, 51, 53, 64, 65, 77, 83, 106, 110, 143–72, 212–13, *see also* al-Ghazālī; Chishtīyya Order; eShaykh; Muʿīn al-Dīn Chishtī; Murīdiyya, Naqshbandiyya; Naqshbandi-Haqqani; Qadiriyya; Rūmī; SufiLive; Sufi Order International; Tijāniyyah; *zāwiyah*
Sufism Reoriented 168
Suhrawardīyya Sufi Order 152–3
Sulaymānī Bohras 124, 125
Sunnah, *see* ḥādīth
Sunni Islam 32, 42, 75–103
SuraLikeIt 220
Syria 28, 79, 83, 96, 181, 185–7

Tablighi Jamaat 166–7
Tajik language 187
Taliban 173, 174, 176–83, 187, 190, 195
Tanzania 176
Taqī al-Dīn ʾAḥmad ibn Taymiyyah 82–5, 88, 96, 102
Tate, Andrew 197–8, 224
Telegram 102, 175, 178, 182, 190
Tijāniyyah Sufi Order 162–4
TikTok 29, 150, 156, 165, 196, 201, 221
Timol, Nusaiba Mohammad 201
Tor 33
Torah 41
TripAdvisor 54, 79, 90, 119, 120, 155
Tsuria, Ruth 16–17, 22
Turkey 14, 161, 168, 195
Twitter (X) 80, 89, 92, 101, 102, 120, 124, 132–4, 137–40, 154, 156, 159, 161, 174, 178–80, 182, 187, 190, 195, 200, 201, 204, 205, 207, 208, 214

Uganda 188
Ukraine 80
Umar, Ahmed 189, *see also* al-Shabāb
ʿUmar ibn al-Khaṭṭāb 70, 113, *see also* caliphate
ʾUmm Ḥabība (Ramla bint Abī Sufyān) 66–7
ʾUmm Kulthūm bint Muḥammad 71
ʾUmm Salama (Hindah bint ʾAbī ʾUmayyah) 64
United Arab Emirates 14, 204, 208
  General Authority of Islamic Affairs and Endowments in the United Arab Emirates (AWQAF) 102
United Kingdom 20
  England 14
  Scotland 54, 201
  Wales 14, 17
United States 48, 67, 149, 199, 205
Urdu 93, 116, 130, 135, 166, 182, 187
uṣūl al-fiḳh 76, 81, 166
ʿUthmān ibn ʿAffān ibn Abī al-'Ās 63, 71, *see also* caliphate
Uzbek language 187
Uzbekistan 158

Virtual Private Networks (VPNs) 33, 130, 228

'Wahhabism' 87–92, 166
Walī, Baktāš 168
Weber, Max 27
WhatsApp 102, 166, 175, 178, 190
Widodo, Joko 210

X, *see* Twitter

Yassin, Naseir 209
Yemen 81, 88, 115
Younus, Zainab bint 197
YouTube 30, 37, 49, 54, 66, 79, 82, 87, 108, 120, 121, 138, 153, 154, 156, 159, 164, 165, 169, 170, 201, 202, 214, 215
Yusuf, Hamza 150

Zakiyuddin, Saiyedna Abu Saʿeed il-Khayr Haatim 125, *see also* ʿAlawī Bohras
Al-Zarqawi, Abu Musab 85, 119
al-Ẓawāhirī, ʾAyman 99, 183–5
zāwiyah
  Dakar, Senegal (Sid ī Abdel Moutalib Tijāni) 163
  Fez, Morocco (Sidī Aḥmad al-Tijāniyy) 162
Zayd bin Thābit 64
Zayd ibn ʿAlī 115
Zayd ibn Ḥāritha (Zayd ibn Muḥammad) 66
Zaynab bint Jaḥsh 66

www.ingramcontent.com/pod-product-compliance
Lightning Source LLC
Chambersburg PA
CBHW071802300426
44116CB00009B/1177
* 9 7 8 1 3 5 0 4 1 8 3 0 1 *